BARACK
THE ENEM

MW00991408

TREVOR LOUDON
Compiled by
Rodney R. Stubbs
Endorsed by
Glenn Beck

"I'm a political researcher from Christchurch, New Zealand. I believe in freedom with responsibility, not freedom from responsibility. My ideal society is one in which government is confined to protecting its citizens from criminals and external enemies. I believe in working with all those who are moving in broadly the same direction. The views expressed in this book are strictly my own." I am founder and editor of KeyWiki.org, a rapidly growing website with the goal of unlocking the covert side of US and Global politics.

Fair Use/Copyright Notice

The proceeds from the sale of this book are for non-commercial purposes to be used for administration, research and education to expose the covert side of US and Global politics. For the benefit of the reader, names contained herein are available with additional information at KeyWiki.org.

Updates, Errors, Omissions and Redactions of attributed material are welcome. All changes require documentation identifying source, requestors name and address and the page and line number as it appears in this Edition. Changes will be posted when a second edition is published. An example of an update is found on page 376 submitted by Carl Davidson. The redaction policy applies to materials attributed in the book. Redactions will consist of striking through the material and footing the request for redaction by the person or persons responsible for the initial publication. A sample redaction is found on Page 239. Future publications are subject to the approval of the Author.

United States Library of Congress

Loudon, Trevor

Barack Obama and the Enemies Within: How a group of public and private sector unions, environmentalists and radicals entered into the corporatist paradigm to expand government and control America for their own personal gain in money and power. This is a history about what the media refused to report, who they are and what they intend to accomplish in their own words.

Includes attributions and index.

Table of contents

FAIR USE/COPYRIGHT NOTICE II

TABLE OF CONTENTS III

FORWARD VII

ACKNOWLEDGEMENT IX

INTRODUCTION XI

CHICAGO! CHICAGO!! CHICAGO!!!... 3

1.   Forget Islam – Look at Obama's Socialism! 5
2.   Barack Obama Was Endorsed by Chicago Marxists................................... 6
3.   Socialist Unionists Endorse Barack Obama 9
4.   Obama was endorsed by the Far Left "New Party"................................. 11
5.   Did Barack Obama Court Chicago Marxists & Peace Activists?..................... 15
6.   Bolshevik Barbara Bolsters Obama.. 17
7.   Barack Obama and the Democratic Socialists of America 20
8.   Baltimore Communists Back Obama... 23
9.   Communists Explain Backing for Barack Obama 26
10. Barack Obama and the Socialist "Mafia" 29
11. Communists Muster Latino Vote for Barack Obama 32
12. Jan Schakowsky-Barack Obama's Loyal Socialist Supporter....................... 35
13. Top Communist Not Fooled By Obama's Critics................................... 39
14. Socialist Led Mega - Union Backs Barack Obama................................. 40
15. Socialist Octogenarians for Barack.. 44
16. Barack Obama and the Legacy of Harold Washington.............................. 49
17. Major Union Federation Endorses Barack Obama - More Socialist Links 54
18. Will Obama Be the Communist Party's "People's President?" 58
19. Obama '08 "All the Way with DSA".. 66
20. Young Communist League Backs Barack Obama - Again............................. 69
21. Top Communist Criss-Crosses the US for Obama.................................. 72
22. Barack Obama, Danny K. Davis and the Marxist New Party........................ 74
23. Alice Palmer - Obama's Soviet Sympathizing Patroness 79

2008 DEMOCRATIC NATIONAL CONVENTION, DENVER,
COLORADO, USA 84

24. Obama's Major Socialist Supporter... 86
25. Committees for Correspondence for Democracy and Socialism Marxist-Leninists
     Come Out for Obama 89
26. William McNary: Yet another Obama Radical?.................................... 92

27. Reds, Radicals, Terrorists and Traitors - Progressives for Obama 98

28. Top US Communist - Elect Obama "Go On to Change the World"............................104

29. Senior US Socialist Jose Laluz, Manipulates Latino Vote for Obama........................107

30. Who helped launch Barack Obama's political career? 110

31. Grey Power! The Ageing Texan Radicals for Obama 115

32. Ayers, Davidson, Klonsky - the toxic trio! Linked to Pro-Obama Organization.......119

33. More Weathermen for Obama 124

34. Should US voters know this? 129

35. Even More Weathermen for Obama - Connections 135

36. How Socialist Was Obama's "New Party"? 141

37. Obama's Mentor, Frank Marshall Davis - Was He Still a Communist? 148

38. Obama, Davis, Jarrett - One Degree of Separation..151

39. Barack Obama, Carol Moseley-Braun and the Chicago Socialist Machine 158

40. Bill & Bernardine's Buddy Bert, Backs Barack 166

41. Obama Was a New Party Member - Chain of Evidence..169

42. Obama's Socialist Neighbor, Jackie Grimshaw 173

43. Terrorists, Marxists, NP Veterans, Unite Behind Obama 177

44. Barack Obama and the socialist New Party 183

45. The Terrorist Friendly, Socialist Friend and Neighbour, Rabbi Wolf 187

46. The Axelrod Axis – Who is Behind the Man Behind Obama? 192

47. The Paid Soviet Agent behind Axelrod and Obama 199

48. OBAMA'S SUBTLE SERMON - ADVICE TO SOCIALIST ALLIES 209

THE SECOND DAY OF INFAMY!... **216**

49. Communists, Socialists and Obama Can Change America 219

50. The Communist Party Strategy for Obama's America..223

51. Top Communists Used Influence for Obama Victory...226

52. Communists Celebrate Obama Victory!   Plan Steps to Socialism 230

53. Why did Obama Appoint a Socialist to his "Transition Team?".................................233

54. Communist Party Leader on Obama: "We are speaking to a Friend".........................239

55. Terrorist/Comrade Discuss Obama "Lenin Would Be Impressed".............................247

56. Son of Atom Bomb Spy: Do Not Mourn Obama's Leanings, Organize to Push the Other Way 253

57. Obama's Socialist Ally Joins Powerful Congressional Committee..............................258

58. Hilda Solis - Obama Labor Secretary's Socialist Connections....................................262

59. Top Socialist's Memo to Obama 270

60. Institute for Policy Studies Plans Obama's America 276

61. Institute for Policy Studies and the Obama "Movement"..278

62. Obama "Understands What Socialism Is" Works with "Socialists with Backgrounds in the Communist Party"..283

63. Obama's "Energy Czar" and the Socialists Foreign and Domestic 289

THE TRANSFORMATION OF AMERICA!...293

64. Symbolic? Socialist Singer Seeger Serenades Obama 295

65. Obama's "Brains Trust?" More from the Institute for Policy Studies...........................297

66. Socialist Leader: Use Obama Presidency to Create a "Permanent Progressive Majority" 299

67. Communist Leader Claims Obama Considering Nationalization of Finance, Energy, Private Business 307

68. Obama, Antonio Villaraigosa and the Harry Bridges Connection 310

69. The Communists, Obama and the Cesar Chavez Holiday Campaign 314

70. Obama's Socialist Attack Hounds to "Block" Blue Dog Democrats 318

71. Former Terrorist Mark Rudd, Assesses Obama's Progress 322

72. Obama Appoints "Former" Communist to White House "Green Job" 324

73. Weather Alert! Obama's "Green Jobs" Czar Linked to Former Terrorist Supporters? 329

WAKING THE SLEEPING GIANT! 339

74. Communists Honor Obama's Former Pastor – Connecting the Dots...........................341

75. American Rights at Work. Obama's Socialist Labor "Commissars"...............................351

76. Leon Despres Dies. Obama's Socialist "Trailblazer" Moves On to Subvert Heaven..359

77. Sam Webb Lays Out Communist Agenda for Obama Administration........................367

78. Proof That Obama's Hawaii and Chicago Communist Networks Were Linked?......370

79. Filling in the Gaps. More on Obama and Chicago Democratic Socialists of America 378

80. Michelle and Barack's Black Panther Mentor 383

81. Former Weather Underground Terrorists and 60's Maoists Nurtured Obama's "Green Jobs" Czar...388

82. Obama, the Communist Van Jones and the Demos Connection...................................396

83. Obama's Man Van Jones: Many Roads Lead to Cuba, Communism 400

84. Why was Obama's "Brain" Valerie Jarrett so Happy to Hire Communist Van Jones? Was it Fate?...407

85. Security Implications? Obama's Man Axelrod was Mentored by Marxist Radicals..416

86. Obama "Czar" Ron Bloom's Socialist Vision for US Industry......................................429

87. Obama's Socialist Appointees: Where is the Spotlight? 437

88. Parallel Lives? Obama's "Go To" Man, Patrick Gaspard and New York Socialism...446

89. Deepak Bhargava "Advancing Change in the Age of Obama" 454

90. Alice Palmer Re-examined - Was Obama's First Political Boss a Soviet "Agent of Influence?"..460

91. Barack Obama and the Socialist Healthcare Scamsters...469

92. Some Christmas Reading for Your Senators - Obama, Young, Conyers and Socialized Healthcare...477

93. Obama's Marxist Doctor Once Supported Google Health Advisor...........................484

94. Concert or Coincidence? Obama and the Committees of Correspondence Connections 489

95. Obama's Socialist Advisers Push Immigration Reform to "Create a Governing Coalition for the Long Term" 493

96. Coincidence? Obama, Frank Marshall Davis and the Earl Durham Connection 499

97. Obama and the Weissbourds - Was There a Frank Marshall Davis Connection? 503

98. Obama Science Czar Holdren's Pro-Soviet Associations 509

99. Security Risk? Obama "Science Czar" John Holdren and the Federation of American Scientists 516

100. Obama's "Faith Adviser" Jim Wallis Mixes With Socialists, Radicals and "Truthers" 523

101. Who's Been Fibbing Then? Evidence That Obama Was Deeply Involved in Socialist New Party "Sister Organization" 529

102. America's Little Lenin? Joel Rogers and the Obama Movement. 536

103. Barack Obama's "Respectable" Socialist Mentor, Abner Mikva 544

104. Radical Royalty - Obama's Federal Reserve Pick - Sarah Bloom Raskin 551

THE CHOICE: FREEDOM OR TYRANNY 559

105. "A Pattern of Socialist Associations" - Obama's Supreme Court Nominee, Elena Kagan (the Early Years) 560

106. Obama's Supreme Court Nominee, Elena Kagan's Socialist Associations (the Middle Years) 567

107. Neil Abercrombie, Yet Another Covert Socialist in the Obama "Orbit" 573

108. Pro Obama "JournoLista" Outed - New "Can of Worms" Opened 578

109. "JournoList" - the Soros, Google, Free Press and Obama Connections 585

110. Collusion! How Socialist Harold Meyerson Kick Started the Obama Propaganda Machine 593

111. Degrees of Separation – Obama, Socialist Scholars and the East German Spy 597

BIBLIOGRAPHY & ATTRIBUTIONS 603

INDEX 631

Foreword

Trevor Loudon is the foremost researcher of the Progressive Movement, a broad group of anti-capitalists that includes Democrats, Republican moderates, Socialists, Communists, "Peace" Activists, the Religious Left, most organized Labor and Environmentalists. His research has formed the basis for explosive news stories about America's radical Left and has been cited extensively in books and articles by Aaron Klein, Brannon Howse, Jerome Corsi and many others. Trevor's diligent efforts have also provided the background material for many of Glenn Beck's ground breaking TV and radio exposés.

I stumbled upon Trevor three years ago while researching then candidate Barack Obama's connection to the Cloward Piven strategy. Discovering Trevor was like hitting the mother lode. With the Obama Files, I instantly found unimpeachable references proving that which before could only be classified as conjecture. Thereafter, Trevor became my most frequently cited source regarding Obama's radical roots.

Trevor, I and many other commentators, were very concerned about a potential Obama Presidency, and that concern drove our collective efforts to alert the voting public. Unfortunately, these efforts were insufficient to overcome the American press' tidal wave of deception, misinformation and fact suppression that allowed Obama to get elected. Yet, the American public has since awoken to the danger and this can be attributed in no small measure to Trevor's efforts.

It was Trevor Loudon who first exposed the Obama administration's "Green Jobs Czar," Van Jones, as a self-described communist, leading to Jones' expulsion from the White House. It was Trevor who first discovered that the "Frank" mentioned in Obama's autobiography *Dreams from My Father* was in fact the Communist Party USA member Frank Marshall Davis. It was Trevor who exposed Obama's early membership in the New Party, a communist spin-off group. Trevor has so many "firsts" they are impossible to list.

Spanning over twenty-five years, Trevor has researched the Progressive movement like few others, reading mind-numbing treatises and out-of-print journals, examining the Left's own reporting on its many conferences, seminars and organized celebrations, and traveling the nation to unknown libraries erected by the Left to celebrate its obscure heroes. His articles provide a treasure trove of information unavailable anywhere else. He is an unsung hero for the cause of American freedom.

What you learn within these pages will hopefully motivate you to join us in the Herculean effort necessary to stop the Leftist juggernaut – personified by Barack Obama – that threatens our freedom and indeed our very existence on this earth today.

James Simpson,

Baltimore, Maryland

Easter, 2011

Acknowledgement

I wish to extend my gratitude to:

- Cliff Kincaid - (Of America's Survival, who supported my efforts from the earliest days)
- Max Friedman - (A great friend and lifelong anti-communist fighter) Herb Romerstein - (A devoted communist researcher)
- Bob Chandler - (a friend and a patriot, may he rest in peace)
- Unnamed activist friends - (Who have been fighting the good fight all their lives. Without you, hope would have long deserted us)
- Rodney R. Stubbs - (For your generosity, patience and commitment)
- Glenn Beck - (A true American hero and patriot)
- Special thanks to those who helped in the review and editing of the work including Tracey Loudon, Betty Freauf, Jerry Eggers, and Terresa Monroe-Hamilton.

My great friend Jim Simpson; and to, Andy Olsen, Brenda Elliott, Aaron Klein, Robin, Kathie, Nachum, Scott, Liz, and the many others that have helped promote my work.

A special acknowledgement goes to my dear wife, Tracey.

Thank you all.

Compiler's Comments

First, thank you Trevor and Tracey for giving me the honor of helping you publish this work.

The name Stubbs is synonymous with the fight for Freedom. My family descended from Richard Stubbs, born 1676 in Virginia, Colonial America, 100 years before the Declaration of Independence. The family migrated from the Cheshire region of Great Britain.

Other Stubbs' gained notoriety for Freedom of religion and speech. We may not be related to one another other than in spirit but we share our love for freedom and liberty.

John Stubbs received his moment of immortality when Queen Elizabeth ordered his right hand to be struck off on November 3, 1579, as punishment for his "lewd and seditious" pamphlet, *The Discovery of a Gaping Gulf*. A few months before, a thousand copies of the book had been printed to oppose Queen Elizabeth a protestant and her intended marriage with Francis, Duke of Alencon a papist.

Another John Stubbs, a Quaker who faithfully worked with George Fox to teach the Protestant Bible, traveled from England to America in 1761. The book penned by John Stubbs mixed hieroglyphs (sketches of apples, trees and bumble bees) with the English language characters. The book or the Battledore was used to teach the English language and reading of the Bible.

William Stubbs, wrote *The Constitutional History of England*. William went on and became the Bishop of Oxford. The book is the history of Constitutions from Caesar to then modern day England in the late 1800s.

My name too is Stubbs, and I am privileged to compile this work for Trevor Loudon. This is an important reference for future historians.

My dedication is driven by God and a personal prayer as I stood one morning, overlooking the runway in Plieku in the Central Highlands of Vietnam. Before me were more than two-hundred fallen American men, taken from Landing Zones XRay and Albany located in the Ia Durang valley. Their mangled bodies were being off loaded from helicopters and laid side by side as a crew was trying to match arms and legs and arrange them in body bags for transport to the morgue in the coastal city of Qui Nohn.

They lay as they stood, side by side. My effort in compiling this book is dedicated to the memory of all the men and women who reluctantly sacrificed their lives to help their fellow man survive. I swore then, that their loss would not be taken in vein.

Barack Obama and the Enemies Within is a snapshot of how the American Republic was subdued by a corrupt media, lazy citizens, bumbling politicians who also took an oath and then claimed they support a moderate social and progressive agenda and clearly take credit for leading a secular movement to destroy our great Nation.

The result if not stopped, will lead mankind into slavery and erase any memory of God and His gift of Freedom.

My work is dedicated to Dina, my wife and our children and grandchildren who I pray see the American Dream and live in Freedom.

Rodney R. Stubbs, US Army, Capt.

Introduction

Many people have asked why a researcher from New Zealand would be interested in America's internal politics.

They also ask how someone from so far away could possibly uncover facts about some of the country's most powerful political leaders. Why professionals of the US mainstream media are unaware of, or chose to ignore, these simple facts?

The answer to the first question is simple. For the last 60 years, the West and much of the rest of the world has enjoyed the longest period of comparative peace and rising prosperity in world history.

This has been possible only because the United States benevolently used its wealth and military might and held the world's worst tyrants and empire builders at bay.

If the US sinks economically, it will be unable to defend the free world as it has in the past. This will create massive instability that will certainly be exploited by the Russians, Chinese, Iranians, Syrians, Cubans, North Koreans and Islamic militants.

If the US loses its prosperity and military advantage, it will be highly vulnerable to both external attack and internal subversion.

If America loses its freedom, freedom will die everywhere. Who will stand up to China, Russia and Iran? Do you expect Canada, Britain, Australia, France or New Zealand to fill this role? If an all-powerful US Navy is no longer patrolling the Pacific, how long will it be until China makes that entire lake its own? How long will my country maintain its independence and freedom under those circumstances?

All Westerners have a vital interest in American internal politics. As America goes, so goes the free world.

To answer the second question of how a New Zealand blogger could break significant stories, such as the connection of a young Barack Obama to the Hawaiian-based communist Frank Marshall Davis, or the communist roots of Obama's 'short-lived "Green Jobs Czar," Van Jones, my success lies in my tenacity and research.

The stories have been cited in several books, dozens of magazine articles and countless blog posts.

Glenn Beck, Rush Limbaugh and many other broadcasters have

used my material. Postings from my former blog, New Zeal, are now part of the US Congressional Record.

Here is how it all came about. My story goes back to the 1980's.

Until 1984, New Zealand had been a committed and reliable member of the Australia/New Zealand/United States military alliance (ANZUS). New Zealand troops had fought alongside American troops in World War I, World War II, Korea and Vietnam. The military and cultural ties were strong and deep.

Then in 1984, New Zealand threw out the "conservative" government of Sir Robert Muldoon and elected the socialist Labor government of David Lange.

Within a few months, ANZUS was on the rocks. The mouse had roared. New Zealand stood up to the mighty US war machine and said "enough" - no more dirty nukes in our clean harbours. US ships were welcome - nuclear armed ships not. Kiwis had spoken. We were all so proud of our government's brave stand that it was taught in schools and became part of our folklore. No conservative government dared even think of changing the policy.

At the time, I was in a minority. I was incensed and so were several of my friends. Together, we began investigating the New Zealand "peace" movement. What we found shocked us.

Part of our research involved interviewing a former New Zealand communist. This man had joined the pro-Soviet Socialist Unity Party (SUP) during the late 1970's in the country's capital, Wellington. He quickly rose through the ranks. In 1983, he accepted an offer to study in Moscow at Lenin's Institute for Higher Learning.

In Moscow, our comrade helped plan New Zealand's anti-nuclear policy. He trained with 7,000 communists from all over the world in trade union activism, racial agitation, social psychology, crowd manipulation and Soviet history. He worked alongside the more than 200 South Africans, who would later take over that country, Danes, who were tasked with closing off the Baltic in the event of future war, Swedes, Canadians, Chileans, Indians, Palestinians, Lebanese, Syrians, Iraqis, Spaniards and Frenchmen. You name it. Americans, however, were conspicuous by their absence.

Why were there no Americans? Just where was the Soviets "Main Enemy"?

Because, our comrade reports, the US had warned the Soviets, if any

Americans were found training in Moscow, there would be war. The Soviets respected this threat.

What the crafty Soviets did to get around this though, was to train comrades from other nations (New Zealand included) in the desired American policy. They would then instruct those comrades to indoctrinate the appropriate US comrades.

How did the Soviets and their New Zealand agents, the SUP, manage to re-align the foreign policy of a once staunchly loyal US ally?

The SUP went from almost nowhere in the 1970's, to become the dominant force in the trade union movement by the beginning of the 1980's. In 1976, the SUP, as did virtually every other western communist party at the time, set up an affiliate of the Moscow controlled World Peace Council - the New Zealand Council for World Peace.

The Soviets wanted to break an ally away from the protective umbrella in order to encourage others in the NATO alliance to do the same. For a variety of reasons, they selected New Zealand as the most likely country to lead the way. The order went out to build up the New Zealand peace movement and expand its influence into all sectors of society. The SUP Auckland Regional Newsletter reported on November 12, 1980:

> To date in the region the Peace Council has made good progress among trade unions but more effort must be made to build on this and take the peace question to the factory floor. Also needed now is to broaden the Peace Council into other areas of the Community, join up prominent personalities including MPs, increase church involvement, university involvement, other peace groups, community clubs etc. Here branches and comrades can act as catalysts.

> We must be extremely careful that in building the Peace Council it does not become overburdened with "SUP" people or be labelled just another "SUP" front. If our Party is working correctly, only a few comrades, reporting back to the Region and Branches and taking forward issues from the same sources, are necessary to ensure effective involvement in the Peace movement. The broadest possible base is needed if we are to make the Council effective. (SUP Auckland Regional Newsletter 1980)

Oleg Gordievsky, a former high-ranking officer of the Soviet security Service, the KGB, who from 1974 worked as a long-serving undercover agent for MI6 until his formal defection in 1985, recalled:

KGB activity in Australasia was... increased as the result of the election of David Lange's Labor government in New Zealand on an antinuclear programme in 1984... The [KGB] Centre... was jubilant at Lange's election... In its attempts to draw New Zealand into nuclear-free activities, the Soviet authorities had made tremendous efforts to penetrate and strengthen the Labor Party, partly through the local Party of Socialist Unity… and partly through the Trades Union Congress. (Andrew and Gordievsky 1990)

Gordievsky alleged that the New Zealand communists operate under the control of the International Department of the CPSU. He said:

I know the situation in New Zealand very well; only 500 members of the Socialist Unity Party, but they are invaluable because each was ready to do something. It was like the KGB had 500 agents in the country… Plus some of them penetrated the trade unions, and then they penetrated the left wing of the NZ Labor Party. (Andrew and Gordievsky 1990)

SUP members studied at Lenin's Institute of Higher Learning (a.k.a. the Institute for Social Sciences) in Moscow during the early 1980s where indoctrination was extensive by Soviet tutors on the advantages that could accrue to the Soviet Union from the election of a Labor Government in New Zealand.

The Soviets taught and instructed in the way to bring this about; a time honored method practiced by Western communist parties for decades. The trick was to use New Zealand communists to make Soviet designed policies into Labor Party policies, and consequently New Zealand law implementing the following five steps:

- New Zealand's anti-nuclear policies formulated to favor Moscow.
- SUP members, indoctrinated by their Soviet tutors, then sent back to New Zealand to promote anti-nuclear policies through the peace movement, the unions, the environmental movement, their secret members and through sympathizers in the Labor Party.
- SUP members to cite this "public groundswell" as a reason why Labor should adopt the SUP's anti-nuclear policies.
- Get the anti-nuclear policies adopted as official Labor Party policy.
- Keep SUP/union/peace movement pressure on the Labor government to ensure that the policies become a part of New Zealand's law.

By that time, the SUP had gained substantial influence in Labor's executive and policy council, so this process was not overly difficult. The propaganda then needed to be kept up to achieve maximum public acceptance of Moscow's policies without revealing their original source.

The Soviets were amazed at how easily their SUP minions could co-opt Labor to the anti-nuke cause.

By carefully playing all of its many strings in tune, the SUP could turn Soviet policy into Labor Party policy. By playing the patriotic and anti-American cards, the SUP could organize large numbers of New Zealand voters in the name of peace.

Virtually, all Kiwis regard New Zealand's anti-nuclear policies as an indigenous response to US "warmongering" and Cold War madness. Only the tiniest percentage would have any inkling at all of the Soviet origins of those policies.

That is the real "secret" of communism. It is the ability of communist or socialist parties to influence and infiltrate moderate leftist or liberal parties so that they become the unknowing conduit for communist policies.

It has been done countless times - through the British, Australian and New Zealand Labor parties, the French Socialist party, the German Social Democrats, the Canadian Liberals and of course, the US Democratic Party.

Major public policy includes Roosevelt's "New Deal" and Johnson's "Great Society – the two greatest expansions (pre-Obama) of Federal Government power in US history.

While the hundreds of spies in Roosevelt's administration were a huge threat to US security, even more damaging were the legions of legal and illegal communists working through the government and the Democratic Party to move America left. Much of their work exists to this day. Much of it is now part of the American mainstream.

Move forward to the early 1990's.

The Soviet bloc has collapsed. The Communist Party USA is nearly extinct and the AFL-CIO is under anti-communist control. Nobody cares about Reds anymore.

Fast forward, five short years to 1995. SEIU leader John Sweeney has become president of the AFL-CIO. He has joined the Marxist leaning Democratic Socialists of America and has removed the bar on known communists holding office in his unions.

The Communist Party is slowly growing, re-colonizing the unions and is strengthening ties to Cuba and China. Democratic Socialists of

America is working with both organisations, in the unions, in the peace movement and through the Democratic Party's Congressional Progressive Caucus, which now boasts more than 50 members.

Former 1960's radicals, Students for Democratic Society activists, including Weathermen terrorists, are now in their 50's and 60's. They are at the peak of their careers in the Labor unions, academia media, non-profits, Democratic Party, the churches and synagogues.

Their revolution failed "back in the day..." They have one last chance to "fundamentally transform America" and they do not mean to blow it.

The stage is almost set for a new leader to arrive out of the US progressive movement, one who can lead America into socialism while the country is still basking in post-communist euphoria.

Alerted to Soviet infiltration of mainstream political parties by my New Zealand comrade, I began researching the Communist Party USA and other US radical organizations. By the early 2000's, I had a good understanding of American radicalism and its worldwide support networks. I learned much more when I made contact with knowledgeable historians of the American left, particularly my good friend, Max Friedman.

On March 29, 2007, *Rethinking the History and Future of the Communist Party*[1] appeared on the Communist Party USA (CPUSA) website, written by leading communist historian Gerald Horne. I had only vaguely heard of Barack Obama at that point, but Horne pointed out that young Obama had spent some time as a teen in Hawaii with an elderly black poet named Frank Marshall Davis. Horne pointed out that Davis was at least "in the orbit" of the Communist Party.

A little research revealed that Davis was a secret member of the Communist Party USA, which resulted in a report dated March 29, 2009 about Barack Obama's Marxist Mentor[2] on the New Zeal blog.

I got zero response to this post, but I continued my research. I found that Barack Obama had enjoyed the support of the Communist Party USA right up until the 2008 election. In fact he still does. I also found out that Obama had close ties to two allied Marxist organisations, Democratic

[1] http://politicalaffairs.net/rethinking-the-history-and-future-of-the-communist-party-41925/
[2] http://trevorloudon.com/2007/03/barack-obamas-marxist-mentor

Socialists of America and Committees of Correspondence for Democracy & Socialism. As I already knew much about these organizations, I knew where to look for more links - they were not hard to find. I soon discovered that Barack Obama was well "connected" to the Chicago far left.

I published this information in a series of twenty posts,[3] from January 12 to February 29, 2008, which appear as the first twenty files of this book. This information started to get a little interest on the US blogosphere.

In February 2008, Cliff Kincaid of Accuracy in Media picked up the Frank Marshall Davis story and wrote *Obama's Communist Mentor*[4] on February 18, 2008. Readership snowballed. Hundreds of blogs and websites picked up Cliff's article.

The Chicago branch of Democratic Socialists of America noted this on their ejournal *New Ground* of March 2008:

> Right-wing bloggers have discovered Chicago DSA's 1996 endorsement of Obama for the Illinois State Senate and Obama's participation[5] that same year in a University of Chicago Young Democratic Socialists townhall meeting on "Economic Insecurity." This news started in New Zealand (it is the Wide Web indeed) where a local libertarian has been obsessing over Chicago DSA's links to mainstream Chicago politics.

> The news gradually (by web standards) spread to right-wing blogs here in the States. It even managed to pop up in a few conservative mainstream venues. More recently, the conservative Accuracy in Media combined this with some juicy Communist Party associations (communist mentor unmasked!) and threw it out as an example of how the news media has a liberal bias for not reporting the story.

> Of course, many right-wingers had been convinced Obama is a "socialist" already. If you're wondering why, it's mostly because the term "socialist" for these folks have about as much content as "fascist" does for many lefties; it's an insult not a description. So the news from New Zealand was greeted with an "Aha" by these folks more than anything else. (Roman, Other News 2008)

---

[3] Chapter 20 - Young Communist League Backs Barack Obama - Again
[4] http://www.aim.org/aim-column/obamas-communist-mentor/
[5] http://www.chicagodsa.org/ngarchive/ng45.html

At one point, even the pro-Clinton Democrats were distributing our material in an effort to de-rail Obama's campaign.

In April, Cliff Kincaid, through America's Survival,[6] organized a press conference in Washington, DC to release two dossiers on Obama regarding the communist network in Hawaii and Chicago.

Herb Romerstein, regarded as the primary expert on US Communism, wrote "*Communism in Hawaii and the Obama Connection.*[7]" A youthful communist himself, Herb later served as investigator with the US House Committee on Un-American Activities, and in the same capacity with the House Committee on Internal Security and the House Permanent Select Committee on Intelligence. He was the head of the Office to Counter Soviet Disinformation for the US Information Agency. Romerstein is also co-author of the influential book "*The Venona Secrets: Exposing Soviet Espionage and America's Traitors*," which included extensive documentation of the communist activities of Roosevelt administration staffer Alger Hiss.

Cliff Kincaid presented the second dossier "*Communism in Chicago and the Obama Connection*".[8]

I was invited to participate, as was the fourth member of our team, my US communist-historian friend, Max Friedman.

Since the trip, Cliff has published several more articles on Obama's radical ties, which have been re-published thousands of times.

I made many contacts in the US and did some hands on archival research in Chicago, New York, Los Angeles and other cities. This led to another ninety Obama files – now compiled in this book.

These reflect a constant process of discovery. They are not linear. They zig and zag, jump backwards and forward and sometimes repeat key information so that each file stands on its own.

They are a history of the discovery of Obama's radical ties. Like a jigsaw puzzle, key pieces would fill in whole portions of the picture while other sections remained blank. Right up to the 2008 election, Cliff, Max, Herb, others and myself worked overtime to fill in the gaps.

After the election, the pace never slackened as Obama confounded

---

[6] http://www.usasurvival.org/ck05.22.08.html

[7] http://www.usasurvival.org/docs/hawaii-obama.pdf

[8] http://www.usasurvival.org/docs/chicago-obama.pdf

the optimists and began appointing all sorts of radicals to positions of authority.

After the initial breakthrough, more and more blogs, websites, books and broadcasters began referencing the Obama Files. Glenn Beck appeared and with amazing clarity, researched and reduced volumes of information to a series of forty-minute presentations broadcast to millions of Americans all across the United States

By the middle of 2009, it became apparent that Fox News TV host, Glenn Beck, was using some Obama File material.

Glenn honed in on so-called "Green Jobs Czar" Van Jones profiled on my New Zeal blog.

Night after night, Glenn Beck hammered Jones – revealing his vey recent communist past and a whole host of radical statements preserved on YouTube. A virtual Van Jones industry sprang up. People all over began scouring the internet, looking for more and more embarrassing statements by Jones.

After it was revealed that Van Jones had signed a 2004 statement raising the possibility that the 9/11 attack was linked to the US government, the game was up.

Late on the first Saturday night of December 2009, Van Jones quietly resigned his White House position.

Despite an obvious desire on the part of the White House to hush things up, the event made world headlines. Even my local Christchurch Press gave it the front-page treatment – without mentioning that a local blogger had set the ball rolling.

More importantly, many who had been willing to give Obama the benefit of the doubt, now saw the president for what he actually was. Who else but a committed socialist would appoint a radical communist to a senior White House position?

From that point, the Obama Files spread relentlessly over the internet.

I hope you will read these files in the spirit written as a process of discovery, education and filling in gaps on the way to gaining a deeper understanding of the movement that has given America its most radical president ever.

Obama did not make a movement. A movement made Obama.

I hope my Obama Files help lead to a greater general understanding of that truth.

Trevor Loudon

BARACK OBAMA AND THE ENEMIES WITHIN

TREVOR LOUDON
Compiled by
Rodney R. Stubbs
Endorsed by
Glenn Beck

"I'm a political researcher from Christchurch, New Zealand. I believe in freedom with responsibility, not freedom from responsibility. My ideal society is one in which government is confined to protecting its citizens from criminals and external enemies. I believe in working with all those who are moving in broadly the same direction. The views expressed in this book are strictly my own." I am founder and editor of KeyWiki.org, a rapidly growing website with the goal of unlocking the covert side of US and Global politics.

CHICAGO! Chicago!! chicago!!!

1. Forget Islam – Look at Obama's Socialism!

Trevor Loudon © Saturday, January 12, 2008

No doubt, Barack Obama is an engaging and charismatic individual. Whatever the outcome of the 2008 presidential race, Barack Obama will be an influential figure for some time to come. What does Barack Obama believe? Where does he fit on the political spectrum? What would he do in office? Whom would he promote? What would he support?

Few seem to know during the early days of the election process. Some libertarians even seem to think[9] he is one of us!

1-1 Barack Obama

While many have focused on Obama's boyhood Islamic ties[10] and his extreme left voting record, many have overlooked his Marxist ties. The documentation of Hillary Clinton's radical past[11] is well known; Barack Obama's much more recent links remain uncovered. Barack Obama's opponents in the Clinton and Republican camps Google his name in vain. The following reports demonstrate the Communist Party's love of Obama, but that does not prove that Obama supports Communists.

- Barack Obama's Marxist Mentor[12]
- Why Do The Communists Back Barack?[13]
- Young Communist League Infiltrates US Democrats[14]
- American (Communist) Idol-Barack Obama[15]
- Is Barack Obama a Marxist Mole?[16]

[9] http://liberalvaluesblog.com/2008/01/10/the-libertarianism-of-barack-obama/
[10] http://www.brookesnews.com/070801obama.html
[11] http://www.aim.org/publications/aim_report/2003/15.html
[12] http://trevorloudon.com/2007/03/barack-obamas-marxist-mentor/
[13] http://trevorloudon.com/2007/06/why-do-the-communists-back-barack/
[14] http://trevorloudon.com/2007/06/young-communist-league-infiltrates-us-democrats/
[15] http://trevorloudon.com/2007/06/american-communist-idol-barack-obama/

The rest of these files cover aspects of Obama's links to the far left, in his home town of Chicago. The files are not in chronological sequence, but the files do reflect the period when Obama arrived in Chicago and became a State Senator. The citizens of Illinois elected Obama to serve as a Senator for their state in the US Congress. Obama then decided to be a candidate for the office of the President of the United States and ran a successful campaign. President-elect Obama engaged in the process of selecting a transition team to establish his Administration. The final chapters will look into the people and policies that administer his regime. Each file will focus on Obama's links to Democratic Socialists and Communists both in the past and present.

Is there anyone who finds this enlightening?

2.   Barack Obama Was Endorsed by Chicago Marxists

Trevor Loudon © Saturday, January 12, 2008

Barack Obama came to Chicago in 1983, inspired by the city's new Mayor Harold Washington.[17] A long time Communist Party associate, Washington staffed the city's administration with communists and socialists. Mayor Washington died in office in 1987.

Washington was close to the Democratic Socialists of America (DSA) when they formed a coalition of former Trotskyite, "new left" activists, ex-Socialist Party and Communist Party members in 1983. Democratic Socialists of America (DSA) is now the US's largest Marxist organization and its moderate name has allowed it to infiltrate other parties, including the New Party, the Working Families Party, the Greens and the Democratic Party. Democratic Socialists of America (DSA) is strong in Chicago where it has real influence in the left wing of the Democratic Party. It was in these incestuous circles of the Chicago Democratic Party and Socialist leaders where a young lawyer, Barack Obama, began his political career. Chicago Democratic Socialists of America (DSA) endorsed[18] four candidates for the Illinois elections in

[16] http://trevorloudon.com/2008/01/barack-obama-marxist-mole/
[17] http://trevorloudon.com/2007/10/chicagos-redblack-alliance-targets-white-house/
[18] http://www.chicagodsa.org/ngarchive/ng45.html

March 1996.

Danny K. Davis

This is not Danny K. Davis's first run for Representative of the seventh Congressional District any more than 1983 was Harold Washington's first campaign for Mayor of Chicago. This time he is going to win the Democratic ballot and go on to Congress. And Danny is not foreign to Chicago Democratic Socialists of America (DSA).

From the very beginning, he has always been willing to help appearing as a speaker with Michael Harrington, serving as a Master of Ceremonies without peer at the annual Debs-Thomas-Harrington Dinner.

The Seventh Congressional District runs from the lakefront straight west to the Cook County border. If you would like to get involved, contact the Davis for Congress headquarters. (Davis 1996)

2-1 Danny K. Davis

Democratic Socialists of America (DSA) does not say it, but US Representative Danny K. Davis is a Democratic Socialists of America (DSA) member. He was also a member of the New Party, which founded the electoral front by the Democratic Socialists of America (DSA) and the Communist Party breakaway organization, Committees of Correspon-dence.[19]

William Delgado

William Delgado a candidate to win the Democratic ballot line for the Illinois House of Representatives in the third District out on the west side of Chicago. He is a longtime community activist with an academic background in criminal justice and social work. Mr. Delgado is a real firebrand and a member of the New Party. (Davis 1996)

2-2 William 'Willie' Delgado

Barack Obama

Barack Obama is running to gain the Democratic ballot for the Illinois Senate's 13th District.

---

[19] http://www.cc-ds.org/

The 13th District is Alice Palmer's old district, encompassing parts of Hyde Park and South Shore.

Mr. Obama graduated from Columbia University and went into community organizing for the Developing Communities Project in Roseland.

Altgeld Gardens on the far south side of Chicago. In 1992, a Director of Illinois Project Vote, voter registration campaign that made possible US Senator Carol Moseley Braun (D-IL) election to the US Senate. (Davis 1996)

2-3 Barack Obama

What best characterizes Barack Obama is a quote from an article in *Illinois Issues,* a retrospective look at his experience as a community organizer while he was completing his degree at Harvard:

Community organizations and organizers are hampered by their own dogmas about the style and substance of organizing." They practice a 'consumer advocacy' approach, with a focus on wrestling Services and resources from outside authorities. Few are thinking of harnessing the internal productive capacities, both in terms of money and people in the communities. (Obama, *Illinois Issues*)

Luckily, Mr. Obama does not have any opposition in the primary. His opponents have all dropped out or were ruled off the ballot. (Davis 1996)

The New Party granted their endorsement, solicited by Barack Obama...

Alice Palmer was a leftist who worked with some DSA members.

Carol Moseley Braun

US Senator Carol Moseley Braun (D-IL) was elected to a Senate seat by the Communist Party and Democratic Socialists of America (DSA). Barack Obama helped her win the Senate seat and later took it over when Moseley Braun ran for the US Presidency in 2004.

3.   Socialist Unionists Endorse Barack Obama

Trevor Loudon © Saturday, January 12, 2008

While US labor unions are not the force they once were, Democratic Party candidates live or die on union endorsements. Union approval means publicity, campaign volunteers and money.

In the battle for the Democratic US Presidential nomination, both Hillary Clinton and Barack Obama are each trying to lock in as many union endorsements as possible.

In recent years, the hard left has recaptured the US labor movement. The President of the AFL-CIO, John Sweeney, is also a member of the Marxist Democratic Socialists of America. Sweeney presided over the conquest of the US labor movement by the socialists and communists.

The Democratic Socialists of America (DSA) and the Communist Party used their considerable influence to steer union support behind their favored candidates.

Barack Obama has had a long relationship with Democratic Socialists of America (DSA) and the Illinois labor movement.

It is not, surprising to see Democratic Socialists of America (DSA) linked unionists throwing their support Barack Obama's way. From PolitickerNV.com, December 3, 2007:

3-1 The late DSA member Carl Marx Shier (r) presents Henry Bayer (l) with the 2001 Debs Award

Senator Barack Obama's presidential campaign held a conference call for Nevada reporters today to highlight Obama's record of support both by and for organized labor.

On the call were Tom Balanoff, President of the Illinois SEIU State Council; and Local 1; Henry Bayer, Executive director of the AFSCME Council 31; Margaret Blackshere, former President of the Illinois AFL-CIO; Den Gannon, President of the Chicago Federation of Labor; and Henry Tamarin, President of UNITE HERE Local 1.

He comes from us," said Balanoff on Obama. He understands our problems. We could count on Barack on all issues important to working families. Healthcare, general economic justice, jobs… Barack was there, not only there but often times leading.

3-2 Socialist Roberta Lynch (l), presents the 2002 Debs Award to Tom Balanoff (r)

The conference call came at a difficult time for Obama's campaign in his effort to court organized labor in the state. (Damore 2008)

What is interesting here is that at least three of the five unionists named include Bayer, Balanoff and Tamarin, all with connections to Democratic Socialists of America.

Every year, Chicago Democratic Socialists of America hosts the Debs-Thomas-Harrington Dinner,[20] a major event on the Illinois socialist calendar.

The dinner honors outstanding "community leaders," activists and unionists.

Many, if not most, of the honorees are DSA members. All have done their bit for the socialist cause.

In the '70s, Bayer was organizer for the Chicago Socialist Party (a forerunner of Democratic Socialists of America and a member of the Young Peoples Socialist League National Executive Committee.)

The Illinois chapter of the country's major government-employees union broke with its national organization Saturday to endorse Barack Obama for President.

Bayer is a strong backer of Barack Obama:

Nationally, the American Federation of State, County and Municipal Employees are backing Hillary Rodham Clinton. But the union's Illinois leaders decided to make their own endorsement.

"It is an unusual step, but we've had a long relationship with Senator Obama," said Henry Bayer, executive director AFSCME Council 31. "We've had a better opportunity to observe him up close than people in other parts of the country." (Chicago Sun Times 2007)

Balanoff is a longtime friend and supporter of Barack Obama.

Tom Balanoff, President of the SEIU Illinois State Council, said:

---

[20] http://www.chicagodsa.org/dthdin.html

Obama's voting record is sound, with votes against trade deals like the Central America Free Trade Agreement and support for issues as the Employee Free Choice Act. "We know that he's the real thing." (Holland 2007)

Henry Tamarin is a former student leftist,

3-3 Henry Tamarin accepts the Debs Award

involved with Barack Obama in the socialist dominated Independent Voters of Illinois.[21]

Chicago Democratic Socialists of America (DSA) endorsed Barack Obama in his first election - the 1996 contest for a seat in the Illinois State Senate. It seems Chicago Democratic Socialists of America (DSA) is backing Obama again.

4.   Obama was endorsed by the Far Left "New Party"

Trevor Loudon © Friday, January 18, 2008

When Barack Obama ran for the Illinois State Senate in 1996 (as a Democrat), he was endorsed by the Democratic Socialists of America (DSA).[22]

A Marxist organization, Chicago Democratic Socialists of America (DSA) also endorsed three other candidates that year - US Representative Danny K. Davis, a Democratic Socialists of America (DSA) member, current US congressional Representative, Willie Delgado, and Patricia Martin.

4-1 State Senator Barack Obama, ACORN's lawyer

The Chicago branch of the New Party also endorsed Obama.

What was the New Party?[23]

The New Party was an electoral alliance dedicated to electing leftist

---

[21]http://en.wikipedia.org/wiki/Independent_Voters_of_Illinois-Independent_Precinct_Organization

[22] http://en.wikipedia.org/wiki/Democratic_Socialists_of_America

[23] http://en.wikipedia.org/wiki/New_Party_%28USA%29

4-2 Barack Obama the ACORN man

candidates to office - often through the Democratic Party. Two organizations formed the backbone of the New Party, the Democratic Socialists of America and the US's largest radical organization, Association of Community Organizations for Reform Now (ACORN).[24]

Back in Chicago, ACORN is more important than Iraq or Washington. ACORN and its associated Midwest Academy, both founded in the 1970s, continue to train and mobilize activists throughout the country, often using them to manipulate public opinion through "direct action" a code for illegal activities.

Prior to law school, Barack Obama worked as an organizer for their affiliates in New York and Chicago. He has always been an ACORN person - meeting and working with them to advance their causes. Through his membership on the Board of the Woods Fund for Chicago and, his friendship with Teresa Heinz Kerry, Obama has helped ensure that they remain well funded. (Trib Live Opinion 2007)

Since he graduated from law school, Obama's work with ACORN and the Midwest Academy has ranged from training and fundraising, to legal representation and promoting their work.

In Chicago, the New Party consisted of ACORN, Democratic Socialists of America (DSA), and the Committees of Correspondence.[25] A breakaway from the Communist Party USA, COCDS worked with Democratic Socialists of America (DSA) and many activists were members of both organizations. (Trib Live Opinion 2007)

Well known leftist Chomsky is a case in point.

From *New Ground* #38 Jan/Feb 1995:

On Saturday, January 14, the New Party in Chicago took another step in its effort to establish itself as a political force by holding a major outreach meeting directed at Chicago's Left. About 100 people, with sizable delegations from Democratic Socialists of America (DSA) and COCDS,

---

[24]http://en.wikipedia.org/wiki/Association_of_Community_Organizations_for_Reform_Now

[25] http://en.wikipedia.org/wiki/Committees_of_Correspondence

heard Bruce Colburn and Elaine Bernard preach the gospel of the New Party.

Elaine Bernard,[26] a Labor Studies lecturer at Harvard, is a Democratic Socialists of America (DSA) member.

The meeting held at the meeting hall of SEIU Local 880, a local that is tackling the difficult task of organizing home health care workers in Illinois. SEIU Local 880 and ACORN share office space. (Roman, New Party Organizes 1995)

Democratic Socialists of America (DSA) and their COCDS comrades saw the New Party as a vehicle for major political change - to both move the Democratic Party leftward and to prepare the ground for a new third party.

From *New Ground* #39 March/April 1995:

On January 27, forty-five people attended the Chicago Democratic Socialists of America (DSA) and Chicago COCDS organized public forum at the ACTWU hall on Ashland Ave. Each organization had two Representatives on the panel to present their particular elections '94 post-mortem perspectives. Co-Chair, Kurt Anderson and Political Education Officer, Bob Roman represented the Chicago Democratic Socialists of America (DSA). Carl Davidson, a member of COCDS's National Coordinating Committee, and Ronelle Mustin, an activist from the 22nd ward represented the Committee of Correspondence. Sandi Patrinos Chaired the event; she is also the Chair of Chicago COCDS.

Carl Davidson wanted to focus on "voting patterns." There were essentially two winners. Naturally the Republicans, but so were the most left in Congress as the Progressive and Black Caucuses. The Progressives and Black Caucuses are re-elected while the neo-liberal and conservative Democrats were voted out. More importantly this election was the de facto defeat of the elitist Democratic Leadership Council who do not care about the poor or Labor.

To win elections, Davidson emphasized that there are two necessary coinciding factors. A passive majority and a militant minority came to fruition for the Right wing with the Christian Coalition.

Hence, Davidson emphasized that in this historical period the Left's strategy must be electoral politics not revolution. Consequently, the Left

---

[26] http://en.wikipedia.org/wiki/Elaine_Bernard

must galvanize the "majority" - the working class and poor... Moreover, the democratic left needs get active in the New Party, which has won 20 of 30 local elections. A short-term strategy leading with the Democratic Party; and in the long-term, the New Party. (Roman, New Ground 39 1995)

Barack Obama saw the potential of the New Party, because he was soon seeking their support.

From *New Ground* #42 Sep/Oct 1996:

About 50 activists attended the Chicago New Party membership meeting in July. The purpose of the meeting was to update members on local activities and to hear appeals for NP support from four potential political candidates. The NP is being active in organization building and politics.

The political entourage included Alderman Michael Chandler, William Delgado, chief of staff for State Rep Miguel del Valle), and spokespersons for State Sen. Alice Palmer, Sonya Sanchez, chief of staff for State Sen. Jesse Garcia, who is running for State Rep in Garcia's District; and Barack Obama, chief of staff for State Sen. Alice Palmer. Obama is running for Palmer's vacant seat.

Although ACORN and SEIU Local 880 were the harbingers of the New Party there was a strong presence of COCDS and DSA (15%), four political candidates were "there" seeking NP support.

Barack Obama won the 1996 election, by using legal technicalities to get all his opponents disqualified-but he still used New Party volunteers in his campaign. (Bentley 1995)

From *New Ground* #47 July/August 1996:

The NP's '96 Political Program has been enormously successful with 3 of 4 endorsed candidates winning electoral primaries. All four candidates attended the NP membership meeting on April 11th to express their gratitude.

Representative Danny K. Davis, winner in the 7th Congressional District, invited NPers to join his Campaign Steering Committee.

Patricia Martin, who won the race for Judge in 7th Subcircuit Court, explained that due to the NP she was able to network and get experienced adVice from progressives like Davis.

Barack Obama, victor in the 13th State Senate District, encouraged New Party members to join in his task forces on Voter Education and Voter Registration. (Bently 1996)

The young Barack Obama had no aversion to enlisting Marxist help to further his political career.

5. Did Barack Obama Court Chicago Marxists & Peace Activists?

Trevor Loudon © Saturday, January 19, 2008

Carl Davidson[27] is a leading US Marxist. He is a former member of the 60s radical group Students for a Democratic Society (SDS) (which spawned the terrorist Weather Underground)[28] and spent many years working in various Maoist organizations. Around 1992, Davidson joined hundreds of former Maoists, Trotskyites and about a third of the Communist Party USA in a new Marxist coalition - the Committees of Correspondence (COCDS). Davidson remains a leading member of this organization, now known as the Committees of Correspondence for Democracy and Socialism (COCDS).[29]

Davidson serves on the steering committee of the communist dominated[30] US peace umbrella organization, United for Peace & Justice[31] and is co-Chair of the radical Chicagoans Against War & Injustice.[32]

5-1 Carl Davidson

He is also a major US advocate of radical cyber-activism.

In the mid '90s, Davidson played a key role in the Chicago branch of the New Party.

The New Party was a Marxist led political coalition designed to endorse and elect leftist public officials. The bulk of its members came from COCDS, the radical Democratic Socialists of America[33] and the US largest militant left grass-roots organization, ACORN.[34]

It was through the New Party that Davidson first met the aspiring

---

[27] http://carldavidson.blogspot.com/
[28] http://en.wikipedia.org/wiki/Weatherman_(organization)
[29] http://www.cc-ds.org/
[30] http://trevorloudon.com/2007/01/us-communists-organise-huge-anti-war-rally/
[31] http://www.unitedforpeace.org/downloads/2007steering committee.pdf
[32] http://www.noiraqwar-chicago.org/?page_id=2
[33] http://trevorloudon.com/2006/11/the-socialists-behind-the-progressive-caucus/
[34] http://www.acorn.org/

Illinois State Senator, Barack Obama.

Davidson was an ardent supporter of Obama for several years and helped organize the famous peace rally in Chicago where Obama pinned his colors to the anti-Iraq War cause.

As Obama has modified his (public) antiwar position in recent times, Davidson became disillusioned with his former hero.

In 2007, Davidson penned the following piece on Obama.

From the Marxism Mailing List archive:

> I'm from Chicago, too, and known Obama from the time he came to the New Party to get our endorsement for his first race ever. I've been in his home, and as an IL legislator, he's helped or community technology movement a number of times. He said all the right things to the ACORN and New Party folks, and we endorsed him, but I noticed too, that he seemed to measure every answer to questions put to him several times before coming out with it.

> That was in 1996.

> He spoke at our first antiwar rally. He spent most of his speech detailing all the wars in history he supported, then finally made a distinction between just wars and 'dumb' wars, and going into Iraq, which was still six months down the road then, was a 'dumb war,' and he flatly opposed it. Good, that put him on our side, and some of us organized a fundraiser for him for his Senate race. (Davidson 2007)

The antiwar rally was in 2002. Obama's Senate race was in 2004.

> After he visited Iraq when the war was on, he turned. Now we had to set aside whether it was right or wrong to invade, now we had to find the 'smart' path to victory, not Bush's 'dumb' path. Also, in dealing with Iran, we had to leave on the table bombing their nuclear sites. For this, a lot of the local antiwar activists started calling him 'Barack 'Obomb 'em''. He was not listening much to us anymore, but to folks much higher up in the DLC orbit. He had bigger plans.

> To be fair, I read a recent speech he gave to laid-off workers from a plant closing out in Galesburg, IL, around globalization, corporate responsibility, the safety net, the third wave, and so on. It was good. Save for not mentioning the war, I probably could not write a better one myself.

> Giving the current crisis and developments in Congress, he may move back to our side on the war, and get as far as, say, Murtha's position. But right now he's not in the 'Out Now' camp, not as good as Murtha, and a triangulator par excellence. I've watched him do it up close. The press

and his publicists put him in our camp, but if you look at his speeches and votes since his trip to Iraq, I think you will find he has a way to go.

Our peace groups here are sending a bunch of us to visit him soon, and get on his case. Perhaps he is still a work in progress, as Jesse Jackson says, but he still has a way to go to get back in my good graces, and those of many more of us here also. Carl Davidson, Chicago (Davidson, Marxism) (Davidson 2007)

Barack Obama is smart enough to know that what worked to mobilize the Chicago Marxist left for their cause, will not translate to the national stage.

It is interesting that a leading Marxist like Carl Davidson backed Barack Obama for so long.

6.   Bolshevik Barbara Bolsters Obama

Trevor Loudon © Friday, January 25, 2008

Before Christmas, US Representative Barbara Jean Lee (D-CA-9th)[35] became the first California Democrat to endorse Barack Obama.

Three of the US main Marxist organizations have supported Obama:

- Communist Party USA[36] (CPUSA)
- Democratic Socialists of America (DSA)
- Committees of Correspondence for Democracy and Socialism (COCDS)

US Representative Barbara Jean Lee (D-CA-9th) is associated with all three; her ringing endorsement of Obama comes as no surprise.

Lee inherited her Congressional seat upon the retirement of her former boss US Representative Ronald Vernie "Ron" Dellums D-CA-9th District.

Mayor of Oakland CA., Ronald Vernie "Ron" Dellums (and a Hillary Clinton supporter), is a longtime associate of the Communist Party USA.

Both Dellums and Lee were encouraged to enter politics by

---

[35] http://trevorloudon.com/2006/11/s-i-c-o-s-1-barbara-lee/
[36] http://trevorloudon.com/2007/06/american-communist-idol-barack-obama/

longtime Berkeley Councilwoman and Communist Party USA supporter, Maumelle Shriek.

Lee and Dellums are regarded as two of the most socialist Congressmen in recent history.

Dellums was Vice-Chair of Democratic Socialists of America.

In 1983, Dellums was guest of honor at Chicago Democratic Socialists of America (DSA)'s 1983 Thomas-Debs Dinner, an event later associated with several Barack Obama appearances.

Democratic Socialists of America (DSA) has supported US Representative Barbara Jean Lee (D-CA-9th)'s election campaigns.

From San Francisco DSA:

> The Democratic Socialists of America (DSA) national convention passed a resolution condemning the September 11 attacks, supporting in principle the selective use of multilateral armed force, and calling for a halt to the bombing. Its text, along with previous statements by Democratic Socialists of America (DSA) on the war, will presumably be available at the national web site soon. The Sacramento local and the anti-racism commission issued a prior statement.

> The East Bay local will be working for the re-election of US Representative Barbara Jean Lee (D-CA-9th) 37 the sole member of Congress to oppose a resolution granting sweeping, vaguely specified war powers to our illegitimate President. (Campbell 2001)

6-1 Ron Dellums Guest of Honor at Chicago DSA's 1982 Debs Dinner

Representative Barbara Jean Lee (D-CA-9th District) is also co-Chair of the Congressional Progressive Caucus,[38] a grouping of more than seventy left wing Congressmen and one US Senator Bernie Sanders.[39]

Several Communist Party members link to Democratic Socialists of America (DSA) (including US Senator Bernie Sanders (I-VT) and many have Communist Party connections.

[37] http://en.wikipedia.org/wiki/Barbara_Lee
[38] http://trevorloudon.com/2006/11/mark-my-words-readers-this-is-the-most-socialist-us-government-in-decades/
[39] http://en.wikipedia.org/wiki/Congressional_Progressive_Caucus

From Detroit DSA:

> Since 1982, Democratic Socialists of America (DSA) has been working for progressive change. As a national organization, Democratic Socialists of America (DSA) joins with its allies in Congress' Progressive Caucus and in many other progressive organizations, fighting for the interests of the average citizen both in legislative struggles and in other campaigns to educate the public on progressive issues and to secure progressive access to the media. (Ebel 2007)

Many commentators believe that the Congressional Progressive Caucus is an offshoot of Democratic Socialists of America (DSA) which played a role in its formation.

According to Chicago DSA:

> US Senator Bernie Sanders (I-VT) has been charging that these bailouts to regimes that violate worker and civil rights are illegal under a law passed last year by US Senator Bernie Sanders (I-VT) and Barney Frank (D-MA-4th District), both leaders of the Progressive Caucus in Congress, which Democratic Socialists of America (DSA) has helped to organize. (Baiman, New Ground 56 1998)

In 1991/92, the Communist Party USA split, with a third of its members joining forces with other Marxists to found the Committees of Correspondence.

Lee was a member of the COCDS national coordinating committee, alongside her longtime friend, former Communist Party Vice-Presidential candidate, Angela Davis.[40]

In recent years, many COCDS members have drifted back to the Communist Party's orbit, including Rep. Barbara Jean Lee (D-CA-9th District).

In December 2006, US Representative Lee appeared at a Communist Party post-Congressional election function in Northern California.

From the CPUSA *People's Weekly World*:

> Dec. 3 was a day the *People's Weekly World* can celebrate with pride. Still celebrating the results of the Nov. 7 elections, readers held banquets and dinners in various places across the country, attracting elected officials,

---

[40] http://trevorloudon.com/2007/06/angela-davis-to-speak-in-nz/

leaders of people's movements and rank-and-file fighters for justice and democracy. (Bechtel and Johnson)

A highlight of the Northern California banquet in Oakland was...

Other honored guests included anti-nuclear-weapons leader Jackie Cabasso, the Blue Diamond Workers Organizing Committee and two Sacramento-based immigrant rights coalitions. All received certificates from US Representative Barbara Jean Lee (D-CA-9th) as well as from Friends of the *People's Weekly World*/Nuestro Mundo. (Bechtel and Johnson 2006)

Why would a militant socialist like US Representative Barbara Jean Lee (D-CA-9th) want to back a "moderate" like Barack Obama?

7. Barack Obama and the Democratic Socialists of America

Trevor Loudon © Saturday, January 26, 2008

The USA's largest Marxist organization, Democratic Socialists of America,[41] has supported Barack Obama - through its influential Chicago branch.

Ronald Reagan said of the Ku Klux Klan, "Just because they support me, that don't mean I support them."

While Obama has mixed with Democratic Socialists of America (DSA) members for many years, whether in a social or a political context, Obama is careful to avoid Democratic Socialists of America (DSA) sponsored events.

Obama makes an apparent, if obscure, reference to Democratic Socialists of America (DSA) in his 1995 autobiography *"Dreams from My Father."*

Discussing his time studying political science at New York's Columbia University in the 80s, Obama reveals that he "went to socialist conferences at Cooper Union and African cultural fairs in Brooklyn."

---

[41] http://en.wikipedia.org/wiki/Democratic_Socialists_of_America

---

"Cooper Union" is the Cooper Union for the Advancement of Science and Art, a college in Downtown Manhattan that relies on private funds.

For many years, from the 80s until 2004, Cooper Union was the usual venue of the annual Socialist Scholars Conference (SSC).[42]

Was this what Obama referenced? The Socialist Scholars Conference (SSC) was for many years the largest socialist gathering in the USA, attracting up to 2,000 participants.

A group of socialists from City University of New York, led by sociology professor Bogdan Denitch,[43] founded the SSC.

Since Democratic Socialists of America (DSA)'s formation in 1982, its City University branch has sponsored and organized the Socialist Scholars Conference.

Socialist Scholars Conference (SSC)'s organizing committee was populated by Democratic Socialists of America (DSA) members, as were many conference speakers.

Socialist Scholars Conference (SSC) was no love-in for aging hippies and peace loving "democratic" socialists.

Speakers often included members of the Communist Party USA and its offshoot, the Committees of Correspondence, as well as Maoists, Trotskyists, black radicals, gay activists and radical feminists.

Barack Obama speaks of "conferences" plural, indicating his attendance was not the result of accident or youthful curiosity.

In 1983, Obama moved to Chicago to work as a community organizer.

Harold Washington, the city's new Mayor, a longtime associate of the Communist Party and Chicago's socialist community,[44] inspired Obama.

7-1 Bogdan Denitch, a Professor Emeritus at the City University of NY Graduate School Program in Sociology

[42] http://www.pbs.org/heavenonearth/interviews_socialistscholars.html
[43] http://keywiki.org/index.php/Bogdan_Denitch
[44] http://www.chicagodsa.org/d1981/index.html

In 1988, Obama left Chicago to study at Harvard Law School.

Obama returned in 1992 and in 1996, ran for the Illinois State Senate with the endorsement of the Democratic Socialists of America (DSA).

Obama earned the endorsement based on his performance at a Democratic Socialists of America (DSA) sponsored forum held at Chicago University in 1996.

From Chicago DSA's *New Ground* March 1996:

> Over three hundred people attended the first of two Town Meetings on Economic Insecurity on February 25 in Ida Noyes Hall at the University of Chicago. Entitled "Employment and Survival in Urban America," the meeting was sponsored by the University of California Democratic Socialists of America (DSA) Youth Section, Chicago Democratic Socialists of America (DSA) and University Democrats.
>
> The panelists were Toni Preckwinkle, Alderman of Chicago's 4th Ward; Barack Obama, candidate for the 13th Illinois Senate District; Professor William Julius Wilson, Center for the Study of Urban Inequality at the University of Chicago; Professor Michael Dawson, University of Chicago; and Professor Joseph Schwartz, Temple University and a member of Democratic Socialists of America (DSA)'s National Political Committee. (Roman, A Town Meeting on Economic Insecurity: Employment and Survival in Urban America 1996)

7-2 Chicago Socialist Dinner - 1981. Carl Marx Shier (l) a DSA leader and future leader of the Chicago DSA, Egidio Clemente (c) former Socialist Party USA leader, Congressman Harold Washington (r) future Mayor of Chicago.

Toni Preckwinkle and William Julius Wilson (voted one of the twenty-five most influential people in the USA in 1996) have links to Democratic Socialists of America (DSA). Michael Dawson has been a leader of the Democratic Socialists of America (DSA) and Communist Party infiltrated Black Radical Congress.

Barack Obama's flirtation with Democratic Socialists of America (DSA) began in the 80s and continues to this day.

8. Baltimore Communists Back Obama

Trevor Loudon © Monday, January 28, 2008

Baltimore, Maryland man, Tim Wheeler, is one of Barack Obama's biggest fans. He is on the campaign trail with Senator Obama, blogging as he goes.

Wheeler canvassed for his idol[45] in the recent South Carolina primary.

8-1 Barack Obama and Michell on the campaign trail

It is chilly and threatening rain but the media is predicting a record voter turnout of people fired up by Obama's message of hope. I rode down from Baltimore on a bus with 40 other volunteers. Three members of the Maryland General Assembly who have kept us working diligently since we arrived chartered it. Nights we sleep on the gymnasium floor of the Y, strewn with mostly youthful volunteers from as far away as California.

I have been canvassing with a friend, Rev. Pierre Williams, a United Methodist minister in Baltimore. We got a vivid feel for just how deeply Obama's message is resonating here going door-to-door in a working class neighborhood yesterday. (Wheeler, Live Blogging from South Carolina 2008)

Tim Wheeler was in Obama's campaign[46] HQ as the primary results came in:

The Obama people are over the moon. I was at a precinct some four or five miles outside of Columbia, mainly a rural area. And it was a steady stream of over whelming African American voters. There was a feeling of victory in the air.

I'm at the Obama headquarters and you can hear the cheering all over. It's really exciting. (Wheeler, Obama wins big in South Carolina 2008)

Nevertheless, who is this dedicated Obama-fan? Is he a seasoned

---

[45]http://paeditorsblog.blogspot.com/2008/01/live-blogging-from-obamas-campaign-in.html

[46] http://paeditorsblog.blogspot.com/2008/01/obama-wins-big-in-south-carolina.html

8-2 Joyce Wheeler & son

Democratic Party activist or a new convert inspired by the charismatic young Senator from Illinois?

Tim Wheeler[47] is neither; he is a second-generation member of the Communist Party USA. Wheeler is a member of the Communist Party USA National Board and has been a mainstay of the party's Baltimore Club since the '70s. From 1991 to 2003, Tim Wheeler served as editor of the party paper *People's Weekly World* .[48] He is the PWW's national political correspondent.

Does a communist paper have as much right to cover Obama's campaign as any other?

I have posted several times on the CPUSA's long term support for Barack Obama.

This is not historical. This is current. All over the USA Communist Party, members and supporters are swinging in behind Barack Obama. They have been working with and inside[49] the Democratic Party.

The Obama '08 website[50] displayed a copy of the January 21, 2008 - 'Baltimore for Barack' meeting minutes.[51]

Listed are Tim and Joyce Wheeler as prominent members, involved in organizing local canvassing and visibility events.

Joyce Wheeler is a retired schoolteacher and a long time Communist Party activist.

Two other prominent members of "Baltimore for Barack" are Jim and Margaret Baldridge.

Jim Baldridge is a peace activist and Communist Party member.[52] He has also been active in the Democratic Party.

---

[47] http://keywiki.org/index.php/Tim_Wheeler
[48] http://www.peoplesworld.org/
[49] http://trevorloudon.com/2007/06/young-communist-league-infiltrates-us-democrat
[50] http://www.barackobama.com/index.php
[51] http://my.barackobama.com/page/community/blog/timchng
[52] http://keywiki.org/index.php/Jim_Baldridge

In 2004, Baltimore hospital worker, Baldridge, ran as a US Representative Dennis Kucinich (D-OH-10th District)[53] delegate in Maryland's March 2nd Super Tuesday primary.

From the Peoples Weekly World:[54]

> I see the poverty and unemployment up close," Baldridge wrote in an open letter distributed to his neighbors. "A vote for Kucinich is a vote to take back our country from the Halliburton corporate looters, to make the rich pay their share of the taxes … Our school deficit cries out for a President like Representative Dennis Kucinich (D-OH-10th District who will deliver on the promise, 'Leave no child behind.' (Wheeler, Kucinich: the most unreported story of 2004 2004)

Margaret Baldridge[55] is a former executive secretary of the Maryland Communist Party. She has been active in the party since the '70s and was a founder of the Baltimore Committee to Free Angela Davis and another party front, the National Alliance against Racial and Political Repression.

The Wheelers and the Baldridge's are the backbone of the Baltimore Communist Party. In a small town like Baltimore it is inconceivable that the local Democrats do not realize that they have four prominent Communist Party activists working in their midst.

Do they know, but do not care?

The Communist Party has been infiltrating the Democratic Party for decades. In some areas, the Communist Party runs the local Democratic Party machine.

The Communist Party favors Barack Obama over Hillary Clinton or John Edwards.

Why do the Communists favor Obama? How many Party members are working in the Obama campaign? Why do the Democrats not seem to care?

---

[53] http://keywiki.org/index.php/Dennis_Kucinich
[54] http://www.peoplesworld.org/kucinich-the-most-unreported-story-of-2004/
[55] http://keywiki.org/index.php/Margaret_Baldridge

9. Communists Explain Backing for Barack Obama

Trevor Loudon © Friday, February 01, 2008

Why did the Communist Party USA abandon its pretense of neutrality? It is throwing all its energies behind US Senator Barack Obama (D-IL) in the race for the Democratic Party Presidential nomination.

9-1 Terrie Albano

Three top US Communists explain this according to Terrie Albano,[56] editor of the Communist Party USA *People's Weekly World* :

The movement that has exploded around Obama is so important. It is antiracist in essence. It is deep, broad, multiracial, and multigenerational. It has insightful and sophisticated everyday people active in it. It is the cream rising to the top after the long horrendous period of the Bush administration and ultra-right rule since Reagan.

However, even if Obama does not win and Hillary Clinton does, getting rid of any ultra-rightist will take this country forward. Moreover, the movement around Obama will influence Clinton.

This kind of upsurge comes around just once in a lifetime. I hope for all progressives - each of us - get involved. Do not stand on the sidelines. Be active. Do not let history pass you by. (T. Albano 2008)

9-2 Pepe Lozano

Pepe Lozano[57] is a leader of the Chicago Young Communist League and is a People's Weekly World editorial Board member. Pepe Lozano's late father, Rudy Lozano,[58] was a leading Chicago activist until his murder in 1983. Before Lozano's death, Chicago Mayor,

---

[56] http://paeditorsblog.blogspot.com/2008/01/will-progressives-respond.html
[57] http://keywiki.org/index.php/Pepe_Lozano
[58] http://keywiki.org/index.php/Rudy_Lozano

Harold Washington enlisted him as his liaison to the Latino community.

Rudy Lozano played a big role in building the white "progressive" Black-Latino coalition that elected Washington, the first black Mayor of a major US city.

The Communist Party[59] and Chicago's socialist community, which would later coalesce into the Chicago branch of the Democratic Socialists of America, organized this coalition.

Harold Washington was a long time supporter of both groups and a probable secret member of the Communist Party USA. On taking office, he proceeded to stack City Hall with communists, socialists and "progressives."

This socialist "golden age" ended with Washington's death in office in 1987, but the alliance that elected him went on to elect US Senator Carol Moseley Braun (D-IL)[60] to the US Senate in 1992.

It has also supported US Senator Barack Obama (D-IL) at least since his successful State Senate race in 1996.

According to Teresa Albano:

> African Americans and Mexican Americans - and all Latinos - have much to gain in the 2008 elections. There are opportunities for both communities to work together and lead the growing movement for political change in Washington.
>
> The Black-Latino alliance is a major force that brings our communities closer in a world where racism, economic injustice, and inequalities are deeply rooted throughout every aspect of our past and present.
>
> One example of how unity brought progress for everyone was the campaign to elect Harold Washington Mayor of Chicago...
>
> Washington made history that year and put Chicago on the map due to the coalition of Black, Latino, and white progressive forces that culminated in a record turnout of voters...

---

[59] http://trevorloudon.com/2007/10/chicagos-redblack-alliance-targets-white-house/
[60] http://trevorloudon.com/2007/12/carol-moseley-braun-did-clinton-send-us-a-socialist-part-1/

The multiracial coalition for political unity that put Washington in office was in large part due to the Latino vote, which by itself had a record turnout of 62 percent, 82 percent of whom voted for Washington.

Like Harold Washington, US Senator Barack Obama (D-IL), on a much larger scale, could make political history by becoming the first African American President. Moreover, if it wasn't for Washington's example and the coalition forces in Chicago at that time, Obama might not be in the position he is in today. (T. Albano 2008)

While modern Latino's lean heavily towards Hillary Clinton, Lozano believes they can and should be turned Obama's way:

There have been some talk that Mexican Americans and other Latinos aren't going to vote for Obama, that we "aren't ready" to vote for a Black man or we have nothing in common.

It is false to assume that Latinos are not prepared to vote for Obama or that Latinos and Blacks have nothing in common.

Latinos of all nationalities, US born or immigrant, men and women, younger and older, have to be agents of change too and reach out to others. That is what was done during the historic Washington election - and the whole city won with that victory.

9-3 Norman Markowitz

In order to do that we must continue to fight for multiracial unity, and the African American and Latino communities together have to be in the forefront pushing a pro-people agenda.

So let the reactionaries tremble at our unity in action. Together we have nothing to lose but our common oppression. And we have an election to win! (T. Albano 2008)

Contributing editor to the Communist Party USA Political Affairs, Norman Markowitz,[61] hopes that Obama will change the course of US politics.

Progressives seeking to build a national majority coalition that would both end and dismantle nearly thirty years of right-wing political power in the United States suffered a setback (that is all. I think. It can be called) with

---

[61] http://paeditorsblog.blogspot.com/2008/01/edwards-withdraws-some-thoughts-about.html

the apparent announcement that John Edwards is withdrawing his candidacy.

Some, myself included, had hoped that Edwards would stay in, continue to win delegates, and form a coalition with Senator Obama's delegates at the convention to develop both a program and a Presidential slate that would decisively defeat the right-wing Republicans and begin to enact in the 21st century programs like national public health care, substantial increases in minimum wages and other labor and social programs, funded through progressive taxation. (Markowitz, Edwards Withdraws: Some Thoughts About What it Means 2008)

Markowitz believes that Obama will repeat the 1930's. At that time, the Communist Party USA flooded into Franklin Roosevelt's 'New Deal' and pushed the USA far to the left.

Senator Obama has attracted people of progressive views, many of whom have been alienated from politics or are having their first experience with political activities, in a way that few candidates have for a long time.

He is far less of a known commodity, will bring into government independents and progressives from the mass organizations and the communities along with the traditional Democratic organization politicians, as Franklin Roosevelt did during the depression.

Nevertheless, he can, turn his status as an African American, a member of the minority group most stigmatized in US history, into a positive force, becoming in effect a real unifying leader for working class and progressive people of all colors, ethnicities and sexual orientations... (Markowitz, Edwards Withdraws: Some Thoughts About What it Means 2008)

All of these conjectures may be meaningless if Clinton win a large victory in the" "Super Tuesday," which is a good reason for progressives to both vote for and get out the vote for Barrack Obama.

10. Barack Obama and the Socialist "Mafia"

Trevor Loudon © Saturday, February 02, 2008

Most readers have seen Mafia funerals depicted on "*The Sopranos*" or "*The Godfather*" movies.

The FBI is always there, photographing every dapper suited "don" and thuggish looking "soldier." In its war against the Mafia, the FBI knows that funerals are a great opportunity to learn more about the Mob's "order of battle," hierarchy and internal relationships.

Socialist funerals and memorial Services are like that.

In politics, as in other forms of crime, the company you keep may judge you.

On March 13, 1998, Saul Mendelson, a lifelong socialist activist died in Chicago.

Mendelson had been a member of various Trotskyist factions in the 1930's and '40s before joining the US Socialist Party.

In 1958, Mendelson founded the Debs Dinner, an ongoing annual event and highpoint of the Chicago socialist calendar.

Over the years, the dinner has served as a focal point for Chicago's socialist, ex-Trotskyist, ex-communist and left wing Democratic Party community.

In 1983, many of the Debs Dinner crowd helped found a new Marxist organization, the Democratic Socialists of America.

The Debs Dinner crowd consisting of Democratic Socialists of America (DSA) members, in conjunction with the Communist Party, helped elect Chicago's leftist Mayor Harold Washington in 1983, Carol Moseley Braun to the US Senate in 1992 and Barack Obama to the Illinois State Senate in 1996 and to the US Senate in 2004. The same crowd continues to back US Senator Barack Obama (D-IL) in his current bid for the US presidency.

Saul Mendelson was a leader of the Chicago Democratic Socialists of America (DSA) and played a large role in the election of Harold Washington.

The Saul Mendelson Memorial[62] was held on Sunday, March 29, 1998, at the First Unitarian Church, Chicago.

10-1 Saul Mendelson

According to Chicago Democratic Socialists of America (DSA) leader, Carl Marx Shier, who addressed the gathering:

> At the memorial Service held at the 1st Unitarian Church on South Woodlawn, speaker after speaker recounted Saul's contributions.

---

[62] http://www.chicagodsa.org/ngarchive/ng58.html#anchor868634

The Service was ably MC'd by a retired colleague, Bob Clark. I spoke first and was followed by Saul's friend Deborah Meier, a MacArthur Genius Grant recipient who is now starting a new school in Boston. Amy Isaacs, National Director of the ADA, spoke of what Saul had meant on foreign affairs to the ADA.

Other speakers included US Senator Carol Moseley Braun (D-IL), Alderman Toni Preckwinkle, State Senator Barak Obama, Illinois House Majority Leader Barbara Flynn Currie, and a good friend from New York, Myra Russell.

An old friend, Harriet Lefley, who is now Professor of Psychology at the University of Miami Medical School, made the concluding remarks. (Shier 1998)

Deborah Meier was a former Trotskyite and Socialist Party comrade of Saul Mendelson's and a leader of Chicago and Boston Democratic Socialists of America (DSA).

Amy Isaacs was national director of Americans for Democratic Action.[63] In recent years, ADA has close links to Democratic Socialists of America (DSA) and the Democratic Socialists of America (DSA) initiated Congressional Progressive Caucus.[64]

US Senator Carol Moseley Braun (D-IL) [65] was then a US Senator with strong links to both Democratic Socialists of America (DSA) and the Communist Party. Barack Obama helped get her elected in 1992 and then took over her old Senate seat in 2004.

State Senator Barack Obama probably knew Saul Mendelson through his ties to the old communist/socialist infiltrated, Independent Voters of Illinois,[66] in which Mendelson played a leading role.

Alderman Toni Preckwinkle and Illinois House Majority Leader Barbara Flynn Currie are both leftist Democrats with ties to Chicago's socialist community. Both endorsed US Senator Barack Obama (D-IL) in his successful 2004 bid for the US Senate.

Harriet Lefley was a Trotskyist in the 1940s with Saul Mendelson.

---

[63] http://www.adaction.org/pages/about/ada-leadership.php

[64] http://trevorloudon.com/2006/12/progressive-caucus-to-dominate-new-us-congress/

[65] http://trevorloudon.com/2007/12/carol-moseley-braun-did-clinton-send-us-a-socialist-part-1/

[66] http://www.iviipo.org/

Eulogies also came from Quinn Brisben, (Socialist Party Presidential candidate 1976, 1992) and David McReynolds (Socialist Party Presidential candidate 1980, 2000). (Shier, *New Ground*)[58]

Both Brisben and McReynolds are also members of Democratic Socialists of America (DSA).

Ten short years ago, US Senator Barack Obama (D-IL) was up to his ears in the Chicago socialist mafia.

Like the criminal mafia, the socialist version gets what it wants through fraud and other covert means. Deception and underhanded political maneuverings are the socialists' stock in trade.

The US would not want a President who had ties to the criminal mafia.

Why would they want a President with links to the socialist "mob"?

11. Communists Muster Latino Vote for Barack Obama

Trevor Loudon © Wednesday, February 06, 2008

The Communist Party is out to get the Latino vote for US Senator Barack Obama (D-IL).

11-1 Rep. Xavier Becerra (D-CA) (l) and Senate Majority Leader Gloria Romero (D) at east LA college rally for Obama in the East LA Obama office voters Monday (Feb 4). (Photo (c) Rosalio Munoz/Peoples Weekly World

It is an uphill battle, but a crucial one.

Latino Democrats tend to support Hillary Clinton, while Republicans lean towards John McCain because of his liberal positions on immigration and citizenship.

Nevertheless, the Communists are going all out to turn Latino voters into Democratic voters in general and Obama voters in particular.

Senior Communist Party USA member Rosalia Muñoz posted this report today on a party blog:

I'm active in East LA Obama activities, outreach to the neighbor-hoods by phone and shoe leather is mushrooming Obama support, and mania is here it's time to get out the vote all day Super Tuesday. Xavier Becerra is a member of the Communist Party USA Democratic Socialists of America. (R. Munoz 2008)

Gloria Romero is the leftist majority leader of the California State Senate.

Rosalío Muñoz is no party hack, but is an influential communist leader in the USA.

Entrusted by the Communist Party USA, Rosalío campaigned for Obama, to get out the Latino vote for Obama and the Democrats.

11-2 Rosalío Muñoz

Before the 2004 US Presidential elections, the Southern California district of the Communist Party USA organized a "*Socialism, Democracy, and Defeating Bush in 2004*" conference.

Rosalio Muñoz, a Communist Party USA Southern California organizer stated, "It may be possible to trounce Bush in California and, if so, defeat right-wingers in Congress."

He added that ending right-wing control of both houses would create possibilities for real policy changes.

Muñoz is also secretary of the Communist Party USA Mexican American Equality Commission, the party organ dedicated to spreading Communist Party USA influence among Americans of Mexican descent.

The Commission has influence in major trade unions, "community organizations" and Latino organizations across the US South West and California.

From the *People's Weekly World,* March 6, 2004:

> TUCSON, Ariz. - Communist Party leaders and activists met here to discuss plans to bring out the broadest possible Mexican American and Latino vote to defeat the ultra-right in the November elections and to strengthen the Communist Party USA work among this section of the population. The participants at the meeting, held in the Salt of the Earth Labor College on May 15-16, came chiefly from the Southwest and the West Coast.
>
> Lorenzo Torrez, Chair of the Party's Mexican American Equality Commission, reviewed the Commission's work in the recent period. He proposed the organizing of a left-center Latino coalition to mobilize the progressive sentiments of US Latinos.
>
> Rosalío Muñoz, Communist Party USA organizer in Southern California, reported on Latinos and the elections. He noted that the

Presidential race will be decided in key "battleground states.." Arizona, New Mexico, and Colorado, are states where Mexican Americans are concentrated, he said.

> Muñoz proposed that the Communist Party USA put out literature in both Spanish and English explaining what is at stake for Latinos in the upcoming elections. (R. Munoz 2004)

In October 2007, Rosalío Muñoz and Evelina Alarcon, both members of the Communist Party USA Mexican American Equality Commission, joined up to support Obama and the Democrats.

According to an article written for Communidad by Muñoz and a Communist Party USA colleague, Joelle Fishman:

> Some 2000 Latino leaders and activists from throughout the United States came together in Los Angeles October 5-9 to iron out a plan of action and a social justice program of issues for the 2008 elections with the goal of bringing out 10 million Latino voters that can play a decisive role in the Presidential and congressional elections.

> Latinos can be decisive in determining the Presidential electoral in the key battle ground states of "Florida, New Mexico, Arizona, Colorado and Nevada … and congressional elections in twenty states" that can change the political direction of the country said Antonio Gonzalez President of the Southwest Voter Registration Project in opening up the 2nd National Latino Congreso convened by 10 national Latino organizations and hundreds of state and local groups from 22 states.

> "We are going to mobilize massively to reach record levels of Latino vote" on the key issues of immigration reform, the war, greening cities, health care and climate change declared Gonzalez. While recognizing that "today we don't have a critical mass to affect that change," Gonzalez said this can be achieved with "conscious thinking, planning and organizing" leading up to the 2008 elections." "We have big issues not only as Latinos but as citizens of the world," he concluded. (11)

Rosalío Muñoz is a leader of the Southern California Latino activist community. He is active in the peace movement and on immigration issues.

His relationships with the Southern California Democratic Party and the influential Los Angeles labor movement are strong.

If anyone can muster the Latino vote for Barack Obama (D-IL), it is Rosalío Muñoz and his loyal comrades.

12. Jan Schakowsky-Barack Obama's Loyal Socialist Supporter

Trevor Loudon © Sunday, February 10, 2008

At the 2004, 46th Annual Eugene V. Debs-Norman Thomas dinner[67] in Chicago, Illinois, US Representative Jan Schakowsky (D-IL-9th District) tells the story of a meeting in Washington with US President George W. Bush. The Congressional Black Caucus had demanded a meeting with President Bush to discuss the situation in Haiti.

An invitation extended to Schakowsky because of her strong interest in the issue.

> Bush finally, at the insistence of caucus members, made it to this meeting and spent enough time to display his ignorance of the issue. He noticed Jan, a lone white face, and seemed to "jump back" when he saw her button Osama? No, Mr. President Barack Obama, and you'll be hearing from him when he becomes the Senator from Illinois. (Baiman, The Dump Bush Dinner 2004)

US Representative Jan Schakowsky (D-IL-9th District) supported US Senator Barack Obama (D-IL) in his 2004 US Senate bid. She continues to be one of his most ardent supporters today.

Schakowsky does everything to help her hero, from organizing phone banks[68] in Obama's Chicago HQ, to praising his anti-Iraq War stance on YouTube.

According to Wikipedia:

> Schakowsky has been outspoken in her opposition to the Iraq War. She was one of the earliest and most emphatic supporters of US Senator Barack Obama (D-IL) prior to his victory in the 2004 Illinois Democratic primary election, and is actively supporting his bid for the 2008 Democratic Presidential nomination. (Wikipedia contributors 2008)

The purpose of this series is to show that US Senator Barack Obama (D-IL) is no moderate.

He comes from and is supported by the far left of the Democratic

---

[67] http://www.chicagodsa.org/d2004.html
[68] http://my.barackobama.com/page/event/detail/4vr3w

Party and their Marxist allies in Democratic Socialists of America.[69]

> Schakowsky is one of the most liberal members of Congress, and one of the most (by some accounts, the most) liberal members of the Illinois delegation. She is a member of the Congressional Progressive Caucus. She frequently gains ratings of between 90 and 100 from liberal and progressive interest groups and ratings in the low single digits from conservative groups. (Wikipedia contributors 2008)

US Representative Jan Schakowsky (D-IL-9th District) is an influential politician and knows how to trade favor for favor.

She is close to Speaker of the House, Nancy Pelosi.[70]

From Discover the Networks:

> Schakowsky is a close ally of fellow Progressive Caucus member Nancy Pelosi and was an early backer of the San Francisco Congresswoman's successful bid to become House Minority Leader. Pelosi rewarded Schakowsky with the powerful position of Chief Deputy Minority Whip and a seat on the Democratic Steering Committee that decides which committee assignments go to each House Democrat. Schakowsky sits on the Energy & Commerce Committee and is ranking member of its Trade & Consumer Protection Subcommittee. (Horowitz 2008)

The Congressional Progressive Caucus,[71] seventy or more leftist US Congressmen and women, were partially organized by Democratic Socialists of America.

US Representative Jan Schakowsky (D-IL-9th District) has been moving in socialist circles since at least the '70s. A young Farm Workers union leader named Eliseo Medina then recruited her to help with the famous Chicago grape boycott.

A lifelong socialist, Medina is today Executive Vice President of the Service Employees International Union (SEIU), an honorary Chair[72] of Democratic Socialists of America and a supporter of the Communist Party USA newspaper, *People's Weekly World*.

---

[69] http://www.dsausa.org/dsa.html
[70] http://trevorloudon.com/2006/11/a-plane-crash-and-a-decent-heart-attack-away/
[71] http://trevorloudon.com/2006/12/progressive-caucus-to-dominate-new-us-congress/
[72] http://www.dsausa.org/about/structure.html

Medina and Schakowsky crossed paths again at the 2004 Debs-Thomas-Harrington Dinner. Organized by the Democratic Socialists of America, the annual dinner is a major annual gathering of Chicago's Marxist left, much of whom are US Senator Barack Obama (D-IL) supporters. Eliseo Medina[73] is at the dinner while US Representative Jan Schakowsky (D-IL-9th District) was keynote speaker.

12-1 Elseo Medina (l) and Carl Marx Shier (r)

From Chicago DSA's *New Ground*:

> Carl Shier introduced the second honoree, SEIU Executive Vice President Eliseo Medina. Shier first met Medina when Medina was a young man sent to Chicago by Cesar Chavez to organize the UFW's grape boycott in Chicago on $5 dollars a week. Medina worked miracles (including roping young suburban women like US Representative Jan Schakowsky (D-IL-9th District) into the effort). (Baiman, The Dump Bush Dinner 2004)

Neither Medina nor Schakowsky were strangers to the Debs Dinner socialist set.

Eliseo Medina,[74] while in Chicago organizing the grape boycott, thanked US Representative Jan Schakowsky (D-IL-9th District)[75] for her work in Congress and the community.

According to Discovering the Networks:

> Schakowsky in 2004 co-sponsored a bill to ease trade restrictions against the Communist dictatorship in Cuba. In 2002 Schakowsky joined 44 other members of Congress, all but two of whom were Democrats, in signing a letter to Secretary of State Colin Powell alleging human rights violations by the Government of Colombia

12-2 Jan Schakowsky receiving her 2000 Debs Dinner Award from DSA leader the late Carl Marx Shier

---

[73] http://www.chicagodsa.org/d2004.html#anchor1365566
[74] http://www.chicagodsa.org/d1975/index.html
[75] http://www.chicagodsa.org/d2000.html

in its war against the drug-running guerrilla terrorist Colombian Revolutionary Armed Forces, FARC, established as the military wing of the Colombian Communist Party.

This letter, published worldwide and used as pro-FARC anti-Government of Colombia propaganda, made no mention of FARC's thousands of murders, atrocities and support from Fidel Castro and from Venezuela's Marxist caudillo Hugo Chavez. The letter urged Secretary Powell "to take our concerns into account when determining whether to approve additional military aid for Colombia this year."

Like most leftwing members of Congress, Schakowsky voted against the use of force in Iraq but also against allowing oil drilling on a scant 20 acres of the 1.2 million acre Arctic National Wildlife Refuge (ANWR), thus voting to keep America dependent on Middle Eastern oil while opposing efforts to make that region politically democratic and stable.

Nearly 60 percent of Schakowsky's Political Action Committee (PAC) contributions come from organized labor. Among her biggest individual donors are the Teamsters Union, public employee unions as the American Federation of State, County and Municipal Employees (AFSCME) and the Service Employees International Union (SEIU), the Association of Trial Lawyers of America (ATLA), and the AFL-CIO, whose President John Sweeney is a card-carrying member of Democratic Socialists of America.. (Horowitz 2008)

US Representative House Speaker Nancy Pelosi (D-CA-8th District) gave US Representative Jan Schakowsky (D-IL-9th District) some powerful positions in return for her support. If Jan Schakowsky were not a Congresswoman, she would struggle to get a security clearance to clean latrines at any US military base.

What high position might President Barack H. Obama give his loyal supporter US Representative Jan Schakowsky (D-IL-9th District)?

Schakowsky and Obama's Chicago socialist friends will be happy.

13. Top Communist Not Fooled By Obama's Critics

Trevor Loudon © Wednesday, February 13, 2008

Norman Markowitz[76] is a professor of history at Rutgers University, New Jersey.

He is also a leading member of the Communist Party USA and a contributing editor to the party theoretical journal Political Affairs. He is also, like the rest of his party,[77] a strong supporter of US Senator Barack Obama (D-IL). Those stupid or naive souls who call Barack Obama a centrist, a moderate or a tool of big business, do not fool him. Norman Markowitz knows better.

13-1 Norman Markowitz

He knows that US Senator Barack Obama (D-IL) stands with the socialists. Norman Markowitz writing in the Political Affairs editor's blog:

> Senator Obama Continues to Mobilize People for Progressive Change

> Elections are, among other things exercises in mobilizing masses of people to advance politically, not only electing individuals and parties to ostensibly represent the people. Barack Obama is campaigning for substantive progressive change and he is making change, confounding mass media week to week...

> Obama's speech in the aftermath of the primary was a continuation of his clear, focused and eloquent call for unity and active commitment to a progressive program. The people were listening if the media was not.

> I wrote an article recently on Obama's background and policies... let me say that I was surprised, in doing research for it, on how really progressive a candidate Obama is, and how the media and especially

---

[76]
http://history.rutgers.edu/index.php?option=com_content&task=view&id=174&Itemid=140
[77] Chapter 1 - Forget Islam – Look at Obama's Socialism!

sections of the left have refused to take him seriously, preferring instead to play out their fixed ideas as the political landscape changes before them.

I was surprised because I had listened to the endless comments about his vagueness, the rich and powerful among his supporters...

But, like Robert Wagner who came out of New York's Tammany Hall and was the major sponsor of the National Labor Relations Act (still the most significant piece of pro-labor legislation in history). (Markowitz, Senator Obama Continues to Mobilize People for Progressive Change 2008)

Obama is convincing more and more people that he can answer Lenin's question, "What is to be Done?" with the answer that Franklin Roosevelt gave when he rallied American workers to win the battle of production during World War II, "It Can be Done because It Must be Done."

14. Socialist Led Mega - Union Backs Barack Obama

Trevor Loudon © Saturday, February 16, 2008

Socialists and the Marxists from Democratic Socialists of America[78] and the Communist Party USA now dominate the US union movement.

Their intention is to use union money, muscle, and labor to move the US government further down the socialist road.

US Senator Barack Obama (D-IL)[79] and the Chicago branch of the Democratic Socialists and their Communist Party allies[80] support one another.

The Democratic Socialists of America (DSA) and Communist Party USA[81] regard Barack Obama as sympathetic to their cause. For that reason, many socialist led unions[82] are backing US Senator Barack Obama's (D-IL) Presidential bid.

Now one of the United States largest and most influential labor

---

[78] http://www.dsausa.org/dsa.html
[79] Chapter 7 - Barack Obama and the Democratic Socialists of America
[80] Chapter 1 - Forget Islam – Look at Obama's Socialism!
[81] Chapter 9 - US Communists Explain Backing For Barack Obama
[82] Chapter 3 - Socialist Unionists Endorse Barack Obama

organizations, the Service Employees International Union (SEIU),[83] has thrown its weight behind Obama's campaign.

14-1 Andy Stern

From the Communist Party USA Political Affairs Editors Blog, Andy Stern, the Service Employees International Union (SEIU)'s President:

"There has never been a fight in Illinois or a fight in the nation where our members have not asked Barack Obama for assistance and he has not done everything he could to help us." (Wendland 2008)

SEIU announced today its endorsement of Barack Obama for President.

A press statement by the union adds:

Nurses, childcare workers, janitors, and other Service workers endorsed Sen. Barack Obama for President today, calling him the candidate with the best vision, best plan, and best strategy to lead the country to a new American Dream. (SEIU 2008)

SEIU members are supporting Obama with an aggressive political effort. With more than 150,000 members in the upcoming primary states, including Wisconsin, Ohio, Pennsylvania, Rhode Island and Texas, SEIU will mobilize thousands to go door-to-door, work the phones and will send mail about their support for Obama. SEIU also will have a substantial presence on television and radio in every critical state.

Stern stated:

"Barack Obama is creating the broadest and deepest coalition of voters we've ever seen." (Wendland 2008)

Anna Burger, secretary-treasurer of SEIU and Chair of the Change to Win federation of unions that includes SEIU, said:

"This is one of the most important Presidential elections workers have faced. Families are struggling, we're fighting two wars, and majorities of Americans are now worried that their children will be worse off than

---

[83] http://www.seiu.org/

they are. Obama is the right person at the right time to lead the change we so desperately need in our country." (Wendland 2008)

14-2 Gerry Hudson

This is a huge coup in Obama's struggle with the Clinton's, but the SEIU leadership links to the Democratic Socialists of America (DSA).

According to Discover the Networks:

Some SEIU activists boast that they are the "new CIO," referring to the radical, class-warfare Congress of Industrial Organizations (CIO) before Walter Reuther purged it of its most toxic Communist leaders as a condition of merging with the more moderate, boost-worker-wages-oriented American Federation of Labor to create the AFL-CIO in 1955. Today's SEIU "leaders tend to be radical, even socialist," wrote Ryan Lizza, Associate Editor of The New Republic in 2003. (Ponte 2004)

SEIU President Andy Stern gained his current position when his mentor, "card carrying" Democratic Socialists of America (DSA) member John Sweeney, left the job to take on the US labor movement's top job - President of the AFL-CIO.

Stern is a former New Leftist who came out of the University of Pennsylvania. Steve Max gave one of the eulogies at a Democratic Socialists of America memorial after the death of Democratic Socialists of America (DSA) co-founder Michael Harrington., Steve Max, the Midwest Academy's Director of Organizing, and Training, gave tribute to "the people who worked with or fought with Mike who now staff high councils of the American Federation of Labor (AFL), like Andy Stern of SEIU."

Stern is one of many radical union organizers who came out of the Midwest Academy. The Academy founded by onetime Students for a Democratic Society (SDS) members Paul and Heather Booth to train community organizers and infiltrate the labor movement. (Ponte 2004)

According to the Freedom Road Socialist Organization, the Midwest Academy:[84]

---

[84] http://www.midwestacademy.com/

Probably the most well-known organizing method is Alinskyism, named after Saul Alinsky, a Chicago-born community organizer who helped set up the Back of the Yards Neighborhood Council and later the Industrial Areas Foundation in the 1930s. (Today in New York Alinskyism can be found in groups that do neighborhood-based organizing like ACORN, Mothers on the Move, TICO as well as NYPIRG).

The Mid-West Academy is a training center set up by members of Democratic Socialists of America (DSA) [Democratic Socialists of America] that draws heavily from Alinskyism. (Freedom Road Socialist Organization 2008)

Barack Obama was a disciple of Alinsky while working as a "community organizer" in Chicago in the '80s. Later Obama did considerable legal work for the radical community group ACORN, linked to the Midwest Academy.

ACORN and Chicago Democratic Socialists of America (DSA) formed the backbone of the leftist New Party, which Obama worked with during his successful 1996 Illinois State Senate bid.

Steve Max, associate director for the Midwest Academy, is a Democratic Socialists of America (DSA) Vice-Chair, while academy founder Heather Booth[85] and current executive director Jackie Kendall[86] both have close ties to Chicago Democratic Socialists of America (DSA).

SEIU Vice-President Gerry Hudson is also close to DSA.

The January 2007 Boston Democratic Socialists of America (DSA) newsletter advertised the Young Democratic Socialists of America (DSA) conference in New York.

"Democracy and Socialism in the 21st Century." Speakers include Noam Chomsky, Barbara Ehrenreich, former Boston Democratic Socialists of America (DSA) Chair Joe Schwartz and possibly Jerry Hudson of SEIU 1199, among others. (Freedom Road Socialist Organization 2008)

Chomsky and Ehrenreich are also Democratic Socialists of America (DSA) members and it is likely that Hudson is at least a sympathizer. In February 1996, Schwarz spoke alongside Barack Obama at a Young Democratic Socialists of America (DSA) organized forum at the

---

[85] http://www.chicagodsa.org/d1987/index.html
[86] http://www.chicagodsa.org/d1999.html#anchor703644

University of Chicago.

Another SEIU Vice President, Eliseo Medina, is both an honorary Chair of Democratic Socialists of America (DSA)[87] and a supporter of the Communist Party newspaper, *People's Weekly World* . Medina was involved with Chicago Democratic Socialists of America (DSA) in 1975,[88] working on the farm workers union "grape boycott".

While there, he recruited a young US Representative, Jan Schakowsky (D-IL-9th District), to the union cause. Schakowsky also has close ties to Chicago Democratic Socialists of America (DSA) and is one of Barack Obama's key supporters in the US Congress.

Such is the incestuous world of US labor/left politics.

---

15. Socialist Octogenarians for Barack

Trevor Loudon © Wednesday, February 20, 2008

Barack Obama is a creation of the Chicago far left. He is the product of a radical alliance[89] that elected Chicago's Marxist Mayor, Harold Washington in 1983 and Illinois' socialist US Senator Carol Moseley

Braun (D-IL)[90] in 1992. Since Obama's first Illinois State Senate race in 1996, the coalition supported his campaigns.

Though a Democrat, he has long been supported by Chicago members of the Communist Party,[91] its offshoot, the Committees of Correspondence for Democracy and Socialism and the extreme Democratic Socialists of America.

14-3 Eliseo Medina, Vice President SEIU

Two of Obama's Chicago comrades have supported him for many years. Both are octogenarian icons of the Chicago far left. They move in the same circles

---

[87] http://www.dsausa.org/about/structure.html

[88] http://www.chicagodsa.org/d1975/index.html

[89] http://trevorloudon.com/2007/10/chicagos-redblack-alliance-targets-white-house/

[90] http://trevorloudon.com/2007/12/carol-moseley-braun-did-clinton-send-us-a-socialist-part-1/

[91] http://trevorloudon.com/2007/06/why-do-the-communists-back-barack/

and have crossed paths in many campaigns. One has backed off in disappointment at Obama's movement to the "right." The other still stands behind their man.

Dr. Quentin Young is a leading national campaigner for "Single Payer" socialized medicine. Young has been active in Chicago socialist circles since the 1930's. In the 1960's, he was Martin Luther King's personal physician. In the '80s, Young was rewarded with the post of President of the Chicago Board of Health and was a leading member of Harold Washington's inner circle.

15-1 Dr. Quentin Young at the 1992 Debs dinner

In 1992, Chicago Democratic Socialists of America awarded their most well-known member[92] with their highest honor - the Debs Award[93]:

> You have been there in the struggles for Civil Rights, for social and economic justice, and against all forms of discrimination. You were there in 1951 to fight against discrimination in Chicago medical institutions. You were there in 1983 for Harold Washington to win the Mayoralty. You were there when Carol Moseley Braun announced her intention to run for the US Senate. You have demonstrated your understanding that trade unions are a social force for Progress and Justice in our country.

> For your dedication in the fight for universal and comprehensive health care for all and for your lifetime commitment to change our society to the better, the Debs-Thomas-Harrington Dinner Committee hereby presents to you its annual award this First Day of May 1992. (Chicago Democratic Socialist of America 1992)

In the 1990's and 2000's, Obama and Young were on the same page.

Obama also advocated "Single Payer" health case. As a State Senator, Obama and another leftist colleague and Illinois State Representative, William Delgado, presented The Health Care Justice Act to the Illinois House and Senate.

According to blog Thomas Paine's Corner:

---

[92] http://keywiki.org/index.php/Quentin_Young
[93] http://www.chicagodsa.org/d1992/index.html

Barack Obama is familiar with the concepts and the specific merits of Single Payer. Back in the late 1990s, when he was an Illinois State Senator representing a mostly black district on the south side of Chicago, he took pains to consistently identify himself publicly with his neighbor Dr. Quentin Young.

He signed on as co-sponsor of the Bernardin Amendment, named after Chicago's late Catholic Archbishop, who championed the public policy idea that medical care was a human right, not a commodity. At that time, when it was to his political advantage, Obama didn't mind at all being perceived as an advocate of Single Payer. (Dixon 2007)

In an interview with *Healthcare Now*,[94] Quentin Young explains his changed relationship with Barack Obama:

"I knew him before he was political," Young says of Obama. "I supported him when he ran for State Senate. When he was a state Senator he did say that he supported Single Payer. Now, he hedges. Now he says, if we were starting from scratch, he would support Single Payer."

"Barack's a smart man," Young says. "He probably calculated the political cost for being for Single Payer - the shower of opposition from the big boys - the drug companies and the health insurance companies. And so, like the rest of them, he fashioned a Hodge podge of a health insurance plan." (Goodman 2009)

Young said that the last time he spoke with Obama was in 2005. In January 2005, Obama voted to confirm Condoleeza Rice as Secretary of State.

"When I heard about the vote, I wrote him a letter," Young said. "I told him I was disappointed in him. Rice was the embodiment of everything that was wrong with this administration. So, he called me back and he said - why didn't you pick up the phone and call me? In addition, he said - do you think Bush would ever send to the Senate a nominee for Secretary of State who I could vote for? I said - you are the Constitutional lawyer. It's about advice and consent, right? You should have denied him your consent."

Young says that none of the leading Democratic Presidential candidates supports Single Payer. (Goodman 2009)

---

[94]
http://www.democracynow.org/2009/3/11/dr_quentin_young_obama_confidante_and

Dr. Young is looking for an alternative.

One who is not looking for an alternative is Chicago historian, Timuel Black, a longtime friend and admirer of Barack Obama.

Young Timuel Black became interested in socialism in the 1930's. He was inspired by Communist Party street speakers Claude Lightfoot and Ishmael Flory.

Black became an active unionist in the late 1930's and associated with Communists and Trotskyites.

On joining, the US Army in World War II denied Black officer training because military intelligence claimed he had joined the Communist Party, a charge Black still denies.

After the war, the Chicago Police Department's anti-radical "Red Squad" monitored Black's activities for many years.

Black was active in the Communist Party infiltrated Progressive Party in the late 1940's.

Later, he served as Assistant Coordinator of the National Teacher Corps, the Teachers Committee for Quality Education and the Congress of Racial Equality.

He became President of the local chapter of the communist controlled Negro American Labor Council.

In the '80s, Timuel Black led the campaign to register 250,000 voters to help elect Chicago Mayor Harold Washington.

Black also held leadership roles in the Justice Coalition of Greater Chicago and the Chicago Committee to Defend the Bill of Rights. He is active in the anti-Iraq War, Peace Action Committee.

In the 1970s, Timuel Black was involved with the annual Chicago Debs Day Dinners,[95]

15-2 Timuel Black

the highpoint of the Illinois socialist calendar. At that time, dinner was run by remnants of the Socialist Party USA. After 1982, the event was

---

[95] http://www.chicagodsa.org/dthdin.html

taken over by the newly formed Democratic Socialists of America. Timuel Black helped sponsor the event in 1970 (with well-known writer Saul Bellow,) 1976 and 1977.

At the 1989 Debs Dinner,[96] Timuel Black presented an award to ex-communist Democratic Socialists of America (DSA) member Milton Cohen, while the speaker was Democratic Socialists of America (DSA) member Quentin Young. The Master of Ceremonies for the evening was Chicago Alderman Danny K. Davis, a Democratic Socialists of America (DSA) member, current US Congressman and associate of Barack Obama. Democratic Socialists of America (DSA) leader Carl Marx Shier also presented an award to Democratic Socialists of America (DSA) member William Winpisinger. While not revealed at the time, Timuel Black too, is a DSA member. Mr. Black has not abandoned socialism.

Timuel Black serves on the advisory Board[97] of the Communist Party breakaway organization, Committees of Correspondence for Democracy and Socialism, alongside former communists black radical Angela Davis and leftist folk singer Pete Seeger. COCDS has long worked with Democratic Socialists of America (DSA) and there is considerable cross membership.

Another COCDS advisory Board member, Manning Marable, is a former Democratic Socialists of America (DSA) leader, while yet another, linguist and activist Noam Chomsky, is a Democratic Socialists of America (DSA) member. Timuel Black has known Barack Obama since at least 1996. That year he attempted to mediate a dispute between leftist Illinois State Senator Alice Palmer and her anointed successor Obama.

Alice Palmer promised Obama the seat if she was successful in a run for the US Congress. She lost her bid for office and Obama refused to stand aside. Obama, unopposed, went on to win the seat after getting all his opponents (including Palmer) disqualified on the grounds of voting technicalities:[98]

---

[96] http://www.chicagodsa.org/d1989/index.html
[97] http://www.keywiki.org/index.php/Timuel_Black
[98]http://www.chicagotribune.com/news/politics/obama/chi-070403obama-ballot-archive,0,5693903.story

"I liked Alice Palmer a lot. I thought she was a good public servant," Obama said. "It was awkward. That part of it I wish had played out entirely differently." (Jackson and Long 2008)

His choice divided veteran Chicago political activists.

"There was friction about the decision he made," said City Colleges of Chicago professor emeritus Timuel Black, who tried to negotiate with Obama on Palmer's behalf. "There were deep disagreements." (Jackson and Long 2008)

Timuel Black became an admirer of the ambitious young politician, despite the mess. For most Americans, the 2004 Democratic National Convention was their introduction to Obama. "My first impression is this is a brilliant young man," Black said.

Black said Obama's biggest obstacle would not be from whites, but from blacks.

The biggest thing he has to face is the accusations by some blacks that he is not black enough," he said. "He has to overcome that without being so black that he alienates potential white supporters. (Black 2007)

Timuel Black addressed a black audience at the Woodson Regional Library auditorium on Feb. 11, 2007.

Speaking of US Senator Barack Obama (D-IL)'s Presidential campaign, Timuel Black said:

Obama is the test of how deep racism is in this country...Barack is the recipient of the struggle of other generations...That means that you feel proud of your ancestors, your successes...(Obama), based on the opportunities that were opened to him by others, is in the position to prove to the world whether the United States of America is a true democracy, or is a continuing hypocrisy. (Holderness 2008)

US Senator Barack Obama (D-IL)'s political heritage comes not from the struggles of Black America, but from the street agitators, back-room dealers and influence peddlers of Red Chicago.

16. Barack Obama and the Legacy of Harold Washington

Friday, February 22, 2008

Barack Obama did not rise to prominence from nowhere.

An alliance of Chicago socialists groomed Obama for the national

16-2 Pepe Lozano

stage.

This coalition,[99] comprised of the Communist Party USA, their Marxist comrades from Democratic Socialists of America and the far left of the Democratic Party, has been influential in Chicago since the 1980's.

The coalition came together in 1982/83 to elect Chicago's first black Mayor Harold Washington. A Democratic Party Congressman, Washington bravely and successfully ran for Mayor against the previously invincible Daley machine.

Washington died in office in 1987, but his coalition remained intact and went on to elect US Senator Carol Moseley Braun (D-IL)[100], to the US Senate in 1992.

That same coalition groomed the young Barack Obama. It has broadened out across the USA and plans to put their man into the White House.

Writing in the latest *People's Weekly World* , Chicago Young Communist League leader, and US Senator Barack Obama (D-IL) fan, Pepe Lozano gives some history of the 1983 Washington campaign and touches on its relevance to Obama's campaign:

> Washington's election was the outcome of a multi-racial citywide coalition beginning within the African American community. Then immediately he included the involvement of Latino and white working-class communities representing a progressive and independent reform movement that eventually carried him to victory.
>
> One thing that has been unsung was how the Chicago labor movement, especially Black trade unionists, led the way in registering tens of thousands of

16-1 Carl Marx Shier, Egidio Clemente and Harold Washington

[99] http://trevorloudon.com/2007/10/chicagos-redblack-alliance-targets-white-house/
[100] http://trevorloudon.com/2007/12/carol-moseley-braun-did-clinton-send-us-a-socialist-part-1/

new voters, including a recruitment drive of petition signers, door knockers, phone bankers and an army of volunteer foot-soldiers on Election Day.

It was precisely labor's role in Chicago that helped shape Washington's campaign turning it into a broad people's movement that revolutionized the city's Democratic machine politics under former Chicago Mayor Richard J. Daley.

Washington was a progressive leader who stood up for working people's causes including the peace movement, civil, immigrant rights, and especially the rights of workers.

By 1983 when Washington decided to run for Mayor, he was a respected member of Congress and became an important ally in progressive political circles throughout Chicago. Still, many people in the city's political machine just didn't believe an African American could win. And some - deeply influenced by racism - were extremely hostile to the idea of a Black Mayor. (Lozano 2008)

Washington had ties to the Communist Party since the 1940s and was also closely associated with the Marxists who went on to form Democratic Socialists of America in 1982.

These Marxists organized a major dinner every year to honor US socialist leaders, Eugene Debs, Norman Thomas and Michael Harrington.

Mayor Harold Washington MC'd the 1981 Debs Dinner,[101] but had to cancel out of the 1983 event.[102]

The 1983 Norman Thomas - Eugene V. Debs Dinner held at the McCormick Inn on Saturday, May 7, Mayor Harold Washington was unable to attend at the last minute. Carl Shier, who was to have introduced him, read a message from him instead, and spoke of Democratic Socialists of America (DSA)'s considerable role in Washington's election campaign.

Despite the racism, Black unionists formed a labor coalition for Harold Washington.

Before the 1983 Mayoral primary, the Chicago Teachers Union held a delegates' meeting where pro-Washington campaign literature including

---

[101] http://www.chicagodsa.org/d1981/index.html
[102] http://www.chicagodsa.org/d1983/index.html

"Washington for Mayor" buttons were passed out before a motion was made to have the union endorse his run.

During the meeting, teachers were chanting Washington's name, and the white and Black union leadership had no choice but to endorse him with overwhelming support. After that, support for Washington started steam rolling within some of the city's unions.

Leaders of the Coalition of Black Trade Unionists (CBTU), including Service workers and Teamsters, endorsed Washington. CBTU made up of integrated unions with white, Black, Latino, and Asian memberships that pressed the Chicago Federation of Labor to endorse Washington in the 1983 general election.

We saw Washington as a viable candidate and we endorsed him wholeheartedly, and we felt he was more qualified than those before him," said Elwood Flowers who just retired as Vice President of the Illinois AFL-CIO and was a close friend of Washington. "But we as labor were just one arm of the Washington movement." (Lozano 2008)

Union endorsements and support are a large part of the momentum building behind US Senator Barack Obama (D-IL) in his campaign for the Democratic nomination. Obama's campaign is Chicago 1983 "up sized."."

A number of African American labor leaders who were important allies for Washington and played influential roles in his administration, Flowers said. For example, he cited Charles Hayes, Vice President of the United Packinghouse Workers Union (now known as the United Food and Commercial Workers union), who won Washington's seat in the 1st District, a powerhouse African American community on the city's south side, after Washington was elected Mayor.

Other notable allies of Washington at that time included Addie Wyatt, who was the first African American woman Vice President of the Packinghouse Workers, and Jim Wright, who was the first Black director of United Auto Workers Region 4. Jackie Vaughn, the President of the Chicago Teachers Union and first African American to hold that post, was also instrumental in Washington's administration. All were leading members of CBTU.

The Coalition of Black Trade Unionists[103] is a Communist Party/socialist front.

Charles Hayes helped Washington win the Mayoralty and take over

---

[103] http://keywiki.org/index.php/Coalition_of_Black_Trade_Unionists

his congressional seat. Less than a decade later, Barack Obama helped Carol Moseley Braun win a seat in the US Senate; he occupied the same seat in 2004.

Like many black trade unionists of the era, Hayes was a long time secret member of the Communist Party, whilst Harold Washington had a long record with Communist Party fronts.

From the late '70s on, Hayes was also involved with the Debs Dinner socialist set.

Addie Watt was a regular sponsor of the Debs Dinners in the late '70s and was herself honored with a Debs Award in 1979.[104]

Jackie Vaughn headed the re-elect Harold Washington Campaign in 1986 and was honored for her work at that year Debs Dinner:[105]

> In the predominantly Latino communities of Pilsen and Little Village, my father, the late Rudy Lozano was also a key ally in Washington's labor-based coalition.
>
> He was also a community activist and decided to run for alderman in the 22nd Ward, a predominantly Mexican and Mexican American neighborhood. Although he narrowly lost, Lozano was a rising political star and leader that advocated for multi-racial coalitions and worker unity. He rallied and mobilized the Latino constituent base to vote for Washington.
>
> Lozano understood the need for Black, Latino and white working class unity, the importance of union solidarity including undocumented immigrant workers. Lozano's independent and grassroots-based organizing, along with Washington's Mayoral victory, sparked a movement throughout Chicago's Latino communities, which did not have any representation in City Council. Washington's victory galvanized the majority of the Latino electorate and soon new Latino leaders emerged as viable elected officials under his administration. (Lozano 2008)

16-3 Congressman Charles Hayes (l), Jacque (Jackie) Vaughn (c) and DSA founder Michael Harrington at the 1986 Debs Dinner

---

104 http://www.chicagodsa.org/d1979/index.html
105 http://www.chicagodsa.org/d1986/index.html

In 1983, Rudy Lozano,[106] known to be close to the Communist Party, was murdered.

> Twenty-five years later the struggle for workers' rights and the fight for multi-racial unity continues - perhaps not on the same level that Washington was able to achieve - but it continues. Witness the 2007 aldermanic elections where labor-backed candidates won and helped to strengthen the City Council. (Lozano 2008)

The Communist Party backed several successful candidates in last year's Chicago municipal elections.

> The movement to elect US Senator Barack Obama (D-IL) today is almost identical to Washington's, but nationwide, said Flowers. "Our members wanted to be involved in the political process, similar to people today for Obama," said Flowers.

> "What Obama can do for the country will help all communities including providing jobs and health care. And the number one issue is stopping the Iraq War, which is draining our economic resources. If those things bear fruit, then they will benefit all working-class communities," he added.

> It was Washington's example and the power of working people that will always remind us about what is possible. The greatness is in our hands. (Lozano 2008) Harold Washington's Chicago Mayoral campaign victory inspired a young Barack Obama to move to Chicago. (Lozano 2008)

Will Harold Washington's political legacy, now send US Senator Barack Obama (D-IL) to the Whitehouse?

17. Major Union Federation Endorses Barack Obama - More Socialist Links

Trevor Loudon © Saturday, February 23, 2008

A major labor union federation, Change to Win (CtW),[107] endorsed US Senator Barack Obama (D-IL).[108]

---

[106] http://www.chicagotribune.org/Markers/Lozano.htm
[107] http://www.changetowin.org/
[108]
http://www.changetowin.org/connect/2008/02/fired_up_ready_to_go_change_to.html

---

Their six million members, muscle and money, may be enough to clinch the Democratic nomination for Obama. That is their stated objective.

From the Communist Party USA's *People's Weekly World* 02/22/08:

17-1 Make the American Dream a Reality

Citing his promise to re-negotiate the North American Free Trade Agreement (NAFTA) and saying that it is time for the race for the Democratic Presidential nomination to end, the seven unions, six million members *Change to Win* federation, on Feb. 21, endorsed Sen. Barack Obama.

In a telephone conference with reporters, CtW Chair Anna Burger said the federation acted now, essentially, to push Obama to wins in the coming primaries, including Texas and Ohio.

"One reason we endorsed now is because we think we can make a difference," Burger said. "It's time to bring this process to a close. There's a movement building here and the winds of change are blowing for Barack Obama, and it could possibly be time for Hillary Clinton to recognize they're blowing for him. We're hoping to get to that point sooner than later."

"Obama's stands on trade, on achieving the American Dream and on the war in Iraq - he was against it even while in the Illinois state senate before entering the US Senate - really resonated with our members," Burger continued.

The CtW endorsement means that four of its seven unions - SEIU, UFCW, Teamsters and UNITE HERE - are joining forces now to make phone calls, leaflet and canvass in the upcoming primary states. The Laborers and Carpenters have yet to complete their internal canvassing while the seventh CtW union, the Farm workers, endorsed Clinton.

"But they're comfortable with our decision?" Burger asked.

Ohio, Rhode Island, and Texas vote March 4. Pennsylvania votes April 22. The biggest impact of the CtW endorsement may be in Ohio where Burger said CtW has staffers on the ground and where member unions are mobilizing in different cities. CtW unions have 175,000 members in Ohio and Burger said the federation intends to get 110,000 votes for Obama out of that total. CtW unions have 60,000 members in Texas and 20,000 in Rhode Island. (Wojcik 2008)

Change to Win's endorsement is no surprise as one of its major

17-2 Andy Stern, President SEIU, Founder "Change to Win"

constituents, the Service Employees International Union (SEIU), came out for Obama last week.

SEIU President Andy Stern founded Change to Win in 2005 and is considered a leader of the federation.

Change to Win's declaration for Obama follows a pattern of strategic endorsements by leftist politicians and unions - many connected in some way to Democratic Socialists of America.[109]

Change to Win's seven constituent unions are not all leftist controlled, but two members of the organization's governing council have links to Democratic Socialists of America (DSA) – the Chicago Branch that helped young Barack Obama.

Andy Stern leads the SEIU in conjunction with two Democratic Socialists of America (DSA) affiliated Vice-Presidents, Eliseo Medina[110] and Gerry Hudson.[111]

Stern worked with Democratic Socialists of America (DSA) founder Michael Harrington.

Stern also trained at the Democratic Socialists of America (DSA) founded Midwest Academy[112] in Chicago, founded by former Students for a Democratic Society (SDS) radicals Paul and Heather Booth that trains militant community organizers and union officials.

Heather and Paul Booth were regular sponsors of the Chicago Debs Dinners in the late 1970s. The Debs Dinners were organized by the Democratic Socialist Organizing Committee, which in 1982 became Democratic Socialists of America.

Heather Booth was honored for her work at the 1987 Debs Dinner.[113]

Steve Max, associate director the Midwest Academy, is a

---

[109] http://www.dsausa.org/dsa.html
[110] http://www.dsausa.org/about/structure.html
[111] http://keywiki.org/index.php/Gerry_Hudson
[112] http://www.midwestacademy.com/
[113] http://www.chicagodsa.org/d1987/index.html

Democratic Socialists of America (DSA) Vice-Chair, while current executive director Jackie Kendall[114] is a close associate and probable member.

Bruce Raynor, President of UNITE, has direct ties to Chicago DSA.

Chicago Democratic Socialists of America's (DSA) *New Ground* of May/June 1999, carries the following report[115] of that years Debs Dinner. Jackie Kendall, Heather Booth, Bruce Raynor and US Representative Jan Schakowsky (D-IL-9th District), are Barack Obama supporters.

> The 41st Annual Debs-Thomas-Harrington Dinner was on May 7 at the Holiday Inn City Centre. It was a resounding success. The Program Book, 40 pages of congratulations to Awardees Jackie Kendall of the Midwest Academy and James Tribble of UNITE, was a record.

> First presenter was past Awardee, Heather Booth, founder of Midwest Academy. Heather spoke of Jackie Kendall's organizational ability, and how she inspired people to live up to their potential by giving them confidence in themselves. Jackie will go anywhere to help an organization draw up programs and help facilitate them. With Representative Jan Schakowsky (D-IL-9th District) who attended, she fought for, and got, consumers the right to know the freshness of their food by having dates put on all perishable items.

> In accepting the Award, Jackie Kendall told how grateful she was to receive the Debs - Thomas - Harrington Award; how, at Catholic school, she became aware of socialism (for years, she said, she thought all socialists were nuns); and how one's life should be about what they can do to make life better through a just society. The Midwest Academy, Kendall said, gave her the opportunity to train women and men to stand up for themselves and work in good causes.

17-3 Bruce Raynor

> The presenter of the Award to James Tribble was UNITE's secretary - treasurer, Bruce Raynor. Raynor established a great record of militant organizing in the South, and is likely to be the next President of UNITE. Raynor spoke of Jim Tribble's

[114] http://www.chicagodsa.org/d1999.html#anchor703644
[115] http://www.chicagodsa.org/ngarchive/ng64.html

leadership on the front lines in organizing and negotiating, and his contributions at the International Board meetings of UNITE by being a union man who spoke his mind. (C. Shier 1999)

Bruce Raynor also presented the Debs award to union activist Lynn Talbot at Chicago Democratic Socialists of America (DSA)'s 2004 Debs Dinner.[116] In between the two Chicago events, Bruce Raynor served on the awards committee[117] for Boston Democratic Socialists of America (DSA)'s Debs–Thomas–Bernstein Award Dinner in 2001.

When it comes to Barack Obama, all roads seem to lead back to Chicago Democratic Socialists of America.

18. Will Obama Be the Communist Party's "People's President?"

Trevor Loudon © Tuesday, February 26, 2008

Far from being dead as most Americans imagine, the Communist Party USA remains an important political player. While a few thousand

18-1 Mayor Harold Washington

strong, the Communist Party USA's influence in labor unions, the peace movement, black and Latino mass organizations and the Democratic Party, gives the communists a significant say in US politics. The Communist Party USA is strong in several large cities, including Chicago, where it has influenced city and state politics for decades.

In 1983, the party and its Marxist allies from Democratic Socialists of America, was a driving force behind the election of a very sympathetic[118] Chicago Mayor, the late Harold Washington.

In 1992, the Communist Party USA and Democratic Socialists of America (DSA) helped elect another sympathizer, US Senator Carol Moseley Braun (D-IL).[119] For several years, the Communist Party USA[120]

---

[116] www.chicagodsa.org/2004book.pdf

[117] http://www.dsaboston.org/2001DTB.htm

[118] http://trevorloudon.com/2007/10/chicagos-redblack-alliance-targets-white-house/

[119] http://trevorloudon.com/2007/12/carol-moseley-braun-did-clinton-send-us-a-socialist-part-

[120] Chapter 1 - Forget Islam – Look at Obama's Socialism!

and Democratic Socialists of America (DSA) have backed another Chicago rising star-Barack Obama. The Communist Party USA learned a lot from Harold Washington's successes. Indeed, the Harold Washington campaign appears to be almost a blueprint for US Senator Barack Obama (D-IL)'s spectacular Presidential campaign.

The Communist Party USA is optimistic about US Senator Barack Obama (D-IL). The Party still calls their protégé, Harold Washington - the "People's Mayor."

Now, the Communist Party USA wants to make US Senator Barack Obama (D-IL), the "People's President."

Joel Wendland, managing editor of the Communist Party USA theoretical journal, outlines Harold Washington's successful campaign and its significance for Barack Obama and America's future.

> The 1980s opened with a huge transformation in American political and social life unseen since the Great Depression. The New Deal was decimated. Reagan and his successors shifted national resources to military spending and war, weakened federal oversight of consumer goods and worker protections, eliminated and stripped education, housing, health care, Affirmative Action and welfare programs...

> But in this wave of Reagan reaction and corporate greed, there stood an island of hope, a city with a new idea for fighting back. At the helm of that city was a people's Mayor named Harold Washington, the first African American Mayor of Chicago... In Chicago in the run-up to the 1983 election, the coalition Washington helped bring together included the labor movement infuriated over the loss of jobs and plant closings, reformers tired of corrupt and racially divisive machine politics, and growing African American and Latino communities struggling for civil rights and a voice in city government. One former 7th ward coordinator for Washington's 1987 campaign said, "I loved the Washington days; it was magical."

> Throughout this early period of his political life, Washington worked hard to breakdown racial barriers for young African American political hopefuls in the city government using coalition politics, shrewd political maneuvering, and mobilizing new participants in the process. Mostly, however, Washington confronted hostility in Chicago's Democratic machine toward any challenge to the "way things are done."

> In 1964, Washington won election to the Illinois state house of Representatives where he served until 1976... Elected to the state senate in 1976, he turned in 1977, following the death of Chicago Mayor Richard J. Daley, to a failed attempt to win the Democratic nomination for Chicago

18-2 Beatrice Lumpkin

Mayor. In 1981, Washington won election to the US House of Representatives from Chicago's predominantly African American 1st district.

Along the way, Washington was an advocate for the labor movement, the peace movement, and a variety of people's causes. Long-time Chicago peace and labor activist Beatrice Lumpkin, recalled a rainy afternoon in the early 1970s at which a few hundred Chicago residents gathered at a rally sponsored by the Chicago Peace Council to protest the war in Vietnam. Lumpkin recalled, "Harold spoke strongly against the war. He was one of the more progressive legislators. I was impressed that he spoke in the rain and grateful to him for coming and giving our rally greater impact." (Wendland, Harold Washington: The People's Mayor 2008)

Beatrice Lumpkin was a leader of the Chicago Communist Party. The Chicago Peace Council, like its parent body the US Peace Council, was a front for the Communist Party USA.

Washington's relationship to the labor movement went back a long way. When plant closings in northern Illinois, Indiana, and southern Wisconsin pounded the Chicago region economically in the late 1970s and early 1980s with no relief in sight, Washington was part of the struggle to save jobs and provide relief...

The 1980 closure of Wisconsin Steel located in Chicago's east side was the final straw for many disaffected workers...

Retired African American steel workers Frank Lumpkin, who had also campaigned for Harold Washington in his earlier state and federal campaigns, along with other laid off workers and angry retirees, formed the "Save our Jobs" committee.

They organized public protests, demanding relief for workers in the form of the benefits that Harvester, the billion dollar operation that owned Wisconsin Steel, refused to pay after the mill closed and the organization of resources to keep the mills opened. The committee circulated a petition, gathering some 4,000 steelworkers' signatures, and delivered it to the Illinois state legislature and to members of Congress, including US Representative Harold Washington (Wendland, Marxist Thought Online 2008)

Frank Lumpkin was of course Bea Lumkin's husband. He was also a leader of the Illinois Communist Party.

By the middle of 1981, the struggle to re-open Wisconsin Steel, win back benefits and to re-gain lost jobs, shifted as Ronald Reagan took power. It seemed clear that Reagan would simply defund the federal Economic Development Administration, which held the Wisconsin Steel plant, and force its closure.

In the end, the struggle was partially victorious, retirees were paid partial benefits, but the plant never re-opened. According to Beatrice Lumpkin in Always Bring a Crowd, the biography of Frank Lumpkin, Washington won the support of Chicago's steelworkers with his strong support for their struggle. Washington's determination to speak up on this issue enabled him to win labor's endorsement in the campaign for Mayor even as the party machine set up obstacles to that labor endorsement

Having been soundly defeated in the 1977 Mayoral primaries, Washington made his 1983 candidacy for Mayor contingent on the success of registering 100,000 new Black voters and raising a certain amount of funds before an official campaign would be put together. However, he refused to confine his appeal to African Americans. In the summer before the 1983 primary, he said, "As a practical politician, I would seek to build a coalition of Black and white campaign workers throughout the city. The issue would not be anti-race, but anti-greed and anti-corruption." After the 1983 victory, Washington stated:

In our ethnic and racial diversity, we are all brothers and sisters in a quest for greatness. Our creativity and energy are unequalled by any city anywhere in the world. We will not rest until the renewal of our city is done. ... [W]e is going to do some great deeds here together.

Washington felt that white voters who initially resisted his candidacy could be won over if a dominant theme of his campaign and his administration of the city was to eliminate corrupt forces that also hurt the city's white residents as much as its people of color.

Chicago journalist Ron Dorfman, who edited the published photographic essay of Washington's career, Harold: Photographs from the Harold Washington Years, said...

"Harold brought together different factions in the Black community."" Uniting labor progressives, nationalists, and traditional civil rights people in the African American community, Dorfman suggested, was a key element of Washington's candidacy, and "there

18-3 Frank Lumpkin

really wasn't anybody else who could pull that part of the coalition together."

Within three months, organizations like Operation PUSH, welfare rights organizations, African American churches, and labor unions helped register over 200,000 new African American voters in the city. Public figures like Stevie Wonder, Rev. Jesse Jackson, Sr., African American elected officials state US Senator Carol Moseley Braun (D-IL)Moseley Braun and US Representative Danny K. Davis, and US Representative Gus Savage (D-IL-2nd District) appeared at many public events to promote the voter registration drive. (Wendland, Marxist Thought Online 2008)

US Representative Danny K. Davis is a member of Democratic Socialists of America (Democratic Socialists of America (DSA). Danny Davis and Obama were endorsed by Democratic Socialists of America (DSA)[121] in 1996. US Representative Gus Savage was close to the Communist Party.

African American educator and activist and Chicago resident Dee Myles, said:

"Initially there was concern about whether or not Washington's candidacy would take hold in the African American community. But when it did, "the support for Washington in the African American community grew quickly. Literally you could feel it, you could cut it with a knife it was so thick."

Myles, who worked in the 1983 campaign as a precinct worker and in the 1987 campaign as a ward coordinator in the independent political committee in the 7th ward, described the campaign of 1983 as a real people's movement. She remembered people riding the bus to work in south Chicago wearing their blue Washington for Chicago buttons. "After his election, Harold Washington repealed a city ban on public musicians, and there was more music in the city," Myles said. "It was really a period of engagement that was astonishing." (Wendland, Harold Washington: The People's Mayor 2008)

Dee Myles, is a Chicago based member of the National Board and National Committee of the Communist Party USA. She is also head of the Communist Party USA Education Commission.

---

[121]Chapter 2 - Barack Obama Was Endorsed by Chicago Marxists

Washington did not rely on the Democratic Party either to win Mayoral elections or to govern with his reform program.

"It was understood that if stability was going to be produced, and progress and building support was going to be maintained from election to election, an independent operation was needed, and that he wouldn't have to depend on the regular Democratic Party machine," said Myles. (Wendland, Harold Washington: The People's Mayor)

Indeed, after his victory in the 1983 primary, the Democratic machine remained aloof to his candidacy and even proposed running Mayor Jane Byrne, whom Washington had defeated in the primary, as a write-in candidate.

Washington appealed to independent voters from a large cross-section of the city's electorate: a broad coalition of Democrats, independent-minded Democrats, others on the left, and still others who held no specific ideological viewpoint but alienated from the process by corruption in or the ineffectiveness of city government. To succeed at this unorthodox approach to politics, Washington encouraged the formation of independent political organizations to boost his campaign and to promote his program.

Important elements of the Washington campaign were the drive for interracial, inter-ethnic unity. Washington found in racial diversity a source of strength. In his first inaugural speech, he said, "We are a multiethnic, multiracial, multilanguage city and that is a source of stability and strength."

While all observers of those events seem to agree that the unique unity of Latino and African American voters helped send Washington to City Hall, it is also true that a growing number of whites who came to see his program and accomplishments as beneficial to all Chicagoans. According to former Chicago Alderman and Washington supporter Dick Simpson, though Washington never received more than 20 percent of the white vote, it was clear that had he lived, Washington's share of that vote would have grown.

Washington's Republican opponents, and even some within the Democratic machine, promoted white city residents with fears that handing power to an African American would cause the city to fall apart or promote "retribution against whites," Simpson noted:

"That Washington did diffuse that sentiment. There was no longer fear of African Americans in positions of power by the time his regime ended," Simpson recalled. "He was successful in diffusing that racial animosity, but not successful enough by 1987 to win over a majority of

18-5 Rudy Lozano

white ethnic voters." Still, the trend favored an anti-racist majority in the city. (Wendland, Harold Washington: The People's Mayor 2008)

Chicago Alderman Dick Simpson[122] was, in the late '70s, a close associate of the Marxists who went on to form Democratic Socialists of America.

Here again, the labor movement played a key role. The Coalition of Black Trade Unionists pressed the Chicago Federation of Labor to endorse Washington during the general election battle.

The Coalition of Black Trade Unionists is heavily influenced by the Communist Party. Latino community leader and garment workers union organizer Rudy Lozano and other organizers within the growing Latino community helped forge support from Latinos and put together a strong base of support both for Washington's candidacy and in the battle to win Washington's reform platform in the city council. Lozano, who had also been a key figure in the "Save Our Jobs" campaign, based in the 22nd ward and led the formation of that ward's independent political organization.

18-4 Chicago Alderman Dick Simpson

A battle over redistricting had begun. Machine politicians fought redistricting in order to block Washington's reform platform. They had succeeded in the past of forcing Chicago Mayor Jane Byrne, who had also run as a reform candidate, to back off ethics reform by keeping control of the city council and browbeating her into submission. However, Washington and his supporters, armed with the independent political forces and a broad multiracial coalition as the tool for winning popular support, took their stand.

The organization that Lozano and his allies put together in the 22nd Ward was an unrivaled model of grassroots organizing. Get-out-the-vote campaigns mobilized huge sections of the population who had not participated before behind Washington's reform program. Some people

---

[122] http://keywiki.org/index.php/Dick_Simpson

close to Lozano also suspect that his assassination in June 1983 linked to his efforts on Washington's behalf. (Wendland, Harold Washington: The People's Mayor 2008)

18-6 Senator Obama on the Campaign trail

Rudy Lozano was a probable member of the Communist Party USA. His son Pepe Lozano is now a leader of the Chicago Young Communist League and is a strong advocate of mobilizing the Latino vote for US Senator Barack Obama (D-IL).

April 2008 will mark the 25th anniversary of Washington's inauguration as Mayor of Chicago. In honor of the anniversary, of Chicago Mayor Harold Washington Commemorative Year was established to celebrate his life and work by holding dozens of public events around the city, church Services, music programs, and university symposia as well as the publication of the book Harold!: Photographs of the Washington Years. The Commemorative Year is headed by numerous prominent Chicago elected officials as well as many of the people who fought by Washington's side all those years ago.

Some of Washington's accomplishments are tangible and remain part of the political life of Chicago to this day. With the people behind him, organized and willing to fight, Washington won many of the battles in the city council...

Washington's Affirmative Action policies were another key change he brought to city government. "He opened city hall to African Americans and Latinos, women, gays, Asians - everybody that had been locked out," said Simpson. Leadership and management positions in the city government included more women and people of color. "It is now just a part of the city fabric," said Dorfman. "Absent Harold, it wouldn't have happened. Harold did it and it stuck." Another part of Washington's legacy is his enduring influence on national politics. About everyone interviewed for this story came around to talking about another emerging Chicagoan - Barack Obama. Perhaps it is no accident that he too talks in broad, hopeful terms about change, reform, and empowering the people to reclaim democracy.

Indeed, is it mere chance that Obama's main campaign image is a rising sun over a flag and the words "Obama for America"?

Those blue buttons that dotted Chicago's landscape in those exciting days of 1982 and 1983 showed rays of the sun like hope rising above the words "Washington for Chicago."

Perhaps Washington's greatest legacy is the insurgent challenge to politics as usual Obama represents on a national stage. Perhaps "the peoples' Mayor" will inspire the making of "the Peoples' President." (Wendland, Harold Washington: The People's Mayor 2008)

The same organizations that backed Harold Washington -the Communist Party USA and Democratic Socialists of America - are now backing Obama.

They were successful with Chicago Mayor Harold Washington, so it is no surprise they are using the same tactics with Barack Obama.

Will they succeed in making US Senator Barack Obama (D-IL), the "People's President"?

19. Obama '08 "All the Way with DSA"

Trevor Loudon © Wednesday, February 27, 2008

If US Senator Barack Obama (D-IL)'s campaign for the US presidency has an unofficial slogan, it should be "All the way with DSA."

The Marxists of Chicago Democratic Socialists of America (DSA) helped launch Obama's political career and have supported him ever since.

Democratic Socialists of America (DSA) linked unions have endorsed Obama's campaign for the Democratic nomination.

DSA linked figures such as US Representative Jan Schakowsky (D-IL-9th District) and US Representative Barbara Jean Lee (D-CA-9th) have come out for the Senator.

While the iron disciplined Communist Party USA has committed itself to the Obama cause, the looser Democratic Socialists of America (DSA) is less obvious about its support.

Democratic Socialists of America (DSA) allows its members more freedom to back candidates of their choice, but several prominent Democratic Socialists of America (DSA) members have stood up for Obama in recent times.

These range from senior union officials, to street level supporters, to well-known academics.

An interesting example of Obama union political solidarity occurred in Chicago on March 3, 2007.

Speaking in a vernacular and cadence that showed the Harvard Law School and Columbia University trained Barack Obama can connect with working class people, the third year U. S. Senator wowed and energized a mostly labor union crowd of about 1600 supporters this morning...

The event attracted some of Labor's big hitters to join Obama on the dais and speak, including John Sweeney, President of the AFL-CIO and Gerald McEntee, President of AFSCME. Representative Jan Schakowsky (D-IL-9th District) [D-Evanston, 9th CD], an early and big-time supporter of Obama's in the 2004 Senate Primary and US Senator Dick Durbin [D-IL] also spoke...

Eight other individuals spoke at the rally, including local labor leaders and health care workers, as well as a local favorite for liberals, Dr. Quentin Young.

Cong. Representative Jan Schakowsky (D-IL-9th District):

Employers can intimidate, fire, threaten to move people from the day shift to the graveyard...it is a new day in our nation's capital, it's a new day for Resurrection workers and their friends, it's a new day for immigrant workers, it's a new day for all our working Americans who dream of the justice that ONLY the Union Movement can deliver. And, to the doubters I say, you ain't seen nothing yet. Just wait until we have a Labor Department under President Barack Obama. (Berkowitz 2007)

At the time, it was a safe bet that US Representative Jan Schakowsky (D-IL-9th District) was angling to head the US Labor Department under President Obama.

John Sweeney, President of the AFL-CIO, is the USA's most powerful labor leader. He is also a longtime Democratic Socialists of America (DSA) member.

19-1 John Sweeny

Gerald McEntee, the nation's top public sector unionist, is an ally of Sweeney. Is he also a Democratic Socialists of America (DSA) member?

According to San Francisco Democratic Socialists of America (DSA)

19-2 Senator Dick Durbin (l)
and Senator Barack Obama (r)

member Michael Pugliese:[123]

BTW, for what it's worth McEntee is one of the Democratic Socialists of America (DSA) notables in the labor bureaucrat column as is John Sweeney. (Publiese 1999)

Quentin Young is a well-known Chicago Democratic Socialists of America (DSA) member and an early Obama backer who seems to have come back to the cause after a period of disillusionment with his friend and neighbor.

US Representative Jan Schakowsky (D-IL-9th District) has close ties to Democratic Socialists of America (DSA). US Senator Dick Durbin (D-IL) is a strong Obama backer and regarded as one of the most far left members of the US Senate.

The Young Democratic Socialists online magazine, the Activist, stated:

- It is true that Obama has delivered a lackluster performance in the Senate and that there are some bizarrely conservative people in his campaign. However, Barack has some real left-wing street creed in Chicago. Let this inaccurate right-wing attack on Obama (associating him with a certain organization near and dear to us) speak for itself:

He is probably the only person running for President who could identify, say, Antonio Gramsci, and that should count for something shouldn't it?

He has often attacked for being less outspoken than the Senior Senator from Illinois is, Dick Durbin is, but Obama actually takes his cues from Durbin who, along with Democratic Socialists of America (DSA)-friendly Representative Jan Schakowsky (D-IL-9th District), has been his main political sponsor. (Prados 2008)

A leading academic Obama backer is Princeton University professor of Religion and African American Studies, Cornel West.[124]

An honorary Chair of Democratic Socialists of America (DSA),[125] West was a Clinton backer and cool towards Obama.

---

[123] http://mailman.lbo-talk.org/1999/1999-December/021208.html
[124] http://keywiki.org/index.php/Cornel_West
[125] http://www.dsausa.org/about/structure.html

Now Cornel West is an unabashed Obamaphile and introduces US Senator Barack Obama (D-IL) at the Apollo Theater, November 29, 2007.

19-3 Duane Campbell

West describes Obama as his "companion and comrade."

Further, down the socialist academic food chain is California State University, Sacramento, Professor Duane Campbell.

A leader of Democratic Socialists of America (DSA) Anti-Racism and Latino Commissions,[126] Campbell is an Obama zealot.

His blog Choosing Democracy[127] focuses more on Obama. Duane Campbell[128] is a leading activist in the Sacramento area Obama campaign, including the Sacramento Obama Meet Up group.

> US Senator Barack Obama (D-IL)'s Presidential campaign was brought to the attention of those who walked by a booth that was set up on the Library Quad today.
>
> Bilingual and multicultural education professor Duane Campbell, who has been involved with political activities since the 70's, volunteers his time three days a week to educate students of the presidential candidate's campaign. (Garnace 2007)

Democratic Socialists of America (DSA) members worked hard to put their man in the White House.

20. Young Communist League Backs Barack Obama - Again

Trevor Loudon © Friday, February 29, 2008

> The Young Communist League129 is the youth wing of the Communist Party USA. Like its parent body, the YCL is backing US Senator Barack Obama (D-IL) for the Democratic Presidential nomination.

---

[126] http://antiracismdsa.blogspot.com/

[127] http://www.choosingdemocracy.blogspot.com/

[128] http://keywiki.org/index.php/Duane_Campbell

[129] http://www.yclusa.org/

If Obama fails, the YCL will line up behind Clinton-anything to defeat the hated Republicans.

But even though the ultra-right is in retreat, kicking and screaming and even calling Senator Hillary Clinton's half public-half private healthcare proposal "socialist," they still haven't been defeated. As Communists, we have to finish the task of isolating the ultra-right and completely removing them from power-using the Democrats to finish the job. (Smiley 2007)

For now, the Democrats have their uses - but that will change when it suits the Communists. Communist Party USA has infiltrated the Democratic Party to support Obama, all over the US, including in Baltimore and Los Angeles.

In 2004, the Chicago Communist Party[130] and the Chicago YCL also helped[131] campaigned for Obama in his successful US senate race.

In 2008, the YCL has mobilized across the US, from New York to Chicago to Missouri, to ensure US Senator Barack Obama (D-IL) clinches the Democratic nomination. In the knife-edge world of US elections, the combined efforts of thousands of dedicated Communists and several hundred enthusiastic YCLers is enough to push the US to the left.

The Young Communist League is the stuff of the late-US Senator Joseph McCarthy' (R-WI)'s worst nightmares: Several hundred motivated

young people organized in 17 chapters in cities that include New York, Chicago and Milwaukee. But unlike McCarthy's Red witch hunts of the 1950s, when communists were lying low to avoid persecution, Reds are openly pushing their agenda these days by campaigning for mainstream presidential candidates.

20-1 YCL leader Erica Smiley hands out Obama brochures in Brooklyn

This election, the league is largely banking on the candidacy of the junior Senator from Illinois, Barack Obama. Erica Smiley, who has been at the helm of the league for the past two years, noted that they will support any Democratic candidate who may potentially loosen labor laws and pass broad social reforms.

---

[130] http://trevorloudon.com/2007/06/why-do-the-communists-back-barack/
[131] http://trevorloudon.com/2007/06/young-communist-league-infiltrates-us-democrats/

"Obama is an excellent candidate, but it's not about Obama or Clinton," she said recently over a breakfast bagel in a coffee shop down the street from the Obama campaign office in Brooklyn. "It's about beating the extreme right wing; at the end of the day, they're just playing their roles."

The league doesn't claim official ties to the Obama campaign, and the Obama campaign did not respond to repeated phone calls and e-mails to its Chicago headquarters seeking comment.

Rather than introducing its own candidate, as Communist Party USA last did in 1984 with Gus Hall, the league decided to back the Democratic Party candidate who members believe supports the most proletariat-friendly platform.

"If we were to run our own candidate this year," Smiley said, "some people would vote for him, taking away votes from Clinton or Obama, and McCain might jump in. That would be terrible!"

Smiley, who sported a red T-shirt with the words "Troublemakers Union," said the league members fear that an official endorsement of Obama could hurt the senator's chances to become President because a stigma is still attached to communists.

"It's better than it used to be in my parents' generation," Smiley said, "but it's still taboo. The Bush administration puts communists and fascists together."

Even within the league, not all members refer to themselves by "the C-word." Hector Gerardo, 24, co-Chair of the league for Harlem and the Bronx, prefers to call himself a socialist. (Smiley, YCL leader, Erica Smiley hands out "Vote for Obama" leaflets in Brooklyn)

Outside New York, league comrades also are outraged.

Docia Buffington, co-Chair of the Chicago chapter, which has about 30 members, said in a phone interview that they have concentrated their campaign efforts on Little Village, a Latino area of the Windy City.

"I think it was clear that most people were excited about Obama than other candidates," Buffington said. "I think that he does represent a certain kind of change, or it seems so."

The leadership of the Young Communist League is honest about its long-term goals: to home in on the ultra-right Republicans by supporting Democrats now, and then to carry on their struggle—eventually against their former allies.

For some of the group, the excitement of Super Tuesday has faded along with hopes of a decisive Obama victory that day. Regardless, Smiley vowed that her organization will unify behind whoever wins the nomination in August.

"We don't want to sit on the sidelines," she said. (Farberov 2008)

The Democrats are in a bind. If they admit that the Communists have infiltrated their party to help Obama, the publicity could be hugely damaging.

If someone else exposes it, the results could be even worse.

The Republicans will not have the guts to do it. The main stream media is almost as bad as the Democrats are.

That leaves the independent media and the blogosphere.

Do your duty, patriotic American bloggers.

21. Top Communist Criss-Crosses the US for Obama

Trevor Loudon © Saturday, August 16, 2008

Communist Party USA Number two man, Jarvis Tyner, has been criss-crossing America, rallying party members, converting wavering Democrats and building support for Democratic Presidential candidate, US Senator Barack Obama (D-IL).

It's time to stand up and be counted if you're a Democrat in Maine. Yes, I am a registered Democrat and have had periods of actual participation in Party activities over the years...But I have made up my mind for Obama and I will stand for him at the caucus on Sunday.

Why? Well, it happened today at a talk I went to record in Orono at the University. It was by Jarvis Tyner, executive Vice-Chair of the Communist Party USA, and former candidate for Vice President of the US Tyner made the case in favor of the social movement building behind Obama...

I am sold, not because I put any special weight on the Communist Party, but because I do believe in social movement, as Tyner helped me understand. (Tyner, Obama for President 2008)

21-1 Jarvis Tyner Communist Party USA

From the West Coast, Communist Party USA led Willamette Reds

21-2 SEIU Local 503 Oregon Public Employees Union

of Oregon:[132]

> The Civil and Human Rights Committee of SEIU Local 503, Oregon Public Employees Union sponsored and hosted a talk by Communist Party Vice Chair Jarvis Tyner, Local 503 retiree activist Ann Montague and union organizer Bob Novick on Friday, August 8 in Portland, Oregon.

> The Friday meeting was one of four events held in Oregon featuring Jarvis Tyner and discussions about the Party and the elections. A Thursday night dinner brought together Communication Workers of America (CWA), SEIU and American Federation of Teachers (AFT) members. A Saturday educational discussion involved the Oregon club and several friends, and was followed by a reception, which brought together a mix of union and gay activists and some people from a West Salem neighborhood. (Willamette Reds of Oregon 2008).

What is the Communist Party USA trying to build around US Senator Barack Obama (D-IL)?

Who was Jarvis Tyner?

---

[132]http://willamettereds.blogspot.com/2008/08/jarvis-tyner-on-presidential-election.html

Jarvis Tyner was inspired[133] in his radical activities in the '60s by communist singer and activist Paul Robeson. Robeson had, in the mid '40s, helped persuade a prominent poet (and secret communist), Frank Marshall Davis, to move from Chicago to Hawaii. In the late '70s, the poet became a mentor to a young man[134] sent to High School in Hawaii from his home in Indonesia. The question is - to what extent did Frank Marshall Davis inspire the young Barack Obama?

22. Barack Obama, Danny K. Davis and the Marxist New Party

Trevor Loudon © Tuesday, August 19, 2008

When Barack Obama ran for the Illinois State Senate in 1996 on the Democratic Party ticket, he was endorsed by two interrelated organizations, Democratic Socialists of America and the Chicago branch of the New Party. Two groups formed the backbone of the New Party Democratic Socialists of America (DSA) and the related radical grassroots organization the Association of Community Organizations for Reform Now (ACORN). In some areas, the Communist Party is involved, and in Chicago, there was considerable input from the Communist breakaway group Committees of Correspondence. Together, the New Party Marxists worked through the Democratic Party in order to move it leftward.

In 1996, a New Party document entitled "Who's Building the New Party," lists several prominent COCDS and Democratic Socialists of America (DSA) activists in the national New Party leadership.

They included two of COCDS's five co-Chairs:

• Raphael Pizzaro - (also a Democratic Socialists of America (DSA) member and a former communist)

• Manning Marable - (a former Democratic Socialists of America (DSA) official)

Other Democratic Socialists of America (DSA) members listed include:

• Noam Chomsky - (activist who now serves on the COCDS advisory

---

[133] http://keywiki.org/index.php/Jarvis_Tyner
[134] http://www.aim.org/aim-column/obamas-communist-mentor/

Board)
- Elaine Bernard Gloria Steinem – (Labor academic)

And five contemporary Obama supporters[135]:
- Cornel West - (Black activist and academic)
- Frances Fox Piven - (Sociologist credited as the theoretician behind ACORN)
- Bill Fletcher - (Former Maoist)
- Barbara Ehrenreich - (Feminist)
- Dr. Quentin Young – (Chicago physician and "Single Payer" advocate)

The New Party exploited the concept of electoral "fusion," which enabled candidates to run on two tickets at the same time.

If a candidate ran as a Democrat and for the New Party, he or she would be on the ballot twice and attract the votes of both centrist Democrats and leftist New Party supporters. The total of both votes gave the candidate a much greater chance of winning the election.

Using this tactic, the New Party succeeded in electing hundreds of candidates to local offices in several states.

A Supreme Court decision on April 28 1997, written by Justice William H. Rehnquist rendered "Fusion" ineffective and led to the collapse of the New Party and similar efforts nationwide.

Barack Obama had worked with ACORN Affiliates for many years in New York and Chicago. He also had close ties to Democratic Socialists of America (DSA) and was a natural fit for the New Party.

Obama's links to the New Party went well beyond accepting their nominal support. Obama sought the New Party's endorsement and urged members to join his campaigns.

The New Party claimed Obama as an official member of their organization.

Former Chicago Alderman Danny K. Davis joined the New Party during his successful Congressional 1996 campaign on the Democratic Party ticket.

---

[135] http://progressivesforobama.blogspot.com/

A New Party News article from the spring of 1996, page 1, celebrated the Davis' congressional victory and went on to say:

"New Party members won three other primaries this spring in Chicago: Barack Obama (State Senate), Michael Chandler (Democratic

22-1 New Party Candidates Patricia Martin (l), Danny K. Davis (c), Barack Obama (r), New Party News Spring 1992, Page 2

Party Committee) and Patricia Martin (Cook County Judiciary). "These victories prove that small 'd' democracy can work' said Obama". (New Party News 1996)

Barack Obama saw the potential of the New Party, because he sought their support well before the scheduled election.

"About 50 activists attended the Chicago New Party membership meeting in July. The purpose of the meeting was to update members on local activities and to hear appeals for New Party support from four potential political candidates.

The political entourage included Alderman Michael Chandler, William Delgado, Chief of Staff for IL State Representative Miguel del Valle (D), and spokespersons for IL State Senator Alice Palmer, Sonya Sanchez, chief of staff for IL State Senator Jesse Garcia, who is running for IL State Representative in Garcia's District; and Barack Obama, chief of staff for IL State Senator. Alice Palmer. Obama is running for Palmer's vacant State Senate seat. Although ACORN and SEIU Local 880 were the harbingers of the New Party there was a strong presence of COCDS and Democratic Socialists of America (DSA) (15% DSA)... Four political candidates were "there" seeking NP support." (Bentley, Chicago New Party News Update 1995)

The next year, the New Party socialists were celebrating their campaign successes.

"The NP's '96 Political Program has been enormously successful with 3 of 4 endorsed candidates winning electoral primaries. All four candidates attended the NP membership meeting on April 11 to express their gratitude.

Representative Danny K. Davis, winner in the 7th Congressional District, invited NPers to join his Campaign Steering Committee.

Judge Patricia Martin, who won the race for Judge in seventh Subcircuit Court, explained that due to the NP she was able to network and get experienced adVice from progressives like Davis.

IL State Senator Barack Obama, victor in the 13th State Senate District, encouraged NPers to join in his task forces on Voter Education and Voter Registration..." (Bentley, New Ground 42 1995)

In the end, Obama did not need the New Party to win the election. Serving under Alice Palmer, Obama stood against her for the State Senate seat - after Palmer lost a bid for the US Congress and decided she wanted her old job back. Obama won by using legal technicalities to get all his opponents, including IL State Senator Alice Palmer (D-IL), disqualified.

Obama and his New Party associate, US Representative Danny K. Davis, formed a strong relationship that has endured to this day. The pair has worked on several projects in the Illinois Legislature and congressional Representative Davis has played a significant role in Obama's Senate and Presidential campaigns. He is now a Democratic Party "super delegate" pledged to Obama. In this 2004 speech to the Chicago Teamsters Union, Obama describes Davis as "one of our best congressmen" because "he shares our values."

But what are US Representative Danny K. Davis' values?

Around the time the New Party was alive, Davis was linked to no fewer than three Marxist organizations.

An email from Democratic Socialists of America (DSA) membership officer, Solveig Wilder, dated December 29, 1998, stated:

Ron Dellums (who recently retired from Congress) is a Vice Chair of Democratic Socialists of America (DSA), and Representative Danny K. Davis, John Conyers, and Major Owens are all Democratic Socialists of America (DSA) Members. (Free Republic LLC 2008)

US Representative Danny K. Davis has MCed several Democratic Socialists of America (DSA) run Debs Dinner functions in Chicago in recent years and was named as a Democratic Socialists of America (DSA) member in the organization's newsletter *"Democratic Left,"* Summer 2006 edition.[136]

Davis also had ties to COCDS:

> Over five hundred delegates and observers (including one hundred and forty from Chicago) attended the founding convention of the Committees of Correspondence (COCDS) held here in Chicago in July.
>
> Speakers…included Charles Nqukula, General Secretary of the South African Communist Party; Dulce Maria Pereira, a senatorial candidate of the Workers Party of Brazil; Angela Davis of COCDS; and Andre Brie of the Party of Democratic Socialism of Germany (a revamp of the old East German Communist Party)
>
> Other guests during the Convention included Cook County Commissioner Danny Davis, Alderman Helen Schiller and Rick Muñoz, a Representative of the Green Left Weekly of Australia, and a Representative of the Cuban Interest Section. (Williams 2000)

Rick Muñoz is an Illinois Democratic Party delegate for Obama.

Davis was also associated with the Communist Party USA. In Chicago, Communist Party USA holds annual a fund raising banquet for its paper, the *People's Weekly World* (formerly the People's "Daily" World).

The July 28 1990, edition of the People's "Daily" World, reported that Chicago Alderman Danny K. Davis attended that year's banquet:

> Davis applauded those at the banquet, who, he said, are always in the midst of struggle. PDW readers, he said, are "steadfast in the fight for justice." The affair netted $2,500 for the PDW fund. (People's Daily World 1990)

According to the *People's Weekly World* 's October 3, 1998 issue, Representative Danny K. Davis interrupted his campaign work for Senate Candidate Carol Moseley Braun,[137] to present an award at the Chicago annual *People's Weekly World* banquet.

This event raised a more respectable $10,000 towards keeping the Communist Party USA paper afloat.

---

[136] http://www.dsausa.org/dl/Summer_2006.pdf

[137] http://trevorloudon.com/2007/12/carol-moseley-braun-did-clinton-send-us-a-socialist-part-1/

US Representative Danny K. Davis' values are socialist. What are Barack Obama's values?

23. Alice Palmer - Obama's Soviet Sympathizing Patroness

Trevor Loudon © Saturday, August 23, 2008

At every point in Barack Obama's spectacular career, there has been a socialist ready to help. Few people have done as much to help Barack Obama as did Alice Palmer; however, when the cards were turned, Obama abandoned Alice for his own good will.

The story of how Illinois State Senator Alice Palmer anointed the up and coming Barack Obama as her chosen successor is well known. In 1995, Palmer introduced Obama to many of Chicago's radical elite in the home of former Weather Underground terrorists Bill Ayers and Bernadine Dohrn. In addition, present was Obama's longtime friend, neighbor and supporter, Quentin Young, a member since 1983 of Democratic Socialists of America.

23-1 Illinois State Senator Alice Palmer

The House of Un-American Activities Committee accused Young of being a member of Communist Party USA and the North Chicago based communist doctor's branch, the Bethune Club.

Alice Palmer promoted Obama to a much wider audience than the Ayers/Dohrn circle.

> On September 19th, Obama invited some two hundred supporters to a lakefront Ramada Inn to announce his candidacy for the State Senate...Alice Palmer introduced Obama, and an account in the Hyde Park Herald quoted more from her speech than from his; it was, after all, chiefly her endorsement that certified him as a plausible candidate. "In this room, Harold Washington announced for Mayor," Palmer said. "Barack Obama carries on the tradition of independence in this district. . . . His candidacy is a passing of the torch." (Lizza 2008)

A passing of the torch it was.

Harold Washington, Chicago's first black Mayor, who had died in office in 1987, was elected by a coalition[138] led by Communist Party USA and a group of Marxists, who went on to form Democratic Socialists of America.

Harold Washington's success inspired Barack Obama to come to Chicago in the first place.

Why did Alice Palmer choose Obama as her successor? What impressed her enough to support the young left wing lawyer?

Did she see in Obama, a kindred soul?

Palmer began working at Malcolm X College in Chicago in the late '60s. She received her Master's degree from the University of Illinois at Chicago Circle Campus and her Ph.D. from Northwestern University where she later became Director of African American Student Affairs.

Palmer, with her husband, was also involved in the Chicago based Black Press Institute (BPI). It was as a Representative of this organization that Palmer served on the executive Board of the US Peace Council[139] from 1983 to 1985.

23-2 Obama during his 1995 campaign

The US Peace Council was, according to Rob Prince of the Colorado Federation of Teachers, created by the Communist Party USA.

In Lawrence S. Wittner's 2003 book, *The Struggle Against the Bomb, Prince*[140], a 15 year veteran of the Communist Party USA National Council, describes how he was "part of a nucleus of Communist Party activists" that set up the US Peace Council in 1978/79.

Several known communists worked with Palmer on the Peace Council Executive Board.

---

[138] http://trevorloudon.com/2007/10/chicagos-redblack-alliance-targets-white-house/
[139] http://www.uspeacecouncil.org/
[140]
http://books.google.co.nz/books?id=4ouQhNthlHgC&pg=PA39&lpg=PA39&dq=rob+Prince+US+peace+Council&SOURCE=web&ots=6EYFLeeU6I&sig=RMLNoM0gdsV7syUog_2ClFMdIq8&hl=en&sa=X&oi=book_result&resnum=8&ct=result

Known Party members included Rob Prince, Sara Staggs of the Chicago Peace Council, Frank Chapman[141] of the National Alliance Against Racial and Political Repression, Pauline Rosen of Women's Strike for Peace and Council executive director Mike Myerson.

Several other executive members later joined the Communist Party USA offshoot Committees of Correspondence for Democracy and Socialism,[142] including Mayor of Berkeley, Gus Newport, Boston academic Mark Solomon, Otis Cunningham of the Chicago Peace Council and current US Representative Barbara Jean Lee (D-CA-9th) .

The US Peace Council and the Soviet controlled and funded[143] World Peace Council are affiliated.

In 1983, Palmer travelled to Czechoslovakia to the World Peace Council's Prague Assembly, in time for the launch of the Soviet Union's "nuclear freeze" movement - designed to cement Eastern bloc military superiority over the West.

No doubt, that Alice Palmer was a Soviet sympathizer.

In June 1986, the Black Press Institute (BPI) contributed an article:

> "An Afro-American Journalist in the USSR," to the Communist Party USA's newspaper People's Daily World. The article detailed how Alice Palmer had recently attended the 27th Congress of Communist Party USA of the Soviet Union and had been greatly impressed by the Soviet system. (Gilbert and Loud 2008)

From Palmer's statements in the following article, it is clear that she was seduced by what she saw:

> We Americans can be misled by the major media. We're being told the Soviets are striving to achieve a comparatively low standard of living compared with ours, but actually they have reached a basic stability in meeting their needs and are now planning to double their production."

> Palmer said that America's white-owned press "has tended to ignore or distort the gains that have been made [by the Soviets] since [the Russian Revolution of 1917]. But in fact the Soviets are carrying out a policy to resolve the inequalities between nationalities, inequalities that they say

---

[141] http://trevorloudon.com/2008/01/barack-obama-marxist-mole/
[142] http://trevorloudon.com/2008/01/barack-obama-marxist-mole/
[143] http://archive.peacemagazine.org/v08n3p16.htm

were inherited from capitalist and czarist rule. They have a comprehensive Affirmative Action program, which they have stuck to religiously – if I can use that word – since 1917.

There is no second-class 'track' system in the minority-nationality schools as there is in the inferior inner city schools in my hometown, Chicago, and elsewhere in the United States.

The Soviet government and people have always sided with the Africans in South Africa and Namibia against apartheid…. I saw this, too, at the Patrice Lumumba Friendship University in Moscow, where students from underdeveloped countries are trained to become engineers, doctors, nurses, teachers, agricultural specialists and skilled workers. There is no brain drain going on; the students receive a free education and then return to use their talents to build up their own countries. (Gilbert and Loud 2008)

By the mid '90s, Palmer was involved in another leftist organization, the Illinois Public Action (IPA). The IPA fronts as a consumer group and is one of 'Illinois' leading leftist pressure groups. Communist Party members Bea and Frank Lumpkin were prominent as were several Democratic Socialists of America (DSA) members, including Board member Quentin Young. Other key activists included Bill McNary and US Representative Jan Schakowsky (D-IL-9th District), both of whom became key Obama allies.

In 1995, Alice Palmer decided to relinquish her Illinois State Senate seat to run for Congress. Barack Obama served as Palmer's chief of staff during the campaign, but Palmer failed to win the Democratic Party primary, losing the three-way race to Jesse Jackson Jr.

Jesse Jackson Sr., approached Alice J. Palmer with a deal where they supported her for Congress and she support Junior for her seat in the Illinois State Senate, but Jackson Jr. did not agree with that plan...he decided to run for the seat. Palmer ran and endorsed Barack Obama for her old State Senate seat.

Jackson has a lengthy relationship with Barack Obama. The two have collaborated on issues, stood together against the party slate on certain reform-minded candidates, and sought each other's advice. Additionally, Jackson's sister Santita Jackson was a close friend of Michelle Obama and served as a bridesmaid at the Obama wedding. (Wikipedia 2003)

Jesse Jackson Jr. co-Chaired Obama's national campaign 2007.

In 2007, Jesse Jackson Jr.'s wife, Sandi Jackson, ran for the Chicago City Council - backed by Communist Party USA.

After losing to Jackson, Palmer decided to rest and run for her State Senate seat and asked Obama to stand aside - he refused.

Timuel Black, Palmer's friend, was asked to mediate the rift between Obama and Palmer. He was unsuccessful, but ended up becoming a friend and supporter of Obama's. When Timuel Black joined the Army during World War Two, his background check alleged him to be a member of the Communist Party. Today he serves on the advisory Board of the Committees of Correspondence for Democracy and Socialism[144] with Gus Newport.

> Palmer resolved to run against him (and two other opponents who also had declared their candidacy) in the 1996 Democratic primary. To get her name placed on the ballot, Palmer hastily gathered the minimum number of signatures required. Obama promptly challenged the legitimacy of those signatures and charged Palmer with fraud. A subsequent investigation found that a number of the names on Palmer's petition were invalid, thus she was knocked off the ballot. (Horowitz, Alice Palmer 1986)

Obama knocked out the other two candidates by the same method, winning the Democratic primary by default.

Alice Palmer is now a Hillary Clinton supporter.

---

[144] http://keywiki.org/index.php/Timuel_Black

2008 Democratic National Convention, Denver, Colorado, USA

24. Obama's Major Socialist Supporter

Trevor Loudon © Thursday, August 28, 2008

US Senator Barack Obama (D-IL) is the Democratic Party candidate for the US presidency because of the support of two Marxist organizations - Democratic Socialists of America and the Communist Party USA.[145]

Together these two groups have ties to the seventy members of the Congressional Progressive Caucus,[146] the largest power bloc inside the US Congress.

Many Congressional Progressive Caucus members are supporters of Obama, including US Representative John Conyers and caucus co-Chair US Representative Barbara Jean Lee (D-CA-9th). Conyers and Lee have longstanding ties to Democratic Socialists of America (DSA) and the Communist Party USA.

Another strong Obama supporter, Major Owens, was also, until his retirement in 2007, a leading member of the Congressional Progressive Caucus.

While the Brooklyn Democratic Party backed Hillary Clinton in the primary race, he was among the first to back US Senator Barack Obama (D-IL).

In October 2007, one day after Senator Hillary Clinton received the endorsement of the Brooklyn Democratic Party, former congressional Representative Owens released this statement:

> "Obama stands for the concerns of the masses in the black community who have been let down by the broken promises of past leadership. Our leadership on both sides of the aisle has continued to fail us by supporting the war in Iraq and by standing by while poverty, disparities in our healthcare system and lack of affordable education opportunities for young people weaken our communities. It is time to shake loose from the past and Senator Obama's record shows that he will deliver on his promise to stand up for us in the White House." (Rauh 2007)

---

[145] http://trevorloudon.com/2007/06/why-do-the-communists-back-barack/
[146] http://trevorloudon.com/2006/11/mark-my-words-readers-this-is-the-most-socialist-us-government-in-decades/

US Representative Major Owens was destined to be an Obama supporter. In 1983, Owens inherited his seat in the 11th District of New York, Brooklyn, from another African American, the late Senator Shirley Chisholm. From a Communist Party background, Chisholm was the first black woman to enter Congress. In 1972, she made an unsuccessful run for the Democratic Party Presidential nomination against Senator George McGovern. One of her campaign workers was US Representative Barbara Jean Lee (D-CA-9th), who was inspired by the experience to seek out her own political career.

24-2 Shirley Chisholm

Owens was regarded as a far left Democrat in the House. The Democratic Socialists of America (DSA) infiltrated Americans for Democratic Action rated his latter voting record at 90-95 percent on the left

24-1 US Representative Major Owens

side of legislation. Owens also helped found the Congressional Black Caucus, which he Chaired in 1995-96.

Like fellow congressional Representatives (and Obama's supporters), Danny K. Davis and John Conyers, Major Owens has long been a card-carrying member of Democratic Socialists of America (DSA). In 1997, he participated in the annual Democratic Socialists of America (DSA)-sponsored Socialists Scholars Conference at the City University of New York - the same conferences Obama attended when studying in New York in the '80s.

Like Davis, Conyers[147] and US Representative Barbara Jean Lee (D-CA-9th), Owen has a history of supporting Communist Party linked organizations.

In March 1985, Owens endorsed the National Preparatory

147 http://trevorloudon.com/2007/01/s-i-c-o-s-3-john-conyers/

Committee for the 12th World Festival of Youth and Students in New York - established to send delegates to an international gathering organized by the Soviet front World Federation of Democratic Youth.

In 2006, while still a congressional Representative, Owens showed his true colors at the national convention[148] of the Communist Party USA youth wing, the Young Communist League.

> BROOKLYN, N.Y. - Determined to fight for a better future and to beat back the ultra-right, over 250 members, friends, and allies of the Young Communist League USA gathered at the Marriott Hotel here May 27-29 for the YCL's eighth National Convention. (Margolis, Young Communists League)
>
> US Representative Major Owens welcomed participants "on behalf of all the progressive forces of the nation and the world." "To hell with employers who exploit and cause poverty," he told the crowd.
>
> "There are people who care about humanity, to stop exploiting workers, who want health care instead of a war in Iraq. I hope your youthful energy can provide the spirit to confront the tough politics ahead." (Margolis, Young Communist League 2006)

The same year, Owens was honored at a Communist Party function[149] in New York.

> The Communist Party honored Congressional Representative Major Owens at the annual "Better World Awards" for his years of progressive struggle in Congress. Also honored is Betty Smith, President of International Publishers and longtime fighter for peace and democracy. Elena Mora, Chair of the N.Y. State Communist Party, will discuss the recent election results. (Margolis 2006)

If US Representative Major Owens were 30 years younger, perhaps US Senator Barack Obama (D-IL) wouldn't have had to search so long for a Vice Presidential running mate.

---

[148] http://www.pww.org/article/articleview/9242/
[149] http://www.pww.org/article/articleview/10231/

25. Committees for Correspondence for Democracy and Socialism Marxist-Leninists Come Out for Obama

Trevor Loudon © Saturday, August 30, 2008

The Committees for Correspondence for Democracy and Socialism (COCDS), after the Democratic Socialists of America and Communist Party USA, is the third largest Marxist group in the USA. Formed in 1992 from a large split in the Communist Party USA, COCDS is influential in Chicago, New York, California and some other centers in the union movement and in black communities.

All three organizations are backing US Senator Barack Obama (D-IL) in the coming US election.  committees of correspondence for democracy and socialism

The Communist Party USA is using its own resources in the unions and the social movements, while Democratic Socialists of America (DSA) and COCDS (which have a large cross membership) are working together through Progressives for Obama (P40).

Chicago COCDS has long supported Barack Obama.

COCDS National Committee member Carl Davidson worked with Obama in the New Party in the mid/late '90s and helped organize the famous 2002 peace rally where Obama first came out against the Iraq War.

25-1 Carl Davidson

COCDS Advisory Board member Timuel Black is a long-term friend and supporter of the Senator from Illinois. Timuel Black's wife Zenobia Johnson - Black is one several, COCDS linked endorsers of the Progressives for Obama (P4O) website.

Other long-term Obama supporters such as US Representative Barbara Jean Lee (D-CA-9th) and US Representative Danny K. Davis also have COCDS connections.

25-2 CCDS Advisory Board Member Timuel Black

COCDS revealed just how committed they are to an Obama presidency in this recent statement:

A Critical Moment

A Message to COCDS Membership

August 10, 2008

With less than three months remaining before the November 4th general election, COCDS members together with all left and progressive forces are urged to work wholeheartedly to ensure a massive defeat at the polls for John McCain and his war-mongering, neo-conservative, right-wing sponsors.

Only a massive turnout of new, young, African American, Latino, Asian American, trade union, and progressive voters casting a ballot for Senator Barack Obama can insure this defeat. We must find ways to argue the stakes inherent in a McCain win on key issues: ending the war, the faltering economy, creating "green" jobs, a sustainable environment, universal health care, and restoring the right to organize unions.

The various smears, racism, and fear mongering surrounding the first viable African American Presidential candidacy are making inroads among large segments of the public. COCDS members have a role to play in challenging the racism, joining with broad efforts like that of the petition campaign against Fox TV's racist characterizations of the Obamas organized by the Color of Change. Hip-hop artist, Das, and 150 others delivered 620,000 signatures to Fox TV's studios in Manhattan in July.

It is important to find ways to pressure the Obama campaign from an independent platform, and resist efforts to demoralize, sidetrack, and divide the movement to elect Obama. Progressives for Obama (P4O) is one vehicle. It emerged in March 2008 during the primary campaign and has become a viable voice of critical support from the left, aiming to countervail the growing right-wing pressures on the Obama campaign.

We urgently ask COCDS members to link up with local campaigns and organizations like Progressives for Obama" (P4O) to infuse the election campaign with the issues that matter most - and making the campaign at the base a deeply progressive project.

The NEC, at its most recent meeting, discussed issuing a message urging members in local areas to help build Progressives for Obama (P4O). At the launch of P4O, Tom Hayden, Bill Fletcher, Barbara Ehrenreich, and Danny Glover issued a draft call. Carl Davidson, a member of the NCC of COCDS, is a key organizer and moderator of the P4O web blog. The list of endorsers has grown impressively to include leaders of labor, peace and justice organizations, and leading progressive individuals. (CCDS)

In a message from Carl Davidson about what you do with P4O, he writes:

In addition to signing up and giving us some financial support:

Work locally to expand the electorate in a younger, more progressive direction. Register new voters, and work with other groups, including the young people around the Obama campaign. If it's a normal election, McCain can win. If it's not, and turnout is new and different, we have a good shot. It really boils down to that.

Get out the vote. Registering doesn't help if they don't go to the polls. Again, work with others and the Obama youth, to do this. Be resolute, don't get sidetracked by the bumpy ride, stick to the slogan, "Stop McCain, Stop the War, Vote Obama 2008!"

Get outside the usual comfort zones and make new allies. We're going to need them to wage struggle with the Obama White House in 2009.

Hook all this up with a local progressive blog or two or three, or start one yourself. For example see: www.beavercountyblue.org. Be a public face, then link to others across the country and with us nationally. This is the scaffolding of a national network.

If you're up for adventure, come to Denver for the Democratic National Convention. Hook up with Tent State, P4O, PDA (Progressive Democrats of America), UFPJ and the Nation Magazine. We'll put you to work!

COCDS members have a lot to contribute as an independent force committed to advance the fight for peace and for a massive jobs program in this year's crucial elections. From this perspective we urge members to consider joining and or supporting Progressives for Obama (P40) with our ideas, activism and financial support. For those members and friends who are supporting other independent candidates, we urge that we go forward together to register new voters, fight hard on the issues and lay the groundwork for expanding and consolidating the progressive majority.

Let us know what you are doing and share your stories. Write a note on the COCDS membership list serve or send to the national office for the next issue of the Mobilizer (deadline: end of August). Address: COCDS, 545 Eighth Ave, Rm 1420, NY, NY 10018. (Committees of Correspondence for Democracy and Socialism 2008)

26. William McNary: Yet another Obama Radical?

Trevor Loudon © Tuesday, September 2, 2008

Since his youth,[150] Barack Obama has seldom been without a communist or socialist in his life. Obama has been supported his entire political career by people connected to several Marxist organizations; the Democratic Socialists of America, the Communist Party USA and the Committees of Correspondence for Democracy & Socialism (COCDS).

This post looks at a close associate of Obama's; a friend, longtime colleague and political supporter - William McNary.

Who is this man? What are his connections to Obama? Why does it matter?

According to the website USAction:

> William McNary has been called one of the most electrifying and inspirational speakers of our time. McNary serves as the President of US Action, the nation's largest coalition of progressive grassroots organizations working together to win social, racial, economic and environmental justice. (US Action 2008)

26-1 William McNary

Before joining US Action, McNary served for 12 years as Legislative Director of Illinois Public Action (IPA) - known as Citizen Action/Illinois.

Marxists, several of whom have close connections to Barack Obama, infiltrated both Illinois Public Action (IPA) and US Action.

In the mid-90s Illinois Public Action (IPA)'s Board included Obama's longtime friend, Democratic Socialists of America (DSA) member Dr. Quentin Young, his onetime boss and Communist Party USA front activist Alice Palmer, longtime supporter, Democratic Socialists of America (DSA) US Representative Jan Schakowsky (D-IL-9th District) and Obama supporting Democratic Socialists of America (DSA) linked unionist Tom Balanoff.

---

[150] http://trevorloudon.com/2007/03/barack-obamas-marxist-mentor/

Frank and Bea Lumpkin, members of Chicago Communist Party USA, and several other Democratic Socialists of America (DSA) members get the credit for major roles in building the IPA organization.

Heather Booth, who now serves as Vice President under McNary, founded US Action. A former member of the 1960's radical organization Students for a Democratic Society (SDS), Booth was connected in the '70s to the Chicago socialists who went on to help found Democratic Socialists of America (DSA) in 1982. Booth went on to found the Democratic Socialists of America (DSA) run Midwest Academy, an infamous training school for agitators, unionists and activists. Obama was close to the Midwest Academy before and after entering politics.

26-2 Heather Booth

US Action's Board seats several radicals including former Chicago Democratic Socialists of America (DSA) activist John D. Cameron. US Action Program Director Alan Charney was Democratic Socialists of America (DSA)'s National Director.

How well does William McNary know Barack Obama?

In May 2008, McNary told the Huffington Post:[151]

> I am also a voter. And in this election, I am supporting Barack Obama, whom I've known and worked with for years. I am also an elected delegate to the Democratic Convention for Barack Obama. (McNary 2008)

Obama has worked with McNary for some years.

> He collaborated with United Power for Action and Justice (UPAJ), a metropolitan Chicago faith-based organization formed in 1997 by the IAF, to expand children's health insurance in Illinois. For its part, UPAJ gave Obama a prominent platform to address its multiracial, metropolitan membership during his 2004 bid for the US Senate. William McNary, co-director of Citizen Action/Illinois, a coalition of labor, community and citizen groups, says, "Barack was not just willing to meet with community-

---

[151]http://www.huffingtonpost.com/william-mcnary/womens-voices-women-vote_b_99548.html

based groups, not only to be a good vote for us, but he also strategized with us to help move our position forward. (Moberg 2007)

From David Moberg again, writing In These Times:

William McNary, President of US Action, a national network of statewide progressive citizen groups, personally - but not organizationally-supports Obama as a "genuine progressive" who will "expand the boundaries of American democracy," and heal the rupture with the rest of the world Bush caused with the war in Iraq." . (Moberg 2007)

According to the pro-Democratic Party[152] blog TPM Cafe:

William McNary is...one of Obama's personal friends and longtime supporters - someone Obama went to when considering his run for Senate and for President. William loves Obama and I know beyond the shadow of a doubt he would not serve on an organization Board that was trying to favor Clinton over Obama. (TPM Cafe 2008)

At last week's Democratic Convention in Denver, McNary compared his friend to Dr. Martin Luther King:

When this country was first started, the only ones who could vote were white men with property. Then we extended the boundaries of democracy to include women and people of color and religious minorities. Who would have thought we would have expanded the boundaries of democracy so wide that someone like Barack Obama, an African American, could run and win. So Barack Obama is not just a culmination of King's dream, he's the culmination of the American dream. (City Room 2008)

Clearly, McNary is a supporter of Obama's, a former colleague and a friend. He is even someone Obama turned to when making his biggest political decisions.

Why should that concern us? We should be concerned because while a Democrat, McNary has close and recent ties to several Marxist organizations.

Every year, Chicago Democratic Socialists of America (DSA) hosts a major awards dinner,[153] named after prominent socialists Eugene Debs,

---

[152]http://www.talkingpointsmemo.com/talk/2008/05/compendium-of-hillarys-dirty-t.php

[153] http://www.chicagodsa.org/dthdin.html

Norman Thomas and Michael Harrington. Most of the speakers and award recipients are Democratic Socialists of America (DSA) members, sympathetic socialists or communists.

From the Chicago DSA website:

> The 47th Annual Debs-Thomas-Harrington Dinner was held on Friday evening, May 6, 2005, at the Holiday Inn Mart Plaza in Chicago... Our featured speaker was William McNary, who spoke on the theme of the Dinner, "A Perfect Storm Rising: The Crisis in Health Care, Defending Social Security." The Dinner also heard from Frank Llewellyn, the National Director of Democratic Socialists of America (DSA) (Chicago 2005 Debs-Thomas-Harrington Dinner 2005)

In June 2008, McNary attended a Democratic Socialists of America (DSA) Communist Party USA organized[154] demonstration in support of striking workers at Chicago's Congress Hotel.

McNary works with several Chicago socialists in opposition to the Iraq War.

From the CPUSA's *People's Weekly World:*

> Joe Moore is a leftist Democrat and a strong Obama supporter. Carl Davidson is a leader of the Communist Party USA breakaway organization, Committees of Correspondence for Democracy and Socialism (COCDS). Like Heather Booth he was active in Students for a Democratic Society and has worked closely with Barack Obama.

> He helped organize the famous 2002 Chicago peace rally where Obama first made his name as an opponent of the Iraq War. In 1994 Ricardo Muñoz attended the founding conference of COCDS in Chicago with long time Obama friend and supporter, US Representative Danny K. Davis. Muñoz was a pledged Obama delegate to the Democratic Convention. (McNary, Presidents proposal protects drug profits 2002)

Even more concerning are McNary's ties to Communist Party USA.

McNary wrote an article opposing Drug Company profiteering for the February 16, 2002 edition of the Communist Party USA newspaper People's World:[155]

---

[154] http://www.chicagodsa.org/c20080612/index.html
[155] http://transitional.pww.org/president-s-proposal-protects-drug-profits/

CHICAGO - Honoring legendary fighters for social justice, the annual Illinois *People's Weekly World*/Nuestro Mundo banquet raised $6,100 for the 2002 Fund Drive here Oct. 20. William McNary, President of US Action and veteran of countless successful union and community battles, gave the keynote address. In his speech McNary told of his own personal tragedies, from which he has found the strength to fight until social justice is won, and gave a call to all present, "We must be in it to win it." (McNary, Presidents proposal protects drug profits 2002)

People's Weekly World interviewed McNary in October 2002:

No matter the issue, if it affects working people, William McNary, President of US Action, is there, fighting the good fight for social and health security, quality public schools and against the right-wing agenda.

"That's a big order but it can be won with leadership and organization. If we had elected leaders who would stand as firmly for these issues as others stand for Wall Street, we'd be well on the road to winning them," he said in a recent interview. "If we are to win these things we must build political power at the grass roots (Gaboury 2002)

McNary and the Communist Party USA[156] both supported Obama in his 2004 Senate race. Outside the Democratic Party mainstream, Obama organized a coalition of socialist - communist dominated unions and community organizations to win.

From the February 2004 issue of *People's Weekly World:*

The race for the Democratic nomination for the open US Senate seat in Illinois has boiled down to a three-person race, according to polls. Millionaire Blair Hull has a slight lead after pouring $18 million of his own money into an advertising blitz. IL State Senator Barack Obama and State Controller Dan Hynes trail him, with a large undecided vote remaining. The primary will be held March 16.

At several campaign rallies across this city on Feb. 21, Obama said that after the Presidential race, the Senate race in Illinois might be the most important. He noted the historic potential of his campaign, aside from helping break the Republican majority. If successful, he would be only the third African American since Reconstruction elected to the US Senate.

Of all the candidates, Obama can boast the most diverse support. While Hynes has the backing of the state AFL-CIO and the bulk of the

---

[156] http://trevorloudon.com/2007/06/why-do-the-communists-back-barack/

Democratic machine, Obama has the support of several key unions including the American Federation of State, County, and Municipal Employees; Service Employees International Union; Hotel Employees and Restaurant Employees; the state American Federation of Teachers; Chicago Teachers Union and Teamsters Local 705, the second largest in the country. Obama has a 90 percent voting record on labor issues in the Illinois Senate.

In addition to widespread support in the African American community, Obama has also received the backing of several independent Latino elected officials led by IL State Senator Miguel del Valle), IL State Representative, Cynthia Soto and Chicago Alderman Ray Colon, Chicago Alderman Joe Moore from the North Side is also backing him.

Many progressive organizations have thrown their support to Obama, including the Sierra Club and League of Conservation Voters. In its endorsement, Citizen Action/Illinois praised Obama's 96 percent voting record on consumer issues. President William McNary said Obama "will be a strong voice in Washington on behalf of working families." (Bachtell 2007)

In July 2005, William McNary was a keynote speaker at the Communist Party USA Convention in Chicago. Of the fifteen speakers and panelists listed, McNary and James Thindwa were not confirmed Communist Party members.

McNary gives the impression of being among friends.

The paper's former editor, Communist Party USA National Board member Tim Wheeler, is active in Obama's Baltimore organization and covered the 2008 conference for *People's Weekly World*.

William McNary, President of US Action, told the World he believes the nation is on the verge of sweeping change not seen in a generation. He emphasized, "Real change can only happen when real, ordinary people get in motion." (Wheeler, 2008 Take back America Conference 2008)

Change! Where have we heard that word before?

27. Reds, Radicals, Terrorists and Traitors - Progressives for Obama

Trevor Loudon © Thursday, September 11, 2008

Barack Obama did not rise to prominence on his own merits.

For many years, support for Obama's career came from a socialist network, based in Chicago, but now reaching into every state of the US.

The network is an activist matrix led by former members of the '60s radical organization Students for a Democratic Society (SDS) and supporters of Democratic Socialists of America, the Communist Party USA (CPUSA)[157] and the Committees of Correspondence for Democracy and Socialism (COCDS).[158]

The network has links to hundreds of leftist organizations including the Black Radical Congress,[159] Progressive Democrats of America, United for Peace & Justice, US Action, ACORN and several major trade unions.

27-1 Barack Obama Anti-Military Speech

The network has been co-operating since at least the 1980s. Parts of it came together behind Jesse Jackson's failed 1988 US Presidential bid and again in the late '90s the New Party helped launch Barack Obama's successful bid for the Illinois State Senate.

Now the network has come together to put US Senator Barack Obama (D-IL) in the White House.

Their ambition does not end there, however. The network wants to build a movement that will be able to pressure an Obama presidency into legislating for massive social change. They want to relive the 1930s and 1960s with a new "New Deal" and a new civil rights movement.

They want a socialist America.

Progressives for Obama (P40) are a new organization representing

---

[157] Chapter 18 - Will Obama Be the Communist Party's "People's President"?
[158] Chapter 25 - CCDS Marxist-Leninists Come Out for Obama
[159] http://en.wikipedia.org/wiki/Black_Radical_Congress

one prominent tip of the socialist iceberg.

> We agree that Barack Obama is our best option for President in 2008, and that an independent grassroots effort can help strengthen his campaign.
>
> It can also strengthen the mandate for his programs for stopping war, promoting global justice, and securing our rights, liberties, and economic well-being. More important, independent organization at the base is needed for compelling social change no matter who is in the White House.
>
> We have understood, from the beginning that Senator Obama is not a consistent progressive, and often speaks to and from the center of our country's political spectrum-sometimes well, sometimes not. Even more reason, we think, to organize a strong progressive pole, independent of his campaign, to counter rightward drift and push him to do better on issues that will win him more solid and wider support.
>
> We do not attempt to define 'progressive' here. We're open to all trends, from the socialist left to moderate liberals, who want not only to defeat McCain, but also build the grassroots organizations and networks for wider and deeper change over the longer term. (Tom, et al. 2008)

Writing in The Nation,[160] PGO founder Tom Hayden explained:

> During past progressive peaks in our political history – the late Thirties, the early Sixties – social movements have provided the relentless pressure and innovative ideas that allowed centrist leaders to embrace visionary solutions. We find ourselves in just a situation today.
>
> We intend to join and engage with our brothers and sisters in the vast rainbow of social movements to come together in support of Obama's unprecedented campaign and candidacy. Even though it is candidate-centered, there is no doubt that the campaign is a social movement, one greater than imagined by the candidate. (Hayden 2008)

---

[160] http://www.thenation.com/doc/20080407/hayden_et_al

The four founders of Progressives for Obama are:

Tom Hayden

27-2 Tom Hayden

Tom Hayden the author of *"Ending the War in Iraq,"* a five-time Democratic convention delegate, former state senator, and Board member of the Progressive Democrats of America. Hayden was also a founder in 1964 of Students for a Democratic Society.

According to Discover the Networks:

During the Vietnam War, Hayden traveled many times to North Vietnam, Czechoslovakia, and Paris to strategize with Communist North Vietnamese and Viet Cong leaders on how to defeat America's anti-Communist efforts. He came back from Hanoi proclaiming he had seen "rice roots democracy at work." According to people who were present at the time...Hayden offered adVice on conducting psychological warfare against the US. (Horowitz, Tom Hayden 2008)

27-3 Bill Fletcher

Bill Fletcher

Bill Fletcher is the originator of the call for founding "Progressives for Obama" and the executive editor of Black Commentator and founder of the Center for Labor Renewal. Bill Fletcher is a former Maoist and is currently a leader of Democratic Socialists of America (DSA). In 1998, he was also a founding member of the Communist Party USA-COCDS-Democratic Socialists of America (DSA) dominated Black Radical Congress.[161]

27-4 Barbara Ehrenreich

Barbara Ehrenreich

Barbara Ehrenreich is a member of The Nation's editorial Board. She is an honorary Chair of Democratic Socialists of America (DSA) and was active in the New American

[161] http://en.wikipedia.org/wiki/Black_Radical_Congress

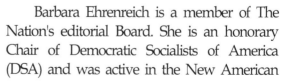

Movement - led by former Students for a Democratic Society and Communist Party USA activists. According to Discover the Networks:[162]

> Communist Manifesto re-released on its 150th anniversary in 1998, Ehrenreich celebrated the event. She noted that in producing the Manifesto as a commercial product, capitalists were – as Lenin had once predicted – providing the rope that eventually would hang them. (Horowitz, Barbara Ehrenreich 2008)

Danny Glover

Danny Glover is an actor, activist, and Chair of the Board of TransAfrica.[163] He worked with two former Communist Party front activists: Harry Belafonte and Johnetta Cole. Glover is close to former Berkeley Mayor Gus Newport, once linked to Communist Party USA and now active in both Democratic Socialists of America (DSA) and COCDS. He has also been involved with the Black Radical Congress. Glover has close ties to Cuba and according to Discover the Networks:[164]

27-5 Danny Glover

> On several occasions, Glover has visited Venezuela and made guest appearances on President Hugo Chavez's television and radio talk show, Hello, President. Glover is a Board member of Venezuela's "TeleSUR" news network, which Chavez created in 2005. (Horowitz, Danny Glover 2008)

The list of endorsers on the Progressives for Obama (P40) website further illustrates the socialist nature of the organization.

They include:

- Rosalyn Baxandall – (Marxist)
- Paul Buhle – (A former member of SDS, one time editor of the original SDS journal Radical America. Currently a DSA leader)
- Malcolm Burnstein – (Progressive Caucus, California Democratic Party. Formerly active in the communist front National Lawyers Guild. Formerly a partner in the CPUSA linked San Francisco Bay

---

[162] http://www.discoverthenetworks.org/individualProfile.asp?indid=1058
[163] http://www.transafricaforum.org/about-us/our-board
[164] http://www.discoverthenetworks.org/individualProfile.asp?indid=1119

Area law firm of Truehaft, Walker and Burnstein, that once employed a young Hillary Rodham (Clinton))

- Duane Campbell – (Sacramento Progressive Alliance, Anti-Racism and Latino Commission of DSA)
- Jim Campbell – (CCDS National Co-Chair)
- Steve Cobble – (Progressive Democrats of America, formerly with the New Party and affiliated with the ultra-radical, Cuban linked, Institute for Policy Studies)
- Barry Cohen – (NJ Institute of Technology, CCDS member, formerly with CPUSA)
- Carl Davidson - (PFO webmaster. Former SDS later involved with Maoist groups and in the '90s with Barack Obama in the New Party. On the national council of CCDS)
- Peter Dreier – (Occidental College, DSA member)
- Thorne Dreyer – (former SDS member)
- Mickey Flacks – (former SDS member)
- Richard Flacks – (Husband of Mickey, SDS founder member. Active in Santa Barbara DSA)
- Jane Fonda – ("Hanoi Jane," former wife of Tom Hayden)
- Aviva Futorian – (Associated with Obama in the DSA infiltrated Independent Voters of Illinois)
- Christine George – (Researcher and University Teacher. Associated with Chicago DSA)
- Todd Gitlin – (Columbia University. Former SDS leader)
- Jorge Gonzalez – (Cuba Journal)
- Thomas Good – (Communist turned anarchist)
- David Hamilton – (Ex-SDS)
- Harold Jacobs – (Historian of the SDS terrorist offshoot, the Weather Underground)
- Michael James – (Heartland Cafe, 49th Ward Democrats Chicago, Former SDS member)
- Zenobia Johnson – (Black National Organisation of African-Americans in Housing, Chicago. Wife of Obama's friend and supporter of Timuel Black of the CCDS Advisory Board)
- Marilyn Katz – (Former Chicago SDS chief of security. Helped found Chicagoans Against War on Iraq, with Carl Davidson. The pair organised the 2002 peace rally where Obama came out publicly against the Iraq War. Both of Katz's parents were CPUSA members)
- Robin D. G. Kelly – (Historian. Formerly a member of the

Communist Workers Party. Now close to CPUSA and active in the Black Radical Congress)

- Fred Klonsky – (former SDS member, son of leading CPUSA member Robert Klonsky)
- Susan Klonsky – (Chicago based education writer, former SDS member)
- Jay Mazur – (A leader of the CPUSA/DSA infiltrated New York Working Families Party)
- Joe Moore – (49th Ward Alderman, Chicago)
- Frances Fox Piven – (DSA honorary Chairman, formerly active in the New Party and closely linked to ACORN)
- Christine Riddiough – (A former Chicago DSA activist and national leader. Active in soliciting gay support for the Obama campaign.
- Mark Rudd - A former leader of both SDS and the terrorist Weather Underground)
- Jay Schaffner – (Local 802 American Federation of Musicians. Active in CCDS, formerly active in the Chicago CPUSA)
- Andy Stern – (President, SEIU. Assistant to DSA member and AFL-CIO president John Sweeney. Stern was trained in the DSA controlled Midwest Academy in Chicago.)
- Harry Targ – (Leading CCDS member, Purdue University)
- Jonathan Tasini – (National Writers Union. Endorsed by DSA in his unsuccessful 2006 US Senate primary race against Hillary Clinton)
- John Trinkl – (Former writer for the Maoist oriented journal, The Guardian)
- Immanuel Wallerstein – (Marxist professor, Yale University)
- Cornel West – (Honorary Chairman of DSA, calls Obama "comrade")
- Mildred Williamson – (CCDS leader. Formerly a leader of Chicago CPUSA)
- Betty Willhoite – (Chicago DSA member, Independent Voters of Illinois activist)
- Tim Wise – (Author, Anti-Racism Educator. Has attended DSA and CCDS conferences)

Why do people like this back Barack Obama? What do they hope to gain from an Obama Presidency?

28. Top US Communist - Elect Obama "Go On to Change the World"

Trevor Loudon © Saturday, September 13, 2008

Libero Della Piana is New York State Chair of the Communist Party

USA, former national organizer of the party and a member of the Communist Party USA, 140 strong National Council.

Like all the Communist Party USA several thousand members and supporters, Della Piana is working to elect US Senator Barack Obama (D-IL) to the US Presidency.

Following the Communist Party USA "line," Della Piana supported Barack Obama in the Primaries against Hillary Clinton.

28-1 Libero Della Piana at CPUSA HQ in New York, March 2007.

Libero Della Piana writing in the Political Affairs Editors blog[165] after Hillary Clinton's victory in the New York State Democratic primary:

> I am here with a group of folks watching the election results in Manhattan. Many of us worked on the Obama campaign here in the city, so we have been a little disappointed by the big victory for Clinton here tonight...
>
> Moments ago, Associated Press declared the state of Utah for Obama.
>
> I grew up in Salt Lake City, Utah. Growing up African American in Utah, you can believe me when I say the state is overwhelmingly white and more than a little conservative. (Utah had the biggest Bush vote in 2004.)
>
> To me this is truly amazing and exciting. It represents a huge shift in the consciousness of the country and an amazing moment for the democratic forces too. Obama appears to be sweeping many of the Prairie States (North Dakota, Kansas, etc.) as well as other parts of the Mountain West (Idaho, Colorado).

---

[165] http://paeditorsblog.blogspot.com/2008/02/new-york-obama-victories-signal-huge.html

To me this represents a victory in and of itself. (Piana 2008)

Comrade Della Piana sees the upcoming US election as an opportunity to change the direction of the US.

From the Communist Party USA *People's Weekly World* blog:[166]

Della Piana:

This Labor Day working people and their families in New York State are in an exciting and challenging moment. For the first time in years, the labor movement together with its broad movement allies has the potential to change the course of the country in a more positive direction.

The 2008 Presidential election is historic. The Democratic Party nominated an African American as its candidate for the first time, but there have also been record turnouts in the primaries and a vibrant grassroots movement has developed. (Piana, NY Labor Day: Time to Make a Change 2008)

Libero Della Piana sees the election as a choice between Republican conservatism and a new people/union driven movement for social change.

Della Piana:

What's at stake for working people in the election couldn't be starker.

McCain represents four more years of the failed Bush policies of war and aggression, tax-breaks for the rich and big corporations, and destruction of social Services vital to working-class communities. On the other hand, the candidacy of Barack Obama reflects and represents the massive desire for change: for a livable environment and a sustainable world, for jobs with justice, for peace and progress, for fair taxes and a program to rebuild our cities and towns.

Let's be clear, there is a big difference between these two choices. McCain is no "maverick." He is a real conservative who puts the "rights" of the rich and corporations ahead of the needs of the working majority. McCain received a dismal zero percent pro-labor voting record for 2007 while Obama has a stellar 100 percent record and said he looks forward to signing the Employee Free Choice Act into law as our next President. (Piana, CPUSA People's World Blog)

---

[166] http://peoplesweeklyworldblog.blogspot.com/2008/09/ny-labor-day-time-to-make-change.html

Twenty-five percent of the Democratic Party's Convention delegates were union members, while the GOP Convention speakers took turns bashing unions and blaming them for the economic crisis in the country. (Piana, NY Labor Day: Time to Make a Change 2008)

Libero Della Piana looks beyond Obama. The election is a chance to shift the whole US government to the left. By electing leftist Democrats, the Communist Party USA hopes to tilt the direction of the US government towards socialism. The Communist Party USA, through their influence in the US union movement, wants to transform the US political landscape.

Della Piana:

Of course, deeper Democratic majorities in the House and Senate and in an increase in progressives in the Congress will also shift the terrain in Washington, opening the way for legislation to turn-back the damage of the Bush years, and to repair the country from 30 years of right-wing rule. This is no time to sit out the election.

We not only have a chance to undo the Bush Agenda, but to win big transformative victories and set the stage for higher levels of struggle. A decisive electoral victory in November will lead the way to passage of the Employee Free Choice Act, the end of the occupation of Iraq and implement some form of national health care. The working-class has been on the defensive for decades, this election has the chance to put the movements back on offense, to set the agenda for the country.

A big people's victory in November is not the end of the struggle, but a new beginning on more favorable ground. The mass movements of the people: the peace movement, student movement, civil rights movement, women's movement, and labor movement have to keep the pressure on to ensure a new Democratic Administration and Legislature keep the promise to meet the people's needs. (Piana, NY Labor Day: Time to Make a Change 2008) Change the US government and world revolution has no significant opposition.

Della Piana:

Together, we can win in November and together we can go on to change the world. (Piana, NY Labor Day: Time to Make a Change 2008)

Libero Della Piana is right. The entire direction of the planet depends on the outcome of the US election. Several thousand communists and socialists directing several million unionists, peace activists and "community workers" could be enough to tip the balance.

In a knife-edge election, Della Piana and his comrades may hold the balance of power.

29. Senior US Socialist Jose Laluz, Manipulates Latino Vote for Obama

Trevor Loudon © Thursday, September 18, 2008

Communist Party USA has been working hard to muster the crucial Latino vote for US Senator Barack Obama (D-IL) for many months.

Key Marxists, Democratic Socialists of America, are trying to manipulate the must win Latino vote through their Chairmanship of Latinos for Obama.

Latino Voters Key to Obama Win in Battleground States

The historic Nov. 4 Presidential election is less than two months away, and a monumental battle is heating up in a few crucial swing states, as some nine million Latino voters prepare to cast their ballot, which could be the deciding factor for an Obama win.

Latinos are the fastest growing minority group in the US at 15 percent of the population and represent nine percent of eligible voters. However, many agree the Latino vote could be the key bloc that could lead to an Obama victory, especially in battleground states where Latinos make up at least 10 percent of the voting population...

Latino voters represent 35 percent of the electorate in New Mexico, 11 percent in Colorado, 12 percent in Nevada and 14 percent in Florida. According to the poll, Obama expects to win the majority of Latino voters in California, which is the state with the largest Latino population...

In New Mexico, Obama leads McCain 56 percent to 23 percent among Latino voters. Among non-Latino voters, McCain leads 50 percent to 34 percent.

In Colorado, Obama has a 56 percent lead over McCain's 26 percent among Latinos. And among non-Latino voters Obama has a narrow 45 percent lead over McCain's 41 percent.

In Nevada, Obama leads McCain at 62 percent to 20 percent among Latinos. Yet McCain leads among non-Latino voters at 46 percent to 37 percent. (Lozono 2008)

Jose Laluz, Chairperson for Latinos for Obama, campaigned in Colorado and New Mexico registering, educating and mobilizing voters until Election Day. He is also the director of the Leadership Academy with the American Federation of State, County and Municipal Employees Union (AFSCME).

LaLuz spoke with the Peoples Weekly World during an AFL-CIO Labor forum at the Democratic National Convention in Denver.

The *People's Weekly World* went on to say:

> Well over 60 percent of Latino voters are supporting Obama - closer to 66 percent now, the right wing is pulling all its dirty tricks even in the Latino community. We all realize that Bush used appeals to 'family values,' religion and the sanctity of marriage, etc. to get white workers and Reagan Democrats to back him last time...Well they are using the same stuff, the same tactics in the Latino communities. When you combine this with their attention on swing states we find they are waging an especially big push against Obama in the Mexican and Chicano communities in Colorado and New Mexico... (Lozano, CPUSA People's World)

LaLuz explained his tactics to the *People's Weekly World*:

> The Obama campaign is working in both New Mexico and Colorado, among other states, telling Latino voters about McCain's terrible stands on the economy and about the horrible role Republicans have played and continue to play on immigration... "We are showing how the companies and outfits that exploit Latino workers are the people behind McCain, (Lozono 2008)

Between now and Election Day, LaLuz said that the Obama campaign is registering voters in New Mexico and Colorado and developing lists of tens of thousands of Latino supporters for Obama.

> Those lists will constitute the people we bring out on Election Day.

> President Bush won 40 percent of the Latino vote in 2004, a key factor in his win. Even though John Kerry lost Ohio then, many Democrats feel if Kerry had won Nevada, New Mexico, and Colorado, he would be President today. Things have changed since then and the margin of victory is in the Latino vote, particularly in these states, respectively, Democrats say. Polls across the country concur and find that Latinos are fed up with the Bush administration and the Republican Party represented by McCain and see Obama as the person to change course for the better. (Lozono 2008)

Who is Jose Laluz? Why has he left his Puerto Rican base to campaign across the Southwest for US Senator Barack Obama (D-IL)?

In the '70s, Jose Laluz was active in the Connecticut branch of the Puerto Rican Socialist Party (PSP). Allied to Castro's Cuba, the Marxist-Leninist PSP agitated for Puerto Rican independence and committed several bombings and other terrorist acts on US soil.

LaLuz, expelled from the PSP in 1976, went on to join the Democratic Socialist Organizing Committee (DSOC) the following year.

He became Chairman of the Hispanic Commission of DSOC, before the merger with the New American Movement that created Democratic Socialists of America (DSA) in 1983.

Like many in the DSOC/Democratic Socialists of America (DSA) LaLuz also supported the Communist Party USA initiated and dominated US Peace Council - an affiliate of the Soviet front World Peace Council.

LaLuz rose through Labor movement ranks and today serves as Executive Director of Servidores Publicos Unidos de Puerto Rico/AFSCME.

Jose Laluz, an influential socialist in America, is also Vice Chair of the several thousand strong Democratic Socialists of America (DSA).

29-1 Jose Laluz

Like many Democratic Socialists of America (DSA) linked unionists[167] backing Obama, La Luz has ties to the Chicago socialists who have supported Barack Obama since his earliest days in the "Windy City." In 1992, La Luz addressed the Democratic Socialists of America (DSA) sponsored 1992 dinner in Chicago.[168]

> The 34th Annual Dinner held on May 1, 1992 at the Congress Hotel in Chicago. The Master of Ceremonies was Michael Lighty, who was the Executive Director of Democratic Socialists of America (DSA), Sue Purrington, and the Executive Director of Chicago NOW, and Dr. Quentin Young, President of Physicians for a National Health Program, was the honorees. The speaker was Jose La Luz, who was the National Education Director of the Amalgamated Clothing and Textile Workers Union. (Chicago DSA Debs Dinner 1992)

Democratic Socialists of America (DSA) member Quentin Young is

---

[167]Chapter 2 - Barack Obama Was Endorsed by Chicago Marxists
[168] http://www.chicagodsa.org/d1992/index.html

a long time neighbor, friend and supporter of US Senator Barack Obama (D-IL). Young attended the famed 1995 gathering in Chicago with US Peace Council activist Alice Palmer in the home of former Weather Underground terrorists Bill Ayers and Bernardine Dohrn.

Bernadine Dohrn was one of the first radicals to travel to Castro's Cuba with one of the Venceremos Brigades.[169] Some of Quentin Young's children are also Brigade veterans.

Jose Laluz might struggle to win the patriotic Cuban American vote for Obama, if they knew how many Castroites had helped launch the good Senator's career.

30. Who helped launch Barack Obama's political career?

Trevor Loudon © Sunday, September 21, 2008

In 1995, former Weather Underground terrorists Bill Ayers and Bernardine Dohrn helped launch Barack Obama's political career at a small function in their Chicago home.

Bill Ayers also hired Obama to head the Annenberg Challenge, a $50 million fund that enabled Obama to fund organizations which could enhance his political career.

30-1 Bernardine Dohrn and William "Bill" Ayers

Later Ayers worked with Obama on the board of the Woods Fund, together doling out millions to leftist causes.

Obama has consistently tried to minimize his relationship with Ayers and Dohrn. The couple themselves seems intent on maintaining a low profile - until at least after the election. Both parties realize that Obama's opponents will seize on any links to Ayers and Dorhn in order to discredit the Senator.

However, are Ayers and Dohrn really out of the picture? Could they still be helping their friend from "underground?"

The profile for Progressives for Obama includes the following

---

[169] http://www.venceremosbrigade.org/

information. Founded earlier this year, Progressives for Obama unites all the main leftist currents behind the Obama campaign - the Communist Party USA (CPUSA), the CPUSA offshoot Committees of Correspondence for Democracy and Socialism (COCDS), Democratic Socialists of America and former members of the '60s radical organization Students for a Democratic Society (SDS) and its terrorist splinter group the Weather Underground Organization.

Progressives for Obama aims to not only put Obama in the White House, but to build a huge united "progressive" movement that can force the new President to move America massively to the left.

The influence of the CPUSA on the Roosevelt administration that produced the "New Deal" and the pressure of the CPUSA and Students for a Democratic Society/New Left that pressured Johnson into the great social changes of the '60s are the model for this new movement.

Nevertheless, this begs the question who founded Progressives for Obama?

In early 2006, a group of former Students for a Democratic Society members and sympathizers, led by Democratic Socialists of America (DSA) activist Paul Buhle, joined with a new generation of college students to re-found Students for a Democratic Society. The movement now has over 130 chapters across the USA.

More importantly, Buhle and company also founded the Students for a Democratic Society support group for older activists - Movement for a Democratic Society (MDS). Students for a Democratic Society are the muscle behind the new protest movement and were very prominent in the recent violence at

30-2 Movement for a Democratic Society

the Republican National Convention at St. Paul, Minnesota. Movement for a Democratic Society is the brains behind the Students for a Democratic Society brawn.

A review of the 2006 Movement for a Democratic Society board reveals some interesting connections:

- Elliott Adams - (leader of the Communist Party USA front Veterans for Peace)
- Senia Barragan - (Student Representative - new Students for a

Democratic Society)

- David Barsamian - (a leftist broadcaster with close ties to Noam Chomsky)
- Noam Chomsky - (Well known linguist, writer and activist. A member of both Democratic Socialists of America (DSA) and the COCDS Advisory Board)
- Carl Davidson - (A founder member of Students for a Democratic Society, later a Maoist activist before becoming a leader of COCDS in 1992)
- Bernardine Dohrn
- Bill Fletcher Jr. – (A former Maoist. A leader of Democratic Socialists of America (DSA) and the AFL-CIO)
- Bert Garskof - (Involved with Students for a Democratic Society of the 60s, a close friend of Bill Ayers and Bernadine Dohrn)
- David Graeber - (Former member of the Students for a Democratic Society, turned anarchist)
- Tom Hayden - (Founder and leader of the Students for a Democratic Society)
- Gerald Horne - (A member of the editorial Board of Political Affairs, theoretical journal of the Communist Party USA)
- Michael James - (A former member of Students for a Democratic Society)
- Robin D.G. Kelley - (A former member of the Communist Workers Party, close to Communist Party USA)
- Michael Klonsky - (Son of Communist Party USA member Robert Klonsky. A former member of Students for a Democratic Society, who later led the pro-Chinese Communist Party (Marxist-Leninist).)
- Mike Klonsky - (Works with Bill Ayers on educational projects)
- Ethelbert Miller - (Chairman of the Board of the leftist and Cuban linked Washington based think tank, Institute for Policy Studies)
- Charlene Mitchell - (A leader of COCDS, former high ranking member of Communist Party USA)
- Michael Rossman (deceased) – (A Californian New Leftist, with close ties to Students for a Democratic Society)
- Mark Rudd - (A former leader of the Students for a Democratic Society and the Weather Underground)
- Howard Zinn - (A well-known Marxist historian and former secret member of the Communist Party USA)

The connections between those listed above, Obama and

Progressives for Obama (P40) are many fold.

Carl Davidson worked with Obama. In Chicago in the mid-'90s with former Students for a Democratic Society activist Marilyn Katz, they organized the famous 2002 peace rally in Chicago where Obama first came out against the Iraq War. Davidson is the webmaster for the Progressives for Obama (P40) website.

30-3 Moving Obama Left

Bert Garskof is active in the Obama campaign in Connecticut. He recently wrote this comment on the website Foreign Policy in Focus.

> We must realize that the only way to hold Obama, as President, to the progressive agenda is to maintain and build the grass-roots state/County organizations that were built only to elect him...We must remember that the most significant progressive changes have only been instituted into law after grass-roots activism forced the issue...we can maintain our more progressive values and work as organizers within the grass-roots election campaigns.

> We need to convince the new people and the many veterans of electoral wars that this is a unique opportunity. we can create 2-way communication with the People's President - truly make him the People's President if we create methods and structures that work to connect in an on-going way - the President, his staff and grass-roots Obama groups for discussion of what the grass-roots thinks and wants. (Zunes 2008)

Gerald Horne, a historian who has studied the Hawaiian Communist Party, was first to reveal[170] the connection between Barack Obama and his boyhood mentor, secret Communist Party USA member Frank Marshall Davis.

Mike Klonsky was a blogger on Obama's website until negative publicity forced his withdrawal. Klonsky's brother Fred and wife Susan are endorsers of the Progressives for Obama (P40) website.

Bill Fletcher was the initiator of the Progressives for Obama (P40) project, which he co-founded with Tom Hayden. The other two founders

---

[170] http://trevorloudon.com/2007/03/barack-obamas-marxist-mentor/

of Progressives for Obama were writer Barbara Ehrenreich, who is a member of both Democratic Socialists of America (DSA) and Movement for a Democratic Society and actor/activist Danny Glover who is close to some Democratic Socialists of America (DSA) members.

Mike James, Robin D.G. Kelley, and Mark Rudd listed as endorsers of the Progressives for Obama (P40) website.

A quick trawl of the internet[171] reveals several other Movement for a Democratic Society linked activists listed as endorsing Progressives for Obama (P40).

They include:

- Paul Buhle and Thomas Good – (Movement for a Democratic Society founders, former communists turned anarchists who have referred to themselves as an unrepentant Weather supporters)
- David Hamilton and Thorne Dreyer – (Texan former Students for Democratic Society activists)
- Marilyn Katz – (Chicago based Obama fundraiser)
- Rosalyn Baxandall and Immanuel Wallerstein – (Marxist academics)
- Cornel West – (an academic and Democratic Socialists of America (DSA) member refers to Obama as his "comrade")
- Rashid Khalidi - (was a close friend of Obama's from his time in Chicago in the 90s. Khalidi is accused of ties with the Palestinian Liberation Organization and has written for the pro-Obama, Chicago based Democratic Socialists of America (DSA)/IPS linked journal "In These Times.")

Three of the four founders of Progressives for Obama, Bill Fletcher, Tom Hayden and Barbara Ehrenreich have served on the MDS board, as has the PFO webmaster Carl Davidson. Several MDS activists are endorsers of PFO.

Obviously, Progressives for Obama is an MDS creation.

While Bernardine Dohrn's high level role as an MDS board member is clear, Bill Ayers's is less so.

From the MDS website:

> Movement for a Democratic Society (MDS) held its first national convergence at Loyola University, from November 8 through 11 (2007)

---

[171] http://antiauthoritarian.net/NLN/?p=179

with the participation of the newly inspired SDS, Students for a Democratic Society. (Topo 2007)

One of the events listed is:

> Thomas Good, Bill Ayers, Elaine Brower, Alan Haber, David Hamilton, Devra Morice and others representing New York, Chicago, Austin, and Ann Arbor discussed current forms of popular resistance against the war and then joined a necessary and long needed discussion of the
> future of MDS. (Topo 2007)

Bernardine Dohrn and Bill Ayers spoke at the November 2007 SDS reunion at Michigan State University.

Dorhn made reference to the new SDS and MDS. She also made references to the overthrow of capitalism, visits to Chavez's Venezuela and building a "new movement." These people are still revolutionaries.

Bill Ayers and Bernardine Dohrn are involved in an organization uniting three Marxist parties, a host of '60s radicals and terrorists, and a new generation of militant activists.

That organization has spawned a spin-off organization designed to put US Senator Barack Obama (D-IL) in the White House and to bring about massive social change across the US.

Ayers and Dohrn helped launch Barack Obama's political career. Do they still guide Obama's political future?

31. Grey Power! The Ageing Texan Radicals for Obama

Trevor Loudon © Tuesday, September 23, 2008

There are numerous links between Movement for a Democratic Society (MDS)[172] and Progressives for Obama (P4O).[173]

Both organizations link former members of Students for a Democratic Society (SDS) and its terrorist splinter the Weather Underground with Marxists from the Committees of Correspondence for Democracy, Socialism and Democratic Socialists of America

---

[172] http://www.movementforademocraticsociety.org/
[173] http://progressivesforobama.blogspot.com/

Movement for a Democratic Society

(COCDS) and Democratic Socialists of America (DSA).

All of these groups are using their influence in the Democratic Party, media, unions, churches, academia, protest organizations and social movements to make US Senator Barack Obama (D-IL) the next President of the USA.

This chapter looks at two activists involved with the Movement for a Democratic Society from Texas, Thorne Dreyer and David Hamilton.

Both are former members of the original Students for a Democratic Society and are endorsers of the Progressives for Obama (P40).[174]

Dreyer and Hamilton are active Movement for Democratic Society members from the Austin, Texas branch,[175] one of the most active in the US.

31-1 Thorne Dreyer (2dL) former Weather Underground terrorist, Progressives for Obama

The Movement for a Demo-cratic Society (MDS) is a multi-issue activist organization affiliated with the revived Students for a Democratic Society (SDS). Many of its members are veterans of the New Left in the 60's and 70's.

The goal of Movement for a Democratic Society is the creation of a more egalitarian society in both the political and economic spheres. Movement for a Democratic Society believes in participatory democracy, the expansion of human rights, universal healthcare, and the rejection of discrimination based on race, gender, or sexual preference, the

---

[174] Obama File 27 - Reds, Radicals, Terrorists and Traitors – Progressives for Obama
[175] http://mds-austin.pbwiki.com/

preservation of the earth's environment, the expansion of workers' rights, a more equitable distribution of wealth, and the rejection of militarism and war as a way of resolving differences between peoples and nations. (Embree 2008)

Both men are dedicated, practical supporters of Barack Obama. Hamilton has served as an Obama delegate at a Travis County Democratic Convention.

Both believe that Obama is like them, a socialist and that an Obama presidency would place more socialists in key governmental positions.

They believe that communist/socialist/Democratic Party unity is necessary to elect Obama and to change society. To win election, they accept that Obama will have to lie about his true beliefs.

They are OK with that.

Excerpts from Hamilton and Dreyer's Rag Blog of March 23, 2008:

Most of the activists I work with in Austin, those of us in Movement for a Democratic Society/Austin... and other progressive groups, have chosen to support and, in many cases to actively participate in the campaign of Democrat Presidential candidate Barack Obama, for a number of reasons. For this writer at least, those reasons include the following:

We find Barack Obama to be sincerely left leaning and personally inspiring, and believe him worthy of trust, with the requisite reservations. We see the massive, enthusiastic, and largely radical-leaning movement that his campaign has engendered to be a surprisingly positive sign in largely lethargic times and at the least a fertile ground for future activism...

31-2 Obama - All hat no horse

We believe the election of a progressive Democrat at this time in history would result in a quick end to the tragic War in Iraq, the introduction of progressive measures as universal (or virtually universal) health care, and would produce judicial and other governmental appointments that would make a real difference in people's lives.

This would result in real, tangible changes in the lives of struggling lower income citizens, of racial minorities, of those rotting in jail because of race or victimless crimes, and, significantly, of oppressed peoples in other parts of the world.

31-3 Che Obama Poster

And, taking into account that both major parties, in the long haul, represent similar if not identical vested interests, we believe that the Republicans, with their corporate masters, with their oppressive and mean-spirited politics at times verging on the neo-fascist, must be stopped.

It is of critical importance that we never latch on to a political candidate in this electoral system and herald him or her as some kind of a savior. Bottom line, the problems in this country are not based in who runs the system. The system itself is the problem. The shameful disparity in distribution of wealth between the obscenely rich and those left to struggle for their daily needs.

All that taken into account, we believe that there is much to like about Barack Obama, and that there are substantial and valid reasons to work for his election.

In 1936, the French Communist Party ended years of conflict with the French Socialist Party and established a united front that elected Leon Blum as the first socialist prime minister of France. That united front passed reforms that have characterized the socialist aspect of French society ever since.

I am not a Democrat. I have not voted for the Presidential nominee of the Democratic Party since 1972 and have not participated in their primary process since the Jackson campaign of 1988.

I support Barack Obama enthusiastically. I do not do so because I don't find things to criticize in what he says. I do so because, to a much greater degree than any other major party politician, I trust him. I trust him to do what he promises and talk to our supposed "enemies" instead of threaten them. In that, there is the kernel of the rejection of the militarism that is intrinsic to US imperialism...

I expect to be disappointed. I expect to have to criticize him and exert pressure on him from the left. I also expect him to make statements in order to get elected that I disagree with. But this time, I see a chance for a transformational figure that might just change the course of US history and I'm taking that chance...

Purists who reject him have no alternative other that "build an anti-imperialist movement." That is a false dichotomy. In November, hopefully you will have the opportunity to vote for Barack Obama for President. The ideal anti-imperialist won't be on the ballot. Relate to that reality. He may disappoint somewhere along the way, but he is by far the best major party candidate I've ever seen. (Dreyer and Hamilton 2008)

Thorne Dreyer and David Hamilton are not Movement for a Democratic Society bosses. They are not in the league of Bernardine Dohrn, Mark Rudd, Bill Fletcher, Tom Hayden, Carl Davidson, Robin D.G. Kelley, Charlene Mitchell or Gerald Horne.

32-1 Bill Ayers

They are good soldiers, working hard for Barack Obama and the revolution.

32. Ayers, Davidson, Klonsky - the toxic trio! Linked to Pro-Obama Organization

Trevor Loudon © Saturday, September 27, 2008

US Senator Barack Obama (D-IL) has tried to minimize his relationship to former Students for a Democratic Society (SDS) activist and Weather Underground terrorist Bill Ayers.

Meanwhile, Obama's political opponents are racing the clock to uncover the Senator's links to his radical friend and colleague.

Let us try a different tack. Are there any current links between Ayers and organizations supportive of Obama?

It was revealed that Ayers's wife and fellow former terrorist, Bernadine Dohrn, was a Board member of Movement for a Democratic Society (MDS) - an alliance of former Students for Democratic Society members and several Marxist organizations. Ayers also had ties to Movement for a Democratic Society and that a membership overlap between Movement for a Democratic Society and Progressives for Obama (P40) exists.

This will confirm Ayers's ties to Movement for a Democratic Society and his long term and ongoing links to two key pro-Obama activists and former Students for Democratic Society members, Carl Davidson and Mike Klonsky.

Carl Davidson criticized these findings about Obama and his radical ties.

From February this year, another commenter "Spitfire," called

Davidson out:

> Gee, Carl, why don't you talk a little about your background? ... Make sure you mention your recent relationships with Bill Ayers and Mike Klonsky. (Spitfire 2008)

Carl Davidson replied...

> Bill and Mike and I have been friends since the Students for a Democratic Society days of the 1960s–although Mike and I bitterly opposed the Weather underground nonsense back then when it counted... What's silly is the notion that any of us shape the politics of Barack Obama. Carl's comments establish the relationship. Who are Carl Davidson and Mike Klonsky? (Davidson, Carl Davidson replies to Trevor Loudon 2008)

Carl Davidson

Carl Davidson served on the Movement for a Democratic Society Board after its founding in August 2006. He serves as webmaster of Progressives for Obama (P40) which he founded with three fellow Movement for a Democratic Society Board members: Bill Fletcher Jr., Tom Hayden and Barbara Ehrenreich.

According to Discover the Networks:

> Davidson is an American Marxist who serves as a national steering committee member of United for Peace & Justice, a field organizer for the Solidarity Economy Network, and co-Chair of Chicagoans Against War & Injustice. The latter organization has formed alliances with groups as the League of Women Voters, Rainbow/PUSH, Citizen Action, People for the American Way, the Congressional Progressive Caucus, the Congressional Black Caucus, and the Congressional Hispanic Caucus. Aiming ultimately to transform the United States into a socialist nation, Davidson advocates the mobilization of "new grassroots majorities required for progressive, systemic change." (Horowitz, Carl Davidson 2008)

In the 1960s, Davidson was a national secretary of Students for a Democratic Society and a key leader of the anti-Vietnam War campaign. With Tom Hayden, Davidson helped launch, in 1969, the "Venceremos Brigades," which according to Discover the Networks:

> ...covertly transported hundreds of young Americans to Cuba to help harvest sugar cane and interact with Havana's communist revolutionary leadership. (The Brigades organized by Fidel Castro's Cuban intelligence agency, which trained "brigadistas" in guerrilla warfare techniques, including the use of arms and explosives.) (Horowitz, Carl Davidson 2008)

After the Students for a Democratic Society broke up, Davidson became involved in Maoist politics until 1992 when he became a leader of the Committees of Correspondence (COCDS), a Marxist-Leninist coalition of former Maoists, Trotskyists and former Communist Party USA (CPUSA) members. The organization has since changed its name to the Committees of Correspondence for Democracy and Socialism (COCDS). Davidson remains a prominent figure in COCDS alongside several Movements for Democratic Society Board members including Noam Chomsky and Manning Marable.

In the mid-1990s Davidson was a leader of the Chicago branch of the New Party, a Marxist political coalition, whose objective was to endorse and elect leftist public officials. Most New Party members were also involved in the COCDS, the Democratic Socialists of America or the militant leftist "community" organization ACORN.

Other leaders of the New Party later included Movement for Democratic Society Board members Bill Fletcher, Jr. and Barbara Ehrenreich (both Democratic Socialists of America (DSA) leaders and Progressives for Obama (P40) founders) Noam Chomsky and Manning Marable.

Obama joined the New Party in 1995, before his Illinois State Senate run, where he met Davidson. The New Party endorsed Obama, while Davidson and other Party members helped Obama's campaign.

Davidson wrote in 2007:

> I'm from Chicago ... and [I've] known Obama from the time he came to the New Party to get our endorsement for his first race ever.... He said all the right things to the ACORN and New Party folks, and we endorsed him... (Davidson, Marxism)

In 2002, Davidson and fellow former Students for a Democratic Society member (now Obama fundraiser and Progressives for Obama (P40) endorser) Marilyn Katz, organized a large Chicago anti-War rally where Obama first came out against the Iraq War.

32-2 Carl Davidson with Kathy Kelly

32-4 1978 CP-ML poster, Klonsky's name bottom left.

32-3 Klonksky's Blog on Obama's campaign website. Removed June 2008

Michael Klonsky

Mike Klonsky joined the Movement for a Democratic Society Board in 2006. Klonsky's father Robert was a leading activist in the Communist Party USA. In 1968, Mike Klonsky was the national secretary of Students for a Democratic Society and in May 1969 was one of five Students for a Democratic Society members arrested when police raided Students for a Democratic Society offices in Chicago.

In late 1969, Klonsky founded the October League, a pro-Mao communist organization that in 1977 became Communist Party USA, Marxist-Leninist. Klonsky Chaired the Communist Party-ML, recognized by the Chinese Communist Party as their US fraternal party. Klonsky made several trips to China beginning in July 1977, vetted by Communist Chinese officials.

In 1991, Klonsky co-founded the Small Schools Workshop in Chicago with Bill Ayers.

The Workshop received a grant of at least $175,000 from Chicago's Annenberg Challenge. Barack Obama, recruited for the job by a group, which included Bill Ayers, Chaired this organization.

Until June this year, Klonsky ran a Blog on Obama's campaign website.

On short notice, after publicity began surfacing in the blogosphere about Klonsky, someone pulled the blog from Obama's website.

Unlike several movements for Democratic Society Board members, Mike Klonsky DID NOT endorse the Progressives for Obama (P40) campaign.

However, his wife Susan and his brother Fred (both former Students for Democratic Society members) did.

In November 2007, Movement for a Democratic Society held a "Convergence" in Chicago.

Speakers included:

- Manning Marable - (Movement for a Democratic Society Chairman, Obama supporter, COCDS, Democratic Socialists of America)
- Mark Rudd - (Movement for a Democratic Society Board and Progressives for Obama (P40), former Students for a Democratic Society/Weather Underground)

32-5 Mike James (l), Franklin Rosemont (2), Mike Klonsky (3) Muhammad Ahmad (r)

- Marilyn Katz
- Mike James - (Movement for a Democratic Society Board, Progressives for Obama (P40), former Students for a Democratic Society)
- Paul Buhle - (Democratic Socialists of America (DSA), Progressives for Obama (P40), former Students for a Democratic Society)
- Al Haber - (Founder of Students for a Democratic Society)
- Franklin Rosemont - (former Students for a Democratic Society)
- Tom Good - (Movement for a Democratic Society Board, Progressives for Obama (P40)
- Muhammad Ahmad aka Max Stanford (A former leader of the Students for a Democratic Society, aligned with the black militant organization the Revolutionary Action Movement)

Bill Ayers as usual was a star, one of the few speakers whose thoughts were committed to video.

Ayers's refers to Movement for a Democratic Society as "our work." Ayer's was enthusiastic for building alliances and using the US elections to enlist "hundreds of thousands" of young people to his cause.

It was noted that there was a reference to Rashid Khalidi, an Movement for a Democratic Society linked, pro-Palestinian activist, a close friend of Barack Obama.

Ayers chided Obama for adopting centrist positions. Ayers referred to Progressives for Obama (P40) founder Tom Hayden's call for Obama to stay true to his anti-Iraq War position.

All of this is in line with Movement for a Democratic Society and Progressives for Obama (P40) strategy.

It is clear that the movement behind both organizations is not new. It has roots in the Students for a Democratic Society of the '60s, the New Party of the '90s and leading strands of the American Marxist movement. Davidson, Klonsky and Ayers have all played significant roles - sometimes in concert.

The Davidson, Klonsky, Ayers "Toxic Trio" have all put their lives into the communist movement. They have all paved the way for Obama's political advancement.

What do these committed activists expect from Obama in return for their considerable investment?

33. More Weathermen for Obama

Trevor Loudon © Tuesday, September 30, 2008

In the last three chapters we have reviewed Movement for a Democratic Society and the organization's relationship to US Senator Barack Obama (D-IL) and his campaign.

Despite its innocuous sounding name, Movement for a Democratic Society (founded August 2006) is a coalition of former members of the Students for a Democratic Society (SDS), its terrorist splinter the Weather Underground and three Marxist organizations; Communist Party USA, Committees of Correspondence for Democracy and Socialism (COCDS) and Democratic Socialists of America.

33-1 Power to the Weathermen

Every one of these strands has supported Barack Obama since at least the mid-'90s - some even further back.

Today many Movement for Democratic Society activists are working in the Obama campaign, through the Movement for a Democratic Society offshoot Progressives for Obama (P40).

The links between Barack Obama and his "patrons" former Weather Underground terrorists Bill Ayers and Bernardine Dohrn are covered in several writings.

These files clearly show that Dohrn has been a Movement for a Democratic Society Board member, while her husband Ayers is at least an active supporter.

That's two known former terrorists involved in Movement for a Democratic Society, but there are at least three more in the Movement for a Democratic Society - Progressives for Obama (P40) orbit - Jeff Jones, Howie Machtinger, and Mark Rudd.

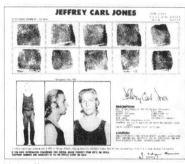

33-2 Jeff Jones

Ayers, Dohrn, Jones, Machtinger, and Rudd are old revolutionary comrades. In the late '60s, the five were key leaders of the faction of Students for a Democratic Society (SDS) that split to form the Weather Underground. All attended the famous 1969 Flint War Council that gave birth to the Weathermen faction of Students for a Democratic Society.

All were anti-American in their radical heyday.

Bernardine Dohrn has been accused of planting a bomb that killed San Francisco police officer Brian V. McDonnell. When police raided a Weathermen bomb factory in Pine Street San Francisco in 1970, they found the fingerprints of Ayers, Machtinger, and Rudd.

All are still radicals today and all proven Obama supporters.

This post profiles the three neglected Weathermen in the Movement for a Democratic Society/Progressives for Obama (P40) network-Jones, Machtinger and Rudd.

Jeff Jones

Who is Jeff Jones? According to his website:

> Jeff Jones went to his first rally against the Vietnam War in 1965. Within a year, he had quit Antioch College to become a fulltime organizer for Students for a Democratic Society (SDS).

In 1966, he traveled to Cambodia to meet with high-level Viet Cong leaders of the National Liberation Front (NLF).

In 1967 and 1968 he served as Students for a Democratic Society Regional Organizer for New York City. In 1969, he was elected, along with Bill Ayers and Mark Rudd, to Students for a Democratic Society national office.

Then, in the spring of 1970, he disappeared. As a leader of the Weather Underground, Jeff evaded an intense FBI manhunt for more than a decade. In 1981, they finally got him. Twenty special agents battered down the door of the Bronx apartment where he was living with his wife and four-year-old son. (Jones 2008)

Jeff Jones serves on the Board of Movement for a Democratic Society and is a signed up supporter of Progressives for Obama (P40).

Howie Machtinger

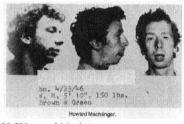

bn. 4/23/46
W, M, 5' 10", 150 lbs.
Brown & Green

Howard Machtinger.

33-3Howard Machtinger

Who is Howie Machtinger?

Today Howard Machtinger is director of Teaching Fellows at the University of North Carolina.

Machtinger was on the barricades at Columbia University in 1968 and was one of the founders of the Weather Underground. He co-authored a tome that stated, "At the right moment, revolutionaries within the United States were to wage a 'people's war' and attack from within. The government would fall and 'world Communism' would eventually be instituted." He also spoke about "how the black liberation movement is so far advanced at this point that the only thing left for white revolutionaries is to support blacks by fighting cops as a diversionary tactic." (Kaplan 2004)

Machtinger is not a confirmed member of Movement for a Democratic Society, but does contribute to Next Left Notes, edited by Movement for a Democratic Society Board member and Progressives for Obama (P40) endorser Tom Good.

Ayers, Dohrn and Rudd are also Next Left Notes contributors.

Machtinger has signed on as a supporter of Progressives for Obama (P40), on the same page with another former Weatherman, Steve Tappis. Further along Jennifer Dohrn sister of Bernardine Dohrn has also signed up.

Machtinger is also the author of a distributed essay entitled Obama and the Left:

> If we, as a Left, are content to critique the Obama phenomenon, we trade self-fulfilling sectarianism for the chance at political impact. A victory for Obama will be a boon for the African-American community and for people of color, it will offer a unique opportunity for the development of an organized and aggressive Left movement that retains its independence at the same time that it is willing to risk everyday involvement in the strange world of American politics.

> If we only critique Obama, we will miss a moment that may not come again for a while. If our politics are, effective, and get to the root of problems, we should put them to the test in political work that connects to large numbers of people struggling to find direction in a dangerous world. Something wonderful is happening. We must be alive to it. I hope we figure out how to relate to it before we consign ourselves to continued marginalization. (Machtinger 2008)

Mark Rudd

Who is Mark Rudd?

As he traveled the country, from the fall of 1968 to the summer of 1969, Mark met many other activists in Students for a Democratic Society who were thinking along the same lines as he, that Students for a Democratic Society could move from anti-war resistance to full-scale socialist revolution...

33-4 Mark Rudd, New Mexico school teacher

White students would reject their "white skin privilege" and actually begin armed struggle against the US government; this, in turn, would attract broad youth support as the struggle increased, following the Cuban model. This theory became fully articulated in a paper presented to the Students for a Democratic Society National Convention in Chicago in June, 1969, authored by a collective of eleven, of which Mark was a member. Its title was "You Don't Need a Weatherman to Know Which Way the Wind Blows," from which Mark's faction of Students for a Democratic Society became known as "The Weathermen."

The convention proved to be Students for a Democratic Society' last. Following a titanic ideological battle concerning "the correct revolutionary direction," a split occurred between the Weathermen and allies grouped around the National Office and a competing faction of Maoist Progressive Labor Party members and their allies. When it was all over, Mark found

33-5 Mark Rudd at MDS Conference New York, NY Feb 2007

himself elected National Secretary of Students for a Democratic Society, along with comrades Billy Ayers as Educational Secretary, and Jeff Jones as Inter-organizational Secretary, and the Weathermen in control of the National Office backed by a small number of chapters around the country... (Rudd 2008)

More from his Mark Rudd's website:

A few national Students for a Democratic Society leader had met with Vietnamese and Cubans to find out about their resistance to US imperialism. Out of these meetings came an invitation for Students for a Democratic Society to send a group of students to Cuba in January, 1968. Because of his active work with the chapter, Mark was invited by the National Office to join the trip, which was openly defying the US government's ban on travel to Cuba. He accepted, working out a month-long absence with his professors...

Mark met young Cubans in positions of responsibility as running schools, farms, and medical institutions with revolutionary enthusiasm: they were remaking society along non-capitalist lines, creating socialism! Meeting with Vietnamese delegates in Cuba, he learned about the nature of the resistance to American aggression, that these people believed they would drive the Americans from their country, no matter how long it took. As if to prove their point, the Tet Offensive was raging at the time in Vietnam, giving the lie to the American military's claims that they were winning the war. A Vietnamese diplomat in Havana, "The American people will eventually tire of the war and the troops will have to be withdrawn," told his group. (Rudd 2008)

According to the FBI, Mark Rudd's trip to Cuba involved terrorist training in camps set up by Soviet KGB Colonel Vadim Kotchergine.

Today Mark Rudd serves on the Board of Movement for a Democratic Society.

Rudd is also an endorser of Progressives for Obama (P40).

Bill Ayers, Bernardine Dohrn and other former Weathermen backed the Senator from Illinois.

Add their old comrades Jeff Jones, Howie Machtinger, Mark Rudd and even Steve Tappis to the mix and you are starting to get beyond coincidence.

That former terrorists are working with Marxist groups to elect US Senator Barack Obama (D-IL) is beyond doubt.

34. Should US voters know this?

Trevor Loudon © Saturday, October 04, 2008

We looked at the Movement for a Democratic Society (MDS) and its offshoot organization, Progressives for Obama (P40).

The two organizations unite all the main radical strands behind the Obama movement. Democratic Socialists of America, Communist Party USA, Committees of Correspondence for Democracy and Socialism (COCDS), former members of the ultra-radical Students for a Democratic Society and its terrorist splinter the Weather Underground.

34-1 Black Radical Congress banner

Several of these currents came together in the mid-1990s to form the New Party. Barack Obama joined the New Party in Chicago in 1995 and received their support and endorsement in his successful 1996 Illinois State Senate race.

In June 1998, radical black activists including many key leaders of the New Party came together in Chicago to form a new organization - the Black Radical Congress.[176]

According to BRC documents:

It seemed to us the idea of bringing together the varied sections of the Black radical tradition - Socialists and Communists, revolutionary nationalists, and radical Black feminists and womanists - was long

---

[176] http://www.afrocubaweb.com/brc.htm

overdue. We began talking with others about the idea and possibilities for a gathering. (Black Radical Congress)

In March of 1997, some seventy activists from more than twenty cities across the country came together in Chicago to begin planning for a Black Radical Congress. Those who gathered reflected a broad spectrum of the radical tradition. Participants came as individuals but represented connections to groups ranging from New Afrikan People's Organization, Black Workers for Justice, The Labor Party, Communist Party USA, The Malcolm X Grassroots Movement, African American Agenda 2000, The Chicago Ida B. Wells Forum and the Committees of Correspondence.

This group agreed to host a Black Radical Congress and constituted itself as the continuations committees. Three subsequent national meetings of the continuations committee occurred in Washington, D. C., in May of 1997, in Atlanta in September 1997, and in New York City in January of 1998. They drafted a "Call for the Congress" and issued the names of over 100 conveners.

Some of those who endorsed the call and have participated in the process include: Abdul Alkalimat, Bill Fletcher, Jr., Manning Marable, Leith Mullings, Barbara Ransby, Barbara Smith, Cornel West, Salim Muwakkil, Charlene Mitchell, Angela Y. Davis, Amiri and Amina Baraka, Sonia Sanchez, Sam Anderson, Evelynn Hammonds, Julianne Malveaux, Jarvis Tyner, General Baker, Ahmed Obafemi, Cathy Cohen, Robin D. G. Kelley, and many others... (Arm the Spirit 1998)

The Black Radical Congress (BRC) organizers issued a call[177] to support their project:

Sisters and Brothers, we stand at the edge of a new century. The moment for a new militancy and a new commitment to the liberation of all Black people, at home and abroad, has arrived. Let us build a national campaign toward the Black Radical Congress, setting in motion a renewed struggle to reclaim our historic role as the real voice of democracy in this country. Spread the word: Without struggle, there is no progress! Now's the time! (Kupendua 1998)

The Struggle Continues: Setting a Black Liberation Agenda for the 21st Century.

Those answering the call included:

- Akbar Muhammad Ahmad - (Instructor of African-American history

---

[177] http://www.hartford-hwp.com/archives/45a/524.html

& political science, Cuyahoga Community College, Cleveland)

- Abdul Alkalimat - (League of Revolutionaries for a New America) Amina Baraka (CPUSA)
- Amiri Baraka - (Unity & Struggle newspaper, affiliated with the CPUSA for a number of years in the late 90's/early 2000s)
- Debbie Bell - (CPUSA)
- Lisa Brock - (Chicago, wife of Committees of Correspondence leader Otis Cunningham)
- Humberto R Brown - (Afro Latino Network;
- Ida B. Wells – (W.E.B. Du Bois Network, alleged CPUSA)
- Linda Burnham - (Women of Color Resource Center, Berkeley, CA, from a Communist Party family, close to Committees of Correspondence)
- James E Campbell - (Retired educator, Committees of Correspondence)
- Angela Y Davis - (Professor, University of California at Santa Cruz; Committees of Correspondence, former CPUSA Vice presidential candidate)
- Michael Dawson - (Chicago)
- Bill Fletcher, Jr. - (Labor activist and writer, Washington, DC, affiliated with "Crossroads" publications and "Transactions" Maoist group in the early 1990's, leading DSA member)
- Arturo Griffiths - (African-American Human Rights Foundation, Washington, DC, editorial board of CPUSA theoretical journal Political Affairs)
- Gerald Horne - (Professor of African-American studies, University of North Carolina, Chapel Hill, editorial board of CPUSA theoretical journal Political Affairs)
- Gerry Hudson - (Executive Vice President, Local 1199 – National Health & Human Services Union, New York City, Close to DSA)
- J.J. Johnson - (DC 1707, AFSCME, New York City) CPUSA
- Robin DG Kelley - (Historian, Africana Studies, New York University; Ida B. Wells-W.E.B Du Bois Network, formerly with the Communist Workers Party, latterly close to CPUSA
- Manning Marable - (Co-Chair, Committees of Correspondence; Ida B. Wells-W.E B. Du Bois Network)
- Togi Marshall - (Washington, DC, alleged CPUSA)
- Denice (Dee) Myles - (Chicago, CPUSA)
- Charlene Mitchell (Co-Chair, Committees of Correspondence; staff,

Local 371, AFSCME, former CPUSA presidential candidate)

- Leith Mullings - (Professor of Anthropology, City University of New York Graduate School; Ida B. Wells-W.E.B Du Bois Network, was in CPUSA, close to CCDS)
- Salim Muwakkil - (Chicago, writer for the DSA linked magazine In These Times)
- Prexy Nesbitt - (Chicago, alleged CPUSA)
- Barbara Ransby - (Chicago)
- Joe Sims - (CPUSA; Editor, Political Affairs)
    - Lasker Smith - (Ecorse, MI, CPUSA)
    - Jarvis Tyner - (CPUSA)
    - Cornel West - (Cambridge, MA, DSA)

34-2 Manning Marble, MDS, Feb 2007

There is some continuity with this group.

Manning Marable, Bill Fletcher, and Cornel West were all leaders of the New Party.

Bill Fletcher, Robin D.G. Kelley, Gerald Horne, Charlene Mitchell, Angela Y. Davis and Akbar Muhammad Ahmed have all served on the Board of Movement for a Democratic Society.

Manning Marable was elected Movement for a Democratic Society Chair[178] in February 2007. Bill Fletcher was the initiator of Progressives for Obama (P40), while Robin D.G. Kelley, Cornel West and James Campbell are endorsers of the organization. Prexy Nesbitt is a signatory of Progressives for Obama's online petition.

Michael Dawson spoke with Obama at a 1996 forum on Economic Insecurity sponsored by the University of Chicago Democratic Socialists of America (DSA) Youth Section, Chicago Democratic Socialists of America (DSA) and University Democrats.

Gerald Horne, who studied the Communist Party USA in Hawaii, linked[179] Barack Obama with his boyhood mentor, long time Communist Party USA member Frank Marshall Davis in the Communist Party USA journal of Political Affairs.

---

[178] http://antiauthoritarian.net/NLN/?p=179
[179] http://trevorloudon.com/2007/03/barack-obamas-marxist-mentor/

Gerry Hudson is a senior official of the Service Employees International Union (SEIU), which endorsed US Senator Barack Obama (D-IL). Robin D.G. Kelley will deliver[180] Hampshire College's eleventh annual Eqbal Ahmad Lecture on October 15th in the Robert Crown Center. His talk will be titled *"Confronting Obama: A Primer on Race and Empire for the New US President."*

Manning Marable strongly endorsed Obama in a January 2008 article entitled *"Barack Obama's Problem - And Ours"*.

Dee Myles[181] penned an Obama piece for the Illinois Communist blog.

Leith Mullings is a signatory of the February 2008 Feminists for Peace and US Senator Barack Obama (D-IL)

Salim Muwakkil is a prominent propagandist[182] for US Senator Barack Obama (D-IL).

Barbara Ransby spoke at the forum in Chicago at The Center for Public Intellectuals and The University of Illinois-Chicago (UIC) April 19th-20th, 2002 with Bill Ayers, Salim Muwakkil and US Senator Barack Obama (D-IL).

Intellectuals in Times of Crisis: Experiences and applications of intellectual work in urgent situations:

- William Ayers – (UIC, College of Education; author of Fugitive Days)
- Douglass Cassel – (Northwestern University, Center for International Human Rights)
- Cathy Cohen - (University of Chicago, Political Science)
- Salim Muwakkil - (Chicago Tribune; In These Times)
- Barack Obama - (Illinois State Senator)
- Barbara Ransby - (UIC, African-American Studies moderator)
- Joe Sims - (Wrote a pro-Obama article for the Communist Party USA Political Affairs)
- Jarvis Tyner - (Criss-crossed the USA drumming up support for

---

[180] http://www.hampshire.edu/news/9668.htm
[181] http://communistpartyillinois.blogspot.com/2008/02/joyous-magnificence-african-american.html
[182] http://www.democracynow.org/2004/7/15/barack_obama_a_look_at_the

Obama)

- Cornel West - (Obama's "comrade")

There is one more significant link between the Black Radical Congress and US Senator Barack Obama (D-IL). One session[183] at the Congress was entitled:

> Faith as a Weapon: Spirituality and the Role of the Church in the Radical Movement. What are the lessons we learn from Nat Turner, Absalom Jones, Sojourner Truth, Malcolm X, Martin Luther King Jr. and other Black ministers as leaders in the struggle? What is the history of spiritual motivation in the radical/liberation movement?

> Panelists: Michael Eric Dyson, Cornel West, Rev Jeremiah Wright, Linda Thomas, Kevin Tyson (Black Radical Congress 1998)

Well fancy that, Obama's pastor discussing "faith as a weapon" with Michael Eric Dyson and Cornel West, both members of the Religion and Socialism Commission[184] of Democratic Socialists of America - not to mention Kevin Tyson, involved with the youth wing of the Communist Party USA.

Cornel West, (Progressives for Obama (P40), advisor to Obama) was a strong defender[185] of Rev Jeremiah Wright when the pastor's extremist views became a public scandal. Likewise, his comrade Michael Eric

34-3 Barack Obama (l) Rev. Jeremiah Wright

Dyson has been a strong defender of both Rev Jeremiah Wright and a prominent supporter of US Senator Barack Obama (D-IL).

Obama's pastor of 20 years was an associate of some of the most radical communists and socialists in the US. Did Obama get some of his ideas, which he did not notice?

Many of those radicals are now prominent Obama supporters.

What a tiny world we live in.

---

[183] http://mailman.lbo-talk.org/1998/1998-June/002946.html

[184] http://www.religioussocialism.com/

[185] http://www.time.com/time/politics/article/0,8599,1735662,00.html

35. Even More Weathermen for Obama - Connections

Trevor Loudon © Wednesday, October 08, 2008

In recent posts I have examined former Weather Under-ground Organization (WUO) involvement in two interlinked organizations, Movement for a Democratic Society" (MDS)[186] and Progressives for Obama (P40).[187]

In the mid-1970s the Weather Underground published a 158-page statement entitled, "Prairie Fire" calling for the:

> Uniting of all revolutionary forces in this country with the ultimate aim to overthrow the Government. (Ayers 1974)

Founded in August 2006, Movement for a Democratic Society embodies the type of revolutionary unity the WUO was striving for back in the '60s.

The Movement for a Democratic Society Board includes Representatives from three of the United States' most influential (and pro-Obama) Marxist organizations, Democratic Socialists of America[188], the

35-1 From Weather Underground to Movement for a Democratic Society, Bernardine Dohrn (l) and Bill Ayers (r)

Communist Party USA (CPUSA)[189] and Committees of Correspondence for Democracy and Socialism (COCDS),[190] plus many former members of Students for a Democratic Society (SDS) and its terrorist splinter, the Weather Underground Organization (WUO).

Former Weathermen and their allies dominate Movement for a Democratic Society.

It was revealed that three former

---

[186] Chapter 30 – Former Terrorists Bill Ayers and Bernardine Dohrn Involved in Key Pro-Obama Organization

[187] Chapter 27 - Reds, Radicals, Terrorists and Traitors – Progressives for Obama

[188] Chapter 7 - Barack Obama and the Democratic Socialists of America

[189] Chapter 25 - CCDS Marxist-Leninists Come Out for Obama

[190] Chapter 25 - CCDS Marxist-Leninists Come Out for Obama

Weathermen, Bernardine Dohrn,[191] Mark Rudd and Jeff Jones have served on the Movement for a Democratic Society Board, as have two close friends of Dohrn's husband, Bill Ayers, former Students for a Democratic Society Maoists Carl Davidson and Mike Klonsky[192] - both familiar names to Obama watchers.

Bill Ayers, himself, is a prominent Movement for a Democratic Society activist, while another Board member, Thomas Good, describes himself as an "unrepentant Weather supporter."

A Progressives for Obama (P4O) and intimately tied to Movement for a Democratic Society. Four of the six original Progressives for Obama founders are Movement for Democratic Society Board members:

- Carl Davidson - (CCDS member)
- Tom Hayden - (former Students for a Democratic Society leader)
- Bill and Barbara Ehrenreich - (both Democratic Socialists of America (DSA) leaders)
- Mark Rudd and Thomas Good – (PFO endorsers as are Klonsky's wife Susan and brother Fred)

Good edits the Movement for a Democratic Society "unofficial" ejournal Next Left Notes[193] that carries a prominent link to Progressives for Obama. Jeff Jones and two former" Weathermen, Howie Machtinger (a Next Left Notes contributor) and Steve Tappis have signed a Progressives for Obama supporter's petition.

Another Progressive for Obama petition signatory is Jennifer Dohrn, sister of WUO leader Bernardine Dohrn. The list includes other Movement for Democratic Society Board members including Steve Tappis, Bernardine Dohrn and Bruce Rubenstein.

It turns out that Bruce Rubenstein is one of three key players in Movement for a Democratic Society.

According to an article on Movement for a Democratic Society and the re-born Students for a Democratic Society in The Nation April 2007:

---

[191] Chapter 30 – Former Terrorists Bill Ayers and Bernardine Dohrn Involved in Key Pro-Obama Organization
[192] Chapter 33 - More Weathermen For Obama
[193] http://www.antiauthoritarian.net/NLN/

Power has resided with three figures: historian Paul Buhle, once editor of the original Students for a Democratic Society journal Radical America; Thomas Good, a 48-year-old Communist-turned-anarchist who created the new Students for a Democratic Society website and Bruce Rubenstein, a Connecticut personal-injury attorney. (Phelps 2007)

The Nation goes on to comment on tensions within Movement for a Democratic Society caused by the dominance of the Weatherman clique:

The Weather controversy erupted when Bernardine Dohrn, a Weather leader who now teaches law at Northwestern University, was invited to speak at the first new Students for a Democratic Society conference, held in Providence, Rhode Island, in April 2006. Dohrn received a rousing welcome, but when Bob Ross, associated with the Students for a Democratic Society, used his talk to lament that "the largest legal and unarmed movement in the history of the West" turned " violent and useless."

At the first new Students for a Democratic Society national convention in Chicago, in August, Good opened the proceedings by reading greetings from Dohrn. Moreover, Rubenstein, Movement for a Democratic Society's treasurer, is unapologetic about his Weather history and says that if it were 1969 he would "do it all over again..." (Phelps 2007)

35-2 Bruce Rubenstein

Bruce Rubenstein

Bruce Rubenstein[194] and former WUO member Mark Rudd are to the Movement for a Democratic Society.

It also turns out that Rubenstein may also be an Obama supporter.

From the Hartford Courant.com:[195]

Barack Obama's Connecticut campaign drew a capacity crowd of 250 to a kickoff event at Yale's Afro-American Cultural Center today, while Hillary Rodham Clinton rolled out an endorsement by Stamford Mayor Dannel Malloy...Bruce Rubenstein of West Hartford, a fundraiser who likes to play both radical and insider, dropped by. (Pazniokas 2008)

Rubenstein was also involved in countering a fake Obama blog,

---

[194] http://keywiki.org/index.php/Bruce_Rubenstein
[195] http://blogs.courant.com/capitol_watch/2008/01/obama-kickoff-is-sro-hillary-a.html

Down with Tyranny[196] June 1, 2006:

> Everyone who has paid any attention at all to Joe Lieberman's political career knows he is one of the slimiest and low down dirty players in American politics...But posting fake blogs in the name of Barack Obama and Harry Reid is downright bizarre.

> According to today JOURNAL INQUIRER from north-central Connecticut, the FBI has been brought in on the case. "A Hartford lawyer says the FBI has agreed to investigate postings promoting Sen. Joseph I. Lieberman's re-election on a popular Connecticut-based Internet 'blog' in the names of Senate Minority Leader Harry Reid, D-Nev., and Sen. Barack Obama, D-Ill. Bruce D. Rubenstein, a former finance Chairman for the Democratic State Central Committee and a Lieberman critic, said Wednesday that an agent in the FBI's Meriden office told him the agency would probe the postings on the 'Connecticut Local Politics' Web log.

> Obama confirms that Lieberman's postings were fake and that he never authorized Lieberman to use his name for anything. (Down iwth Tyranny 2006)

Chalk up one more Weatherman for Obama.

Jennifer Dohrn

35-3 Jennifer Dohrn

Jennifer Dohrn was never a proven WUO member, but she was a national leader of the Prairie Fire Organizing Committee, the WUO's above ground support network and a spokesperson for her terrorist sister. Later, she was married to radical lawyer Haywood Burns, founder of the legal arm of the black revolution, the National Conference of Black Lawyers - an affiliate of the Soviet front International Association of Democratic Lawyers.

Burns had close ties to Cuba and was involved in several other communist fronts including the National Lawyers Guild, Center for Constitutional Rights and the Emergency Civil Liberties Committee.

---

[196] http://downwithtyranny.blogspot.com/2006/06/desperate-lieberman-campaign-being.html

Burns successfully defended CPUSA radical Angela Davis, who was acquitted of kidnapping and murder charges after the 1970 invasion of a California courthouse which killed four people including the presiding judge. Angela Davis is now a leader of COCDS and was a founding Movement for a Democratic Society Board member with Bernadine Dohrn.

Steve Tappis

An original leading Weatherman, with Bill Ayers, Bernardine Dohrn, Mark Rudd, Jeff Jones and Howie Machtinger, Steve Tappis was also one of the earliest dropouts.

He has stayed radical all the way, however, and in September 2008 was involved in a TEACH IN ON THE IRAQ WAR at the University of California Berkeley.

Speakers included Progressives for Obama (P4O) founder Tom Hayden and Progressives for Obama website endorsers Daniel Ellsberg and Immanuel Wallerstein.

Described as a "Sixties activist in Chicago," Tappis was a member of the "Teach In" organizing group.

Rick Ayers

35-4 Rick Ayers

Another group member was Berkeley PhD student Rick Ayers - another former Weatherman and brother of Bill Ayers - fancy that.

Crossroads

Chicago is home to the Crossroads Fund[197], a foundation that channels money to organizations such as the:

- Ad Hoc Committee on Chicago Police Torture
- Feminist Response in Disability Activism
- Female Storytellers Igniting Revolution to End Violence
- Illinois Safe Schools Alliance
- Coalition for Education on Sexual Orientation

---

[197] http://www.crossroadsfund.org/

- Communist Party USA/Democratic Socialists of America (DSA) linked organizations such as the Chicago Committee to Defend the Bill of Rights and Jobs with Justice

Do you get the picture?

The Fund is co-Chaired by leading Chicago Democratic Socialists of America (DSA) member Bill Barclay,[198] while Ali Abunimah, a claimed Obama associate, serves on the Board. Steve Tappis is a donor to the Crossroads fund. Other donors in recent times might also be familiar to keen Obama watchers. A view of Crossroad 2007 Annual Report and 2005 Annual Report[199] reveal some interesting names.

They include:

- Timuel Black – (Obama's personal friend (COCDS member and husband of Progressives for Obama (P40) endorser Zenobia Black)
- Quentin Young – (Democratic Socialists of America (DSA) member - present at the famous 1995 meeting at the home of Bill Ayers and Bernardine Dohrn which launched Obama's political career)
- Bettylu Saltzman (Obama financier)
- Carl Davidson and Tim Carpenter – (Progressives for Obama (P40) founders)
- Aviva Futorian and Susan Klonsky - (Progressives for Obama endorsers)
- Mike Klonsky - (Movement for a Democratic Society Board member)
- Barbara Ransby[200] - (An unsuccessful Board nominee)
- Ted Pearson - (Progressives for Obama petition signers COCDS, former Illinois Communist Party USA Chairman)
- Prexy Nesbitt[201] - (Communist Party USA and Black Radical Congress connections)
- Bill Ayers and Bernardine Dohrn - (Listed in 2005. Ayers and Dohrn are Crossroads donors, and they are active fundraisers)

In the Fall, of 2005, Crossroads Fund worked with donors and Board members to put together house parties to discuss critical community issues and to raise money for the Crossroads Fund. Bill Ayers and

---

[198] http://www.chicagodsa.org/ngarchive/ng120.html#anchor434300
[199] http://www.scribd.com/doc/2367930/Crossroads-Fund
[200] http://keywiki.org/index.php/Barbara_Ransby
[201] http://keywiki.org/index.php/Prexy_Nesbitt

Bernardine Dohrn, along with Yvonne Welbon and Dorian Warren, hosted a group of donors and friends as they engaged in discussions about political participation in Chicago. When Crossroads held anniversary celebrations last year, they established a 25th Anniversary Host Committee.

Honorary Hosts included US Representative Danny K. Davis and Alderman Helen Schiller[202], Alderman Joseph A. Moore[203] Cook County Clerk David Orr[204] and of course US Senator Barack Obama (D-IL).

Do you suppose Barack hosted Bill and Bernardine?

36. How Socialist Was Obama's "New Party"?

Trevor Loudon © Saturday, October 11, 2008

There has been a big buzz in the blogosphere since US mega-blog Powerline noticed evidence proving that Barack Obama was, in the mid-'90s, a member of a short-lived socialist organization, the Chicago New Party.[205]

Democratic Socialists of America, which also endorsed Obama that year, and to which the Senator has longstanding and ongoing ties, has also been dragged into the fray.

The Obama camp has countered in two ways: (1) claiming that the New Party endorsed Obama, and (2) he was never a member of the New Party.

36-1 Barack Obama (far right) celebrate with Chicago New Party members Ted Thomas and Ruth Schools after their victories in the Democratic primary last month.

[202] http://keywiki.org/index.php/Helen_Shiller
[203] http://keywiki.org/index.php/Joseph_A._Moore
[204] http://www.chicagodsa.org/d1988/index.html
[205]
http://keywiki.org/index.php/Barack_Obama_and_the_New_Party/Progressive_Chicago

36-2 Carl Davidson

That lie is disposed of.

First, from the front page of *New Ground* 42[206] and page 2 includes this paragraph:

> The political entourage included Alderman Michael Chandler, William Delgado, chief of staff for State Rep Miguel del Valle, and spokespersons for State Sen. Alice Palmer, Sonya Sanchez, chief of staff for State Sen. Jesse Garcia, who is running for State Rep in Garcia's District; and Barack Obama, chief of staff for State Senator Alice Palmer. Obama is running for Palmer's vacant seat...Although ACORN and SEIU Local 880 were the harbingers of the NP there was a strong presence of COCDS and Democratic Socialists of America (DSA) (15% DSA)... Four political candidates were "there" seeking NP support." (Bentley, New Ground 42 1995)

Second, supporters claim that the New Party was not socialist.

Long time Obama associate and former Chicago New Party activist Carl Davidson has posted this statement on several blogs.

> The New Party in Chicago was never a socialist party. Democratic Socialists of America (DSA) in Chicago had little to do with it in any practical way. It was a pragmatic party of 'small d democracy' mainly promoting economic reforms like the living wage and testing the fusion tactic, common in many countries but only operational in New York in the US. The main trend within it was ACORN, an Alinskyist outfit, which is hardly Marxist. Most socialist left groups either ignored it or opposed it, even if a few of their members took part in it. That's the truth of the matter. (Horowitz, Carl Davidson 2008)

This is far from the truth.

The New Party was the creation of Democratic Socialists of America (DSA) and the radical community organization ACORN - which was something of a Democratic Socialists of America (DSA) front. In some areas, the Communist Party USA was involved, but in Chicago, the Communist Party USA splinter group Committees of Correspondence (COCDS) was more prominent. Carl Davidson is well aware that Marxists set up the Chicago New Party because he was one of them.

---

[206] http://www.chicagodsa.org/ngarchive/ng42.html#anchor792932

On January 27th approximately forty-five people attended the Chicago Democratic Socialists of America (DSA) and Chicago COCDS organized public form at the ACTWU hall on Ashland Ave... Chicago Democratic Socialists of America (DSA) was represented by Co-Chair, Kurt Anderson and Political Education Officer, Bob Roman. Committee of Correspondence (COCDS) was represented by Carl Davidson, who is a member of COCDS's National Coordinating Committee and Ronelle Mustin, an activist from the 22nd ward. The event was Chaired by Sandi Patrinos, Chair of Chicago COCDS...

Carl Davidson wanted to focus on "voting patterns." ...To win elections, Davidson emphasized that there are two necessary coinciding factors. First, a passive majority; and second, a militant minority.

Davidson emphasized that in this historical period the Left's strategy must be electoral politics not revolution. Consequently the Left must galvanize the "majority" - the working class and poor... Moreover the democratic left needs to get active in the New Party which has won twenty of thirty local elections. Thus a short-term strategy of working with the Democratic Party; and, in the long-term work with the New Party. (Bentley, Where Does the Left Go from Here? 1995)

If that is not clear enough, the Chicago Democratic Socialists of America (DSA)'s *New Ground*[207] of September/October 1995:

The political entourage included Alderman Michael Chandler, William Delgado, chief of staff for State Rep Miguel del Valle), and spokespersons for State Sen. Alice Palmer, Sonya Sanchez, Chief of Staff for State Sen. Jesse Garcia, who is running for State Rep in Garcia's District; and Barack Obama, chief of staff for State Sen. Alice Palmer. Obama is running for Palmer's vacant seat...Although ACORN and SEIU Local 880 were the harbingers of the NP there was a strong presence of COCDS and Democratic Socialists of America (DSA) (15% DSA)... Four political candidates were "there" seeking NP support." (Bentley, New Ground 42 1995)

---

[207] http://www.chicagodsa.org/ngarchive/ng42.html#anchor792932

Danny K. Davis

36-3 Danny K. Davis

Obama's 1996 New Party running mate, US Rep. Danny K. Davis (D-IL-7th District) was elected to the US Congress as a Democrat - the highest office won by a New Party candidate.

An NPer and a Democrat, Davis was, and is, a Democratic Socialists of America (DSA) member. Links exist that the Congressman supported both the COCDS and Communist Party USA.

"Over 500 delegates and observers (including 140 from Chicago) attended the founding convention of the Committees of Correspondence (COCDS) held here in Chicago in July.

Speakers…included:

- Charles Nqukula – (General Secretary of the South African Communist Party)
- Dulce Maria Pereira - (A senatorial candidate of the Workers Party of Brazil)
- Angela Davis - (COCDS)
- Andre Brie - (Party of Democratic Socialism of Germany, a revamp of the old East German Communist Party)
- Danny Davis – (Cook County Commissioner)
- Helen Schiller - (Alderman)
- Rick Muñoz – (A Representative of the Green Left Weekly of Australia, and a Representative of the Cuban Interest Section)

The Chicago Communist Party held an annual fund raising banquet for its paper, the *People's Weekly World* (now the People's "Daily" World)

The People's Daily World reported in the July 28, 1990 issue that Chicago Alderman Danny K. Davis attended that year's banquet on July 15, 1990.

Davis applauded those at the banquet, who, he said, are always in the midst of struggle. PDW readers, he said, are "steadfast in the fight for justice."

According to the *People's Weekly World* of October 3, 1998,

Representative Danny K. Davis interrupted his campaign work for Senate candidate Carol Moseley-Braun[208] to present an award at the Chicago annual *People's Weekly World* banquet.

Obama helped get the Communist Party USA-COCDS-Democratic Socialists of America (DSA) connected Moseley-Braun elected in 1992 and then inherited her former Illinois Senate seat in 2004.

US Representative Danny K. Davis remains one of Obama's most loyal supporters.

Carl Davidson is correct in that the Chicago New Party was not OPENLY socialist. It was designed as a vehicle for socialists to infiltrate leftist candidates into positions of power through the Democratic Party.

The Chicago New Party was socialist dominated, but what about other chapters across the Nation?

A New Party document from 1995 or 1996 is entitled *"Who's Building the New Party?"*

It lists one hundred "community leaders, organizers, unionists, retirees, scholars, artists, parents, students, doctors, writers and other activists who are building the NP."

Those listed include:

- Elaine Bernard – (A Labor academic and prominent DSA member)
- Noam Chomsky – (Linguist and activist, member of both DSA and CoC)
- Steve Cobble – (Political consultant, now a leader of the DSA linked Progressive Democrats of America)
- Barbara Ehrenreich – (Author, activist and DSA leader)
- Bill Fletcher – (Former Maoist, a Labor activist and leading DSA member)
- Maude Hurd – (Long-time ACORN president. Awarded for her work by Boston DSA)
- Manning Marable – (A founder of both DSA and CoC. Regarded as a driving force within the New Party)
- Frances Fox Piven – (A DSA member, regarded as the brains behind ACORN)

---

[208] http://trevorloudon.com/2007/12/carol-moseley-braun-did-clinton-send-us-a-socialist-part-1/

- Raphael Pizzaro – (New York Labor activist and former CPUSA member. An official of both CoC and DSA)
- Gloria Steinem – (Author and DSA member)
- Cornel West – (Academic and prominent DSA member)
- Quentin Young – (Chicago doctor, prominent DSA member, formerly allegedly involved with CPUSA)
- Howard Zinn – (Historian who describes himself as an anarchist/democratic socialist)

Is there a pattern here?

While the New Party helped launch Obama's political career, the connections did not end there.

Dr. Quentin Young

36-4 Dr. Quentin Young

Quentin Young[209] is a long time friend, near neighbor and political supporter of Obama. He attended the famous 1995 meeting in the Chicago home of former terrorists Bill Ayers and Bernardine Dohrn where Illinois State Senator Alice Palmer introduced Barack Obama as her chosen successor.

Cornel West is now one of the two members of Obama's "Black Advisory Council."

Movement for a Democratic Society

36-5 Austin, TX and the MDS

In August 2006, several former Weather Underground terrorists, including Ayers and Dohrn, joined leaders of Democratic Socialists of America (DSA), Communist Party USA and COCDS to form a new organization - Movement for a Democratic Society (MDS).

Several former New Party leaders joined the Movement for a

---

[209] http://keywiki.org/index.php/Quentin_Young

Democratic Society Board,[210] including Noam Chomsky, Carl Davidson, Barbara Ehrenreich and Bill Fletcher and, since January 2007, Chairman Manning Marable.

Unsuccessful Board nominees included former New Party leaders Cornel West and Howard Zinn.

This year, Movement for a Democratic Society Board members Davidson, Ehrenreich and Fletcher, joined with former Students for a Democratic Society (SDS) leader Tom Hayden and Democratic Socialists of America (DSA) linked actor/activist Danny Glover, to form a satellite organization, Progressives for Obama (P40).

> In its creed, first published in March in the Nation magazine, the Progressives for Obama (P40) founders state their organization descended from the "proud tradition of independent social movements that have made America a more just and democratic country." (Klein 2008)

Is this a reference to the New Party?

> Progressives for Obama (P40) stated it can help the Illinois senator's ascent to highest office by contributing funds, using the Internet to reach "millions of swing voters;" defending Obama against negative attacks and making its agenda known at the Democratic National Convention.

> "Progressives can make a difference in close primary races like Pennsylvania, North Carolina, Oregon and Puerto Rico, and in the November general election," the founders state. (Klein 2008)

The Progressives for Obama website carries a long list of endorsers, many of whom are from Democratic Socialists of America (DSA), COCDS, Students for a Democratic Society or the Weathermen.

They include former New Party leaders Steve Cobble, Frances Fox Piven and Cornel West.

Is this all coincidence?

Alternatively, are the same socialists who supported Obama in his 1996 State Senate race now trying to put their man into the White House?

---

[210] http://antiauthoritarian.net/NLN/?p=179

---

37. Obama's Mentor, Frank Marshall Davis - Was He Still a Communist?

Trevor Loudon © Thursday, October 16, 2008

Since the New Zeal blog first publicized[211] the connection, the late communist poet Frank Marshall Davis' relationship to Barack Obama has been the subject of thousands of articles, blog posts and talk back calls.

37-1 Frank Marshall Davis

Obama's apologists first attempted to minimize the Obama/Davis relationship. As evidence mounted however, it became apparent that Davis was indeed a mentor to Obama. The relationship lasted from 1970, when Obama was ten, until he left Hawaii for college on the mainland at age 18.

Next, the Obamaphiles tried to minimize Davis's communism, portraying him as a benevolent civil rights activist and therefore, if anything, a positive influence on the young Obama.

Some have acknowledged that Davis did indeed join Communist Party USA in Chicago in the 1940s, but all that was well behind him by the time he met the young Obama.

As is common with Obama, the truth is distinct from the appearance.

Information from Davis' 601-page FBI file[212] reveals that Davis (born 1905) became interested in Communist Party USA as far back as 1931.

From the mid/late '30s to the '40s, Davis was involved in several Communist Party fronts including the National Negro Congress, the League of American Writers and the National Federation for Constitutional Liberties and the Civil Rights Congress.

The FBI first began tracking Davis in 1944, when they identified him

---

[211] http://trevorloudon.com/2007/03/barack-obamas-marxist-mentor/
[212] http://www.usasurvival.org/docs/davis.FBI.File.pdf

as a member of Communist Party USA's Dorie Miller Club in Chicago - card number 47544.

Davis taught courses at the Communist Party controlled Abraham Lincoln School in Chicago and attended meetings of the party's Cultural Club until he left for Hawaii in 1948.

In Hawaii, Davis became a columnist for a union financed, communist controlled newspaper, the Honolulu Record.

Choose a building block. Despite going underground in 1950, the Hawaiian Communist Party was the most dynamic in the United States at the time. The mainland put huge resources into the Hawaiian party because the Soviets wanted the US military presence on the islands shut down. The Hawaiian Communist Party was charged with agitating against the US military bases at every opportunity. Several times the FBI observed Davis photographing obscure Hawaiian beaches, for espionage purposes.

Through its control of the International Long Shore Workers Union (ILWU), the Hawaiian Communist Party had huge influence on the local Democratic Party. In the mid-'50s, while still a confirmed communist, Davis like many of his comrades became an official in the local Democratic Party. The communist influence is present in the Hawaiian Democratic Party today.

At the time, the underground Communist Party divided into two or three person independent cells. Davis led one cell, "Group 10," with his wife and one other comrade.

An extensive Senate Security Investigation in 1956 shattered the

Figure 37-2 Letter Head ACFPFB

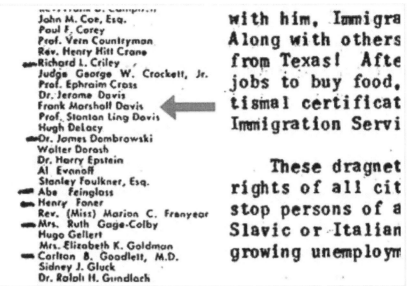

Figure 37-3 Enlarged Letterhead ID Frank Marshall Davis (arrow)

Hawaiian Communist Party, driving the remnants underground where it remains to this day. The FBI continued to monitor Davis into the '60s and though they found little, if any, party activity on the islands, Davis is regarded as a "believer." The FBI monitored Davis for at least 19 years. They marked him down for immediate arrest should war break out between the United States and the Soviet Union; an honor reserved for the most dangerous subversives.

One of the longest-lived communist fronts was the American Committee for Protection of Foreign Born (ACFPFB). Active from 1935 until 1980, the ACFFPBP was charged with preventing foreign communists like Davis's friend ILWU leader, Harry Bridges, from deportation.

Davis was a longtime supporter of the ACFPFB, at least until 1973, three years after meeting the young Obama. Hawaiian lawyer, party member and longtime Davis comrade, Harriet Bouslog, appears on the list.

Others of the several known party members listed above, include civil rights activists Carl and Anne Braden and Dirk J. Struik, a mathematician, whose peace activist daughter Gwen lives in New Zealand. US Representative Hugh DeLacy (D-WA-1st District), a secret party member who became a Democratic Congressman for Washington

State and three prominent Chicago activists, Richard Criley, Frank Wilkinson and Abe Feinglass.

When Obama decided to go to Chicago in 1983 to become a "community organizer," he was inspired by that year's election of Chicago's first black Mayor, Harold Washington.

A long time friend of the Chicago Communist Party, Washington would have known Frank Marshall Davis from his post-War student days.

It would be interesting to know if Frank Marshall Davis ever told the young Obama about Harold Washington and his leftist connections.

What connection did Obama have to Chicago other than his boyhood mentor, Frank Marshall Davis?

38. Obama, Davis, Jarrett - One Degree of Separation

Trevor Loudon © Friday, October 17, 2008

Why did Barack Obama move to Chicago? Why did he choose a city famous for its corruption and distrust of outsiders as a launching pad for his political career?

Did Obama's boyhood mentor, lifelong communist, Frank Marshall Davis influence that choice?

38-1 Frank Marshall Davis

Obama admits he was inspired to first move to Chicago in 1983 by the election of the city's first black Mayor Harold Washington. Obama even unsuccessfully wrote away for a job in Washington's administration.

Frank Marshall Davis[213] had lived in Chicago for many years until moving to Hawaii in 1948. He had been active in Chicago's post-War Communist Party while Harold Washington was a left leaning young law student. Had the two ever met?

---

[213] Chapter 37 - Obama's Mentor, Frank Marshall Davis- Was He Still a Communist?

38-3 Chicago's South Side Community Art Center

38-2 Vernon Jarrett

38-4 Vernon Jarrett with Harold Washington and Cicely Tyson

Possibly not, but there was only one degree of separation.

Frank Marshall Davis was involved in Chicago's South Side Community Art Center,[214] "a meeting place for young African American writers and artists during the 1940s." An outgrowth of the Federal Art Project, the Art Center was a hangout for Communist Party members and sympathizers, including Richard Wright, Margaret Burroughs, Marion Perkins and Arna Bontemps.

Another center regular was a young journalist named Vernon Jarrett. Davis and Jarrett also worked together on the black run newspaper, the Chicago Defender.

By the 1940s, many of the themes, slogans, demands, and cultural icons of this would-be Negro People's Front were hegemonic on the South Side; the Chicago Defender, for example,

without ever referring to the Communists or other left organizations, presented the race-and-class based radicalism of Communist Party USA. (Wald 2000)

Vernon Jarrett went on to forge an impressive career in journalism. He became the Chicago Tribune's first black syndicated columnist and was a founder of the National Association of Black Journalists. He became an icon to Chicago's black community.

According to a Washington Post obituary May 25, 2004:

Mr. Jarrett continually shone a light on African American history and pertinent issues in Chicago and throughout the country. He stoked the

---

[214] http://www.newberry.org/outspoken/exhibit/objectlist_section2.html

political embers in Chicago that led to the 1983 election of the city's first African American Mayor, Harold Washington. (Lamb 2004)

Vernon Jarrett was a key influence in Washington's decision to run for the Chicago Mayoralty and remained a key supporter through his four-year tenure.

Harold Washington defeated the Daley machine to win the Mayoralty backed by a coalition[215] led by Chicago's Communist Party and the local branch of Democratic Socialists of America.

38-5 Future DSA leader the late Carl Marx Shier (l), veteran socialist Egidio Clemente (c), and Harold Washington (r) at the 1981 Debs Dinner

Historian Paul Buhle wrote in a 1992 article for the Encyclopedia of the American Left:

> Communists also gained from long-standing political relationships in the black community. Victories of black Mayoral and congressional candidates with decades - old ties to the Communist Party - a short list would include Coleman Young and George Crocket in Detroit, Gus Newport in Berkeley, and, Harold Washington in Chicago (Buhle and Georgakas 1992)

Paul Buhle knows his socialists.

A former member of the Students for a Democratic Society, Buhle is now a leader of Democratic Socialists of America (DSA). He also serves on the Board of Movement for a Democratic Society (MDS) where he works with former Weather Underground terrorists Bill Ayers, Bernadine Dohrn, Jeff Jones and Mark Rudd. Buhle and Rudd are also involved with the Movement for a Democratic Society offshoot Progressives for Obama (P40).

Washington was close to Chicago Democratic Socialists of America (DSA), which in turn went on to endorse Barack Obama during his 1995/96 Illinois State Senate race.

Chicago Democratic Socialists of America (DSA) organized a major dinner every year to honor US socialist leaders, Eugene Debs, Norman

---

[215] http://trevorloudon.com/2007/10/chicagos-redblack-alliance-targets-white-house/

Thomas, and Michael Harrington known as the Debs-Thomas-Harrington Dinner.

Harold Washington MC'd the 1981 Debs-Thomas-Harrington Dinner[216] but had to cancel out of the 1983 event.

> The 1983 Debs-Thomas-Harrington Dinner held at the McCormick Inn on Saturday, May 7... Mayor Harold Washington was unable to attend at the last minute. Carl Shier, who was to have introduced him, read a message from him instead, and spoke of Democratic Socialists of America (DSA)'s considerable role in Washington's election campaign. (Chicago DSA 1983)

The Chicago Communist Party was right behind Harold Washington and they later supported his "proxy protégé" Barack Obama.

Remarks by Illinois Communist Party organizer John Bachtell to a "Special District Meeting on African American Equality and Building of the Communist Party USA and Young Communist League, Chicago," IL September 30, 2007:

> The legacy of Harold Washington's election and his administration is in the collective consciousness of the African American community, but the entire city. Many of his democratizing achievements endure 20 years later.

> The historic election of Washington was the culmination of many years of struggle. It reflected a high degree of unity of the African American community and the alliance with a section of labor, the Latino community, and progressive minded whites. This legacy of political independence also endures...

> The struggle for African American representation and political independence also led to the historic election of US Senator Carol Moseley-Braun (D-IL) for Senate and many African American state legislators and local elected officials.

> The African American community and trade unionists have played a crucial role in the struggle to defeat the ultra-right. This includes massive voter turnout in election after election, but also the swing state mobilizations in 2004.

---

[216] http://www.chicagodsa.org/d1981/index.html

This was reflected in the historic election of Barack Obama. The Party supported Obama during the primary election. Once again, Obama's campaign reflected the electoral voting unity of the African American community, but also the alliances built with several key trade unions, and forces in the Latino and white communities.

It also reflected a breakthrough with white voters. In the primary, Obama won 35 percent of the white vote and seven north side wards, in a crowded field. During the general election, he won every ward in the city and all the blue-collar counties. This appeal has continued in his Presidential run. (Bachtell, Speical District Meeting on African American 2007)

Chicago Communist Party member and pro-Obama activist, Pepe Lozano, quoted black trade unionist Elwood Flowers in a February 23, 2008 article from the People's Daily World:

The movement to elect Barack Obama today is almost identical to Washington's, but nationwide, said Flowers, "Our members wanted to be involved in the political process, similar to people today for Obama," said Flowers.

38-6 Pepe Lozano

"What Obama can do for the country will help all communities including providing jobs and health care. And the number one issue is stopping the Iraq War, which is draining our economic resources. If those things bear fruit, then they will benefit all working-class communities," he added.

It was Washington's example and the power of working people that will always remind us about what is possible. The greatness is in our hands. (Lozano, Harold Washington wore a Union Label 2008)

Vernon Jarrett was also a fan of Barack Obama. He watched his career from its beginning and became an ardent supporter.

In 1992, Barack Obama worked for the ACORN offshoot Project Vote to register black voters to aid the Senate Campaign of Carol Moseley-Braun. US Senator Carol Moseley-Braun (D-IL) had strong Communist Party and Democratic Socialists of America (DSA) ties[217]

---

[217] http://trevorloudon.com/2007/12/carol-moseley-braun-did-clinton-send-us-a-socialist-part-1/

38-7 State Senator Carol
Moseley-Braun

and were Harold Washington's legislative floor leader.

Obama helped Moseley-Braun win her Senate seat, took it over himself in 2004 - backed of course by the same set that had elected his political "ancestors" Mayor Harold Washington and US Senator Carol Moseley-Braun (D-IL).

Commenting on the 1992 race, Vernon Jarrett wrote in the Chicago Sun-Times of August 11 1992:

Good news! Good news! Project Vote, a collectivity of ten church-based community organizations dedicated to black voter registration, is off and running. Project Vote is increasing its rolls at a 7,000-per-week clip. Just last Saturday it registered 2,000 during the Chicago Defender's annual Bud Billiken Parade. But now, the not-so-good news: If Project Vote is to reach its goal of registering 150,000 out of an estimated 400,000 unregistered blacks statewide, "it must average 10,000 rather than 7,000 every week," says Barack Obama, the program's executive director... (Jarrett 1992)

Dee Myles is a Chicago activist and Chair of the Education Commission of the Communist Party USA. In 2004, after Vernon Jarrett's death from cancer, she penned this tribute for the *People's Weekly World* of June 5 that year:[218]

Vernon Jarrett: a Partisan Journalistic Giant

Readers like me can be extremely selective of the journalists we read habitually... We are selective about the journalists to whom we become insatiably addicted, and once hooked we develop a constructive love affair without the romance...

Such was my experience with Vernon Jarrett, an African American journalist in Chicago who died at the age of 86 on May 23. I became a Vernon Jarrett addict, and I am proud of it!

Vernon Jarrett's career as a journalist in Chicago began and ended at the Chicago Defender, the African American daily paper. In between, he

---

[218] http://www.pww.org/article/articleview/5331/

was the first Black journalist at the Chicago Tribune, and I first began to read his articles during his tenure at the Chicago Sun-Times.

Jarrett's claim to fame is that he was a partisan of the cause of African Americans in the broad democratic tradition of Paul Robeson and W.E.B. DuBois... (Myles 2004)

Robeson and DuBois were both Communist Party members. On April 9, 1998, at Chicago's South Shore Cultural Center, Jarrett hosted a Paul Robeson Citywide Centennial Celebration event with his old comrade Margaret Burroughs and former Communist Party members Studs Terkel and Oscar Brown Jr.

Dee Myles continues:

Jarrett was fanatical about African Americans registering and voting in mass for socially conscious candidates. He championed Harold Washington like a great warrior, and this March, from his hospital bed, wrote an article appealing to Black Chicago to turn out to vote for Barack Obama in the Illinois primaries. Obama astounded everyone with an incredible landslide victory as the progressive, Black candidate for the Democratic Party nomination for the US Senate seat from Illinois. From his sickbed, Vernon Jarrett issued a clarion call, and the people responded.

I think Black Chicago was passionately in love with Vernon Jarrett...His unrelenting drive kept us reminded of a sense of purpose and helped to instill the courage of our convictions in struggle as a people. We will forever be indebted; we will never forget. (Myles 2004)

Not forgotten is Vernon Jarrett's legacy. Much of it lives on in the work of his daughter-in-law Valerie Jarrett.

Another former Mayor Harold Washington staffer, Valerie Jarrett is a close friend of both Barack and Michelle Obama.

Jarrett met Barack Obama when she hired Michelle to work with her in Mayor Daley's City Hall. Valerie Jarrett ran the finances for Obama's 2004 Senate bid and served as treasurer of Obama's HOPEFUND.

"She's always been the other side of Barack's brain." That's how an Obama insider described Valerie Jarrett as an Obama campaign aide announced Thursday night the former CTA chief and current Habitat Co. CEO is taking on a larger role to help her close friend win his White House

38-8 Valarie Jarrett daughter in law to Vernon Jarrett

bid.

The development comes as Jarrett, a charter member of Sen. Barack Obama's kitchen cabinet, has been formalizing her portfolio and stepping up the pace within the past few weeks as a top advisor within the campaign.

Though she will be part-time, Jarrett will be one of the most visible and powerful African-Americans in the top rungs of the Obama operation... (Blount 2008)

Valerie Jarrett has been tipped for a top post in an Obama administration.

Did this all start with Frank Marshall Davis; an almost forgotten communist?

39. Barack Obama, Carol Moseley-Braun and the Chicago Socialist Machine

Trevor Loudon © Monday, October 20, 2008

39-1 Campaign Poster

Barack Obama's spectacular rise in Chicago politics is not a one-time affair. It is part of a long established pattern.

The left side of Chicago politics likes to come together to back promising candidates[219] for high office.

Democratic Socialists of America, the Communist Party USA and the Party offshoot Committees of Correspondence, have worked together on several occasions to elect "Progressive" Democrats. This alliance started in 1983 with the election of Chicago's first black Mayor Harold Washington.

It has worked since to elect Barack Obama to the Illinois State Senate, the US Senate and now the US presidency.

In between Washington and Obama, it helped elect Carol Moseley-Braun to the Illinois State Legislature and the US Senate. In some ways

---

[219] http://trevorloudon.com/2007/10/chicagos-redblack-alliance-targets-white-house/

Moseley-Braun, the first black female Senator in US history, was a trial run for the future Obama phenomenon.

US Senator Carol Moseley-Braun (D-IL)'s rise in politics links to both Washington and Obama. Like them, she was the product and protégé of the far left side of Chicago politics.

Born in 1947, Carol Moseley-Braun was raised by a medical technician mother and a "socialist" father who worked as a guard in the Cook County Jail.

While still in high school, Carol Moseley-Braun staged a one-person sit-in at a restaurant that refused to serve her, she succeeded in integrating an all-white beach and marched with Martin Luther King.

After law school, Moseley-Braun worked as a prosecutor in the United States Attorney's office in Chicago. In 1978, she won a seat in the Illinois State Legislature.

Later she worked for Judson Miner's law firm, as did Barack Obama, Michelle Obama and former Weather Underground terrorist Bernardine Dohrn.

Moseley-Braun became Chicago Mayor Harold Washington's legislative floor leader and sponsored bills to reform education, to ban discrimination in housing and private clubs and to bar the State of Illinois from investing funds in Apartheid South Africa.

Harold Washington was a lifelong Communist Party associate, elected to Chicago's Mayoralty in 1983, by a communist/socialist led black/white "liberal"/Latino coalition.

Moseley-Braun also had ties to Communist Party USA.

In November 1979, she was a co-sponsor of the founding conference of the US Peace Council, a Communist Party USA front and an affiliate of the Soviet controlled World Peace Council.

Moseley-Braun's Peace Council co-sponsors included US Representative Danny K. Davis, both lifelong Communist Party USA front operatives and later Democratic Socialists of America (DSA) members and US Congressmen John Conyers.

In May 1987, Moseley-Braun helped sponsor, with Communist Party USA leaders Angela Davis and Herbert Aptheker, a benefit for Chicago Communist Party veterans Claude Lightfoot and Jack Kling.

Furthermore, in 1987, Moseley-Braun joined Mayor Harold

39-2 Chicago CPUSA
Chairman Frank Lumpkin

Washington's multi-ethnic, multi-racial and gender-balanced "Dream Ticket" to run for the office of Recorder of Deeds. Washington died in office after the election.

While serving as a recorder of deeds, Moseley-Braun decided to run for US Senate in the 1992 election with Communist Party USA backing.

I quote Communist Party USA official and Obama activist[220] Tim Wheeler, who wrote in a 1999 issue of *People's Weekly World* " on Chicago Communist Party Chair and Save Our Jobs (SOJ) committee leader, Frank Lumpkin:

> Lumpkin also led SOJ into independent political action. They played an important role in the election of Harold Washington as Mayor of Chicago, a historic victory over the most entrenched, reactionary political machine in the US Bea (Lumpkin's wife) writes that "At that time, Washington and Lumpkin had a special relationship ... Washington seemed to draw strength from Lumpkin's participation. At meetings rallies, street encounters, whatever, Washington would call Frank over and say, 'When I see you, I know things are in good hands." (Wheeler, Whose World is it? 1999)

Lumpkin was appointed by Harold Washington to taskforces on hunger and dislocated workers.

Wheeler continues:

> Save Our Jobs was also an important factor in the election of Charles Hayes, African-American leader of the Meat cutters union, (a covert member of the Communist Party USA to take the Congressional seat vacated by Congressman Harold Washington, and the election of Carol Moseley-Braun, the first Black woman to serve in the US Senate. (Wheeler, Whose World is it? 1999)

While US Senator Carol Moseley-Braun (D-IL) was close to Chicago's Communist Party, other socialist groups also helped her to win elections.

In 1991/92, about a third of the members of the Communist Party

---

[220] Chapter 8 - Baltimore Communists Back Obama

USA broke away to form a new organization, the Committees of Correspondence (COCDS). Well known members of COCDS include black academic Angela Davis, linguist/activist Noam Chomsky and Timuel Black, Professor (emeritus) City College of Chicago and longtime friend and associate of both US Senator Carol Moseley-Braun (D-IL) and Barack Obama.

One lifelong Communist Party USA member to join the COCDS was Chicago activist Hannah Cohen.

From the CoC's Portside:

> Hannah was active in Chicago, in what became a lifetime of political and electoral activism. Throughout the new upsurge of the 60s, 70s and 80s, Hannah was an active participant. She was active in teachers' union, peace and community groups in Chicago and later in the international campaign that won the freedom for Angela Davis.
>
> Hannah became a community volunteer in the Mayoral campaigns of Harold Washington, and was one of the key volunteers in the election campaign of Carol" Moseley" Braun. The first African American woman elected to the United States Senate. (Committees of Correspondence for Democracy and Socialism 2008)

Democratic Socialists of America (DSA) also backed Moseley-Braun.

One woman associated with the Democratic Socialists of America (DSA) was long time Chicago Democratic Party activist. Sue Purrington, who played a role in Moseley-Braun's decision to run for Senate.

From the Chicago DSA website:

> The 34th Annual Dinner on May 1, 1992 at the Congress Hotel in Chicago. The Master of Ceremonies was Michael Lighty, who was then the Executive Director of Democratic Socialists of America (DSA). Sue Purrington, Executive Director of Chicago NOW, a Dr. Quentin Young, President of Physicians for a National Health Program, were honorees. The featured speaker was Jose Laluz, was the National Education Director of the Amalgamated Clothing and Textile Workers Union

39-3 Sue Purrington

> We honor you as a career fighter for women's rights and equality...

Quentin Young and Jose Laluz are Democratic Socialists of America (DSA) members. Young is a longtime friend, neighbor and political supporter of Obama's. He was present at the famous meeting in Chicago in 1995 at the home of Bill Ayers and Bernardine Dohrn where State Senator Alice Palmer introduced Obama as her chosen successor.

Jose Laluz, also a leader of Committees of Correspondence and a Peace Council supporter, is President of Latinos for Obama.

Another Democratic Socialists of America (DSA) activist associated with Moseley-Braun was Milt Cohen.

A long time Chicago Communist Party activist, Cohen later joined the New American Movement and Democratic Socialists of America (DSA).

According to the Chicago DSA's New Ground, Cohen was a friend of Harold Washington's:

In 1982, Rep. Harold Washington issued a challenge to register 50,000 new voters in preparation for the coming Mayoral election. Milt helped organize a grassroots movement, which met the challenge by more than double. Later he chaired the Chicago Coalition for Voter Registration.

Milt joined the 1983, Washington campaign full-time. He later said that hard-won victory was his greatest satisfaction. The Washington movement reflected Milt's long-time priorities: anti-racism, political independence, and progressive multi-racial coalitions.

A few months after his election, Washington issued a proclamation declaring Milton M. Cohen Day a day for Chicagoans to honor a man, "who has dedicated his life to the unceasing struggle for the civil and economic rights of all people and has worked for 50 years in the cause of progressive change and reform politics in Chicago and a more democratic, humane and peaceful America and world."

Mayor Washington noted that to honor Milt Cohen is to honor "thousands of rank-and-file activists that worked day and night in the struggle for jobs, justice, and peace." (C. Black 1994)

And of Moseley Braun's:

US Senator Carol Moseley-Braun (D-IL)'s election to the Senate in 1992 was another landmark for Milt. He had helped recruit Braun for her first legislative race in 1978, and one of his last projects before leaving Chicago was soliciting Democratic Socialists of America (DSA) members to participate in the Braun campaign. (C. Black 1994)

Chicago Democratic Socialists of America (DSA) put a big effort into Senator Carol Moseley-Braun's successful Senate campaign.

From Chicago's DSA's *New Ground 28*:

Progressive forces in Illinois made history November 3 by electing Senator Carol Moseley-Braun as the first African-American woman to the US Senate.

Braun beat Republican millionaire Rich Williamson soundly, 57%-43%. Former Democratic Socialists of America (DSA) Youth Organizer Jeremy Karpatkin directed Braun's field operations. Chicago Democratic Socialists of America (DSA) contributed volunteers and money to Braun's campaign. (Democratic Socialists of America 1992)

Barack Obama also played a role in US Senator Carol Moseley-Braun's Senate victory - perhaps the decisive role.

From *Chicago Magazine* January 1993:

A huge turnout in November 1992 altered Chicago's electoral landscape-and raised a new political star: a 31-year-old lawyer named Barack Obama...

The most effective minority voter registration drive in memory was the result of careful handiwork by Project Vote!, e local chapter of a not-for-profit national organization. "It was an efficient campaign I the best have seen in my 20 years in politics," says Sam Burrell, a Alderman of the West Side's 29th Ward and a veteran of many registration drives.

At the head of this effort were a little-known 31-year-old African-American lawyer, community organizer, and writer: Barack Obama. In 1984, after Columbia, but before Harvard, Obama moved to Chicago. "I came because of Harold Washington," he says. "I wanted to do community organizing, and I couldn't think of a better city than one as energized and hopeful as Chicago was then."

By 1991, when Obama, law degree in hand, returned to Chicago, black voter registration and turnout in the city were at their lowest points since record keeping began.

Six months after he took the helm of Chicago's Project Vote!, those conditions had been reversed. Within a few months, Obama, a tall, affable workaholic, had recruited staff and volunteers from black churches, community groups, and politicians.

He helped train 700 deputy registrars, out of a total of 11,000 citywide. And he began a saturation media campaign with the help of black-owned Brainstorm Communications...The group's slogan-"It's a Power Thing"-was ubiquitous in African-American neighborhoods. It is overwhelming," says Joseph Gardner, Commissioner of the Metropolitan Water Reclamation District and the director of the steering committee for Project Vote! "The black community in this city had not been so energized and single minded since Harold died."

"I think it's fair to say we reinvigorated a slumbering constituency," says Obama. "We got people to take notice."

As for Project Vote! Itself, its operations in Chicago have officially closed down. Barack Obama has returned to work on his book, which he plans to complete this month..."We won't let the momentum die," he says. "I'll take personal responsibility for that. We plan to hold politicians' feet to the flames in 1993, to remind them that we can produce a bloc of voters large enough that it cannot be ignored."

Nor can Obama himself be ignored. The success of the voter-registration drive has marked him as the political start the Mayor should perhaps be watching for. "The sky's the limit for Barack," says Burrell.

Some of Daley's closest advisers are similarly impressed. "In its technical demands, a voter-registration drive is not unlike a mini-political campaign," says John Schmidt, Chairman of the Metropolitan Pier and Exposition Authority and a fundraiser for Project Vote! "Barack ran this superbly. I have no doubt; he could run an equally good political campaign if that's what he decided to do next."

Obama shrugs off the possibility of running for office. "Who knows?" he says, "But probably not immediately," He smiles. (Reynolds 1993)

Project Vote of course was an affiliate of the radical community group ACORN, to which Obama was long connected.

In 1995/96, Democratic Socialists of America (DSA) endorsed Obama for his run for an Illinois State Senate seat. He also joined and was endorsed by the New Party, a front for ACORN, Democratic Socialists of America (DSA) and the Committees of Correspondence.

Saul Mendelson

On March 13, 1998, Saul Mendelson, a lifelong socialist activist, died in Chicago.

Mendelson had been a member of various Trotskyist factions in the 1930s and '40s before joining the US Socialist Party and later Democratic Socialists of America (DSA).

In 1983, Saul Mendelson played a significant role in the election of Harold Washington.

The Saul Mendelson Memorial Service was held on Sunday, March 29, 1998, at the First Unitarian Church, Chicago.

Figure 39-4 Saul Mendelson

According to Chicago DSA leader, the late Carl Marx Shier (who addressed the gathering):

> At the memorial Service held at the 1st Unitarian Church on South Woodlawn, speaker after speaker recounted Saul's contributions, speakers included Deborah Meier, Senator Carol Moseley-Braun, Alderman Toni Preckwinkle, State Senator Barack Obama, Illinois House Majority Leader Barbara Flynn Currie and a good friend from New York, Myra Russell.
>
> The concluding remarks were made by an old friend, Harriet Lefley, who is now Professor of Psychology at the University of Miami Medical School. (Shier, *New Ground* 58)

Deborah Meier was a former Trotskyist and Socialist Party comrade of Saul Mendelson's and a leader of Chicago and Boston Democratic Socialists of America (DSA).

Alderman Toni Preckwinkle and Illinois House Majority Leader Barbara Flynn Currie, are both leftist Democrats with ties to Chicago's socialist community. Both endorsed Barack Obama in his successful 2004 bid for the US Senate.

Harriet Lefley was a Trotskyist in the 1940s with Saul Mendelson.

Eulogies also came from Quinn Brisben, (Socialist Party Presidential candidate 1976, 1992) and David McReynolds (Socialist Party Presidential candidate 1980, 2000).

Both Brisben and McReynolds are also Democratic Socialists of America (DSA) members.

39-5 Carol Moseley Braun lost her Senate seat in 1998

State Senator Barack Obama knew Saul Mendelson through their mutual activism in Independent Voters of Illinois, an organization investigated for communist infiltration as far back as the 1940s.

Ambassador Carol Moseley-Braun

In 1998, Senator Carol Moseley-Braun, mired in constant scandal, lost her US Senate seat.

President Bill Clinton looked after Carol, appointing her as ambassador to an unsuspecting New Zealand. By 2004, she was back in Chicago talking of running for her old Senate seat.

After considering her options, Ambassador Carol Moseley-Braun instead made a short-lived run for the Democratic Party's Presidential nomination.

Seizing the opportunity, Barack Obama ran for Senator Carol Moseley-Braun's old Senate seat and was elected-with the active support of the Chicago Communist Party and the Young Communist League. Perhaps the timing was right.

40. Bill & Bernardine's Buddy Bert, Backs Barack

Trevor Loudon © Tuesday, October 21, 2008

Bert Garskof was a mentor to the '60s radical organization Students for a Democratic Society. Bert has been pursuing his ideals through the Green Party.

According to the New York Times of November 17, 2000:

Professor Bert Garskof, a research psychologist at Quinnipiac University in Hamden, Conn., was an architect of the Green Party's national political strategy and Ralph Nader's first run for President in 1996. He was a Connecticut party leader and remains a registered Green. He is also US Senator Joseph I. Lieberman's brother-in-law.

Although he campaigned for the Democrats this year, even helped organize a final Greens-for-Gore effort, does he share in the blame? Didn't the ragtag pro-environment, anti-free-trade movement that he helped channel into organized electoral politics deny Mr. Lieberman – the brother of his third wife, Ellen, 50 – a clear victory and perhaps the Vice Presidency? (Herszenhorn 2000)

40-1 Bill Ayers (l) and buddy Bert Garskof (r)

Bert Garskof

Bert Garskof is also a longtime friend of former Students for a Democratic Society leaders and Weather Underground terrorists Bill Ayers and Bernardine Dohrn.

Like Ayers, Dohrn and former Weathermen Jeff Jones,[221] Mark Rudd and Bruce Rubenstein,[222] Garskov is a leader of the Movement for a Democratic Society, a support network for the 2006 vintage new Students for a Democratic Society.

Movement for a Democratic Society links senior members of modern Marxist organizations with the Democratic Socialists of America, Communist Party USA and Committees of Correspondence for Democracy and Socialism with former Students for a Democratic Society and several former Weathermen.

Movement for a Democratic Society is also the parent organization of a new group founded in 2008, the Progressives for Obama (P4O).

Like Ayers, Dohrn and most of his old comrades, Bert Garskof has learned little in the last 40 years.

He is still fighting against the Vietnam War.

Garskof posted this defense of Bill Ayers in the comments section of this blog post:

> Senator McCain suffers from a convenient historic amnesia as he carps about Bill Ayers. Nothing that supposed urban terrorist Bill Ayers said or did could compare to the mass destruction, the death and tragedy brought to the Vietnamese by McCain and the armed forces he blindly served. Better patriots than he saw the war on Vietnam for what it was mass murder from the air and on the ground. Murder most foully

---

[221] http://keywiki.org/index.php/Jeff_Jones
[222] http://keywiki.org/index.php/Bruce_Rubenstein

unjustified. The Vietnam War was not justified by international law, the US Constitution, or the Charter of the United Nations.

Nor were our chances of winning the war supported by the long history of the conflict, or by the wishes of the masses of Vietnamese people. In fact, President Eisenhower said that if we allowed an election (something we never did) in Vietnam, 90% of the people would elect Ho Chi Min, the man at the head of the forces opposing us. Nor was the war supported by the American people as a whole. Most of us were horrified at the deadly force and murderous weapons of mass destruction brought down on the Vietnamese.

From high altitude bombing to napalm to rapid firing multiple barrel machine guns, our air and ground forces killed an estimated 2 million people. We actually rained down more bombs on the small country of Vietnam than were dropped by all participants in World War II on the whole planet. Nor was it, by the end, supported by many of the young men and women serving in that un-winnable and morally untenable war. Many Service men refused to fight the Vietnamese. Many young men fought the draft, fought the intrusion of ROTC on campuses. Pilots refused to take part in this immoral action. One was a friend of mine, Captain Dale Noyd, who was Court Martialed. Were Dale, now deceased several years, to come back and run for President, and were he to point to his war record, I would say here is a man who could serve the country as he did during the Vietnam War.

Whereas, Senator McCain represents today, all that was sordid and cowardly in those years. He reaps no glory for, nor brings any moral rectitude to his campaign because of his years flying high tech missions over Vietnam. His actions then against the Vietnamese, as his rah-rah support of the war in Iraq and Afghanistan now, most profoundly, condemn him. (Garskof 2008)

In November 2007, several former Students for a Democratic Society spoke at a reunion event at Michigan State University. Speakers on a video taken at the event include Students for a Democratic Society founder Al Haber, Bill Ayers, Bernardine Dohrn and Bert Garskof.

Do I hear the ghost of Jimi Hendrix playing *"All Along the Watchtower"* or is it the way the wind is blowing?

Garskof spoke of revolution and socialism and declared that he may work "for Obama." Bill Ayers and Bernardine Dohrn share the panel.

Well perhaps Bert Garskof has learned something after all, no more Green Party futility for Bert. Now Comrade Garskof is pursuing his socialist ideals through the Democrats.

Bert did go to work for Obama. He is active in the Obama campaign in Connecticut.

He also supports the aims of Progressives for Obama (P40).

In March 2008, Garskof contributed this comment to The Nation article on Progressives for Obama (P40):

> I agree that we people to the left of the Democratic Party should join the Obama campaign. We need to do the hard work of electoral organizing alongside the thousands of volunteers who have created the Obama movement. I think that we should, along with jumping into the work of the electoral campaign, argue that the Obama volunteers could become the base of a mass ongoing movement that lives on after Obama wins, a movement that would be in place to give the Obama Administration direct, on-going, immediate information from the base up and hear what Obama thinks from the Government down.
>
> We can try to create grassroots advisory committees in every district. Even if we cannot make these ideas realities everywhere or even anywhere, raising the ideas is a good thing. And in some places we may be able to do it. Every town, or ward or even neighborhood that succeeds in creating a post-election advisory committee would be a great lesson, a great guide for others to build more participatory democracy. (Garskof, Bert Garskof Bethany CT 2008)

What do you bet that basement bomb builders Bill and Bernadine will be backing Bert backing Barack?

41. Obama Was a New Party Member - Chain of Evidence

Trevor Loudon © Thursday, October 23, 2008

This post is for journalists who care about the future of their country more than their careers.

Senator Barack Obama's involvement in the socialist led Illinois New Party is outlined in Chapter 4, 22 and 36.

The images in this chapter are from The New Party News Spring 1996.

They prove that Barack Obama was a member of the Illinois New Party and was endorsed by them in his 1996 Illinois State Senate race.

The New Party drew a distinction. Obama was on the wrong side of the dividing line.

The New Party was the creation of the quasi-Marxist Democratic Socialists of America,

41-4 Page 2 New Party News

the radical community organization ACORN and the Communist Party USA splinter group Committees of Correspondence (COCDS).

From the Chicago DSA's *New Ground* of September-October 1995:

41-3 Page 1, New Party News

41-2 Page 1, Article on Obama and the New Party

New Party members won three other primaries this Spring in Chicago: Barack Obama (State Senate), Michael Chandler, (Democratic Party Committee) and Patricia Martin (Cook County judiciary). Unfortunately, NP-endorsed State Representative candidate Willie Delgado lost a tight primary challenge, although he won 5 of the 6 precincts that the NP worked through the election.

41-1 Enlarged Lower Left of Page 1

The political entourage (The Gang of Five) included Alderman Michael Chandler, William Delgado, Chief of Staff for State Rep Miguel del Valle), and spokespersons for State Sen. Alice Palmer, Sonya Sanchez, Chief of Staff for State Sen. Jesse Garcia, who is running for State Rep in Garcia's District; and Barack Obama, Chief of Staff for State Sen. Alice Palmer.

Obama is running for Palmer's vacant seat. Although ACORN and SEIU Local 880 were the harbingers of the New Party, there was a strong presence of Committees of Correspondence

41-5 Building a New Party with all types of Professionals

41-6 Barack Obama and the Gang of Five

(COCDS) and Democratic Socialists of America (DSA) (15% DSA)... Four political candidates were "there" seeking New Party support." (Bentley, New Ground 42 1995)

Here is part of an undated New Party document, probably from 1995.

Those listed include:

- Blaine Bernard - (A Labor academic and prominent Democratic Socialists of America (DSA) member)[223]

- Noam Chomsky - (Linguist and activist, member of both Democratic Socialists of America (DSA))[224]

- Barbara Ehrenreich - (Author, activist and Democratic Socialists of America (DSA) leader. This year Ehrenreich was one of the four founders of Progressives for Obama (P40))[225]

- Bill Fletcher - (Former Maoist, a Labor activist and leading Democratic Socialists of America (DSA) member.[226] This year Fletcher was one of the four founders of Progressives for Obama (P40))

- Maude Hurd - (Long-time ACORN President. Awarded for her work by Boston Democratic Socialists of America (DSA).[227] ACORN is involved in the Obama campaign)

- Manning Marable - (A founder of Democratic Socialists of America (DSA) and a leader of COCDS. Regarded as a driving force within the New Party, now an Obama supporter)

- Frances Fox Piven - (A senior Democratic Socialists of America (DSA) member.[228] Regarded as the brains behind ACORN. Piven is now an endorser of the Progressives for Obama (P40) website)

- Raphael Pizzaro - (New York Labor activist and former Communist Party USA member. An official of both COCDS and Democratic Socialists of America (DSA))[229]

- Gloria Steinem - (Author and senior Democratic Socialists of America (DSA) member.[230] An Obama supporter[231] and volunteer)

- Carl Davidson - (former Chicago COCDS National Committee

---

[223] http://www.dsausa.org/minutes/NPC2007sep15.pdf

[224] http://www.dsaboston.org/aboutdsa.htm

[225] http://progressivesforobama.blogspot.com/

[226] http://theactivist.org/blog/2007-democratic-socialists-of-americas-dsa-convention-in-atlanta-ga

[227] http://dsaboston.org/2003DTB.htm

[228] http://www.dsausa.org/about/structure.html

[229] http://www.chicagodsa.org/ngarchive/ng37.html

[230] http://www.dsausa.org/about/structure.html

[231] http://time-blog.com/real_clear_politics/2008/06/gloria_steinem_supporting_obam.html

member, New Party activist, associate of Barack Obama and friend of Bill Ayers, now serves as Progressives for Obama (P40) webmaster)

- Cornel West - (Academic and prominent Democratic Socialists of America (DSA) member.[232] West now serves as an advisor to the Obama campaign)
- Quentin Young - Chicago doctor, prominent Democratic Socialists of America (DSA) member. Quentin Young is a neighbor, friend and supporter of Barack Obama he attended the famous 1995 meeting[233] in the home of Bill Ayers and Bernadine Dohrn where Barack Obama was introduced by Alice Palmer as the chosen successor to her Illinois State Senate seat)

42. Obama's Socialist Neighbor, Jackie Grimshaw

Trevor Loudon © Saturday, October 25, 2008

Most big cities have them. An enclave where the radicals and leftists live, socialize and plan the subversion of their unsuspecting neighbors. Decades ago, these often bordered industrial areas, now they tend to surround universities.

Barack Obama's Chicago neighborhood, Hyde Park, is an enclave. The ultra-liberal Democratic Party stronghold is the home to Nation of Islam leader Louis Farrakhan, former Weather Underground terrorists Bill Ayers[234] and Bernardine Dohrn, Obama confidante Valerie Jarrett[235] and lots and lots of socialists.

One socialist is Jackie Grimshaw, Barack Obama's next door neighbor - opposite the Tony Rezko side of Obama's home.

42-1 Jackie Grimshaw the Obama's Next Door Neighbor

---

[232] http://www.chicagodsa.org/CornelWest.html

[233] http://trevorloudon.com/2008/10/cnn-exposes-some-of-obamaayers-links/
[234] http://keywiki.org/index.php/Bill_Ayers
[235] http://keywiki.org/index.php/Valerie_Jarrett

42-2 Dinner Invitation for Leading Socialists

42-3 Heather Booth

Obama's neighbor on the less famous side of his house is Jacky Grimshaw who ran Harold Washington's successful campaign for Mayor. Her husband Bill is a University of Chicago professor. The Grimshaw's sometimes baby sit the Obama girls. Jacky and Michelle Obama are close. (Daily Kos 2008)

Jackie Grimshaw served as a Senior Advisor Director of Intergovernmental Affairs under Harold Washington. Bill Grimshaw, the author of *"Bitter Fruit: Black Politics and the Chicago Machine, 1931-1991,"* was also a political adviser to Washington.

The connection to Harold Washington is significant.

With backing from Communist Party USA and Democratic Socialists of America, Washington won the Chicago Mayoralty in 1983. His victory inspired the young Obama's original move to Chicago.

Jackie Grimshaw, Barack Obama's next-door neighbor:

One of the things that Harold started was going out to the community with the budget, listening to what people wanted in their communities, and then responding.

I think, you know, Barack coming in fresh out of school, seeing this kind of leadership, I think, helped to shape him in terms of people being empowered. Like her late boss, Harold Washington, and her neighbor, Barack Obama, Jackie Grimshaw also has close ties to Democratic Socialists of America (DSA). (PBS Online Newshour 2008)

Every year, Chicago Democratic Socialists of America (DSA) hosts an awards dinner[236] named in honor of US socialist icons Eugene Debs and Norman Thomas. Jacquelyne D. Grimshaw received an award for her political work:

> You have been a stalwart in the Chicago independent political movement for years, and firm in your belief that building coalitions will make changes and reform possible.
>
> In both the 1983 and 1987, campaigns to elect and re-elect Mayor Harold Washington, you made your contribution by providing inspiring leadership in the victorious coalition.
>
> For all this, the Thomas - Debs Award is presented to you on this 9th day of May, 1987.
>
> To Heather Booth for her radical educational activities.
>
> Through the Midwest Academy, you have inspired and trained thousands of new activists in the Citizen Action movement, the peace movement, and the women's movement.
>
> You have reached across the generations to connect with and maintain the best traditions of the old radical movement while reaching out to upcoming student activists with a new vision and strategy for a better future... (Democratic Socialists of America 1983)

After Democratic Socialists of America (DSA) leader Michael Harrington died in 1989, his name was added to the socialist honor roll.

The 1991 Debs-Thomas-Harrington Dinner was held at the Congress Hotel in Chicago on Saturday, May 11, 1991. The MC was Jackie Grimshaw.

The Chicago Democratic Socialists of America (DSA)'s *New Ground* Archive Spring 1992 issue includes an article entitled:

> "Heather Booth, Jackie Grimshaw, and Michael Dyson Wow Crowd at the University of Chicago" (Roman, Progressive Potential 1999)

Michael Dyson is a leading Democratic Socialists of America (DSA) member and strong supporter of both Barack Obama and the Rev. Jeremiah Wright.

---

[236] http://www.chicagodsa.org/dthdin.html

Some 200 people attended a panel presentation on "The Progressive Potential of Chicago City Politics" this last December 8th at the University of Chicago. The panelists included Jacquelyn Grimshaw, Alderman Toni Preckwinkle, Alderwoman Helen Shiller, Bernard Craighead, and others. The event was sponsored by the University of Chicago Democratic Socialists of America (DSA) Youth Section and the Hispanic Association for Cultural Expression and Recognition. (Roman, Progressive Potential 1999)

The pair have served together on the Board of the Chicago based Midwest Academy,[237] Booth as Chair, Grimshaw as secretary/treasurer.

The most well-known organizing method is Alinskyism, named after Saul Alinsky, a Chicago-born community organizer who helped set up the Back of the Yards Neighborhood Council and later the Industrial Areas Foundation in the 1930s. The Mid-West Academy is a training center set up by members of Democratic Socialists of America (DSA) that draws from Alinskyism. (Freedom Road Socialist Organization 2008)

Other Midwest Board members included:

- Heather Booth[238] – (Together in the 1970s, Paul and Heather Booth were regular sponsors[239] of the annual Debs-Thomas Dinner. Also worked alongside Barack Obama when she directed field operations for Carol Moseley-Braun's successful, "Democratic Socialists of America (DSA) and Communist Party backed Senate campaign in 1992"

- Paul Booth – (Is a former President of Chicago's Citizen Action Program, formed in 1969 by trainees from Saul Alinsky's Industrial Areas Foundation. He is now an assistant to alleged Democratic Socialists of America (DSA) member[240] Gerald McEntee,[241] President of the public employees union AFSCME, which has endorsed Obama. A founder and former secretary/treasurer of the radical Students for a Democratic Society (SDS))

- Robert Creamer – (Husband of the "Democratic Socialists of America (DSA) friendly" Representative Jan Schakowsky (D-IL-9th District)[242] - a loyal Obama supporter)

---

[237] http://www.midwestacademy.com/

[238] http://keywiki.org/index.php/Heather_Booth

[239] http://www.chicagodsa.org/d1975/index.html

[240] http://mailman.lbo-talk.org/1999/1999-December/021208.html

[241] http://keywiki.org/index.php/Gerald_McEntee

[242] http://keywiki.org/index.php/Jan_Schakowsky

- Jackie Kendall[243] - (Also a Debs-Thomas award winner.[244] Kendall knew Obama when he first worked in Chicago)
- Nancy Shier – (Daughter of Chicago Democratic Socialists of America (DSA) leader, Midwest Academy tutor and regular Debs-Thomas Dinner MC,[245] the late Carl Marx Shier)
- Barack Obama - Also an Alisnsky disciple and has ties to Midwest Academy through the allied radical organization ACORN)

Obama's ties to Jackie Grimshaw are more than neighborly.

In May, Grimshaw was named to represent US Senator Barack Obama (D-IL) on the Credentials Committee for the Illinois Democratic Delegation to the Democratic National Convention in Denver.

The pair also linked up through the Center for Neighborhood Technology, a Chicago based Environmental group, where Grimshaw serves as Vice President for Policy, Transportation and Community Development.

According to GOP.com:

> Over A Two-Year Period In The US Senate, Obama Requested $3.2 Million In Earmarks For The Center For Neighborhood Technology.[246] (GOP 2008)

For what return?

> Former Employees from the Center for Neighborhood Technology Ben Helphand and Paul Smith have, "Done multiple tours of duty in the political trenches-for Obama..." Neighborhood Technology contributed $20,688 to Obama's campaigns. (GOP 2008)

43. Terrorists, Marxists, NP Veterans, Unite Behind Obama

Trevor Loudon © Sunday, October 26, 2008

Before you bother to read this, first ask yourself these questions.

If I told you that in 2006, several former Weather Underground terrorists linked up with Communist Party USA, Committees of Corre-

---

[243] http://keywiki.org/index.php/Jackie_Kendall

[244] http://www.chicagodsa.org/d1999.html

[245] http://www.chicagodsa.org/d1983/index.html

[246] http://www.cnt.org/board

43-1 The Austin Texas MDS

spondence for Demo-cracy and Socialism (COCDS) and Demo-cratic Socialists of America to form an activist support group, would you do any more than yawn?

If two of those former terrorists were Bill Ayers and his wife Bernardine Dohrn, would your ears prick up?

If several leaders of this organization went on to create a satellite group, designed to help US Senator Barack Obama (D-IL) win the US presidency, would you start to get interested?

The organization in question is Movement for a Democratic Society (MDS)[247] - the namesake of the '60s support group for the ultra-radical Students for a Democratic Society (SDS).

The new Movement for a Democratic Society is in fact a lot like the old Movement for a Democratic Society; it even has many of the same people. Movement for a Democratic Society is a community support group for the new Students for a Democratic Society (also founded in 2006), which now has 130 chapters in colleges and high schools nationwide.

What distinguishes the new Movement for a Democratic Society from the old is the wider composition of its leadership. Movement for a Democratic Society links old Students for a Democratic Society and Weathermen to old line Marxists-Leninists from the Communist Party USA, Committees of Correspondence, anarchists and Marxists from Democratic Socialists of America (DSA).

The 2006 Movement for a Democratic Society Board included:

- Noam Chomsky – (Well known linguist, writer and activist. A member of both DSA and the CCDS)

- Carl Davidson – (A founder member of SDS, later a Maoist activist before becoming a leader of CCDS in 1992. Based in Chicago, Davidson is a long time personal friend of Bill Ayers)

---

[247] http://www.movementforademocraticsociety.org/

- Angela Davis – (A leader of CCDS, formerly prominent in the CPUSA)
- Bernardine Dohrn – (Former SDS and a core leader of the Weather Underground)
- Bill Fletcher Jr. – (A former Maoist. A leader of DSA and an official in the AFL-CIO)
- Bert Garskof – (Involved with SDS the '60s, a close friend of Bill Ayers and Bernadine Dohrn)
- David Graeber – (Former member of the SDS, turned anarchist)
- Al Haber – (Original founder of SDS)
- Tom Hayden – (Founder and former leader of the SDS)
- Gerald Horne – (A member of the editorial board of Political Affairs, theoretical journal of the CPUSA)
- Michael James – (A former member of SDS)
- Robin DG Kelley – (A former member of the Communist Workers Party, more recently close to the CPUSA)
- Michael Klonsky - (Son of CPUSA member Robert Klonsky. A former member of SDS, who later led the pro-Chinese, Communist Party (Marxist-Leninist). Mike Klonsky is a long-time friend of Bill Ayers and works closely with him on educational projects)
- Ethelbert Miller – (Chairman of the board of the notoriously leftist and Cuban linked Washington based think tank, Institute for Policy Studies)
- Charlene Mitchell – (A leader of CCDS, formerly a high ranking member of the CPUSA)
- Mark Rudd – (A former leader of the SDS and a core leader of the Weather Underground)
- Howard Zinn – (A well-known leftist historian and self-described democratic socialist)

The 2007 board added some new names, including:;

- Manning Marable – (MDS Chairman. A founder of DSA and now a leader of CCDS)
- Barbara Ehrenreich – (An honorary Chair of DSA)
- Jeff Jones – (Former SDS and a core leader of the Weather Underground)
- Paul Buhle – (Former SDS, now prominent in DSA)

Other known board members include:

- Bruce Rubenstein – (MDS treasurer and a former Weatherman)
- Thomas Good – (A communist turned anarchist who describes himself as an "unrepentant Weather supporter")

Bill Ayers's wife Bernardine Dohrn, comrades and others are all here - but where's Bill?

43-2 MDS board members Bert Garskof, Al Haber, Bernardine Dohrn and Bill Ayers at the November 30, 2007 Michigan State University SDS Reunion

Although not a known Board member, Ayers is involved in Movement for a Democratic Society.

Ayers's referenced the Movement for a Democratic Society as "our work" and his enthusiasm for building alliances and using the US elections to enlist "hundreds of thousands" of young people to his cause. Ayers also referenced Rashid Khalidi, an unsuccessful Movement for a Democratic Society Board candidate, pro-Palestinian activist and close friend of Barack Obama.

It is clear that former Weather supporters form a significant bloc in Movement for a Democratic Society.

Many of the others are also connected. Several worked together in the mid-1990s in the New Party.

A front for the radical community organization ACORN, Democratic Socialists of America (DSA) and Committees of Correspondence, the short lived New Party was set up to help elect left wing candidates through the Democratic Party.

Who's Building the New Party?

Movement for a Democratic Society Board members Noam Chomsky, Bill Fletcher, Barbara Ehrenreich, Manning Marable and Howard Zinn, were all named as New Party leaders according to a (circa 1995) New Party document.

Barack Obama joined the New Party in Chicago and enlisted New Party help for his successful 1996 Illinois State Senate campaign.

43-3 Who's Building the New Party?

43-4 Carl Davidson

Though not listed above, Movement for a Democratic Society Board member, Carl Davidson, was also a leader of the New Party in Chicago, where he worked closely with Obama. After the New Party folded, Bill Ayers continued to support Obama. Davidson, in conjunction with another Movement for a Democratic Society supporter, Marilyn Katz, organized the 2002 Chicago peace rally where Obama first came out against the Iraq War.

It is well known that Bill Ayers and Bernardine Dohrn hosted a party for Barack Obama's political career in their Chicago living room in 1995. The Chicago New Party also helped Obama's career that year. Interesting that the two factions should come together 13 years later.

In 2008, Movement for Democratic Society Board members Tom Hayden, Bill Fletcher and Barbara Ehrenreich, joined with radical actor/activist Danny Glover to set up a new organization - Progressives for Obama (P4O).

> We intend to join and engage with our brothers and sisters in the vast rainbow of social movements to come together in support of Obama's unprecedented campaign and candidacy. Even though it is candidate-centered, there is no doubt that the campaign is a social movement, one greater than the candidate himself ever imagined.

> Progressives make a difference in close primary races like Pennsylvania, North Carolina, Oregon and Puerto Rico and in the November general election. We can contribute our dollars. We have the proven online capacity to reach millions of swing voters in the primary and general election. We can and will defend Obama against negative attacks from any quarter. We will seek Green support against the claim of some that there are no real differences between Obama and McCain. We will criticize any efforts by Democratic super delegates to suppress the

winner of the popular and delegate votes, or to legitimize the flawed elections in Michigan and Florida. We will make our agenda known at the Democratic National Convention and fight for a platform emphasizing progressive priorities as the path to victory. (Hayden, Key Task: Isolate and Divide the Right 2008)

It is clear that Movement for a Democratic Society and Progressives for Obama (P40) are connected.

Movement for a Democratic Society Board member, Carl Davidson, runs the Progressives for Obama (P40).

Movement for Democratic Society Board members Paul Buhle, Robin D.G. Kelley, Thomas Good, Michael James and former Weatherman Mark Rudd endorse the site.

Movement for a Democratic Society supporter Marilyn Katz has also signed up, as has Frances Fox Piven, a Democratic Socialists of America (DSA) activist and former New Party leader.

Unlike several Movements for Democratic Society Board members, Mike Klonsky, DID NOT endorse the Progressives for Obama (P40) website. However his wife, Susan, and his brother, Fred, (both former Students for Democratic Society members) did.

The website also links to an online petition where you sign up to support the cause.

Signatories include Movement for a Democratic Society Board member Jeff Jones and two other former members of the Weatherman inner circle, Howard Machtinger and Steve Tappis. Jennifer Dohrn, a former Weather supporter and sister of Bernardine Dohrn, has also lent her name to the Obama cause.

Movement for a Democratic Society linked news site Next Left Notes,[248] (edited by Thomas Good) also carries a prominent link to Progressives for Obama (P40).

Movement for a Democratic Society and Progressives for Obama (P40) link several strands of the pro-Obama movement. They connect at least seven former Weathermen, (including Ayers and Dohrn), with the former core leadership of Barack Obama's New Party. Communist Party

---

[248] http://www.antiauthoritarian.net/NLN/

USA, Committees of Correspondence and Democratic Socialists of America, all of which have backed Obama also form part of the matrix. This is NOW, not when Obama was eight years old.

How smoky does the gun need to get?

44. Barack Obama and the socialist New Party

Trevor Loudon © Monday, October 27, 2008

Despite documentary evidence[249] to the contrary, US Senator Barack Obama's (D-IL)[250] website continues to deny that Barack Obama was a member of the ACORN/Democratic Socialists of America initiated New Party.

Let us delve into the matter to see what more information we might find.

You should visit the website of Barack Obama's old law firm Miner, Barnhill & Galland, you will find this short profile,[251] the home of his Madison, Wisconsin based partner, Sarah Siskind.

It seems that a few years ago Ms. Siskind represented ACORN in a successful class action against sub-prime mortgage lender Household Finance Corporation.

44-1 Sarah Siskind

For the last ten years, the firm, Sarah Siskind also represents individual consumers and organizational plaintiffs in class action lawsuits challenging predatory lending practices. These include a series of deceptive practices actions brought in Illinois, California, and Massachusetts against Household Finance Corporation, and consolidated in Household Lending Litigation, (Case No. C-02-1240 and Related Cases, N.D. Ca.), and settled for $152 million in benefits and future practice change relief. (14)

Ms. Siskind represents ACORN (Association of Community Organizations for Reform Now) and individual plaintiffs in three

---

[249] Chapter 41 - Obama Was a New Party Member - Documentary Evidence
[250] http://fightthesmears.com/articles/28/KurtzSmears
[251] http://www.lawmbg.com/index.cfm/PageID/2783

deceptive practices actions against Wells Fargo Financial, Inc. in state court class actions pending in California (ACORN, et al v. Household International, Inc. 2002)

According to this November 25, 2003, press release:

Household, ACORN and consumers reach proposed settlement.

CHICAGO – Household International, Inc., a wholly owned subsidiary of HSBC Holdings plc. (NYSE:HBC), the Association of Community Organizations for Reform Now (ACORN), and a series of borrowers from across the United States, announced today they have reached a proposed settlement of nationwide class action litigation relating to the mortgage lending practices of Household's two US branch -based businesses, Household Finance Corporation and Beneficial Corporation. (United States Securities and Exchange Commission)

The core of the proposed settlement is a Foreclosure Avoidance Program (FAP). The Foreclosure Avoidance Program will provide relief to Household borrowers who are delinquent on their payments and at risk of losing their homes.

Components of FAP include:

- Interest rate reductions.

- Waivers of unpaid late charges.

- Deferral of accrued unpaid interest.

- Principal reductions.

(Household International, Inc 2003)

Sounds like a great deal all round. Sarah Siskind and Miner, Barhill & Galland make money. ACORN strikes it rich and gets to force another mortgage lender to make even softer loans, which will help scuttle the US economy. The communists certainly got a revolutionary win-win.

According to this report,[252] Sarah Siskind is a generous donor to the Barack Obama campaign. Sarah Siskind donation to Obama for America in 2008:

---

[252] http://www.campaignmoney.com/political/contributions/sarah-siskind.asp?cycle=08

- 53726 Miner Barnhill/Attorney, $ 200 01/29/2008 G
- 53726 Miner Barnhill/Attorney, $-200 01/29/2008 P
- 53726 Miner Barnhill/Attorney, $1,000 01/29/2008 P
- 53726 Miner Barnhill/Attorney, $ 500 12/19/2007 P
- 53726 Miner Barnhill/Attorney, $1,000 10/10/2007 P

With possible electoral chaos, justices of the US Supreme Court expressed skepticism Wednesday over an effort to overturn forty state laws that forbid nominations of the same candidate by more than one political party.

The high court heard arguments in a case from Minnesota orchestrated by a Wisconsin couple Joel Rogers, a University of Wisconsin-Madison law professor, and his wife, Madison attorney Sarah E. Siskind.

Rogers is a co-founder and national Chair of the New Party, which describes itself as progressive and claims 10,000 members nationwide.

It also turns out that Sarah Siskind fought another important case in 1997.

It involved the New Party. Siskind took a case to the Supreme Court to overturn state bans on "fusion" voting. The New Party wanted to use fusion voting, whereby candidates run on both Democratic Party and New Party tickets, combining the vote from both.

44-2 Joel Rogers m. Sarah Suskind

Barack Obama signed up for this in 1996 when he ran as both a Democrat and New Party member for the Illinois State Senate.

The case failed and the New Party consequently went into sharp decline.

The case did however, reveal an interesting connection.[253]

How about that, Obama's legal partner and ACORN lawyer Sarah Siskind is married to Joel Rogers, the founder and Chairperson of the ACORN initiated New Party; which Barack Obama claims he did not join.

---

[253] http://www.highbeam.com/doc/1P2-6483435.html

Many Obama supporters have argued that the New Party was not socialist anyway.

Every year for decades, Democratic Socialists of America ran an annual Socialist Scholars Conference at the Cooper Union in New York.

These were almost certainly the "socialist conferences at Cooper Union" that Obama wrote of attending in his 1995 autobiography *"Dreams from My Father."* This is the introduction to the program for the 1997 conference:

> RADICAL ALTERNATIVES ON THE EVE OF THE MILLENNIUM
>
> 1997 Socialist Scholars Conference, March 28, 29, 30, 1997
>
> Borough of Manhattan Community College
>
> Changes in the labor movement, Marxist theory, the state of the economy, market socialism, and other areas where theory and practice meet.
>
> Listen to the United States' only independent and socialist, US Senator Bernie Sanders (I-VT) , dialogue with Joel Rogers of the New Party and In These Times' Salim Muwakkil on independent politics *"In These Times"* has strong links to Democratic Socialists of America. . (Neff 1997)

Frances Fox Piven is a prominent Democratic Socialists of America (DSA) member and regarded as the brains behind ACORN. She was a leading activist in the New Party and is now an endorser of the Progressives for Obama (P40).

Manning Marable, Bill Fletcher and Barbara Ehrenreich, also addressed the 1997 conference. All three were Democratic Socialists of America (DSA) activists and New Party leaders. In 2008, Fletcher and Ehrenreich were two of the four founders of Progressives for Obama (P40), while Marable Chairs the organization's parent body Movement for a Democratic Society" (MDS).

Democratic Party congressman Major Owens, a Democratic Socialists of America (DSA) member, Communist frontiersman and avid Obama supporter, also spoke.

In 2004, Socialist Scholars changed its name to Left Forum.

Speakers at the 2005 conference included Barbara Ehrenreich,[254] Bill Fletcher, Manning Marable and Frances Fox Piven, plus Robin D.G. Kelley of Movement for a Democratic Society and Progressives for Obama (P40), Gerald Horne from the Communist Party USA and Movement for a Democratic Society and of course Joel Rogers.

It is a small world that Barack Obama wants to rule.

45. The Terrorist Friendly, Socialist Friend and Neighbor, Rabbi Wolf

Trevor Loudon © Tuesday, October 28, 2008

Though Barack Obama does not dare admit it, he has long-standing ties to Democratic Socialists of America.

Despite their innocuous name, these people are Marxists, extremists, many of them former Communist Party supporters.

Obama has personal ties to several Democratic Socialists of America (DSA) members or supporters including US Representative Danny K. Davis,[255] US Representative Jan Schakowsky (D-IL-9th District),[256] William McNary,[257] Quentin Young and his next door neighbor Jackie Grimshaw.[258]

Rabbi Wolf is a member of Rabbis for Obama,[259] he has held Obama fundraisers in his home and is an ardent propagandist for the Senator.

In an interview with the June 2008 *Weekly Standard*, Rabbi Wolf explained Obama's place in the neighborhood.

> "Barack is perfect for the neighborhood!" Rabbi Arnold Wolf told me, when I stopped by his Hyde Park house one afternoon for a talk.

45-1 Rabbi Arnold Jacob Wolf

---

[254] http://www.leftforum.org/events/leftforum_2005_speaker_bios.html

[255] http://keywiki.org/index.php/Danny_Davis

[256] http://keywiki.org/index.php/Jan_Schakowsky

[257] http://keywiki.org/index.php/William_McNary

[258] http://keywiki.org/index.php/Jackie_Grimshaw

[259] http://keywiki.org/index.php/Arnold_Jacob_Wolf

He's as round and white-bearded as Santa, with the same twinkle. He came to Hyde Park before urban renewal and saw its effects firsthand. For 25 years, he led the congregation at KAM Isaiah Israel, a synagogue across the street from Obama's mansion.

You can't say Barack's a product of Hyde Park. He's not really from here. But everybody saw the potential early on. We had a party for him at our house when he was just starting, back in the Nineties. I said right away: 'Here's a guy who could sell our product, and sell it with splendor!'

I asked him what the Hyde Park product was:

'People think we're radicals here, wild-eyed!" he said. "Bill Ayers—I know Bill Ayers well. Bill Ayers is an aging, toothless radical. A pussycat, and his wife, too. I sat on a commission with his wife a few years ago. My god, she was more critical of the left than I was! The two of them, they're utterly conventional people. They had a violent streak at one time. But now—they're thoroughly conventional, just nice, well-educated people from the neighborhood." (Pallasch 2008)

Nevertheless, back to the product Obama could sell:

"The thing is, it's not what you might think," Rabbi Wolf said. "It's not radical. It's not extreme. It's a rational, progressive philosophy based on experience. You see it here. This neighborhood is genuinely integrated. We did it here, we really did it! Not just talk about it. Look around. And Barack and his family fit right in. This is their neighborhood." (Pallasch)

Rabbi Arnold Jacob Wolf knew Ayers in the 1960s and re-met Ayers and Dohrn decades later. He describes Ayers as "wonderful, compassionate, thoughtful, serious," Wolf said. I asked him to help reconcile the past and the present.

"What we want is not to let bygones be bygones, but to transform ourselves into the kind of people we want to be and ought to be," Wolf said. (Sweet 2008)

The famous 1995 meeting in the home of Bill Ayers[260] and Bernardine Dohrn was one of several functions designed to introduce Obama to the Hyde Park set.

---

[260] Chapter 23 - Alice Palmer – Obama's Soviet Sympathizing Patroness

Around this time, Obama started to attend a series of coffees in the Hyde Park community where he lived, standard operating procedure for political rookies running in the neighborhoods surrounding the University of Chicago.

"I was certainly (hosting) one of the first," said Rabbi Arnold Jacob Wolf, Rabbi Emeritus at Chicago's KAM Isaiah Israel

"There were several every week," he recalled... "I remember what I said to him: 'Someday you are going to be Vice President of the United States.' He laughed and said, 'Why not President?'" (Sweet, Sun Times Media)

But it's not neighborly instinct that's led me to support the Obama candidacy:

I support Barack Obama because he stands for what I believe what our tradition demands.

I've worked with Obama for more than a decade, as has my son, a lawyer...

45-2 Bernardine Dohrn and Bill Ayers

I am proud to be his neighbor. I hope someday to visit him in the White House. (Wolf 2008)

If Obama stands for what Rabbi Wolf believes, it may be helpful to know what those beliefs actually are.

Rabbi Wolf believes in socialism.

In 2000, Rabbi Wolf was named as a member of Democratic Socialists of America in the Democratic Socialists of America (DSA) publication Religious Socialism.[261]

Rabbi Wolf sent a "Shalom" to Chicago Democratic Socialists of America (DSA)'s 50th annual Debs-Thomas-Harrington Dinner.

Rabbi Wolf's activism goes back to the 1940's when:

Rabbi Wolf served as the American Representative to Brit Shalom, joining other renowned Jewish leaders including Judah Magnes, Martin Buber, and Henrietta Szold in calling for "Jewish-Arab cooperation, as both

---

[261] http://www.religioussocialism.com/pdf/2000.sum.pdf

45-3 Rabbi Arnold Jacob Wolf

necessary and possible." In 1949, he was instrumental in founding Israel's Givat Haviva Educational Institute, created to educate for peace, democracy, coexistence and social solidarity.

In 1973, Rabbi Wolf served as founding Chair of the American Jewish Movement "Breira: A Project of Concern in Diaspora-Israel Relations."

Breira called for discussions with the Palestine liberation Organization, for US recognition of the PLO and for PLO participation at all peace talks.

According to Michael E. Stab in his, book: *Torn at the Roots: The Crisis of Jewish Liberalism in Postwar America*:

"Breira survived four tumultuous years. Its proposals on Israeli-Diaspora Jewish relations and Palestinian nationalism generated fierce international debate over the limits of public dissent and conflict in Jewish communal life, and virtually every major American Jewish organization took a public stand on the group and what it advocated" (Staub)

Breira attacked from the beginning:[262]

Major Jewish organizations denounced Breira members as PLO supporters; some rabbis and other Jewish professionals threatened with dismissal. A campaign in the Jewish press isolated Breira from the larger Jewish community. The organized Jewish community's attacks on Breira as it sought to build support for Israeli doves and dissidents, and provide them with a forum here to win support, is now legend.

Breira destroyed after five leaders including Rabbi Wolf and Arthur Waskow met in secret with PLO Representative in Washington DC.

The Jerusalem Post leaked details of the meeting and Breira collapsed in the subsequent uproar. (Staub 2002)

---

[262] http://en.wikipedia.org/wiki/Breira_(organization)

Rabbi Wolf told the Chicago Jewish News:

> "I met with PLO people as long as 30 years ago. Two of them were assassinated for meeting with me and other Jews. Now I'm careful. I don't want to risk any lives on any side." (Yearwood 2007)

45-4 Dr. Quentin Young and Barack Obama

Arthur Waskow was involved with the radical Washington think tank, Institute for Policy Studies, an organization connected to both Cuba and the Democratic Socialists of America.

Like a lot of older Democratic Socialists of America (DSA) members, Rabbi Wolf has, what used to be described in a more honest era, a "communist front record as long as your arm."

One of the more interesting associations was Rabbi Wolf's 1970's involvement in the Chicago Communist Party.

The Alliance was set up to abolish the Chicago Red Squad, the police unit charged with monitoring communist and radical organizations.

Rabbi Wolf served as the organization's Vice Chair. The Alliance's executive director was Richard Criley, a well-known member of the Communist Party USA.

Other Communist Party members involved included Abe Feinglass, Jack Spiegel, Jesse Prosten and Norman Roth.

Other radicals active in the Alliance were former Communist Party member Milton Cohen (later a founder of Chicago Democratic Socialists of America (DSA)) and two governments accused communists, Quentin Young and Timuel Black.

Young went on to join Chicago Democratic Socialists of America (DSA) where he still works with Rabbi Wolf.

Timuel Black went on to join Communist Party USA offshoot Committees of Correspondence for Democracy and Socialism.

Both Young and Black are close friends of Barack Obama.

Another key Alliance to End Repression activist was journalist Donald C. Rose - himself later an Obama supporter. Rose went on to mentor an up and coming young Chicago journalist named David Axelrod - that is right, the same David Axelrod who ran Obama's Presidential campaign in 2008.

Rabbi Wolf's hoped for trip to the White House has been a long time in the making.

46. The Axelrod Axis – Who is Behind the Man Behind Obama?

Trevor Loudon © Thursday, October 30, 2008

David Axelrod

46-1 Barack Obama (l) and David Axelrod (r)

Chicago based political consultant, David Axelrod, is chief strategist and media adviser for US Senator Barack Obama (D-IL)'s 2008 Presidential campaign.

He has known Obama since 1992 and helped Obama win his 2004 Senate race. He is the ideas man of the campaign - the man behind Obama.

> "I thought that if I could help Barack Obama get to Washington, then I would have accomplished something great in my life." (The Independent 2008)

Great, by what standard, is the obvious question.

Many key figures in Obama's political life come from the far left. Does David Axelrod conform to this pattern?

Axelrod was born in New York in 1955 to leftish parents Joseph and Myril Axelrod.

In the 1940s, Myril Axelrod wrote for a left leaning magazine *PM*, though not a communist publication, several Marxists (including Labor editor Leo Huberman) and Communist Party members worked on the paper.

According to the *Traditional Values Coalition*:

> Former Communist Eugene Lyons, writing in The Red Decade: The Stalinist Penetration of America, noted that PM's staff included a former editor of the Daily Worker; another was former editor of The Communist; and a third was a leader of the Communist Youth League; a fourth was a Soviet government official; and a fifth was the former staff cartoonist for the

Daily Worker, the official newspaper of the Communist Party, USA. (The Traditional Values Coalition 2008)

PM's Washington DC correspondent I.F. Stone was later identified as involved in Soviet Intelligence operations.

One of PM's writers, Earl Conrad, also wrote for the leftist magazine Negro Story, as did Frank Marshall Davis, the Communist Party USA member, who was later to mentor the teen-age Barack Obama in Hawaii.

Don Rose

David Axelrod's own mentor was a well-known Chicago journalist/political activist named Don Rose.

> In his early years as a political consultant, Axelrod, following in the footsteps of his mentor, the political strategist Don Rose, carved out a reputation for himself as a skillful specialist working for local progressive candidates...says Rose. "I think he's a principled, generally progressive guy... ." (Reardon 2007)

Axelrod first met Rose in the 1970's while studying political science at the University of Chicago and working as a reporter on the Hyde Park Herald.

46-2 Don Rose

Around that time, Rose edited and co-owned a small newspaper called the *Hyde Park Kenwood Voices*. The paper's radical tone suited the neighborhood. It tended to follow Communist Party USA line campaigning e.g. to abolish the House on Un-American Activities Committee. The Voice's co-owner, the late David S. Canter, appeared before the committee and was named as a Communist Party member in the late 1960's.

Canter and Don Rose took the young David Axelrod under their wing. They took it upon themselves to "mentor" and "educate...politically," the young journalist. Don Rose later wrote a reference letter for Axelrod that helped win him the internship at the Chicago Tribune, which launched his career.

Don Rose[263] was a member of a Communist Party front at the time, the Alliance to End Repression.[264]

The Alliance was set up to abolish the Chicago Red Squad, the police unit charged with monitoring communist and radical organizations.

Rose's personal Red Squad file accused him of being a "member of the anarchists."

The Alliance's executive director was Communist Party member Richard Criley. Further Party members involved included Abe Feinglass, Jack Spiegel, Jesse Prosten and Norman Roth.

Other radicals active in the Alliance included former Communist Party member Milton Cohen, later a founder of Chicago Democratic Socialists of America (DSA), Quentin Young,[265] Timuel Black[266] and Rabbi Arnold Wolf.[267] All three went on to join or support Democratic Socialists of America (DSA) and to form close personal friendships with Barack Obama.

Quentin Young became the physician to both Obama and Bill Ayers.[268]

Don Rose also went on to Chair another Communist Party front, the Chicago Committee to Defend the Bill of Rights, succeeding comrade Richard Criley.

Rose had been radical since the 1940's when he joined Henry Wallace's communist controlled Progressive Party.

In the 1950's, Rose was involved in the campaign for nuclear disarmament and in the 1960's was involved in the civil-rights movement. He was Dr. Martin Luther King's Chicago press secretary for several years.

---

[263] http://keywiki.org/index.php/Don_Rose
[264] The Communist Takeover Of America - 45 Declared Goals recorded in the Congressional Record, Vol. 109, 88th Congress, 1st Session Appendix Pages A1-A2842 Jan. 9-May 7, 1963 Reel 12

[265] http://keywiki.org/index.php/Quentin_Young
[266] http://keywiki.org/index.php/Timuel_Black
[267] http://keywiki.org/index.php/Arnold_Jacob_Wolf
[268] http://keywiki.org/index.php/Bill_Ayers

In 1968, Rose was asked to serve as press secretary to the Chicago Mobilization Committee, the Students for a Democratic Society (SDS)/Communist Party influenced alliance that wreaked havoc at the Chicago Democratic Party Convention. It was during these violent times that Rose coined the famous phrase - "the whole world is watching."

Marilyn Katz

Through the Mobilization Committee Don Rose met Marilyn Katz, the Students for a Democratic Society security officer for the demonstrations.

By the late 1970s, Rose was linked to[269] the Chicago coalition of former Trotskyists, Socialist Party members and communists that would in 1982 form Democratic Socialists of America.

In 1982, David S. Canter and nine others invited black Democratic US Representative, Harold Washington, to stand for the Chicago Mayoralty. Washington had a long history[270] with Chicago's communists and socialists. When he accepted, Communist Party USA and Democratic Socialists of America (DSA) formed a multi-racial alliance behind Washington.

46-3 Marilyn Katz, Chicago 1968

The alliance targeted black voters in a huge voter registration drive on the city's south side.

Rose, Katz and Canter all worked on the successful campaign and all later secured jobs in Washington's administration.

In 1987, Washington won his election, aided by a young political adviser, David Axelrod.

Though Washington died in office after his election the communist socialist alliance lived on.

In 1992, the alliance elected the Communist/Democratic Socialists of America (DSA) friendly US Senator Carol Moseley-

46-4 Washington (r) at a 1981 Democratic Socialist dinner in Chicago

---

[269] http://www.chicagodsa.org/d1977/index.html
[270] http://keywiki.org/index.php/Harold_Washington

Braun (D-IL).[271]

In 2004, it helped put US Senator Barack Obama (D-IL) into the same Senate seat. In 2008, it is campaigning hard to put Obama in the White House.

When Barack Obama was 22 years old, just out of Columbia University, he took a $10,000-a-year job as a community organizer on the South Side of Chicago. It was a shrewd move for a young black man with an interest in politics...

The politician who set the stage for Obama's rise was also a South Side congressional Representative: US Representative Harold Washington, who was elected Mayor of Chicago in 1983...In New York, Obama read about Washington's victory and wrote to City Hall, asking for a job. He never heard back, but he made it to Chicago months after Washington took office...

Washington dropped dead of a heart attack in his second term. But the confidence he instilled in black leaders became permanent in Chicago politics. His success inspired Jesse Jackson to run for President in 1984, which in turn inspired Obama, who was impressed to see a black man on the same stage as Vice President Walter Mondale and Gary Hart. Washington also strengthened the community organizations in which Obama was cutting his teeth, says Ransom. Obama's Project Vote, which put him on the local political map, was a successor to the South Side voter registration drive that made Washington's election possible.

Chicago has two unique advantages, says political consultant Don Rose. First, it's in Cook County, which contains half of Illinois' voters. Second, the local Democratic Party is a countywide organization. After Chicago's Carol Moseley-Braun beat two white men to win the 1992 Democratic Senate primary, precinct captains in white Chicago neighborhoods and the suburbs whipped up votes for her in the general election.

"They had to go out and sell the black person to demonstrate that the party was still open," says Rose, who sees "direct links" from Washington to Moseley-Braun to Obama. (McClelland 2008)

---

[271] http://keywiki.org/index.php/Carol_Moseley_Braun

Rose, Canter and Axelrod all worked on Moseley Braun's 1992 campaign. Marilyn Katz worked with Obama on Project Vote, the huge voter registration drive that ensured Moseley-Braun's victory.

By the 2000s, Rose, Katz and another Obama associate and former Students for a Democratic Society member, Carl Davidson,[272] had formed Chicagoans against the War in Iraq.

This group organized the 2002 Chicago anti-war rally where Obama came out against the Iraq War.

The speech was a major turning point in Obama's career. Obama consulted David Axelrod before staking out his position.

46-5 The Braun Campaign

Katz is now an Obama fundraiser and an endorser of the Progressives for Obama (P40)[273] website. Carl Davidson helped found the organization and moderates its website.

In August this year, Don Rose and Marilyn Katz gave an interview to the Democratic Socialists of America (DSA) linked journal *In These Times*, before Obama's "coronation" at the Democratic Party Convention in Denver. Here are some excerpts:

> Don Rose (ITT):40 years ago this week, Chicago police battled protesters at the DNC. Two '60s radicals remember the madness, and look to Denver for change...
>
> The '68 Democratic National Convention debacle remains a symbol of everything that went wrong with American politics, society and culture in that tumultuous and iconic year. It was five days of mayhem in the Windy City. Five days that left the Democratic Party in shambles.
>
> In August 1968, those explosive battles put Chicago at the epicenter of one of the most searing political and social upheavals of the 20th century. In August 2008, a US senator from Chicago anointed the first black major-party nominee for the presidency of the United States.

---

[272] http://keywiki.org/index.php/Carl_Davidson
[273] http://keywiki.org/index.php/Progressives_for_Obama

Don Rose...the political wise man has helped elect Mayors and Senators since then, from Harold Washington to Paul Simon. Rose now 77, was a mentor to David Axelrod, Obama's top campaign strategist.

The 1983 election of Harold Washington as Chicago's first black Mayor came courtesy of a progressive coalition of blacks, Latinos, and so-called "Lakefront liberals." Katz and Rose were there, once again, as advisors and operatives.

Katz: My straight line goes from '66/'68 to the folks who began to work together and formed the core group of the Harold Washington campaign. (Almost) everyone I worked with in 1982 I had met as a kid in '68. I believe that Barack Obama could only have emerged in Chicago. Why? Because since '68 there was a web of relationships between black civil rights groups, anti-war groups, women's activities, immigrant rights activities, that has sustained and grown...

Don Rose (ITT): What we did here in Chicago had international implications: In '68 there was a workers' movement in Paris, there was a worldwide movement of students. We lost that in the intervening 40 years. Now in 2008, with Barack Obama, we have a renewed sense that the whole world is watching again.

Katz: I think that millions of young people are flocking to Barack, as we did to the anti-war movement...

Don Rose (ITT): The Democratic Party will gather once again later this month. Everybody is expecting a big party in Denver. Will it be an Obama coronation? Is that what we should be looking for?

How do you resolve Obama's move to the center? What about holding Obama's feet to the fire? Don't we need to keep him true to progressive issues?

Katz: We have to get him into office so then we can be the left opposition. I think it is a delicate balance between those of us who are progressive, how much you push, how much you don't want to put him in difficult positions that would embarrass him or give John McCain some advantage...

Don Rose (ITT): I believe that almost everything the Obama people do, like the McCain people, like the Hillary people, is a well-tested proposition.

Given that, I think Obama's positions, the ones we like, do not like and applaud, are all well tested. I know the people who are doing these things, and they have run a flawless campaign. Therefore, I have a lot of confidence that they know what they are doing when they trim their sails and when they attack this way and attack the other way. I believe they are doing what will win and I think they have a concept of what will win. (Washington 2008)

Indeed Don Rose does "know the guys who are doing these things" He mentored their leader.

47. The Paid Soviet Agent behind Axelrod and Obama

Trevor Loudon © Friday, October 31, 2008

US Senator Barack Obama (D-IL)'s chief campaign strategist David Axelrod,[274] once worked for a man who was an identified member of the Communist Party USA, a registered agent of the Soviet Union and a paid disseminator of Soviet black propaganda.

This man went on to become a key Chicago political fixer who helped elect communist linked politicians including the late Chicago Mayor Harold Washington and former US Senator Carol Moseley-Braun (D-IL).[275]

This man knew Barack Obama and was a key member of an organization which endorsed Barack Obama in his 2004, US Senate race. Barack and Michelle Obama were active members of this organization, which was investigated by the FBI over claims of communist infiltration.

Who was this man? What was his background?

David Simon Canter

The individual in question was late Chicago lawyer David Simon Canter (1923/2004).

Born in Boston, David Canter was the son of Harry J. Canter, an activist with the Industrial Workers of the World who later became secretary of the Boston Communist Party.

Communist Party candidate for Massachusetts Secretary of State, Harry Canter

47-1 David Simon Canter

---

[274] http://keywiki.org/index.php/David_Axelrod
[275] http://keywiki.org/index.php/Carol_Moseley_Braun

was arrested for carrying a placard "FULLER-MURDERER OF SACCO AND VANZETTI." Canter is attacking Governor Fuller for the execution of anarchists Sacco and Vanzetti. Harry Canter was tried, convicted and jailed for a year for criminal libel in May 1929.

After his release, Canter Senior moved his family, including son David, to the Soviet Union. The boy must have stayed in the "workers' paradise" for some time because according to his obituary in the Chicago Sun-Times of August 30, 2004:

> "After his release, Mr. Canter's father moved the family from Boston
> to Russia, where the young man developed a love for Russian literature,
> (Sydney) Bild said." (Thomas 2004)

By 1946, the family had turned up in Chicago, where Harry Canter worked for many years as Secretary of Chicago Local 16 of the International Typographical Union.

Harry Canter later moved to San Francisco, where he remained active in leftist causes. David Canter however remained in Chicago.

David Canter was the left's choice for editor of the University of Chicago student newspaper "*Maroon*" in 1948.

In 1958, David Canter graduated from the John Marshall Law School. He also edited the Packinghouse Workers Union newspaper "*Champion.*"

The Packinghouse Workers Union was a long time CPUSA-influenced, if not controlled, union that later merged with the Meatcutters to form the CPUSA run Amalgamated Meatcutters & Butcher Workmen Union, led by identified CPUSA labor leader Abe Feinglass, who was also a VP of the Soviet-KGB front the World Peace Council. The House Un-American Activities Committee held some hearings on the Packinghouse Workers and one revealed that the future Illinois State Representative Charles Hayes (D-Ill, Chicago) was a high-ranking member of the CPUSA in the Meatcutters Union along with Feinglass. (Friedman, Free Republic)

By 1960, David Canter had teamed with Chicago Communist Party member and later founder of Veterans for Peace, Leroy Wolins.

Translation World Publishers

The pair owned a company, Translation World Publishers, which specialized in publications from and about the Soviet Union.

The company soon attracted the attention of the House Un-American Activities Committee, which suspected Canter and Wolins of being conduits for Soviet propaganda.

COMMUNIST OUTLETS FOR THE DISTRIBUTION OF
SOVIET PROPAGANDA IN THE UNITED STATES
PART 1

HEARINGS
BEFORE THE
COMMITTEE ON UN-AMERICAN ACTIVITIES
HOUSE OF REPRESENTATIVES
EIGHTY-SEVENTH CONGRESS
SECOND SESSION

MAY 9, 10, AND 17 AND JULY 12, 1962
INDEX IN PART 2

Printed for the use of the
Committee on Un-American Activities

47-2 House Committee on Un-American Activities

The committee questioned Canter and Wolins on payments received from the Soviet Union.

The committee also questioned Canter about his membership in the Communist Party.

The committee went on to find that:

Mr. CANTER. My answer to that question is the same answer as I have given to your question No. 2 and the legal grounds cited therefor.

Mr. WALSH. Well, in Exhibit B (Wolins Exhibit No. 2), it is stated that you received from the Soviet Embassy in Washington the sum of $2,400, which was allegedly advance payment for 2,400 copies of a *Geography of the USSR*, which the Translation World Publishers was to produce and publish. Was this the real purpose for which the money was received?

Mr. CANTER. My answer to that question is the same answer I have given to you in response to your question No. 2 and the legal ground cited therefor.

Mr. WALSH. How did the individuals, the partners in the Translation World Publishers, use this $2,400?

Mr. CANTER. My answer to that question is the same answer as I have previously given the committee in response to its question No. 2 and the legal ground cited therefor.

47-3 Canter's Congressional Testimony

Translation World Publishers was an outlet for the distribution of Soviet propaganda...this publishing house was subsidized by Soviet funds and was created by known Communists to serve the propaganda interests of the U.S.S.R. (Committee on Un-American Activities) In 1963/64, the Soviet Union tried to undermine Republican Presidential candidate Senator Barry Goldwater, in favor of Democrat Lyndon B Johnson. Goldwater lost the election paving the way for Johnson's "Great Society. (US House of Representatives 1962)

Mr. WALSH. According to the record this committee has, it shows you, the Translation World Publishers, did receive $3,400 from the Soviet Embassy in Washington, D.C., and for which you allegedly delivered to them 1,000 copies of the booklet *The Trial of the U-2*. Is that correct?

Mr. CANTER. My answer to that question is the same answer as I have given in response to your question No. 2 and the legal ground cited therefor.

Mr. WALSH. On the same date that the Translation World Publishers filed under the Foreign Agents Registration Act the fact that they were the agent for a foreign power, you also filed on the same day a notice of the termination of the registration. Is that correct? (Wolins Exhibit No. 4.)

Mr. CANTER. My answer to that question is the same as I have given in response to your question No. 2 and the legal grounds cited therefor.

Mr. WALSH. Now, has the Translation World Publishers engaged in any activity on behalf of the Soviet Government since February 13, 1961?

Mr. CANTER. My answer to that question is the same as I have given in response to your question No. 2 and the legal grounds cited therefor.

Mr. WALSH. Do you know a Carl Nelson of Chicago?

Mr. CANTER. My answer to that question is the same as I have previously answered to your question No. 2, and the legal reasons cited therefor.

Mr. WALSH. Well, Mr. Nelson, Carl Nelson, appeared before this committee and identified himself as a member of the Communist Party. Did you know that Carl Nelson was a member of the Communist Party at any time?

Mr. CANTER. My answer to that question is the same as I have answered your previous question No. 2 and the legal reasons cited therefor.

Mr. WALSH. Mr. Nelson told this committee that he knew you to be a member of the Communist Party. Is that true or false?

Mr. WILLIS. And that statement was under oath?

Mr. WALSH. Yes, sir.

Mr. WILLIS. All right.

Mr. WALSH. Was he telling the truth when he stated under oath that he knew you to be a member of the Communist Party?

Mr. CANTER. My answer to that question is the same as I have answered in response to your question No. 2 and the legal reasons cited therefor.

Mr. WILLIS. Well, are you now, or have you ever been, a member of the Communist Party?

Mr. CANTER. My answer to that question is the same as I have previously stated in response to your question No. 2 and the legal reasons cited therefor.

47-4 Canter's Testimony about Communist Party affiliations

In their 1989 book, "*THE KGB AGAINST THE MAIN ENEMY-How the Soviet Intelligence* Service *Operates against the United States,*" the US's premier communist researcher Herbert Romerstein and former KGB officer Stanislav Levchenko examined Soviet attempts to blacken Goldwater's name and other Soviet campaigns of the time:

> The false charge that Goldwater was a racist was only one of the smear campaigns used against his candidacy by the Soviets and their

surrogates. The American Communists covertly assisted in this "active measures" campaign.

A 1963, booklet claimed that Goldwater was conspiring with the John Birch Society to organize a "putsch," or violent insurrection to take over the United States in 1964. The booklet is entitled, *Birch Putsch*. (Romerstein and Levchenko 1989)

The committee went on to find that:

Plans for 1964, contained no address for the publisher, Domino Publications. The author used the not-very imaginative pseudonym, "John Smith, as told to Stanhope T. McReady." There was nothing to tie this publication to the communists until an ad for the book in the pro-communist National Guardian for April 25, 1963, listed the publisher as "Domino Publications, Suite 900, 22 West Madison Street, Chicago, Illinois."

This was in fact the address of Translation World Publishers, which was registered under the Foreign Agents Registration Act as an agent of the Soviet Union. The co-owners, LeRoy Wolins and David S. Canter, were identified by the House Un-American Activities Committee as members of the Communist Party USA.

In 1965, Domino Publications of Chicago published a pamphlet attacking the NATO Multilateral Nuclear Force (MLF). The pamphlet, by David S. Canter, was titled MLF-Force or Farce? It presented the Soviet arguments against the NATO nuclear defense. (US House of Representatives 1962)

By the late 1960s, David Canter was publishing a small politically oriented Chicago neighborhood newspaper *Hyde Park Kenwood Voices*. Canter's partner and the paper's editor was Don Rose, a journalist active in at least two Communist Party fronts.

In one of them, the Chicago Committee to Defend the Bill of Rights, Rose worked with Quentin Young,[276] Timuel Black[277] and Rabbi Arnold Jacob Wolf[278] - all now personal friends and supporters of Barack Obama.

The Chicago Committee to Defend the Bill of Rights was set up to

---

[276] http://keywiki.org/index.php/Quentin_Young
[277] http://keywiki.org/index.php/Timuel_Black
[278] http://keywiki.org/index.php/Arnold_Jacob_Wolf

abolish the Chicago Red Squad,[279] the police unit charged with monitoring communist and radical organizations.

The paper also campaigned against the House Un-American Activities Committee.

> The one issue that I have from early 1969, featured several major stories about attempts in Chicago and elsewhere to abolish the above-mentioned internal-security groups as well as the history of the Chicago "Red Squad" from the leftist Columbia Journalism Review of late 1968. (Friedman 2008)

David Canter's late wife Miriam Canter was of similar mind. She was an active fundraiser for a Defense committee for prominent medical researcher and Communist Party affiliate, Dr. Jeremiah Stamler, who was also under investigation by House Committee for Un-American-Activities.

The Hyde-Park Kenwood Voices folded in 1975. David Canter and Don Rose began to "mentor" and "educate...politically,"[280] a young University of Chicago political science student and Hyde-Park Herald reporter named David Axelrod.

The young journalist spent time "hanging around" the Canter household. Don Rose wrote a reference letter for Axelrod that helped him win the internship at the Chicago Tribune that would launch his stellar career.

In the 1980s, David Canter was trying to change the Chicago political scene. The Daley era was ending and Canter saw an opportunity to move City Hall to the left.

With nine others, Canter approached Democratic Party congressional US Representative Harold Washington about standing for the Chicago Mayoralty. Canter had known Washington for many years, not surprising as the congressional Representative had ties to Chicago's communists and socialists dating back until the 1940s.

Washington accepted the proposal. Charles Hayes, the secret Communist Party member from Canter's old Packinghouse Workers

---

[279] http://americanfraud.com/Communist Partyredsquad.aspx
[280] http://blog.broadbandmechanics.com/2008/11/my-family-has-been-outed-were-dam-commies-but-we-aint-paid-to-be

Union, took up his vacant congressional seat.

In October 2004, David Canter's son, Chicago IT consultant Marc Canter,[281] described his father's relationship with Harold Washington:

47-5 David Canter and Harold Washington

> One day I stumbled downstairs into our kitchen to meet US Representative Harold Washington talking to my father. Harold was the Congressman from our district and my father was explaining to him how he could split the white vote and become the first black Mayor of the city of Chicago.
>
> My father had been mentoring, encouraging and working with Harold for 15 years by then and it worked. They won the election and Harold became history...
>
> My father encouraged black politicians to get their piece of the pie...
>
> My father never charged for helping anyone out - and it was only until he was 65 did he ever accept a job from anyone he helped. He was one of those idealistic reds. (Canter 2004)

Indeed, David Canter would not take a job under Washington, but after his 1987 re-election, Canter relented and became Deputy Commissioner of Streets and Sanitation.

Marc Canter has also written:

> My brother worked for Harold in D.C. when he was still a Congressman and got a job as a lawyer prosecuting crooked cops - when Harold came to power. My father remained in the inner circle and helped out on all sorts of political and community activities. (Canter 2004)

Don Rose and David Axelrod also worked for Harold Washington. Rose served as an adviser to the Mayor, while Axelrod served as a campaign consultant.

From *The Nation* February 6, 2007:

> Axelrod and Forest Claypool...opened their own consulting shop, handling mostly long-shot candidates until 1987, when Chicago Mayor Harold Washington hired the firm to help with his re-election. Four years

---

[281] http://blog.broadbandmechanics.com/2004/09/who_was_david_s

earlier, Washington had won a historic victory...As the Tribune's city hall bureau chief, Axelrod had ringside seats. "Nineteen eighty-three, that was a phenomenal election. Harold Washington—extraordinary guy. I mean, he was the kinetic campaigner and politician that I've ever met. It was inspiring the way the African-American community came alive around the prospect of electing Harold...

Axelrod sees Obama, who was working in Chicago as a community organizer during the Washington years, as a marker of progress, writing the second act of a story that Washington started. "In 1983, after Harold won the primary, he went to the northwest side of Chicago with Walter Mondale. They went to a place called St. Pascal's Catholic Church. And what ensued there was so ugly—the protests—that it became a national story.

Twenty-one years later, when Barack ran for the US Senate in the primary against six strong candidates, he carried every ward on the northwest side except one, and carried the ward that St. Pascal's is in...That's what he was thinking about on primary night. I was thinking, and I told Barack, that Harold Washington is smiling down on us." (Hayes 2007)

Harold Washington died shortly after starting his second term, the coalition that elected him endured. The Chicago Communist Party was a key component of this alliance as was the Democratic Socialists of America. By the late 70s, Don Rose had become close to the Chicago socialists as had US Representative Charles Hayes and Harold Washington[282] himself.

From the Chicago Democratic Socialists of America:[283]

The 1983 Thomas - Debs Dinner was held at the McCormick Inn on Saturday, May 7...Newly elected Mayor Harold Washington was unable to attend at the last minute. Carl Shier, who was to have introduced him, read a message from him instead, and spoke of Democratic Socialists of America (DSA)'s considerable role in Washington's election campaign. US Representative Danny K. Davis provided the Thomas - Debs address.

Charles Hayes, who (regardless of whether he had actually announced at the time of the Dinner) was already running for the

[282] http://keywiki.org/index.php/Harold_Washington
[283] http://www.chicagodsa.org/d1983/index.html

Congressional seat left vacant when Harold Washington won the Chicago Mayoral election. (Chicago DSA 1983)

When Communist Party - Democratic Socialists of America (DSA) associate US Senator Carol Moseley-Braun (D-IL)[284] ran for US Senate in 1992, the coalition swung into action. While the communists and socialists worked on the ground, Canter, Rose and Axelrod played senior roles in the successful campaign.

47-6 David Orr and Charles Hayes at Chicago's DSA's 1983 Thomas Debs Dinner

Barack Obama ran the successful voter registration drive that secured Moseley-Braun's victory.

Marc Canter has told me that David Canter "knew Barack."

They met through the Moseley campaign and the two were both active in Independent Voters of Illinois (IVI).[285]

David Canter had become active in the organization in the 1940s and remained involved up to his death in 2004.

Independent Voters of Illinois (IVI) campaigns for endorsed "progressive" candidates.

The government took an interest in IVI[286] as far back as 1944. The FBI prepared a more extensive intelligence report on an active political group, the Independent Voters of Illinois, because it was the target of Communist "infiltration." The Independent Voters group was reported to have been formed:

."....for the purpose of developing neighborhood political units to help in the re-election of President Roosevelt and the election of progressive congressmen. IVI endorsed or aided democrats for the most part, although it was stated to be "independent."

Other prominent IVI activists included Communist Party member Milton Cohen and alleged member Timuel Black (who both later joined

[284] http://keywiki.org/index.php/Carol_Moseley_Braun
[285] http://www.iviipo.org/
[286] http://ftp.fas.org/irp/ops/ci/docs/ci1/ch4d.htm

Don Rose's Alliance to End Repression) and Trotskyist turned Socialist Party member Saul Mendelson. (Roosevelt 1939)

Cohen and Mendelson both went on to join Democratic Socialists of America.

When Mendelson died in 1998, US Senator Carol Moseley-Braun (D-IL)[287] and Barack Obama both spoke at his memorial Service.

Both Barack and Michelle Obama[288] were members of IVI and the organization endorsed Obama during his 2004 US Senate race.

In 2004, IVI celebrated its 60th anniversary. Members of the event committee included:[289]

Timuel Black

Leon Despres[290]

Betty Wilhoitte – (Socialist Party veteran member)

A whole host of Democratic Socialists of America (DSA) connected activists and politicians:

Dick Simpson, Bernice Bild, Barbara Flynn Currie, Bob Mann, Joe Moore, David Orr, Toni Preckwinkle, Sue Purrington, US Senator Carol Moseley-Braun (D-IL) and of course David Canter and Barack Obama.

That may have been the last time Canter and Obama met. Canter died the following month.

On September 30, 2008 Marc Canter[291] wrote:

> My father was an old-time politico in Chicago and one of his old buddies - Don Rose writes a column for a Chicago web site called the 'Chicago Daily Observer'.
>
> In today's column he writes that Obama has taken a 50-42 lead in the polls.
>
> I'm saying this in honor of my father who fought for civil rights, against the Vietnam War and would be tickled pink to see what Barack is up to.

---

[287] Chapter 10 - Barack Obama and the Socialist "Mafia"

[288] http://www.iviipo.org/iviipodec2003-rev.pdf

[289] http://www.iviipo.org/IDD60-archivedinfo2.htm

[290] Chapter 27 - Reds, Radicals, Terrorists and Traitors – Progressives for Obama

[291] http://blog.broadbandmechanics.com/2008/09/50-42

I know he's looking down from wherever he is - and laughing right now. (Canter, 50-42 2008)

I will bet he is.

48. Obama's Subtle Sermon - Advice to Socialist Allies

Trevor Loudon © Sunday, November 02, 2008

US Senator Barack Obama (D-IL)[292] posted a piece to a leftist blog the Daily Kos from September 30, 2005, just after the nomination of John G. Roberts to the US Supreme Court.

It is an important piece because here Obama is talking to friends - not voters. Obama makes it clear that he shares "Kos" readers "progressive" values and suggests how to be realistic by a more subtle and inclusive approach.

This is Obama's true vision. There is nothing "centrist" about it. Here is Obama's grand plan for bringing about a socialist America.

Tone, Truth and the Democratic Party:

> US Senator Barack Obama (D-IL) I read with interest your recent discussion regarding my comments on the floor during the debate on John Roberts' nomination. I do not get a chance to follow blog traffic as regularly as I would like, and rarely get the time to participate in the discussions. I thought this might be a good opportunity to offer some thoughts about not only judicial confirmations, but how to bring about meaningful change in this country.

48-1 Anti War Speech by Obama

> Maybe some of you believe I could have made my general point more artfully, but it's precisely because many of these groups are friends and supporters that I felt it necessary to speak my mind.

> There is one way, over the long haul, to guarantee the appointment of judges that are sensitive to issues of social justice, and that is to win the right to appoint them by recapturing the presidency and the Senate. And I

---

[292] http://www.dailykos.com/story/2005/9/30/102745/165

don't believe we get there by vilifying good allies, with a lifetime record of battling for progressive causes, over one vote or position. I am convinced that, our mutual frustrations and strongly-held beliefs notwithstanding, the strategy driving much of Democratic advocacy, and the tone of much of our rhetoric, is an impediment to creating a workable progressive majority in this country. (Obama 2005)

Trevor Loudon: Is Obama a man who wants to appoint Supreme Court judges "sensitive to the issues of social justice" and has a "lifetime record of battling for progressive causes" a true centrist?

Does Obama use language – addressing heartland America? If not, why not?

Is it because Obama sees that "the strategy driving much of Democratic advocacy, and the tone of much of our rhetoric, is an impediment to creating a workable progressive majority in this country?"

> US Senator Barack Obama (D-IL): According to the storyline that drives many advocacy groups and Democratic activists - a storyline often reflected in comments on this blog - we are up against a sharply partisan, radically conservative, take-no-prisoners Republican party. They have beaten us twice by energizing their base with red meat rhetoric and single-minded devotion and discipline to their agenda. In order to beat them, it is necessary for Democrats to get some backbone, give as good as they get, brook no compromise, drive out Democrats who are interested in "appeasing" the right wing, and enforce a more clearly progressive agenda. The country, finally knowing what we stand for and seeing a sharp contrast, will rally to our side and thereby usher in a new progressive era.

> I think this perspective misreads the American people. From traveling throughout Illinois and more recently around the country, I can tell you that Americans are suspicious of labels and suspicious of jargon. They don't think George W. Bush is mean-spirited or prejudiced, but have become aware that his administration is irresponsible and often incompetent. They don't think that corporations are inherently evil (a lot of them work in corporations), but they recognize that big business, unchecked, can fix the game to the detriment of working people and small entrepreneurs. They don't think America is an imperialist brute, but are angry that the case to invade Iraq was exaggerated, are worried that we have unnecessarily alienated existing and potential allies around the world, and are ashamed by events like those at Abu Ghraib which violate our ideals as a country. (Obama 2005)

Trevor Loudon: Obama shares the views and aims of the Kos "progressives," but he is trying to tell his socialist friends that more subtlety and less obvious partisanship are required:

> US Senator Barack Obama (D-IL): It's this non-ideological lens through which much of the country viewed Judge Roberts' confirmation hearings. A majority of folks, including a number of Democrats and Independents, don't think that John Roberts is an ideologue bent on overturning every vestige of civil rights and civil liberties protections in our possession. Instead, they have good reason to believe he is a conservative judge who is (like it or not) within the mainstream of American jurisprudence, a judge appointed by a conservative President who could have done much worse (and probably, I fear, may do worse with the next nominee). While they hope Roberts doesn't swing the court too sharply to the right, a majority of Americans think that the President should probably get the benefit of the doubt on a clearly qualified nominee.

> A plausible argument can be made that too much is at stake here and now, in terms of privacy issues, civil rights, and civil liberties, to give Judge John Roberts the benefit of the doubt. That certainly was the operating assumption of the advocacy groups involved in the nomination battle.

> I shared enough of these concerns that I voted against Roberts on the floor this morning. But short of mounting an all-out filibuster – a quixotic fight I would not have supported; a fight I believe Democrats would have lost both in the Senate and in the court of public opinion; a fight that would have been difficult for Democratic Senators defending seats in states like North Dakota and Nebraska that are essential for Democrats to hold if we hope to recapture the majority; and a fight that would have effectively signaled an unwillingness on the part of Democrats to confirm any Bush nominee, an unwillingness which I believe would have set a dangerous precedent for future administrations – blocking Roberts was not a realistic option. (Obama 2005)

Trevor Loudon: Pick your fights people, we are not Ralph Nader or US Representative Dennis Kucinich (D-OH-10th District) here. We want to win the big ones, not alienate the voters over unwinnable battles...

> US Senator Barack Obama (D-IL): In circumstances, attacks on Pat Leahy, Russ Feingold and the other Democrats who, after careful consideration, voted for Roberts make no sense. Russ Feingold, the only Democrat to vote not only against war in Iraq but also against the Patriot Act, doesn't become complicit in the erosion of civil liberties simply because he chooses to abide by a deeply held and legitimate view that a President, having won a popular election, is entitled to some benefit of the doubt when it comes to judicial appointments. Like it or not, that view has strong support in the Constitution's design.

The same principle holds with respect to issues other than judicial nominations. My colleague from Illinois, Dick Durbin, spoke out forcefully - and voted against - the Iraqi invasion. He isn't somehow transformed into a "war supporter" - as I've heard some anti-war activists suggest - just because he hasn't called for an immediate withdrawal of American troops. He may be simply trying to figure out, as I am, how to ensure that US troop withdrawals occur in a way that we avoid all-out Iraqi civil war, chaos in the Middle East, and much more costly and deadly interventions down the road. A pro-choice Democrat doesn't become anti-choice because he or she isn't absolutely convinced that a twelve-year-old girl should be able to get an operation without a parent being notified. A pro-civil rights Democrat does not become complicit in an anti-civil rights agenda because he or she questions the efficacy of certain Affirmative Action programs. And a pro-union Democrat doesn't become anti-union if he or she makes a determination that on balance, CAFTA will help American workers more than it will harm them. (Obama 2005)

Trevor Loudon: No enemies on the left. Tolerate some dissent. Do not criticize your own team. Work for Progressive unity for the sake of the bigger picture...

US Senator Barack Obama (D-IL): Or to make the point differently: How can we ask Republican senators to resist pressure from their right wing and vote against flawed appointees like UN Ambassador John Bolton, if we engage in similar rhetoric against Democrats who dissent from our own party line? How can we expect Republican moderates who are concerned about the nation's fiscal meltdown to ignore Grover Norquist' threats if we make similar threats to those who buck our party orthodoxy? (Obama 2005)

Trevor Loudon: A recognition that a progressive majority needs to at least neutralize the opposition by reaching out to independents and the Republican left. Build bridges not burn them. Keep the bigger picture in mind.

US Senator Barack Obama (D-IL): I am not drawing a facile equivalence here between progressive advocacy groups and right-wing advocacy groups. The consequences of their ideas are vastly different. Fighting on behalf of the poor and the vulnerable is not the same as fighting for homophobia and Halliburton. But to the degree that we brook no dissent within the Democratic Party, and demand fealty to the one, "true" progressive vision for the country, we risk the thoughtfulness and openness to new ideas that are required to move this country forward. When we lash out at those who share our fundamental values because they have not met the criteria of every single item on our progressive "checklist," then we are essentially preventing them from thinking in new ways about problems. We are tying them up in a straightjacket and forcing them into a conversation only with the converted. (Obama 2005)

Trevor Loudon: Do not worry, I am as committed to socialism as you are, but we will not achieve our goals if we indulge ourselves in self-righteous attacks on our less committed allies.

US Senator Barack Obama (D-IL): Beyond that, by applying tests, we are hamstringing our ability to build a majority. We won't be able to transform the country with a polarized electorate. Because the truth of the matter is this: Most of the issues this country faces are hard. They require tough choices, and they require sacrifice. The Bush Administration and the Republican Congress may have made the problems worse, but they won't go away after President Bush is gone. Unless we are open to new ideas, and not just new packaging, we won't change enough hearts and minds to initiate a serious energy or fiscal policy that calls for serious sacrifice. We won't have the popular support to craft a foreign policy that meets the challenges of globalization or terrorism while avoiding isolationism and protecting civil liberties. We certainly won't have a mandate to overhaul a health care policy that overcomes all the entrenched interests that are the legacy of a jerry-rigged health care system. And we won't have the broad political support, or the effective strategies, required to lift large numbers of our fellow citizens out of numbing poverty. (Obama 2005)

Trevor Loudon: The socialists appeal to "serious sacrifice" and Obama wants to "lift large numbers of our fellow citizens out of numbing poverty" without sacrificing. Who will sacrifice?

Conditioning people to accept sacrifice is essential to meet Obama's objectives. Obama knows that people will embrace sacrifice when motivated by an ideal, the promise of something better - "change." Obama does not dare state the result of the change.

US Senator Barack Obama (D-IL): The bottom line is that our job is harder than the conservatives' job. After all, it's easy to articulate a belligerent foreign policy based solely on unilateral military action, a policy that sounds tough and acts dumb; it's harder to craft a foreign policy that's tough and smart. It's easy to dismantle government safety nets; it's harder to transform those safety nets so that they work for people and can be paid for. It's easy to embrace a theological absolutism; it's harder to find the right balance between the legitimate role of faith in our lives and the demands of our civic religion. But that's our job. And I firmly believe that whenever we exaggerate or demonize, or oversimplify or overstate our case, we lose. Whenever we dumb down the political debate, we lose. A polarized electorate that is turned off of politics, and easily dismisses both parties because of the nasty, dishonest tone of the debate, works perfectly well for those who seek to chip away at the idea of government because, in the end, a cynical electorate is a selfish electorate. (Obama 2005)

Trevor Loudon: Exactly how Obama has run his campaign positive, inclusive and respectful of the opposition. Nevertheless, what does he believe in?

US Senator Barack Obama (D-IL): Let me be clear: I am not arguing that the Democrats should trim their sails and be more "centrist." In fact, I think the whole "centrist" versus "liberal" labels that continue to characterize the debate within the Democratic Party misses the mark. Too often, the "centrist" label seems to mean compromise for compromise sake, whereas on issues like health care, energy, education and tackling poverty, I don't think Democrats have been bold enough. But I do think that being bold involves more than just putting more money into existing programs and will instead require us to admit that some existing programs and policies don't work well. And further, it will require us to innovate and experiment with whatever ideas hold promise (including market- or faith-based ideas that originate from Republicans).

Our goal should be to stick to our guns on those core values that make this country great, show a spirit of flexibility and sustained attention that can achieve those goals, and try to create the sort of serious, adult, consensus around our problems that can admit Democrats, Republicans and Independents of good will. This is more than just a matter of "framing," although clarity of language, thought, and heart are required. It's a matter of actually having faith in the American people's ability to hear a real and authentic debate about the issues that matter. (Obama 2005)

Trevor Loudon: Luring as many as possible into the "progressive tent" is essential for his personal success.

US Senator Barack Obama (D-IL): I am not arguing that we "unilaterally disarm" in the face of Republican attacks, or bite our tongue when this Administration screws up. Whenever they are wrong, inept, or dishonest, we should say so clearly and repeatedly; and whenever they gear up their attack machine, we should respond quickly and forcefully. I am suggesting that the tone we take matters, and that truth, as best we know it, be the hallmark of our response.

My dear friend Senator Paul Simon used to consistently win the votes of much more conservative voters in Southern Illinois because he had mastered the art of "disagreeing without being disagreeable," and they trusted him to tell the truth. Similarly, one of Senator Paul Wellstone's greatest strengths was his ability to deliver a scathing rebuke of the Republicans without ever losing his sense of humor and affability. In fact, I would argue that the most powerful voices of change in the country, from Lincoln to King, have been those who can speak with the utmost conviction about the great issues of the day without ever belittling those who opposed them, and without denying the limits of their own perspectives. (Obama 2005)

Trevor Loudon: Name-dropping US Senator Paul Simon (D-IL) and the late US Senator Paul Wellstone (D-MN), two of the most extreme left Senators in recent US history, is a clear signal to the "Kos"-ites. I am one of you. I am with Simon and Wellstone. Like them, I charm the moderates and con the conservatives.

US Senator Barack Obama (D-IL): In that spirit, let me end by saying I don't pretend to have all the answers to the challenges we face, and I look forward to periodic conversations with all of you in the months and years to come. I trust that you will continue to let me and other Democrats know when you believe we are screwing up. And I, in turn, will always try and show you the respect and candor one owes his friends and allies. (Obama 2005)

Trevor Loudon: How many American voters know that Barack Obama regards the far left "Kos" people as "friends and allies?"

The Second Day of Infamy!

49. Communists, Socialists and Obama Can Change America

Trevor Loudon © Tuesday, November 11, 2008

The Communist Party USA and their allies in the Democratic Socialists of America[293] have backed Barack Obama for many years.

How can a couple of fringe Marxist sects with a combined membership of fewer than 10,000 effect a country as powerful as the United States of America?

Here is how.

49-1 Barack Obama (l) John Sweeney (r)

In this report from the Communist Party USA's Political Affairs website entitled: "*Special Interest or Class Consciousness? How Labor Put Obama in the White House,*" the communists explain how socialist led unionists elected a President.

Political Affairs explains the importance union backing played in the

Obama campaign and goes on to quote AFL-CIO President and well-known Democratic Socialists of America (DSA) member, John Sweeney, and AFL-CIO Political Committee Chair and AFSCME President, Gerald McEntee,[294] a Democratic Socialists of America (DSA) supporter.

49-2 Gerald McEntee, President AFSCME

New polling data released this week by the AFL-CIO revealed the extent of union support for US Senator Barack Obama (D-IL) in the Presidential election.

The data showed that a high turnout of working class union voters in states like Ohio, Pennsylvania, and Michigan formed a foundation of support for Obama. In addition, union voters in key battleground states

---

[293] http://keywiki.org/index.php/Democratic_Socialists_of_America
[294] http://newzeal.blogspot.com/2008/02/obama-file-19-obama-08-all-way-with-dsa.html
Chapter 19 - Obama '08 "All the Way With DSA"

like Colorado, Virginia, North Carolina, and Florida proved influential as well, an AFL-CIO press statement on the new data indicated.

Union members supported Obama by a 68-30 margin and influenced their members, according to an election night survey conducted for the AFL-CIO by Peter D. Hart Research Associates.

According to exit polling by major media outlets, voters from union households totaled one in five voters. (Gruenberg 2007)

AFL-CIO President John Sweeney said:

"We have taken the first crucial steps to build a better future for our children and grandchildren. And what we've seen - the stunning voter participation and the common call for change - is an indication of the history we can continue to make together."

"More than 250,000 union volunteers took to the streets in the largest independent voter mobilization in history," AFL-CIO Political Committee Chair and AFSCME President Gerald McEntee said.

Union education and mobilization efforts turned in impressive statistics for the Obama-Biden ticket, the data revealed.

Obama won white men who are union members by 18 points. Union gun-owners backed Obama by 12 points. Union veterans voted for Obama by a 25-point margin. In the general population, Obama lost these groups by significant margins.

In addition, labor leaders stated that an immediate goal is to pass an economic stimulus package that provides direct relief for working families by strengthening the social safety net, creating jobs through public infrastructure investments, and directing financial relief to states to help cover costs of health care and education programs:

The election is just step one in delivering the change we need, Sweeney said. Working men and women are poised to keep the energy pumping to help the Obama administration lead the change we need. There will be no gap or letdown.

The AFL-CIO mobilized 250,000 volunteers in 24 battleground states. In its final get out the vote push, the AFL-CIO boasted, union volunteers contacted 1 million union voters. Throughout the campaign, the union said, the labor movement made 76 million calls, knocked on 14 million doors, and circulated 29 million fliers at work sites and union households. The effort identified a total of 3 million "undecided" voters and helped convince many of them to support Barack Obama (PA Staff Writers 2008)

Step one. Use union muscles to get whom you want elected, elected.

Step two. Use front groups and unions to push socialist policy inside the Democratic Party. Make communist/socialist policies "respectable" by giving them a Democratic Party label.

Step three. Use your sympathizers, allies and secret members inside the Democratic Party to get your socialist policies passed into law.

Political Affairs covers Dr. Quentin Young's call for a "Single Payer" health care system. "Single Payer" or socialized medicine is a long time platform issue for both CPUSA and Democratic Socialists of America (DSA):

> "A group of over 15,000 US physicians has called on President-elect Barack Obama and the new Congress to "do the right thing" and enact a single-payer national health insurance plan, a system of public health care financing characterized as "an improved Medicare for all." (Political Affairs)

> "Our country is hailing the remarkable and historic victory of President-elect Barack Obama and the mandate for change the electorate has awarded him," said Dr. Quentin Young, national coordinator of Physicians for a National Health Program.

> "In large measure President-elect Obama's victory and the victories of his allies in the House and Senate were propelled by mounting public worries about health care," he said. "Yet the prescription offered during the campaign by the President-elect and most Democratic policy makers - a hybrid of private health insurance plans and government subsidies - will not resolve the problems of our dangerously dysfunctional system." Young said.

> "The only effective cure for our health care woes is to establish a single, publicly financed system, one that removes the inefficient, wasteful, for-profit private health insurance industry from the picture," he said. "Single Payer has a proven track record of success - Medicare being just one example - and is the only medically and fiscally responsible course of action to take."

> "A solid majority of physicians endorse an approach," Young said. "An April 2008 study in the Annals of Internal Medicine shows 59 percent of US physicians support national health insurance. Opinion polls show two-thirds of the public also supports a remedy. Now, with strong political leadership, this reform is within reach."

> Young said the adoption of a single-payer health system is a "major component of the new President's economic rescue of Main Street." (Young M.D., et al. 2008)

Young noted that Obama has said more than once that he is a supporter of a single-payer universal health care program. If he were "starting from scratch," he would favor adopting one. In 2003, Young said, and Illinois State Senator Obama remarked that:

> "First we have to take back the White House, we have to take back the Senate, and we have to take back the House." (Political Affairs)

Young remarked:

> "Tuesday's election has made all of these conditions happen. In his first 100 days, President Obama has a window of opportunity to inspire the nation by championing the enactment of single-payer national health insurance under the slogan, 'Everybody in, nobody out.' a plan is embodied in the US National Health Insurance Act, H.R. 676, introduced by Congressman John Conyers Jr. (D-MI) and co-sponsored by more than 90 others, more than any other health reform legislation."

> "Adopting a nationwide single-payer system will build on the great achievement of Medicare, further unify our people, strengthen our country's economic competitiveness and assure President Obama's legacy as an American hero," Young said. (Young M.D., et al. 2008)

Quentin Young is a leading member of Chicago Democratic Socialists of America (DSA). Before joining Democratic Socialists of America (DSA) in the 1980's, Young was involved in Communist Party fronts and in the 1970's was accused by a Senate Internal Security body of once belonging to the North Chicago based Bethune Club of the Communist Party USA.

Quentin Young[295] is a longtime friend and political supporter of Barack Obama. He was present at the famous 1995 meeting[296] in the home of former Weather Underground terrorists Bill Ayers[297] that helped launch Obama's political career.

49-3 Dr. Quentin Young (l)
Barack Obama (r)

Quentin Young has treated both the Obama and Ayers/Dohrn families.

---

[295] http://keywiki.org/index.php/Quentin_Young
[296] http://keywiki.org/index.php/Alice_Palmer
[297] http://keywiki.org/index.php/Bill_Ayers

"Single Payer" advocate US Representative John Conyers[298] is a Democratic Socialists of America (DSA) member[299] and is a strong Obama supporter.

Democratic Socialists of America (DSA) and CPUSA controlled unions got Barack Obama (and dozens of other socialist Democrats) elected.

Democratic Socialists of America (DSA) and CPUSA fronts use politicians to promote socialist policies inside the Democratic Party.

By using front groups like Quentin Young's "Physicians for a National Health Program," the communists and socialists advance their agenda under a false flag. Their sympathizers and allies in the Democratic Party promote and vote on those policies, claiming them as their own - leaving the public in the dark as to their true source.

The socialist threat to America comes not from abroad, but from the Democratic Socialists of America (DSA)/CPUSA controlled unions, their front groups and their allies in the Democratic Party.

That is how a few thousand dedicated activists influence and in some cases control the political direction of the mightiest country on earth.

How much easier will it be now that their man has the top job?

50. The Communist Party Strategy for Obama's America

Trevor Loudon © Friday, November 14, 2008

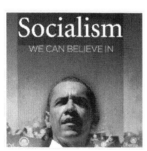

The best way to determine the Obama administration's agenda is to read the communist press.

Very few US voters would have any inkling that the 3,000 members of the Communist Party USA[300] and Committees of Correspondence for Democracy and Socialism

[298] http://keywiki.org/index.php/John_Conyers
[299] http://keywiki.org/index.php/Danny_K_Davis
[300] http://keywiki.org/index.php/Communist_Party_USA
50-1 Barack Obama

(COCDS)[301] have long abandoned violent revolution as the primary means of achieving power in the United States of America.

For many years Communist Party USA, Democratic Socialists of America (DSA) and COCDS have worked to change America through infiltrating and influencing the Democratic Party.

50-2 Norman Markowitz

To accomplish this task it is necessary to move secret socialists into the Democrats, by the infiltration of socialist ideas and concepts into the DP's program.

This is the real secret and the real threat of American socialism.

If the United States ever succumbs to socialism, it will be because Marxist controlled trade unions and pressure groups have managed to insinuate their policies into the Democratic Party and use their sympathizers to pass them into law.

The process is simple:

- The Marxists come up with a policy.
- They promote it through their hundreds of front organizations to build real or pseudo fake public support.
- Their sympathizers and secret members in the Democratic Party pick the policy up and promote it as their own, or as a response to "public opinion."
- The Democrats pass the policy into law, with voters remaining unaware of its communist origin.
- The Marxists move onto the next policy.

The best examples of communist/socialist inspired social change on a major scale were FDR's "New Deal" of the 1930's and Johnson's "Great Society of the 1960's."

The American left sees the Obama presidency as an opportunity for "social change" on a scale never before seen in US history.

The strategy is to introduce socialized medicine, greater union rights

---

[301] http://www.cc-ds.org/

and other social programs to move even conservative voters into the Democratic Party camp. US Marxists want to emulate the communist inspired programs of the post-World War II British Labor Party that locked in the British working class behind Labor for several decades.

The Communist Party wants to make US workers dependent on the Democrats as a step on the road to socialism.

There is an article of note from *Political Affairs*, the theoretical journal of the Communist Party USA by its author, Norman Markowitz, who is a history professor at Rutgers University in New Jersey and a long time Communist Party member.

Markowitz, like the rest of his comrades, is a strong supporter of President elect Barack Obama.

Markowitz explains communist strategy for an Obama presidency and the policy agendas the Communist Party wishes their new President to pursue.

Obama's Mandate for Change:

Obama won a solid victory in both the popular vote and the Electoral College and will have a solid majority in Congress.

Obama has a mandate and it is a mandate for change. Obama's slogan, "Change we can believe in," was reminiscent of slogans like the "New Deal" of Roosevelt's 1932 campaign and the "Great Society" banner under which Johnson won in 1964. In the latter cases, those slogans translated into the major policy domestic agendas of those administrations.

For the people who elected Obama and the increased Democratic majority, "change we can believe in" is not about bailouts for corporations and banks. It is not about wearing American flag pins on your lapel while the military budget continues to escalate and bankers and corporate CEO's wine and dines. "Change we can believe in" is not about a spruced up version of trickledown theory or the same policies behind a fresh face in the White House.

It is about reversing and repealing the policies that have both led to the immediate financial crisis and looming global depression. It is about ending the post-World War II policies that led to the long-term stagnation and decline of the labor movement. It is about creating a national public health care program more than 50 years after it established in other major industrial nations, and handling a national debt, which has increased 10 times since Ronald Reagan became President in 1981.

A "Single Payer" national health system - known as "socialized medicine" in the rest of the developed world - should be an essential part of the change that the core constituencies, which elected Obama, need. Britain serves as an important political lesson for strategists. After the Labor Party established the National Health Service after World War II, conservative workers and low-income people under religious and other influences who tended to support the Conservatives would vote for the Labor Party when labor-supported governments enacted health care, social welfare, education, and pro-working class policies.

In addition, passing the Employee Free Choice Act to make joining a union easier and to expand the base of union voters who supported Obama by 50 points on Nov. 4 seems logical. It would also provide a massive boost for working families struggling with stagnant incomes, high health care costs, retirement costs, and job insecurity.

The best way to win over the portion of the working class in the South or the West that supported McCain and the Republicans is to create important new public programs and improve the social safety net. National health care, higher minimum wages, support for trade union organizing, aid to education should all be on the agenda. These programs will improve the quality of our lives, giving us greater security and establishing the social economic changes that will bring reluctant voters into the Obama coalition. That is how progress works.

The right-wing propaganda machine will scream socialism, and that is a good thing. The more socialism identifies with real policies that raise the standard of living and improve the quality of life for the working class and the whole people, the more socialism considered. A stronger left that follows the tradition of the Communist Party in its unbreakable commitment to a socialist future and to educating people about the value and necessity of socialist policies in the present follow. (People's World 2008)

Who wants to bet against my prediction that all the policy agendas suggested by Markowitz will be "on the table" during Obama's first term?

51. Top Communists Used Influence for Obama Victory

Trevor Loudon © Thursday, November 20, 2008

The unions played a huge role in the election of President Elect Barack Obama.

After John Sweeney of Democratic Socialists of America became

AFL-CIO President in 1996, he oversaw the repeal of the ban on known communists holding office in AFL-CIO unions.

Supporters of Democratic Socialists of America (DSA) and the Communist Party USA now dominate the anti-communist US union movement.

Illinois unionist Scott Marshall is one the most influential socialists in the US. He is Vice Chair of the Communist Party USA and Chair of the Communist Party Labor Commission.

Scott Marshall directs the hundreds of Communist Party members and sympathizers who have re-colonized the US Labor movement in recent years.

This gives Marshall control of millions of dollars of union money and thousands of paid and volunteer union political campaigners.

Scott Marshall used his considerable influence to help get Barack Obama elected President and he is damn happy about it.

From the Communist Party USA Labor Upfront Blog:[302]

Obama Wins!

Labor Wins!

Working Families Win!

The American people reject policies of greed and union-busting!

51-1 Unionist Scott Marshall

President Elect Barack Obama.

Those words ring with meaning. For organized labor they ring with pride, hope, and energy for the struggles ahead. No one feels like "labor's candidate won, so now we can go home and rest," as congratulation messages pour in from all parts of the labor movement, the critical subtext is, we are ready and eager to march with you for change. At the top of labor's change agenda is boots-on-the-ground support for the Obama agenda of a new "New Deal" for economic recovery and passage of the Employee Free Choice Act.

---

[302] http://laborupfront.blogspot.com/2008/11/obama-wins-labor-wins-working-families.html

Organized labor played an amazing role in the election Barack Obama.

Unions played an extraordinary leadership role in winning the working class for Obama.

It's been many years since labor was so totally united behind a Presidential candidate.

Labor raised the struggle against racism and for class unity to a whole new level.

Unions gave vital leadership in building support for Obama on issues like the economy, workers' rights to organize, protecting retiree's pensions and social security, healthcare, and building green manufacturing that protects the environment and puts people back to work.

The labor movement took independent political action to spectacular new levels. Unions broke all previous records in mobilizing it's rank and file for labor walks, phone banks, plant gate distributions, and member to member contact in the workplace. Labor continued to build and develop its own political apparatus and voice. Hundreds, if not thousands, of union halls became campaign central for the Obama campaign as well as for targeted Congressional contests.

As phenomenal as labor's efforts were, the impact of the Obama upsurge and campaign on labor was also incredible. New coalitions were built or strengthened. A new depth was added to ties between labor and all the components of the Obama movement.

Labor's role was hardly mentioned in the mainstream press. All the more reason for labor to have a big showing of celebration and support for our new President. Some in labor have begun to talk about a big mobilization for President Barack Obama's "People's Inaugural." (Marshall 2008)

What a great idea!

Joelle Fishman is Chair of the CPUSA Political Action Commission and Chair of the Connecticut Communist Party. She is also the daughter-in-law of the late senior Soviet spy and former head of the Communist Party Economics Commission, Victor Perlo.[303]

---

[303] http://en.wikipedia.org/wiki/Victor_Perlo

51-2 Joelle Fishman

Fishman's role in the Communist Party's Political Action Commission gives her responsibility for organizing party support for "progressive" Democratic Party candidates at the state, congressional, senate and of course Presidential level.

She has links to Obama friend and US Action leader, William McNary.

Like all of the Communist Party "red army," Joelle Fishman campaigned for President elect Barack Obama.

Joelle Fishman writing in the Connecticut Communist Party's *People before Profits Blog*:[304]

It was enjoyable to knock on doors and find voters who were enthusiastic and inspired by Obama's historic candidacy, like the teacher who said her whole family was spreading the word. There were several families of divided opinion and others who declined to say. The most challenging conversations were with voters who did not want to support Obama because they were caught up in the lies and rumors undermining his integrity and patriotism. Those who were ready to discuss appreciated the comparison of McCain's anti-worker record with Obama's near perfect score.

It was exciting to be part of the quarter million union volunteers across the country, the biggest election mobilization in labor's history, which has influenced the political climate in working class swing states and districts, laying the basis for a much larger labor movement.

The example set by labor's top leaders talking directly with white sisters and brothers about how Obama represents their best chance for a secure future will have a lasting impact...

This year the chance to uproot ultra-right corporate political dominance is much greater. Voters want to be part of history. They see that the policies of the Bush administration, which McCain-Palin would continue, are bankrupting the country and endangering the world.

---

[304] http://ctpeoplebeforeprofits.blogspot.com/2008/11/merrilee-milstein-day-puts-working.html

Labor's giant effort along with massive organizing by African American, Latino, women's and youth groups has turned historically Republican states' House and Senate seats into battlegrounds, including the Senate seat in New Hampshire.

A landslide victory for Obama and Congress will open the door for big new struggles to organize workers into unions and place the needs of working families' front and center in this economic crisis. (Fishman 2008)

The Communist Party has backed Obama electorally since at least 2004. This year the communists put every resource they had behind the Obama's campaign. Why?

52. Communists Celebrate Obama Victory! Plan Steps to Socialism

Friday, November 21, 2008

The Communist Party USA will emerge from the shadows - for at least a while, now that Barack Obama is President,

They are free to gloat over Obama's victory, to boast about the part they played in it and to lay down the agenda they expect Obama to pursue.

The party wants Obama to implement huge social changes.

The party wants to preserve the left wing coalition that brought Obama to power and to use that unity to keep the pressure on Obama's government.

The party wants to put socialism back on the agenda.

52-1 Jarvis Tyner

This is the culmination of decades of hard work. The Communist Party USA does not intend to blow this opportunity.

From the *People's Weekly World* :

NEW YORK - Communist Party USA leaders meeting here Nov. 15-16, 2008 celebrated the election of President elect President Elect Barack Obama, the nation's first African

American President, and of stronger Democratic majorities in Congress, saying it opened the way to progressive advances for America's working families.

They adopted a call to action to carry out the election mandate, including immediate government steps to help Americans hit by the economic crisis and bringing peace to Iraq and Afghanistan. And they said maintaining the unity of the movement that elected Obama will be vital to making gains. Anything that disrupts that unity is "the worst thing that could happen," an Ohio steelworker retiree declared.

The election outcome represented "the biggest political realignment since the 1930s," said Communist Party Political Action Chair Joelle Fishman. "We can think back with pride to decades of hard work toward the goal of a big enough, broad enough and united enough labor and all-people's movement that could overcome the ultra-right blockage to all progress," she said. "That all-people's movement has come to life. It is dynamic and it has the potential to grow."

52-2 Sam Webb

"This election showed magnificently what our people are made of," the party's executive Vice Chair, Jarvis Tyner[305], said with tears in his eyes. "This is not just a campaign, it is a movement," one that has updated and made a reality of the slogan, "black, brown, white, unite and fight," he said. (People's World 2008)

Communist Party USA National Chair Sam Webb said:

"The people have taken a necessary first step toward a new society." Obama is bringing a "reform agenda in a reform era whose character will be decided in the years ahead," he said.

The "biggest challenge" now, he told the meeting, is to "resist efforts by reaction and some on the left" to advocate a break in the coalition that elected Obama and is now led by him. "We will have our differences but they have to be handled so as not to break the overall unity," he said. The elections showed the possibilities for building a bigger and broader coalition to effect progressive change, based in the labor movement and among women, racial and ethnic minorities and young people, and including small businesses and people who did not vote for Obama, Webb said. (People's World 2008)

---

[305] http://keywiki.org/index.php/Jarvis_Tyner

Speakers hailed the role of labor, the African American people, Latinos, women and youth in the stunning Nov. 4 victory.

Activists from battleground states emphasized the key role that trade union leaders and rank-and-file union members played there. Communist Party USA Labor Commission Chair, Scott Marshall, noted the "near-total unity of labor" in backing Obama, saying it bodes well for further labor unity.

Fishman stressed that the election took place in the shadow of the deepest economic crisis since the Great Depression and the endless war in Iraq and Afghanistan.

52-3 Communist Party campaign poster

Now, "people are angry, hopeful and ready to go," she said. "Our program should be strong and decisive. It should call for taking the profits out of basic needs like health care and energy and explore public ownership. At the same time, we should be part of the movement that puts the wind at Obama's back."

Webb said the seeds of today's economic meltdown were planted in the 1970s with a combination of bad government policies, corporate greed and the destabilizing dynamics inherent in capitalism. The result was a ballooning unregulated financial sector and an economy fueled by government and consumer debt. Along with that came the collapse of manufacturing, mass unemployment, union-busting, wage and benefit cuts, and attempts to privatize public education, Social Security and Medicare. These policies, Webb charged, produced the biggest shift in wealth from working people to the rich in our history.

What is needed to reverse this crisis, he said,

"is massive fiscal expansion, large injections of federal money into the economy" to fund public works job programs, extend jobless benefits and food stamps and help Americans hold onto their homes. As immediate priorities, Webb said, "We need to single out jobs and passage of the Employee Free Choice Act, joining with others in the struggle." The EFCA, labor's top priority, will make it easier for workers to join unions.

The party leaders emphasized combining support for immediate and partial measures and for more advanced and longer-term reforms, along with projecting socialism as a fundamental solution, one that Americans are now open to hearing more about. The economic crisis shows that socialism is a necessity for our country, Webb said. "We need to put out our vision of socialism and how it will come about."

Fishman cautioned against bogging down in disputes over Cabinet appointments.

"Our energy and focus should be on building the labor and people's broad movement at the grass roots," she said. "That is how we can give a constructive push in a united way." (People's World 2008)

53. Why did Obama Appoint a Socialist to his "Transition Team?"

Trevor Loudon © Thursday, November 27, 2008

According to the Washington Post,[306] scrutinizing potential appointees to President elect Obama's new administration are undergoing in-depth investigations like never before.

Now, as President Elect Barack Obama assembles his administration, an army of lawyers volunteering on his transition team is

53-1 David Bonior (D-MI)

vetting his potential picks with unprecedented scrutiny of their personal, financial, and professional backgrounds.

Obama is conducting the vetting process much the way he managed his campaign on a prodigious scale. He did not wait until he won the election to vet his favored picks. Soon after he clinched the Democratic nomination, lawyers prepared dossiers of about 150 contenders for senior positions, often without the candidates themselves knowing. (Rucker 2008)

Why did President elect Obama, appoint a socialist to his proto

---

[306]http://www.washingtonpost.com/wp-dyn/content/article/2008/11/17/AR2008111703037.html?hpid=topnews

cabinet - Transition Economic Advisory Board?

The man in question, former Michigan Congressman David Bonior, is a supporter and a "member in good standing" of Democratic Socialists of America.

Despite its name, Democratic Socialists of America is not "democratic" in the traditional American sense. The organization is a several thousand strong alliance of Marxists, anarchists, former communists, Trotskyists and student radicals dedicated to the socialist transformation of American society.

53-2 Kurt Stand

Democratic Socialists of America (DSA) has close ties and some cross membership with both the Communist Party USA and the Communist Party offshoot Committees of Correspondence for Democracy and Socialism; both of which also supported Obama.

Many Democratic Socialists of America (DSA) members have ties to Castro's Cuba, Chavez's Venezuela and Mexico's Zapatista rebels.

One Democratic Socialists of America (DSA) National Political Committee member, Kurt Stand (code name "Junior"), was jailed in 1997 after the FBI discovered he had spied for the former East Germany.

Senior Democratic Socialists of America (DSA) member William (Bill) Moseley still runs The Friends of Kurt Stand support group:

> First elected to the US House of Representatives in 1976, Bonior served as Democratic whip in the House from 1991 to 2002, during which time Democrats were in both the majority (1991-1995) and minority (1995-2002), making Bonior the third and second highest-ranking Democrat in the House, respectively. During his tenure in office, Bonior was the public face of Democratic opposition to the North American Free Trade Agreement (NAFTA). (Bonior 2008)

US Representative David Bonior was a leading member of the Congressional Progressive Caucus,[307] a grouping of around fifty leftist Democratic congressional Representatives, which includes some

---

[307] http://newzeal.blogspottrevorloudon.com/2006/11/the-socialists-behind-the-progressive-caucus.html/

Democratic Socialists of America (DSA) members.

> No, we are not a separate party. Like our friends and allies in the feminist, labor, civil rights, religious, and community organizing movements, many of us have been active in the Democratic Party. We work with those movements to strengthen the party's left wing, represented by the Congressional Progressive Caucus. Maybe sometime in the future, in coalition with our allies, an alternative national party will be viable. For now, we will continue to support progressives who have a real chance at winning elections, which usually means left-wing Democrats (Democratic Socialist of America 2008)

After leaving Congress in 2002, Bonior lost his run for Governor of Michigan where the Detroit Democratic Socialists of America (DSA) backed him.

From DSA's Democratic Left Fall 2002:

> Detroit Democratic Socialists of America (DSA) remains active in the electoral arena. Over the spring and summer, its work focused on Congressman David Bonior 's gubernatorial campaign. The local endorsed Rep. Bonior almost eighteen months ago. He was the keynote speaker at its last Douglass-Debs Dinner. Democratic Socialists of America (DSA) helped with the early fundraising for his campaign, collecting signatures for his nominating petitions, distributing literature at Detroit churches, and walking door to door in Macomb County on his behalf on the weekend before the primary. On the weekend of July 20-21, the local brought Representative Danny K. Davis (an African-American congressman and Democratic Socialists of America (DSA) member from Chicago) to Detroit to campaign for Bonior. (Democratic Left 2002)

US Representative Danny K. Davis is also long time friend and political ally of Barack Obama.

In 2003, US Representative David Bonior was a keynote speaker at Democratic Socialists of America (DSA) national convention in Detroit.[308]

Bonior's speech - *"Towards a North American Parliamentary Union"* called for a political forum or Parliament to address US/Canada/Mexico relations. While Bonior was a leading opponent of the North American Free Trade Agreement, he is not opposed to a North American Political Union.

---

[308] http://www.dsausa.org/dl/Winter_2003.pdf

Bonior told the Democratic Socialists of America (DSA) conference:

> This is a tremendous organization in the Detroit area in [the]living wage campaign's great, great success. They have been one of the stalwarts in it-fighting for a Single Payer healthcare plan and, of course, global justice. And I couldn't be more thrilled to be here with you today and to be associated... (D. Bonior 2003)

Four days after Obama won the presidency, on November 4, 2008, Greater Detroit Democratic Socialists of America (DSA) honored US Representative David Bonior:[309]

> At this year's Douglass-Debs Dinner, we will celebrate the 25th anniversary of the merger of the Democratic Socialist Organizing Committee (DSOC) with the New American Movement to form Democratic Socialists of America . The dinner is at UAW Local 600 at 6 PM on Saturday, November 8. This year we are honoring US Representative David and Judy Bonior and Judge Claudia Morcum... (Newsletter 2009)

Bonior also Chairs the Board of pro-union organization American Rights at Work.[310] Other Board members include AFL-CIO President and Democratic Socialists of America (DSA) member John Sweeney, NAACP Communist Party leader Julian Bond (once a member of Democratic Socialists of America (DSA) ancestor organization Democratic Socialist Organizing Committee) and two Democratic Socialists of America (DSA) connected politicians - former Congressman and NAACP President Kweisi Mfume and US Representative Hilda Solis (D-CA-32nd District).

US Representative David Bonior is close to Democratic Socialists of America (DSA), but is he a member?

From DSA's Democratic Left Spring 2006:

> Democratic Socialists of America (DSA) has formed a Political Action Committee-Democratic Socialists of America PAC (DSA PAC), which will raise funds to enable activity that supports or opposes candidates for federal office. By law, Democratic Socialists of America (DSA) is not permitted to expend its resources in support of or against candidates in partisan elections; however, Democratic Socialists of America (DSA) is permitted to form a PAC for this purpose...

---

[309] http://kincaidsite.com/dsa/newsletter.html
[310] http://www.americanrightsatwork.org/

The PAC is a separate legal entity that will file reports of its activity with the Federal Election Commission (FEC).

Democratic Socialists of America (DSA) members in good standing may contribute to the PAC. Because the law is specific, the screening of all contributions to make sure that they are from members is essential.

"Only Members in good standing may contribute..." (DSA 2006)

According to US Representative David Bonior Political Campaign Contributions 2006 Election Cycle (see Pg. 352), David E. Bonior gave $1,000 to the Democratic Socialists of America (DSA) PAC:

BONIOR, DAVID E

MT CLEMENS, MI

48043 WAYNE STATE UNIV./PROFESSOR $1,000

06/19/2006 P

DEMOCRATIC SOCIALISTS OF AMERICA PAC (Federal Election Commission 2006)

Democratic Socialists of America (DSA), Bonior or both broke US electoral law, or Congressman David E. Bonior was, in 2006, an official member of Democratic Socialists of America.

Other contributors listed with Bonior[311] included confirmed Democratic Socialists of America (DSA) members:

David Green, Ed Clark, Adam Hochschild, Duane Campbell, David Knuttenen, Richard Shoemaker, Milton Tambor, Eric Edel, Oskar Pascal and William Moseley US Representative David Bonior was, or is, a paid up socialist.

Why would Obama appoint US Representative David Bonior to an important post in the country?

It is not as if Bonior and Obama go way back. Bonior is a recent convert to the Obama cause. He was a campaign manager for Obama's Democratic primary rival John Edwards, even though Bonior's conversion was complete.

Why should Obama choose him above all other contenders?

---

[311] http://www.campaignmoney.com/political/committees/democratic-socialists-of-america-pac.asp?cycle=06

The answer may be obvious.

Obama has his own documented ties to Democratic Socialists of America.

Obama began attending Democratic Socialists of America (DSA) sponsored conferences while at Columbia University in the '80s. The Chicago Democratic Socialists of America (DSA) endorsed Obama during his successful 1996 run for Illinois State Senate. At the same time he joined the Democratic Socialists of America (DSA) initiated New Party.

Obama has close personal and political ties to several Democratic Socialists of America (DSA) supporters including Quentin Young,[312] Rabbi Jacob Wolf,[313] Jackie Grimshaw,[314] William McNary,[315] the late Saul Mendelson,[316] and US Congressional members' Representative Danny K. Davis and Jan Schakowsky (D-IL-9th District).[317]

Is it credible that Obama has no knowledge of Bonior's Democratic Socialists of America (DSA) connections? Is it possible that Obama's sleuths missed Bonior's easily found socialist links?

Was Obama aware of Bonior's background before he appointed him?

In appointing US Representative David Bonior to his "Transition Team," was Obama promoting a socialist "comrade?"

There are some important questions to answer here.

Update

The September 2007, report from Boston Democratic Socialists of America (DSA) states[318]:

> It should also be noted that Edward's recent statements on this issue have shown real improvement, which might be due to his key advisor, former House Democratic Whip and recent Democratic Socialists of

---

[312] http://keywiki.org/index.php/Quentin_Young
[313] http://keywiki.org/index.php/Arnold_Jacob_Wolf
[314] http://keywiki.org/index.php/Jackie_Grimshaw
[315] http://keywiki.org/index.php/William_McNary
[316] http://keywiki.org/index.php/Saul_Mendelson
[317] http://keywiki.org/index.php/Jan_Schakowsky
[318] http://www.dsaboston.org/yradical/yr2007-09.pdf

America (DSA) member US Representative David Bonior (D-MI-17th District). (Pattberg 2007)

54. Communist Party Leader on Obama: "We are speaking to a Friend"

Trevor Loudon © Friday, November 28, 2008

"The left can and should advance its own views and disagree with the Obama administration without being disagreeable. Its tone should be respectful. We are speaking to a friend." (Webb 2008)

Now that Barack Obama is President, his Communist Party backers feel confident to come out of the shadows.

Communist Party leader Sam Webb posted a long speech on the Communist Party website - *A Springtime of Possibility.*

Here are some extracts, with commentary from Trevor Loudon:

54-1 Sam Webb Communist Party Chairman

Sam Webb: If the election of President Elect Barack Obama was a monumental victory, election night itself was a magical moment. In Chicago and across the nation, tears of joy and exhilaration mingled with memories of how far we have come. As the President-elect greeted the hundreds of thousands of well-wishers in Grant Park, it was hard not to think of the many struggles for freedom mapping our nation's history...

To say that a sea change occurred on Nov. 4 is no exaggeration. On one side, the arguably worst President in our history leaves Washington disgraced. His party's policies, ideology, and cultural symbols are discredited. The GOP is in disarray and the blame game has begun. The red/blue state paradigm and the southern strategy, a strategy conceived exactly forty years ago to divide the nation along racial lines, are in shambles. And the entire capitalist class, not only its most reactionary section, is weakened.

On the other side of the changing sea, a sense of joy, catharsis and renewal is in the air. Expectations are high. A new era of progressive change is waiting to be set in motion. If the past eight years of the Bush administration seemed like a winter of discontent, Obama's ascendancy to the presidency feels like springtime of possibility... (Webb 2008)

Loudon: Webb has every right to gloat. The left has routed the "right" as represented by George W. Bush's Republican Party. Webb sees this as no temporary blip, but as the beginnings of a great shift to the left.

> Sam Webb: No one, of course, expects that the securing of a better future will be easy. There is, after all, eight years of extreme right-wing misrule to clean up. The economic crisis is widening and deepening. Right-wing extremism, while badly weakened, still retains enough influence in Congress and elsewhere to block progressive measures. And class realities are still embedded in our society.

> Nevertheless, in electing Barack Obama and larger Democratic Party majorities in Congress, the American people have taken the first and necessary step in the direction of building a more just society. We are not on the threshold of socialism for sure, but it is easy to see the further congealing of a growing majority that will realign politics, not incrementally and momentarily, but decisively and enduringly in the direction of economic justice, equality and peace. (Webb 2008)

Loudon: No, not socialism, not yet. This is the beginnings of a permanent shift in that direction and worse.

> Sam Webb: While we should look at the outcome of the elections objectively, I would argue that the biggest danger is to underestimate the political significance of what has happened. I am suspicious of advice that suggests that we temper our understandable joy and enthusiasm as if nothing of great importance has happened.

> The country is in a period of transition. A new potentially transformative President is entering the White House, along with increased Democratic majorities in Congress. Class-consciousness is deeper and reaches into every section of the working class. A spirit of broad unity is palpable. The ideological environment is infused with progressive and egalitarian ideas. Labor and its allies are retrofitting their priorities, message and initiatives to the new political landscape. And millions are ready to energetically back the legislative agenda of the Obama administration...

> This favorable correlation of class and social forces couldn't happen at a better time. The challenges facing the new administration are immense. Some are short term; others longer term; some are national in scope; others global. And all are begging for solution. (Webb 2008)

Loudon: Perfect - a leftist President and Congress, plus an international financial crisis and impending recession/depression. People will accept radical solutions during a time of crises - even socialist solutions.

> Sam Webb: Given the current situation, it is apparent that the Obama administration enters the White House with huge challenges. At the same time, no President in recent memory brings to the job so much popular good will, a Congress dominated by Democrats, an election mandate for progressive change, and an energized movement that supports him.

> As I said earlier, we are in a transitional period in which the broad contours and class relationships of US politics have changed to the point that we have to adjust our strategic policy. Our policy of singling out the extreme right and its reactionary corporate backers and building the broadest unity against them, discussed in these meetings and contained in our Party program, captured the class realities of the past 30 years. In this year's election we applied that policy consistently and creatively. Admittedly, we adjusted this policy at the tactical level in January of this year after concluding that Obama had the potential to bring together, give voice to an all-people's coalition, and win the election by a landslide. (Webb 2008)

Loudon: Communist policy was to demonize and divide the "extreme right" (normal conservative Americans).

It worked. Communists decided that Obama was a potential winner, and Senator Hillary Clinton was never favored.

> Sam Webb: Looking back, it is not immodest to say that both our overall policy and our tactical adjustment were on the money. We should not claim bragging rights, but our strategic and tactical approach captured better than any other organization or movement on the left the political algebra of the election process, including the possibility of a landslide.

> This isn't to say that other left movements and organizations were of no consequence, because they were, but none of them had as much political coherence in their strategic and tactical policies as we did. Nor did they do the day-to-day grassroots work with the same consistency that we did. (Webb 2008)

Loudon: Some well justified boasting from the Communist Party leader.

> Sam Webb: That said, the new political landscape in the election's wake compels us to make strategic as well as tactical changes. Our current strategic policy, I'm sure you will agree, no longer corresponds with the present situation...

> Now and for the near future, the country is in a political transition that interweaves elements of the past and the future. This argues against

attempts to fit the political dynamics of this moment into a rigid and schematic strategic framework. Our strategic policy is a conceptual device (or guide to action) whose purpose is to give social forces and us a first approximation of what is happening on the ground among the main class which of them has the upper hand, and what it will take to move the political process in a progressive direction. It doesn't claim to capture reality in all of its complexity and contradictoriness. And this is especially so in a transitional period as this one. Therefore, the strategic notion of stages of struggle has to be employed judiciously and flexibly, or, as some like to say, dialectically. (Webb 2008)

Loudon: Webb warns that now is not the time to be doctrinaire. Now is the time for dialectics, a flexible approach to a fast moving situation.

Sam Webb: So briefly, how do the various forces line up? Let's begin with Obama. During the election we correctly resisted fitting Obama into a tightly sealed political category. We should continue that practice. I don't think categorizing him as a bourgeois or centrist politician at this moment is helpful, even if he begins by governing from the center.

Obama is an unusual political figure. He has deep democratic sensibilities, a sense of history and modesty, and an almost intuitive feel for the national mood. His political and intellectual depth matches his eloquence. In the wake of the election, he is the leader of a far-flung multiclass "change" coalition that constitutes a new political universe to which everyone has to relate. He embraces a reform agenda in a reform era whose political character will be decided in the years ahead. Many, including ourselves, have used the words "transformational" or "transforming" to describe his candidacy - that is, a candidacy capable of assembling a broad people's majority to reconfigure the terms and terrain of politics in this country in a fundamental way. The same can be said about the potential of his presidency.

Obama isn't finished with Obama. Like other great leaders, he is a work in progress who has demonstrated the capacity to grow as things change and new problems arise. He will undoubtedly feel competing pressures, but he will also leave his own political imprint on Presidential decisions, much like Lincoln and Roosevelt did. It's good that Obama has these qualities because he is inheriting mammoth problems. In consultation with the Democrats in Congress and the main organizations of the people's coalition, he will set the agenda and determine the timing of legislative initiatives next year. (Webb 2008)

Loudon: Keep your eye on the big picture comrades. Do not sweat if Obama has to do some things you do not like. It is the broad changes we communists are after.

> Sam Webb: However, let us not go bananas when he appoints somebody whose politics we do not like. We should not expect that this administration will be free of Representatives of Wall Street or old line Democrats or even some Republicans. Their presence does not necessarily define the political inclinations of the Obama administration, nor does it tell us exactly what its political priorities will be. Nothing would be worse at this moment than to force politics into fixed and frozen categories on the one hand and to ignore the new political dynamics and movements that emerged from the elections on the other. Let us give Obama some space; millions of others will, including, I suspect, the main leaders of the labor and people's movement. Marxism is a guide to action, not a dogma. (Webb 2008)

Loudon: Do not be dogmatic comrades. Give the man a break. He will have to do things we do not like to appease the mainstream. He is on the right track, give him a chance.

> Sam Webb: Then there are the Obama grassroots networks and committees. These web-generated forms of organization and action were formidable in the elections and will in all likelihood continue to be a forceful presence in the coming years. They contain an array of diverse people, including many young people, all of whom are loyal to Obama and will throw their weight behind his program. In some places we are part of "Yes We Can" networks and should remain so; where we aren't, we (along with others) should make connections with them. (Webb 2008)

Loudon: The Communist Party was active in Obama's campaign all over the US. Keep the networks going and expand communist presence into areas where currently weak.

> Sam Webb: The Democratic Party, for sure, isn't an anti-capitalist people's party. Yet it contains a variety of currents. In the recent elections, the center and progressive currents gained in size and influence. While its character is not left in its outlook in the wake of Obama's landslide victory, liberal and progressive, congress people have the wind at their back. Right-wing Democrats, meanwhile, are running into headwinds. This is not 1992 all over again. (Webb 2008)

Loudon: The far left is now dominant in the Democratic Party. We will not let Obama slip out of our control as Clinton did.

> Sam Webb: Then there are the broad people's forces, and Communists are a current among these forces. These forces continue to evolve in positive ways. Unity is on a higher level. Their politics move

along anti-corporate, egalitarian, and anti-militarist lines. They express themselves through a range of organizational forms. In this election these forces walked with seven league boots, kicked butt and took no prisoners. Nothing seemed to knock them off stride.

These loosely grouped forces will energetically participate in struggles in the period ahead. Labor will continue to play a special organizing and political role. (Webb 2008)

Loudon: The communist controlled peace movement, mass organizations, pressure groups and unions are doing well. Expect them to put huge pressure on the Obama administration in the years ahead.

Sam Webb: At the same time, labor and its allies, while vigorously advancing their own agenda, must adjust to the new scope of the post-election change coalition led by Obama that had emerged. Never before has a coalition with breadth walked on the political stage of our country. It is far larger than the coalition that entered the election process a year ago; it is larger still than the coalition that came out of the Democratic Party convention in August.

Moreover, its growth potential is enormous. Significant numbers of white workers and small businesspeople, for example, who didn't cast their vote for Obama, can be won to progressive and anti-racist positions of struggle going forward. (Webb 2008)

Loudon: The communist/socialist trade unions and their affiliates will be used to broaden the "people's movement" behind Obama. They will aim to bring the conservative white working class back to the Democrats.

Sam Webb: As you can see, this change coalition contains various political forces with disparate class loyalties. There are no pure struggles at any stage of struggle. Indeed, in a broad, multiclass coalition, relations will be contested as well as cooperative...

As for us, we can provide leadership only to the degree that we are in the trenches of the wider labor-led people's movement, building this people's upsurge in all directions. Only if we are making practical, on-the-ground contributions to the immediate struggles, and especially in the economic arena, can we help give political coherence to this broad coalition. (Webb 2008)

Loudon: Communists must get their hands dirty, increase dominance of the union movement and the mass organizations. This is not the time to sit on the sidelines.

Sam Webb: Yes, we should bring issues and more advanced positions into the process that go beyond the initiatives of the Obama administration and the broad multiclass, many-layered coalition that supports it. But we should do this within the framework of the main task of supporting Obama's program of action and building breadth, depth and participation of the core forces. We have to master the art of combining partial demands with more advanced ones. The former (partial demands) are the immediate grounds for building broad unity in action. (Webb 2008)

Loudon: Communists must keep pushing to the left whenever possible, but should never do this at the expense of movement unity. Keeping the movement behind Obama united is the number one priority.

Sam Webb: Nevertheless, we shouldn't assume that the Obama administration will inevitably track right. It isn't dialectical because it fails to take into account the election mandate, the new leverage of labor and its allies and, perhaps most important, the broader developments in the economy. We also shouldn't have any truck with people on the left who argue that the main protagonists in the coming period are the Obama administration and Democrats on one side and the people on the other.

Finally, we should take a dim view of some on the left who will wait for the new administration to stumble and then immediately call for a break and attempt to turn broader forces into a hostile opposition. In fact, probably the biggest challenge for the core forces of this multiclass coalition is to resist attempts by reaction and some left forces to pit the Obama administration and Congress against the main sections of the people's movement on one or another issue. Where there are (and will be) differences over appointments, legislation or other actions between the administration and the broad democratic forces, these differences have to be handled in a way as not to break the overall unity. (Webb 2008)

Loudon: Unity is all! Unity is all! Unity is all!

Sam Webb: The left can and should advance its own views and disagree with the Obama administration without being disagreeable. Its tone should be respectful. We are speaking to a friend. When the administration and Congress take positive initiatives, they should be wholeheartedly welcomed. Nor should anyone think that everything will be done in 100 days. After all, main elements of the New Deal were codified into law in 1935, 1936 and 1937.

Although we are not in the socialist stage of the revolutionary process, we are, nevertheless on the road, and the only road, that will lead to socialism - to a society that is egalitarian in the rough sense, eliminates exploitation of working people, brings an end to all forms of oppression, and is notable for the many-layered participation of working people and their allies in the management of the economy and state.

The room for socialist ideas is in the public square has grown enormously. ideas can be easily discussed with many people and people's leaders. Furthermore, the force of economic events will compel millions more to consider socialist ideas that in the past were dismissed out of hand. But our vision of socialism will resonate to the degree that it addresses contemporary sensibilities and challenges... (Webb 2008)

Loudon: Communists must keep their eyes on the big picture. We are on the road to socialism and we must not deviate.

Sam Webb: Our role, as I have tried to say, is to be part of the struggles going forward - beginning with attending the inauguration and encouraging others to do the same. It is going to be a grand event and a public expression of support for Obama and a mass expression for change.

Let us reengage with others (labor, the nationally and racially oppressed, women, and youth) in this struggle. As to precisely what we do, we have to do some brainstorming as well as consult with people and organizations that we worked with in the election campaign.

A couple of ideas come to mind. We should consider initiating meetings to discuss the economic crisis and how to respond to it at the local, state, and national level. Meetings could be broad in their participation and sponsorship. We should also mobilize support for Obama's stimulus package, for aid to the auto corporations – albeit with strings – and for immediate relief for homeowners...

In these and the other struggles, we have to become better at building the Party, press and YCL. I don't want to say the opportunities to build the Party and press are limitless, but they have grown immensely.

Let me finish by saying that it sure feels good to be on the winning side. I'm sure everyone feels the same way. At the same time, because of this historic victory, we -and the broader movement that we are a part of - have our work cut out for us in the coming years. It's a big challenge, but we have met other challenges. So let's go out there and do it with a sense of confidence that the best days for our country lay ahead of us. Yes we can! Si Se Puede! Thank you. (Webb 2008)

Loudon: Thank you, Sam.

55. Terrorist/Comrade Discuss Obama "Lenin Would Be Impressed"

Trevor Loudon © Wednesday, December 03, 2008

A big hat tip to the Real Barack Obama (RBO).

Mark Rudd

Mark Rudd was a leader of the '60s radical organization Students for a Democratic Society (SDS) and its terrorist splinter group - Weather Underground Organization (WUO).

Today Mark Rudd serves on the Board[319] of the Movement for a Democratic Society (MDS).[320]

55-1 Mark Rudd

55-2 Mark Rudd serves on the Board of the Movement for a Democratic Society (MDS)

Movement for a Democratic Society is the parent body of Progressives for Obama (P40),[321] the leading leftist umbrella group behind Obama's Presidential campaign. The purpose of Progressives for Obama (P40) is to unite radicals behind the President elect, defend Obama from attack and "explain" Obama's positions to radicals who do not understand his subtle approach to socialism.

Movement for a Democratic Society unites leaders of the three major socialist organizations behind Obama - Democratic Socialists of America,[322] Communist Party USA[323] and Committees of Correspondence

---

[319] http://keywiki.org/index.php/Mark_Rudd

[320] http://keywiki.org/index.php/Movement_for_a_Democratic_Society

[321] http://keywiki.org/index.php/Progressives_for_Obama

[322] http://keywiki.org/index.php/Democratic_Socialists_of_America

[323] http://keywiki.org/index.php/Communist_Party_USA

for Democracy and Socialism (COCDSDS).[324]

Movement for a Democratic Society also groups together many former leaders of both the Students for a Democratic Society and the WUO.

Several MDS leaders know President elect Barack Obama.

55-3 Obama at the 2002 Chicago peace rally

Movement for a Democratic Society Board member Bernardine Dohrn and her husband Movement for a Democratic Society activist Bill Ayers[325] (both former Students for a Democratic Society and Weathermen Underground Organization leaders) helped launch Obama's political career[326] at a 1995 gathering in their Chicago home.

Ayers worked with Obama for several years and since the election has revealed that the Obama's were "family friends."[327]

Bill Ayers's longtime friend, former Students for a Democratic Society leader and Movement for a Democratic Society Board member, Carl Davidson,[328] who also knows Obama well.

Davidson, a leader of the Communist Party offshoot COCDS, met Obama beginning in 1995 when the aspiring young politician joined the Chicago New Party.[329]

Democratic Socialists of America (DSA) is a front for Committees of Correspondence, Democratic Socialists of America (DSA) and the radical community group ACORN. The New Party endorsed Obama for his successful Illinois State Senate run.

Davidson visited Obama's home and maintained a relationship

[324] http://keywiki.org/index.php/Committees_of_Correspondence
[325] http://keywiki.org/index.php/Bill_Ayers
[326] http://keywiki.org/index.php/Alice_Palmer
[327] http://newzeal.blogspottrevorloudon.com/2008/11/finally-a-little-truth-on-obama-and-ayers.html/
[328] http://keywiki.org/index.php/Carl_Davidson
[329]
http://keywiki.org/index.php/Barack_Obama_and_the_New_Party/Progressive_Chicago

55-4 Thorne Dreyer pushing "The Rag

with him until at least 2002. That relationship included Marilyn Katz, former Students for a Democratic Society member and Don Rose former Communist Party front activist.[330] Don Rose organized the Chicago peace rally where Obama made his name as an opponent of the Iraq War.

Mark Rudd was close to Ayers and Dohrn during their Students for Democratic Society - Weather-men days. Now they all work together in the leadership of Movement for a Democratic Society. They also work with fellow Movement for a Democratic Society Board member Carl Davidson.

Rudd also supports Progressives for Obama (P40), which Davidson helped found with former Students for a Democratic Society leader Tom Hayden and Democratic Socialists of America (DSA) leaders Barbara Ehrenreich and Bill Fletcher Jr. Rudd has discussed Obama with the trio who know the President elect well - Ayers, Dohrn and Davidson.

So if Rudd believes Obama to be a socialist, committed to changing America, a shrewd Marxist tactician of whom "even Lenin would be impressed," can we believe his word? Rudd posted an article on a radical blog, "*The Rag*"[331] run by Austin Texas based former Students for a Democratic Society activist and Movement for a Democratic Society and Progressives for Obama (P40) supporter, Thorne Dreyer.

The original publication, "*The Rag*" was a '70s radical newspaper, also produced by Thorne Dreyer and comrades.

Rudd was writing for friends and let his guard down when he laid out his take on the Obama agenda. It is subtle, it is clever, and it is socialist.

Rudd explains to his wavering radical friends, that Obama is on their side, but must work tactically to achieve his radical goals.

---

[330] http://keywiki.org/index.php/Don_Rose
[331] http://theragblog.blogspot.com/

If you are anything like me, your inbox fills up daily with the cries and complaints of lefties. Just the mere mention of the names Hillary Clinton and Lawrence Summers alone conjure up a litany of horrendous right-wingers appointed to top-level positions.

Betrayal is the name of the game.

However, wait a second. Let us talk about a few things:

55-5 Thorne Dreyer (2d l), Mark Rudd (c) MDS Convergence Chicago November 2007

Obama is a strategic thinker. He knew precisely what it would take to get elected and didn't blow it...But he also knew that what he said had to basically play to the center to not be run over by the press, the Republicans, scare centrist and cross-over voters away. He made it.

So he has a narrow mandate for change, without any direction specified. What he's doing now is moving on the most popular issues – the environment, health care, and the economy. He'll be progressive on the environment because that has broad popular support; health care will be extended to children, then made universal, but the medical, pharmaceutical, and insurance corporations will stay in place...the economic agenda will stress stimulation from the bottom sometimes and handouts to the top at other times. It will be pragmatic...On foreign policy and the wars and the use of the military there will be no change at all. That's what keeping Gates at the Pentagon and Clinton at State and not prosecuting the torturers is saying. (Rudd, Let's Get Smart About Obama)

And never, never threaten the military budget. That will unite a huge majority of congress against him.

And, I agree with this strategy. Anything else will court sure defeat. Move on the stuff you can to a small but significant extent, gain support and confidence. Leave the military alone because they're way too powerful. For now, until enough momentum is raised. By the second or third year of this recession, when stimulus is needed at the bottom, people may begin to discuss cutting the military budget if security is being increased through diplomacy and application of nascent international law.

Obama plays basketball. I'm not much of an athlete, barely know the game, but one thing I do know is that you have to be able to look like you're doing one thing but do another. That's why all these conservative appointments are important. The strategy is feint to the right, move left. Any other strategy invites sure defeat. It would be stupid to do otherwise in this environment.

Look to the second level appointments. There is a whole government in waiting that Podesta has at the Center for American Progress (CAP). They're mostly progressives, I'm told (except in military and foreign policy). Cheney was extremely effective at controlling policy by putting his people in at second-level positions.

Read Obama's first book, "Dreams from My Father." The second section is the story of his three years doing community organizing in Chicago. It's some of the best writing on organizing I've ever seen. That is all it's about, the core of the book. Obama learned many lessons of strategy and patience.

Then read the first section, on his family and growing up in Hawaii and Indonesia. No other President has ever had intimate experience with class and race. The final section is about his trip to Kenya. No other President has ever had an understanding of not only race, but colonialism and neo-colonialism, even using the terms. It is the whole story he tells of his African family and especially his father, a victim of neo-colonialism. As was his step-father in Indonesia. (Rudd, *Let's Get Smart about Obama*)

This is no stupid guy. Had any of the stupid Republicans read his books, they never could have said, "We don't know who this guy is." You know every thought he has ever had.

Our job now is to organize both inside and outside the Demo party. There's already a big battle in the Demo party at every level. Here in the New Mexico State Legislature, the progressives are challenging the conservative Dems for leadership; the same is true in Congress. If you can't stand to work in the party, work on putting mass pressure on issues as healthcare and jobs and the war from outside. Here is my mantra: "Let's put this country on our shoulders and get to work." (Rudd, Let's Get Smart About Obama 2008)

How blatant is that?

"And I agree with this strategy. Leave the military alone because they are excessively powerful. Until achieving projected gains, you have to be able to look like you are doing one thing but do another. That is why all these conservative appointments are important. The strategy is feint to the right, move left. Look to the second level appointments. Podesta controls a new government in waiting at the "Center for American Progress" (CAP). They are progressives." (Rudd, Let's Get Smart About Obama 2008)

Is this a recipe for stealth socialism, or what!

Another "*The Rag Blog*" contributor, Austin activist Jeff Jones (not to be confused with the former Weatherman and Movement for a Democratic Society Board member of the same name) backed up Mark Rudd's analysis and added some telling remarks of his own.

Jeff Jones[332] November 29, 2008:

> I agree with Mark Rudd's perceptive article Let's Get Smart About Obama in The Rag Blog.

> The writing style of Audacity of Hope reveals how complex and perceptive Obama is... He does not interpret reality in black and white terms: he is the nation's first post-modern President.

> All of this leads me to the same conclusion reached by Mark Rudd:

> ...this guy is really SMART. He is setting Secretary of State Hillary Clinton up to be the public face of his effort to end the Iraq War. He is going to successfully extort green concessions from Detroit. He will convince Congress to pass a major stimulus package that will lay the foundation for the development of an alternative energy manufacturing industry. He will do something to help reduce housing foreclosures. He will let the Bush tax cuts for the wealthy expire.

> These various initiatives, which will collectively set the nation on a path towards energy independence, ending the war and redistributing financial resources downward, are presented as unconnected pieces of legislation but actually they are interlocking components of Obama's coherent multi-layered agenda. His centrist appointments are a smokescreen; they co-opt the moderate center, but he's still the commander in chief. Even Lenin would be impressed! (J. Jones 2008)

What is that?

> "Redistributing financial resources downward...Obama's coherent multi-layered agenda...centrist appointments are a smokescreen...Lenin would be impressed"? (J. Jones 2008)

Does that sound like "change" expected by over 60 million Americans voters? Is that your idea of "democracy?"

---

[332] http://theragblog.blogspot.com/2008/11/obama-centrist-appointments-are-smoke.html

---

56. Son of Atom Bomb Spy: Do Not Mourn Obama's Leanings, Organize to Push the Other Way

Trevor Loudon © Friday, December 12, 2008

The son of convicted Soviet atom bomb spies, Julius and Ethel Rosenberg, wants to push President elect Barack Obama further to the left. Michael Meeropol calls for a mass movement to exert pressure on Obama. His model is the communist-led Labor unions and "people's organizations" of the New Deal era, which forced huge concessions from Franklin D. Roosevelt.

Figure 56-1 Abe Meeropol

56-2 Ethel and Julius Rosenberg

Meeropol knows that while Obama has worked with socialists since his teens, he will still need pressure to keep him in line.

All the stories about Obama's economic team and his economic instincts mean is that we on the left have to shout loud and clear to make the policies move in our direction.

That's what the socialists and communists did during the Depression and though the New Deal "saved" capitalism – it also made it a lot more "worker" and "people" friendly.

It wasn't revolution, but that didn't stop the socialists and communists of the 1930s from fighting for the right to organize unions, for anti-lynching legislation, for the minimum wage law, etc. etc. – and it didn't stop the Civil Rights Movements of the 1930s, 40s, and 50s from demanding the most minimal rights already guaranteed under the capitalist constitution.

I think to a large extent, we ought to stop discussing whether Obama is being "good" or "bad" and focus on the POLICIES we want his administration (and Congress) to follow.

Whether he stays in the DLC-Clintonian mode or adopts policies that significantly move away from the right-wing economic consensus depends on US and the progressive wing of the Democratic Party.

Joe Hill said, "Don't mourn for me, and organize." We should say, "Don't mourn Obama's leanings – organize to push him the other way..." (Meeropol 2008)

The reason this is significant is that Meeropol is no lone leftist wailing in the wilderness. He is part of an organization at the heart of Obama's leftist support movement. He is close to people who know Obama well. He is reflecting a strategy that has been in place for some time.

That is - get our man into the White House and mobilize mass pressure to keep him on target.

Meeropol's leftist credentials are impeccable. His parents were both ardent communists tried and executed in June 1953 for passing on atomic bomb secrets to the Soviet Union.

A New York schoolteacher and covert communist, named Abe Meeropol adopted the orphaned Rosenberg boys, Michael and Robert.

56-3 Abe Meeropol

The two brothers have been involved in the left all their lives. Much of it spent campaigning to clear the names of their late parents.

That campaign suffered a major setback earlier this year when a 91-year-old Morton Sobell, the co-defendant in the famous trial, after more than 50 years of denials,

56-4 MDS founder, former SDS and DSA Leader Paul Buhle

admitted that he and Julius Rosenberg had both been Soviet agents..

Michael Meeropol[333] is a leading member of the Movement for a Democratic Society (MDS).[334] It is a family affair. Robert Meeropol is also

[333] http://keywiki.org/index.php/Michael_Meeropol
[334] http://keywiki.org/index.php/Movement_for_a_Democratic_Society

close to Movement for a Democratic Society (he was active in Students for a Democratic Society in college) as is Michael's daughter, Ivy.

Founded in 2006, Movement for a Democratic Society unites all the main leftist currents behind the Obama campaign - the Communist Party USA,[335] the Communist Party USA offshoot Committees of Correspondence for Democracy and Socialism (COCDS),[336] Democratic Socialists of America.[337]

Together with former members of the '60s radical organization Students for a Democratic Society (SDS) and its terrorist splinter group, Weather Underground Organization (WUO).

The DSA board in 2006/2007 included:

- Gerald Horne - (CPUSA)
- Carl Davidson - (CCDS, ex-SDS, ex-Communist Party Marxist-Leninist)
- Manning Marable - (DSA, CCDS)
- Charlene Mitchell - (CCDS, ex-CPUSA)
- Angela Davis - (CCDS, ex-CPUSA)
- Noam Chomsky - (DSA, CCDS)
- Barbara Ehrenreich - (DSA)
- Bill Fletcher -(DSA Freedom Road Socialist Organisation)
- Paul Buhle - (DSA, ex-SDS)
- Mike Klonsky - (ex-SDS, ex-Communist Party Marxist-Leninist)
- Bert Garskof - (ex-SDS)
- David Graeber - (ex-SDS)
- Tom Hayden - (ex-SDS)
- Mike James (ex-SDS)
- Bruce Rubenstein - (ex-Weatherman)
- Bernardine Dohrn - (ex-SDS, ex-WUO)
- Mark Rudd - (ex-SDS, ex-WUO)
- Jeff Jones - (ex-SDS, ex-WUO)

Other prominent Movement for Democratic Society activists

---

[335] http://keywiki.org/index.php/Communist_Party_USA
[336] http://keywiki.org/index.php/Committees_of_Correspondence
[337] http://keywiki.org/index.php/Democratic_Socialists_of_America

includes Marilyn Katz (ex-Students for a Democratic Society) and Bill Ayers (ex-Students for a Democratic Society, ex-WUO).

Of those listed above, it is significant to note that at least five - Carl Davidson, Mike Klonsky, Bernardine Dohrn, Bill Ayers and Marilyn Katz have been close to Barack Obama on a personal basis.

Figure 56-5 Bernardine Dohrn, 2006

Ayers and Dohrn are friends who helped launch Obama's career[338] and, in Ayers' case, has worked in several organizations with the President-elect. Klonsky is a friend of Ayers and Davidson since Students for a Democratic Society days and has worked with Ayers and Obama on "school reform." Davidson worked with Obama in the Chicago New Party and together with Katz, organized the 2002 peace rally where Obama made his name as an opponent of the Iraq War. Katz fundraised for Obama during his campaign and served as an Obama delegate to the 2008 Democratic Party convention.

The pair interviewed for the August 17, 2006 edition of the socialist journal, "*In These Times*:"[339]

> To mount a movement, "let's look at history," said Dohrn between bites of her tuna nicoise salad. "Lyndon B Johnson was not a civil rights leader; Lyndon B Johnson was responding to a civil rights movement. FDR was not a labor leader; FDR was responding to a labor movement. We confuse these things when we think about them today."
>
> Indeed, that's "a great mistake. President Lyndon B Johnson was the most effective politician of his generation, but it took a movement independent of Lyndon B Johnson to get Lyndon B Johnson to use that effectiveness for the good." (L. S. Washington 2006)

Movement for Democratic Society Board members Barbara Ehrenreich, Bill Fletcher, Tom Hayden and Carl Davidson were four of the six founders of Progressives for Obama (P4O). Designed to unite socialists behind the Obama campaign, Progressives for Obama also subscribes to the "mass pressure" policy.

---

[338] http://keywiki.org/index.php/Bill_Ayers
[339] http://www.inthesetimes.com/article/2785/

56-6 Mobilizing millions of Americans from the cadre of public sector unions

According to Progressives for Obama founders Ehrenreich, Fletcher and Hayden:[340]

It was the industrial strikes and radical organizers in the 1930s who pushed Roosevelt to support the New Deal. The civil rights and student movements brought about voting rights legislation under Lyndon B Johnson and propelled Eugene McCarthy and Bobby Kennedy's antiwar campaigns. The original Earth Day led Richard Nixon to sign environmental laws.

And it will be the Obama movement that will make it necessary and possible to end the war in Iraq, renew our economy with a populist emphasis, and confront the challenge of global warming. We should not only keep the pressure on [Obama] but also connect the issues that Obama has made central to his campaign into an overarching progressive vision. (Hayden, ROOTING FOR THE NEW WORLD ORDER 2008)

There is no doubt that Meeropol, Ayers, Dohrn, Rudd and their MDS colleagues have the power to mobilize millions of Americans.

Movement for a Democratic Society's three affiliate socialist organizations: Communist Party USA, COCDS and Democratic Socialists of America (DSA) dominate the AFL-CIO and the rival Change to Win Labor federation. They control the peace movement peak body United for Peace & Justice and dominate or influence dozens of mass organizations including the NAACP, Coalition of Black Trade Unionists, Black Radical Congress,[341] Jobs with Justice, ACORN and US Action.[342]

Therefore, it is a mistake to think that activists like Meeropol and his comrades have no influence. They sit in a powerful position. They helped put their man in the White House. They mobilized millions to push him in the direction they want.

The Movement for a Democratic Society wants to change America forever through the Obama presidency. Movement for a Democratic

---

[340] http://www.thenewblackmagazine.com/view.aspx?index=1318
[341] http://keywiki.org/index.php/Black_Radical_Congress
[342] http://keywiki.org/index.php/USAction

Society unites several thousand hardened activists, many of whom have been working for socialism since the '60s.

This is their last, best chance. They are not going to let it slip by without a fight.

Will Michael Meeropol get to realize his parent's aborted socialist vision?

57. Obama's Socialist Ally Joins Powerful Congressional Committee

Wednesday, December 17, 2008

The left's "long march" through the US government has, since the recent election, broken into a jog.

A good example is the appointment of long time President elect Barack Obama friend, Illinois Representative Danny K. Davis, to the United States House Committee on Ways & Means- the most powerful organ of the US Congress.

> The Committee of Ways and Means is the chief tax-writing committee of the United States House of Representatives. Members of the Ways and Means Committee cannot serve on any other House Committees, though they can apply for a waiver from their party's congressional leadership. The Committee has jurisdiction over all taxation, tariffs and other revenue-raising measures, as well as a number of other programs including Social Security, Unemployment benefits, Medicare... (D. K. Davis 2008)

57-1 Representative Danny K. Davis

The Ways & Means Committee is heavily influenced by members of the Congressional Progressive Caucus,[343] a grouping of leftist Democratic congressional Representatives, many of who have ties to Democratic Socialists of America, the Communist Party USA or both.

---

[343] http://newzeal.blogspottrevorloudon.com/2006/11/the-socialists-behind-the-progressive-caucus.html/

57-2 The New Party Members including Barack Obama

Current Communist Party members on Ways & Means include Chairman Charles Rangel.[344]

Davis' ties with Barack Obama go back at least to their time together in the Illinois New Party in the mid-1990s.

While both Democrats, Davis joined the New Party during his successful run for US congress, Obama joined to help his successful bid for Illinois State Senate.

In Chicago, activists from the radical community group ACORN and members of Democratic Socialists of America (DSA) and the Communist Party USA breakaway group Committees of Correspondence formed the New Party.

Obama has a long history with the Marxist organization, Democratic Socialists of America (DSA), including being endorsed them.

Congressman Davis was then, and still is, a Democratic Socialists of America (DSA) member - one of the few semi-open socialists in the US Congress.

Congressman Davis also had ties to COCDS. According to Chicago Democratic Socialists of America (DSA)'s "New Ground" of September 1994:[345]

> "Over 500 delegates and observers (including 140 from Chicago) attended the founding convention of the Committees of Correspondence (COCDS) held in Chicago in July 2008. (Williams, New Ground 36: Committees of Correspondence Meet in Chicago)

---

[344] http://keywiki.org/index.php/Charles_Rangel
[345] http://www.chicagodsa.org/ngarchive/ng36.html#anchor810069

Speakers…included:

- Charles Nqukula, General Secretary of the South African Communist Party.

- Dulce Maria Pereira, a senatorial candidate of the Workers Party of Brazil.

- Angela Davis of COCDS.

- Andre Brie of the Party of Democratic Socialism of Germany (Formerly the East German Communist Party).

Other guests during the Convention included Cook County Commissioner Danny Davis, Alderwoman Helen Shiller and Rick Muñoz, a Representative of the Green Left Weekly of Australia, and a Representative of the Cuban Interest Section." (Williams, Committees of Correspondence Meet in Chicago 2000).

Davis was also close to the Communist Party USA. In Chicago, the Communist Party held an annual fund raising banquet for its paper, the *"People's Weekly World,"* the former *"People's Daily World."*

According to the *"People's Daily World"* of July 28, 1990, Chicago Alderman Danny K. Davis attended that year's banquet on July 15.

Davis applauded those at the banquet, who, he said, are always in the midst of struggle. PDW readers, he said, are "steadfast in the fight for justice."

According to the *"People's Weekly World"* of October 3, 1998, Representative Danny K. Davis presented an award at the Chicago annual *"People's Weekly World"* banquet.

Recently Davis, along with several other Obama friends and supporters,[346] has been associated with the Chicago Committee to Defend the Bill of Rights COCDS.[347] According to their COCDS website:

"The Chicago Committee to Defend the Bill of Rights (CCDBR) has fought for 41 years against government encroachment on our constitutional rights in all its forms. CCDBR began as part of the struggle to disband the House Un-American Activities Committee (HUAC), played a major role in the opposition to Chicago Police "Red Squad" spying in the

---

[346] http://www.ccdbr.org/events/050821.html
[347] http://www.ccdbr.org/

seventies, and most recently, helped facilitate the passage of the Chicago City Council Resolution against The Patriot Act." (Gage and Myers Jr. 2004)

Frank Wilkinson

Founded by Communist Party USA members Milton Cohen and Richard Criley,[348] CCDBR was led Communist Party veteran, Frank Wilkinson.

When Wilkinson died in 2006, US Representative Danny K. Davis joined the Honoring Committee[349] to celebrate the esteemed comrade's life.

57-3 Frank Wilkerson

Committee Chair was Timuel Black,[350] a Chicago historian, friend of Barack Obama and alleged former communist and CoC member.

Other Committee members included:

• Yolanda Hall – (Accused of CPUSA membership by the House Committee on Un-American Activities in the 60s, with Milton Cohen)

• Peggy Lipshutz – (A one-time CPUSA member)

• Bea and Frank Lumpkin – (both CPUSA members)

• Honorable Abner Mikva – (a well-known mentor to Barack Obama)

• Harold Rogers – (A well-known Chicago CPUSA member in the 1980s)

• Mark Rogovin – (A CPUSA member)

• Frank Rosen (A former official of the CPUSA front, US Peace Council)

• Norman Roth – (A one-time CPUSA member)

• Emile Schepers – (A CPUSA member)

• Alderwoman Helen Schiller – (linked to CoC)

• Studs Terkel – (A secret CPUSA member in the 1940s, later linked to DSA)

---

[348] http://keywiki.org/index.php/Richard_Criley
[349] http://www.ccdbr.org/events/wilkinson/Wilkinson_Committee.html
[350] http://keywiki.org/index.php/Timuel_Black

- Tim Yeager – (A CPUSA member)
- Dr. Quentin Young – (Accused of CPUSA membership by the House Committee on Un-American Activities in the 60s now a prominent DSA member and personal friend of Barack Obama)

Chicago Democratic Socialists of America (DSA) supported the event, as did an old Obama associate and Democratic Socialists of America (DSA) member, Lou Pardo.

US Representative Danny K. Davis has been one of President elect Barack Obama's most consistent supporters and friends in Congress. Davis has endorsed Obama, campaigned for him, even telephone banked for him.

Now as Obama gets set to bring "Change" to America, US Representative Danny K. Davis and his Communist Party comrades will be there to raise all the money needed, from the US taxpayer.

58. Hilda Solis - Obama Labor Secretary's Socialist Connections

Trevor Loudon © Saturday, December 20, 2008

Los Angeles US Representative Hilda Solis (D-CA-32nd District) is to join the Obama Cabinet as Secretary of Labor.

By appointing the pro-union Solis, President Elect Barack Obama has sent a clear signal to his far left support base that he has not abandoned his roots.

According to the Communist Party USA's, "People's World:"[351]

> One labor source said Solis' name was put forward by SEIU President Andrew Stern, whose union – along with the Change to Win coalition – endorsed Obama's Presidential candidacy long before the AFL-CIO did. SEIU is the biggest union in Change To Win.

> But leaders ranging from Change to Win Chair Anna Burger to AFL-CIO President John

58-1 Los Angeles U.S. Congresswoman Hilda Solis58 1 Los Angeles U.S. Congresswoman Hilda Solis

[351] http://www.peoplesworld.org/union-leaders-welcome-solis-choice-as-labor-secretary/

Sweeney to RWDSU President Stuart Appelbaum all welcomed the Solis appointment.

House Minority Whip US Representative David Bonior (D-Mich.), Chair of pro-labor American Rights at Work, and ARW Executive Director Mary Beth Maxwell. Both had been on lists circulated for the job. Bonior dropped out of the running to endorse Solis, who sits on the group's Board...

Bonior, citing his work with Solis since she entered Congress in 2001 -- he was there until 2004 – called her:

."..a terrific leader who I know first-hand will work tirelessly on behalf of America's working families."

Sweeney said the AFL-CIO is "thrilled at the prospect of having Solis as our nation's next Labor Secretary...The AFL-CIO looks forward to working with Solis as she charts new territory for our nation's working men and women." (People's World)

Andy Stern

58-2 Andy Stern

Stern is one of the US labor movement's new breed of leftist leaders trained by the Chicago based and Democratic Socialists of America controlled Midwest Academy.[352]

David Bonior[353] and Sweeney are both Democratic Socialists of America (DSA) members and both serve with US Representative Hilda Solis (D-CA-32nd District) on the Board of American Rights at Work (ARW). Most other ARW Board members have Democratic Socialists of America (DSA) connections, including Julian Bond who was active in the Democratic Socialists of America (DSA)'s predecessor, the Democratic Socialist Organizing Committee and labor academic Harley Shaiken - also touted for the Labor Secretary Job.

The fact that four Board members of a Democratic Socialists of America (DSA) front were the main contenders for the Labor position is

---

[352] http://keywiki.org/index.php/Midwest_Academy
[353] http://keywiki.org/index.php/David_Bonior

revealing.

It does not stop there however.

> "It's extraordinary," SEIU President Andy Stern said in an interview with us a few moments ago. "On every issue that's important to us, she has stood up for an America where everyone's hard work is valued and rewarded."

> Some labor officials had initially thought that an elder statesman type with stature would be best in the gig. But Stern said he thinks the choice of Solis by Obama, who has a keen appreciation of the power of biography, wanted someone with a bio steeped in labor, someone who has the kind of built in dedication and passion that could make her a kind of labor star in a cabinet that is stocked with a fair amount of star power already.

> "As opposed to some candidate [for whom] this would have been just a job, for Hilda Solis it's the fulfillment of a life-long dream," Stern said, adding that that Solis was one of the names that labor officials had privately communicated as acceptable to them in talks with the transition. "Her father was a teamster. She is the American dream." (Sargent 2008)

Stern said that the person who knows Solis perhaps best is writer Harold Meyerson.

Democratic Socialists of America (DSA) Vice Chair Harold Meyerson has written on American Prospect's group blog "Tapped:"

> HILDA SOLIS IS GREAT.

> What does US Representative Hilda Solis, Barack Obama's selection for secretary of labor, bring to the job? Only a record of passionate commitment to working people, a high level of political smarts, and some genuine displays of raw guts that could make her a star of American liberalism...

> In the House, Solis has continued to champion labor causes, immigrants' rights, women's health, and environmental protections. She also worked with Rahm Emanuel in recruiting Democratic House candidates from the Southwest and Latino-dominated districts, she brings to her new job a strong relationship with Obama's incoming chief-of-staff. Now, she is in the key position to promote the Employee Free Choice Act, which seems to be the most contentious issue on Obama's agenda. Nevertheless, Solis is not deterred by controversy. (Boyd 2008)

US Representative Hilda Solis (D-CA-32nd District) is also a leader of the Congressional Progressive Caucus, the seventy left wing Democrats with strong ties to Democratic Socialists of America (DSA).[354]

Democratic Socialists of America (DSA) member Duane Campbell[355] confirms the promotion of US Representative Hilda Solis (D-CA-32nd District) to "Vice-Chair Liaison to the Women's Caucus" of the Congressional Progressive Caucus.

Democratic Socialists of America (DSA) is a friend of US Representative Hilda Solis (D-CA-32nd District), but is Hilda Solis a friend of Democratic Socialists of America (DSA)?

58-3 Midwest Academy founder Heather Booth (l) and Harold

In November 2005, Solis addressed the Democratic Socialists of America (DSA) National Convention in Los Angeles - "The New Capital of Progressive Politics?"[356]

The Twenty-First Century approach to Socialism

While the gathering at the" working convention-one that differed from past meetings in that all convention business happened on the plenary floor for maximum delegate participation, two evening public sessions focused on the big picture, too.

On Friday evening, a panel consisting of ACORN chief organizer Wade Rathke, Kent Wong of the UCLA Labor Center and Roxana Tynan of the Los Angeles Alliance for a New Economy looked at the level of struggles nationwide.

Saturday evening delegates recognized the contributions of Democratic Socialists of America (DSA) Vice Chair and Washington Post columnist Harold Meyerson, Occidental College sociologist and longtime Democratic Socialists of America DSAer Peter Dreier and insurgent California Congress member Hilda Solis (D) in turn provided in-depth perspectives of the political scene. (Solis 2006)

"Insurgent?"

---

[354] http://newzeal.blogspottrevorloudon.com/2006/11/the-socialists-behind-the-progressive-caucus.html/
[355] http://keywiki.org/index.php/Duane_Campbell
[356] http://www.dsausa.org/dl/Winter_2006.pdf

US Representative Hilda Solis (D-CA-32nd District) also has indirect ties to Socialist International. In June this year, the Socialist International Migrations Committee[357] held a Migrations Reform, Integration, Rights forum in Los Angeles.

Democratic Socialists of America (DSA) National Director Frank Llewellyn, plus Duane Campbell and Dolores Delgado Campbell of Democratic Socialists of America (DSA)'s Anti-Racism network and the Latino networks represented Democratic Socialists of America (DSA), the Socialist International's main US affiliate.

California State Senator Gill Cedillo attended.

Elena Henry, a caseworker from Hilda Solis's East Los Angeles Office, represented Solis.

This was not the first time that Solis had sent a Representative to a socialist gathering.

According to the Communist Party's *People's Weekly World* of June 20, 1996:

> The Southern California Friends of the *People's Weekly World* tribute to two of Los Angeles' finest labor leaders, Jerry Acosta and CA State Senator Gilbert Cedillo, became a dynamic rally of elected officials, activists, labor and community leaders in solidarity with labor struggles and in the fight to defeat the ultra-right in November...
>
> The audience clapped, cheered and sometimes shouted out during the spirited tribute to Jerry Acosta, regional director of the Utility Workers Union, and CA State Senator Gilbert Cedillo, long-time leader of Service Employees International Union (SEIU) Local 660 Los Angeles, CA.
>
> "The *People's Weekly World* and all of us in this room feel strongly about whom we honor today," said Evelina Alarcon, Chair of the Southern California District and National Secretary of the Communist Party USA, one of the emcees of the tribute. "Jerry Acosta and CA State Senator Gilbert Cedillo represent the new fight back vision of the Sweeney, Trumka, Chavez-Thompson leadership in the AFL-CIO. They represent the rank and file that is pushing from the bottom for that new vision!"
>
> Alarcon recounted many of Acosta's and Cedillo's achievements, calling them "real live working class heroes in the forefront of struggle"

---

[357]http://www.socialistinternational.org/viewArticle.cfm?ArticleID=1924&ArticlePageID=1252&ModuleID=18

who "take bold initiatives on labor issues" and spearhead mass action in the fight for equality of all people.

If there is any time that we value that kind of leadership, "it is now when we face the greatest electoral challenge of our time," Alarcon said pointing to the necessity "to vote out the Republican ultra-right in the Congress and in the California State legislature."

Rep. Esteban Torres, a UAW labor leader in Congress, wearing his union jacket and standing tall, told the crowd, "This event would have made old Sam Kushner proud," referring to the late World labor reporter.

Los Angeles City Councilman Richard Alarcon, on behalf of the council which adopted a resolution honoring Acosta and Cedillo, said, "Gil Cedillo and Jerry Acosta have changed the whole dynamic of what it means to be for the working class and what it means to fight for workers' rights. Because of them and other labor leaders, we have seen a resurgence of strength of the least empowered in our country."

58-4 National Holiday for César Chávez

Presentations to the honorees were also made by Clara James, Chair of the Community Affairs Commission of the Second Baptist Church, on behalf of Congresswoman Maxine Waters, one of the nation's most distinguished African American leaders; Antonio Aguilar, on behalf of State Senator Hilda Solis, California's first Latina elected to the State Senate, who, along with labor, led the drive to put a minimum wage increase initiative on the ballot;

State Assemblyman Antonio Villaraigoza sent a message and 17 elected officials and more than 50 labor leaders put their names in the program book honoring Cedillo and Acosta. Victoria Castro, a member of the L.A. City Board of Education, sent certificates recognizing the two labor leaders. (Waters, Solis and Henry 1996)

This piece is important because it shows the influence of the Communist Party USA in Southern California Politics. The Communist Party USA has substantial influence in the Los Angeles labor movement and by directing union money and human resources in the right direction, it is able to determine who gets elected and where.

Richard Alarcon is now a Los Angeles City Councilor. Both Richard and his communist big sister, Evelina, are close friends and supporters of Los Angeles Mayor Antonio Villaraigoza, who serves on President elect

Barack Obama's economic transition team alongside Democratic Socialists of America (DSA) member and US Representative Hilda Solis (D-CA-32nd District) supporter, US Representative David Bonior.

The election of Richard Alarcon and Antonio Villaraigoza was the result of strong union support.

Senator Maxine Waters is a stalwart of the Congressional Progressive Caucus.

58-5 Chelsea (l), Hillary Clinton (c) and Dolores Huerta (r)

US Representative Hilda Solis (D-CA-32nd District) also enjoyed strong union (and Communist Party USA backing) when she ran for the US Congress in 2000.

In a report submitted to the Communist Party in November 2000,[358] Evelina Alarcon, Vice Chair Communist Party USA and Chair Southern California District, commented on US Representative Hilda Solis (D-CA-32nd District)'s Congressional victory:

> The monumental victories which are occurring in Los Angeles electorally and in the workplace are because of the coalition building that the labor movement is doing with the Latino and African American community. In Los Angeles, the Labor Federation not only targeted three congressional districts but it had organized 250 volunteers to help State Senator Hilda Solis win her Congressional seat by turning out the union household and Latino vote...

> We in the Party can also be proud because our members were involved in all the targeted electoral efforts... (Alarcon 2000)

In 2007, US Representative Hilda Solis (D-CA-32nd District), endorsed US Senator Hillary Clinton (D-NY) for President and signed on to co-Chair the Clinton campaign's Environmental and Energy Task Force and to co-Chair the National Hispanic Leadership Council.

Her friend and Democratic Socialists of America (DSA) honorary

---

[358]http://cc.bingj.com/cache.aspx?q=%22www+Communist Partyusa+org+index+php+article+articleview+152%22&d=5052552363445174&mkt=en-US&setlang=en-US&w=585de640,c54f3fa4

Chair, Dolores Huerta, former colleague of legendary Farm workers Union leader Cesar Chavez, joined her.

Together Huerta and Solis campaigned for Clinton throughout California and Nevada on a tour themed "Juntas Con Hillary, Una Vida Mejor" (Together with Hillary, A Better Life). By 2008, US Representative Hilda Solis (D-CA-32nd District) was campaigning under a new slogan "Yes we can" -the Anglicized version of Cesar Chavez's old battle cry "Si se puede."

Solis joined Obama's National Latino Advisory Council:[359]

"As the Latino community continues to get to know Senator Obama, it is clear that he is the right candidate for our issues and is the best

candidate to deliver the change that America desperately needs," said Congresswoman Hilda L. Solis. "Senator Obama not only understands the struggles and diversity of our community but because of his personal history and background he will stand with us and be a fighter for our issues. I look forward to continuing to work to elect Senator Obama as the next President of the United States." (National Latino Advisory Council)Solis was not alone. (Democracy for New Mexico 2008)

58-6 Eliseo Medina (l) at the Chicago DSA dinner - 2004

Solis sure wasn't lonely.

Other members of the Advisory Council included five members of the Congressional Progressive Caucus:

- Xavier Becerra[360]
- Raúl Grijalva
- Luis Gutiérrez
- Linda T. Sánchez
- Nydia Velasquez - (D-NY-12th District).

Another member was Service Employees International Union (SEIU) Executive Vice President and Democratic Socialists of America (DSA) honorary Chair Eliseo Medina.[361]

---

[359] http://keywiki.org/index.php/National_Latino_Advisory_Council
[360] http://keywiki.org/index.php/Xavier_Becerra
[361] http://keywiki.org/index.php/Eliseo_Medina

Medina also has close ties to Chicago Democratic Socialists of America (DSA);[362] the same people who endorsed US Senator Barack Obama[363] during his successful bid for Illinois State Senate in 1996.

Democratic Socialists of America (DSA) has supported President elect Barack Obama through his entire political career.

Is appointing US Representative Hilda Solis (D-CA-32nd District) to a key position Obama's way of returning a favor, or is it indicative of a shared agenda?

59. Top Socialist's Memo to Obama

Monday, December 29, 2008

President elect Barack Obama owes his new job to two organizations: Communist Party USA and the allied and much larger Democratic Socialists of America.

These two organizations share similar agendas. A socialized and much weakened America through slashed military expenditure, socialized medicine, massive increase in union power and large-scale redistribution of wealth.

Both organizations see the Obama administration as an opportunity to move the US way to the left through what I describe as the "sandwich strategy."

The plan is to stack Obama's administration with as many sympathizers and socialists as possible to represent one slice of bread. Then create a massive "people's movement" of protest groups, mass organizations and "community groups" the other slice of bread which will continue to pressure Obama into moving in the desired direction.

Obama will be able to implement socialist measures in response to "public demand."

---

[362] http://newzeal.blogspot.com/2008/02/obama-file-12-jan-schakowsky-barack.html
Chapter 12 – Jan Schakowsky – Barack Obama's Loyal Socialist Supporter
[363] http://newzeal.blogspot.com/2008/02/obama-file-19-obama-08-all-way-with-dsa.html
Chapter 19 - Obama '08 "All the Way With DSA"

59-2 Joseph Schwartz

The US taxpaying middle class will of course be the meat in the middle.

In their January-February issue, *"Tikkun Magazine"*[364] asked a number of "liberal and leftist academics and activists" to draft a "Memo to President Obama." Democratic Socialists of America (DSA)'s Labor movement blog *Talking Union*[365] has pre-published a memo drafted by Temple University politics lecturer and Democratic Socialists of America Vice-Chair Joseph Schwartz.

"Tikkun Magazine," is run by former Students for a Democratic Society (SDS) radical and one time Democratic Socialists of America (DSA) member, Rabbi Michael Lerner and Democratic Socialists of America (DSA) honorary Chair and member of Obama's Black Advisory

59-1 Cornel West (l), Rabbi Michael Lerner (c)

Council,[366] Cornel West. Joseph Schwartz and Obama go back.

According to Chicago Democratic Socialists of America (DSA)'s *New Ground* of March/April 1996:[367]

Schwartz: Over three hundred people attended the first of two Town Meetings on Economic Insecurity on February 25 in Ida Noyes Hall at the University of Chicago. Entitled "Employment and Survival in Urban America," the meeting was sponsored by the University of Chicago Democratic Socialists of America (DSA) Youth Section, Chicago Democratic Socialists of America (DSA) and University Democrats. The panelists were Toni Preckwinkle, Alderman of Chicago's 4th Ward; Barack Obama, candidate for the 13th Illinois Senate District; Professor William Julius Wilson, Center for the Study of Urban Inequality at the University of Chicago; Professor Michael Dawson, University of Chicago; and Professor Joseph Schwartz, Temple University

---

[364] http://www.tikkun.org/article.php/jan09
[365] http://talkingunion.wordpress.com/2008/12/17/memo-to-President-obama/
[366] http://news.nationaljournal.com/articles/080331nj1.htm
[367] http://www.chicagodsa.org/ngarchive/ng45.html

and a member of Democratic Socialists of America (DSA)'s National Political Committee. (Roman, A Town Meeting on Economic Insecurity: Employment and Survival in Urban America 1996)

Loudon: What advice does comrade Schwartz have for the President elect?

Schwartz: The impressive depth and breadth of your electoral victory, combined with Democratic gains in both the House and the Senate, provides the possibility of reversing three decades of growing inequality that is the primary cause of an impending depression. But to do so you will have to act boldly and quickly. As a constitutional law scholar, you realize that the system of checks and balances and separation of powers established by our founders consciously aimed to forestall rapid change. Thus, almost all the reforms we identify with the twentieth-century Democratic Party-Social Security, the National Labor Relations Act, the Civil Rights Acts, and Medicare-occurred in the periods 1935-1938 and 1964-1966, the only times when the Democrats controlled the presidency and had strong majorities in both chambers of Congress. (Roman, A Town Meeting on Economic Insecurity: Employment and Survival in Urban America 1996)

Loudon: In other words Schwartz is advising Obama to "blitzkrieg" the system, allowing constitutional checks and balances to be over-ridden or by-passed. There is a rare window of opportunity here to create significant socialist change.

Schwartz: If upon taking office you lead with boldness, your administration could pass major legislation in regard to universal health care, massive investment in green technology, and labor law reform that would transform United States social relations for generations to come. But as a former community organizer you know that reforms did not come from the top down; they arose because moderate elites made concessions to the movements of the unemployed and the CIO in the 1930s and to the Civil Rights, anti-war, women's, and welfare rights movements of the 1960s. While your office cannot conjure up mass social movements, you can call your supporters to ongoing grassroots activism. (Roman, A Town Meeting on Economic Insecurity: Employment and Survival in Urban America 1996)

Loudon: Schwartz is referring here to the communist led union/mass movements of the 1930s, which pushed Roosevelt into the "New Deal" and the communist/New Left led movements of the 1960s, which brought about Lyndon B. Johnson's "New Society." Democratic Socialists of America (DSA) sees the next few years as the next "New

Deal" Schwartz wants Obama to be guided by (and no doubt to finance) this movement. Obama's encouragement of the recent CPUSA/Democratic Socialists of America (DSA) supported Republic strike in Chicago is perhaps an indicator of things to come.

> Schwartz: Even before taking office, you confront the most serious breakdown in the global economy since the Great Depression. Hopefully well before you take office, you and your Treasury Secretary nominee will push the lame-duck Congress to pass a massive stimulus package of at least $500 billion or $600 billion...

> The stimulus package should include major government funding of job training in the inner cities (in green technologies, for example) and of opportunities for both GIs and displaced workers to return to university as full-time students (and for women on TANF to fulfill their "workfare" requirements through secondary and higher education pursuits). While affluent suburbs provide their residents superb public education and public Services, federal cutbacks in aid to states and municipalities has worsened the life opportunities of inner city residents.

> Your election as the first African American President is of inestimable symbolic import; but its promise will be soured if your administration does nothing to address inner city poverty and the massive rise in the incarceration of young youth of color. Only federal funding of pre-K education and of after-school programs for vulnerable youth can begin to redress rampant educational inequalities. (Roman, A Town Meeting on Economic Insecurity: Employment and Survival in Urban America 1996)

Loudon: Redistribute the wealth to the areas where socialists are most influential. Fund government programs that socialists will control. The communists of the 1930s infiltrated and lived off Roosevelt's myriad make-work schemes. The socialists of the new century aim to do the same. Redistribute the wealth to socialists.

> Schwartz: The inefficient and inequitable United States health care system cries out for replacement by a universal and cost-efficient alternative... While the power of the insurance lobby may preclude your backing a national single-payer bill, you must back progressive Democratic amendments for opt-out provisions from your "pay or play" system of private insurance. Opt-outs would allow states to create their own single-payer systems, and allow Medicare or the federal employee's health plan to market to employers as a lower-cost alternative to private group plans. (Roman, A Town Meeting on Economic Insecurity: Employment and Survival in Urban America 1996)

Loudon: Single Payer or socialized medicine is at the top of the

Democratic Socialists of America (DSA)/CPUSA agenda. The socialists see socialized medicine as a way of making the US middle class dependent on the state - the Democratic Party "state."

Chicago physician Quentin Young, a Democratic Socialists of America (DSA) member and friend of Obama's has been pushing this for years through his Physicians for a National Health Program. Obama ally, US Representative John Conyers with lifelong ties to Communist Party USA and an alleged DSA member, has been pushing his HR676 health proposal in Congress and through the union movement.

> Conyers wrote on his blog 12/28/2008. Already nearly Nine thousand people sent a message online to the incoming Obama Administration that Single Payer is the one true health care reform that the country needs. Now there are citizens groups across the country meeting to come together to call upon the President-elect to consider Single Payer health care.

> Schwartz: But how to pay for all this? You should attempt to reverse not only the Bush tax cuts, but also the Reagan-era cuts in marginal rates on high-income earners (approximately $300 billion in revenues, each). In addition, abolishing the 15 percent tax rate on hedge fund and private equity managers' earnings could garner another $100 billion in annual revenues. (Roman, A Town Meeting on Economic Insecurity: Employment and Survival in Urban America 1996)

59-4 Senator Obama and US Representative John Conyers

59-3 Quentin Young (l) Barack Obama (r)

Loudon: Taxes, taxes and more taxes - the socialists answer to every problem.

> Schwartz: Ending the war in Iraq should save $100 billion per annum; a one-third cutback in United States military bases abroad and an end to Cold War era plans to build a next generation of fighters and an anti-ballistic missile defense could save $216 billion in federal revenue per year.

> The military budget is hideously oversized for a nation that claims armaments are necessary for defense, and not defense of empire. (Roman, A Town Meeting on Economic Insecurity: Employment and Survival in Urban America 1996)

Loudon: Maybe it is time to give Russia, China, Cuba, Iran, North Korea, Venezuela and Al Qaida their turn on top.

Schwartz: When the Ponzi scheme of "securitized mortgages" collapsed with the end of the irrational run-up in housing prices, the federal government had to bail out Bear Stearns, then Fannie Mae and Freddie Mac, and then AIG. American capitalism has privatized gain, but socialized risk. Yet if risk is to be socialized, then so should investments. Your administration should not only demand equity shares in the banks and corporations that are bailed out by the public treasury, but should also require that consumer, worker, and government Representatives be added to the Board of directors of corporations receiving government aid. (Roman, A Town Meeting on Economic Insecurity: Employment and Survival in Urban America 1996)

Loudon: Get the unions and "peoples organizations" into the Board rooms. Do not waste this great opportunity to socialize "Big Business."

Schwartz: A "New Deal" would have to restructure international economic institutions so that they raise international labor, living, human rights, and environmental standards. In large part you owe your victory in the key battleground states of Ohio, Michigan, Indiana, and Pennsylvania to the efforts of one of the few integrated institutions in the United States-the American labor movement. Restoring the right to organize unions (which de facto no longer exists in the United States) is a key policy component in the battle against economic inequality. Given the already massive corporate and media offensive already launched against the Employee Free Choice Act, you will have to place the entire prestige of your office behind the legislation... (Roman, A Town Meeting on Economic Insecurity: Employment and Survival in Urban America 1996)

Loudon: You owe us! Schwartz is reminding Obama that the unions got him elected, he owes them (and by extension their communist and socialist leaders) his soul.

Schwartz wants Obama to resist pressure to stop the Employee Free Choice Act, which abolishes secret ballots in the workplace and gives union goons tremendous power to re-unionize the workforce.

It is payback time!

Schwartz: Your victory by no means guarantees the bold policy initiatives necessary to restoring equity with growth to the United States economy. Your campaign did not advocate major defense cuts, progressive tax reform, and significant expansion of public provision. However, FDR did not campaign on bold solutions in 1932. It was pressure from below that forced FDR's hand. Similarly, your victory may provide space for social movements to agitate in favor of economic justice and a democratic foreign policy. But as a President who understands the process of social change, I trust that you will understand that those demanding the most from your administration are those who can best help you succeed in office. (Roman, A Town Meeting on Economic Insecurity: Employment and Survival in Urban America 1996)

Loudon: Okay President elect Obama, we know you did not campaign on socialism, but FDR did not campaign on the "New Deal" either. He did what he did, because the communists forced him to.

Schwartz: We are going to pressure you too. You understand what we are doing. We are not going to attack you, we're trying to help. We are going to give you President-elect Obama the excuse to implement the socialist agenda we all desire. (Roman, A Town Meeting on Economic Insecurity: Employment and Survival in Urban America 1996)

60. Institute for Policy Studies Plans Obama's America

Trevor Loudon © Thursday, January 01, 2009

I urge every person who cares about the freedom of America (and by extension, the Western World) to view a video Post-Election Analysis a six part series[368] filmed after the US election which covers a seminar organized by the Washington based Institute for Policy Studies (IPS).

It is hard to see the three panelists - John Cavanagh, Steve Cobble, and Bill Fletcher Jr., as dangerous people. They are amiable, intelligent and "moderate." These people are not fire breathing, bomb throwing revolutionaries - they are well connected, effective "change agents."

The organization they all represent, the Institute for Policy Studies (IPS), is a subversive organization operating in the US.

60-1 Institute for Policy Studies (IPS)

Founded in 1963, Institute for

---

[368] http://www.youtube.com/watch?v=xlF-ChDdvlk&feature=related

Policy Studies (IPS) has well documented past ties to the Soviet KGB and Cuban Intelligence. It remains supportive of Cuba, Hugo Chavez's Venezuelan revolution and Mexico's Zapatista rebels.

Soviet agent and journalist I.F. Stone once called IPS "the think tank for the rest of us."

Institute for Policy Studies (IPS) has close ties to the two key organizations behind the Obama movement: Democratic Socialists of America and Communist Party USA.

Democratic Socialists of America (DSA) and IPS were the key founders of the Congressional Progressive Caucus, the grouping of now more than eighty far left Congressmen that dominates the US House of Representatives. IPS continues to advise them.

IPS also founded United for Peace & Justice, the US peace movement umbrella group, led by senior members of DSA, CPUSA and the CPUSA offshoot Committees of Correspondence for Democracy and Socialism (CoCDS).

Several IPS members also play leading roles in Movement for a Democratic Society (MDS). A coalition of senior leaders:

- Democratic Socialists of America (DSA)
- Communist Party USA
- Committee of Correspondence
- Students for a Democratic Society (SDS)
- Weather Underground
- Long-time Obama associates Bill Ayers and Bernardine Dohrn.

Movement for a Democratic Society also spawned Progressives for Obama (P4O). Four of the six Progressives for Obama founders include:

- Barbara Ehrenreich - (DSA)
- Bill Fletcher Jr. - (DSA, Freedom - Road Socialist Organization)
- Tom Hayden - (former Students for a Democratic Society leader)
- Carl Davidson - (former Students for a Democratic Society and Communist Party Marxist-Leninist, Committee of Correspondence leader)
- Steve Cobble – (an endorser of the PFO website)

All are Movement for Democratic Society Board members.

Ehrenreich is an Institute for Policy Studies (IPS) trustee; Fletcher is an IPS fellow, while Tom Hayden is a long time IPS affiliate.

Hayden and Cobble are also Board members of Progressive Democrats of America, together with several Communist Party USA members, including Obama supporters US Representative John Conyers and US Representative Barbara Jean Lee (D-CA-9th).

It is also worth noting that John Cavanagh, Steve Cobble, Bill Fletcher Jr., Barbara Ehrenreich, and Carl Davidson were in the '90s, leaders of the Democratic Socialists of America (DSA)/Committees of Correspondence/ACORN front, the New Party. The organization Obama joined to gain support for his 1996 Illinois State Senate race.

That is the history and a glimpse of IPS' vision of the future.

61. Institute for Policy Studies and the Obama "Movement"

Trevor Loudon © Friday, January 09, 2009

It is indisputable that President Elect Barack Obama was groomed and supported by radical Marxists almost his entire life.

It is now well known that three Marxist organizations - Communist Party USA, Committees of Correspondence for Democracy and Socialism (COCDS) and Democratic Socialists of America have supported Obama's political career.

It is also common knowledge that Obama has enjoyed close ties to several former members of Students for a Democratic Society (SDS) and its terrorist splinter, Weather Underground Organization (WUO).

What is less well known is that these entire strands link to one entity, an organization with documented ties to hostile foreign intelligence Services, Washington based "think tank," the Institute for Policy Studies.[369]

This post looks at three organizations that have influenced Obama's career and their ties to IPS.

---

[369] http://newzeal.blogspot.com/2009/01/blog-post.html Chapter 60 - Institute For Policy Studies Plans Obama's America

The New Party

Founded in the '90s, the New Party was an alliance of Democratic Socialists of America (DSA) and the radical community group ACORN, with some input from the Committees of Correspondence (COCDS) and Communist Party USA.

The New Party was designed to assist socialist leaning candidates on the Democratic Party ticket, by using the New Party endorsement as a signal to far left voters. Barack Obama ran successfully for the Illinois State Senate campaign in 1996.

Behind ACORN and Democratic Socialists of America (DSA) stood the Institute for Policy Studies (IPS). The New Party was an IPS creation, one of several similar political party projects dating back to the late 1960s.

New Party documents from 1994 lists one hundred "community leaders, organizers, unionists, retirees, scholars, artists, parents, students, doctors, writers and other activists who are building the New Party."

Those New Party leaders with proven ties to IPS include:

- John Cavanagh - (Listed in the IPS's 1993 30th Anniversary as an IPS Fellow. Cavanagh later became IPS Director and is still with the organization)
- Steve Cobble - (Now an IPS Associate Fellow)

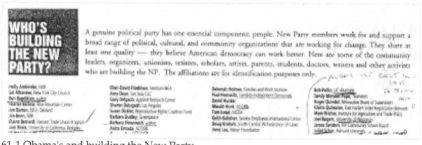

61-1 Obama's and building the New Party

- Noam Chomsky - (A member of both Democratic Socialists of America (DSA) and COCDS. Chomsky was in the late 1970s, a sponsor, with Barbara Ehrenreich, of the socialist IPS magazine In These Times. Chomsky also served on the IPS 20th Anniversary Committee)
- Gary Delgado - (Attended an IPS seminar in 1983 where he was billed as the founder of ACORN)
- Barbara Ehrenreich - (Listed in the IPS's 1993 30th Anniversary as a former IPS Fellow. Ehrenreich is now an IPS Trustee and a

Democratic Socialists of America (DSA) leader)

- Bill Fletcher Jr. – (Now an IPS Scholar and prominent Democratic Socialists of America (DSA) member)

- Manning Marable - (Listed in the IPS's 1993 30th Anniversary as a former IPS visiting scholar or Associate Fellow. Former Democratic Socialists of America (DSA) Board member, COCDS National Committee member)

- Frances Fox Piven - (Listed in the IPS's 1993 30th Anniversary as a former IPS visiting scholar or Associate Fellow. Democratic Socialists of America (DSA) honorary Chair)

- Michael Schuman - (Listed in the IPS's 1993 30th Anniversary brochure as IPS Director)

- Arthur Waskow - (A founding IPS Fellow and one of the organization's most prominent activists. Waskow, A Democratic Socialists of America (DSA) member, active in Students for a Democratic Society, also went on to co-lead with the late Rabbi Arniold Jacob Wolf the controversial Breira Organization, which collapsed after being linked to Palestinian Liberation Organization officials. Rabbi Wolf was also a Democratic Socialists of America (DSA) member and a neighbor, supporter and personal friend of Barack Obama)

- Quentin Young - (Involved in the late 1970s with the Citizens Committee, an IPS attempt to found a new political party. Young is a Democratic Socialists of America (DSA) member and long-time friend, neighbor and supporter of Barack Obama. He has also been the family doctor to former WUO terrorists and Obama associates Bill Ayers and Bernardine Dohrn)

61-2 MDS Board 2007. Manning Marable (c), Mark Rudd (far l) and Jeff Jones (2d from r)

Clearly Obama joined something of an IPS front.

Movement for a Democratic Society (MDS)

In 2006, a group of former Students for a Democratic Society members and sympathizers, led by Democratic Socialists of America (DSA) activist Paul Buhle, joined with a new generation of college students to re-found Students for a Democratic Society.

Buhle and comrades also founded the Students for a Democratic

Society support group for older activists -Movement for a Democratic Society (MDS).[370]

The Movement for a Democratic Society united all the main strands of the Obama movement - Communist Party USA, COCDS, Democratic Socialists of America (DSA), a whole bunch of old Students for a Democratic Society, including long time Obama associates Carl Davidson and Mike Klonsky,[371] and several former WUO terrorists including Bill Ayers and Jeff Jones.[372]

The Movement for a Democratic Society activists with ties to IPS include:

- Tariq Ali - (A British Trotskyist leader. A long time Fellow of the IPS's European wing Transnational Institute)
- Paul Buhle - (Movement for a Democratic Society founder, former Students for a Democratic Society activist. Occasional IPS lecturer in the 1970s)
- Robb Burlage - (A long time IPS Fellow)
- Noam Chomsky - (Movement for a Democratic Society Board member. IPS as above)
- Barbara Ehrenreich - (Movement for a Democratic Society Board member. IPS as above)
- Bill Fletcher Jr. - Movement for a Democratic Society Board member. IPS as above)
- Al Harber - (Movement for a Democratic Society Board member. Original Students for a Democratic Society founder and active in the 1970s in the IPS affiliated Bay Area Institute)
- Tom Hayden - (Movement for a Democratic Society Board member. A former Students for a Democratic Society leader, Tom Hayden was active in the 1970s in the IPS established National Conference for Alternative State and Local Public Policies)
- Manning Marable - (Movement for a Democratic Society Chairman. IPS as above)
- Ethelbert Miller - (Movement for a Democratic Society Board member. Chairman of IPS Board of Trustees)

---

[370] http://keywiki.org/index.php/Movement_for_a_Democratic_Society
[371] http://keywiki.org/index.php/Mike_Klonsky
[372] http://newzeal.blogspot.com/2008/09/obama-file-33-more-weathermen-for-obama.html

- Studs Terkel - (Recently deceased. A former secret Chicago Communist Party member. Terkel served on the IPS 20th Anniversary Committee)
- Immanuel Wallerstein - (Circa 1979 Wallerstein addressed an IPS/Transnational Institute seminar in Amsterdam on "The World Capitalist System)

Clear links exist between IPS and Movement for a Democratic Society.

Progressives for Obama

In 2008, four Movement for a Democratic Society Board members

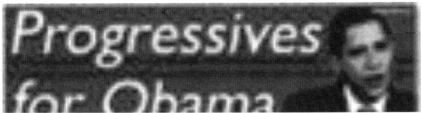

61-3 Progressives for Obama banner

and actor/activist Danny Glover set up a subsidiary organization, Progressives for Obama (P40).[373]

The three Progressives for Obama founders with ties to IPS were:
- Barbara Ehrenreich - (IPS)
- Bill Fletcher Jr.- (IPS)
- Tom Hayden - (IPS)

Progressives for Obama were designed to unify leftist support behind the Obama campaign and again brought together many of the old crowd.
- New Party - (NP)
- Democratic Socialists of America - (DSA)
- Committees for Correspondence for Democracy and Socialism Marxist-Leninists Come Out for Obama– (CCDS)
- Students for a Democratic Society - (SDS, Founded 1959)
- Students for a Democratic Society - (SDS, Founded 2006)
- Weather Underground Organization - (WUO)
- Institute for Policy Studies - (IPS)

---

[373] http://keywiki.org/index.php/Progressives_for_Obama

Several *Institute for Policy Studies (IPS)* connected individuals endorsed the Progressives for Obama website, including:

- Paul Buhle - (IPS)
- Steve Cobble - (IPS)
- Daniel Ellsberg - (In 1970, when Ellsberg stole the famous "Pentagon Papers" from the Rand Corporation, he passed a full set to IPS founder Marcus Raskin, who based a book on them - *"Washington Plans an Aggressive War"*)
- Richard (Dick) Flacks - (Democratic Socialists of America (DSA) member and former Students for a Democratic Society leader. In the 1970s Flacks was active with Tom Hayden in the IPS founded National Conference for Alternative State and Local Public Policies)
- Max Palevsky - (Philanthropist. A major IPS funder)
- Frances Fox Piven - (IPS)
- Jim Hightower - (In 1979 Hightower served on the Board of the IPS founded National Conference for Alternative State and Local Public Policies)
- Immanuel Wallerstein - (IPS)

Is there a pattern here?

It is clear that the Institute for Policy Studies has ties to three organizations with close connections to President elect Barack Obama. Future Chapters will examine further IPS/Obama links and the possible reasons for them.

62. Obama "Understands What Socialism Is" Works with "Socialists with Backgrounds in the Communist Party"

Trevor Loudon © Sunday, January 11, 2009

A leading US Marxist claims that President elect Barack Obama has read some of his books and "understands what socialism is."

Columbia University professor of African American Studies, Manning Marable, writing in the December Issue of British Trotskyist journal *Socialist Review*,[374] also alleges that Obama works with socialists

---

[374] http://www.socialistreview.org.uk/article.php?articlenumber=10628

"with backgrounds in the Communist Party."

According to Dr. Marable:

> Obama represents a generation of post-racial black politicians-by which I mean they espouse a politics that minimizes matters of race. They do not like to talk about race and subsume it under the rubric of poverty and class. Therefore, they are generally left of center, or liberal, on social and economic policy. Obama is a progressive liberal.

> What makes Obama different is that he has also been a community organizer. He has read left literature, including my works, and he understands what socialism is. Many of the people working with him are, indeed, socialists with backgrounds in the Communist Party or as independent Marxists. There are many people like that in Chicago who has worked with him for years. (Marable 2008)

Manning Marable is in a position to know about Obama's views and reading habits. Whether Dr. Marable and Barack Obama have ever met, I am unsure, but they have been "close" for many years.

Since the 1980s, Dr. Marable has been a regular speaker at Democratic Socialists of America (DSA)'s annual Socialist Scholars Conference,[375] at Cooper Union in New York. In the '80s, Obama "went to socialist conferences at Cooper Union and African cultural fairs in Brooklyn."

Perhaps Dr. Marable inspired Obama as Obama inspires Dr. Marable[376] today.

In the mid-1990s, Dr. Marable was a key founder of the New Party,[377] which Obama joined in 1995 to help him with his successful Illinois State Senate bid.

When Dr. Marable voted for Barack Obama, he voted for him not as a Democrat, but on the New York Working Families Party (WFP) line. Manning Marable is a member of the WFP, which is a direct descendant of the now defunct New Party.

Says Dr. Marable:

---

[375] http://keywiki.org/index.php/Democratic_Socialists_of_America
[376]
http://academic.udayton.edu/race/2008ElectionandRacism/RaceandRacism/race86.htm
[377] http://keywiki.org/index.php/New_Party

"Why vote for Obama on a Working Families ticket? You are counted independently of the Democrats and it shows there is a left constituency in the state of New York. It gives us some leverage on decision-making and policy and we run our own candidates at local level." (Marable 2008)

Dr. Marable has been, for at least 20 years, a leading member of Democratic Socialists of America and would know most of the many Democratic Socialists of America (DSA) connected types in Obama's orbit, including Quentin Young, Lou Pardo, Danny K Davis, Jan Schakowsky, Cornel West, David Bonior, Major Owens, the late Rabbi Arnold Wolf, Jackie Grimshaw, William McNary, Jose LaLuz and Hilda Solis.

Several key New Party people knew Obama, including Carl

62-1 Working Family Party (WFP)

Davidson, Obama's friend and neighbor Dr. Quentin Young and longtime colleague US Rep. Danny K. Davis.[378]

Since 1992, Dr. Marable has held leadership roles in the Communist Party offshoot, Committees of Correspondence for Democracy and Socialism (COCDS). He would know fellow COCDS leaders, Carl Davidson and long time Obama friend and supporter, Timuel Black.[379]

In 1998, Manning Marable helped found the Black Radical Congress (BRC),[380] a coalition of black socialists including many members of the Communist Party, Democratic Socialists of America (DSA) and COCDS. In the Black Radical Congress (BRC) Marable worked with two Democratic Socialists of America (DSA) leaders, Cornel West, who went on to become half of Obama's 2008 Black Advisory Council and Bill Fletcher Jr. who founded Progressives for Obama (P40)[381] with Democratic Socialists of America (DSA) member Barbara Ehrenreich and

[378] http://keywiki.org/index.php/Danny_K_Davis
[379] http://keywiki.org/index.php/Timuel_Black
[380] http://keywiki.org/index.php/Black_Radical_Congress
[381] http://keywiki.org/index.php/Progressives_for_Obama

the ubiquitous Carl Davidson.

Obama's long time pastor, the Rev. Jeremiah Wright, was also involved in the Black Radical Congress (BRC).

Since January 2007, Manning Marable has been Chair of Movement for A Democratic Society,[382] a radical alliance of Communist Party, Democratic Socialists of America

Figure 62-2 Dr. Marable (c) MDS conference New York January 2007

(DSA), COCDS activists and former leaders of the radical Students for a Democratic Society (SDS)[383] and its terrorist splinter, the Weather Underground Organization (WUO).

In Movement for a Democratic Society, Dr. Marable worked with several more Obama friends or colleagues including former WUO terrorists, Bill Ayers and Bernardine Dohrn and former Students for Democratic Society leaders, Klonsky and Carl Davidson!

Dr. Marable has also been involved in the radical Washington based think tank Institute for Policy Studies (IPS). Through IPS, Marable may have gotten to know several other Obama friends, colleagues or supporters, including US Representative David Bonior, US Representative John Conyers, Obama mentor US Representative Abner Mikva (D-IL-2nd District),[384] Bill Fletcher Jr., Barbara Ehrenreich, Dr. Quentin Young or even Obama's choice for CIA boss, Leon Panetta.[385]

Dr. Marable may never have met Obama, but he[386] goes on to say:

> Among the post-racial black leadership, Massachusetts Governor Deval Patrick, New York Governor David Paterson, Cory Booker, and US Representative Harold Ford Jr is head of the Democratic Leadership Council;the right wing of the Democratic Party. Obama is a part of that cohort. He is more liberal than most of that group, but he is in it. The group is pragmatic and centrist. It cooperates with Republicans and tries to

[382] http://keywiki.org/index.php/Movement_for_a_Democratic_Society
[383] http://keywiki.org/index.php/New_Students_for_a_Democratic_Society
[384] http://newzeal.blogspot.com/2009/01/blog-post.html
[385] http://www.militantislammonitor.org/article/id/3807
[386] http://keywiki.org/index.php/Manning_Marable

present a non-partisan or post-partisan appeal, the way Obama does. So you will see Republicans in some key positions in Obama's administration. (Marable 2008)

This does not trouble Dr. Marable, as a Marxist tactician, he understands that to win elections and promote his policies Obama has to be subtle. He must bring his opponents on board and be careful not to scare centrist voters.

Obama regularly sends text messages to millions of people. He just sent a message saying, "Don't go away, now I need you to help govern." There is a debate right now within the Obama campaign about whether to move fast or go more slowly. The argument is that there have been 10 elections for President between 1968 and 2004 and Republicans have won seven of them. Obama is looking at the history and so are progressives who worked with him or critically endorsed him, like myself. (Marable 2008)

Again, Dr. Marable is emphasizing that a slow but sure pace is more likely to be successful. Marable lays out the left's agenda for Obama, in order of priorities:

My argument is simple. The left must force him to carry out the agenda he promised, and that includes a national healthcare system. That is the number-three priority. The main priority is ending the war in Iraq. The second is the economic crisis. We need a robust Keynesian approach to employment and investment in infrastructure - a lot of the bridges built by the works projects administration of Franklin D Roosevelt 75 years ago need to be rebuilt and the roads are crumbling.

We also need a solution to the foreclosures, to keep families in their homes. The fourth issue is green energy - a national challenge to be independent of foreign oil in 10 years. In addition, a fifth priority is immigration - essential to Latinos. There are 12-14 million undocumented Americans living in this country as so-called illegal aliens and there has to be a pathway to citizenship for them. (Marable 2008)

Dr. Marable gives the standard "Obama is not a socialist" disclaimer. One seen many times before in Communist Party and Democratic Socialists of America (DSA) literature:

Obama is not a Marxist or a socialist - he is a progressive liberal with a kind of center-left strategy. He will be Keynesian on economic policy. He is an astute politician who is trying to construct a coalition that has striking parallels to the New Deal, built on these core constituencies I have identified - working women, Hispanics and blacks, who are overwhelmingly working class. But he is going to put forward policy that is centrist or "moderate."

In some ways he is a reverse of Reagan, in that Reagan ran a hard-line right campaign but appealed to moderates through certain initiatives. He unified people - the so-called Reagan Democrats - around positions that transcended the Republican Party. Barack is doing the same in reverse. He is anchored to the progressives in the Democratic Party, but reaching to the center on policy and through certain values, for example on faith-based initiatives. (Marable 2008)

Figure 62-3 US Socialist Party leader A Phillip Randolph with Eleanor Roosevelt

Dr. Marable goes on to explain the role of the left - that is the Communist Party, Democratic Socialists of America (DSA), COCDS, Movement for a Democratic Society, Progressives for Obama (P40) and the countless unions and "community organizations" under their control. All these key organizations push the line[387] that they must create a mass movement to push Obama to the left - as the communists and socialists did in the '30s when they forced Roosevelt to adopt their (sometimes justified) policies:

Most of us on the left have taken a position of critical support toward Obama. We have to press him to carry out his own agenda.

The analogy of FDR is appropriate. But someone has to play the role of a Philip Randolph, the black socialist leader who attacked FDR from the left and in 1941 forced him to sign an executive order outlawing racial discrimination in factories producing for the war effort that refused to hire black people. Randolph threatened to bring 100,000 black workers to surround the White House. Roosevelt capitulated and signed an order that was the foundation of Affirmative Action.

We need a network that can do it. That is the challenge for socialists in the US. (Marable 2008)

Manning Marable is in a far better position to know Barack Obama's true thoughts and goals. As a lifelong Marxist, Dr. Marable believes that Obama is on the right track and wants his comrades to show

---

[387] http://newzeal.blogspot.com/2008/12/obama-file-59-top-socialists-memo-to.html
Chapter 59 - Top Socialist's Memo to Obama

understanding and offer support.

Someone is a fool - is it the American voter or is it Manning Marable?

63. Obama's "Energy Czar" and the Socialists Foreign and Domestic

Trevor Loudon © Tuesday, January 13, 2009

The US blogosphere is abuzz with the news that President elect,

Barack Obama's pick for Energy Czar is Carol Browner, who has ties to *Socialist International*.

63-1 President Elect Barack Obama and Energy Czar Carol Browner

This comes after revelations that Obama's proposed Labor Secretary US Representative Hilda Solis (D-CA-32nd District) also has ties to Socialist International (SI) and to its US affiliate, the crypto Marxist Democratic Socialists of America.

In addition, a senior member of Obama's economic transition team is former number two man US Representative David Bonior, is a

63-2 Carol Browner addressing Socialist International's 13th Congress, Athens, Greece - June 30, 2008 - Acting Now on Climate Change

confirmed member of Democratic Socialists of America, an organization that has supported Obama throughout his career.

According to the Washington Times:

Until last week, Carol M. Browner, President-elect Barack Obama's pick as Global Warming Czar, was listed as one of 14 leaders of a socialist group's Commission for a Sustainable World Society, which calls for "global governance" and says rich countries must shrink their economies to address climate change. (Dinan)

By Thursday, the removal of Mrs. Browner's name and biography from Socialist International's Web page, though a photo of her speaking June 30, 2008 to the group's Congress in Greece was still available.

Do not downplay Browner's membership in a senior Socialist International body. Once the Socialist International was staunchly anti-communist, but this has changed dramatically in recent years. Since the fall of communism, several former and "still existing" communist parties, including those of Laos, Cuba and China, now actively participate in the Socialist International (SI). In many ways, the SI has replaced the old Communist International as a key driver of socialist change.

While active on the international stage, Energy Czar, Carol Browner, does not neglect domestic politics.

Earlier this year, Ms. Browner endorsed President elect Barack Obama through her leadership position in the League of Conservation Voters.

Though living in Maryland, Energy Czar, Carol Browner also donated to the 2006 Senate campaign of long-time Vermont US Senator Bernie Sanders (I – VT)[388]:

> CAROL M BROWNER (THE ALBRIGHT GROUP/ ATTORNEY), (Zip code: 20912) $500 to SANDERS FOR SENATE on 05/25/06

US Representative David Bonior[389] also donated to Sanders

63-3 arol M. Browner Member Socialist International

63-4 Deputy Minister Zhang Zhijun, International Department of the Communist Party of China, addressing Socialist International (SI) 13th Congress. Athens, Greece – June 30, 2008

63-5 Carol Browner endorsing Barack Obama

[388] http://www.city-data.com/elec2/06/elec-TAKOMA-PARK-MD-06.html
[389] http://www.newsmeat.com/campaign_contributions_to_politicians/donor_list.php?candidate_id=S4VT00033&li=B

63-6 Sanders: A Thank You note!

campaign.

US Senator Bernie Sanders' (I–VT) political life began as a student in the *Chicago Young Peoples Socialist League*. He has long supported communist and socialist front activities. Though Independent, Sanders caucuses with the Democrats and was a key founder of the now more than eighty strong alliance of leftist Congressmen (and US Senator Bernie Sanders,) the Congressional Progressive Caucus.

US Senator Bernie Sanders (I – VT) is a socialist and has worked with Democratic Socialists of America for years. Like US Representative Hilda Solis (D-CA-32nd District) and US Representative David Bonior, Sanders has attended Democratic Socialists of America (DSA) conferences and the organization supported and financed Sanders' successful Senate campaign.

The Illinois Senator Barack Obama also backed US Senator Bernie Sanders (I-VT)' Senate campaign.

This is great, the way socialists are always helping people.

The Transformation of America!

64. Symbolic? Socialist Singer Seeger Serenades Obama

Trevor Loudon © Tuesday, January 20, 2009

What is symbolic of the Obama presidency?

At President Barack H. Obama's inauguration concert, life long communist Pete Seeger sang with fellow communist Woody Guthrie's socialist anthem *"This Land is Your Land"* on the steps of the Lincoln Memorial.

Fred Klonsky, son of communist Robert Klonsky, former Students for a Democratic Society activist, Progressives for Obama (P4O) supporter and brother of Obama colleague Mike Klonsky,[390] marked the occasion on his blog.[391]

How ironic. Here was the legendary Pete Seeger singing for the President at the Lincoln Memorial. Pete Seeger is a friend of both Republicans and Democrats.

> There was a big high wall there that tried to stop me;
> Sign was painted, it said private property;
> But on the back side it didn't say nothing;
> That side was made for you and me.
> In the squares of the city, in the shadow of a steeple;
> By the relief office, I'd seen my people.
> As they stood there hungry, I stood there asking,
> Is this land made for you and me?
> Nobody living can ever stop me,
> As I go walking that freedom highway;
> Nobody living can ever make me turn back
> This land was made for you and me. (Guthrie 2009)

---

[390] http://keywiki.org/index.php/Mike_Klonsky
[391] http://preaprez.wordpress.com/2009/01/19/pete-seeger-at-the-lincoln-memorial/

He fights for working people he is a defender of the environment and he is a lifelong radical and a one-time communist. For the first time, many got to hear the original Woody Guthrie lyrics to *This Land is Your Land*.

Fred Klonsky did get one thing wrong. Ninety-year-old Pete Seeger remains a communist to this day.

Seeger first subscribed to the Communist Party paper *"New Masses"* in 1932 and joined the party ten years later, under the influence of his party member father.

Seeger says he left the party in 1950, but continued involvement[392] in communist fronts and organs for decades including:

- American Peace Mobilization
- American Youth Congress
- Communist Party; American Youth for Democracy
- Council on African Affairs
- American Committee for Yugoslav Relief
- National Council of American-Soviet Friendship
- Civil Rights Congress
- American Committee for Protection of Foreign Born
- Committee for a Democratic Far Eastern Policy
- Jefferson School of Social Science
- Veterans Against Discrimination of Civil Rights Congress
- New Masses
- Daily World; the Labor Youth League
- California Labor School
- National Lawyers Guild; Veterans of the Abraham Lincoln Brigade
- Committee for the First Amendment
- American Peace Crusade
- National Emergency Civil Liberties Committee
- National Committee to Abolish the House Un-American Activities Committee.

Obama's communist mentor, Frank Marshall Davis, was also active

---

[392] http://www.discoverthenetworks.org/individualProfile.asp?indid=1619

in the Committee for Protection of Foreign Born. Both also moved in Communist Party USA cultural circles in the same frame. It would be fascinating to know if the two ever met.

In 2004, Seeger was still reading[393] the Communist Party paper "*People's Weekly World.*"

64-1 Angela Davis left, Pete Seeger, celebrating gift of Communist Party literature to Tamiment Library New York

Today Pete Seeger[394] and wife Toshi serve on the advisory board of the Communist Party splinter group Committees of Correspondence for Democracy and Socialism - an organization with other COCDS advisory Board members including long time Obama friend and supporter, Timuel Black and radical academics, Angela Davis and Noam Chomsky.

Angela Davis and Noam Chomsky both serve on the Board of Movement for a Democratic Society, which in turn created Progressives for Obama (P40).

Perhaps for an encore Pete Seeger should have sung, "*If I Had a Hammer and a Sickle?*"

65. Obama's "Brains Trust?" More from the Institute for Policy Studies

Trevor Loudon © Wednesday, January 28, 2009

Extreme left, Washington based "think tank" Institute for Policy Studies (IPS) has backed the Obama movement through the New Party in the '90s and Movement for A Democratic Society and Progressives for Obama (P40) during the recent election.

Now that they have their favored son in the White House, IPS plans to turn their radical agenda into legislation that will affect the Liberty and Freedom of every American citizen.

The Institute for Policy Studies has several "transmission belts" into

---

[393] http://www.peoplesworld.org/pete-seeger-standing-tall-at-85/
[394] http://www.cc-ds.org/advisory_bd.html

65-1 (l to r) Lynn Woolsey, John Cavanagh, John Conyers, Barbara Lee

the Obama administration.

Most important is the more than 80 strong grouping of leftist Democrats, the Congressional Progressive Caucus.[395]

Institute for Policy Studies and their allies in Democratic Socialists of America established Communist Party USA in 1991. Now it forms the largest bloc in the US Congress and Communist Party USA members Chair the majority of the most powerful Congressional Committees.

Other avenues of influence include the Institute for Policy Studies founded and guided peace movement "peak" organization United for Peace & Justice, Progressive Democrats of America, and the US's two main labor union federations, Change to Win and AFL-CIO.

Institute for Policy Studies aims to force its agenda into law, through a two-pronged approach - based on the strategy used by communists and socialists to push Roosevelt's administration far to the left during the New Deal era.

Their goal is to infiltrate radical policy ideas and "progressive" activists into the Obama camp through Communist Party USA, AFL-CIO and its linked organization Center for American Progress (CAP); which has supplied several key Obama administration personnel including Energy Czar, Carol Browner.

Institute for Policy Studies has enlisted seventy writers to produce a document "*Mandate for Change Policies and Leadership for 2009 and Beyond*,"

---

[395] http://newzeal.blogspottrevorloudon.com/2006/11/the-socialists-behind-the-progressive-caucus.html/

which is designed to provide a policy blueprint for President Obama's administration.

In other words, influence the Obama administration from WITHIN.

Use its muscle ACORN, AFL-CIO,[396] Democratic Socialists of America (DSA), Communist Party USA,[397] Committees of Correspondence for Democracy & Socialism, United for Peace & Justice, Code Pink etc. to build a huge "people's movement" to march, strike, occupy and agitate for the Institute for Policy Studies agenda. Fill the streets with millions of people all coordinated around specific demands.

Pressure the Obama administration from BELOW.

The four key Institute for Policy Studies demands:

- Healthcare and Socialized medicine.
- Equality International and domestic re-distribution of wealth.
- Climate Change-Zero US CO_2 emissions by 2050 - yes "zero!"
- Peace and ending the Iraq and Afghanistan wars and immediate $60 billion cuts to defense spending.

Institute for Policy Studies has worked with communists and socialists, both in the US and abroad, since its foundation in 1963. The organization has enjoyed documented ties to both the former Soviet Union's KGB and Cuban Intelligence (DGI) Services and to the socialist governments of Venezuela and Nicaragua.

The Institute for Policy Studies stands behind the Obama presidency.

Who stands behind the Institute for Policy Studies?

66. Socialist Leader: Use Obama Presidency to Create a "Permanent Progressive Majority"

Trevor Loudon © Wednesday, February 04, 2009

Retired Massachusetts history professor, Mark Solomon, is co-leader of the US Communist Party breakaway organization, Committees of Correspondence for Democracy and Socialism (COCDS). He is the

---

[396] http://keywiki.org/index.php/AFL-CIO
[397] http://keywiki.org/index.php/Communist_Party_USA

author of "*The Cry for Unity: Communists and African Americans, 1917-1936.*"

While never identified as a Communist Party USA member, Solomon was in the '80s a leading member of the Communist Party USA front US Peace Council (USPC) - an affiliate of the Soviet controlled World Peace Council.

At one point Solomon was US Peace Council national Chair and a Presidential Committee member of the World Peace Council. The position afforded regular contact with agents of the Communist Party and the Soviet Union International Department.

There is no doubt the Communist Party USA controlled the US Peace Council. In 1983/85, Solomon was one of five US Peace Council co-Chairs. Two others (Frank Rosen and Sarah Staggs) were Chicago Communist Party USA leaders, while another, Berkeley Mayor Gus Newport, was at least a party sympathizer who later went on to join COCDS.

Vice Chair Rob Prince was a Colorado communist, while executive director Mike Myerson was a Communist Party USA member who also left to join the Committees of Correspondence (COCDS) as it was known when founded in the '90s.

The US Peace Council Executive Board included Communist Party USA members Pauline Rosen, James Jackson, Frank Chapman and at least one sympathizer, Alice Palmer. Two other Board members went on to join COCDS, Otis Cunningham of Chicago and US Representative Barbara Jean Lee (D-CA-9th).

Figure 66-1 Mark Solomon

When US Representative Barbara Jean Lee (D-CA-9th) joined the COCDS executive board in 1992, she was a serving Democratic Party California state legislator. She was "ousted" by leading US communist researcher Herb Romerstein[398] and cut all (open) ties to COCDS.

---

[398] http://www.usasurvival.org/docs/Wallace_to_Ayers_Communist_Progressive.pdf

Now a California Democratic Party US Representative, Barbara Jean Lee (D-CA-9th) is co-Chair of the more than eighty strong grouping of leftist Democrats, the Congressional Progressive Caucus. She also appears to have mended her fences with Communist Party USA, attending a party function[399] in California in December 2006.

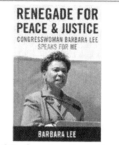

66-2 Barbara Lee Campaign Poster

Lee is of course a major Obama supporter who broke ranks with her Hillary supporting fellow California Democrats to endorse the "Senator from Illinois" in December 2007.

Barack Obama was Alice Palmer's chief-of-staff in mid-90s during her unsuccessful bid for congress. Both joined the COCDS/Democratic Socialists of America (DSA) front New Party at the time, but Obama went on to break with Palmer and run for her former Illinois State Senate seat.

Frank Chapman[400] was the author of a curious letter to the Communist Party USA *Peoples Weekly World* commenting on Obama's historic victory in the Iowa Democratic primary:

> Obama's victory was more than a progressive move; it was a dialectical leap ushering in a new era of struggle. Marx once compared revolutionary struggle with the work of the mole, who sometimes burrows far beneath the ground that he leaves no trace of his movement on the surface. This is the old revolutionary "mole," showing his traces on the surface but also breaking through. (Chapman 2009)

Some old US Peace Council types know Obama and several COCDS types are also close to Obama, it is probable that Prof. Mark Solomon[401] has some insight into Obama's history and political outlook.

Solomon has penned an article, re-produced on the Progressives for Obama (P4O) website - moderated by COCDS leader, former New Party activist and longtime Obama colleague, and supporter Carl Davidson. In

---

[399] http://keywiki.org/index.php/Barbara_Lee
[400] http://keywiki.org/index.php/Frank_Chapman
[401] http://keywiki.org/index.php/Mark_Solomon

the article, Solomon urges his comrades to stay the course with Obama, to build a left wing movement to keep the pressure on the new President and to work for a permanent "progressive majority" in the USA.

Solomon seems in little doubt that Obama is on the side of the "progressives." His article is a blueprint for using Obama's presidency as an opening to move America to the left.

Some extracts with commentary from Trevor Loudon:

> Solomon: Obama's 'Center-Left' Realignment vs. the Right, and our role from below. The election of President Barack H. Obama was historic in innumerable ways. It was a crucial and powerful blow against right-wing reaction, portending a center-left realignment of the nation's politics. Obama's election has opened an emphatic path to progressive change, a path that can lead to deeper, more transforming change. The motor for thoroughgoing progress is the multiracial working class in alliance with a vast array of social forces that worked for Obama's election - youth, African Americans, Latinos, and other people of color, women, and progressive clusters of business and professions.

> The Obama victory reflects changing demographics in every region of the country that is becoming more racially and ethnically diverse. The victory confirms an emerging progressive majority driven largely by a re-energized labor movement - a majority that must become more organized and able to connect the various issues confronting the country into a coherent political force for change. That is decisive for pressing the Obama administration in a more progressive direction. That is the profound challenge before all working people and their allies. (Solomon 2007)

Loudon: "Progressive change" means socialist change. Solomon is calling for a massive socialist movement built around labor unions to keep the momentum going in a leftward direction. Solomon knows that demographics are on the side of the socialists. As the US gets younger and more diverse, Solomon expects the country to become ever more "progressive."

> Solomon: The most significant element for the present and future in Obama's ascension to the presidency is the gathering mass movement that put him in the White House. That movement represents the promise of a permanent progressive majority. It needs to be nurtured, deepened, and strengthened to assure a future of an irreversible path to progress. (Solomon 2007)

Loudon: Note the phrases "permanent progressive majority" and "irreversible path to progress." This is serious stuff. Solomon does not see the reversal of Obama's "opportunity" as another swing of the political pendulum in four or eight years' time. Solomon is exhorting his comrades to work for "permanent" change. If Solomon and his comrades get their way, there will be no going back.

> Solomon: Obama is also no stranger to the symbols and substance of a progressive outlook. As an undergraduate at Occidental College and Columbia University, he became involved in the movement to boycott apartheid South Africa. (Solomon 2007)

Loudon: Interesting that Solomon should mention the Occidental College campaign. The movement refers to the student wing of Tom Hayden's socialist Campaign for Economic Democracy. This in turn links to the radical Cuban/Soviet connected Institute for Policy Studies (IPS). Tom Hayden co-founded Progressives for Obama (P4O) with Carl Davidson, IPS Trustee Barbara Ehrenreich and IPS scholar, Bill Fletcher Jr., in '08.

> Solomon: After winning the nomination, Obama rankled at the assertion that he was now shifting to the center. He ran off a list of progressive measures that he avidly supported - universal health care, fair taxes, and early childhood education...Progressive commentator John Nichols has pointed out that Obama 'knows exactly what it means to say he is a progressive.' That includes understanding the subtle nuances on the left between being called a 'liberal'...and being

> Called a progressive that connotes a principled commitment to social change... Obama's penchant for pragmatic compromises and straddling a line through the center can be traced to important influences on this thought. Obama's three years of community organizing in predominantly black neighborhoods on Chicago's South Side was influenced by famed organizer Saul Alinsky who rejected broad strategic objectives and ideology (including visions of transforming change). Despite much radical posturing, Alinsky perceived a vastly imperfect world that was essentially suitable to cutting deals and compromises with those who hold power... (Solomon 2007)

Figure 66-3 Saul Alinsky

Loudon: It all comes back to Alinsky, who lectured at the IPS back in the '60s.

Solomon: He probably is open to compromises with Russia regarding Bush's push for deployment of an anti-missile system in Central and Eastern Europe. With China, the Obama administration will rhetorically take a hard line on human rights issues; it will complain about the alleged low valuation of Chinese currency, but will not undermine the massive dependence of the collapsing US financial system upon Chinese investment in treasury bonds. He has already advocated the softening (but not the removal) of the repugnant blockade of Cuba. That is a wedge for a coalition of agricultural interests, manufacturers, and peace activists to press for a total lifting of the blockade. (Solomon 2007)

Loudon: This will please Solomon's comrades many of who still have a soft spot for Russia and now look to China as the new leader of the socialist world. Look for a "normalization" of relations with Cuba not far down the track.

Solomon: President Obama's outstretched hand to the Muslim world represents a promising departure from previous US policies. Despite Obama's lavish bows to organizations defending the Israeli occupation of Palestinian lands, and his painful silence as President-elect in the face of the slaughter in Gaza, his appointment of George Mitchell as special envoy to the region (and his apparent rejection of the strongly pro-Israel Dennis Ross) is encouraging...An energized peace movement will need to press its firm opposition to the continuing Israeli occupation of Palestinian lands while calling for and an end to US weapons to Israel as basic requirements in addressing that core issue that lies at the heart of regional tensions. (Solomon 2007)

Loudon: This may not please those who suffer under the illusion that Obama is pro-Israel, but it is music to the ears of the US pro-Palestinian left.

Solomon: There can be no illusion that Obama, without major counter pressures, would depart from the untouchable requirements of the intersecting national security and warfare states, the essential institutions of US imperialism. Given the unchallenged and deeply rooted power of the warfare state and its national security component, he will continue to call for 'rebuilding our military' and advocate selective interventions. Now, it is not possible to occupy White House without obeisance to those institutions. Only a mass movement with a growing grasp of the imperial nature of US global policies and a determination to chart a qualitatively different path can breach that line. Obama's representation of the multilateralist and 'realist' wing of the ruling class offers an opening to an increasingly politically educated public to press for a deeper transformation of US global policies... (Solomon 2007)

Loudon: Solomon is making it clear that Obama will come under tremendous pressure to conform to the status quo. It is therefore imperative that the left must build a mass movement to force Obama to stay true to his socialist ideals.

> Solomon: His willingness to review free trade policies to assure decent labor and environmental standards has earned him crucial support from the union movement. Obama acknowledges the crisis of climate change, advocating large-scale government programs to reduce the use of fossil fuels...By combining urgent environmental and economic issues; Obama has opened a door to a grand alliance of environmental and labor activists. (Solomon 2007)

Loudon: Otherwise known as the "red/green" alliance.

> Solomon: Overriding all domestic considerations is the worldwide economic crisis of unprecedented proportions. The essence of the crisis lies within the capitalist system itself: its exploitation of labor, making it impossible for workers to claim the full fruit of their production - a crucial portion of which is appropriated by capital as profit...Obama has proposed an $825 billion spending program...Leading liberal and progressive economists have stated that at least two trillion dollars in government spending is needed to make a significant dent in unemployment... Despite his present statements, he will have to scale back wasteful and unproductive military spending. (Solomon 2007)

Loudon: Cutting defense spending is a major part of the bailout rationale. Use the "necessity" of massive new social spending as an excuse to slash the defense budget. Remember, this is a former leader of the Soviet controlled World Peace Council talking here.

> Solomon: Many progressives were disappointed with Obama's cabinet appointments...Yet, that disappointment fails to take into account that the Bush neo-conservative cabal is gone; that Obama will be a hands-on President who will guide the policies of his administration...In sum, the center has shifted towards the left. The responsibility of a unified progressive force is to press that center even further leftward as mounting layoffs and spreading economic paralysis worsens. (Solomon 2007)

Loudon: Keep up the pressure comrades. Obama is the boss. He is on our side.

> Solomon: Critical to a positive outcome to the battle is the forging of an effective grass-roots movement. Of great significance is the unprecedented founding of 'Organizing for America' by the Obama organization. Building on a list of over 13 million names and the

experiences of tens of thousands of local organizers, Obama clearly intends to mobilize that huge constituency to press for adoption of his program. That is critically important. But that program falls short of a solidly progressive agenda and compels the left to engage with 'Organizing for Obama' to constructively work for deeper change. (Solomon 2007)

Loudon: "Organizing for America" will become an Obama power base independent of the Democratic Party. The purpose is to help elect more Obama supporters to public office and scare less enthusiastic backers into line. In socialist-speak "engage with" means to "infiltrate." Solomon is advising the left to take over "Organizing for America" and use it as an instrument for socialist change.

Solomon: A united left pole of influence over the Obama movement can oblige it to press for a larger and more working class-oriented stimulus program. The left needs to press for an end to the war in Afghanistan and the occupation of Iraq. It needs to call for an inclusive 'Medicare for All' national health plan. It needs to press Obama to hold firm in support of the Employee Free Choice Act. It must insist on dealing with climate change as a priority; it should press for no loopholes in the ban on torture and prosecution of the crimes of the Bush administration. It needs to vigorously pursue justice for the Palestinians and Palestinian-Israeli peace, it must call for an end to the persecution of immigrants by meeting their just demands with a fair and reliable road to permanent status and citizenship. As the ravages of the Depression spread, the left also has an obligation to advance deeper and more transforming ideas as democratic, public ownership of banks and financial institutions as the way to end the destructive practices of financial capitalism. It can advance the concept of public ownership of energy as the assured way to end the stranglehold of fossil fuels and launch a new era of clean energy. (Solomon 2007)

Loudon: The left wing wish list known as the socialist's agenda for the Obama presidency.

Solomon: In building a progressive majority of left and center, we need a mature, unified left committed to building links to the new, surging movements activated by the Obama phenomenon. We need a movement that integrates seamlessly the triple crises of a collapsing economy (including crises in health care, education housing), climate change and a fruitless, lethal imperial global policy.

The election of President Barack H. Obama is indeed an historic watershed. It holds out the promise of a major realignment of the nation's politics. For the first time in memory, this presidency actually is calling upon a gathering grass roots movement to actively 'make change from the bottom up.' The dangers of the moment are dire. But the opportunities are enormous and compelling.

> Let us seize this moment to end the reign of the right wing and set the country on the road to a progressive, democratic, and peaceful future. (Solomon 2007)

Loudon: Onward, comrades, onward!

67. Communist Leader Claims Obama Considering Nationalization of Finance, Energy, Private Business

Trevor Loudon © Friday, February 06, 2009

The leader of the Communist Party USA claims that the Obama administration is "considering" a radical agenda, which includes nationalizing the US financial system, the Federal Reserve and even certain "problematic" private businesses.

Sam Webb[402] asserts that big defense cuts, expansion of US aid to the underdeveloped world, more "Affirmative Action" for women and ethnic minorities, greater union power, socialization of childcare and healthcare and a

Figure 67-1 Sam Webb Chair Communist Party USA

"massive assault on global warming" are also strong possibilities for the Obama presidency.

In a January 31st speech entitled, *"Off and Running: Opportunity of a Lifetime,"*[403] to party members in Cleveland, Ohio, Communist Party USA National Chairman Webb stated.

The Obama administration and the broad coalition that supports him will almost inevitably have to consider, and they already are, the following measures:

- Public ownership of the financial system and the elimination of the shadow banking system and exotic derivatives.

---

[402] http://keywiki.org/index.php/Sam_Webb
[403] http://www.politicalaffairs.net/article/articleview/8085/

- Public control of the Federal Reserve Bank.
- Counter-crisis spending of a bigger size and scope to invigorate and sustain a full recovery and meet human needs - something that the New Deal never accomplished.
- Strengthening of union rights in order to rebalance the power between labor and capital in the economic and political arenas.
- Trade agreements that have at their core the protection and advancement of international working class interests.
- Equality in conditions of life for racial minorities and women.
- Democratic public takeover of the energy complex as well as a readiness to consider the takeover of other basic industries whose future is problematic in private hands.
- Turning education, childcare and healthcare into "no profit" zones.
- Rerouting investment capital from unproductive investment (military, finance and so forth) to productive investment in a green economy and public infrastructure.
- Changing direction of our nation's foreign policy toward cooperation, disarmament and diplomacy. We can't have threats, guns and military occupations on the one hand and butter, democracy, goodwill and peace on the other.
- Full scale assault on global warming.
- Serious and sustained commitment to assisting the developing countries that are locked in poverty and misery.

Webb went on to claim, "an era of progressive change is within reach, no longer an idle dream."

Webb also said that the "new model of governance wouldn't be

Figure 67-2 Barack Obama and The Unions

socialist, but it would challenge corporate power, profits and prerogatives."

Webb then went on to outline the role of organized labor in ensuring that the Obama administration did not compromise its

agenda.

67-3 President Elect Barack Obama

The old anti-communist US labor movement is no more. Since the mid-1990s, US unions are increasingly dominated by Communist Party USA, their allies in Democratic Socialists of America and veterans of the New Left.

In the meantime, we have some immediate struggles on our hands But the good news is that the broad movement that elected President Obama and larger majorities in the Congress is up and running.

This movement, or if you like, this loose coalition in which labor plays a larger and larger leadership role, can exercise an enormous influence on the political process. Never before has a coalition with breadth walked on the political stage of our country. It is far larger than the coalition that entered the election process a year ago; it's larger still than the coalition that came out of the Democratic Party convention in August.

The task of labor and its allies is to provide energy and leadership to this wide-ranging coalition. Yes, we can bring issues and positions into the political process that go beyond the initiatives of the Obama administration. However, we should do this within the framework of the main task of supporting Obama's program of action.

We can disagree with the Obama administration without being disagreeable. Our tone should be respectful. We now have not simply a friend, but a people's advocate in the White House. (Webb, Off and Running: Opportunity of a Lifetime 2009)

Webb finishes off with a list of missions for his troops that includes supporting Obama's nomination for Labor Secretary, Hilda Solis. Is it coincidental that Solis won her election to Congress with Communist Party support and enjoys close ties to Democratic Socialists of America?

Of course, change will not be easy. The pressures to weaken, even mothball, progressive, anti-corporate measures will come from many quarters.

That said, the opportunities for working class and people's gains are extraordinary. This is a once in a lifetime opportunity.

Starring us in the face are some immediate challenges.

We have to support the passage of the President's stimulus bill in the Senate.

We have to block any Republican efforts to derail the nomination of US Representative Hilda Solis (D-CA-32nd District) , the nominee for the Secretary of Labor. This is the first round in the battle to pass the EFCA. Some may think this is a struggle of only the labor movement. Nevertheless, nothing could be further from the truth. A bigger labor movement in this country would strengthen the struggle on every front.

We have to join others in resisting evictions and foreclosures - not to mention cutbacks and layoffs at the state and city level.

Ending the wars of occupation in Iraq and Afghanistan is a top priority.

In any case, we have our work cut out for us. However, I think we can confidently say that change is coming. In addition, we will build a perfect union.

Yes, We Can! (Webb, Off and Running: Opportunity of a Lifetime 2009)

Damn right, they can.

Some enterprising journalist needs to ask Sam Webb this important question: "How do you know what the Obama administration is considering?"

68. Obama, Antonio Villaraigosa and the Harry Bridges Connection

Trevor Loudon © Wednesday, March 04, 2009

After winning the November 2008 election, President elect Barack Obama appointed Los Angeles Mayor Antonio Villaraigoza to his Transition Economic Advisory Board.

Formerly Hillary Clinton's campaign co-Chair, the Mayor Antonio Villaraigoza appointment was seen as a unifying move, a nod to Clinton Democrats, to Latino voters and to Los Angeles, California and the West Coast.

It was even more than that. It was a gesture of solidarity with the California left, second to Chicago as a crucible of the "people's movement" that brought Obama to power.

It was a salute to a man whose rise to power in many ways paralleled Obama's own.

Obama was born in Hawaii in 1961, Tony Villar was born in Los Angeles in 1953.

Frank Marshall Davis, a writer and Communist Party member who had moved from Chicago to Hawaii in 1948, mentored Obama as a teenager. Davis was close to the communist controlled International Longshore Workers Union (ILWU) that dominated Hawaiian politics for decades. Davis was close to ILWU head, San Francisco based secret party member, Harry Bridges. When contemplating moving to Hawaii, Davis wrote to Harry Bridges, "whom I had met at Lincoln School. Bridges suggested I get in touch with Koji Ariyoshi, editor of the *Honolulu Record*.

The Chicago Communist Party ran the Lincoln School. Koji Ariyoshi was a leader of the Hawaiian party, which controlled the ILWU, affiliated Honolulu Record, where Davis worked.

Australian born Harry Bridges was a longtime leader of the ILWU. The US government fought for years to deport Bridges for his ties to the Communist Party that Bridges would never admit.

The Communist Party front Committee for Protection of Foreign Born (CFPFB) spent considerable time and money keeping Bridges in the US.

Years later it was revealed that Bridges was not only a party

68-1 President Elect Obama (r) and Mayor of Los Angeles Antonio Villaraigosa

68-2 MECHA leader Tony Villa (c. 1974)

68-3 Frank Marshall Davis

member, but served on the party's powerful Central Committee.[404]

Antonio Villaraigoza and Obama grew up without a father and both went off the rails as teens. Obama straightened himself out to study law.

Antonio Villaraigoza has a long friendship with serving California state Senator Gilbert Cedillo - who is a close associate of Obama's new Labor Secretary; Communist Party linked US Secretary of Labor Hilda Solis (D-CA-32nd District):[405]

> Gilbert Cedillo met Villaraigoza at Roosevelt High, and they became close friends.

> Through an Upward Bound program, Cedillo was accepted at U.C.L.A.; Villaraigoza went to East Los Angeles College and then transferred to U.C.L.A... They both became active in Movimiento Estudiantil Chicano de Aztlán , a campus Chicano-rights group. And both attended the Peoples College of Law, a night school dedicated to producing public-interest lawyers. (Villaraigoza took the bar exam four times, but never passed.) (Bruck 2007)

Movimiento Estudiantil Chicano de Aztlán (MECHA) is a radical Chicano separatist group with a strong Marxist-Leninist underpinning.

> Peoples College of Law was founded in 1974, by the Asian Law Collective, the La Raza National Lawyers Association (LRNLA), the National Conference of Black Lawyers (NCBL), and the National Lawyers Guild (NLG). (Bruck 2007)

The NLG was for decades associated with the Communist Party.

> Villaraigoza visited Cuba with the Venceremos Brigade, a radical group. And he and Cedillo became involved in Centros de Acción Social Autónomo, or CASA, an immigrant's-rights organization led by the Mexican-American labor activist Bert Corona, and worked on its newspaper, Sín Fronteras. "At CASA, we wanted to organize the undocumented into unions, instead of seeing them as a threat," Cedillo said. (Bruck 2007)

Activists, many of whom would later join the terrorist Weather

---

[404] http://97.74.65.51/readArticle.aspx?ARTID=5188
[405] http://keywiki.org/index.php/Hilda_Solis

Underground (WUO),[406] founded the Venceremos Brigades in the 1960s. Later it became (and remains) a Communist Party operation and still sends an annual quota to Cuba to harvest sugar cane and at least in the past, undergo terrorist training.

Bert Corona,[407] who died in 2001, was an icon of the California left. Most sources claim that Corona never joined the Communist Party, but did work with party members and fronts for many years.

68-4 Bert Corona

Other sources claim he was indeed a Communist Party member, at least for a time in the 1940s.

During the 1940's, Bert Corona was an organizer for the International Longshoreman's and Warehouseman Union (ILWU)[408] and identified in Congressional testimony[409] as a Communist Party USA member inside that union.

That is right, Frank Marshall Davis' favorite union, the ILWU. How long Corona remained in the Communist Party is unclear, but there is no doubt that Corona was close to Harry Bridges.[410]

> Corona came to Los Angeles to study at the University of Southern California, where he went to work and was caught up in the labor ferment of the late 1930s. He became President of Local 26 of the International Longshore and Warehouse Union, and a political ally of Harry Bridges, one of US labor's most progressive and democratic leaders. (Bacon 2001)

After Corona was fired from his ILWU position union over an internal dispute, Harry Bridges, also a major figure within the communist dominated Congress of Industrial Organizations (CIO), offered Corona a job as a CIO organizer.

President elect Barack Obama and Antonio Villaraigoza have a common benefactor in Harry Bridges. Had Bridges not helped Frank

---

[406] http://keywiki.org/index.php/WUO
[407] http://keywiki.org/index.php/Bert_Corona
[408] http://keywiki.org/index.php/International_Longshore_and_Warehouse_Union
[409] http://www.knology.net/~bilrum/RedTide.htm
[410] http://keywiki.org/index.php/Harry_Bridges

Marshall Davis and Bert Corona back in the 1940s, Obama and Villaraigoza might not hold the positions they do today.

I wonder if that thought ever occurred to them as they sat across a table planning America's future.

69. The Communists, Obama and the Cesar Chavez Holiday Campaign

Trevor Loudon © Thursday, March 05, 2009

For several years, a leading Communist Party USA activist has been campaigning to honor the memory of late Chicano Farm Workers Union leader Cesar Chavez with a national holiday.

The campaign has already been successful in California:[411]

On August 18, the state of California recognized that legacy when Governor Gray Davis signed into law the creation of an official state holiday, which will be celebrated starting in 2001 on Cesar Chavez's birthday March 31st. Also established will be a Cesar Chavez day of learning and Service in the state's public schools where the state's youth will be taught about Cesar and his union. (Alarcon, Cesar E. Chavez: The Farm Worker Leader honored with a California Legal Holiday 2000)

However, the campaign is working to extend the holiday nationwide:[412]

69-1 Campaign Director Evelina Alarcon

The mission of Cesar E. Chavez National Holiday, a public benefit organization, is to work for national recognition of Cesar E. Chavez on his birthday March 31. We are forming national, state and local coalitions; organizing volunteer committees; and providing education about the value to our nation of honoring Cesar E. Chavez. (Alarcon, Cesar E. Chavez: The Farm Worker Leader honored with a California Legal Holiday 2000)

---

[411] http://www.cesarchavezholiday.org/aboutcesarechavez.html
[412] http://www.cesarchavezholiday.org/aboutus.html

The campaign's director is Californian based activist, Evelina Alarcon. She held several senior positions in the Communist Party USA,[413] including Chair of the party's Southern California District and Secretary of its National Mexican American Equality Commission.

Alarcon views the Chavez campaign as a communist campaign with the potential to build the party's influence:[414]

> If someone would have asked me one year ago, "Can my District really lead thousands?" I probably would of hesitated. But today, I say "yes," because a few comrades in my district are literally leading a movement of thousands in California for the Cesar Chavez holiday. We are a key part of the core of leaders who are coordinating the whole campaign...
>
> Our participation has opened many formerly closed doors. The California leaders who agreed to my being the public leader and state coordinator of the Cesar Chavez holiday campaign are prominent statewide and even national leaders. Most of them know that I am a Communist. Has this built the Party's influence? Yes. Has it built the Party's credibility? Yes. Is it opening new doors to us in other areas of labor and people's movements? Yes. (Alarcon, On the Work of Districts and Clubs 2001)

Evelina Alarcon was over the moon in April 2008 when no less a figure than Democratic Presidential primary candidate Senator Barack Obama came out in support of a Cesar Chavez Holiday.

From the Chavez website:[415]

> April 1, 2008 Washington DC–Evelina Alarcon, Executive Director of Cesar E. Chavez National Holiday welcomed the backing for a Cesar Chavez national holiday from Presidential candidate Senator Barack Obama who issued a statement on Cesar Chavez's birthday Monday, March 31, 2008.
>
> "We at Cesar E. Chavez National Holiday appreciate the backing of a national holiday for Cesar Chavez from Presidential candidate Senator Barack Obama. That support is crucial because it takes the signature of a President to establish the holiday along with the Congress's approval,"

---

[413] http://keywiki.org/index.php/Communist_Party_USA
[414] http://www.Communist Partyusa.org/on-the-work-of-districts-and-clubs/
[415] http://www.cesarchavezholiday.org/

stated Evelina Alarcon. (Alarcon, Cesar E. Chavez: The Farm Worker Leader honored with a California Legal Holiday 2000)

Several others in Obama's circle are also big Cesar Chavez fans, including Los Angeles Mayor and appointee to Obama's Transition Economic Advisory Board, Antonio Villaraigosa, who endorses the national holiday campaign.

Villaraigosa marched with Chavez as a teenager and worked for Chavez's friend and colleague, leading Southern California Communist Party member Bert Corona.

69-2 Bert Corona and Cesar Chavez, 1968

Villaraigosa is a close friend[416] of both Evelina Alarcon and her brother Los Angeles Councilman Richard Alarcon.

According to the Communist Party's June 20, 1996 "Peoples Weekly World":

The Southern California Friends of the People's Weekly World tribute to two of Los Angeles' finest labor leaders, Jerry Acosta and Gilbert Cedillo, became a dynamic rally of elected officials, activists, labor and community leaders in solidarity with labor struggles and in the fight to defeat the ultra-right in November.

69-3 Evelina Alarcon declares Barack Obama will make Cesar Chavez's birthday a national holiday.

"The People's Weekly World and all of us in this room feel strongly about whom we honor today," said Evelina Alarcon, Chair of the Southern California District and national secretary of the Communist Party USA, one of the emcees of the tribute...

State Assemblyman Antonio Villaraigoza sent a message and 17 elected officials and more than 50 labor leaders put their names in the program book honoring Cedillo and Acosta...

Presentations to the honorees were also made by...Antonio Aguilar, on behalf of State Senator Hilda Solis, California's first Latina elected to the State Senate... (Alarcon, Evelina Alarcon 2009)

Hilda Solis is now Obama's Labor Secretary and a Cesar Chavez

[416] http://www.mayorno.com/villar.html

admirer. When still in the US Congress, Solis sponsored House Resolution 76[417] that urged the establishment and observation of a legal public holiday in honor of Cesar Chavez.

69-4 Barack Obama's younger sister Dr. Maya Soetoro-Ng

Not content with Presidential candidate Obama's support, Evelina Alarcon went after another member of the Obama family, Barack Obama's younger sister, Maya Soetoro-Ng.

Addressing a largely Latino audience in East Los Angeles yesterday, Dr. Maya Soetoro-Ng shared stories about her childhood with her older brother, Barack Obama, and the effect he has had on her life. Held in El Sereno's Hecho en Mexico restaurant, the event drew more than a hundred enthusiastic community activists, local elected officials, and regular citizens...

Designed to draw support to her brother's Presidential candidacy from two key voting blocs, women and Latinos:

Evelina Alarcon, a notable Obama supporter and the sister of long-time Los Angeles politician Richard Alarcon, presented a poster to Obama's sister commemorating the life of Cesar Chavez.

Figure 69-5 Evelina Alarcon with Soetoro-Ng

Alarcon recounted the accomplishments of the late Chicano leader and argued persuasively for honoring his accomplishments with a national holiday. Reminding those in attendance, that Barack Obama supports the call to make Cesar Chavez's birthday a national holiday. Alarcon trusts that if Obama is elected President the holiday will become a reality.

Obama has been quoted recently to say: "As Farmworkers and laborers across America continue to struggle for fair treatment and fair wages, we find strength in what Cesar Chavez accomplished so many years ago and we should honor him for what he's taught us about making America a stronger, more just, and more prosperous nation.

That is why I support the call to make Cesar Chavez's birthday a national holiday. It's time to recognize the contributions of this American icon to the ongoing efforts to perfect our union." (Kyle and Price 2008)

---

[417] http://www.cesarchavezholiday.org/abouttheholiday.html

The anniversary of Cesar Chavez's birthday is March 31.

It will be interesting to see what President Obama does to progress "notable Obama supporter" Evelina Alarcon's goal of a Cesar Chavez national holiday.

70. Obama's Socialist Attack Hounds to "Block" Blue Dog Democrats

Trevor Loudon © Saturday, March 28, 2009

President Obama's leftist base is rallying to support his upcoming first budget.

With opposition to Obama's massive spending spree growing, the US left is mobilizing to neutralize both Republican and moderate Democratic Party opposition.

Obama's far left allies are targeting moderate "Blue Dog" Democrats in order to force them into line.

70-1 Blue Dog Democrats Targeted by the Left

From the Communist Party USA's *People's World*:[418]

President Obama appealed to the people to throw their support behind his first federal budget to help pull the country out of the deep economic crisis. Speaking at his second White House news conference the President said the $3.5 trillion Fiscal Year 2010 budget "is going to need the support of the American people," adding that it is "inseparable" from his economic recovery program.

He defended the billions allocated for green, renewable forms of energy, for health care, and education... He renewed his call for tax cuts for middle-income families and higher taxes on the wealthy. He called for elimination of wasteful spending on Medicare and in military procurement. (Webb, Pass the Budget! Grassroots Coalition Demands Action 2009)

Obama's base groups together represent most of the leftist mass organizations which helped push him over the line last November.

---

[418] http://www.peoplesworld.org/pass-the-budget-grassroots-coalition-demands-action/

A coalition of 100 organizations initiated by Americans United for Change was already answering Obama's appeal, launching a grassroots campaign to push through Obama's budget in the face of stubborn opposition by the Republican right and a handful of Blue Dog Democrats. (Webb, Pass the Budget! Grassroots Coalition Demands Action 2009)

The coalition includes the AFL-CIO and many of its affiliated unions, ACORN, SEIU, US Catholic Conference, the YMCA and YWCA, NAA, Communist Party and dozens more organizations with tens of millions of members.

Organizing for America, with more than 14 million people who helped elect Obama in its database, launched a door-to-door campaign on March 21 in support of the budget. MoveOn has scheduled a similar effort.

Behind many of these organizations lie the hard red core of the Obama movement - specifically Democratic Socialists of America, Communist Party USA and the ultra-left Washington based "think tank" Institute for Policy Studies.

The *Peoples Weekly World* went on to say:

Robert Baronage, co-Chair of the Campaign for America's Future and William McNary, President of US Action announced a grassroots campaign to pressure Blue Dog Democrats to vote for Obama's budget. Eight of these Democrats joined with Republicans in opposing efforts to win passage of a Budget Resolution that included the $684 billion health care fund and tens of billions more for Obama's green energy program. It requires only a simple majority of 51 senators to pass a Budget Resolution so it is not subject to a Republican filibuster that requires 60 senators' votes to end.

Borosage accused Blue Dog Democrats led by US Senator Evan Bayh (D-IN) (D-Ind.) and US Senator Kent Conrad (D-ND) of "giving away the store." (Webb, Pass the budget! Grassroots coalition demands action)

"If they feel a little heat at home they may see the light in Washington," he said.

McNary said 50,000 members of US Action in the Blue Dogs' districts will mobilize.

"The people voted for change last November," he said. "We cannot allow senators to get cold feet or become unwitting accomplices of those who don't want change." (Webb, Pass the Budget! Grassroots Coalition Demands Action 2009)

Robert Borosage

Robert Borosage[419] is an influential leftist in America. According to Discover the Networks Borosage[420] is:

> A former New Left radical and onetime Director of the Institute for Policy Studies (IPS), Robert Borosage co-founded (with Roger Hickey) both the Campaign for America's Future and the Institute for America's Future. He also founded and currently Chairs the Progressive Majority Political Action Committee, the activist arm of a political networking organization whose aim is to help elect as many leftist political leaders as possible...

> From 1979 to 1988 Borosage was Director of the Institute for Policy Studies. In 1988 he left IPS to work on Jesse Jackson's Presidential campaign, for which he served as a speechwriter and an assistant in framing responses to policy issues.
>
> Borosage also has worked for political figures as Senators Paul Simon (D-IL), US Senator Barbara Boxer (D-CA), and US Senator Carol Moseley-Braun (D-IL). (Horowitz, Robert Borosage 2009)

70-2 Robert Borosage

Wellstone, Boxer and Moseley-Braun were all far leftists. Moseley-Braun in particular was the product of the same Chicago communist/socialist coalition that produced Barack Obama.

Borosage remains at the Institute for Policy Studies[421] alongside leading Democratic Socialists of America member and Progressives for Obama (P40) founder Barbara Ehrenreich.

Institute for Policy Studies has links to Communist Party USA and is close to Democratic Socialists of America. It also has a long history of links to communist intelligence Services and third world revolutionary movements.

IPS is a key component of the Obama machine.

---

[419] http://keywiki.org/index.php/Robert_Borosage
[420] http://www.discoverthenetworks.org/individualProfile.asp?indid=1170
[421] http://www.ips-dc.org/about/trustees

William McNary

William McNary is a long time Obama friend, colleague and advisor. He was also a Democratic Party delegate for Obama at the Democrats 2008 convention in Denver, Colorado. McNary is also close to Democratic Socialists of America.

An article in the January/February 2009[422] "*International Socialist Review*" covered the US anti-war coalition, United for Peace & Justice (UFPJ), national convention in Chicago December 12-14, 2008.

The article's socialist authors complained that UFPJ (controlled by Democratic Socialists of America (DSA), Communist Party USA and Committees for Correspondence for Democracy and Socialism) had neglected the anti-War movement in favor of electoral politics.

70-3 William McNary (l) receives an award at 2005 Chicago DSA dinner

While the US continues to occupy Iraq and is planning a major escalation of forces in Afghanistan and Pakistan. The conference drew only 248 attendees, fewer than at its convention last year. Such a low turnout should come as no surprise; UFPJ has not called a major national antiwar demonstration in close to two years and has invested the bulk of its resources either directly or indirectly into campaigning for the Democratic Party. A low turnout should come as no surprise; UFPJ has not called a major national antiwar demonstration in close to two years and has invested direct or indirect resources into campaigning for the Democratic Party.

The key question facing United for Peace & Justice (UFPJ) and indeed the entire antiwar movement is how to deal with the new challenges and opportunities under the incoming administration of President-elect Barack Obama. At the convention, a majority of UFPJ's leadership and featured speakers argued that the antiwar movement should credit itself for helping get Obama elected and should be encouraged that the peace/antiwar movement had an ally in the White House.

"We have elected the most progressive mainstream politician imaginable," declared William McNary, President of US Action/True

[422] http://www.isreview.org/issues/63/rep-antiwar.shtml

Majority, at the opening plenary. McNary went on to describe Obama as our "quarterback" and that the movement's task is to "block for" him. (Marable 2008)

The football analogy is apt: Obama is the ball carrier for American socialism.

The job of the left is blocking all opposition, so that Obama can score touchdown after touchdown for Team Left with as little opposition as possible.

Even if that means "blocking" some of the President's own Democratic Party teammates.

71. Former Terrorist Mark Rudd, Assesses Obama's Progress

Trevor Loudon © Saturday, April 04, 2009

Former Weather Underground terrorist leader Mark Rudd has passed judgment on the merits of the Obama administration.

So far, he is happy.

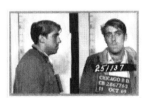

71-1 Mark Rudd

71-2 Tom Hayden (l) Mark Rudd (r)

Now an Albuquer-que algebra teacher and member of the Democratic Party in New Mexico, Rudd is a cog in President Obama's mighty machine.

More than that though, Mark Rudd is a leader of Movement for a Democratic Society (MDS), a grouping of former Weather Underground leaders and senior Communist Party USA, Democratic Socialists of America and Committees of Correspondence for Democracy and Socialism activists - the backbone of the Obama movement.

Several "Movement for a Democratic Society leaders, including Bill Ayers, Bernardine Dorhn, Carl Davidson and Rashid Khalidi know Barack Obama. Several Movement for a Democratic Society leaders including Tom Hayden, Bill Fletcher Jr., Barbara Ehrenreich and Carl Davidson were involved in setting up Progressives for Obama (P4O) an organization tasked with uniting the far left behind the Obama campaign and presidency. Rudd himself is a Progressive for Obama supporter alongside several other Movement for a Democratic Society activists - many of them socialists, communists or former terrorists.

Mark Rudd evaluated the Obama presidency in an interview with Movement for a Democratic Society Board member, anarchist and former communist Thomas Good, in *"Next Left Notes,"*[423] a Movement for a Democratic Society linked website.

He mixes paranoia with astute observation and the occasional lie.

Mark Rudd "knows" Obama and as a key part of the movement that elected the President, his words have "credibility."

Tom Good: What do you think of Obama so far?

> Mark Rudd: I think he has acted in an extremely predictable way, knowing what we already know about him. He is cautious and strategic. He knows that there is no mandate yet for abrupt shifts to the left. I think he is trying to work toward improvement on the economy, healthcare, education, and Israel. On Afghanistan, no. He knows that the biggest internal enemy is the military-industrial-security complex, and he is not going to give them the excuse to organize to defeat him (as they defeated Kennedy). I know that the official left position is that JFK was a cold-warrior, no different from any others, but I've been reading "Brothers," by David Talbot, a good journalist who makes a compelling case that the military and CIA loathed President John F. Kennedy and conspired to kill him. Since Obama is not a leftist (thank God), he isn't hampered by our prejudices. I am sure he believes that Kennedy was killed by the military and CIA. JFK had zero control over both. They rarely carried out his orders. (Good 2009)

Tom Good: What do you make of his appointments?

> Mark Rudd: All terrible at the top level, except maybe Hillary Clinton, whom I'm expecting to win a Nobel prize for forcing the Israelis to accept a settlement. Who but the nation's #1 shiksa, a certified lover of Israel, would the rightwing accept to force the settlement? That was a strategic appointment. All the others are strategic in the same way-giving the right the top positions. The trick is to look at the next level, where Podesta put center-leftists, predominantly. He learned from Cheney.

---

[423] http://antiauthoritarian.net/NLN/?p=577

Actually, the director of CIA, Panetta, a center-leftist, probably gave them conniptions. (A fit of violent emotion, as anger or panic - New Zeal). (Good 2009)

Tom Good: What is your view of the Ayers bashing[424] that started with the election and is ongoing?

Mark Rudd: Obama has almost no chinks in his armor. The right has few ways in, and they are so stupid that they do not realize that the Ayers business has zero traction outside their own circles. Do not ever underestimate the far right's utter stupidity. Rudd praises Obama's deceptive tactics. In an earlier assessment Rudd called this "feinting right, moving left" appeasing the military while moving left on other issues. Try to appear moderate while filling your administration with second tier leftists from John Podesta's Center for American Progress (CAP) the ultra-left Institute for Policy Studies.(CIA director "center-leftist" Leon Panetta also has some history with IPS, as do several of Rudd's Movement for a Democratic Society comrades including Bill Ayers, Tom Hayden, Bill Fletcher Jr, Barbara Ehrenreich, Manning Marable, Paul Buhle, and Ethelbert Miller. (Good 2009)

71-3 Bill Ayers

Rudd's prescription for Israel is a forced settlement that will bring "peace." Using Hillary Clinton is "tactical." Hillary, a supposed friend of Israel will be used to destroy Israel's capacity to defend itself.

It seems that President Obama is living up to Mark Rudd's hopes and expectations.

72. Obama Appoints "Former" Communist to White House "Green Job"

Trevor Loudon © Monday, April 06, 2009

A few short years ago, Anthony (Van) Jones was a Bay Area radical agitator - a committed Marxist-Leninist-Maoist, waging war on the police and capitalist system.

---

[424] http://newzeal.blogspottrevorloudon.com/2009/03/report-on-washington-press-conference.html/

Anthony (Van) Jones

Van Jones held a key position in the US government and has the ear of President Barack H. Obama.

The White House Council on Environmental Quality (CEQ) Chair Nancy Sutley announced yesterday that Van Jones - an early green job will start Monday as Special Advisor for Green Jobs, Enterprise and Innovation at CEQ:

72-1 Van Jones mixes with the cream of the left establishment

Van Jones has been a strong voice for green jobs, we look forward to having him work with departments, and agencies to advance the President's agenda of creating 21st century jobs that improve energy efficiency and utilize renewable resources. Jones will also help to shape and advance the Administration's energy and climate initiatives with a specific interest in improvements and opportunities for vulnerable communities

Jones is the founder of Green for All, an organization focused on creating green jobs in impoverished areas. He is also the co-founder of the Ella Baker Center for Human Rights and Color of Change, and was the author of the 2008 New York Times best-seller, The Green Collar Economy (The White House 2009)

Today, Van Jones mixes not with street level militants, but with the cream of the left "establishment."

Who is Van Jones?[425] In addition, has he really abandoned his communist beliefs? Van Jones first moved to San Francisco in the spring of 1992 while studying law at Yale, when the leftist Lawyers Committee for Human Rights hired several law students to act as legal observers during the trial of police officers charged with assaulting Rodney King.

Not guilty verdicts in the King case led to mass rioting -which Jones joined. Arrested and jailed, Van Jones met a completely new circle of friends.

"I met all these young radical people of color - I mean really radical, communists, and anarchists. And it was, like, 'This is what I need to be a

---

[425] http://keywiki.org/index.php/Van_Jones

72-2 STORM logo

part of... I spent the next ten years of my life working with a lot of those people I met in jail, trying to be a revolutionary...I was a rowdy nationalist on April 28th, and then the verdicts came down on April 29th..By August, I was a communist." (Strickland 2005)

The communist organization Van Jones went on to lead is Standing Together to Organize a Revolutionary Movement (STORM).[426]

According to the leftist blog Machete 48:

> Van Jones, with all the shimmer associated with a rising star, many forget that a man now advising the President was a member of a revolutionary organization in the San Francisco Bay Area called STORM. Throughout the group's history, Van Jones was a public figure within the Bay Area left and a leading member of STORM.

72-3 Van Jones right, "interacting" with San Francisco police.

72-4 Jones supporting International ANSWER, a front for the pro North Korean Workers World Party

> Founded in 1994, STORM had its roots in a grouping of people of color organizing against the Gulf War in the '90's and was. The group's politics had a number of influences, but evolved towards third world Marxism (and an often-vulgar Maoism). The group grew in influence until its disbanding in 2002 amid problems of internal dynamics and controversy around the leadership roles that members played in the youth movement (such as the fight against Proposition 21). The entire membership of the organization was staff members for various social movement non-profits in the Bay Area, many linked to the Ella Baker Center, which Van Jones steered. (Rebel-PWCM-JLA 2009)

While never large, STORM was

---

[426] http://keywiki.org/index.php/STORM

influential and active radical groups in the Bay Area, controlling numerous front organizations including Bay Area Police Watch, one of several anti-police activities Jones was involved in.

Other STORM fronts included a Marxist training organization - School of Unity and Liberation (SOUL) and an unemployed rights group - People Organized to Win Employment Rights (POWER).

Jones and STORM were also active in the anti-Iraq War demonstrations in the early 2000s.

While way out on the left, STORM also worked with "mainstream" communists.

Betita Martinez

Bay Area left identity Elizabeth "Betita" Martinez was close to Jones and helped "mentor" his Ella J. Baker Human Rights Center.

Martinez was a long time Maoist who went on to join the Communist Party USA breakaway organization

72-6 Betita Martinez

Committees of Correspondence for Democracy and Socialism (COCDS) in the '90s.

Martinez still serves on the COCDS advisory Board[427] alongside radicals such as Angela Davis, Timuel Black (a personal friend of Barack Obama who served on his 2004 Senate campaign committee) and musician Pete Seeger (who performed at Obama's Washington Inauguration Concert).

Martinez is also a Board member[428] of Movement for a Democratic Society, the radical parent body of Progressives for Obama (P4O).

Martinez and Jones worked together on several projects including attending a Challenging White Supremacy Workshop,[429] which much impressed Jones:

---

[427] http://www.cc-ds.org/advisory_bd.html

[428] http://antiauthoritarian.net/NLN/?p=179

[429] http://www.cwsworkshop.org/workshops/argj.html

"To solve the new century's mounting social and environmental problems, people of color activist and white activists need to be able to join forces. But all too often, the unconscious racism of white activists stands in the way of any effective, worthwhile collaboration. The Challenging White Supremacy Workshop is the most powerful tool that I have seen for removing the barriers to true partnerships between people of color and white folks. If the CWS trainings were mandatory for all white activists, the progressive movement in the United States would be unstoppable." (V. Jones 2009)

They also both worked together with another STORM member, Adam Gold, on the organizing committee[430] for anti-Iraq War newspaper *War Times*.

STORM also had ties to the South African Communist Party with three "core" comrades attending the South African Communist Party Congress in 1998.

Amilcar Cabral

Figure 72-7 Amilcar Cabral

STORM also much admired[431] Amilcar Cabral, the late revolutionary leader of Guinea-Bissau and the Cape Verde Islands.

STORM may have learned about Amilcar Cabral, from the South African Communist Party, which also revered him.

A tribute to Cabral from the Communist Party's *African Communist*, No. 53, second quarter 1973:[432]

"How is it that we, a people deprived of everything, living in dire straits, manage to wage our struggle and win successes? Our answer is: this is because Lenin existed, because he fulfilled his duty as a man, a revolutionary, and a patriot. Lenin was and continues to be, the greatest champion of the national liberation of the peoples." (Cabral)

These were the words addressed to the delegates attending the seminar on "Lenin and National Liberation" held at Alma Ata, capital of

---

[430] http://www.ratical.org/co-globalize/wartimes.html
[431] http://www.leftspot.com/blog/files/docs/STORMSummation.pdf
[432] http://www.saCommunist Party.org.za/docs/history/dadoo-19.html

Soviet Socialist Republic of Kazakhstan, in 1970. The delegates addressed by Amilcar Cabral, Secretary-General of the PAIGC, who met his death on 20th January 1973 at Conakry, Guinea, at the hands of a traitor, Innocenta Canida, an agent of the Portuguese colonialists who had infiltrated into the ranks of the movement three years ago.

These words reflect the revolutionary thinking and life work of this dedicated patriot, outstanding African revolutionary of our time and the father of the new independent sovereign State of Guinea in the process of birth. It was the cognition of the scientific theory of revolution, of Marxism-Leninism, contacts with the Portuguese Communist Party during his student days in Lisbon. They introduced him to combine within him, in the words of the statement of the Central Committee of the South African Communist Party, "a deep understanding of the processes of the African revolution with an untiring devotion to practical struggle." (Lenin and National Liberation 1970)

Van Jones has named his three-year-old son Cabral in honor of his hero. Jones reportedly uses a quote from Cabral in every email[433] he sends:

"Hide nothing from the masses of our people. Tell no lies. Expose lies whenever they are told. Mask no difficulties, mistakes, failures. Claim no easy victories. . . . Our experience has shown us that in the general framework of daily struggle this battle against ourselves, this struggle against our own weaknesses . . . is the most difficult of all." (Cabral 2009)

Is Van Jones living up to that quote?

Is Van Jones hiding "nothing from the masses of our people?"

73. Weather Alert! Obama's "Green Jobs" Czar Linked to Former Terrorist Supporters?

Trevor Loudon © Wednesday, April 08, 2009

During last year's Presidential election, Senator Barack Obama was quizzed over his connections to former Weather Underground terrorists Bill Ayers and Bernardine Dorhn.

---

[433] http://americanpowerblog.blogspot.com/2009/08/van-jones-revolutionary-communist-in.html

73-1 Barack Obama promoting his friend Bill Ayers

Obama tried to downplay the significance of his ties to the radical couple and told America that their crimes occurred when he was "eight years old."

Now it turns out that Van Jones, President Obama's appointed "Green Jobs" Czar (Special Advisor for Green Jobs, Enterprise and Innovation at the White House Council on Environmental Quality) may also have Weather Underground influence in his background.

While Jones is even younger than Obama, the connections may still have serious security implications.

73-2 Van Jones

Van Jones was, until around 2002, a leader of a Bay Area communist sect, Standing Together to Organize a Revolutionary Movement (STORM). It seems that Jones was linked to or influenced, to some degree, by two former Weather Underground supporters, Bay Area activists, Jon and Nancy Frappier.

Furthermore, Jones was for several years linked to another Bay Area activist, Diana Frappier - related to Jon and Nancy Frappier.

Bay Area lawyer Diana Frappier has been a leftist activist since she was at university in the '90s. While not an identified member of STORM, Frappier worked within the organization's "orbit" for several years. Jones and Frappier ran anti-police organization Cop Watch and in 1996, set up the Oakland California based Ella Baker Center for Human Rights.[434]

Diana has supported the organization's growth from a small-scale operation of one full-time staff member into a grassroots powerhouse. While she is not focused on the Ella Baker Center for Human Rights, she

---

[434] http://www.ellabakercenter.org/page.php?pageid=45

is operating a private community criminal defense practice and serving on the Boards of Bay Area non-profits Machen Center and Together United Recommitted Forever (TURF). This San Francisco native is also a real estate broker, supporting activists and other members of her community to empower themselves through homeownership.

73-3 Diana Frappier

The Ella Baker Center was named after little known civil rights fire brand Ella J. Baker (1903/1986). Baker worked with communists for years including secret party member Stanley Levison[435] for many years, the Communist Party's top money man.

73-4 Nancy Frappier

Why did Van Jones and Diana Frappier name their center after Ella J. Baker?

Here is one possible reason.

By the 1970s, Ella Baker was involved with several far left organizations of the time including the Mass Party Organizing Committee and the Puerto Rican Support Committee. Both groups were close to the Prairie Fire Organizing Committee (PFOC), the "legal" support network for the Weather Underground.

73-5 Ella J. Baker (1903-1986)

Prairie Fire Organizing Committee, led by Bernardine Dohrn's sister Jennifer, organized a large gathering conference in January 1976 in Chicago. The "Hard Times" conference was designed by the Weather Underground to unite the US far left into a new Communist Party.

---

[435] http://www.theatlantic.com/doc/200207/garrow

Invited were The Black Panthers, the Socialist Workers Party, the Workers World Party, the Marxist-Leninist Puerto Rican Socialist Party, the Puerto Rican Support Group and the Mass Party Organizing Committee.

There is a partial list of Hard Times attendees from the 1982 book on the *Weather Underground Outlaws of Amerika*[436] (p33).

Persons Identified as Attending the National Hard Times Conference
January 30-February 1, 1976
(spelling based on phonetics)

Ellen Afterman, PFOC, Chicago
Danny Albert
Miguel Alvarez
Rosa Alvarez
Robert Appel, PFOC
Ella J. Baker, MPOC & PRSC
Joe Barnett, PFOC, Calif.
Nancy Barnett (Frappier), Bay Area PFOC
Dick Becker, WWP
Alan Berkman, N.Y. PFOC
*Vernon Bellecourt, AIM
Arlene Eisen Bergman, Bay Area PFOC
Barbara Bishop, San Francisco

Dennis Cunningham, NLG, Chicago
Jim Dannon, Philadelphia PFOC
Ruth Dear, WWP
Nick DeFreitas, WWP
Mike Deutsch, NLG, Chicago PFOC
*Jennifer Dohrn, PFOC National Committee
Kathy Dorsey, CLUW, N.Y.
Ted Dostal, WWP
David Duboff, Center for Defense Information, D.C.
Kevin Duncan
Deb Dunfield, United Steelworkers

73-6 National Hard Times Conference Attendees

The names Jennifer Dohrn, Prairie Fire Organizing National Committee, Ella J. Baker Mass Party Organizing Committee, Puerto Rican Support Committee and Nancy Barnett (Frappier) Bay Area Prairie Fire Organizing Committee.

Note the names: Jennifer Dohrn PFOC National Committee, Ella J. Baker MPOC & PRSC and Nancy Barnett (Frappier) Bay Area PFOC.

Is this the connection?

Nancy Frappier may have been more

73-7 Nancy Frappier

than the Prairie Fire Organizing Committee. According to the FBI's Weather Underground file, she was associated with many WUO members and her car was parked outside the Weathermen's December 1969, *"War Council"* at Flint,

---

436 http://www.usasurvival.org/docs/Outlaws_Of_Amerika.pdf

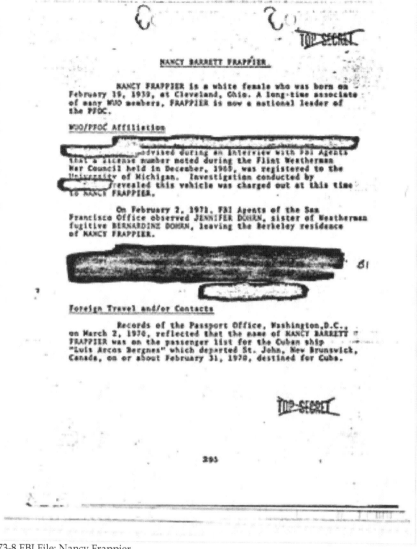

73-8 FBI File: Nancy Frappier

Michigan. In 1971, the FBI also observed Jennifer Dohrn visiting Frappier's home in San Francisco.

The FBI also suspected that Nancy Frappier travelled to Cuba in February 1970.

Today Nancy Frappier works in health Services in the Bay Area. Both Diana and Nancy Frappier donate to the Berkeley YMCA.

Jon Frappier was also close to the Weathermen. Frappier's FBI

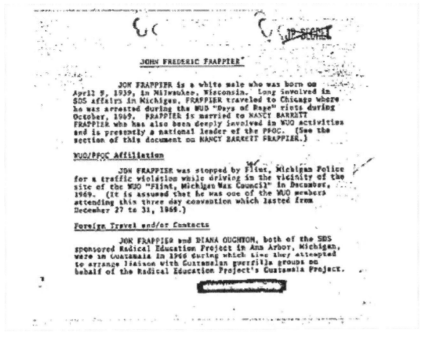

JOHN FREDERIC FRAPPIER

JON FRAPPIER is a white male who was born on April 5, 1939, in Milwaukee, Wisconsin. Long involved in SDS affairs in Michigan. FRAPPIER traveled to Chicago where he was arrested during the WUO "Days of Rage" riots during October, 1969. FRAPPIER is married to NANCY BARRETT FRAPPIER who has also been deeply involved in WUO activities and is presently a national leader of the PFOC. (See the section of this document on NANCY BARRETT FRAPPIER.)

WUO/PFOC Affiliation

JON FRAPPIER was stopped by Flint, Michigan Police for a traffic violation while driving in the vicinity of the site of the WUO "Flint, Michigan War Council" in December, 1969. (It is assumed that he was one of the WUO members attending this three day convention which lasted from December 27 to 31, 1969.)

Foreign Travel and/or Contacts

JON FRAPPIER and DIANA OUGHTON, both of the SDS sponsored Radical Education Project in Ann Arbor, Michigan, were in Guatemala in 1966 during which time they attempted to arrange liaison with Guatemalan guerrilla groups on behalf of the Radical Education Project's Guatemala Project.

73-9 FBI File: John Frederic Frappier

profile claims that he was arrested during the Weathermen's "Days of Rage" rioting in October 1969 in Chicago and that he was also issued a traffic ticket near the 1969 Michigan "War Council."

The FBI also alleges that Frappier travelled to Guatemala in 1966 with future Weather Underground member (and Bill Ayers's late girlfriend) Diana Oughton. The pair was accused of trying to contact Guatemalan guerillas for the Students for a Democratic Society (SDS) Radical Education Project.

John Frappier went on to run the San Francisco office of the North American Congress on Latin America (NACLA), a creation of the Weather Underground's parent organization Students for a Democratic Society (SDS).

According to the website *La Nueva Cuba*:

> North American Congress on Latin America (NACLA) was formed in 1967 after the Tricontinental Congress in Havana by individuals associated with Students for a Democratic Society(SDS). NACLA said it was recruiting "men and women, from a variety of organizations and movements, who not only favor revolutionary change in Latin America, but also take a revolutionary position toward their own society." Students

Data Center
Impact research for social justice

for a Democratic Society leader called NACLA the "intelligence gathering arm" of the radical movement. NACLA's published Methodology Guide recommends supplementing public source information by pretext interviews and phone calls, and NACLA has also planted or developed covert sources in government agencies and private companies...

Particular targets for NACLA information gathering include companies supplying arms, anti-terrorist, and police equipment to Latin America and Mexico; US government defense, counter-insurgent, and anti-terrorist programs; and oil, agribusiness, minerals and other US companies with major Latin American operations. (Cereijo 2006)

In the British edition of *Inside the Company: CIA Diary*, CIA agent turned Cuban intelligence ally Philip Agee admitted that Cuban government agents and Communist Party officials provided "special assistance and data available only from government documentation" and that NACLA staff "obtained vital research materials in New York and Washington, DC."

After North American Congress on Latin America (NACLA), Jon Frappier went on to establish an organization that has become the intelligence hub of the US left.

The Oakland based DataCenter[437], a "national progressive non-profit that provides strategic information & research training to communities advocating for dignity, justice & civil rights." (Data Center Research for Justice)

1977 - DataCenter-an activist library and publication center-is founded in affiliation with the North American Congress on Latin America (NACLA) by Jon Frappier, Fred Goff, Loretta & Harry Strharsky and 40 dedicated volunteers. Further DataCenter activities included;

1979 - Establish Corporate Profile Project for clients as United Nations Centre on Transnational Corporations & customized research Service for

---

[437] http://www.datacenter.org/

immigration attorneys representing Central Americans seeking political asylum.

1980 - Publish press profiles, The Reagan File, on Ronald Reagan and his policies on labor, El Salvador, foreign policy, and military policy in Asia.

1981 - New Right Project tracks the rise of neo-conservatism; launch Right-to-know Project in response to censorship & growing restrictions on access to information; Monitor plant closures and layoffs; Publish press profile Toxic Nightmare for free distribution to leading environmental organizations

1983 - Expand Search Service to include corporate accountability research to support community, labor, and corporate campaigns and political asylees from all over the world. (Data Center 2009)

The Data Center admits to being an information gatherer for Cuban "institutions."

1991 Launch the Cuba Project/Conexiones to respond to information needs of institutions in Cuba & facilitates information exchange between US and Cuban colleagues for the next ten years. (Data Center 2009)

Does that sound scary?

The Data Center also supports Van Jones and Diana Frappier's Ella Baker Center for Human Rights.

2002 Celebrate our 25th Anniversary with a gala celebration honoring Youth United for Community Action, Southwest Organizing Project, and Ella Baker Center for Human Rights and Youth Force Coalition for their Books Not Bars campaign; (Data Center 2009)

Jon Frappier now runs a Northern California security and investigation company, which leads into this story.[438]

Rag Blog contributor Michael D. Nolan recounts a recent trip to Cuba and being guided around the Island by Coqui (Pedro Enrique) Salazar.

"Now 65, Coqui had a full mane of wavy black hair. As a young man, he fought with Castro in the mountains outside his native Guantanamo...a member of the student movement in Havana working to overthrow the Batista regime." (Nolan 2009)

---

[438] http://theragblog.blogspot.com/2009/04/cuban-revolutionary-and-cuban-exile.html

73-10 The Green Jobs Mob

It turns out that "Coqui" has a brother living in the US. Michael D. Nolan offers to help track down the long lost Pedro Salazar.

> I sent a message to Jon Frappier, a detective friend in California, asking if he would search for a Pedro Salazar, or Pedro Eusebio Salazar, or Peter E. Salazar, living in northern California and born in the late 1950s...

> Several days after our return to San Francisco, Jon came to my house. I cleared the paper clutter on the yellow Formica kitchen table so he could spread out lists generated by his online investigation. Among them was a Pedro E. Salazar, born in 1957, living on 21st Street in San Francisco with a phone number. We both agreed it was good bet. (Nolan 2009)

Sure enough, the brothers are united. Jon Frappier got to make a Cuban family happy.

What makes this significant is that the *Rag Blog* is associated with Movement for a Democratic Society (MDS) - which is the "adult" support group for the re-established Students for a Democratic Society.

Movement for a Democratic Society activists include Van Jones' colleague Betita Martinez and several Students for a Democratic Society veterans including former Obama educational colleagues Carl Davidson and Mike Klonsky, plus several former leaders of the Weather

73-11 Green for All

Underground including Bill Ayers, Bernardine Dohrn, Jeff Jones and Mark Rudd.

Rudd and another former Weather Underground member Marilyn Buck[439] are listed as *Rag Blog* contributors. Buck blogs from jail – Federal Corrections Institution (FCI) Dublin in California, where she is serving an 80-year sentence for her role bombing, the Capitol.

Movement for a Democratic Society is also the parent body of Progressives for Obama (P40).

In 2005, Van Jones and Diana Frappier launched the Ella Baker Center's Green - Collar Jobs Campaign. This led to the establishment of the US' first "*Green Jobs Corps*" in Oakland.

In 2007, Van Jones announced a new national organization *Green for All*[440] to take the Green Jobs campaign nationwide.

Diana Frappier[441] serves on the board of Green for All. Jon and Nancy Frappier[442] are listed as donors to the organization.

[439] http://en.wikipedia.org/wiki/Marilyn_Buck
[440] http://www.greenforall.org/
[441] http://keywiki.org/index.php/Diana_Frappier
[442] http://keywiki.org/index.php/Nancy_Frappier

Waking the Sleeping Giant!

I fear all we have done is to awaken a sleeping giant and fill him with a terrible resolve. (Yamamoto)

74. Communists Honor Obama's Former Pastor – Connecting the Dots

Trevor Loudon © Saturday, April 25, 2009

When the pressure came on during last year's Presidential primaries, Senator Barack Obama dropped his pastor and spiritual mentor of twenty years like a hot potato.

While Senator Obama regarded Rev. Jeremiah Wright as a major liability, the now retired pastor still has some friends in Chicago.

Figure 74-1 Barack Obama (l) and Rev. Jeremiah Wright

On April 18, the National Alliance Against Racial and Political Repression (NAARPR)[443] awarded former Rev. Jeremiah Wright its highest honor.

According to a report from the Communist Party USA's *People's World*:[444]

> Human Rights awards were granted to honorees at the event whose work includes ending the death penalty, overturning wrongful convictions, the fight against racism and efforts to help victims of the prison industrial complex. The honorees included:

> Patricia Hill, executive director of the African American Police League; Jane Raley, senior staff attorney with the Northwestern Law School; Judith Stuart, an anti-prison activist; Rev. Jeremiah Wright, retired Pastor with the Trinity United Church of Christ; Karen Yarbrough, Illinois state representative. (A. Davis 2009)

Jane Raley is a colleague at Northwestern Law School of Bernardine Dohrn; Obama's friend and former neighbor.

---

[443]
http://keywiki.org/index.php/National_Alliance_Against_Racist_and_Political_Repression

[444] http://www.peoplesworld.org/angela-davis-not-another-prison/

74-2 Campaign Propaganda

Karen Yarbrough is an Obama supporter who "shares the philosophy" of Obama and US Representative Danny K. Davis (who happens to be a member of Democratic Socialists of America and has close ties to Communist Party USA.)

What is the National Alliance against Racist and Political Repression NAARPR[445] and why does it matter that it should honor a man who helped shape the views of the world's most powerful politician?

What can a study of NAARPR tell us about Senator Barack Obama?

Dr. Barbara Ransby, a professor in the African American Studies Department at the University of Illinois at Chicago, emceed the award ceremony.

Figure 74-3 Dr. Barbara Ransby

"As activists we're always protesting what we're against, but tonight we are celebrating people who are long distance runners in this struggle," said Ransby. "Tonight we're here to seek inspiration and highlight the fight to forge lasting change," she said. Ransby also noted the historic election of President Barack Obama last November was a detrimental blow to racism in this country. (A. Davis 2009)

Barbara Ransby attended Columbia University in New York from 1980 to 1984. Barack Obama was there from 1981 to 1983, while his Chicago friend, former Weather Underground terrorist Bill Ayers (husband of Bernardine Dohrn), studied at nearby Bank Street College of Education during the same period.

Years later, Barbara Ransby was a founder of the Black Radical Congress:[446]

> On June tenth, 1998, on the campus of the University of Illinois at

> Chicago more than 1,000 Black radicals - activists, scholars, and artists will gather to reflect on our collective past, analyze our contemporary reality and explore strategies and visions for the future...We will also celebrate the long and rich tradition of Black resistance from Frederick Douglass and Harriet Tubman to Paul Robeson, Malcolm X, Ella Baker and Audre Lorde.
>
> Participants came as individuals but represented connections to groups ranging from New Afrikan People's Organization, Black Workers for Justice, The Labor Party, The Communist Party, The Malcolm X Grassroots Movement, African American Agenda 2000, The Chicago Ida B. Wells Forum and the Committees of Correspondence. (Ransby 1998)

Add the Democratic Socialists of America to that list. A "Call for the Congress" drafted and issued with the names of over 100 conveners. The following participants endorsed the call and participated in the process:

- Abdul Alkalimat
- Bill Fletcher, Jr.
- Manning Marable
- Leith Mullings
- Barbara Ransby

---

[446] http://www.hartford-hwp.com/archives/45a/228.html

- Barbara Smith
- Cornel West
- Salim Muwakkil
- Charlene Mitchell
- Angela Y. Davis
- Amiri and Amina Baraka
- Sonia Sanchez
- Sam Anderson
- Evelynn Hammonds
- Julianne Malveaux
- Jarvis Tyner
- General Baker
- Ahmed Obafemi
- Cathy Cohen
- Robin D. G. Kelley
- and many others

Jarvis Tyner[447] and Amiri Baraka were Communist Party members. Manning Marable, Charlene Mitchell and Angela Y. Davis were from the

74-4 MDS Board Feb 2007: Mark Rudd (far l), Charlene Mitchell (c w/checker jacket), Manning Marable (to Charlene's l) and Jeff Jones (2d from r)

Communist Party offshoot Committees of Correspondence, while Bill Fletcher and Cornel West represented Democratic Socialists of America (DSA).

Marable, Mitchell, Davis, Fletcher, West, Barbara Ransby and Robin Kelley would all re-unite in 2007 when they joined the Board of Movement For A Democratic Society (MDS) an alliance of Communist Party USA, Committees of Correspondence and Democratic Socialists of America (DSA) with key founders of the Weather Underground including Mark Rudd, Jeff Jones, Bernardine Dohrn and Bill Ayers.

---

[447] http://keywiki.org/index.php/Jarvis_Tyner

In 2008, several Movement for a Democratic Society Board members, including Bill Fletcher, went on to found Progressives for Obama (P40).[448]

> What makes Obama different is that he has also been a community organizer. He has read left literature, including my works, and he understands what socialism is. A lot of the people working with him are, indeed, socialists with backgrounds in the Communist Party or as independent Marxists. There are a lot of people like that in Chicago who have worked with him for years. (D. M. Marable 2008)

In April 2002, a conference was held at the University of Illinois Intellectuals: *Who Needs Them*.[449]

Panel IV. Intellectuals in Times of Crisis featuring:

- William Ayers – (UIC, College of Education; author of *Fugitive Days*)
- Douglass Cassel – (North-western University, Centre for International Human Rights)
- Cathy Cohen - (University of Chicago, Political Science)
- Salim Muwakkil – (Chicago Tribune; In These Times)
- Barack Obama – (Illinois State Senator)
- Barbara Ransby - (UIC, African-American Studies (moderator))

Salim Muwakkil, Cathy Cohen and Ransby were all leading founders of the Black Radical Congress. Ayers, Obama and Ransby were all former New Yorkers.

Panel I. Why Do Ideas Matter? Featuring:

- Timuel Black - (Chicago activist; Prof. Emeritus, City Colleges of Chicago)
- Lonnie Bunch - (President, Chicago Historical Society)
- Bernardine Dohrn - (North-western University Law School, Children and Family Justice Centre)
- Gerald Graff - (UIC, College of Liberal Arts & Sciences)
- Richard Rorty - (Stanford University, Philosophy)

The late Richard Rorty was a member of Democratic Socialists of America (DSA)'s Religion & Socialism Commission. Black, a personal friend of Senator Barack Obama, is a Democratic Socialists of America

---

[448] http://keywiki.org/index.php/Progressives_for_Obama
[449] http://www.uic.edu/classes/las/las400/conferencealt.htm

74-5 Program Announcement

(DSA) supporter and serves on the Committees of Correspondence advisory Board with Movement for a Democratic Society Board members Angela Davis, Manning Marable, Noam Chomsky and Ella J. Baker Human Rights Center supporter Elizabeth "Betita" Martinez.[450]

In 2004, Bernardine Dohrn[451] wrote a glowing review of Barbara Ransby's book *"Ella Baker and the Black Freedom Movement: A Radical Democratic Vision."*

Ella Baker was close to the Weather Underground in the mid-70s. She was also the inspiration for the Oakland based Ella J. Baker Human Rights Center, founded by Obama's appointed "Green Jobs" advisor Van Jones, who in turn is linked to former Weather Underground supporters Jon and Nancy Frappier.

Van Jones also attended the 1998 Black Radical Congress, while still a leader of the communist organization Standing Together to Organize a Revolutionary Movement (STORM). In fact, Van Jones, Angela Davis and Nelson Peery paired up younger activists,[452] Kim Diehl, Kim Springer, Fanon Che Wilkins, Kashim Funny and Quraysh Ali Lansana, respectively.

Even Barack Obama's spiritual guide Rev. Jeremiah Wright participated in the Black Radical Congress. One session at the Congress was entitled:

> Faith as a Weapon: Spirituality and the Role of the Church in the Radical Movement. What are the lessons we can learn from Nat Turner, Absalom Jones, Sojourner Truth, Malcolm X, Martin Luther King Jr. and other Black ministers as leaders in the struggle? What is the history of spiritual motivation in the radical/liberation movement? (Wright 2009)

---

[450] http://keywiki.org/index.php/Elizabeth_Martinez
[451] http://www.monthlyreview.org/0104dohrn.htm
[452] http://www.hartford-hwp.com/archives/45a/230.html

Panelists:

- Michael Eric Dyson
- Cornel West
- Rev. Jeremiah Wright
- Linda Thomas
- Kevin Tyson

74-6 Cornel West (l), Michael Eric Dyson (r)

Kevin Tyson was a leader of the Communist Party's youth wings: the Young Worker's Liberation League. Dyson and West were both active in Democratic Socialists of America (DSA)'s Religion & Socialism Commission.[453]

In 2008, Senator Barack Obama appointed Cornel West to his two members Black Advisory Council.

Angela Davis was keynote speaker at the Chicago NAARPR awards ceremony:

> "The election of Obama was a millennium transformation, and
> we're in a new historical conjunction in 2009," noted Davis. "In a short period of time so much has changed," she said.

> Given the current economy there is a serious crisis erupting in the capitalist system, said Davis. "Many assume Obama is going to save capitalism, but a lot of us here have other ideas about changing the system," said Davis. (A. Davis 2009)

Figure 74-7 Angela Davis

People's Weekly World correspondent Pepe Lozano[454] went on to explain about Angela Davis' background:

> Davis came to national attention in 1969, when she was removed from her teaching position at UCLA as a result of her social activism and her membership in the Communist Party USA. In 1970, she was placed on the FBI's Ten Most Wanted List on false charges of murder, kidnapping, and conspiracy. During her 16-month incarceration, a massive

---

[453] http://www.religioussocialism.com/
[454] http://newzeal.blogspot.com/2008/02/obama-file-16-obama-and-legacy-of.html
Chapter 16 - Barack Obama and the Legacy of Harold Washington

international "Free Angela Davis" campaign was organized, leading to her acquittal in 1972. (A. Davis 2009)

Davis' lawyer was Haywood Burns, founder of the "legal arm of the black revolution," the National Conference of Black Lawyers, an affiliate of the Soviet front International Association of Democratic Lawyers.

Burns had close ties to Cuba and was involved in several other communist fronts including the National Lawyers Guild, Center for Constitutional Rights and the Emergency Civil Liberties Committee.

After defending Angela Davis, Burns went on to marry Jennifer Dohrn, sister and supporter of terrorist Bernardine Dohrn.

The organizations formed to support Angela Davis also founded National Alliance Against Racial and Political Repression (NAARPR). Communist Party members and supporters including Davis herself,

74-8 Wedding notice Jennifer Dohrn to marry Haywood Burns

Charlene Mitchell, Anne Braden and Frank Chapman led it.

By the '80s, Frank Chapman led NAARPR and represented the

organization in another Communist Party front, the US Peace Council.

Chapman served on the Peace Council executive board alongside several party members, including future US Representative Barbara Jean Lee (D-CA-9th) and Chicago activist Alice Palmer.

Later a Democratic Illinois State Senator, Alice Palmer employed Barack Obama as her chief of staff. When considering relinquishing her State Senate seat to run for US Congress, Palmer chose Obama to succeed her. She introduced her aide to the Chicago left, starting with a gathering at the home of Bill Ayers and Bernardine Dohrn. Also in attendance were the Obama family's doctor and friend, Democratic Socialists of America (DSA) member and former communist Dr. Quentin Young.

When Palmer lost her Congressional bid, Obama refused to stand aside and got her disqualified from the ballot on a technicality. Palmer's friend, Timuel Black, was called in to mediate and ended up becoming an Obama supporter. Black even joined Obama's campaign committee during his 2004 US Senate race.

74-10 New Party colleagues Danny Davis and Barack Obama

Before the Palmer-Obama relationship collapsed, both joined the Chicago branch of the New Party. The New Party was an alliance of Democratic Socialists of America (DSA), Committees of Correspondence and the radical community organization ACORN.

The New Party led by familiar names as Manning Marable, Bill Fletcher Jr., Cornel West, Noam Chomsky and Quentin Young.

The New Party was designed to gather left wing support for "progressives" standing on the Democratic Party ticket. In Chicago, Obama worked with New Party activist Carl Davidson (a Committees of Correspondence leader, Progressives for Obama (P40) founder and longtime friend of Bill Ayers) and Democratic Socialists of America (DSA) member Representative Danny K. Davis.

Figure 74-11 NAARPR's strongest branch is in Chicago

74-9 Obama and Quentin Young, 2003

The Communist Party USA leader, Ted Pearson, is the Chair of NAARPR. Ted is a leader of the Committees of Correspondence and a supporter of Progressives for Obama (P40).

National Alliance Against Racial and Political Repression (NAARPR), Treasurer is Norman Roth, once also a leading member of the Chicago Communist Party.

In the 1970s, Roth was a leader of the Communist Party front

Alliance to End Repression with comrades Abe Feinglass, Jack Spiegel and Jesse Prosten.

Other radicals active in the Alliance included Dr. Quentin Young, Timuel Black and Obama friend and across the street neighbor, the late Rabbi Arnold Jacob Wolf, another member of Democratic Socialists of America (DSA)'s Religion & Socialism Commission.

Another leading Alliance member was journalist Don Rose who, with another former communist David Canter, went on to mentor Obama campaign manager and White House advisor David Axelrod.

Rose, Canter and Axelrod all played leading roles in the 1983 election of Chicago's first black Mayor Harold Washington. Democratic Socialists of America (DSA) and the Communist Party both backed Washington, creating a movement that later fell in behind Barack Obama.

Washington's victory inspired Barack Obama to first move to Chicago in 1983.

David Canter and Don Rose worked with Carl Davidson to organize the famous 2002 Chicago peace rally where Obama first achieved fame as an opponent of the Iraq War.

In January 2008, former National Alliance Against Racial and Political Repression (NAARPR) leader Frank Chapman wrote an intriguing letter to the *People's Weekly World:*

Figure 74-12 David Canter with Harold Washington

Now, beyond all the optimism I was capable of mustering, Mr. Obama won Iowa! He won in a political arena 95 percent white. It was a resounding defeat for the manipulations of the ultra-right and their right-liberal fellow travelers. In addition, it was a hard lesson for liberals who underestimated the political fury of the masses in these troubled times.

Obama's victory was more than a progressive move; it was a dialectical leap ushering in a qualitatively new era of struggle. Marx once compared revolutionary struggle with the work of the mole, which sometimes burrows so far beneath the ground that he leaves no trace of his movement on the surface. This is the old revolutionary "mole," not only showing his traces on the surface but also breaking through. (Chapman, Is Barack Obama a Marxist Mole? 2008)

I am inclined to agree with Frank Chapman. What about you?

75. American Rights at Work. Obama's Socialist Labor "Commissars"

Trevor Loudon © Thursday, April 30, 2009

Control of organized labor is a key component of the Obama administration's power plan.

The Communist Party[455] quoted President Obama as saying:

> "I do not view the labor movement as part of the problem. To me, it's part of the solution." (The White House)

Obama wants to unify the labor movement under a centralized socialist leadership, answerable to him.

This will provide President Obama and the Democrats with money and armies of loyal foot soldiers for their battles with the Republicans, "disloyal" Dems and non-compliant businesses.

It will also enable Obama to neutralize resistance to amnesty and citizenship for more than 10 million illegal workers currently in the US - which will almost certainly lock in millions of extra votes for Obama and the Democrats.

One organization, American Rights at Work (ARW),[456] has served as a key transmission belt from Obama to the labor movement. It is now

75-1 Obama and the Union control of the Rank and File

[455] http://www.pww.org/article/view/14378
[456] http://www.americanrightsatwork.org/

becoming Obama's key control mechanism over the union movement.

American Rights at Work (ARW) has strong ties to Obama's old friends: Democratic Socialists of America, the ultra-left "think tank" Institute for Policy Studies (infamous in the '70s and '80s for its reported links to Soviet and Cuban intelligence Services and one of the US' largest mosques.)

Here is a "who's who" of key American Rights at Work personnel.

US Representative David Bonior (D-MI-17th District)

US Representative David Bonior, ARW President, was a confirmed Democratic Socialists of America (DSA) member at its 10th annual Debs Dinner in December 2008.

According to Talking Union:

US Representative David Bonior served in Congress for 26 years rising through the leadership to become the Democratic Caucus Whip. During his tenure in Congress, Bonior fought to raise the minimum wage, protect pensions, support unions, and extend unemployment benefits. He led the fight to oppose NAFTA in 1993. He worked to prevent war in Central America in the 1980s and again to prevent the Iraq War in 2002. After leaving Congress, Bonior co-founded American Rights at Work, a labor advocacy and research organization, which has made passage of the Employee Free Choice Act its major legislative priority. Bonior was recently appointed to the Obama economic team. (Green 2008)

75-2 US Representative David Bonior

Bonior was touted as a likely Obama Labor Secretary,[457] but withdrew his name from contention. Obama then delegated Bonior to broker a re-unification of the US labor movement, bringing the Change To Win grouping and the AFL-CIO back together under one banner.

According to RBO:

The New York Time's David Greenhouse reported that, on January 7, the union Presidents first met with Bonior, a member of Obama's

---

[457] http://www.mnrem.org/news/2008/12/2/bonior-considered-for-labor-secretary

economic transition team...Bonior helped "arrange and oversee" the meeting.

The union Presidents issued their joint call after the transition team for President-elect Barack Obama signaled that it would prefer dealing with a united movement, than a fractured one that often had two competing voices. (Elliott 2009)

In 2002, Bonior and two other Democratic Congressmen Jim McDermott and Mike Thompson traveled to Iraq on a fact finding mission. Iraqi intelligence funded the trip through a Michigan based Muslim group headed by Muthanna Al-Hanooti.[458]

US Representative David Bonior   75-3 Congressmen visit Sadam Hussein (D-MI-17th District)[459] also has Institute for Policy Studies (IPS) connections.

Representative David E. Bonior (D-Michigan), House Democratic Whip, presented the 1997 Letelier-Moffitt Memorial Human Rights Domestic Award to Carlos and Alicia Marentes from Sin Fronteras, during a joyful and moving ceremony held at the historic Lincoln Theatre in Washington, D.C., on Saturday September 27, 1997. The Institute for Policy Studies (IPS}... organizes this event to honor the memory of Orlando Letelier and Ronni Karpen Moffitt, who were murdered in 1976, when a bomb exploded in their car near Sheridan Circle in Washington, D.C. Letelier, a former Chilean ambassador to the Unites States and Moffitt were at that time working in the IPS. (Marentes and Marentes)

Letelier reportedly was an agent for the Cuban intelligence.[460]

Hilda Solis

[458] http://www.investigativeproject.org/628/exclusive-photos-show-al-hanootis-political-clout
[459] http://www.farmworkers.org/let-mofi.html
[460] http://www.heritage.org/Research/Reports/1979/11/Latin-American-Terrorism-The-Cuban-Connection

75-4 Barack Obama (l) Hilda Solis (r)

Until her appointment as Obama's Labor Secretary, Solis was a California Congress woman and ARW Treasurer. US Rep. Hilda Solis (D-CA-32nd District) has ties to DSA, the Socialist International and Communist Party. She travelled to Cuba, "purpose not disclosed," in April 2001 sponsored by the radical William C. Velasquez Institute,[461] to the tune of $1,214.50.

Mary Beth Maxwell

75-5 Mary Beth Maxwell

Mary Beth Maxwell was a potential candidate to serve as Obama Labor Secretary. Maxwell was ARW executive director until recently appointed as a senior adviser to Labor Secretary Hilda Solis.[462] Prior to her 5 years at ARW, Maxwell was National Field Director for Jobs with Justice,[463] the IPS organization known for employing DSA and Communist Party USA activists.[464]

Julian Bond

75-6 Julian Bond (l) Barack Obama (r)

Julian Bond serves on the American Rights to Work (ARW), Board of Directors and is a long serving Chairperson of the NAACP, and is a veteran of the Communist Party/Students for a Democratic Society (SDS) that organized the Venceremos Brigades to Cuba. In the late 1970s, Bond was Vice President of the Democratic Socialist Organizing Committee - predecessor of Democratic Socialists of America (DSA). Bond was honored at Chicago Democratic Socialists of America (DSA)'s 1993 Debs Dinner.[465] In November 2006, Bond returned to Cuba "to take a first-hand look at the

[461] http://www.legistorm.com/trip/1903.html
[462] http://blogs.wsj.com/washwire/2008/12/02/union-activist-mary-beth-maxwell-on-list-for-labor-secretary/
[463] http://www.ips-dc.org/about/partners
[464] http://www.ips-dc.org/about/partners
[465] http://www.chicagodsa.org/ngarchive/ng30.html

island's health system and especially to find out about the Latin American Medical School (ELAM) and its 90 US students." During the 1970s, Bond was an occasional lecturer at IPS and a Board member of the IPS spin-off Institute of Southern Studies.

Carl Pope

Carl Pope is on the ARW Board of Directors and the Executive Director of the Sierra Club. In 1966, Pope was active in Students for a Democratic Society (SDS) protests at Harvard University.[466] Pope is a Board member of the green/labor coalition, the Apollo Alliance[467] with Democratic Socialists of America (DSA) member Gerry Hudson and IPS Trustee and former director Robert Borosage. Pope also works with another former Apollo Alliance member, Van Jones. A "former" revolutionary communist, Jones worked with Hilda Solis as a "green jobs" advisor to President Obama. In

75-7 Carl Pope (l) and Van Jones (r)

September 2007, Pope addressed an IPS organized Teach In,[468] Confronting the Global Triple Crisis at George Washington University.

Wade Henderson

Wade Henderson is on the American Rights to Work (ARW) Board of Directors and is President of the Leadership Conference on Civil Rights, a coalition of some 200 organizations. Henderson was presented the IPS' 2007 Letelier-Moffitt human rights award for his anti-Iraq War stance. Wade Henderson, the President of the Leadership Conference on Civil Rights, described the domestic award winner Appeal for Redress as "a democratic movement within the military" calling for an immediate US withdrawal from the war in Iraq. The organization is composed of more than 2,000 active duty Service members, war veterans and military families and "has rapidly

75-8 Wade Henderson

---

[466] http://bravenation.com/jones_pope.php
[467] http://apolloalliance.org/about/board/
[468] http://www.ifg.org/events/Triple_Crisis_Speakers.pdf

become the most influential force within the US armed Services to challenge the US occupation of Iraq," according to IPS.

Harley Shaiken

Harley Shaiken is a Director on the ARW Board and is director of the Center for Latin American Studies at the University of California, Berkeley. Shaiken is a leading anti-globalization activist and advocate for relaxing US sanctions against Cuba.

Shaiken has worked closely on "disarmament, economic conversion and economic democracy"[469] with IPS founder Marcus Raskin and IPS scholar and Democratic Socialists of America (DSA) member Noam Chomsky.

Shaiken also has close ties to US Representative David Bonior:[470]

Seventy people attended the eighth annual Douglass- Debs Dinner held at UAW Local 600 in Dearborn on Saturday, November 18th.(2006).

75-9 Harley Shaiken

The dinner is the major fundraising event each year for Detroit Democratic Socialists of America (DSA). The keynote speaker was globalization expert Harley Shaiken who gave a chilling description of the consequences of corporate globalization as well as some suggestions as to how progressive activists fight this phenomenon.

Shaiken was also widely touted as a potential Obama Labor Secretary.[471]

Imam Sayed Hassan Al Qazwini

Imam Sayed Hassan Al Qazwini serves on the ARW Board of Directors and is leader of the Dearborn, Michigan (US Representative David Bonior's old congressional district) based Islamic Center of America (ICOA) and founder of the Young Muslim Association. Born in Karbala, Iraq, Qazwini's family moved

75-10 Imam Sayed Hassan Al Qazwini (l) Barack Obama (r)

---

[469] http://en.wikipedia.org/wiki/Seymour_Melman
[470] http://kincaidsite.com/dsa/nl-archive.html
[471] http://www.dailykos.com/story/2008/12/17/22306/238/983/674307

to Iran after the 1979 Islamic Revolution. After a religious education in Iran, Qazwini followed his family to the US in 1992.

According to Discover the Networks:

On November 15, 1998, Qazwini's Islamic Center of America sponsored an event – attended by more than 1,000 primarily Arab Muslim-Americans – where the featured speaker was Nation of Islam leader Louis Farrakhan. Qazwini and his fellow organizers introduced Farrakhan as "our dear brother," "a freedom fighter," and "a man of courage and sacrifice." (Qazwini)

According to political journalist Debbie Schlussel, Qazwini professes to oppose al Qaeda but nonetheless maintains a close affiliation with the Iranian government of Mahmoud Ahmadinejad Qazwini is friendly with Hezbollah spiritual leader Sheikh Mohammed Hussein Fadlallah, who issued the 1983 fatwa that resulted in the bombing of the US Marine barracks in Beirut, which killed 241 American Service members; and, openly supports both Hamas and Hezbollah. Qazwini met with then Presidential candidate Senator Barack Obama.[472]

Imam Hassan Qazwini, head of the Islamic Center of America, said in an email that he met with Obama at Macomb Community College. A mosque spokesman, Eide Alawan, confirmed that the meeting took place. During the meeting, the two discussed the Presidential election, the Arab-Israeli conflict, and the Iraq War, according to Qazwini.

At the end of the meeting, Qazwini said he gave Obama a copy of new book, "American Crescent," and invited Obama to visit his center.

The meeting with Obama came about after Qazwini had asked David Bonior, the former US Rep. from Michigan, if he could meet with Obama during his visit. Qazwini was not selected to be part of a group of 20 people who met with Obama, but Qazwini later got a private meeting with Obama, Alawan said.

"They gave him an opportunity for a one-on-one," Alawan said. (Schlussel 2008)

---

[472] http://alqazwini.org/qazwini_org/news/news_page/news_051408.htm

75-11 John Sweeney,
President, AFL-CIO

John Sweeney

John Sweeney is President of the US' largest labor federation the AFL-CIO and serves on the ARW Board of Directors. Sweeney joined Democratic Socialists of America (DSA) around 1995 before becoming AFL-CIO President. Sweeney soon reversed the ban on Communist Party members holding office in AFL-CIO affiliated unions. Sweeney now heads a federation almost dominated by communists, socialists and former "new lefters." Sweeney is also a member of the powerful Trilateral Commission and enjoys close ties to IPS, even honoring Brazil's Marxist President "Lula" on their behalf.

> September 23, 2003, 27th annual Letelier-Moffitt Memorial Human Rights Awards, The Institute for Policy Studies invites you to celebrate the legacy of Orlando Letelier & Ronni Karpen Moffitt; and, Tuesday, September 23, 2003, The Organization of American States, 6 pm Reception / 7 pm Dinner and Human Rights Program, International Award Recipient: Nancy Sanchez Mendez, Presented by Representative Jan Schakowsky (D-IL-9th District), Special Recognition Award: Luiz Inácio Lula da Silva, President of Brazil, Presented by John Sweeney, President, AFL-CIO (Cavanagh 2005)

There are several clear threads running through American Rights at Work - pro-Cuba, anti-Iraq War, pro-Democratic Socialists of America (DSA) and pro-Institute for Policy Studies (IPS). Most American Rights at Work (ARW) officials would struggle to get a security clearance to clean latrines at any US military base. Yet three AWR alumni - Bonior, Solis and Maxwell, now work with President Obama at the heart of the US government. No less than four ARW Board members were touted for the Labor Secretary Job. Talk about socialist nepotism - did anyone else have any chance at all? Several ARW figures are close to Democratic Socialists of America (DSA), IPS or both. Democratic Socialists of America (DSA) and IPS both have close ties to the Communist Party USA and the militant Committees of Correspondence for Democracy and Socialism (COCDS).

All four organizations have had members or associates convicted or accused of spying for foreign governments. All are anti-American and pro-Marxist socialists. ARW is positioned to build a socialist led, Obama labor movement.

However, will Obama's Labor "Commissars" be tough enough to keep America's "proletariat" in their place?

76. Leon Despres Dies. Obama's Socialist "Trailblazer" Moves On to Subvert Heaven

Trevor Loudon © Saturday, May 16, 2009

Chicago political icon and former city Alderman, Leon Despres,[473] died at the age of 101.

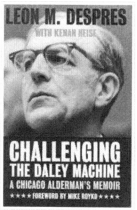

Though not known outside Illinois, Despres created a political movement in Chicago's affluent Hyde Park enclave that propelled Barack Obama to the US presidency.

From the leftist blog, *Daily Kos*:

President Barack Obama recognized this trailblazer whose contributions to Hyde Park's politics set the stage for our President's own ascent.

76-1 Alderman Leon Despres

In a statement Wednesday, President Obama said, "Through two decades on the Chicago City Council and a

---

[473] http://keywiki.org/index.php/Leon_Despres

long lifetime of activism, Leon Despres was an indomitable champion for justice and reform. With an incisive mind, rapier wit and unstinting courage, he waged legendary battles against the corruption and discrimination that blighted our city, and he lived every one of his 101 years with purpose and meaning. I have been blessed by his wise counsel and inspired by his example." (Nuisance Industry 2009)

According to the *Chicago Tribune*:

> Despres and his South Side neighborhood, which he represented in the City Council from 1955 to 1975, were long the city's liberal conscience, and both were part of President Barack Obama's original political base.

> "Michelle and I were saddened by the passing of our dear friend and a towering giant in Chicago history, Leon M. Despres," Obama said in a statement. "With an incisive mind, rapier wit and unstinting courage, he waged legendary battles against the corruption and discrimination that blighted our city." (Trevor and Grossman 2009)

Stone Cipher Report[474] put it another way:

> He (Despres) strongly supported Obama, seeing him bring "a breadth of integrity not in that office in a long time." He also said, "[Obama] is a good man, highly intelligent, but not an elitist. And I see him staying that way." (Sweeney 2009)

Moreover, a key for the former Alderman was watching the rise of this young community organizer, then state Senator in the same neighborhood that Despres once represented and still knew so well. With Obama being supported and then elected by the same core mixed group of progressives who had emerged in the '50s (and solidified through the '60s and '70s) supporting his independent Democratic candidacy.

Alderman Leon Despres was a key figure in the movement that nurtured Obama's career. Despres helped found a coalition that united the Chicago left against the mighty Daley machine. It put Chicago's first black Mayor Harold Washington into power. It boosted Jesse Jackson's Presidential ambitions and it elected the US' first black female US Senator Carol Moseley-Braun (D-IL). It gave the far left a say in the running of Chicago and it gave the US its first black President.

---

[474] http://stonecipher.typepad.com/the_stonecipher_report/2009/05/leon-m-despres-19082009-the-liberal-conscience-of-chicago.html

Who was Leon Despres?

Born in 1908, Leon Mathis Despres moved as an infant to Chicago's Hyde Park area and lived there almost his entire life. Despres studied law at the University of Chicago, gaining his degree in 1929 and linking up with the radical father of US "community organizing," Saul Alinsky.

76-2 Saul Alinsky

Centenarian Despres gave a speech on Alinsky at their old Alma Mater early this year that revealed much about both men:

> But palling around with street toughs convinced Alinsky that social problems had to be tackled head-on, not by gathering statistics, said Leon Despres, a former 5th Ward alderman, and a classmate of Alinsky's at U. of C.
>
> He and Alinsky went to a shooting range to prepare for the revolution that seemed inevitable, as the Great Depression appeared to be the end of capitalism.
>
> However, socialism and the revolution never came, and Alinsky afterward became intolerant of ideology... (Grossman 2009)

Alinsky went on to radicalize much of South Chicago before his death in 1972. Eleven years later, a young Barack Obama moved to the same area to cut his political teeth with Alinsky trained people and organizations.

Following his brief tenure with the Democrats, Despres joined the Hyde Park branch of the Socialist Party USA in 1933, serving four years.

Despres was a union lawyer by 1937 and became heavily involved in supporting strikers at Republic Steel in Chicago through the Lawyers Constitutional Rights Committee. The strike ended in tragedy when 14 strikers died and many were wounded in a hail of police bullets.

According to the Illinois Labor History Society:

> Len (Leon) was among the lawyers who took depositions from the many witnesses to the carnage inflicted by the Chicago police at the 1937 Memorial Day Massacre at Republic Steel. Later, Len helped the La Follett Congressional Investigating Committee to gather information used in its scathing criticism of the police conduct on the field that day. (Balanoff 2008)

The Communist Party USA orchestrated the ill-fated strike, working through the party dominated Congress of Industrial Organizations (CIO). Lee Pressman, the CIO lawyer, played a major role. It revealed that Pressman was a secret communist and Soviet spy - part of the Ware ring, founded in the US Department of Agriculture.

Despres' colleague on the Lawyers Constitutional Rights Committee, John Abt, was also a secret communist and Ware ring member.

From 1931 to 1935, Despres also worked with another Communist Party front, the Chicago Civil liberties Committee, but left because of the "Stalinism."[475]

76-3 John Abt

Almost certainly, this was a signal, that like many on the US left at the time Despres was breaking with Stalinism to embrace the rival Trotskyites movement.

According to this biography of Despres' wife Marian:

In 1937, a fellow lawyer asked Leon Despres to deliver a suitcase of clothing to Leon Trotsky, the exiled Bolshevik living in Mexico. The Despreses traveled south and met not only Trotsky but his ally, artist Diego Rivera. Mrs. Despres sat for a portrait with Rivera while her husband escorted Rivera's wife, the artist Frida Kahlo, to a movie (Jensen 2007)

Trotsky at the time was under tight security, fearing Stalin dispatched assassins. Despres must have been trusted by the Trotskyites to get anywhere near their leader.

Marian Despres

From 1946 to 1951, she was an assistant psychology professor at Roosevelt University, where she urged a young student named Harold Washington to run for the student council presidency, which he won. As Mayor of Chicago, Washington often said that, "Despres had launched his political career."

[475] http://www.schwarzreport.org/yct/04ycttc.htm

Representative Harold Washington (D-IL-1st-District) went on to serve Illinois in the US Congress and the Communist Party in a variety of front organizations.

Obama credits the election of Representative Harold Washington (D-IL-1st-District) in 1983 as the reason he first moved to Chicago. Obama even applied for a job with Washington's administration.

76-4 Harrington (l) Despres at microphone

Back in Hyde Park, Despres was building the coalition of communists, socialists, leftist Democrats, unionists and black radicals that would first change Chicago and the US.

In 1955, Despres was elected to the Chicago City Council as an independent Alderman from Hyde Park. Despres, who served until 1975, was a left wing maverick, the sole dissenter against Mayor Daley's invincible "machine."

Despres never abandoned the left and by the late 1950s was back in the Socialist Party orbit.

In 1958, the Chicago leftists' Party established an annual dinner in honor of Socialist icon Eugene Debs.[476]

The Dinner began as the Debs Day Dinner in 1958 under the auspices of the old Socialist Party of America.

In 1969, the Dinner became the Thomas-Debs Dinner in honor of Norman Thomas. It became an awards dinner in 1971. In 1973, the Democratic Socialist Organizing Committee (DSOC) took over the Dinner's sponsorship. In 1983, DSOC and the New American Movement merged to form the Democratic Socialists of America. Democratic Socialists of America (DSA) has sponsored the Dinner ever since.

Democratic Socialists of America (DSA) leader Michael Harrington's name was added to the event's title after his death in 1989.

Leon Despres[477] MCed the first Debs Dinner in 1958 and was on the podium again in 1962. In 1975, Despres was the honoree.

---

[476] http://www.chicagodsa.org/dthdin.html
[477] http://www.chicagodsa.org/ngarchive/ng59.html

76-5 Citizens Committee

In 1976, Leon Despres[478] introduced Michael Harrington and Dolores Huerta, Vice President of Cesar Chavez's United Farmworkers Union, now a prominent Democratic Socialists of America (DSA) member.

Cesar Chavez's "Si Se Puede!" slogan behind Despres is the origin of the Obama campaign's "Yes We Can!"

The Debs-Thomas-Harrington Dinners feature Democratic Socialists of America (DSA) members, many of whom are ex-communists. Many speakers and awardees have gone on to work for Obama or play some significant role in his life or career, including:

Quentin Young has been Obama's friend, neighbor and physician. He has also been Despres' doctor and a friend for 50 years. Young was in the Young Communist League in the '30s, the Communist Party for many years before joining Democratic Socialists of America (DSA) in 1982.

Timuel Black is also a long time Obama friend and supporter. He is a member of the Communist Party splinter group Committees of Correspondence for Democracy, Socialism and a Democratic Socialists of America (DSA) donor.

Despres knew Timuel Black well. The pair organized a delegation of Chicagoans to march with Dr. Martin Luther King in Selma, Alabama in 1965. At the time, Black was a member of the Socialist Party. Later Despres served on a "Citizen's Committee" supporting Black's campaign for State Representative in the 22nd District. The "Citizen's Committee"

---

[478] http://www.chicagodsa.org/d1976/index.html

was Chaired by Communist Party member Harold Rogers.

Also serving with Despres were former communist Charles Hayes, DSA members Saul Mendelson (former Trotskyist), Danny Davis, Milton Cohen (former communist) and journalist Don Rose.

Harold Rogers, Charles Hayes, Harold Washington, Carol Moseley Braun, Danny Davis, Milton Cohen and Timuel Black were all leaders in 1981 of another far left organization, the Chicago Committee in support of Southern Africa.

76-6 David Canter

Despres and Don Rose also went back to the 1970s when Rose, a veteran of several communist controlled organizations, set up a newspaper, the *Hyde Park-Kenwood Voices*. Rose's business partner was David Canter, a long time Communist Party member, raised in the Soviet Union and at one time a registered agent of that country.

Alderman Despres published *"Voices"* a weekly column from local contributors with articles by and about Hyde Park radicals, socialists, peace activists, Students for a Democratic Society rioters, Cuba sugar cane cutters, and communists.

It campaigned against the Chicago Police's "Red Squad" the section dedicated to gathering intelligence on communists and radicals.

Despres was also active against the "Red Squad" because he was one of their targets.

According to the Illinois American Civil Liberties Union[479] (of which Despres was a leading member):

> Unlawful surveillance of political and religious organizations and community groups by the FBI and Chicago police was rampant in Chicago for many decades up through the mid-1970s, when federal lawsuits by the ACLU of Illinois and other organizations resulted in court supervision over these intelligence-gathering activities. Groups like the

---

[479] http://www.aclu-il.org/news/press/2004/12/prominent_chicago_area_organiz.shtml

76-7 David Canter and Harold Washington

League of Women Voters, Operation PUSH and the Independent Voters of Illinois as well as individuals including former Chicago City Council member Leon Despres, Jesse Jackson Jr., Studs Terkel, Dick Simpson and Dr. Quentin Young were subjected to unlawful surveillance and the disruption of lawful political (American Civil Liberties Union of Illinois 2004)

The late Studs Terkel, (who attended Despres's 100th birthday celebration), was a long time secret Communist Party member, Jesse Jackson supported by communists and Dick Simpson was involved with the Debs Dinner set.

Independent Voters of Illinois was heavily infiltrated by socialists such as Milton Cohen, Saul Mendelson, Betty Wilhoitte (all DSA) and a who's who of the Chicago left including Dick Simpson, David Canter, Bernice Bild, Bob Mann, Joe Moore, David Orr, Sue Purrington, Carol Moseley Braun and Michelle and Barack Obama.

After "*Voices*" folded in 1975, Rose and Canter embarked on a new project mentoring a young student journalist named David Axelrod who was later to serve as Obama's Presidential campaign boss and White House advisor.

By the '80s, Mayor Daley was dead and gone and Canter and several others persuaded Harold Washington to stand for the Chicago Mayoralty.

Rose, Axelrod, Canter and Despres all worked on the successful campaign that was an alliance between the Chicago Communist Party and Democratic Socialists of America (DSA).

Rose, Axelrod and Canter all worked for Washington's administration, while Despres served on the new Mayor's Chicago Plan Commission and as City Council Parliamentarian until Washington's death in 1987.

After the Washington era, Despres returned to his law practice but maintained strong political interests.

His last major political act came this year when Illinois Congressional Representative Rahm Emanuel gave up his seat to serve as Obama's Chief of Staff in a bye-election called in Illinois' fifth District.

Leon Despres' law partner, Tom Geoghegan, threw his hat in the ring. He was endorsed by Leon Despres, Dr. Quentin Young and Don Rose, but lost the Democratic primary race.

Even Leon Despres and the Hyde Park socialists could not win 'em all.

77. Sam Webb Lays Out Communist Agenda for Obama Administration

Trevor Loudon © Friday, May 22, 2009

Barack Obama has been beholden to the Communist Party USA. From the boyhood mentoring he received from Frank Marshall Davis, ongoing work in Chicago and mass party support in his 2008 Presidential run.

Now it is payback time.

The Party wants Obama to deliver a new "New Deal" - a massive extension of government and union power that will transform US society.

By using pressure from the "bottom up and the top down," the Communist Party aims to squeeze the US middle class into accepting its socialist program.

The following is a speech[480] given by Communist Party National Chair Sam Webb at the PWW's Better World Awards banquet in New York City, May 17, 2009.

77-1 Sam Webb

THE IMPOSSIBLE BECOMES POSSIBLE

On the heels of the first 100 days of our new President, we heard nearly endless commentary and analysis. Much of it was favorable; and some wasn't.

I would like to briefly add my two cents

After the first 100 days I would say without hesitation or qualification that the political atmosphere, landscape, conversation and agenda

---

[480] http://www.peoplesworld.org/speech-the-impossible-becomes-possible/

compared to the previous eight years of the Bush administration have changed dramatically.

To borrow an expression of Jarvis Tyner, the executive Vice Chair of our party, "What was once impossible during the Bush years has become possible, thanks to the election of Barack Obama."

In this new political climate, we can foresee winning a public option, like Medicare, in the current legislative fight over health care reform.

We can visualize enacting tough regulatory reforms on the financial industry that brought the economy to ruin.

We can imagine bringing the troops home from Iraq and Afghanistan, while being part of a regional process that brings peace and stability to the entire region.

In this new political climate, the expansion of union rights in this legislative session is not only sensible, it is doable.

Much the same can be said about winning a second stimulus bill, and we sure need one, given the still rising and likely long term persistence of unemployment with the heaviest burden, as usual, falling on communities of color.

Isn't it possible in the post-Bush era to launch a vigorous attack on global warming and create millions of green jobs in manufacturing and elsewhere?

Can't we envision taking new strides in the long journey for racial and gender equality in this new era, marked at its beginning by the election of the first African American to the presidency?

And isn't the overhaul of the criminal justice and prison system - a system steeped in racism and employing punitive treatment as it organizing principle - no longer pie in the sky, but something that can be done in the foreseeable future?

All these — and many other — things are within our reach now!

We can dream again, knowing that the gap between our dreams and reality is bridgeable.

We can turn King's words — that "justice roll down like a mighty stream" — into a living reality for every American.

We can re-bend the arc of history in the direction of justice and peace.

But only if we, and millions like us, do our part in these struggles, much like we did last year.

Neither President Obama nor progressive congress people can do it by themselves — they can't be the only change agents.

After all, they are up against formidable opposition.

On the one hand the extreme right is badly weakened, but is still a poisonous and reactionary political presence in our nation.

On the other hand, the Obama change coalition includes people and groups that want to cut down on the scope and sweep of the reform agenda.

So both the new President and new congress need our help. Our responsibility is support them as well as prod and constructively take issue with them when we have differing views.

But more importantly - and this is the nub of the problem - we have to reach, activate, unite and turn millions of Americans into change agents who can make the political difference in these struggles.

Changes of a progressive nature, especially major ones— if history is any guide —usually combine the bottom up and the top down.

So the challenge facing the discontented of our land is to be the bottom up change agents this year and in the years to come.

Our parents and grandparents did exactly that in the Depression years. Not happy with the pace and substance of change, they sat down in plants and in the fields, marched on Washington, petitioned local relief agencies, lobbied for a social safety net, established unemployed and nationality (immigrant) groups, organized industrial workers, opposed discrimination and racism, elected New Dealers to Congress and re-elected Roosevelt in a landslide in 1936, and turned (not all at once and not perfectly) multi-racial unity into an organizing principle.

I am confident the American people in their millions - reeling under the weight of this terrible economic crisis and yearning for a more decent, equal, peaceful and just world - will follow their example and turn this country into a more perfect union.

Yes we can — Si se puede! (Webb, The Impossible becomes Possible 2009)

Now you know every major item on the Communist Party's agenda. Socialized healthcare, increased union power, massive controls on the finance sector, ending the Iraq and Afghanistan Wars, a regulated "green economy," a second "stimulus" bill and a weakening of the "racist" prison system.

Put the Communist Party list on your office wall.

Tick the items off as the Obama administration acts on each one of them.

78. Proof That Obama's Hawaii and Chicago Communist Networks Were Linked?

Trevor Loudon © Monday, June 01, 2009

Barack Obama links to the Hawaiian Communist Party network is through his boyhood-teenage mentor, Frank Marshall Davis.

After moving to Chicago, Obama linked up with the local communist networks.

Manning Marable, a leader of the Communist Party offshoot Committees of Correspondence for Democracy and Socialism, claims that Obama:

> "understands what socialism is. Many of the people working with him are, indeed, socialists with backgrounds in the Communist Party or as independent Marxists. There are a lot of people like that in Chicago who have worked with him for years...." (Marable 2008)

78-1 Frank Marshall Davis

This leads to two key questions.

Were the Hawaii and Chicago networks connected?

Did Obama's connection to Frank Marshall Davis in any way influence his progress up the Chicago political ladder?

If the answer is yes to both, there are significant implications.

It means that the Communist Party USA was watching Obama from his youth and was willing to help his political career.

Frank Marshall Davis was active in the Chicago Communist Party until he moved to Hawaii in late 1948.

Speculation in Chapter 38 made the point that Davis might have known left wing journalist Vernon Jarrett. A connection would be significant because the Jarrett family has played an important role in Obama's rise to power.

Both Jarrett and Davis worked in the communist dominated South Side Community Art Center and on the communist influenced *Chicago Defender* newspaper in the late 1940s in Chicago.

There is conclusive evidence that Davis and Jarrett knew each other, but they also worked together in another Communist Party dominated organization - The Citizen's Committee to Aid Packing House Workers "organized to support the united packing-House workers of America C.I.O. now on strike."

78-2 Partial List of CCAPW officials

A letter dated April 12, 1948, notes that CIO (Congress of Industrial Organizations) was at the time a communist controlled labor federation.

The letterhead includes a partial list of Citizen's Committee to Aid Packinghouse Workers officials, including the names Oscar C. Brown (Treasurer), Louise T. Patterson (Assistant Treasurer), F.M. Davis, and Vernon Jarrett.

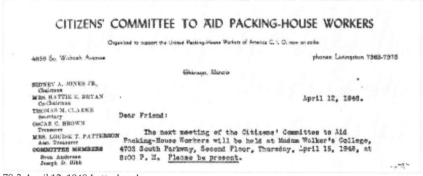

78-3 April 12, 1948 Letterhead

To confirm the connection, below is a close-up of the committee's publicity committee. The committee, Chaired by Vernon Jarrett includes

78-4 Oscar C. Brown

78-5 Ishmael Flory

Frank Marshall Davis.

That the Citizen's Committee was communist influenced is beyond doubt.

Louise T. Patterson was the wife of Illinois Communist Party Vice-Chairman and attorney William Patterson. A prominent Party member in her own right Louise T. Patterson was a leader of the Illinois Communist Party well into the 1970s.

Further down the page appears a list of the organization's "Food and groceries committee."

One of the eulogists at Flory's funeral was Timuel Black, a well-known member of Committees of Correspondence for Democracy & Socialism and a long time friend and political supporter of Barack Obama.

Oscar C. Brown, later a famous jazz

Vernon Jarrett
Joseph Jefferson
Horace Johnson
Mrs. Marjorie Joyner
K. F. Jones
Sidney A. Jones Jr.
Ulysses S. Keyes
Rev. William Latham
Theophilus Mann
Mrs. Jackie Ormes
Mrs. Bertha Keith Payne

PUBLICITY COMMITTEE: Vernon Jarrett, Chairman; Joseph D. Bibb, Theodore Coleman, Charles A. Davis, Frank Marshall Davis, Mrs. Rebecca Styles Taylor.

The duty of this Committee is to give publicity to the facts with reference to the strike, the plight of the workers and the work of the Citizens Committee.

78-6 Committee's Publicity Committee

78-7 Louise T. Patterson

musician under the name Oscar Brown Jr., was also at the time a Communist Party member. He joined in 1946 and was expelled around 1954.

In 1948, Vernon Jarrett left his job as journalist at the *Chicago Defender* to start a black oriented radio show *"Negro Newsfront"* with Oscar Brown.

Jarrett was on the far left and like his colleague Frank Marshall Davis, a covert member of the Communist Party.

Jarrett worked hard promoting socialist causes including the communist controlled Progressive Party.

Vernon Jarrett went on to become the *Chicago Tribune's* first black syndicated columnist and was a founder of the National Association of Black Journalists.

According to a *Washington Post*[481] obituary May 25, 2004:

78-8 Vernon Jarrett and Henry Wallace

> Mr. Jarrett continually shone a light on African American history and pertinent issues in Chicago and throughout the country. He stoked the political embers in Chicago that led to the 1983 election of the city's first African American Mayor Harold Washington.
>
> Vernon Jarrett was a key influence in Washington's decision to run for the Chicago Mayoralty and remained a key supporter through his four year tenure. (Lamb, Vernon Jarrett, 84, Journalist, Crusader - Obituaries 2004)

Mayor Harold Washington defeated the Daley machine to win the Mayoralty backed by a coalition led by Chicago's Communist Party and the local branch of Democratic Socialists of America.

78-9 Communist Party Organizer Paul Buhle

Democratic Socialists of America (DSA) member and socialist historian Paul Buhle[482] wrote in a 1992 article for the *Encyclopedia of the American Left*:

> Communists also gained from long-standing political connections in the black community. Victories of black Mayoral and congressional candidates with old ties to the Communist Party that lasted decades. A short list would include Coleman Young and George Crocket in Detroit, Gus Newport in Berkeley, and Mayor Harold Washington in Chicago. (Buhle and Georgakas, History of the Comintern Sections Communist Party USA 1992)

Washington was involved in

78-10 Vernon Jarrett with Harold Washington and Cicely Tyson

---

[481] http://www.washingtonpost.com/wp-dyn/articles/A53239-2004May24.html
[482] http://eprints.cddc.vt.edu/marxists//history/usa/parties/Communist Partyusa/encyclopedia-american-left.htm

Communist Party fronts such as the US Peace Council and the Chicago Committee on Southern Africa, right up to winning the Mayoralty with Party support. After victory he stacked his administration full of communists, socialists and sympathizers to create one of the most far left administrations in US history, cut short by his pre-mature death after four years in office.

I quote from remarks by Illinois Communist Party organizer John Bachtell to a "Special District Meeting on African American Equality and Building the Communist Party and Young Communist League," Chicago, IL September 30, 2007.[483]

> The legacy of Mayor Harold Washington's election and his administration is in the collective consciousness not only of the African American community, but the entire city. Many of his democratizing achievements endure 20 years later.

> The historic election of Washington was the culmination of many years of struggle. It reflected a high degree of unity of the African American community and the alliance with a section of labor, the Latino community, and progressive minded whites. This legacy of political independence also endures... (Bachetell 2007)

The following paragraph includes a redacted sentence from the original publication resulting in a claim that the Communist Party and Young Communist League of Chicago deny they supported Obama.

> This was also reflected in the historic election of Barack Obama. ~~Our Party actively supported Obama during the primary election.~~ Once again, Obama's campaign reflected the electoral voting unity of the African American community, but also the alliances built with several key trade unions, and forces in the Latino and white communities.

> It also reflected a breakthrough among white voters. In the primary, Obama won 35% of the white vote and 7 north side wards, in a crowded field.

> During the general election he won every ward in the city and all the collar counties.

---

[483] http://www.Communist Partyusa.org/special-district-meeting-on-african-american-equality/

This appeal has continued in his Presidential run. (Bachtell, Communist Party USA: Special District Meeting on African American Equality) Barack Obama has stated that Mayor Harold Washington's victory in 1983 was the spur that made him leave New York to move to Chicago. (Bachtell, Speical District Meeting on African American 2007)

Vernon Jarrett was also a fan of Barack Obama. He watched his career from its early stages and became an ardent supporter.

In 1992, Obama worked for the ACORN offshoot, Project Vote, to register black voters in support of the Senate Campaign of Carol Moseley-Braun also had strong Communist Party ties and was Harold Washington's legislative floor leader.

Obama helped Moseley-Braun win her Senate seat and took it over himself in 2004 - backed of course by the same communist/socialist alliance that had elected his political predecessors Harold Washington and Carol Moseley-Braun.

78-11 Moseley Braun also had strong Communist Party ties

Commenting on the 1992 race, Vernon Jarrett wrote in the *Chicago Sun-Times* of August 11, 1992:

> Good news! Good news! Project Vote, a collectivity of 10 church - based community organizations dedicated to black voter registration, is off and running. Project Vote is increasing its rolls at a 7,000-per-week clip...If Project Vote is to reach its goal of registering 150,000 out of an estimated 400,000 unregistered blacks statewide, "it must average 10,000 than 7,000 every week," says Barack Obama, the program's executive director... (Jarrett, Project Vote brings Power to the People 1992)

Dee Myles is a Chicago activist and Chair of the Education Commission of the Communist Party USA. In 2004, Myles stated the following after Vernon Jarrett passed away:

> Readers like me can be extremely selective of the journalists we read habitually... We are selective about the journalists to whom we become

insatiably addicted, and once hooked we develop a constructive love affair without the romance...

Such was my experience with Vernon Jarrett, an African American journalist in Chicago who died at the age of 86 on May 23. I became a Vernon Jarrett addict, and I am proud of it!

Vernon Jarrett's career as a journalist in Chicago started at the Chicago Defender, the African American daily paper. In between, he was the first Black journalist at the Chicago Tribune, and I first began to read his articles during his tenure at the Chicago Sun-Times

Jarrett's claim to fame is that he was a partisan of the cause of African Americans in the broad democratic tradition of Paul Robeson and W.E.B. DuBois... (Myles 2004)

Robeson and DuBois were both Communist Party members. On April 9, 1998, at Chicago's South Shore Cultural Center, Jarrett hosted a Paul Robeson Citywide Centennial Celebration event, with his old comrade and Party sympathizer Margaret Burroughs and former Communist Party members Studs Terkel and his old friend Oscar C. Brown.

Jarrett was fanatical about African Americans registering and voting in mass for socially conscious candidates. He championed Harold Washington like a great warrior, and this March, from his hospital bed, wrote an article appealing to Black Chicago to turn out to vote for Barack Obama in the Illinois primaries. Obama astounded everyone with an incredible landslide victory as the progressive, Black candidate for the Democratic Party nomination for the US Senate seat from Illinois. From his sickbed, Vernon Jarrett issued a clarion call, and the people responded.

The Jarrett/Obama connection did not end with Vernon Jarrett's death. It moved to a higher level with his famous daughter-in-law Valerie Jarrett. (Myles 2004)

A former Deputy Corporation Counsel for Finance and Development under Mayor Harold Washington, Jarrett continued to work in the Mayor's office into the 1990s.

In 1991, while Deputy Chief of Staff for Chicago Mayor Richard J. Daley, Jarrett hired Michelle Robinson, who was engaged to Barack Obama.

Later, Valerie Jarrett ran the finances for Obama's 2004 Senate bid and served as treasurer of Obama's HOPEFUND.

The relationship is more than professional because Jarrett, regarded as one of the Obamas' closest friends and advisors.

Figure 78-12 Valerie Jarrett (l) Barack Obama (r)

"She's always been the other side of Barack's brain." That's how an Obama insider described Valerie Jarrett as an Obama campaign aide announced Thursday night the former CTA chief and current Habitat Co. CEO is taking on a larger role to help her close friend win his White House bid.

The development comes as Jarrett, a charter member of Sen. Barack Obama's kitchen cabinet, has been formalizing her portfolio and stepping up the pace within the past few weeks as a top advisor within the campaign.

Though she will be part-time, Jarrett will be one of the most visible and powerful African-Americans in the top rungs of the Obama operation... (Blount 2008)

Today Valerie Jarrett serves as one of three Senior Advisors to President Obama. She is Assistant to the President for Intergovernmental Affairs and Public Engagement and Chairs the White House Commission on Women and Girls.

Frank Marshall Davis works in communist causes with Vernon Jarrett in Chicago. Davis moves to Hawaii where he meets and mentors a young Barack Obama. Obama moves to Chicago where both Davis' old colleague Vernon Jarrett promotes his career and the Communist Party. Vernon Jarrett's daughter-in-law employs Barack Obama's fiancé, befriends the family and becomes one of President Obama's most trusted advisors. The Communist Party throws its entire weight behind Obama's Presidential campaign.

Are we to believe that this is all mere coincidence?

Would there be an Obama/Jarrett relationship today, if there had been no Frank Marshall Davis/Jarrett connection through the Communist Party of post war Chicago?

What role, if any, has the modern Communist Party USA played in fostering that relationship? The Communist Party openly considers

Barack Obama their "friend."

How has the Communist Party been involved in advancing Obama's political career through other parties and the Jarrett family?

The answers to these questions will have major implications for the future of what is left of the free world.

79. Filling in the Gaps. More on Obama and Chicago Democratic Socialists of America

Wednesday, June 17, 2009

Barack Obama's association with the Marxists of Democratic Socialists of America is deep and enduring.

Democratic Socialists of America (DSA), founded in the '80s, continues to this today.

Obama makes an apparent reference to Democratic Socialists of America (DSA) in his 1995 autobiography *"Dreams from My Father."*

Discussing his time at New York's Columbia University in the '80s, Obama reveals that he "went to socialist conferences at Cooper Union and African cultural fairs in Brooklyn."

For many years, from the early '80s until 2004, Cooper Union was the usual venue of the annual Socialist Scholars Conference (SSC).[484] Was this what Obama was referring to in his book?

Since Democratic Socialists of America (DSA)'s formation in 1982, its

City University branch has sponsored and organized the Socialist Scholars Conference (SSC) (now called Left Forum) featuring Democratic Socialists of America (DSA) speakers such as Frances Fox Piven, Leo Panitch, Bogdan Denitch, Stanley Aronowitz, Stephen Eric Bronner, Cornel West, Bill Fletcher Jr., Noam Chomsky and Barbara Ehrenreich as well as guests from the Communist Party, Committees of Correspondence for Democracy & Socialism and other militant groups.

---

[484] http://www.pbs.org/heavenonearth/interviews_socialistscholars.html

In 1996, Obama addresses a Democratic Socialists of America (DSA) sponsored forum[485] held at Chicago University in 1996. Later that year Chicago Democratic Socialists of America (DSA) endorses Obama for his run for Illinois State Senate.

79-1 Lou Pardo

It begs the question as to why the gap of fourteen years? Was there really a long break in Obama/Democratic Socialists of America (DSA) relations?

It seems that Democratic Socialists of America (DSA) contacted Obama after he returned to Chicago, from his studies at Harvard in 1992:

> I first heard of Barack back in 1992. The year 1992 was a little like 2008. Then, as now, we needed to save the country from the misguided policies of a President named Bush. I was working with my old friend, Lou Pardo, a retired machinist, on an effort to register Latino voters in Chicago. One day, we were talking about how we could reach more voters and cover more ground, but we needed more resources. Lou told me we should go see Barack Obama, who was directing a voter-registration drive called Project Vote. So Lou met with Barack and, without missing a beat, Barack Obama helped us out. Barack Obama made sure that the thousands of Latinos in Chicago were registered to vote. He helped empower the Latino community and ensure that we were full participants in our democracy. (Valle 2009)

Lou Pardo is indeed a retired machinist, but he is also a socialist.

> Lou Pardo, a volunteer with Senator Del Valle, Democratic Socialists of America (DSA) member and activist with the Midwest-Northeast Voter Registration Education Project, emphasized how important it was to support independent progressive democrats. (Baiman, What I Saw of the Revolution: the 1995 Midwest Radical Scholars and Activists Conference)

Pardo was honored by Chicago Democratic Socialists of America (DSA) at their 1994 Debs-Thomas-Harrington awards dinner[486] for his work on turning out the vote for leftist Democrats.

[485] http://www.chicagodsa.org/ngarchive/ng45.html
[486] www.chicagodsa.org/d1994/index.html

79-3 Chicago City Clerk
Miguel Del Valle

79-2 Illinois State Senator
Miguel Del Valle

Your voter registration efforts have been recognized. In 1990, you were given the William C. Velasquez Volunteer of the Year Award at the 8th Annual US Hispanic Leadership Conference. You have worked in the Midwest-Northeast Voter Registration Education Project in Senator Miguel del Valle's district. This project was a tremendous success, and on August 20, 1992, you were the recipient of an award by the Illinois State Democratic Convention for "historic efforts in registering thousands of new Illinois voters." (Democratic Socialists of America)

Illinois State Senator Miguel Del Valle presented the Democratic Socialists of America (DSA) award.

In 2001, Miguel Del Valle was again guest speaker[487] at a Chicago Democratic Socialists of America (DSA)'s Debs Dinner indicated a more than passing relationship with the "Windy City" Marxists.

The 2001 Debs-Thomas-Harrington Dinner was held Friday, May 4 at the Holiday Inn Mart Plaza in Chicago. The honorees were Kim Bobo and Henry Bayer. The speaker was Miguel del Valle.

Illinois State Senators Miguel Del Valle and Barack Obama worked together with Project Vote's radical partner organization ACORN.

Joined by three state elected officials, Association of Community Organizations for Reform Now (ACORN) leaders Tuesday called for the passage of energy assistance legislation they say will help the poor pay their heating bills.

During a press conference held outside of the James R. Thompson Center, IL State Representative Mary Flowers , Sens. Barack Obama (D-13th) and Miguel del Valle (D-5th) along with ACORN member April Troope, urged legislators to approve Senate Bills 2240 and 2180 and House Bill 668.

---

[487] http://www.chicagodsa.org/d2001.html

The Flowers and del Valle bill (HR 668) calls on President Bush to release the $600 million in emergency Low-Income Home Energy Assistance (LIHEAP) funds that are already appropriated by the US government for heating crisis...

Senate Bill 2180 (del Valle's) increases eligibility for LIHEAP from about $26,000 for a family of four to about $37,000 (from 150 percent of the federal poverty level to 60 percent of the state median income). (Chicago Defender 2002)

Obama's bill, SB 2240, increases the state's allocation to LIHEAP by about $10 million:

"I recognize that we are in a budget crunch right now and allocating an additional $10 million may seem inappropriate at this time, but there is a rationale as to why we need to transfer this money," Obama said. (I. S. Obama 1996)

Obama was elected to the Illinois State senate in 1996, joined and

79-4 Barack Obama and the New Party

gained endorsement from the New Party, a radical coalition of Democratic Socialists of America (DSA), ACORN, and the Communist Party offshoot Committees of Correspondence (COCDS) which aimed to leftist candidates through the Democratic Party machine.

Obama was Chief of Staff to pro-communist Illinois State Senator Alice Palmer, who anointed him to take over her State Senate seat while she ran for US Congress. After her Congressional bid failed, Palmer changed her mind and asked Obama to stand aside. He refused and got her knocked off the ballot by challenging the validity of her nomination signatures.

The New Party had initially courted Alice Palmer.

In the next two elections in the city -... the New Party has taken a slightly different approach. It organized a citywide candidate's forum and

79-5 Senator Barack Obama endorses
Miguel Del Valle

invited a number of progressive candidates. Of those responding, two were of special interest, Alice Palmer and Willie Delgado. Alice Palmer is an Illinois state senator and Willie Delgado is an activist with an anti-Machine coalition of Latinos led by State Senator Miguel del Valle.

Both of these campaigns have strong local organizations that run as Democrats but are consistently opposed by the regular Democrats. Both are rooted in working-class communities with a large percentage of labor and left activists in their organizational structures. Alice Palmer especially has a long history with the African American left. Lou Pardo, a labor leader and New Party activist, is a strategist and organizer for Delgado.

Both Palmer and Delgado attended the forum and were thoroughly questioned by seventy or so New Party members. At the close, both publicly signed a "contract" with the New Party... Two weeks later, the New Party formally endorsed them and is now mobilizing support. (Palmer 2009)

Obama won the election unopposed and went on to the US Senate in 2004 and the Presidency.

Despite his rise to power, Obama has not forgotten his friends. When Miguel Del Valle won the Chicago County Clerk's job in 2006, the second most powerful job in the city, Obama was there in support.

From Del Valle's MySpace page:[488]

"I am thrilled that Miguel del Valle is now our City Clerk and I can think of nobody better to serve out a full term than Miguel del Valle" US Senator Barack Obama. (Valle 2009)

I am sure Chicago's socialists would agree.

---

[488] http://www.myspace.com/migueldelvalle

80. Michelle and Barack's Black Panther Mentor

Trevor Loudon © Friday, July 24, 2009

US President Obama has waded into a controversy over the arrest[489] in his own house of black Harvard academic Henry Louis Gates.

Why would Obama risk a public backlash defending this man and criticizing the police?

Well, it turns out that Obama regards Gates as a friend and they have several acquaintances in common on the black left.

Gates co-wrote two books with Obama's "comrade," Democratic Socialists of America member Cornel West. Gates is also close to another Democratic Socialists of America (DSA) supporter who Obama once shared a Democratic Socialists of America (DSA) organized forum with - academic William Julius.

Gates' lawyer Charles Ogletree is a longtime friend and mentor to both Michelle and Barack Obama.

It also turns out that Ogletree was a hard-core radical with roots in the Maoist influenced Black Panthers movement. Ogletree is still a militant leftist and called on by the Obama's for advice.

In 1970, Charles Ogletree enrolled at Stanford University near San Francisco, a major center of black activism. Ogletree became a campus radical,[490] organizing an Afrocentric dormitory and editing a campus Black Panthers newspaper called "*The Real News.*" He also traveled to Africa and Cuba with student activist groups. In 1973, Ogletree was President of the radical Black Student Union.[491]

Ogletree's first interest in the law came when he attended the trial of Black Power activist and Communist Party USA member Angela Davis.

---

[489] http://www.peoplesworld.org/the-henry-louis-gates-jr-arrest-uppity-in-2009/
[490] radicalhttp://biography.jrank.org/pages/2366/Ogletree-Jr-Charles.html
[491] http://dynamics.org/SWOPSI/WEB/v216i0025_08.html

80-2 Michelle Obama and Charles Ogletree

By 1986, Ogletree was director of Harvard's introduction to trial advocacy workshops, where teaching students that law could be:

"An instrument for social and political change; a tool to empower the dispossessed and disenfranchised, and a means to make the privileged more respectful of differences," (Ogletree 1986)

Ogletree also began a Saturday School Program to teach "African-American students how to learn from other professionals of their own heritage." Barack Obama became one of his regular students.

80-1 Barack Obama and Charles Ogletree

Ogletree claims to have mentored both Michelle and Barack Obama. According to Ogletree, the Obama's have called on him for advice since that time.

"I met Michelle when she started her legal career here at Harvard in the fall of 1985, and I was able to watch her develop into a strong and powerful student leader.

She was an active member of the Harvard Legal Aid Bureau, where she served as a student attorney for indigent clients who had civil cases and needed legal help..."

"I met Barack three years later when he arrived at Harvard Law School in fall of 1988. He was quiet and unassuming, but had an incredibly sharp mind and a thirst for knowledge. He was a regular participant in a program that I created called the Saturday School Program, which was a series of workshops and meetings held on Saturday mornings to expose minority students, in particular, to critical issues in the study of law. Even then, I saw his ability to quickly grasp the most complicated legal issues and sort them out in a clear, concise fashion.

80-3 A gaggle of lawyers: James Lloyd; Alfred L. Brophy; Michele Roberts; Kimberly Ellis (at back); Johnnie Cochran; Randall Robinson; Charles J. Ogletree; Dennis Sweet; Adjoa Aiyetoro; Eric J. Miller; Sharon Cole; James O. Goodwin

I was faculty adviser to the Harvard Black Law Student Association. I routinely gave career advice, and often personal advice, to students who would come in with questions about where they should work, how they should use their legal skills and talent, and was it possible to do well and do good...My advice to people like Barack and Michelle was that they could easily navigate the challenges of a corporate career and find a variety of ways to serve their community-through financial support, through volunteer legal Services, and through getting involved in community efforts. So this advice started then, and I guess it must have been useful enough. They have not hesitated to call on me over the past 20-plus years as needed.

It's one thing to see Michelle and Barack keep their promises by going back to Chicago and serving those communities. It's another thing to see them have the dream of leading the nation as the President and First Lady and to see that happen. I was most deeply touched during Barack's acceptance speech at the Democratic National Convention in Denver...It was a moment of deep reflection that I will never forget, and it is an incredible reality today to realize that not only are the President and First Lady younger than me, but they are two people that I've had the honor and pleasure of mentoring over the past 20 years." (Ogletree 1986)

80-4 Bowman, Jones, Boudreaux

After the election, Ogletree had messages for both of his protégés.

"For the President, it was a personal message about the things that he needed to do. Without getting into any details, the central point was: Make sure you keep your promises. With Michelle, it was more my sense and my hope, that has now been realized, that she would not just be a great First Lady and a phenomenal First Mom, but that she would also be able to use her many gifts and talents in the community in ways that were natural to her. I've been particularly pleased this past week to see her not only out building support for her husband's stimulus package, but talking about families and children and education and health care, where she's going to be incredibly helpful." (Zagaroli 2009)

As Ogletree seems not to have abandoned his youthful radicalism, it might be interesting to know what advice he has given the first couple over the years.

In 2000, Ogletree joined[492] the Reparations Coordinating Committee, a group pursuing a lawsuit to win reparations for descendants of African slaves.

TransAfrica Forum, a partner organization[493] and the radical Institute for Policy Studies, convened the committee. Ogletree[494] led the TransAfrica Forum, alongside long time Communist Party USA front activist, Johnetta Cole and Board Chair and Progressives for Obama (P4O) founder Danny Glover.

The committee's objectives were to ascertain, document and report comparative repair and restitution in the United States and abroad on behalf of the contemporary victims of slavery and the century-long practice of de jure racial discrimination which followed slavery:

- To detail a range of feasible relief, reform, reconciliation and restitution initiatives to make America better for everyone.
- To identify and structure causes of action that would be cognizable in domestic and international tribunals and courts.

---

[492] http://homepage.mac.com/millerej11/Personal8.html
[493] http://www.ips-dc.org/about/partners
[494] http://www.transafricaforum.org/about-us/our-board

- To begin a comprehensive review of initiatives with leading domestic and international institutions, and

- To work cooperatively with other groups pursuing reparation claims.

80-5 Cornel West (l) Charles Ogletree (r)

The committee, which Ogletree co-Chaired, was a mixture of top trial layers and seasoned radical activists. It included Johnnie Cochran of O.J. Simpson fame, Randall Robinson and Ogletree's co-Chair Adjoa Aiyetoro; in the 1990s involved with the Communist Party splinter group Committees of Correspondence.

On December 8, 2005, Former Black Panther members, John Bowman, Hank Jones and Ray Boudreaux held a meeting at the Washington, D.C. office of TransAfrica Forum. They were complaining about renewed police investigations of a 1971 police killing in San Francisco that they stood accused of.

The three Panthers indicted at the time by a grand jury and released when the court rendered a decision stating the methods used to obtain information were unlawful.

Danny Glover, reparations activist, Ron Daniels, Democratic Socialists of America activist and Progressives for Obama (P40) co-founder Bill Fletcher, Jr. and Charles Ogletree flanked the former Panthers.

Ogletree said that the community should protect the rights of the former Panthers with their lives.

> "These gentlemen, Ray Boudreaux, Hank Jones and others have been victims of the most vicious forms of American terrorism and torture...It takes a village to protect its elders. We tell them today, through our presence here and through our commitment that we will provide a protective blanket over them. They will not come in this village and take these elders, except over our dead bodies." (About Time 2005)

Barack Obama called on Ogletree and Democratic Socialists of America member Cornel West, during his 2008 Presidential campaign.

Ogletree and West both joined Obama's Black Advisory Council.[495]

> "Ogletree has advised Obama on reforming the criminal-justice system as well on constitutional issues. He is a member of the Obama campaign's black advisory council, which also includes Cornel West, who teaches African-American studies at Princeton University. The group formed after Obama skipped a conference on African-American issues in Hampton, Va., to announce his Presidential candidacy in Illinois." (Barnes 2008)

Maybe Obama was sticking up for old friends.

81. Former Weather Underground Terrorists and 60's Maoists Nurtured Obama's "Green Jobs" Czar

Sunday, August 09, 2009

Fox News focused attention on President Obama's "Green Jobs Czar Van Jones,"[496] his background and ties to the influential Apollo Alliance.[497]

A grouping of Green, labor union and social "justice organizations," the Apollo Alliance has had a huge influence on the Obama administration and has succeeded in getting Apollo founder and long time Board member Van Jones a job in the White House. Van Jones collaborated with Gerry Hudson of Democratic Socialists of America, former Students for a Democratic Society (SDS) supporter, Carl Pope of the Sierra Club and Joel Rogers the founder of the radical New Party.

81-1 Van Jones

Despite its power, Apollo is a relatively small organization on the ground with only fourteen affiliates[498] nationwide - one of them

---

[495] http://news.nationaljournal.com/articles/080331nj1.htm
[496] http://keywiki.org/index.php/Van_Jones
[497] http://apolloalliance.org/what%E2%80%99s-new/apollo-board-member-van-jones-accepts-white-house-post/
[498] http://apolloalliance.org/state-local/

being Van Jones' tiny Oakland, California based Ella Baker Center for Human Rights.

According to Apollo's website:

> Jeff Jones campaigned to remove PCBs from the Hudson River, clean up toxic pollution in inner-city and rural neighborhoods and reverse global warming. From 1995-2005, he was the Communications Director of Environmental Advocates of New York. Previously, he was a reporter covering state politics and policy for a variety of news organizations.

> Mr. Jones has devoted much of his time to researching and confronting federal and state energy policies that contribute to global warming and catastrophic climate change. In 2006, he represented the state Apollo Alliance on the governor's Energy and Environmental Transition Task Force. He serves on the Boards of directors of several organizations, including the Healthy Schools Network, the Mohawk Hudson Land Conservancy and West Harlem Environmental Action (We Act for Environmental Justice). (Apollo Alliance 2008)

That is right! Jeff Jones is a former member of the 1970s terrorist organization, the Weather Underground. More than that, Jones was a founder and one of four key leaders of the organization with Mark Rudd, Bill Ayers, and Bernardine Dohrn. Remember those names.

81-2 Jeffrey Carl Jones

If the name Jeff Jones rings a few bells - this may be why.

What is the Weatherman connection to Apollo?

Van Jones had links in San Francisco to two other former Weather-men supporters, Jon and Nancy Frappier.

Jon Frappier[499]'s organization DataCenter worked with Jones' Ella J. Baker Center for Human Rights. Nancy Frappier attended a Weather Underground organized "Hard Times" conference in 1976 with the late Ella J. Baker herself.

Jon and Nancy Frappier have both donated to Jones' later creation, Green for All.

---

[499] http://keywiki.org/index.php/Jon_Frappier

Diana Frappier is believed to be a relative of Jon and Nancy. She has worked with Van Jones in Copwatch and helped Jones found and run both Ella Baker and Green for All.

Jon Frappier lists its contributor's former Weather Underground leader, Mark Rudd.[500]

Van Jones was a leader of the Bay Area Marxist-Leninist-Mao group and the organization Standing Together to Organize a Revolutionary Movement (STORM).

Composed of young activists "of color," STORM worked with a grouping of older Maoists - veterans of Line of March and the Venceremos Brigades to Cuba, most of whom in the '90s joined the Communist Party USA offshoot Committees of Correspondence (COCDS).

Betita Martinez

Jones was close to COCDS activist Betita Martinez and her friend of thirty years Roxanne Dunbar-Ortiz. Martinez and Dunbar-Ortiz have worked together on countless projects in the Bay Area including

supporting Van Jones' *War Times* - anti Iraq War publication in 2002. The pair are now both advisors to the Catalyst Project,[501] a Bay Area radical organization.

Our advisory Board brings together long time mentors and comrades who have supported our political and organizational development over the years.

81-3 Betita Martinez

Van Jones[502] and the Catalyst Project, Challenging White Supremacy Workshop:

"To solve the new century's mounting social and environmental problems, people of color activists and white activists need to be able to join

[500] http://theragblog.blogspot.com/2009/04/cuban-revolutionary-and-cuban-exile.html
[501]
http://collectiveliberation.org/index.php?option=com_content&task=view&id=24&Itemid=40
[502]
http://collectiveliberation.org/index.php?option=com_content&task=view&id=46&Itemid=62

forces. But all too often, the unconscious racism of white activists stands in the way of any effective, worthwhile collaboration. The Challenging White Supremacy Workshop is the most powerful tool that I have seen for removing the barriers to true partnerships between people of color and white folks. If the CWS trainings were mandatory for all white activists, the progressive movement in the United States would be unstoppable." Van Jones, Executive Director of the Ella J. Baker Center for Human Rights. (V. Jones 2009)

When former Students for a Democratic Society, Line of March leader and Committees of Correspondence member, Max Elbaum, released his book "*Revolution in the Air: Sixties Radicals Turn to Lenin, Mao and Che*" in 2002; he listed Dunbar-Ortiz, Martinez and Van Jones:[503]

"In the many contentious interpretations of the volatile 1960s and their aftermath, one key element is virtually excluded: the independent Marxists who tried to develop a new collective revolutionary project...Finally, here is a book that tells their story, and mine.

Here is the first in-depth account of the New Communist Movement of the 1970s, from its roots to its demise, and finally we can understand why it inspired thousands of Americans at the time."

By unearthing a hidden history of radical US politics, Max Elbaum has erected an invaluable bridge between the generations. Finally, we have one book that can successfully connect the dots between the battles of the 1960s and the emerging challenges and struggles of the new century."

A book also reveals some connection between Dunbar-Ortiz, Martinez and Jon Frappier. Susanne Jonas the author of The Battle for Guatemala: Rebels, Death Squads, and US Power

"Thanks Elizabeth Martinez...Jon Frappier, who first introduced me to Guatemala in 1967... Roxanne Dunbar-Ortiz, Richard Adams, Jorge Castafieda, Barbara Epstein.... for their help with the book." (Westview Press, 1991)

Roxanne Dunbar-Ortiz reveals on her website:

Dunbar-Ortiz was also a dedicated anti-war activist and organizer throughout the 1960s and 1970s. During the war years she was a fiery, indefatigable public speaker on issues of patriarchy, capitalism,

---

[503] http://www.blythe.org/nytransfer-subs/Media/The_Real_Sixties:_Book_Examines_The_Other_New_Left

imperialism, and racism. She worked in Cuba with the Venceremos Brigade and formed associations with other revolutionaries across the spectrum of radical and underground politics, including the Students for a Democratic Society, the Weather Underground, the Revolutionary Union.... (Elbaum)

As a footnote to the same piece, former Students for a Democratic Society and Weather Underground leader Mark Rudd adds:

> Roxanne Dunbar gives the lie to the myth that all New Left activists of the '60s and '70s were spoiled children of the suburban middle classes. (Elbaum)

In 2006, a group of activists from Democratic Socialists of America, Committees of Correspondence, Communist Party USA and former members of Students for a Democratic Society and the Weathermen joined forces to create a new organization, Movement for A Democratic Society (MDS).

Key figures in Movement for a Democratic Society included all four of the key Students for a Democratic Society - Weather Underground leaders Bill Ayers, Bernardine Dorhn, Jeff Jones and Mark Rudd, plus several former Students for Democratic Society comrades who had rejected the Weathermen in the late 1960s to take the Maoist road to Revolution.

Dorhn, Jones and Rudd were all Movement for Democratic Society Board members, as were former Students for a Democratic Society leaders turned Maoist, Carl Davidson, Mike Klonsky and Betita Martinez.[504] Several Movement for a Democratic Society leaders have known or worked with Obama in Chicago - including Ayers, Dorhn, Carl Davidson, Mike Klonsky and Rashid Khalidi. As has Movement for a Democratic Society Chair and Committees of Correspondence leader Manning Marable.

> What makes Obama different is that he has also been a community organizer. He has read left literature, including my works, and he understands what socialism is.

---

[504] http://nextleftnotes.org/NLN/?p=179

In 2008, Movement for a Democratic Society Board members Barbara Ehrenreich and Bill Fletcher Jr. (both Democratic Socialists of America members), Tom Hayden (former leader of Students for a Democratic Society) and Carl Davidson established Progressives for

81-4 Mark Rudd, far left, Marable center, black shirt, Jeff Jones second from right MDS conference New York January 2007.

Obama (P40) to rally far left support behind the Obama campaign. Mark Rudd has endorsed the organization.

Movement for a Democratic Society and Progressives for Obama (P40) took a strong interest in Obama administration appointments.

Shortly after the November 2008 election, Mark Rudd wrote a column in *The Rag Blog*,[505] to reassure leftists alarmed at some of Obama's appointments.

> If you are anything like me, your inbox fills up daily with the cries and complaints of lefties. Just the mere mention of the names Hillary Clinton and Lawrence Summers alone conjure up a litany of horrendous right-wingers appointed to top level positions.

[505] http://theragblog.blogspot.com/2008/11/mark-rudd-lets-get-smart-about-obama.html

81-5 Carl Davidson

Betrayal is the name of the game.

But wait a second. Let's talk about a few things:

Obama is a strategic thinker. He knew precisely what it would take to get elected and didn't blow it...But he also knew that what he said had to basically play to the center to not be run over by the press, the Republicans, scare centrist and cross-over voters away. He made it.

Obama plays basketball. I'm not much of an athlete, barely know the game, but one thing I do know is that you have to be able to look like you're doing one thing but do another. That's why all these conservative appointments are important: the strategy is feint to the right, move left. Any other strategy invites sure defeat. It would be stupid to do otherwise in this environment.

Look to the second level appointments. There's a whole govt. in waiting that Podesta has at the Center for American Progress (CAP). They're mostly progressives, I'm told (except in military and foreign policy). Cheney was extremely effective at controlling policy by putting his people in at second-level positions.... (Rudd, The Rag Blog: Mark Rudd : Let's Get Smart About Obama)

In a March 2009, *The Rag Blog*[506] review of Van Jones' book *'Green Collar Economy: How One Solution Can Fix Our Two Biggest Problems,'* Carl Davidson wrote:

It's time to link the newly insurgent US Green Jobs movement with the worldwide efforts for the solidarity economy. Both are answering the call to fight the deepening global recession, and both face common adversaries in the failed "race to the bottom," environment-be-damned policies of global neoliberalism.

That's the imperative facing left-progressive organizers with connections to these two important grassroots movements. It's even more important in the wake of the appointment of a key leader of one of these movements, Van Jones of "Green for All," to a top environmental and urban policy post in the Obama administration.

---

[506] http://theragblog.blogspot.com/2009/03/books-van-jones-green-collar-economy.html

"Green Collar Economy" was instantly a powerful voice in policy circles. It gained a wider and deeper significance in light of the financial crises that hit the fan soon after it reached the bookstores. Just as the voter revolt against Wall Street helped lift Obama to the Oval Office, so too was Van Jones's urban policy monograph raised into a *"What Is To Be Done"* manifesto for deep structural reforms capable of busting the onset of a major depression. (V. Jones, 'Green Collar Economy')

Where Van Jones' approach to both the green and solidarity economies most compels our attention is that he starts where the need is greatest, the millions of unemployed and underemployed inner city youth. The structural crises of neoliberal capitalism has long ravaged this sector of our society through deindustrialization, environmental racism and a wrecking ball approach to schools in favor of more prisons. To borrow from Marx, these young people are bound with radical chains, and when they break them with the tools suggested in Green Collar Economy, they free not themselves, but the rest of us are set in a positive direction as well.

However, Green Collar Economy's core mass base remains a united Black and Latino community in close alliance with organized labor, the same engine of change that put Obama in the White House. In addition, by asserting the interests and needs of that base, the green jobs and infrastructure proposals in Obama's stimulus package serve to drive the entire recovery effort in a progressive direction.

Davidson also promoted Van Jones' April 2009 Left Forum[507] at Pace University in New York.

I had to quickly get to the next panel, since I was on it, and there was only about five minutes between sessions. "Building a Progressive Majority and Advancing a Vision of Socialism" was the title, and it was pulled together by my group, Committees of Correspondence for Democracy and Socialism, and Chaired by Pat Fry, an SEIU staffer.

I led off by presenting Van Jones's program for Green Jobs for inner city youth, but framing it as a larger structural reform project that could, if done right, unite a progressive majority and help get us out of the current crisis. At the same time, we had to unite a militant minority around socialist tasks, so I offered the solidarity economy movement and its projects as practical examples of cooperative forms that could, within the

---

[507] http://www.zmag.org/znet/viewArticle/21276

81-6 Green Jobs - Van Jones

capitalist present, point to a socialist future. (Davidson, Keep on Keepin' On 2009)

There you have it - sextegenarian Maoists, unfulfilled Weathermen, socialists and communists are pushing their agenda in the White House through a mouthpiece they have promoted and nurtured over many years.

"Green Jobs" is a cover for increased socialization of the US economy, driven by a man who seven years ago was an ultra-militant San Francisco street communist. Do you have more understanding as to why Van Jones (and Barack Obama) hold the positions they do today?

82. Obama, the Communist Van Jones and the Demos Connection

Trevor Loudon © Monday, August 17, 2009

Why did President Obama choose a communist, Van Jones, to be his "Green Jobs Czar?"

Why did Obama risk controversy by appointing a well-known street radical to a senior position in the White House?

Exploring Jones' links to former Weather Underground[508] '60s Maoists and the Committees of Correspondence for Democracy and Socialism, it becomes clear these are connections that both men have in common.

There is another connection however, one untouched by either the mainstream media or the blogosphere.

82-1 Van Jones

In a September 26, 2008, in an article, posted on the website of the radical Institute for Policy Studies (IPS),[509] two IPS staffers Phyllis Bennis and Chuck Collins posted twenty-two names they thought would make

---

[508] http://newzeal.blogspot.com/2009/08/obama-file-81-former-weathermen.html Chapter 81 - Former Weather Underground Terrorists and '60s Maoists Nurtured Obama's "Green Jobs" Czar
[509] http://newzeal.blogspot.com/2009/01/blog-post.html Chapter 60 - Institute For Policy Studies Plans Obama's America

suitable appointments for an Obama administration.

Take note this was several weeks before Obama won the election.

Collins recommended:[510]

> Van Jones, of the Ella J Baker Center of Human Rights, to direct the Commerce Department's new "green jobs initiative,"

82-2 Chuck Collins

Six months later, on March 10, 2009, Van Jones is appointed "Green Jobs Czar;" and more officially Special Adviser for Green Jobs, Enterprise and Innovation at the White House Council on Environmental Quality.

What is the connection here?

One organization unites Barack Obama, Van Jones[511] and Chuck Collins, DEMOS, a Fifth Avenue New York based think tank.

An influential organization, DEMOS is a key component of the "progressive" machine that brought Obama and the Democrats to power in 2008.

Besides being Director,[512] Program on Inequality and the Common Good at the Institute for Policy Studies, Chuck Collins[513] worked as Director of the Tax Program, Business for Shared Prosperity.

In the mid-1990s, Collins was one of several IPS people who helped organize the New Party in 1995 in Chicago.

Van Jones[514] serves on the Demos Board of Trustees.

Where does Obama fit in?

According to the Demos website:

---

510 http://www.ips-dc.org/articles/742

511 http://www.DEMOS.org/

512 http://www.ips-dc.org/staff/chuck

513 http://www.DEMOS.org/people.cfm

514 http://www.DEMOS.org/board.cfm#jones

DEMOS began as a vision of Charles Halpern--then the President of the Nathan Cummings Foundation and a veteran non-profit entrepreneur. He was troubled by the narrow conversation about America's future. On the eve of the 21st century, it seemed that America no longer had the imagination to tackle its largest problems and build a more just society.

Halpern set out to challenge the status quo with a new institution. He envisioned a dynamic hub for creative scholars and cutting-edge practitioners--an organization that combined ideas and action to chart a new set of priorities for America.

82-3 DEMOS ACORN Project Vote –
Motor voter Registration program

By 1999, Halpern had assembled a talented working group to develop DEMOS. Among them were::

- David Callahan – (a fellow at the Century Foundation)

- Rob Fersh - (a long-time policy advocate)

- Stephen Heintz – (Vice-President of the East-West Institute)

- Sara Horowitz - (founder of Working Today)

- Arnie Miller - (a leading executive recruiter)

- Barack Obama – (then a state senator from Illinois)

- David Skaggs - (a congressman from Colorado)

- Linda Tarr-Whelan – (an internationally recognized expert on women and economic development)

This working group would eventually form the core of DEMOS' staff and Board of Trustees. (DEMOS 2000)

The question here is obvious. Why would an obscure Illinois State Senator with a funny name be "cherry picked" to help set up a new "think tank" in New York?

All the others had records of accomplishment: Heintz was even a member of the "prestigious" Council on Foreign Relations.

Why humble Barack Obama?

One possible connection was Obama's work in the '90s leading Illinois Project Vote and his strong connections to the radical community group ACORN.

DEMOS worked with ACORN and its voter registration wing

Project Vote on several projects.

In fact, the three organizations are almost "partners."

In 2005, a report on DEMOS/ACORN/Project Vote motor registration project surfaced.

DEMOS[515] Lorraine Minnite served on the Project Vote[516] Board.

DEMOS President Miles Rapoport was one of ACORN's most ardent defenders when the organization was accused of widespread voter registration fraud during the 1008 election.

Another possible connection is through the Institute for Policy Studies (IPS) itself.

The IPS website lists DEMOS as a "partner" organization.

Several DEMOS personnel have IPS connections including founder "father of public interest law" Charles Halpern.

In the 1960s, Halpern became Corporate Secretary to IPS. He began to attend IPS seminars and parties at the Institute and at the home of founder Marcus Raskin, where he mixed with radicals Paul Goodman and Ivan Ilich.

82-4 Institute for Policy Studies: Partner Organizations

Raskin and several other activists were arrested for conspiring to obstruct the military draft during the Vietnam War. Halpern helped with their defense. Halpern even flew with Raskin to a meeting with the other defendants and their lawyers at the Greenwich Village home of radical lawyer and secret Communist Party USA member Leonard Boudin; father of future Weather Underground terrorist Cathy Boudin.

Halpern later served as President of the left leaning Nathan Cummings Fund, a significant IPS donor.

Several people around Obama have IPS connections including his Chicago mentor, former US Representative Abner Mikva (D-IL-2nd

[515] http://www.DEMOS.org/people.cfm
[516] http://www.projectvote.org/home.html

District).

In 1979, Don Rose and Obama's right hand man David Axelrod served in the leadership of the IPS spinoff Conference on Alternative State and Local Policies, with Miles Rapoport.

The four founders of Progressives for Obama (P4O) Barbara Ehrenreich, Bill Fletcher Jr., Danny Glover and Tom Hayden all have IPS ties.

Ehrenreich is an IPS Trustee, Bill Fletcher Jr. is an IPS Scholar, both are members of Democratic Socialists of America and both helped found the New Party.

Danny Glover Chairs the Board of IPS "partner organization" TransAfrica Forum and Tom Hayden is a long-term IPS associate, going back to Conference on Alternative State and Local Policies days.

Saul Alinsky's radical methods helped Obama learn the ropes in his "community organizing days." Alinsky was an occasional IPS lecturer back in the 1960s.

Seven years ago, Van Jones was a San Francisco hardcore Alinskyite street communist. After hooking up with the Committees of Correspondence for Democracy and Socialism, Democratic Socialists of America, former '60s Maoists, the Weather Underground and DEMOS managed to land a job in the White House.

Twenty-two years ago, Barack Obama was a Chicago Alinskyite "community organizer." After hooking up with the Committees of Correspondence for Democracy and Socialism, Democratic Socialists of America, former '60s Maoists, Weather Underground and DEMOS he managed to land a job in the White House.

Could there be a connection?

83. Obama's Man Van Jones: Many Roads Lead to Cuba, Communism

Trevor Loudon © Thursday, August 27, 2009

There are two big questions that hang over President Obama's radical "Green Jobs Czar" Van Jones.

Is he still a communist? And is he a security threat?

Did Van Jones' commitment to communism end when STORM dissolved in 2002?

A 2004 treatise: *Reclaiming Revolution: History, Summation, and Lessons from the Work of Standing Together to Organize a Revolutionary Movement* written and endorsed by a majority of former STORM members, makes it clear that most ex- STORMers are still committed to the revolutionary movement.[517]

83-2 Reclaiming Revolution

From page 49:

> When the last sixteen STORM members decided to dissolve, each committed as an individual revolutionary to helping this emerging trend continue to consolidate.
>
> Some are building organizations in working class communities of color...Some are promoting revolutionary ideas. Some are developing revolutionary cadre...
>
> Some are finding other ways to serve the people. (Westerfield 2009)

Most former STORM members are still active in San Francisco or New York. The STORM created or staffed organizations Ella J. Baker Center for Human Rights,[518] POWER,[519] SOUL,[520] FIERCE,[521] War Times[522] and Women of Color Resource Center[523] are all going strong and still receiving mega-bucks from multiple left wing foundations.

All these organizations are still networked with former STORM associates such as Harmony Goldberg, Raquel Lavina, Maria Poblet, Adam Gold, Cindy Wiesner, Jason Negron-Gonzales, Mei-ying Williams or Steve Williams who are active in one group while serving on the board of another.

---

[517] http://www.leftspot.com/blog/files/docs/

[518] http://www.ellabakercenter.org/page.php?pageid=45

[519] http://therealbarackobama.wordpress.com/2009/04/13/more-storm-stories/

[520] http://therealbarackobama.wordpress.com/2009/04/09/storm-stories/

[521] http://www.fiercenyc.org/media/docs/9700_fiercenewsletter_12.06_final.pdf

[522] http://www.war-times.org/

[523] http://therealbarackobama.wordpress.com/2009/04/19/storm-story-women-of-color-resource-center/

Most former Bay Area STORMers are working with cadre from the Communist Party USA offshoot Committees of Correspondence for Democracy and Socialism (COCDS).

Van Jones himself has long worked with people from the CCDS orbit including Betita Martinez, Roxanne Dunbar-Ortiz, Linda Burnham, Max Elbaum, Felicia Gustin and Bob Wing.

In February 2006, three years after STORM folded and three years before appointment to his White House position, Van Jones was keynote speaker[524] at a Committees of Correspondence fundraiser in Berkeley.

> The second annual COCDS and Kendra Alexander Foundation Banquet will take place on Sunday, February 19 at the Redwood Gardens community room in Berkeley with Van Jones, a pioneering human rights activist known as a steadfast opponent of police brutality and mass incarceration, as keynote speaker.
>
> Jones is now working to create, "green-collar" jobs for incarcerated persons.
>
> The banquet is titled "Towards Building a Progressive Majority" and benefits the Committees of Correspondence for Democracy and Socialism and the Kendra Alexander Foundation. The Foundation, named in honor of the visionary leader of the Committees of Correspondence. (V. Jones, Second Annual Banquet Gathers to Build Progressive 2006)

Maybe Jones did not realize he was addressing a Marxist-Leninist function. Maybe he thought it was a Rotary or PTA group.

Of even more concern are the close ties between STORM, the Bay Area COCDS, foreign communists and Cuba.

According to "Reclaiming Revolution," several STORM members traveled to Cuba in 1999 as part of the notorious Venceremos Brigades.

> One of the most formative "political education sessions" of this period was a group trip to Cuba in the summer of 1999.
>
> Several STORM members participated in the Venceremos Brigade to see and support one of the world's few surviving socialist states.
>
> Members came back with a heightened understanding of both socialism and capitalism and a stronger commitment to red politics.

---

[524] http://lists.portside.org/cgi-bin/listserv/wa?A2=ind0601d&L=portside&P=1708

As STORM seldom exceeded 20 members, Van Jones, as a leader of the organization was on that, or another, Cuba trip.

Is this a good question for some enterprising journalist?

Three STORM leaders also travelled to South Africa in 1998 for the South African Communist Party conference.

Students founded the Venceremos Brigades in 1969. The following is by Students for Democratic Society (SDS) radical Carl Davidson:[525]

> Davidson and Tom Hayden take credit for having launched in 1969 the "Venceremos Brigades," which covertly transported hundreds of young Americans to Cuba to help harvest sugar cane and interact with Havana's communist revolutionary leadership. (The Brigades were organized by Fidel Castro's Cuban intelligence agency, which trained "brigadistas" in guerrilla warfare techniques, including the use of arms and explosives.) (Davidson, Discover the Networks 2009)

83-3 Venceremos Brigadistas entering US from Canada

Hayden and Davidson were two of the five founders of a new organization in 2008 - Progressives for Obama (P40). Davidson has a personal history with Obama when they worked together in the Chicago New Party and in anti-Iraq War activism.

STORM associate Mei-ying Ho traveled to Cuba with the 2004 Venceremos Brigade. Now married to another STORM associate, Steve Williams, Mei-ying Williams is involved with the Women of Color Resource Center where she works with Linda Burnham and well-known radical and COCDS leader Angela Davis.

Steve Williams, who has been to South Africa, Cuba and Venezuela, now runs People Organized to Win Employment Rights (POWER).

He worked on the organizing committee of anti-Iraq War magazine *War Times* with Van Jones, Betita Martinez, Linda Burnham, Max Elbaum, Felicia Gustin, Bob Wing and Adam Gold in the '00s.

In July 2009, Steve Williams represented POWER at the COCDS

---

[525] http://www.discoverthenetworks.org/individualProfile.asp?indid=2322

National Convention in San Francisco.

According to Carl Davidson[526]-elected as one of COCDS's four new co-leaders at the conference:

> The panel featured responses to the "Democracy Charter" by Bill Fletcher, Jr., editor of Black Commentator, Michael Eisenscher of US Labor Against the War, Jacqueline Cabasso from Western States Legal Foundation, Frank del Campo from the Labor Council for Latin American Advancement, and Steve Williams of People Organized to Win Employment Rights (POWER). Bill Fletcher, Jr. cast the Charter as a political and social guide for mass struggle." (Davidson, Keep on Keepin' On 2009)

Jacqueline Cabasso is a Communist Party USA supporter. Bill Fletcher Jr. is with Democratic Socialists of America and was with Davidson and Tom Hayden, one of the five key founders of Progressives for Obama (P40).

The conference attracted several international guests:

> International guests included Chris Matlhako from the South African Communist Party and Marcos Garcia from the Venezuelan Embassy in DC gave a picture of protracted

83-4 Steve Williams

> battles against neo-liberalism and their efforts to build and maintain unity on the left in their countries.

> Helmut Scholz, a leader of Die Linke (The Left Party) of Germany, described the unity efforts between groups in East and West Germany that brought together its forerunner, the Party of Democratic Socialism, made up of the former East German Communists, and groupings of Left Social Democrats from the West. Their common task now, he explained, was making sure the burden of the capitalist crisis was not placed on the working class.

> Jackeline Rivera, an FMLN deputy to the legislature of El Salvador, was warmly received. She revealed how, in their recent electoral victory, the FMLN saw two left groups break away, and the national unity efforts that followed.

---

[526] http://carldavidson.blogspot.com/2009/08/socialism-and-emerging-progressive.html

Solidarity messages to COCDS were read to from Cuba and Vietnam and "The Internationale" was sung. (Davidson, Keep on Keepin' On 2009)

Carl Davidson is of course also a big fan and promoter of Van Jones' work.

Van Jones associates Linda Burnham, Bob Wing, Betita Martinez, Roxanne Dunbar-Ortiz, Linda Burnham, Max Elbaum and Bob Wing are veterans of the Venceremos Brigades or multiple trips to former East Bloc countries.

83-5 Helmut Scholz of Die Linke, Germany; Chris Matlhako of the Communist Party of South Africa, and Angela Davis of CCDS

Jones' friend Betita Martinez is a Cuban visitor.

In 1959, three months after the Cuban Revolution claimed victory; Martinez went to Cuba to witness a successful anti-colonial, socialist struggle. This trip to Cuba had a profound impact on her.

In addition to Cuba, Martinez later traveled to the Soviet Union, Poland, Hungary, Vietnam (during the war), and China to witness and observe how people were implementing socialism.

Roxanne Dunbar Ortiz worked in Cuba with the Venceremos Brigades and with other revolutionaries including the Students for a Democratic Society (SDS) and its terrorist offshoot the Weather Underground. She also worked in London in the 1960s with the South African Communist Party controlled African National Congress.

Not to mention over a hundred trips to Nicaragua, in Sandinista times. In addition, another Cuban connection is even more concerning.

When Van Jones ran the "Ella J. Baker Center for Human Rights," the organization was close to another Bay Area institution - DataCenter.[527]

---

[527] http://www.datacenter.org/

Impact research for social justice

83-6 Data Center is essentially the intelligence hub of the US left

Founded by Jon Frappier, a former supporter of the Weather Underground Organization, Datacenter is the intelligence hub of the US left.

The Oakland California based organization provides strategic information & research training to communities advocating for dignity, justice & civil rights.

According to a history published on Data Center:[528]

> 1977   Data Center—an activist library and publication center—is founded in affiliation with the North American Congress on Latin America (NACLA) by Jon Frappier, Fred Goff, Loretta & Harry Strharsky and 40 dedicated volunteers.

> 1979   Establish Corporate Profile Project for clients including the United Nations Centre on Transnational Corporations & customized research Service for immigration attorneys representing Central Americans seeking political asylum.

> 1980   Publish press profiles, The Reagan File, on Ronald Reagan and his policies on labor, El Salvador, foreign policy, and military policy in Asia.

> 1983   Expand Search Service to include corporate accountability research to support community, labor, and corporate campaigns and political asylees from all over the world. The DataCenter also admits to being an "information" gatherer for Cuban "institutions."

> 1991   Launch the Cuba Project/Conexiones to respond to information needs of institutions in Cuba & facilitates information exchange between US and Cuban colleagues for the next ten years (Data Center 2009)

Data Center's ties to Jones' Ella J. Baker Center for Human Rights are

---

[528] http://www.datacenter.org/about/history/

close. Diana Frappier, who helped Jones establish and run the Center, is believed to be a relative of Jon Frappier.

Celina Ramirez worked as a Policy Director at the Ella J. Baker Center for Human Rights in 2006. In 2006-2007 served on the DataCenter Board.

In 2002, DataCenter celebrated its 25th Anniversary with a gala celebration honoring:

83-7 Diana Frappier

> Youth United for Community Action, Southwest Organizing Project, and Ella J Baker Center for Human Rights and Youth Force Coalition for their Books Not Bars campaign (Data Center 2009)

Van Jones sprang from this environment. These are his "roots."

Has Jones abandoned the values he held and the people he worked with up until a few months ago, because he now has more power, money and influence?

Working in the White House is (or should be) a high security job.

Van Jones now has access to all sorts of high-level information and gossip.

He has President Obama's ear on economic and social matters that could influence the US economy and US military power and security.

Has Van Jones abandoned his core convictions and past associations during the last 6 months?

After all, the Obama White House claims to have vetted all appointments. So he must be OK, right?

84. Why was Obama's "Brain" Valerie Jarrett so Happy to Hire Communist Van Jones? Was it Fate?

Trevor Loudon © Wednesday, September 09, 2009

Why was President Barack Obama's friend and senior adviser Valerie Jarrett happy to recruit Bay Area communist Van Jones to the White House?

Van Jones' radicalism was well known on the US left. His links to

STORM and Committees of Correspondence for Democracy and Socialism were no secret.

Why would Valerie Jarrett be happy about a socialist advising her friend and President?

Barack Obama links to the Hawaiian Communist Party network through his boyhood/teenage mentor Frank Marshall Davis.

After moving to Chicago, Obama linked up with the local communist networks.

Manning Marable, a leader of the Committees of Correspondence for Democracy and Socialism, claims that Obama:

> "Understands what socialism is. Many of the people working with him are, indeed, socialists with backgrounds in the Communist Party or as independent Marxists. There are a lot of people like that in Chicago who has worked with him for years."

84-1 Vernon Jarrett

It seems that Valerie Jarrett is following a family tradition - one of promoting up and coming radical politicians.

In the '40s, Valerie Jarrett's future father-in-law, Vernon Jarrett was a rising activist and journalist on the South Side of Chicago.

Vernon Jarrett

Vernon Jarrett worked in the South Side Community Art Center and on the black run *Chicago Defender* newspaper.

The Communist Party had several cadres in both organizations, including a covert member, the black poet and journalist, Frank Marshall Davis.

Jarrett and Davis also had a third organization in common, Communist Party dominated Citizen's Committee to Aid Packinghouse Workers, which in 1948 was "organized to support the United Packing-House workers of America C.I.O. now on strike."

A letter dated April 12, 1948, notes that CIO Congress of Industrial Organizations was at the time a communist controlled labor federation.

CITIZENS' COMMITTEE TO AID PACKING-HOUSE WORKERS

Organized to support the United Packing House Workers of America C. I. O. now on strike

4859 So. Wabash Avenue   phone: Livingston 7365-7275

Chicago, Illinois

SIDNEY A. JONES JR.,
   Chairman
MRS. HATTIE E. BRYAN   April 12, 1948.
   Co-Chairman
THOMAS M. CLARKE   Dear Friend:
   Secretary
OSCAR C. BROWN
   Treasurer   The next meeting of the Citizens' Committee to Aid
MRS. LOUISE T. PATTERSON   Packing-House Workers will be held at Madam Walker's College,
   Asst. Treasurer   4735 South Parkway, Second Floor, Thursday, April 15, 1948, at
COMMITTEE MEMBERS   8:00 P. M. Please be present.
   Sven Anderson
   Joseph D. Bibb

84-2 Letterhead Committee to Aid Packing - House Workers

In the left margin of the letterhead is a partial list of Citizen's Committee to Aid Packinghouse Workers officials.

The names that appear include Oscar C. Brown (Treasurer), Louise T. Patterson (Assistant Treasurer), F.M. Davis and Vernon Jarrett.

To confirm the connection, there is a close-up of the organization's publicity committee. It is Chaired by Vernon Jarrett and includes Frank Marshall Davis.

That the Citizen's Committee was communist influenced is beyond doubt.

Louise T. Patterson was the wife of Illinois Communist Party Vice-Chairman William Patterson and a prominent Party member in her own right.

SIDNEY A. JONES JR.,
   Chairman
MRS. HATTIE E. BRYAN
   Co-Chairman
THOMAS M. CLARKE
   Secretary
OSCAR C. BROWN
   Treasurer
MRS. LOUISE T. PATTERSON
   Asst. Treasurer
COMMITTEE MEMBERS
   Sven Anderson
   Joseph D. Bibb
   Oscar C. Brown
   Mrs. Mattie E. Bryan
   Thomas M. Clarke
   Theodore Coleman
   Charles A. Davis
   Frank M. Davis
   George Dorsey
   Hilliard Ellis
   Si Falk
   Albert George
   Mrs Irene M. Gaines
   Rev. Arthur D. Gray
   John M. Gray
   Dr. C. Stanley Hough
   Dr. Jenkins Hightower
   Mrs. Margaret Hayes
   Dr. Maurice Hebert
   Vernon Jarrett
   Joseph Jefferson
   Horace Johnson
   Mrs. Marjorie Joyner
   B. F. Jones
   Sidney A. Jones Jr.
   Ulysses S. Keyes
   Rev. William Latham
   Theophilus Mann

84-3 Left Edge of Letterhead

Further down the page was a list of the organization's "Food and groceries committee" including Ishmael Flory, a leader of the Illinois Communist Party from the late 1930s until his death in 2004.

Oscar C. Brown, Jr.

Oscar C. Brown, later a famous jazz musician under the name Oscar Brown Jr., was also at the time a Communist Party member. He joined in 1946 and was expelled around 1954.

84-4 Oscar C. Brown, Jr.

In 1948, Vernon Jarrett left his job as journalist at the *Chicago Defender* to start a black oriented radio show "*Negro Newsfront*" with Oscar Brown.

Late the same year, Frank Marshall Davis moved to Hawaii where he was active in the underground Communist Party. At one point, like many of his comrades, Davis became a Democratic Party official.

Later in 1970, Frank Marshall Davis met and mentored a fellow future Democrat named Barack Obama.

Vernon Jarrett was on the left and, like his colleague Frank Marshall Davis, a covert member of the Communist Party.

Vernon Jarrett went on to become the *Chicago Tribune's* first black syndicated columnist and was a founder of the National Association of Black Journalists.

According to a Washington Post obituary May 25, 2004:

> Mr. Jarrett continually shone a light on African American history and pertinent issues in Chicago and throughout the country. He stoked the political embers in Chicago that led to the 1983 election of the city's first African American Mayor Harold Washington.
>
> Vernon Jarrett was a key influence in Washington's decision to run for the Chicago Mayoralty and remained a key supporter through his four-year tenure. (Lamb, Vernon Jarrett, 84, Journalist, Crusader - Obituaries 2004)

Harold Washington defeated the Daley machine to win the Mayoralty backed by a coalition led by Chicago's Communist Party and the local branch of Democratic Socialists of America.

Democratic Socialists of America (DSA) member and socialist historian, Paul Buhle, wrote in a 1992 article for the *Encyclopedia of the American Left*:[529]

---

[529] http://eprints.cddc.vt.edu/marxists//history/usa/parties/Communist Partyusa/encyclopedia-american-left.htm

Communists also gained from long-standing political contacts in the black community. Victories of black Mayoral and congressional candidates with decades - old ties to the Communist Party - a short list would include Coleman Young and George Crocket in Detroit, Gus Newport in Berkeley, and more ambiguously, Harold Washington in Chicago. (Buhle and Georgakas, History of the Comintern Sections Communist Party USA 1992)

Washington was involved in Communist Party fronts, including the US Peace Council and the Chicago Committee on Southern Africa, right up to winning the Mayoralty with Party support. After victory, he stacked his administration full of communists, socialists and sympathizers to create the greatest far-left administration in US history only to be cut short by his pre-mature death in 1987.

Illinois Communist Party organizer, John Bachtell, remarked to a Special District Meeting on African American Equality and Building the Communist Party and Young Communist League:[530]

The legacy of Harold Washington's election and his administration is in the collective consciousness not of the African American community, but the entire city. Many of his democratizing achievements endure 20 years later.

The historic election of Washington was the culmination of many years of struggle. It reflected a high degree of unity of the African American community and the alliance with a section of labor, the Latino community, and progressive minded whites. This legacy of political independence also endures, reflected in the historic election of Barack Obama. Our Party supported Obama during the primary election.

Once again, Obama's campaign reflected the electoral voting unity of the African American community, but also the alliances built with several key trade unions, and forces in the Latino and white communities.

It also reflected a breakthrough with white voters. In the primary, Obama won 35 percent of the white vote and seven north side wards, in a crowded field. During the general election, he won every ward in the city and all the collar counties. This appeal has continued in his Presidential run. (Bachetell 2007)

Barack Obama has stated that Harold Washington's victory in 1983

---

[530] http://www.Communist Partyusa.org/article/articleview/858/1/39/

was the spur that made him leave New York for a $13,000 a year job as a "community organizer" in South Chicago.

Vernon Jarrett was also a fan of Barack Obama. He watched his career grow and became an ardent supporter.

In 1992, Obama worked for the ACORN offshoot, Project Vote, to register black voters in support of the Senate Campaign of Carol Moseley-Braun. Moseley-Braun also had strong Communist Party ties and was Harold Washington's legislative floor leader.

Obama helped Moseley-Braun win her Senate seat and then won the seat in 2004 - backed by the same communist/socialist alliance that had elected his political predecessors, Harold Washington and US Senator Carol Moseley-Braun (D-IL).

Commenting on the 1992 race, Vernon Jarrett wrote in the *Chicago Sun-Times* of August 11, 1992:

> Good news! Good news! Project Vote, a collectivity of ten church-based community organizations dedicated to black voter registration, is off and running. Project Vote is increasing its rolls at a 7,000-per-week clip...If Project Vote is to reach its goal of registering 150,000 out of an estimated 400,000 unregistered blacks statewide, "it must average 10,000 rather than 7,000 every week," says Barack Obama, the program's executive director...
> (Jarrett, Project Vote brings Power to the People 1992)

Dee Myles is a Chicago activist and Chair of the Education Commission of the Communist Party USA. In 2004, after Vernon Jarrett's death from cancer, she penned this tribute for the *People's World* of June 5[531]:

> Readers like me can be extremely selective of the journalists we read habitually. We are selective about the journalists to whom we become insatiably addicted, and once hooked we develop a constructive love affair without the romance.

> Such was my experience with Vernon Jarrett, an African American journalist in Chicago who died at the age of 86 on May 23. I became a Vernon Jarrett addict, and I am proud of it!

> Vernon Jarrett's career as a journalist in Chicago began and ended at the Chicago Defender, the African American daily paper. In between, he

---

[531] http://www.peoplesworld.org/vernon-jarrett-a-partisan-journalistic-giant/

was the first Black journalist at the Chicago Tribune, and I first began to read his articles during his tenure at the Chicago Sun-Times

Jarrett's claim to fame is that he was a partisan of the cause of African Americans in the broad democratic tradition of Paul Robeson and W.E.B. DuBois...

84-5 Barbara Bowman greets Barack Obama

Robeson and DuBois were both Communist Party members. On April 9, 1998, at Chicago's South Shore Cultural Center, Jarrett hosted a Paul Robeson Citywide Centennial Celebration event, with his old comrade and Party sympathizer Margaret Burroughs and former Communist Party members Studs Terkel and his old friend Oscar C. Brown. (Myles 2004)

Paul Robeson encouraged Frank Marshall Davis to move to Hawaii. Dee Myles continues:

Jarrett was fanatical about African Americans registering and voting in mass for socially conscious candidates. He championed Harold Washington like a great warrior, and this March, from his hospital bed, wrote an article appealing to Black Chicago to turn out to vote for Barack Obama in the Illinois primaries. Obama astounded everyone with an incredible landslide victory as the progressive, Black candidate for the Democratic Party nomination for the US Senate seat from Illinois. From his sickbed, Vernon Jarrett issued a clarion call, and the people responded. (Myles 2004)

The Jarrett/Obama connection did not end with Vernon Jarrett's death, it moved to a higher level.

A former Deputy Corporation Counsel for Finance and Development under Harold Washington, Valerie Jarrett continued to work in the Mayor's office into the 1990s.

In 1991, while Deputy Chief of Staff for Chicago Mayor Richard J. Daley, Valerie Jarrett hired Michelle Robinson. At that time, she was engaged to Barack Obama.

Later Valerie Jarrett ran the finances for Obama's 2004 Senate bid and served as treasurer of Obama's HOPEFUND.

Jarrett became one of the Obamas' closest friends and advisers and sometimes even described as the "other side of Barack's brain."

Valerie Bowman's marriage to Vernon Jarrett's late son lasted five years, but the Bowman and Jarrett families had been lifelong friends.

Valerie Jarrett's mother and early childhood education author Barbara Taylor Bowman, also has some interesting connections.

For several years she has run the Chicago based Erikson Institute. An Erikson Board member was Chicago businessperson and "liberal" activist Tom Ayers, father of Weather Underground terrorist leader and long time Obama colleague Bill Ayers.

Bernardine Dohrn, wife of Bill and the real leader of the Weather Underground, has also served on the Erikson Board in recent years.

According to World Net Daily's Brad O'Leary:

> Tom Ayers served as a trustee of the Erikson Institute. The Institute distributed $46,025 in Northern Trust scholarships. At the time, the Erickson Institute Board of Trustees also included Ayers' convicted felon daughter-in-law, Bernadine Dohrn Ayers. In addition, the Institute's co-founder, Barbara Bowman, is the mother of close Obama adviser Valerie Jarrett. (O'Leary 2008)

In an obvious reference to Barbara Taylor Bowman, Bill Ayers wrote on page 82 of his book, "*A Kind and Just Parent*," describing his Hyde Park neighborhood:

> Just south I see the Robert Taylor Homes named for the first head of the Chicago Housing Authority, whose daughter, a neighbor and friend is President of the Erikson Institute. (Norris 2009)

Bill Ayers and Bernardine Dohrn have both been leaders of the radical Movement for a Democratic Society alongside Van Jones' associates Roxanne Dunbar-Ortiz and Betita Martinez.

Barbara Bowman was interviewed for Timuel Black's "*Bridges of Memory: Chicago's First Wave of Black Migration-an Oral History*." Timuel Black serves on the advisory Board of Committees for Correspondence for Democracy and Socialism[532] alongside Manning Marable and Van Jones' mentor and friend, Betita Martinez.

Timuel Black is also a longtime friend of Barack Obama.

---

[532] http://www.cc-ds.org/advisory_bd.html

The Erikson Institute, named after pioneering child educationalist Erik Erikson, an errant disciple of Sigmund Freud and coiner of the phrase "identity crisis." In 1950, Erikson became a cause célèbre on the left after leaving the University of California refusing to sign an anti-communist loyalty oath.

Larry Friedman, activist and author of the 1999 book, "*Identity's Architect: A Biography of Erik H. Erikson,*" also had ties to communism and California.

> Both my parents were very active in the Communist Party...So that's much where I picked up the activism." (Formwalt)

> In the late 1940s, Larry's family moved from Ohio to California for health reasons as Larry "was always getting sick. The real reason, as Dorothy Healy later explained to me, is the Party reassigned my father to California to organize." (L. Friedman 1999)

84-6 Eric Erikson

Larry Friedman[533] states that he been in contact with Erikson since the 1960s. Did the introduction come through his Communist parents?

Dorothy Healey, once the top communist in Southern California, later attended the 1992 founding conference of the Committees of Correspondence in Berkeley alongside later Van Jones' associates Betita Martinez, Roxanne Dunbar-Ortiz, Max Elbaum, Arnoldo Garcia and Bob Wing.[534]

In March 2009, the Communist Party's "*People's World*"[535] reprinted an Institute for Policy Studies article on the prospects for children under Obama.

Some are hopeful that the new administration of President Barack Obama, who appears focused on children's welfare and education, will reverse this decline.

---

[533] http://www.oah.org/pubs/nl/2007feb/friedman.html
[534] http://www.usasurvival.org/docs/COCDSbckgrnd.pdf
[535] http://www.peoplesworld.org/one-in-five-children-sinking-into-poverty/

"It is important to remember that for the first time in a long time we have a person who gets it," said Barbara Bowman, a consultant to the US Secretary of Education, praising Obama for "(understanding) the importance of early childhood care and education." (Litvinsky 2009)

It is almost as if it was fated that Jones, Jarrett's, and Obama's paths would cross.

85. Security Implications? Obama's Man Axelrod was Mentored by Marxist Radicals

Trevor Loudon © Friday, September 11, 2009

Few would dispute that Valerie Jarrett and David Axelrod are two of President Barack Obama's key advisors.

Valerie Jarrett's father-in-law Vernon Jarrett, worked with Communist Party member Frank Marshall Davis, in at least three communist dominated organizations in late 1940s Chicago.

85-1 Barack Obama and David Axelrod

Davis went on to mentor the young Barack Obama in Hawaii.

David Axelrod too has connections that stretch back to post war Chicago communism.

While a New Yorker by birth, David Axelrod studied political science at the University of Chicago in the '70s.

Later, while a start-out journalist with the *Hyde-Park Herald*, Axelrod was mentored by two older journalists cum political activists, Don Rose and David S. Canter.

According to the Chicago Tribune:

> In his early years as a political consultant, Axelrod, following in the footsteps of his mentor, the political strategist Don Rose, carved out a reputation for himself as a skillful specialist working for local progressive candidates...says Rose. "I think he's a principled, generally progressive guy." (Reardon 2007)

![VOICES - Hyde Park-Kenwood]

Published monthly by Voices Press. **Mailing address:** 1525 E. 53rd Street, Chicago, Illinois 60615. Telephone **(312) 667-7838.** Offices open by appointment only. Subscriptions: $2.50 per year.

Co-Publishers: David S. Canter, Don Rose. **Editor:** Don Rose. **Managing Editor:** Jody Parsons. **General Manager:** David S. Canter. **Business Manager:** Ray Sherman. **Community Organizations Editor:**

Don Rose

From 1966 until 1975, Don Rose and his partner David S. Canter co-owned a small newspaper called the *Hyde-Park Kenwood Voices*. The paper's radical tone suited the neighborhood. It tended to follow the Communist Party line campaigning for example to abolish the House Un-American Activities Committee.

The paper covered the Students for a Democratic Society (SDS) riots at the 1968 Chicago Democratic Party convention and the Students for a Democratic Society convention that gave birth to the Weather Underground.

It gave a voice to prominent figures of the Hyde Park left. These included several future Obama mentors; US Representative Abner Mikva (D-IL-2nd District), Leon Despres, Timuel Black and Quentin Young.

Chicago Students for a Democratic Society activist Paul Booth and Rennie Davis were *"Voices"* contributors. Davis wrote a November 1967 article about his visit to communist North Vietnam with future Progressives for Obama (P40) founder Tom Hayden.

The paper covered Quentin Young's 1972 trip to North Vietnam and his son Ethan's 1970 sojourn in Cuba with the Venceremos Brigades.

85-2 Don Rose

"Essentially what I see myself working for

is socialism in the United States," said Ethan, "Exactly how it will emerge, I'm still not sure...but that's what I'll be working for." (R. Davis 1967)

Don Rose and David Canter took the young David Axelrod under their wing. Axelrod was a regular visitor to the Canter household and the radical duo[536] took it upon themselves to "mentor" and "educate...politically," the young journalist.

Don Rose later wrote a reference letter for Axelrod that helped win the internship at the Chicago Tribune launching his career.

At the time, Rose was active in a Communist Party front, the Alliance to End Repression.[537]

The Alliance was set up to abolish the Chicago "Red Squad," the police unit charged with monitoring communist and radical organizations.

Rose's personal Red Squad file accused him of being a "member of the anarchists."

The Alliance's Executive Director was Communist Party member Richard Criley. Other Party members involved in the organization included Abe Feinglass, Jack Spiegel, Jesse Prosten and Norman Roth.

In addition, active in the Alliance was former Communist Party member Milton Cohen, Quentin Young, Timuel Black and Rabbi Arnold Wolf. All four went on to join Democratic Socialists of America, while Young, Black and Wolf all became close friends of Barack Obama.

Don Rose also chaired another Communist Party front, the Chicago Committee to Defend the Bill of Rights, succeeding comrade Richard Criley.

Rose had been radical since the 1940s when he joined Henry Wallace's communist controlled Progressive Party.

In the '50s, Rose was involved in the campaign for nuclear disarmament and in the 1960s was active in the civil-rights movement. He was Dr. Martin Luther King's Chicago press secretary for several

---

[536] http://blog.broadbandmechanics.com/2008/11/my-family-has-been-outed-were-dam-commies-but-we-aint-paid-to-be

http://www.archive.org/stream/nationwidedrivea02unit/nationwidedrivea02unit_djvu.txt

years.

In 1968, Rose asked to serve as press secretary to the Chicago Mobilization Committee; the Students for a Democratic Society (SDS)/Communist Party influenced alliance that wreaked havoc at the Chicago Democratic Party Convention. It was during these violent times that

85-3 Marilyn Katz, Chicago 1968

Rose coined the famous phrase - "the whole world is watching."

Through the Mobilization Committee, Rose met Marilyn Katz, the Students for a Democratic Society security officer for the demonstrations.

By the late 1970s, Rose was linked to[538] the Chicago coalition of former Trotskyists, Socialist Party members and communists that would, in 1982, form Democratic Socialists of America.

In 1982, David S. Canter and nine others invited black Democratic Party US Representative Harold Washington to stand for the Chicago Mayoralty.

Vernon Jarrett also played a role in persuading Washington to stand, but whether he was part of the 'nine' is unclear.

Washington had a long history with Chicago's communists and socialists. When he accepted, the

85-4 Harold Washington (r) at a 1981 Democratic Socialist dinner in Chicago

Communist Party and Democratic Socialists of America formed a multi-racial alliance behind Washington.

The alliance targeted black voters in a huge voter registration drive on the city's south side. Rose, Katz and Canter all worked on the successful campaign and all later secured jobs in Washington's administration.

In 1987, Washington won his election, aided by a young political

---

[538] http://www.chicagodsa.org/d1977/index.html

adviser - David Axelrod.

Though Washington died in office, the communist - socialist alliance lived on.

In 1992, the alliance elected the Communist - Democratic Socialists of America (DSA) US Senator Carol Moseley-Braun (D-IL) to the US Senate.

In 2004, it helped put Barack Obama into the same Senate seat.

According to *Salon*, January 2008:

> When Barack Obama was 22 years old, just out of Columbia University, he took a $10,000-a-year job as a community organizer on the South Side of Chicago. It was a shrewd move for a young black man with an interest in politics.
>
> The politician who set the stage for Obama's rise was also a South Side congressional US Representative Harold Washington elected Mayor of Chicago in 1983. In New York, Obama read about Washington's victory and wrote to City Hall, asking for a job. He never heard back, but he made it to Chicago months after Washington took office.
>
> Washington dropped dead of a heart attack in his second term. Nevertheless, the confidence he instilled in black leaders became a permanent factor in Chicago politics. His success inspired Rev. Jesse Jackson to run for President in 1984, which in turn inspired Obama. Washington also strengthened the community organizations in which Obama was cutting his teeth. Obama's Project Vote, which put him on the local political map, was a successor to the South Side voter registration drive that made Washington's election possible.
>
> Chicago has two unique advantages says political consultant, Don Rose. First, it is in Cook County, which contains half of Illinois' voters. Second, the local Democratic Party is a countywide organization. After Chicago's Carol Moseley-Braun beat two white men to win the 1992 Democratic Senate primary, precinct captains in white Chicago neighborhoods and the suburbs whipped up votes for her in the general election.
>
> "They had to go out and sell the black person to demonstrate that the party was still open," says Rose, who sees "direct links" from Washington to Moseley-Braun to Obama. (McClelland 2008)

Rose, Canter and Axelrod all worked on Moseley-Braun's 1992 campaign. Marilyn Katz worked with Obama on Project Vote, the huge voter registration drive that ensured Moseley-Braun's victory.

85-6 Obama's Anti-War Speech

By the '00s, Rose, Katz and another Obama associate and former Students for a Democratic Society member, Carl Davidson, had formed Chicagoans against the War in Iraq.

This group organized the 2002 Chicago anti-war rally where Obama came out against the Iraq War.

The speech was a major turning point in Obama's career. Obama consulted David Axelrod before staking out his position.

Katz was an Obama fundraiser in 2008 and is an endorser of the Progressives for Obama (P40) website. Carl Davidson helped found the organization and moderates its website.

In August 2008, Don Rose and Marilyn Katz gave an interview to the Democratic Socialists of America (DSA) linked journal "In These Times" before Obama's "coronation" at the Democratic Party Convention in Denver.

85-5 Campaign Poster

> ITT: Forty years ago this week, Chicago police battled protesters at the DNC. Two '60s radicals remember the madness, and look to Denver for change. The '68 Democratic National Convention debacle remains a symbol of everything that went wrong with American politics, society and culture in that tumultuous and iconic year. It was five days of mayhem in the Windy City. Five days that left the Democratic Party in shambles. In August 1968, those explosive battles put Chicago at the epicenter of one of the most searing political and social upheavals of the 20th century. In August 2008, a US senator from Chicago anointed the first black major-party nominee for the presidency of the United States. Don Rose...the political wise man has helped elect Mayors and senators since then, from Harold Washington Chicago to Paul Simon. Now 77, Rose, a mentor to David Axelrod, Obama's top campaign strategist the 1983 election of Harold Washington Chicago as Chicago's first black Mayor came courtesy of a progressive coalition of blacks, Latinos, and so-called

"Lakefront liberals." Katz and Rose were there, once again, as advisors and operatives.

Katz: My straight line goes from '66/'68 to the folks who began to work together and formed the core group of the Harold Washington campaign. (Almost) everyone I worked with in 1982 I had met as a kid in '68. I believe that Barack Obama could only have emerged in Chicago. Why? Because since '68 there was a web of relationships between black civil rights groups, anti-war groups, and women's activities, immigrant rights activities that has sustained and grown...

ITT: What we did here in Chicago had international implications: In '68 there was a workers' movement in Paris, there was a worldwide movement of students. We lost that in the intervening forty years. Now in 2008, with Barack Obama, we have a renewed sense that the whole world is watching again.

Katz: I think that millions of young people are flocking to Barack, as we did to the anti-war movement...

ITT: The Democratic Party will gather once again later this month. Everybody is expecting a big party in Denver. Will it be an Obama coronation? Is that what we should be looking for? So how do you resolve Obama's move to the center? What about holding his feet to the fire? Don't we need to keep him true to progressive issues?

Katz: We have to get him into office so then we can be the left opposition. I think it is a delicate balance between those of us who are progressive, how much you push, how much you don't want to put him in difficult positions that would embarrass him or give John McCain some advantage. (L. S. Washington, The Whole World was Watching 2008)

David J. Canter

The other half of the David Axelrod mentoring team, David S. Canter (1923/2004) had an even more exotic background.

Born in Boston, David Canter[539] was the son of Harry J. Canter, secretary of the Boston Communist Party.

---

http://www.archive.org/stream/partogourtime006520mbp/partogourtime006520mbp_djvu.txt

Whilst the Communist Party candidate for Massachusetts Secretary-of-State, Canter was arrested for carrying a placard "FULLER-MURDERER OF SACCO AND VANZETTI," attacking Governor Fuller for the execution of anarchists Sacco and Vanzetti. Harry Canter was tried, convicted, and jailed for a year for criminal libel in May 1929.

85-7 David J. Canter

After his release, Canter Senior moved his family, including son David, to the Soviet Union. The boy must have stayed in the "workers' paradise" for some time because according to his obituary in the *Chicago Sun-Times* of August 30, 2004:

> "After his release, Mr. Canter's father moved the family from Boston to Russia, where the young man developed a love for Russian literature..." (Chicago Sun Times 2004)

By 1946, the family had turned up in Chicago, where Harry Canter worked for many years as Secretary of Chicago Local 16 of the International Typographical Union.

Harry Canter later moved to San Francisco, where he remained

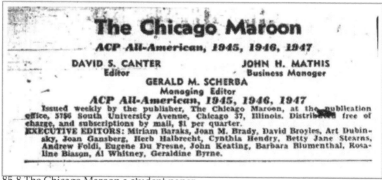

85-8 The Chicago Maroon a student paper

active in leftist causes. David Canter however remained in Chicago, where he was active in Communist Party circles and as editor of the student paper *Chicago Maroon*.

In 1958, David Canter graduated from the John Marshall Law School. He also edited the Packinghouse Workers Union newspaper *"Champion"*.

According to communist historian Max Friedman:

> The Packinghouse Workers Union was a long time Communist Party-influenced, if not controlled union that later merged with the Meatcutters to form the Communist Party-run Amalgamated Meatcutters & Butcherworkmens' Union, led by identified Communist Party labor leader Abe Feinglass, who was also a Vice President of the Soviet-KGB front, the World Peace Council. The House Un-American Activities Committee held some hearings on the Packinghouse Workers and one revealed that the future US Representative Charles Hayes (D-IL-1st District) was a high-ranking member of the Communist Party in the Meatcutters Union along with Feinglass. (M. Friedman 2008)

By 1960, David Canter had teamed up with well-known Chicago Communist Party member and colleague from *Chicago Maroon* days, LeRoy Wolins.

The pair owned a company, Translation World Publishers, which specialized in publications from and about the Soviet Union. The company soon attracted the attention of the House Un-American Activities Committee, which suspected Canter and Wolins of being conduits for Soviet propaganda.

85-9 House Un-American Activities report

The committee questioned Canter and Wolins on payments received from the Soviet Union.

The committee went on to find that:

> Translation World Publishers was an outlet for the distribution of Soviet propaganda...this publishing house subsidized by Soviet funds and was created by known Communists to serve the propaganda interests of the U.S.S.R. (US House of Representatives 1962)

In 1963/64, the Soviet Union tried to undermine Republican

85-10 Canter being questioned on payments received from Soviet Union

Presidential candidate Senator Barry Goldwater in favor of Democrat Lyndon B. Johnson. Goldwater lost the election paving the way for Johnson's "*Great Society*."

In their 1989 book, "*THE KGB AGAINST THE MAIN ENEMY-How the Soviet Intelligence Service Operates against the United States*" the US'

85-11 Canter questioned about membership in the Communist Party

premier communist researcher Herbert Romerstein and former KGB officer Stanislav Levchenko examined Soviet attempts to blacken Goldwater's name and other Soviet campaigns of the time.

> The false charge that Goldwater was a racist was one of the smear campaigns used against his candidacy by the Soviets and their surrogates. The American Communists covertly assisted in this "active measures" campaign.

> A 1963 booklet claimed that Goldwater was conspiring with the John Birch Society to organize a "putsch," or violent insurrection to take over the United States in 1964. The booklet, Birch Putsch Plans for 1964, contained no address for the publisher, Domino Publications. The author used the not-very imaginative pseudonym, "John Smith." There were no ties this publication linking the communists until an ad for the book in the pro-communist National Guardian for April 25, 1963, listed the publisher as "Domino Publications, Suite 900, 22 West Madison Street, Chicago, Illinois."

> This was in fact the address of Translation World Publishers, registered under the Foreign Agents Registration Act as an agent of the Soviet Union. The House Un-American Activities Committee identified the co-owners, LeRoy Wolins and David S. Canter, as members of the Communist Party USA.

> In 1965, Domino Publications of Chicago published a pamphlet attacking the NATO Multilateral Nuclear Force (MLF). The pamphlet, by David S. Canter, titled MLF-Force or Farce. It presented the Soviet arguments against the NATO nuclear defense. (Romerstein, Herbert and Levchenko, Stanislav 1989)

David S. Canter

By 1966, David Canter was working as an insurance sales representative and publishing *Hyde-Park Kenwood Voices* with Don Rose.

Great-West Life
congratulates
David S. Canter

85-12 David S. Canter

As stated above, by the '80s David Canter was trying to move Chicago to the left through Harold Washington's Chicago.

Charles Hayes, the secret Communist Party member from Canter's old Packinghouse Workers Union, took up his vacant congressional seat.

From the Chicago Democratic Socialist of America website:

The 1983 Thomas-Debs Dinner was held at the McCormick Inn on Saturday, May 7...Newly elected Mayor Harold Washington Chicago was unable to attend at the last minute. Carl Shier, who was to have introduced him, read a message from him instead, and spoke of Democratic Socialists of America (DSA)'s considerable role in Washington's election campaign. Congressman Danny K. Davis provided the Debs Thomas Dinner address.

Figure 85-13 David Canter and Harold Washington

A majority of the "grip & grin" shots included Charles Hayes, who (regardless of whether he had announced at the time of the Dinner) was running for the Congressional seat left vacant when Harold Washington Chicago won the Chicago Mayoral election. (Democratic Socialists of America 1983)

In October 2004, David Canter's son, Chicago IT consultant Marc Canter[540] reflected on his memory:

One day I stumbled downstairs into our kitchen to meet Harold Washington Chicago talking to my father.

Harold was the Congressman from our district and my father was explaining to him how he could split the white vote and become the first black Mayor of the city of Chicago.

My father had been mentoring, encouraging and working with Harold for 15 years by then and it worked. They won the election and Harold became history...

My father encouraged black politicians to get their piece of the pie.

---

[540] http://blog.broadbandmechanics.com/2004/09/who_was_david_s

> My father never charged for helping anyone out, and it was only until he was 65 did he ever accept a job from anyone he helped. He was one of those idealistic reds. (Canter, Who was David S. Canter #1 2004)

Indeed David Canter would not initially take a job under Washington, but after his 1987 re-election, Canter relented and became Deputy Commissioner of Streets and Sanitation.

Marc Canter has also written:

> My brother worked for Harold in D.C. when he was still a Congressman and got a job as a lawyer prosecuting crooked cops - when Harold came to power. My father remained in the inner circle and helped out on all sorts of political and community activities. (KeyWiki 2009)

Barack Obama was later a beneficiary of the work done for Washington.

From *The Nation* February 6, 2007:

> Axelrod and Forest Claypool...opened their own consulting shop, handling mostly long-shot candidates until 1987, when Chicago Mayor Harold Washington Chicago hired the firm to help with his re-election. Four years earlier, Washington had won a historic victory...As the Tribune's city hall bureau chief, Axelrod had ringside seats. "Nineteen eighty-three, that was a phenomenal election. Harold Washington Chicago —extraordinary guy. I mean, he was the most kinetic campaigner and politician that I've ever met. It was inspiring the way the African-American community came alive around the prospect of electing Harold...

> Axelrod sees Obama, who was working in Chicago as a community organizer during the Washington years, as a marker of progress, writing the second act of a story that Washington started.

> Twenty-one years later, when Barack ran for the US Senate in the primary against six strong candidates, he carried every ward on the northwest side except one. I was thinking and I told Barack, "that Harold Washington is smiling down on us." (Hayes 2007)

While David Canter and Barack Obama met through the 1992 Moseley-Braun campaign, the two were also both active in Independent Voters of Illinois.[541]

David Canter had become active in the organization in the 1940s

---

[541] http://www.iviipo.org/

85-14 Saul Mendelson

and remained involved up to his death in 2004.

Independent Voters of Illinois (IVI) was established to campaign for endorsed "progressive" candidates.

The government took an interest in IVI[542] as far back as 1944.

In 1944, the FBI prepared a more extensive intelligence report on an active political group, the Independent Voters of Illinois, because it was the target of Communist "infiltration." The Independent Voters group organized:

.".for the purpose of developing neighborhood political units to help in the re-election of President Roosevelt and the election of progressive congressmen. Apparently, IVI endorsed or aided democrats for the most part, although it was stated to be "independent." (Roosevelt, Presidential Directive of September 6, 1939 1944)

Other prominent IVI activists included familiar faces Milton Cohen, Timuel Black, and Trotskyist turned Socialist, Party member Saul Mendelson.

Like Cohen and Black, Mendelson also went on to join Democratic Socialists of America.

When Mendelson died in 1998, US Senator Carol Moseley-Braun (D-IL) and Barack Obama both spoke at his memorial Service.

Both Barack and Michelle Obama[543] were members of IVI and the organization endorsed Obama during his 2004 US Senate race.

In July 2004, IVI celebrated its 60th anniversary. Members of the event committee[544] included:

Timuel Black and Socialist Party veteran Leon Despres, DSA and Progressives for Obama member Wetty Wilhoitte, a whole host of DSA connected activists and politicians, Dick Simpson, Bernice Bild, Barbara Flynn Currie, Bob Mann, Joe Moore, David Orr, Toni Preckwinkle, Sue

---

[542] http://ftp.fas.org/irp/ops/ci/docs/ci1/ch4d.htm

[543] http://www.iviipo.org/iviipodec2003-rev.pdf

[544] http://www.iviipo.org/IDD60-archivedinfo2.htm

Purrington, Carol Moseley Braun and of course David S. Canter and Barack Obama.

That may have been the last time Canter and Obama met. Canter died the following month.

> My father was an old-time politico in Chicago and one of his old buddies, Don Rose writes a column for a Chicago web site called the 'Chicago Daily Observer'.

> In today's column he writes that Obama has taken a 50-42 lead in the polls.

> I'm saying this in honor of my father who fought for civil rights, against the Vietnam War and would be tickled pink to see what Barack is up to.

> I know he's looking down from wherever he is and laughing right now. (Canter, Marc's Voice: 50-42)

Damn right he is!

86. Obama "Czar" Ron Bloom's Socialist Vision for US Industry

Trevor Loudon © Wednesday, September 16, 2009

Czar Ron Bloom was named the Manufacturing Czar for the United States by President Barack Obama on September 8, 2009 - two days after communist "Green Jobs Czar" Van Jones resigned under pressure.

To understand Ron Bloom and his assigned role, it helps to know the environment he comes from.

The Obama Administration has emphasized Bloom's investment banking and business background.

86-1 Ron Bloom

Bloom has spent far longer in the labor and socialist movements than he has on Wall Street. There is even some evidence that Bloom went into banking to serve organized labor.

Like Obama himself, Bloom has moved in circles close to Democratic Socialists of America - an organization far more "socialist" than "democratic."

To illustrate Democratic Socialists of America (DSA)'s radicalism, I cite their journal *Democratic Left*, Spring 2007.[545] The article by Detroit Democratic Socialists of America (DSA) Chair and National Political Committee member David Green supports the Employee Free Choice Act (EFCA) - or "card check."

> What distinguishes socialists from other progressives is the theory of surplus value. According to Marx, the secret of surplus value is that workers are a source of more value than they receive in wages. The capitalist is able to capture surplus value through his ownership of the means of production, his right to purchase labor as a commodity, his control over the production process, and his ownership of the final product. Surplus value is the measure of capital's exploitation of labor
>
> Our goal as socialists is to abolish private ownership of the means of production. Our immediate task is to limit the capitalist class's prerogatives in the workplace...
>
> In the short run we must at least minimize the degree of exploitation of workers by capitalists. We can accomplish this by promoting full employment policies, passing local living wage laws, but most of all by increasing the union movement's power...
>
> The Employee Free Choice Act (EFCA) provides an excellent organizing tool through which we can pursue our socialist strategy while simultaneously engaging the broader electorate on an issue of economic populism. (Green, The Employee Free Choice Act - A Democratic Socialist of America Priority 2007)

Green explained how Democratic Socialists of America (DSA) could play a role in getting the Act passed through the Senate after the 2008 elections:

> The fact that we face an uphill battle in the Senate does not detract from the value of Democratic Socialists of America (DSA) doing organizing work around EFCA. At a minimum, we can force conservative senators to place themselves on record as opposed to EFCA. This would then make these incumbents even more vulnerable in the 2008 elections. If we replace only a few of these anti-labor senators in 2008, we should be able to pass EFCA in the next Congress.

---

[545] http://www.dsausa.org/dl/Spring_2007.pdf

Democratic Socialists of America (DSA) could play a role in organizing support for EFCA. We have locals and activists across the country capable of organizing successful public events as demonstrated by our Sanders house parties. We have "notables" capable of attracting non-Democratic Socialists of America (DSA) members to public events. We have academics, writers and speakers capable of elucidating public policy issues in clear and simple language. We have a solid relationship with several major unions-UAW, USW, and IAM. (Green, The Employee Free Choice Act - A Democratic Socialist of America Priority 2007)

Green went on to explain how Democratic Socialists of America (DSA)'s EFCA campaign could work - Democratic Socialists of America (DSA) could organize public meetings in coalition with other groups, including the AFL-CIO's Voice at Work Department, state AFL-CIOs and central labor councils, American Rights at Work, America Votes, Progressive Democrats of America, Committees of Correspondence, ACORN and state Democratic parties.

Green also listed individuals who could be invited to speak in support including John Edwards, John Sweeney, Cornel West, Barbara Ehrenreich, Leo Gerard, Ron Gettlefinger, David Bonior and openly socialist Vermont Senator Bernie Sanders.

Green emphasizes Democratic Socialists of America (DSA)'s ties to USW-United Steel Workers of America - also that the list of speakers included four Democratic Socialists of America (DSA) members AFL-CIO President John Sweeney, Cornel West, Barbara Ehrenreich and US Representative David Bonior (D-MI-17th District), plus Steel Workers Union President Leo Gerard.

Leo Gerard[546] recruited Czar Ron Bloom into the USW in 1996.

I said, "Why don't you come work at what you really believe in. He could play a lead role in bargaining, play a role in a number of different sectors in the economy and shape policy." (Carty 2009)

Bloom served as an adviser to the union President George Becker and to Leo Gerard when he took leadership in 2001.

---

[546] http://www.usatoday.com/money/autos/2009-03-18-auto-task-force-ron-bloom_N.htm

George Becker was close to Democratic Socialists of America (DSA) - serving on the Board of the Economic Policy Institute under Democratic Socialists of America (DSA) member Larry Mishel.

In 1996, Becker also helped found campaign for America's Future with Democratic Socialists of America (DSA) linked activists: John Atlas,

Barry Bluestone, Julian Bond, Richard Cloward, Peter Dreier, Barbara Ehrenreich, Jackie Kendall, Nelson Lichtenstein, Steve Max, Jay Mazur, Gerald McEntee, Harold Meyerson, Larry Mishel, Frances Fox Piven, Joel Rogers, Richard Rorty and John Sweeney.

86-3 Leo Gerard

In 1997, Chicago Democratic Socialists of America honored Becker at their annual Debs–Thomas-Harrington Dinner, the first Steelworker to be an honoree at the event.

George Becker spoke with pride about his birthplace, Granite City, Illinois. In the 1920s, they had a Socialist Mayor and a Socialist Council and Eugene Debs was an honored speaker at many events. He also spoke of a relative of his wife, in Missouri, who ran for office as a Socialist when Norman Thomas ran for President." (C. M. Shier, 39th Annual Dinner Makes the Organization Proud 1997)

86-2 George Becker

Leo Gerard, Czar Ron Bloom's most recent boss, is also well within the Democratic Socialists of America (DSA) "orbit."

Gerard serves on the Board of the Democratic Socialists of America (DSA) led Economic Policy Institute and on the advisory Board of Wellstone Action with Georgia State Representative Julian Bond, Gerald McEntee and Frances Fox Piven. Wellstone Action, named after late US Senator Paul Wellstone (D-MN), once faculty adviser to a Democratic Socialists of America (DSA) student group.

Leo Gerard also serves on the Board of the Apollo Alliance with Joel Rogers and SEIU Vice President and Democratic Socialists of America (DSA) member, Gerry Hudson. It is unclear if Gerard has ever worked with Apollo founder Van Jones, or New York director, former Weather Underground terrorist leader, Jeff Jones.

When Gerard became President of the United Steel Workers of America in 2001, Bob Roman[547] commented:

> The USWA has a long tradition of militant, good mostly leadership. Now they have someone both militant and radical, which is not surprising as Girard is a Canadian export with ties to the Canadian New Democratic Party. The New Democratic Party is the Canadian counterpart of Democratic Socialists of America. Both organizations are Socialist International affiliates. (Roman, Chicago Anti-FTAA Action 2001)

86-4 Galil Post Card

In May 2007, Chicago Democratic Socialists of America (DSA) honored Leo Gerard with its annual Debs-Thomas-Harrington Award - the second Steelworker to be an honoree at the event.

> For your lifetime of Service to your union and its members;
>
> For your leadership in building working class solidarity across borders;
>
> For your advocacy of fair trade over free trade;
>
> For your work in seeking public policies that support a healthy environment and energy independence;
>
> For your commitment to finding a better way to run the economy for working people everywhere;
>
> The Debs-Thomas-Harrington Dinner Committee does hereby present you with its annual award this 4th day of May 2007. (Roman, Where Do We Go From Here? 2007)

Czar Ron Bloom's background is similarly socialist.

Much of Bloom's childhood revolved around Habonim,[548] "a progressive Labor Zionist youth movement that emphasizes cultural Judaism, socialism and social justice."

---

[547] http://www.chicagodsa.org/ngarchive/ng76.html

[548]

http://www.jewishtimes.com/index.php/jewishtimes/article/ron_bloom_car_czar_in_the_labor_zionist_tradition/

At age 10, Bloom traveled with his two siblings to Camp Galil, a movement-run summer camp in Pennsylvania. He returned each season for the next four years becoming a camp counselor.

Bloom remembers his Habonim experience, "That's part of what I try to do in my work life... That's one of the things that made me want to work for Obama."

After graduating from Wesleyan University in 1977, Bloom worked as an organizer, researcher and negotiating specialist for the SEIU, working for a time under John Sweeney.

He later worked as Executive Director of the Massachusetts Coalition for Full Employment and as New England Regional Director of the Jewish Labor Committee.

The contact for the Detroit Jewish Labor Committee, Selma Goode, works in Greater Detroit Democratic Socialists of America (DSA) with David Green, author of the Democratic Left tract that opened this post.

While at SEIU, Czar Ron Bloom[549] concluded, that those unions lacked the technical skills to negotiate with management teams and their advisers at the bargaining table.

> "Unions were being backed into corners by companies and couldn't understand on a sophisticated level, the company's arguments...Labor needed to be armed with the equivalent skills." (Cohan 2009)

Bloom's next mission was to learn the ways of Wall Street.

Bloom went to Harvard Business School and became an investment banker with Lazard Freres, in New York.

According to future business partner Gene Keilin:

> "He recruited himself to Lazard...Unlike most young bankers; he was fully formed by the time he got here. He worked really hard. He came as a strong technical analyst. He understood valuation and financial

---

[549] http://money.cnn.com/2009/02/25/autos/Obama_car_czar.fortune/index.htm

instruments. The fact is he was a 24x7 guy long before that term was ever coined." (Cohan 2009)

After a period in partnership with Keilin, Bloom took a pay cut in 1996 to join the Steel Workers Union as a Special Assistant to the President and later head of the Union's Corporate Research, Industry Analysis and Pattern Bargaining Departments.

That Wall Street did not dampen Bloom's socialist zeal is evident in an article he contributed to the Fall 2006[550] edition of Democratic Socialists of America (DSA)'s *Democratic Left*.

Based on remarks delivered to the metal industry's Steel Success Strategies XXI Conference in New York in June 2006, Bloom revealed a strong antipathy towards America's traditional competitive free enterprise system.

> The Steelworkers have some advice for industry execs on how to make sure there's plenty for both shareholders and workers. The theme of this adVice will be really simple, be hard-headed and pragmatic capitalists, run the companies and actively participate in the political process on the basis of what is good for your shareholders, and not based on outmoded nostrums about unions, free enterprise, deregulation, free markets and free trade.

> In today's world, the blather about free trade, free-markets, and the joys of competition is nothing but pabulum for the suckers. The people making the real money know that outsized returns are available to those who find the industries that get the system to work for them and the companies within those industries that dominate them. (Perazzo 2009)

Bloom promoted the virtues of business/union "partnership:"

> The starting point is that companies need to get along with the union. Companies that establish a constructive partnership with their unions do far better for their shareholders than those that do not. (Perazzo 2009)

Socialized health care:

> Health Care Costs-The first is one where conflicts between labor and management do still exist, and that is health care. On that issue, however, given that the shareholders want us to get along, the answer is to get it out of collective bargaining and into the public sphere. That means that

---

[550] http://www.dsausa.org/dl/Fall_2006.pdf

management must support universal single-payer national health care...
(Perazzo 2009)

Industry "protection:"

Historically, the industry has focused on the threat from unfairly traded imported steel. And while that threat is real and should continue to be monitored, today the more immediate threat comes from the demand for steel being lost because those who use the steel will use it somewhere else...

The steel industry, in its own self-interest, needs to engage in the fight to save the overall manufacturing sector. Every other nation in the world has a specific and targeted strategy to preserve or expand its manufacturing base...

The growth of China and India can be a great opportunity. But not if we, as Lenin so aptly put it, sell them the rope with which to hang us.

86-6 David Bonior with Detroit DSA chair David Green, 2008

Steel industry managers need to repudiate the race-to-the bottom model of globalization. We need world trade that brings the bottom up, not the top down, and we need to tell the American government to do what every one of its trading partners does, stand up for those who operate on their soil. (Perazzo 2009)

State control of energy:

The steel industry and manufacturers in general need to stop worrying about offending their business school classmates, political soul mates, and friends at the country club and to stand up for their owners. It is time to support a comprehensive national energy program... (Perazzo 2009)

As Manufacturing Czar, Ron Bloom will almost certainly push for a more centralized, unionized, government dependent manufacturing base - exactly what Democratic Socialists of America is calling for.

He will almost certainly try to sell big business on socialized health care to make business more competitive. He will drive the labor union agenda from on high.

Bloom will work with Labor Secretary Hilda Solis.

The pair will also be aided by John Bonior - a paid up Detroit Democratic Socialists of America (DSA) member (and colleague of David

Green) who President Obama has delegated to re-unite the US' two major labor federations, AFL-CIO and Change to Win, under one banner.

Three of the most influential union affiliated officials of the Obama administration have connections to Democratic Socialists of America - an organization whose "goal as socialists is to abolish private ownership of the means of production."

This does not appear to worry the Obama administration known for its vigorous vetting procedures.

Perhaps it concerns you?

87. Obama's Socialist Appointees: Where is the Spotlight?

Trevor Loudon © Tuesday, September 22, 2009

Obama's long-term association with Democratic Socialists of America is documented in these Chapters titled: "So what, you say, they're democratic aren't they? They are socialists, not communists, or militant radicals?"

Some facts:

- 02 - Barack Obama Was Endorsed by Chicago Marxists
- 03 - Socialist Unionists Endorse Barack Obama
- 07 - Obama and the Democratic Socialists of America
- 10 - Barack Obama and the Socialist "Mafia"
- 12 - Jan Schakowsky – Barack Obama's Loyal Socialist Supporter
- 14 - Socialist Led Mega-Union Backs Barack Obama
- 15 – Socialist Octogenarians for Barack
- 19 - Obama 08' "All the Way with DSA"
- 26 – William McNary, Yet Another Obama Radical?
- 29 – Senior US Socialist Jose LaLuz, Manipulates Latino Vote for Obama
- 41 - Obama Was a New Party Member - Documentary Evidence
- 42 – Obama's Socialist Neighbour – Jackie Grimshaw
- 43 - Former Weatherman Terrorists, Marxists, New Party Veterans, United Behind Obama
- 45 - Obama's Cuddly Old, Terrorist Friendly, Socialist Friend and Neighbor-Rabbi Arnold Wolf

- 57 - Obama's Socialist Ally Joins Powerful Congressional Committee
- 58 - Hilda Solis - Obama Labor Secretary's Socialist Connections
- 59 - Top Socialist's Memo to Obama
- 79 - Filling In the Gaps - More on Obama and Chicago Democratic Socialists of America
- 80 - Michelle and Barack's Black Panther Mentor

President Obama has close personal and political ties to several Democratic Socialists of America (DSA) members including Dr. Quentin Young, Timuel Black, the late Rabbi Arnold Jacob Wolf, the late Saul Mendelson, Lou Pardo, US Representative Danny K. Davis and Democratic Socialists of America (DSA) honorees Jackie Grimshaw, Jackie Kendall and US Representative Jan Schakowsky (D-IL-9th District).

Democratic Socialists of America (DSA)'s several thousand strong memberships have grown militant over the years until the point its policies are almost indistinguishable from those of the Communist Party USA.

87-1 Dr. Quentin Young and Barack Obama, c. 2002

In an article in Democratic Socialists of America (DSA)'s *Democratic Left*, spring 2007,[551] Democratic Socialists of America (DSA) National Political Committee member David Green wrote:

> Our goal as socialists is to abolish private ownership of the means of production. Our immediate task is to limit the capitalist class's prerogatives in the workplace...

> In the short run we must at least minimize the degree of exploitation of workers by capitalists. We can accomplish this by promoting full employment policies, passing local living wage laws, but most of all by increasing the union movements power... (Green, The Employee Free Choice Act - A Democratic Socialist of America Priority 2007)

---

[551] http://www.dsausa.org/dl/Spring_2007.pdf

Democratic Socialists of America (DSA) has some cross-membership with the Communist Party and considerable cross-membership with the militant Committees of Correspondence for Democracy and Socialism.

87-2 Kurt Stand

Democratic Socialists of America (DSA) has close ties to many Congressmen, including US Representative John Conyers, Representative Danny K. Davis, US Representative Jan Schakowsky (D-IL-9th District) (all close Obama supporters,) US Representative Jerrold Nadler and Bob Filner.

Democratic Socialists of America (DSA) has key personnel or allies at the top of AFL-CIO, SEIU, United Auto Workers, United Steelworkers of America, and other major unions.

Democratic Socialists of America (DSA) has considerable influence in ACORN, Working Families Party, Green Party, Democratic Party, US Action, Jobs with Justice, Economic Policy Institute, Campaign for America's Future, DEMOS (which Obama helped found), the Black Radical Congress and many other mass organizations, including some churches.

Democratic Socialists of America (DSA) is affiliated with the Socialist International which now includes several "former" communist parties - Mongolia, Mozambique, Bulgaria, Latvia, Belarus, Ukraine, Estonia, Angola, Hungary and Poland, as well as the   Nicaraguan Sandinistas and the still-existing Communist Parties of Laos, Cuba and China ("observer" only).

Former Democratic Socialists of America (DSA) National Political Committee member, Kurt Stand, is serving a 17-year jail sentence for spying for the former East Germany and offering to spy for the South African Communist Party. His wife and co-conspirator Theresa Squillacote, a former Pentagon lawyer and a Committees of Correspondence member, served 22 years.

Several Democratic Socialists of America (DSA) members have long term ties to the Washington based Institute for Policy Studies, which was linked some years back to Soviet and Cuban intelligence officers and many third world revolutionary movements.

In 2006/7, several Democratic Socialists of America (DSA) leaders, including Paul Buhle, Barbara Ehrenreich and Bill Fletcher Jr., held leadership roles in Movement for a Democratic Society with leaders of the Communist Party USA, the Committees of Correspondence and four former key leaders of the terrorist Weather Underground, Bill Ayers,

Bernardine Dohrn, Jeff Jones and Mark Rudd.

Ehrenreich and Fletcher Jr, together with another two Movement for a Democratic Society leaders, Carl Davidson of Committees of Correspondence and Tom Hayden, went on to form Progressives for Obama (P40).

Do you still think Democratic Socialists of America (DSA) is harmless and insignificant?

87-3 Ron Bloom

Next, I list seven members of President Obama's administration who have had some ties to Democratic Socialists of America (DSA)/Socialist International, ranging from paid up DSA membership, to signing a DSA petition, to addressing one DSA sponsored event, related to a DSA member.

Some may be innocent, but some may not. Does any or all of these emerging facts warrant further investigation? You judge.

Ron Bloom Manufacturing Czar

Czar Ron Bloom, a socialist since his teens, has worked for several Democratic Socialists of America (DSA) linked organizations including SEIU, Jewish Labor Committee and United Steelworkers of America.

Bloom wrote in an article for the fall 2006[552] edition of Democratic Socialists of America (DSA)'s *Democratic Left*:

> In today's world, the blather about free trade, free-markets and the joys of competition is nothing but pabulum for the suckers. (Bloom 2006)

David Bonior

US Representative David Bonior is a Member of the Obama Economic Transition Team. President Obama has delegated the Economic Transition Team to negotiate the unification of the AFL-CIO

---

and Change to Win labor federations. Former Democratic Speaker of the House, US Representative David Bonior, has been linked to DSA for many years and had joined the organization by 2006.

Detroit Democratic Socialists of America (DSA) celebrated the 10th Annual Douglass-Debs Dinner, November 8, 2008. Co-Chairs were United Auto Workers official, Rory Gamble and International Union of Operating Engineers Business Manager, Phillip Schloop. The Douglass-Debs Award winners were US Representative David and Judy Bonior.

> US Representative David Bonior served in Congress for 26 years rising through the leadership to become the Democratic Caucus Whip. During his tenure in Congress, Bonior fought to raise the minimum wage, protect pensions, support unions, and extend unemployment benefits. He led the fight to oppose NAFTA in 1993. (Roman, Other News 2008)

He worked to prevent war in Central America in the 1980s and again to prevent the Iraq War in 2002. After leaving Congress, Bonior co-founded American Rights at Work, a labor advocacy and research organization, which has made passage of the Employee Free Choice Act its major legislative priority. Bonior was appointed to the Obama economic team.

In his remarks at the dinner, US Representative David Bonior stressed the importance of building social movements to pressure the new Obama administration for bold progressive changes as, single-payer national health insurance, significant public investment in infrastructure and green technology, fair trade, progressive taxation, massive cuts in the military budget, ending the war in Iraq and passing the Employee Free Choice Act.

Rosa Brooks

The senior advisor to the Under Secretary of Defense for Policy, Michele Flournoy is Rosa Brooks.

Named after communist radical Rosa Luxemburg, Brooks is the daughter of prominent Democratic Socialists of America (DSA) member, Movement for a Democratic Society Board member and Progressives for Obama (P40) founder, Barbara Ehrenreich.

87-4 Rosa Brooks

Rosa Brooks is a known "liberal"

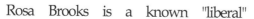

newspaper columnist and writer on defense and international relations.

Brooks has served as Special Counsel to the President at George Soros' Open Society Institute.

Energy Czar Carol Browner

Energy Czar - Carol Browner is the Director of the White House Office of Energy and Climate Change Policy.

Until summer 2008, Energy Czar - Carol Browner was a member of Socialist International Commission for a Sustainable World Society.

The other US delegates to the Athens conference above were DSA leaders Frank Llewellyn, Corey Walker, George Roberts, David Duhalde, Alejandro Duhalde and Andrew Hammer.

In the 1970s Energy Czar-Carol Browner worked for Citizen's Action, founded by former Students for a Democratic Society (SDS) radicals, Steve Max and Heather Booth, both later affiliated to Democratic Socialists of America (DSA).

Browner is also a financial supporter of US Senator Bernie Sanders (I-VT), a socialist, aligned with Democratic Socialists of America (DSA).

Heather Higginbottom

87-6 Heather Higginbottom (l) William Julius Wilson, Dottie Stevens, Jack Clark and Robert J Hayes (r)

Heather Higginbottom is the Deputy Assistant to the President for Domestic Policy with the Obama for America campaign.

From 1999 to 2007, Higginbottom served as Legislative Director for Senator John Kerry of Massachusetts. Heather has a relationship with Boston Democratic Socialists of America (DSA).

On October 30, 2001, while working for Senator Kerry, Heather Higginbottom addressed a Boston Democratic Socialists of America

(DSA)[553] organized forum "Welfare, Children and Families: The Impact of Welfare Reform." Of those listed above Jack Clark was Boston Democratic Socialists of America (DSA) Chair William Julius. Wilson is a longtime

87-5 Carol Browner

---

[553] http://www.dsaboston.org/2001Wilson.htm

Democratic Socialists of America (DSA) affiliate and in 1996 addressed a Democratic Socialists of America (DSA) forum[554] in Chicago with Barack Obama.

Robert Haynes is President of the Massachusetts AFL-CIO, with whom Democratic Socialists of America (DSA) works[555] "frequently."

Samantha Power

Samantha Power is the National Security Council Director for Multilateral Affairs.

After the 2008 Presidential election, Power was a member of Obama's Transition Team, working for the Department of State.

In April 2003, Samantha Power[556] signed her name to an open letter, initiated by prominent Democratic Socialists of America (DSA) member[557] Leo Casey, calling for normalization of relations with Cuba.

87-7 Samantha Power

The letter is in line with Democratic Socialists of America (DSA) and Communist Party aims to remove the trade embargo on Cuba. Democratic Socialists of America (DSA) uses the subtle approach of claiming that sanctions are encouraging Cuba to violate human rights and easing restrictions would make Cuban authorities more tolerant of dissent.

> Democratic Left Against Cuban Repression:
>
> Below is a statement circulating among democratic left/socialist folks, largely by members of Democratic Socialists of America, condemning the recent trials and convictions of non-violent dissenters in Cuba.
>
> The petition sharply criticized Cuba's poor human rights record, but shared the blame for Cuba's failures with "reactionary elements of the US administration..."

---

[554] http://www.chicagodsa.org/ngarchive/ng45.html
[555] http://www.dsausa.org/dl/sum2k/07.html
[556] http://archives.econ.utah.edu/archives/pen-l/2003w15/msg00095.htm
[557] http://www.nathannewman.org/log/archives/000912.shtml

The democratic left worldwide has opposed the US embargo on Cuba as counterproductive as, more harmful to the interests of the Cuban people as helpful to political democratization. The Cuban state's current repression of political dissidents amounts to collaboration with the most reactionary elements of the US administration in their efforts to maintain sanctions and to institute even more punitive measures against Cuba. (Sherman 2003)

Many of the petition's 120 odd signatories were known members of DSA - including Theresa Alt, Dave Anderson, Stanley Aronowitz, Leo Casey, Bogdan Denitch, Bill Dixon, Nancy Fraser, Andrew Hammer, Richard Healey, Michael Hirsch, James Hughes, Maurice Isserman, Mark Levinson, Maxine Phillips, Michael Pugliese, Michele Rossi, Joseph Schwartz, Jason Schulman, Timothy Sears and Ian Williams.

Samantha Power is married to Obama "Regulatory Czar" Cass Sunstein.

Hilda Solis

US Representative Hilda Solis (D-CA-32nd District) is now the Secretary of Labor.

Before she was appointed to her new role, Solis served on the Board of American Rights at Work with several Democratic Socialists of America (DSA) supporters including US Representative David Bonior, AFL-CIO President John Sweeney, labor economist Harley Shaiken and NAACP leader Julian

87-8 Hilda Solis

Bond.

Hilda Solis was a keynote speaker at the DSA national conference "21st Century Socialism" in Los Angeles in November 2005.

Saturday evening delegates recognized the contributions of Democratic Socialists of America (DSA) Vice Chair and Washington Post columnist Harold Meyerson, Occidental College sociologist and longtime Democratic Socialists of America (DSA) member, Peter Dreier and insurgent California Congress member US Representative Hilda Solis (D-

CA-32nd District) who, in turn, provided in-depth perspectives of the political scene. (Democratic Socialists of America 2005)

In June 2008, the Socialist International Migrations Committee held a Migrations Reform, Integration, Rights forum[558] in Los Angeles. Present were Democratic Socialists of America (DSA)'s National Director Frank Llewellyn, Duane Campbell and Dolores Delgado Campbell of Anti-Racism and Latino networks.

Elena Henry, a caseworker from Solis' East Los Angeles Office, represented Hilda Solis. In 2008, US Representative Hilda Solis (D-CA-32nd District) served on Barack Obama's National Latino Advisory Council alongside Democratic Socialists of America (DSA) honorary Chair and SEIU Vice President Eliseo Medina.

The seven officials profiled above include some of the most powerful and influential people in America today.

Several have the power to influence the future prosperity and security of the world's most powerful nation. Some have access to secret information.

The MSM went through Sarah Palin's underwear drawers when she sought the US Vice Presidency. Why do the media not give Obama appointees even a cursory level of scrutiny?

After the Van Jones fiasco, public faith in the Obama Administration's much vaunted vetting procedures is at rock bottom.

Should the spotlight now shine on President Obama's socialist affiliated appointees? If not, why not?

88. Parallel Lives? Obama's "Go To" Man, Patrick Gaspard and New York Socialism

Trevor Loudon © Wednesday, October 07, 2009

In June 2009, Patrick Gaspard, a Brooklyn-based, 41-year-old Democratic operative, became White House Director of the Office of Political Affairs.

Patrick Gaspard's official responsibility is to provide the President with an "accurate assessment of the political dynamics affecting the work of his administration" and to "work with powerbrokers around the country to help push the President's agenda."

88-1 Patrick Gaspard

According to US Representative Gregory Meeks (D-NY-6th District):

> He is a low key, behind-the-scenes, no-fingerprints person. I need something I call Patrick. In addition, if he calls, it is a big deal. He's close to the President." (KeyWiki 2009)

Considerable attention has been focused on Gaspard's ties to the radical community group ACORN.

This chapter looks at Gaspard's ties to the groups behind ACORN. Also the groups that helped President Obama during his Chicago days - Democratic Socialists of America and the Communist Party offshoot Committees of Correspondence for Democracy and Socialism.

Patrick Gaspard was born in Kinshasa, Zaire, after his father, a political opponent of the Duvalier dictatorship in Haiti, fled there.

88-2 Aime Cesaire

Patrick Gaspard's father moved with his wife from Haiti to "post-liberation" Zaire when its pro-communist leader, Patrice Lumumba, appealed to French-speaking academics of African descent to teach there.

Three years after Patrick Gaspard's birth, the family moved to New York.

Like Obama, Patrick Gaspard wrote poetry. Like Obama, Patrick Gaspard grew up admiring third world leftists and revolutionaries. He reportedly idolized Aime Cesaire,[559] a radical poet/politician from the French colony of Martinique.

---

[559] http://www.politickerny.com/4185/patrick-gaspard-writes-poems-collects-comics-kills-obama

Cesaire was elected to the French Parliament with the French Communist Party. When Cesaire left the parliament, he formed his own leftist party in Martinique.

Cesaire also taught the anti-colonialist Marxist theorist Frantz Fanon, of whom Obama wrote admiringly in his autobiography, *Dreams from My Father*.

Patrick Gaspard got his start in politics in the mid-1980s. Gaspard organized demonstrations in New York City for "social justice" in Haiti.

Gaspard got his first taste of campaign work in the 1988 Presidential campaign of Jesse Jackson. Jesse, like Obama, is a product of the Chicago socialist machine.

Patrick Gaspard went on to NY Mayor David Dinkins' first New York Mayoral race as an intern in Dinkins' office and to City Hall when Dinkins won the New York Mayoralty.

Dinkins was at the time a member of Democratic Socialists of America.

In 1997, outgoing Manhattan borough President Ruth Messinger, also a member of Democratic Socialists of America, enlisted Gaspard for her doomed Mayoral campaign against NY Mayor Rudy Giuliani.

After the Messinger debacle, Gaspard became Chief of Staff to New York Councilwoman Margarita Lopez, a radical feminist from the Lower East Side.

88-3 SEIU Local 1199 New York

In 1999, Lopez loaned Gaspard out to help Local 1199 of the Service Employees International Union (SEIU) to organize a march in protest of the police shooting death of Amadou Diallo, a Guinean immigrant.

Gaspard was allegedly a key organizer of the civil disorder that followed Diallo's death.[560]

---

[560] http://keywiki.org/index.php/Patrick_Gaspard

The union was one of the central organizers of the civil disobedience that followed and 1199 President, Dennis Rivera and Political Director, Bill Lynch asked Gaspard to coordinate those efforts.

Dennis Rivera, President of Local 1199, recruited Gaspard to the union where, after some time, he rose

to the rank of union Executive Vice President.

88-4 Manhattan borough President Ruth Messinger

It is important to realize that SEIU Local 1199 is one of New York's most powerful and militant labor unions.

Founded in 1932, the union leaned to the left from the start and was investigated in 1948 by the House Un-American Activities Committee for Communist "infiltration."

At a March 2007,[561] meeting to celebrate the Communist Party USA donation of its papers to New York's Tamiment Library, Steve Kramer, Executive Vice President of Service Employees Union Local 1199, spoke of the Communist Party's role in building and maintaining his union.

Recounting SEIU Local 1199's disastrous 1984 strike and internal strife in which "the union almost tore itself up," Kramer said, "That but for the party's efforts, SEIU Local 1199 would have been a small union." Today, with 300,000 members, it is the world's largest union local.

When the Communist Party split in 1991, several SEIU Local 1199 officials joined the dissenting faction and took many comrades into the breakaway Committees of Correspondence.

The Local 1199 officials signing the Communist Party dissenter's "An initiative to *Unite and Renew the Party*" document, which brought tensions to crisis point, were:

- Paul Friedman - (Local 1199 Vice President)
- Raphael Pizzaro - (Local 1199 organizer)
- Geoffrey Jaques - (Associate Editor 1199 News)
- Marshall Garcia - (Local 1199 Executive Vice President) .

Friedman, Pizzaro, Jacques and Garcia all went on to support

[561] http://www.peoplesworld.org/-party-of-hope-archives-show-living-history/

Committees of Correspondence. Pizzaro also went on to help found the radical New Party, which Obama joined in Chicago in 1995. Many other 1199ers also supported Committees of Correspondence, including:

- Lenore Colbert - (Local 1199 Vice President)
- Pat Harris - (Local 1199 Vice President)
- David Kranz
- Socorro Laguerra - (Local 1199 rank and file)
- Pam Mills - (Local 1199 Seattle)
- Bruce Richard - (SEIU San Francisco, now a Local 1199 Vice President)
- Angela Doyle - (Local 1199 Vice President)
- Nelson Valdez - (Local 1199 Vice President}

Doyle, Valdez and Richard still hold senior positions with the union.

In addition, leading Committees of Correspondence member Mael Apollon[562] is involved with the Local 1199 Child Care Fund.

Also of note is the late Merrilee Milstein, who was from 1972 to 1994, Vice President of the New England Local 1199. Milstein was a hard left activist in her own right and was married to Communist Party member Brian Steinberg.

Milstein left SEIU Local 1199 to become Assistant to Connecticut Secretary of State Miles Rapoport - now President of the ACORN supporting, Democratic Socialists of America (DSA) linked, New York think tank DEMOS.

Barack Obama was one of DEMOS' first Trustees when established in 1999.

Gerry Hudson, now a Vice President of SEIU, also got his start at Local 1199 in New York. Hudson is a member of Democratic Socialists of America and serves on the Board of the Apollo Alliance founded by Obama's departed "Green Jobs" Czar Van Jones.

In 2003, Patrick Gaspard was granted leave from Local 1199 to work as the Deputy National Field Director for the Presidential campaign of Howard Dean. After Dean was eliminated from the race, Gaspard became National Field Director for George Soros' political action group,

---

[562] http://keywiki.org/index.php/Mael_Apollon

America Coming Together.

Later Gaspard helped Yvette Clarke win the Congressional seat vacated by Democratic Socialists of America member and Communist Party supporter Major Owens.

Clarke is now a member of the leftist Congressional Progressive Caucus which has long and deep ties to Democratic Socialists of America (DSA).

In 1995, Patrick Gaspard[563] led the New Jersey chapter of the New Party, a creation of ACORN, Democratic Socialists of America

88-6 Bertha Lewis

(DSA) and Committees of Correspondence. By 2001, Gaspard was a leading activist in the New Party offshoot, the New York Working Families Party, linked to the Democratic Socialists of America (DSA), ACORN, and Committees of Correspondence Communist Party collaboration.

Gaspard and Bertha Lewis of ACORN wrote a letter to the July 2, 2001, issue of "*The Nation.*" In the course of their letter, Gaspard and Lewis describe their extensive joint involvement in "Working Families Party"

88-5 Working Family Party

activities. The letter is signed, "Bertha Lewis, ACORN, WFP; Patrick Gaspard, SEIU State Council, WFP."

Veterans of the left will remember that the 1968 Peace and Freedom Party and the 1980 Citizens Party arose at moments of greater left-wing strength and did not significantly alter the national electoral landscape. Nor has, unfortunately, the New Party, which many Democratic Socialists of America (DSA) workers with in states where "fusion" of third party and major party votes is possible (such as the Democratic Socialists of America (DSA)

563

http://corner.nationalreview.com/post/?q=NjljYzYyMDhlY2Y4MTRhZTI4NGQ5OGVlM
GE5YmIzYTI=

co-sponsored Working Families Party in N.Y. State). (Lewis and Gaspard 2001)

The Democratic Socialists of America (DSA) youth wing's 2004 *"Life After Bush"* Conference[564] included:

> A series of well-attended workshops detailed the nuts-and-bolts of electoral activism, led by veteran campaigners from trade unions and the NY Democratic Socialists of America (DSA)-affiliated fusion Working Families Party. (KeyWiki 2009)

Speakers at *"Life after Bush"*[565] included:

- Cornel West (an active Democratic Socialists of America (DSA), New Party founder, 2008 member of Barack Obama's Black Advisory Council and Progressives for Obama (P40) endorser)

- Frances Fox Piven - (Democratic Socialists of America (DSA), New Party founder, co-creator of the famous Cloward-Piven Strategy[566] for wrecking the US economy. A Progressives for Obama (P40) endorser)

- Steve Max - (Democratic Socialists of America (DSA) Director of Organizing and Training, Midwest Academy Chicago)

- Leslie Cagan (Committees of Correspondence, National Coordindator, United for Peace & Justice)

- Ian Williams - (Democratic Socialists of America (DSA), a correspondent for *In These Times* and *The Nation*)

- Bertha Lewis – (Co-Chair, Working Families Party, Executive Director, New York ACORN)

- Jay Mazur[567] - (a prominent in the Working Families Party and an endorser of the Progressives for Obama (P40) website and the Democratic Society of America)

- Patrick Gaspard - (listed on the advisory Board[568] of the WFP aligned Working Families Center along with Working Families Party co-Chair Bob Master)

- Jon Kest – (Working Families Party Secretary and New York ACORN head)

---

[564] http://www.ydsusa.org/confs/nyc_0204_report.html
[565] http://www.dsausa.org/LatestNews/2004/nyc04.pdf
[566] http://truthandcons.blogspot.com/2009/03/links-to-all-three-manufactured-crisis.html
[567] http://www.ydsusa.org/confs/nyc_0204_report.html
[568]http://cc.bingj.com/cache.aspx?q=%22http+www+centerforworkingfamilies+info+abou t+php%22&d=4842360963793083&mkt=en-US&setlang=en-US&w=91f276ec,e2f5a040

- Hector Figueroa - (SEIU a regular speaker at Democratic Socialists of America (DSA)'s Socialist Scholars Conferences, including the 2004 event where Van Jones also spoke)

88-7 Nathan Newman

- Andrea Batista Schlesinger (On the Board of the Oakland based Applied Research Center which is closely aligned with Van Jones' Ella J. Baker Human Rights Center)

Former Committees of Correspondence National Coordinating Committee member Nathan Newman, who recently wrote in the *Daily Kos*:[569]

> I knew Van (Jones) well back in the early 90s when we were both involved in community organizing efforts, including involvement in a variety of left-leaning groups. (Newman 2009)

Barack Obama, as a young man, admired third world revolutionaries like Frantz Fanon. He went into community organizing and the Democratic Socialists of America (DSA) - Committees of Correspondence aligned Chicago left, before moving on to the White House.

Van Jones, as a young man, admired third world revolutionaries like Amilcar Cabral. He went from radical community organizing into the San Francisco Committees of Correspondence and the New York DSA aligned left (like Obama, Jones was a Trustee of the DSA aligned DEMOS), before moving on to the White House.

Patrick Gaspard, as a young man, admired third world revolutionaries like Aime Cesaire. He went into radical organizing and mixed with the DSA/CoC aligned New York left, before moving on to the White House.

Parallel lives. Alternatively, the way US socialism works.

---

[569] http://www.dailykos.com/story/2009/9/4/776855/-Defending-Van-Jones-from-the-McCarthyites

89. Deepak Bhargava "Advancing Change in the Age of Obama"

Trevor Loudon © Wednesday, October 07, 2009

89-1 Deepak Bhargava

Indian born, New York raised, Harvard educated, Deepak Bhargava may have seldom crossed paths with Barack Obama, but he is a key player in the 44th President's movement to transform America.

Deepak Bhargava is connected to almost every aspect of the Obama movement - from George Soros to ACORN, to Democratic Socialists of America, to The Nation, to the communist dominated United for Peace & Justice, to a whole raft of "progressive" non-profits.

Deepak Bhargava opened the Heartland Democratic Presidential Forum, December 10, 2007, an exclusive forum for thousands of community organizers including ACORN personnel.

At the Forum, Obama promises to invite community organizers to the White House even before his inauguration, to contribute to setting his "Agenda for Change."

Deepak Bhargava[570] joined the Center for Community Change (CCC) in 1994, after several years as legislative director for ACORN.

Bhargava became the Center's Executive Director in 2004. He successfully pushed[571] the organization to develop the power and capacity of low-income people and low-income people of color, to change the policies and institutions that affect their lives.

Deepak Bhargava has sharpened the Center's focus on grassroots community organizing as the central strategy for social justice and on public policy change as the key lever to improve poor people's lives.

Bhargava conceived and led the Center's work on immigration reform, which has resulted in the creation of the Fair Immigration Reform Movement, a leading grassroots network pressing for changes in the

---

[570] http://www.communitychange.org/
[571] http://www.communitychange.org/who-we-are/our-staff/bios/deepak-bhargava

country's immigration laws.

He has spearheaded the creation of innovative new projects like Generation Change, a program that recruits, trains and places the next generation of community organizers, and the Community Voting Project, which brings large numbers of low-income voters into the electoral process.

89-2 Heather Booth

Helping Bhargava change America, is CCC Board member Heather Booth,[572] the former Students for a Democratic Society (SDS) radical, turned Democratic Party power player.

Booth runs the Midwest Academy out of Chicago - churning out hundreds of "community" and union organizers.

Booth and her husband Paul, a labor union power broker, both have close ties to the US' largest Marxist organization, Democratic Socialists of America, as does Deepak Bhargava.

Over September 20-22, 2002, Frances Fox Piven, Deepak Bhargava and Holly Sklar were billed as keynote speakers[573] at "Confronting the Low-Wage Economy" at the First Congregational Church in Washington, DC, organized by Democratic Socialists of America.

This conference will kick off Democratic Socialists of America (DSA)'s Low Wage Justice Project, designed to bring the human consequences of the low wage economy to the attention of the American people.

Democratic Socialists of America (DSA) member, Frances Fox Piven, is the co-author of the famous *Cloward-Piven Strategy*[574] developed in the 1960s; used by ACORN, Democratic Socialists of America (DSA) and US "community organizers" ever since.

The strategy calls for organizers to encourage the "poor" to enroll for every entitlement possible, in order to bankrupt the US government, to bring about chaos and eventual social revolution.

---

[572] http://www.communitychange.org/who-we-are/our-board
[573] http://www.dsausa.org/dl/Summer_2002.pdf
[574] http://www.americanthinker.com/2008/09/barack_obama_and_the_strategy.html

In his speech to the conference, Deepak Bhargava[575] credited the work of Democratic Socialists of America (DSA) founder Michael Harrington and his book, *"The Other America,"* which is credited with sparking the massive growth of US welfare in the 1960s under Kennedy and Johnson.

> I do want to say that I enter this new period with a tremendous amount of optimism. Before nine-eleven we saw larger numbers mobilized in the streets on a whole range of issues, immigration, living wages than we'd seen in a long, long time. There is no question that nine-eleven has taken the wind to some degree out of those sails, but I think both the demographic, the organizational, the economic realities underneath that momentum at the local level are still present, and it is up to our imagination and our will to rekindle it over the next couple of years. But I think we can make great strides on this anniversary of Michael Harrington's The Other America in doing something serious about it... (Quinn)

Deepak Bhargava's radical ties extend in several directions.

At the higher level, Bhargava is a Board member at George Soros' Open Society Institute (OSI).

On November 29, 2006, Bhargava participated[576] in a roundtable discussion at OSI New York entitled "How Do Progressives Connect Ideas to Action?"

> Individuals and organizations with similarly progressive goals often dilute their power by working alone or even working at cross-purposes. As Americans who are politically left of center move forward, questions of infrastructure, communication, and collaboration are particularly important. The progressivism of the past may contain valuable lessons as we build a strong new movement. (Bhargava 2006)

Participants included:

- Deepak Bhargava – (Center for Community Change)
- Robert Borosage – (A trustee of the far left Washington "think tank" Institute for Policy Studies and founder/CEO of Campaign for America's Future)
- Rosa Brooks – (Daughter of IPS Trustee and DSA member Barbara

---

[575] http://www.dsausa.org/lowwage/Documents/2003/TANF3.html
[576] http://www.soros.org/resources/events/progressives_20061129

Ehrenreich. Now a senior advisor to the Under Secretary of Defense for Policy, Michele Flournoy)

- Anna Burger – (AFL-CIO, later a Progressives for Obama endorser and key player in labor union/Obama White House dealings)
- Eric Foner – (DSA Member)
- Gara LaMarche – (George Soro's Open Society Institute)
- John Podesta – (Center for American Progress founder. CAP is a key source of "progressive" personnel for the Obama Administration)
- Joel Rogers – (Key DSA aligned "progressive" activist. A founder of the radical New Party which Obama joined in Chicago in 1995)
- Katrina vanden Heuvel – (IPS trustee, The Nation editor)

As of July 17, 2007, Deepak Bhargava, Center for Community Change (CCC),[577] was affiliated with United for Peace & Justice (UFPJ), the US peace movement umbrella group.

UFPJ was initiated to oppose the Iraq War by the Institute for Policy Studies and dominated by communists and radicals, which does not seem to bother Bhargava.

Also leading organizations affiliated with UFPJ in July 2007, were Communist Party members:

- Judith LeBlanc
- Rosalío Muñoz
- Alfred Marder
- Erica Smiley

Committees of Correspondence for Democracy and Socialism aligned activists:

- Leslie Cagan
- Attieno Davis
- Howard Wallace
- Van Gosse

Democratic Socialists of America (DSA) leaders:

- Jason Schulman
- Lucas Shapiro

Freedom Road Socialist Organization Maoists:

---

[577] http://www.knology.net/~bilrum/UFPJGroups071607.htm

- Dennis O'Neil
- Juliet Ucelli
- IPSers
- Phyllis Bennis
- Saif Rahman
- Arthur Waskow

Ella J. Baker Center for Human Rights:

- Van Jones

Bhargava serves on the editorial Board of *The Nation* the house journal of the Institute for Policy Studies. Fellow Editorial Board members include:

- Barbara Ehrenreich - (Democratic Socialists of America (DSA) member, IPS Trustee, New Party founder and Progressives for Obama (P40) founder)
- Eric Foner – (Democratic Socialists of America (DSA) member)
- Lani Guinier Daughter of communist Ewart Guinier.
- Tom Hayden - SDS and Progressives for Obama (P40) founder.
- Deborah Meier - Democratic Socialists of America (DSA) member and speaker in 1998, with Barack Obama at the memorial Service of Chicago Democratic Socialists of America (DSA) member Saul Mendelson.
- Victor Navasky - IPS Trustee, The Nation.
- Marcus Raskin - IPS founder.

Deepak Bhargava spoke at a The Nation forum in April 2009 on the prospects for "progressive" gains under Obama's "stealth agenda."

On February 26 2009, Mike Lux, Miles Rapoport of DEMOS, Deepak Bhargava and Gloria Totten of Progressive Majority spoke at the Center for Community Change (CCC)[578] entitled "Progressives in an Obama World: The Role of the Progressive Movement in a Democratically Controlled Washington."

The forum blurb identified Obama as a "progressive" and went on to say:

---

[578] http://theprogressiverevolution.com/2009/02/event-progressives-in-an-obama-world-2/

Since the 2004 election, the progressive movement has built a powerful infrastructure of think tanks, media outlets and advocacy organizations. Frustrated by the conservative ascendancy and the dominance of conservative ideas, individuals and institutions have put forward new paradigms for government and promoted a bold vision for the future.

But now a progressive holds the highest office in the land. As the movement struggles to define its role in the Obama era, important questions remain unanswered: What is the role of organizations in Washington and how can they best create political space for Obama to act? On what issues should the movement compromise and on which take strong stands? How can progressives build consensus to make their efforts more effective?

The panel will feature progressive leaders Deepak Bhargava, Miles Rapoport and Mike Lux; the speakers will draw on two new books, 'Thinking Big: Progressive Ideas for a New Era,' and The Progressive Revolution: How the Best in America Came to Be. They discuss what progressives can do to create momentum for greater boldness at a time when opportunities and challenges abound. (Center for Community Change 2008)

Miles Rapoport is another former Students for a Democratic Society, Democratic Socialists of America (DSA) associate, ACORN defender and ardent Obama supporter. Rapoport became President of New York "think tank" DEMOS in 2000, while Obama was still a founding Trustee of the organization.

Van Jones[579] is a DEMOS Trustee.

Another Bhargava speech from February 2009, given to the Liberty Hill foundation: "*Advancing Change in the Age of Obama.*"

On Wednesday, November 05, 2008, Deepak Bhargava and the Center for Community Change (CCC) issued a statement[580] on the new President elect:

Community Organizers Welcome One of Their Own to the White House

---

[579] http://www.DEMOS.org/board.cfm#jones
[580] http://www.communitychange.org/press-room/press-releases/community-organizers-welcome-one-of-their-own-to

Community organizers across the country congratulate the historic victory of one of our own and herald the role community organizing played in revitalizing participation in our democratic process.

"Community organizing helped mobilize voters like never before with grassroots organizations engaging in electoral politics. Sen. Obama's own campaign was modeled on the tools of organizing, building the national groundswell that got him to this moment.

"Election Day is just the beginning. Community organizing will continue to play an important role in keeping an expectant and motivated electorate working together with the new Administration to find solutions for our shared problems. Together we will strive to realize the dream we voted for, an America that works for all of us."

On December 4, thousands of grassroots leaders will host Realizing the Promise: A forum on Community, Faith and Democracy to lay out a strategy to work with President-elect Obama and the new Congress on the people's "Agenda for Change." (Bhargava, Key Wiki Deepak Bhargava 2009)

Mild-mannered Deepak Bhargava is at the heart of the US social revolution.

Deepak and Obama may never have exchanged more than a few words, but they are working for the same future.

90. Alice Palmer Re-examined - Was Obama's First Political Boss a Soviet "Agent of Influence?"

Tuesday, November 17, 2009

Alice Palmer is a Chicago based academic, activist and former friend, employer and political ally of Barack Obama.

90-1 Alice Palmer

In the mid-1990s, Alice Palmer, an Illinois State Senator, employed Obama as her Chief of Staff when she attempted an ill-fated run for the US Congress.

Obama was part of Friends of Alice Palmer, alongside controversial property developer Tony Rezko and Democratic Socialists of America members US Representative Danny K. Davis, Betty Wilhoitte and Timuel Black, (also a

ALICE PALMER

THE FRIENDS OF ALICE J. PALMER
(IN FORMATION)

HON. JOHN STEELE	HON. ALLAN STREETER
HON. JESSE EVANS	HON. SHIRLEY COLEMAN
HON. ARENDA TROUTMAN	HON. DONNE TROTTER
HON. LOVANA "LOU" JONES	HON. JESUS GARCIA
HON. MIGUEL del VALLE	HON. DANNY DAVIS
HON. CHARLES MORROW	HON. VIRGIL JONES
HON. BOBBIE STEELE	HON. GRACE MARY STERN
HON. VIRGIL JONES	HON. TONI PRECKWINKLE
HON. BARBARA FLYNN CURRIE	HON. JIM BERRARA
HON. CORA McGRUDER	HON. EARLEAN COLLINS
HON. CONSTANCE HOWARD	HON. ETHEL S. ALEXANDER
HON. JERRY BUTLER	HON. DAVID ORR
HON. WILLIAM MAROVITZ	HON. CLEM BALANOFF
MILTON R. DAVIS	DR. VERNON SPHERES
AL JOHNSON	BETTY WILLHOITE
ANTON REZKO	JEAN RUDD
ALLISON DAVIS	HARRIET PARKER
BETTYLU & PAUL SALTZMAN	BARACK OBAMA
TIMUEL BLACK	DEMPSEY TRAVIS

90-3 Friends of Alice Palmer

member of Committees of Correspondence).

Later Palmer introduced Obama as a designated successor to her Illinois State Senate seat in the living room of former Weather Underground terrorists Bill Ayers and Bernardine Dohrn, while Democratic Socialists of America (DSA) member, former communist and longtime Obama friend Quentin Young looked on.

The Palmer/Obama relationship soured after Obama refused to step down when Palmer decided she wanted her State Senate seat back, after her Congressional bid failed.

Obama went on to win the seat unopposed, after he knocked Palmer and his other rivals off the ballot by challenging the legitimacy of their nominating signatures.

Alice Palmer was the first rung of Obama's ladder to power.

Alice Palmer had a known reputation as a communist front activist, as were many in Obama's orbit.

New evidence shows that Alice Palmer had high level connections behind the "Iron Curtain" and may have been a Soviet "agent of influence" - that is, a conduit of Soviet propaganda and policy, to the US and the "third world."

What is the evidence?

Alice Palmer and her husband Edward "Buzz" Palmer had radical connections in Chicago and abroad going back at least into the 1970s. In 1980, Buzz Palmer and Alice Palmer were invited by the Maurice Bishop led government of the Caribbean island of Grenada in 1980. They were invited to attend celebrations marking the first anniversary of the country's Cuban/Soviet backed "revolution." A revolution overturned by US troops three years later.

It is unclear if they attended, but Alice Palmer was to work, a few years later, with Bishop's US educated press secretary, Don Rojas.

Alice and Buzz Palmer established the Black Press Institute {BPI) in Chicago around 1982. In a December 24, 1986, interview with the Communist Party USA paper, *People's Daily World*, Alice Palmer explained BPI's role in influencing decision makers such as the Congressional Black Caucus.

> After the 1960s some of us looked around and observed there was no national Black newspaper...So we started the Black Press Review. We received the Black newspapers from around the country, reprinted articles and editorials that gave a sense of the dynamics and the lives of Black people, and sent them out to the Congressional Black caucus and other opinion leaders, saying "Look, here is what Black America is thinking and doing." (Palmer, People's Daily World 1986)

BPI's journal, *New Deliberations*, carried articles such as "Socialism is the Only Way Forward" and "Is Black Bourgeoise Ideology Enough?"

In 1983, Alice Palmer travelled to Czechoslovakia to the Soviet front, World Peace Council's Prague Assembly - the first of several known trips to East Bloc countries.

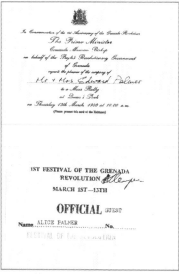

90-4 Official Invitation to Granada

From 1983 to 1985, Alice Palmer was an Executive Board member of the Communist Party USA front group, the US Peace Council - an affiliate of the World Peace Council.

Of the 48 US Peace Council officers in 1983-1985, at least ten - Sara Staggs, Rob Prince, Michael Myerson, Frank Chapman, Otis Cunningham, James Jackson, Atiba Mbiwan, Pauline Rosen, Jose Soler and Denise Young were known Communist Party USA members or supporters.

A further eight, were involved in the 1990s in a Communist Party splinter group - Committees of Correspondence. They were Gus Newport, Mark Solomon, Linda Coronado, Barbara Lee, Kevin Lynch, Anne Mitchell, Arlene Prigoff and Alice Palmer herself.

90-5 Don Rojas

In 1985, Alice Palmer was part of a delegation of sixteen Afro-American journalists to the Soviet Union, East Germany and Czechoslovakia.

Maurice Bishop's former press operator, now International Organization of Journalists executive, Don Rojas organized the trip. Palmer's BPI and the National Alliance of Black Journalists also helped.

Alice Palmer told the *People's Daily World* of December 24:

> The trip was extraordinary because we were able to sit down with our counterparts and with the seats of power in three major capitals- Prague, Berlin and Moscow. We visited with foreign ministers; we talked with the editors of the major newspapers in these three cities...

LIFE UNDER SOCIALISM

An Afro-American journalist in the USSR

Alice Palmer of the Black Press Institute, editor of the Black Press Review, was the only Afro-American to cover the 27th Congress of the Communist Party of the Soviet Union. Following are some of her impressions of the Soviet Union's plans for economic and social development, and affirmative action Soviet-style.

90-6 The article praised Soviet "central planning"

> It was a very unusual trip because we were given access...Every effort was made to give us as much as we asked for...We came back feeling that we could speak well about the interest of the socialist countries in promoting peace. (Palmer, People's Daily World 1986)

In March 1986, Alice Palmer covered the Communist Party of the Soviet Union Congress in Moscow for the Black Press Institute (BPI).

On June 20, 1986, the *People's Daily World* published a Black Press Institute (BPI) article by Alice Palmer on the Communist Party USA conference entitled "*An Afro-American journalist in the USSR*":

> "We Americans can be misled by the major media. We're being told the Soviets are striving to achieve a comparatively low standard of living compared with ours, but actually they have reached a basic stability in meeting their needs and are now planning to double their production." (Palmer, Palmer's trip to the Soviet Union 1986)

Palmer claimed that America's white-owned press:

> "has tended to ignore or distort the gains that have been made [by the Soviets] since [the Russian Revolution of 1917]. But in fact the Soviets are carrying out a policy to resolve the inequalities between nationalities, inequalities that they say were inherited from capitalist and czarist rule. They have a comprehensive Affirmative Action program, which they have stuck to religiously,- if I can use that word- since 1917." (Palmer, Palmer's trip to the Soviet Union 1986)

Alice Palmer, as editor of the Black Press Review, was elected International Organization of Journalists (IOJ) Vice President for North America, at the organization's 10th Congress, October 20-23, 1986, in Prague Czechoslovakia. Palmer's IOJ duties were to include coordinating the activities of chapters in the US, Canada, Mexico and the Caribbean.

The International Organization of Journalists was a documented Soviet front operation, based in Prague, until its expulsion by the new anti-communist Czech government in 1995.

Like other Soviet fronts of the era, the IOJ staff included East Bloc personnel and was directed by the International Department of the Communist Party of the Soviet Union - which in turn was answerable to the Soviet Politburo.

The International Department, often with the assistance of the KGB, used fronts such as IOJ and World Peace Council for "active measures" programs to influence the policies of other nations, to better advance Soviet interests. These might range from spreading propaganda and disinformation to embarrassing publicity stunts or hoaxes, to destroying the career of an enemy of the Soviet Union, or advancing the career of a friend.

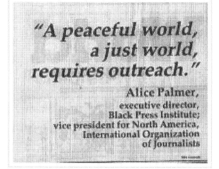

"A peaceful world, a just world, requires outreach."

Alice Palmer,
executive director,
Black Press Institute;
vice president for North America,
International Organization
of Journalists

A summary of a paper by Bob Nowell entitled "*The Role of the International Organization of Journalists (IOJ) in the Debate about the "New International Information Order*," 1958-1978 states:

> This paper examines the International Organization of Journalists (IOJ), which it identifies as a Soviet-dominated organization. The paper suggests that the IOJ has capitalized on "Third World" countries' discontent with Western news media by offering itself as the ideological leader and trainer of anti-Western journalists.

> It examines the function and methods of the IOJ in the context of post-World War II communist international front organizations; reviews the IOJ's structure, publications, and training centers; and explores its role in shaping "Third World" arguments in the debate about the New Information Order. The paper argues that the IOJ's efforts have served Soviet foreign policy on international communications. (Nowell, The Role of the International Organization of Journalists in the Debate about the "New International Information Order," 1958-1978. 1978)

The Sub-Committee on Oversight of the US House of Representatives asserted in February 1980 that, at that time, the IOJ was in receipt of a Soviet subsidy estimated at US $515,000.

Alice Palmer also traveled to the Soviet Union and Bulgaria during the IOJ conference trip, as did the other five US delegates:

- Jan Carew - (BPI, a radical socialist journalist from Guyana)
- Simon Gerson - (USIOJ, a senior member of the Communist Party USA and perhaps significantly, the Party's foremost expert on influencing election outcomes)
- Jose Soler (US IOJ, then a member of the Puerto Rican Socialist Party (PSP) and the US Peace Council, now involved with the Communist Party USA)
- Gwen McKinney - National Alliance of Third World Journalists)
- Leila McDowell - (National Alliance of Third World Journalists)

McKinney and former Black Panther member McDowell went on to work in public relations, including for 10 years as a business partnership. Their clients, collectively or separately, have included the SEIU, ACLU, NAACP, AFL-CIO, TransAfrica, Red Diaper baby Lani Guinier, Haiti's deposed Marxist President Jean Bernard Aristide, the socialist governments of Angola and Mozambique, Chavez's Venezuela and Al Gore's Alliance for Climate Change.

90-7 Randall Robinson
Origins of the Fairness
Doctrine

In the '90s, the McKinney/McDowell team influenced US government policy on Haiti when they organized and publicized a hunger strike by prominent radical activist Randall Robinson.

After twenty-seven publicity-filled days, the Clinton White House caved in to Robinson and demanded of the Haitian military that exiled Marxist President Aristide be re-instated.

TransAfrica's Randall Robinson conducted a dangerous but successful hunger strike that changed the Clinton Administration's policy on Haiti. The DC firm of McKinney & McDowell, whose other clients include President Aristide and the NAACP Legal Defense Fund, handled the PR for the fasting activist.

In a December 24, 1986, *People's Weekly World* interview with Chicago Communist Party USA member Mike Giocondo, Alice Palmer explained the IOJ's use of the concept "media fairness:"

Giocondo: What is the IOJ's approach to the question of fairness in the media? How does it relate to the concept of "objective journalism" which is stressed here in the US?

Palmer: The IOJ believes that there must be fairness in media, which is called for in a proposal for a New Information Order, which the IOJ supports. Fairness is not an abstraction, because journalists are not abstractions; we live in a world, we live in our particular societies, and therefore are caught up in whatever the dynamics of the situation are. This concept of "Objective journalism" that is taught in journalism schools...is not possible...What we are striving for is fairness and balance of information. (Palmer)

To give you a concrete example, the Black Press Institute (BPI) held a media dialogue on Southern Africa in Washington DC on how to make the information more balanced as it comes out of South Africa. The IOJ and the BPI believe there should be balance, that there should be fairness in recognizing the complexities, and that a voice must be given to those who are struggling against oppression." (Palmer, People's Daily World 1986)

Perhaps this is a clue as to the origins of the "Fairness Doctrine" that was long used to stifle conservative media in the US.

During her time as IOJ Vice President, Alice Palmer worked with the highest levels of the Soviet propaganda machine, the Soviet journal *Izvestia*. Palmer also worked with Romesh Chandra, the World Peace Council and the IOJ leadership.

Alice Palmer told the December 24, 1986, *People's Daily World*:

The IOJ has adopted positions on nuclear weapons, trying to do away with the nuclear threat in the world...

I will be heading a taskforce on peace and disarmament. And at the conference I was co-moderator, with the editor of Izvestia (a Soviet government publication) , of a panel on peace and the news media. We came up with some good suggestions. A number of the people complimented the Soviet Union for its efforts towards peace in these past few years-the moratorium and other things. (Palmer, People's Daily World 1986)

The IOJ has worked with the World Peace Council and Kaarle Nordenstreng, Jiri Kubka and other IOJ leaders have worked closely with Romesh Chandra, the President of the World Peace Council.

IOJ delegations visit other countries to report on the peace proposals of the Soviet Union, so that people can hear about it. This by the way is an example of promoting fairness in the media.

The IOJ is the largest journalist organization in the world. Its publications are published in 10 or 15 languages and it reaches many people all over the world. So you can see that being fair in the media is important, particularly in the Third World.

Alice Palmer saw journalists and the US "peace movement" as playing an important role in the struggle for peace:

> At the center of this is that the peace movement must stop the Soviet bashing. That is not productive; it is not a good thing at all. Soviet bashing is a barrier to our ability to work together in the United States and with the people of the Soviet Union for peace. (Palmer, People's Daily World 1986)

After her stint with IOJ had ended, Alice Palmer continued to work with US communists.

Ishmael Flory, a veteran leader of the Illinois Communist Party USA, was honored at a September 21, 1991 function at Chicago's Malcolm X College for his "outstanding contributions to the cause of peace, equality and justice."

"Ishmael Flory is truly a man for all seasons" said State Senator Palmer, noting Flory's unflagging zeal for promoting a progressive, people's agenda for economic security, an end to racism and for world peace. "He never gives up." (Flory 1991)

As late as 1994, when Palmer was known to be working with Barack Obama, she was also working with members of the Communist Party splinter, Committees of Correspondence.

It is now clear that Barack Obama has worked for years with Marxists with backgrounds in the Communist Party USA, Democratic Socialists of America and Committees of Correspondence.

90-8 Ishmael Flory Illinois Communist Party

That is this, only these groups have promoted Obama's career, both in Chicago and nationally, is undeniable.

However, the Alice Palmer case illustrates something even more concerning.

That is this, only a few years before meeting the future President, a key Obama ally had a strong relationship with senior East Bloc officials.

Figure 90-9 Barack Obama (l) Hugo Chavez (r)

Alice Palmer played an active role in promoting Soviet Bloc policy at the height of the Reagan era when the Soviets and their proxies were threatening US interests in every corner of the globe.

A few years later Alice Palmer was promoting the career of a young activist lawyer. That man is now willing and able to negotiate arms control treaties with Alice Palmer's old friends in Moscow.

A man who seems intent on promoting the interests of the former Eastern Bloc and the "third world" over those of the USA.

Is this ironic, or is it catastrophic?

91. Barack Obama and the Socialist Healthcare Scamsters

Thursday, November 26, 2009

Despite little public clamor for government controlled health care, the US Senate is looking to pass a Healthcare Bill in the near future.

How did this happen? Where did the pressure for change come from?

The blunt truth is this. The push to socialize US Healthcare came, not from the "people," but from a small clique of Marxists. This group's goal is socialized, government-run "Single Payer" healthcare long promoted through US Rep. John Conyers National Health Insurance Act, or HR 676.

The leader of this Marxist clique is Dr. Quentin Young, a retired Chicago physician, a life long Marxist activist and long time friend and political ally of Barack Obama.

Young has known and worked with Obama for years in Chicago and has influenced Obama's views on socialized medicine:

> Obama...learned about single-payer health care from his old friend and neighbor Dr. Quentin Young, the longtime coordinator of Physicians for a National Health Program. (Nichols 2009)

Dr. Quentin Young told Amy Goodman of "Democracy Now!"[581]

that while an Illinois State senator, Obama was a strong supporter of "Single Payer":

> Barack Obama, in those early days-influenced, I hope, by me and others-categorically said Single Payer was the best way, and he would inaugurate it if he could get the support, meaning majorities in both houses,

91-1 Quentin Young (l) Barack Obama (r)

which he's got, and the presidency, which he's got. And he said that on more than one occasion.... " (Goodman 2009)

Physicians for a National Health Program

Who is Dr. Quentin Young and his Physicians for a National Health Program (PNHP)? What influence do they have?

PNHP claims to be a national organization of 14,000 doctors advocating single-payer national health insurance.

These are small operations run by Quentin Young and a handful of Marxist comrades.

Dr. Quentin Young

Quentin Young is one of America's most committed socialists, beginning with his time in the Young Communist League in late 1930s' Chicago.

After World War II, into the '70s, Young was associated with the Communist Party and accused of belonging to the Bethune Club (a communist doctor's club) by a US Congressional Committee investigating the riots at the 1968 Democratic Party convention in Chicago.

91-2Quentin Young - leader of this Marxist clique

In the late 1970s, Young was associated with the pro-Marx/Gramsci, New American Movement and in 1982 helped found the Marxist, Democratic Socialists of America to which he still belongs.

581

http://www.democracynow.org/2009/3/11/dr_quentin_young_obama_confidante_and

In 1972, in the dying days of the Vietnam War, Young led a small radical delegation to Communist North Vietnam.

In 1995, Young attended the famous meeting at the Hyde Park home of former Weather Underground terrorists Bill Ayers and Bernardine Dohrn. This is where Alice Palmer introduced Barack Obama as the chosen successor to her position as an Illinois State Senator.

Young was a founder and National Chairman of the Medical Committee for Human Rights, which provided medical care for civil rights workers in the South, but later morphed into a "Single Payer" advocacy organization.

In 1987, Young and Peter Orris founded the Physicians for a National Health Program (PNHP), the US' oldest existing "Single Payer" advocacy organization and is the organization's National Coordinator.

Peter Orris

Peter Orris is the son of Communist Party member and physician Leo Orris. His sister is Maxine Orris, a New York physician who received her medical training in Cuba.

Peter Orris was a leader of Students for a Democratic Society (SDS) at Harvard before going on to join the Communist Party. He was still a Party member in 1987 when he helped Quentin Young form PNHP.

91-3 Peter Orris - Students for a Democratic Society (SDS) at Harvard, Communist Party

In 1992, Peter Orris joined the Communist Party splinter group, Committees of Correspondence, in which he remains a leading activist.

Peter Orris is a strong advocate of "Single Payer." Through PNHP and his associations with:

- International Association of Fire Fighters
- International Brotherhood of Teamsters
- UNITE-HERE
- American Federation of State County and Municipal Employees
- SEIU
- American Public Health Association
- Public Health Committee of the Chicago Medical Society

- Illinois State Medical Society
- American College of Physicians.

On June 25, 2009, Peter Orris was one of several doctors from the Doctors Council of SEIU[582] who traveled to Washington, D.C. for a massive day of action for real health care reform.

The healthcare providers met with their Members of Congress and participated in a rally on Capitol Hill.

Today, Peter Orris[583] is on the National Physicians Advisory Board of the National Physicians Alliance alongside Dr. Quentin Young.

Joanne Landy

Joanne Landy is another key PHNP activist and like Young is a prominent member of Democratic Socialists of America.

In 2005, Landy wrote a pamphlet for PNHP, *"Why Labor Needs Improved, and Expanded Medicare for All."* The pamphlet focused on mobilizing labor union support for US Representative John Conyer's National Health Insurance Act (HR 676).

91-4 Joanne Landy member of Democratic Socialists of America

In 2008, Joanne Landy and Physicians Advisory Board of the National Physicians Alliance (PHNP) President Oliver Fein wrote, *"We Can Do It! The Case for Single Payer National Health Insurance"* a chapter in a book entitled *"Ten Excellent Reasons for National Health Insurance."*

> The time has come for "Single Payer" National Health Insurance in the United States. We have excellent hospitals, skilled practitioners, the technological infrastructure and we are spending enough money to insure everyone and to improve access to care for many who covered today by inadequate plans. All we need is the political will. (O'Brian and Livingston, Martha 2008)

[582] http://www.doctorscouncil.com/admin/Assets/AssetContent/5c916bf5-db1c-4cd7-b302-48e12aa23d94/546bfa9e-94e2-495f-9d30-54cc81f55e47/fa1a4e85-966e-49e8-9316-8354cbbedee0/1/DOCTORS%20COUNCIL%20SEIU-JULY%2022,%202009%20NEWSLETTER.pdf

[583] http://npalliance.org/content/pages/npa_advisory_board

Mark J. Almberg

Mark J. Almberg is PNHP communications director and has been a prominent member of the Illinois Communist Party, since the 1970s.

PNHP President Oliver Fein and Secretary Steffi Woolhandler, have both advocated "Single Payer" at the annual Democratic Socialists of America run Socialist Scholars Conferences in New York City.

Fein, representing Physicians Advisory Board of the National Physicians Alliance (PNHP), addressed the 1992 Socialist Conference, attended by members of Democratic Socialists of America, the Communist Party and Committees of Correspondence, on "The movement for a national healthcare program."

At the 2000 Socialist Conference, Steffi Woolhandler, co-founder of PNHP and Harvard Medical School professor, cited "Single-Payer" health care as the issue in politics where the Left and the American people agree.

Healthcare Now!

In 2004, PNHP joined several other socialist, labor, church and community organizations to form a wider coalition, Healthcare NOW!

Healthcare Now! holds annual national strategy meetings with volunteer organizers and health care activists around the country, including John Conyers.

In 2007, Healthcare NOW launched traveling road shows promoting "Single Payer" reform and also co-sponsored an Annual Health Care Justice Vigil held each September in Washington D.C.

Healthcare-NOW! worked with the California Nurses Association to initiate the National Day of Protest Against Health Insurance Companies.

Dr. Quentin Young is a Healthcare Now! Co-Chair, as is Leo Gerard, President of United Steelworkers of America and Rose Ann DeMauro, Executive Director of the California Nurses Association.

Quentin Young[584] attended the Chicago Democratic Socialists of America at their annual award dinner in 1992. Leo Gerard was the

---

[584] http://www.chicagodsa.org/d1992/index.html

speaker in 2007 and Rose Ann DeMauro, was to have been keynote speaker at the 2008 dinner, until an inter-union dispute caused her to cancel the appearance. The Healthcare Now! Board of Directors[585] includes:

Four leaders of PNHP

- Oliver Fein
- Ida Hellander
- David Himmelstein
- Quentin Young

Other key Board members include:

Medea Benjamin

Medea Benjamin is a member of "peace" group Code Pink. In 1992, Benjamin endorsed the foundation conference of Committees of Correspondence with Peter Orris, mentioned above and in 2002 spoke at a 2002 Committees of Correspondence with John Nichols, also mentioned above.

91-5 Medea Benjamin, right with Hugo Chavez

91-6 Flavio Casoy, revolutionary medicine T shirt

Michael Lighty

Michael Lighty is Director of Public Policy at the California Nurses Association. Lighty is a long time member of Democratic Socialists of America and a former National Director of that organization.

Flavio Casoy

Flavio Casoy is a San Francisco based doctor and Representative of the Medical Students Association. Casoy is also a prominent member of the Communist Party USA. In March 2009, the National Education Commission of the Communist Party USA[586] recorded a podcast by Flavoy

---

[585] http://old.healthcare-now.org/board_of_directors.html
[586] http://www.politicalaffairs.net/article/articleview/8613/

to Party Clubs as a Club Educational/Group Discussion Guide on healthcare reform.

Rev. Lucius Walker

Rev. Lucius Walker is a representative of the Interreligious Foundation for Community Organization.

At the Martin Luther King Center in Havana, Cuban President Fidel Castro embraces the Rev. Lucius Walker, leader of the Friendshipment Caravan.

91-7 Rev. Lucius Walker & Fidel Castro

Walker is a long time supporter of radical and Communist Party USA causes. He has been an organizer of several Pastors for Peace Caravans to Cuba and enjoys a cozy relationship with Cuban leadership. Applications from US citizens to undergo medical training in Cuba, administer their needs through Walker's New York City based Interreligious Foundation for Community Organization.

The British Experience:

Obama's Healthcare Bill is the cornerstone of his Presidency.

Should the Bill pass in almost any form, it will pave the way for more and more legislative changes, which will change American health and political culture beyond recognition.

The Marxist left looks to the British example. They believe that "Single Payer" will lock the stubbornly conservative US worker into near permanent support for the Democratic Party as it did for the British Labor Party after World War II.

Leading Communist Party member Norman Markowitz wrote in the Party journal Political Affairs:[587]

> A "Single Payer" national health system known as "socialized medicine" in the rest of the developed world should be an essential part of the change that the core constituencies that elected Obama need. Britain serves as an important political lesson for strategists. After the Labor Party established the National Health Service after World War II, conservative workers and low-income people under religious and other influences who

---

[587] http://www.politicalaffairs.net/article/articleview/7722/

tended to support the Conservatives were much more to vote for the Labor Party when labor-supported governments enacted health care, social welfare, education, and pro-working class policies. (Markowitz, Obama's Mandate for Change 2008)

Radical journalist John Nichols[588] writes that Obama told an Atlanta town hall audience in 2008:

I am somebody who is no doubt progressive. I believe in a tax code that we need to make more fair. I believe in universal health care. (Nichols 2009)

Nichols also went on to discuss prospects for "Single Payer" under an Obama Administration:

Perhaps most impressive are the moves made by the California Nurses Association/National Nurses Organizing Committee, Physicians for a National Health Program, and Progressive Democrats of America to ensure that the option of single-payer is not forgotten as Obama and House Speaker Nancy Pelosi establish their domestic policy priorities. (Nichols 2009)

To that end, sixty activists from these and allied groups, met one week after election day at the AFL-CIO headquarters in Washington with Michigan US Representative John Conyers, an Obama backer and

the chief House proponent of real reform, to forge a "Single Payer" Healthcare Alliance and plot specific strategies for influencing the new Administration and Congress.

US Representative John Conyers is not an Obama and "Single Payer" zealot. The

91-8 Barack Obama (l) John Conyers (r)

Congressman from Michigan, with a long record of supporting Communist Party fronts, is an honored guest at the founding of Democratic Socialists of America in Detroit in 1982 and at DSA's 2003 National Convention[589] in the same city.

He is also a leading member of the Congressional Progressive

---

[588] http://www.progressive.org/mag/nichols0109.html
[589] http://www.dsausa.org/convention2003/report/index.html

Caucus,[590] an alliance of more than seventy Democratic Congressmen, many of who link to Democratic Socialists of America, the Communist Party or both.

Should Obama succeed in passing any form of Healthcare Bill, will that not be the end of the matter?

US Representative John Conyers, Quentin Young, his Marxist comrades and the alliance they have forged will not rest until the US has a socialized "Single Payer" health system.

There is evidence that that is what Obama wants as well.

Unless stopped, Obama, willing or not, will preside over the "Englandization" of the US health sector and the "Europeanization" of American political life.

Dr. Quentin Young and PNHP have pulled off the greatest socialist "scam" ever perpetrated on the American people.

92. Some Christmas Reading for Your Senators - Obama, Young, Conyers and Socialized Healthcare

Trevor Loudon © Tuesday, December 08, 2009

Dr. Quentin Young served as Barack Obama's Marxist personal physician of more than 20 years and his decade's long campaign to socialize US healthcare.

Young and his comrades in Physicians for a National Health Plan and "Healthcare Now!" have driven the US healthcare debate for years. Now they have a friend in the Oval Office and both Houses of Congress controlled by the Democrats.

92-1 Dr. Quentin Young
Obama's Marxist physician

Soon the Senate may pass a Healthcare Bill, but whatever form it takes, the drive to socialized, government controlled "Single Payer"

http://Communist
Partyc.grijalva.house.gov/index.cfm?SectionID=4&ParentID=0&SectionTypeID=2&Section
Tree=4

healthcare will accelerate.

The socialist's agenda goes far beyond tinkering or minor reforms - they want socialized "Single Payer" healthcare.

Quentin Young is a member of Democratic Socialists of America. He, his Democratic Socialists of America (DSA) comrades and his allies in Committees of Correspondence for Democracy and Socialism (COCDS) and the Communist Party USA, all want socialized healthcare as a major stepping-stone to a socialist America.

Health and Medicine Policy Research Group

This file looks at another arrow in Dr. Quentin Young's "Single-Payer" quiver - his Chicago based Health and Medicine Policy Research Group" (HMPRG)[591]:

> We're a 28-year old 501c3 nonprofit that operates as an independent, freestanding center driven by a singular mission: formulating health policy, advocacy and health systems to enhance the health of the public.

Dr. Quentin Young and John McKnight, a radical community organizer turned academic, founded HMPRG in 1981. McKnight trained Barack Obama for three years in the late '80s and wrote a letter of recommendation which helped the young activist gain entry to Harvard Law School.

HMPRG's Board of Directors[592] includes Yolanda Hall, who was in the Young Communist League with Quentin Young before joining the Communist Party in 1939, plus two more recent Party members, Linda Rae Murray and Mildred Williamson.

Dr. Quentin Young joined the Young Communist League before joining the Communist Party in 1939 with Linda Rae Murray and Mildred Williamson.

On March 7, 2008, HMPRG organized an 85th birthday tribute dinner for Dr. Quentin Young in Chicago. The theme: "Rebel without a Pause."

Guests included Illinois Senator Dick Durbin and Illinois Governor Pat Quinn.

---

[591] http://hmprg.org/
[592] http://hmprg.org/about/board-of-directors/

The Host Committee members included:

- Timuel Black - (formerly with the Socialist Party USA. Now with both Democratic Socialists of America (DSA) and COCDS. Black was Chicago Democratic Socialists of America (DSA)'s Debs-Thomas-Harrington Dinner honoree in 2009. He is a long time friend and supporter of Barack Obama)

- Representative Danny K. Davis - (Illinois Congressman and Democratic Socialists of America (DSA) member, with past ties to both the Communist Party and COCDS. Davis was active with Obama in the Democratic Socialists of America (DSA)/Committees of Correspondence influenced New Party in the mid '90s)

- Leon Despres - (formerly with the Socialist Party USA. Chicago Democratic Socialists of America (DSA) Debs-Thomas Dinner honoree in 1975. A mentor to Barack Obama)

- Miguel del Valle - (Chicago City Clerk. Chicago Democratic Socialists of America (DSA) Debs-Thomas Dinner guest speaker in 2001. Del Valle supported Obama in his 2003 US senate campaign)

- Jacky Grimshaw - (Chicago Democratic Socialists of America (DSA) Debs-Thomas-Harrington Dinner honoree in 1987. Barack Obama's Hyde Park next door neighbor and long time supporter)

- Roberta Lynch - (Democratic Socialists of America (DSA) member. Debs-Thomas-Harrington Dinner speaker in 1983)

- William McNary - (Chicago Democratic Socialists of America (DSA) Debs-Thomas-Harrington Dinner guest speaker in 2005. MacNary also has close ties to the Communist Party and is a close friend and supporter of Barack Obama)

- Calvin Morris - (Chicago Democratic Socialists of America (DSA) Debs-Thomas-Harrington Dinner honoree 2006)

- David Orr - (Cook County Clerk. Chicago Democratic Socialists of America (DSA) Debs-Thomas-Harrington Dinner guest in 1983 and 1993 and guest speaker in 1988)

- Peter Orris - (a founder with Quentin Young of Physicians for a National Health Plan. A Communist Party member until 1991. Now a leader of COCDS)

- Jane Ramsey - (Chicago Democratic Socialists of America (DSA) Debs-Thomas-Harrington Dinner honoree 2009, with Timuel Black)

- Bettylu Saltzman - (A long time Obama supporter and fundraiser)

- Representative Jan Schakowsky (D-IL-9th District) - (Chicago Democratic Socialists of America (DSA) Debs-Thomas-Harrington Dinner honoree in 2000, guest speaker in 2004 and a guest in 1993. A long time Obama supporter)

- Jeremiah Stamler - (A lifelong medical and activist colleague of Quentin Young)
- Yolanda Hall - (A 1960s "Fifth Amendment" Communist)

US Representative John Conyers

One of the key speakers at the Dr. Quentin Young event was Michigan Democratic Congressman John Conyers - a leading proponent of "Single Payer" Healthcare.

Conyers praised Dr. Quentin Young, US Representative Danny K. Davis and US Representative Jan Schakowsky (D-IL-9th District) for their efforts on the health issue.

He stated that "we" were pushing "Single Payer" long before Barack Obama came out in favor of the idea while still an Illinois State Senator.

Socialized healthcare is what Conyers and his comrades want or they will not be satisfied.

Congressman Conyers has a long Communist front record. He is also close to Democratic Socialists of America - addressing their founding conference in Detroit in 1982 and their National Convention in the same city in 2003.

Promoting "Single Payer"

HMPRG personnel promote "Single Payer" in every possible forum, at every possible opportunity.

Claudia Fegan

In June 2008, HMPRG Vice President Claudia Fegan addressed the "How Class Works" conference at Stonybrook, New York on the subject "Putting Single-Payer Health Care in the Mix."

92-2 Claudia Fegan HMPRG Vice President 2008

Other conference speakers included Progressives for Obama founder Bill Fletcher Jr. and Michele Rossi of DSA, Harry Targ, Meta Van Sickle, Carl Bloice, Ira Grupper, Mark Solomon and Manning Marable of CCDS, plus recently elected AFL-CIO president and "Single Payer" advocate, Richard Trumka.

Claudia Fegan spoke on "Single Payer" health care and HR 676, Rep. John Conyers' bill, at the HR 676 Congressional caucus reception during the Democratic National

Convention, August 26, 2008. She is introduced by former Democratic Socialists of America National director, Michael Lighty.

Mildred Williamson

Mildred Williamson, an HMPRG Board member and Illinois Public Health official, was a member of the Communist Party until 1991, when she left to join COCDS.

She is also is an admirer of the Cuban health system. On April 24, 2007, at the School of The Art Institute Auditorium, Chicago, Williamson and COCDS comrade Dr. Peter Orris held a discussion following the screening of "Salud" a documentary exploring Cuba's healthcare system & global initiatives.

Mildred Williamson advocated "Single Payer" at a COCDS Midwest regional meeting in August 2007.[593] The meeting went on to recommend that national COCDS should:

92-3 Mildred Williamson

> ...develop a position paper and a variety of informational materials on the health care crisis, the threat to the basic healthcare infrastructure in the United States, and a single payer national health care system. These materials should be broadly disseminated. (Targ 2007)

Mildred Williamson is one of several COCDS endorsers of the Progressives for Obama (P40) website.

Dr. Linda Rae Murray

Dr. Linda Rae Murray is immediate past President of HMPRG. Like Mildred Williamson, she was a member of the Communist Party until 1991 and has since been close to COCDS and to Democratic Socialists of America (DSA).

> Dr. Murray cautioned about what might be presented as a national health plan and the need for a real radical change in the medical delivery system in our country: the need for public health to be given the consideration it needs, the need to realize that the Canadian Single Payer

---

[593] http://www.cc-ds.org/discussion/midwest_COCDS_meeting_mar07.html

plan was the way to go... The insurance industry and the pharmaceutical industry have to be met head-on. (Shier and Roman, New Ground 30 1993)

In May 2005, Chicago Democratic Socialists of America[594] advocated:

> For your advocacy of universal health care as a right of all citizens;
> For your Service to the community in the field of public health;
> For your willingness to speak out against the injustices of an unequal society;

> The Debs-Thomas-Harrington Dinner Committee does hereby present you with its annual award this 6th day of May, 2005. (Schaps 2005)

Dr. Linda Rae Murray[595] has addressed forums organized by the "Spirit of 1848" caucus within the American Public Health Association that is Marxist and claims that 1848 was the year of many "progressive" social advances including the writing of the Communist Manifesto.

At the October 2008, APHA conference in San Diego, the Medicare, Spirit of 1848, Women's and Socialist Caucuses within APHA, co-sponsored the P. Ellen Parsons Memorial Session, on "Health Access & the Elections: What Happened, What Didn't."

Dr. Linda Rae Murray used the occasion to attack the private healthcare provision and promote the socialist alternative.

Figure 92-4 Linda Rae Murray (r)

> Dr. Linda Rae Murray, a discussant, spoke to the importance of not staying stuck in a complicated policy-wonk mode but instead appealing to people's sense of fairness, framing health care as a human right, and making clear the current system does not work and incremental efforts at reform have made little or no difference. (D. L. Murray 2008)

She also emphasized that one reason that efforts over the past 100 years have failed is that creating a system that provides universal health coverage is a way of redistributing wealth that goes against capitalist ideology. This requires

---

[594] http://www.chicagodsa.org/d2005/index.html#anchor291968
[595] http://keywiki.org/index.php/Linda_Rae_Murray

taking this ideology head-on.

In November 2009, Dr. Linda Rae Murray, a 30-year member of American Public Health Association, the largest public health organization in the world, was elected President of the organization on a platform that stated:

> If we are going to make progress toward a healthy nation, we have to overcome those issues that divide us; issues of racism, immigrant rights, gender discrimination, and workers' rights. It is through unity that we will have the strength to the changes our country needs...

> The United States must join the rest of the industrialized world in guaranteeing the right to medical care to everyone, including those in the country without proper documents. I agree with the APHA position that the best way to accomplish this is through a Single Payer insurance plan. (Murray 2009)

COCDS leader Manning Marable:[596]

> What makes Obama different is that he has also been a community organizer. He has read left literature, including my works, and he understands what socialism is. (M. Marable 2008)

Many of the people working with him are, indeed, socialists with backgrounds in the Communist Party or as independent Marxists. There are many people like that in Chicago who have worked with him for years.

Socialists won't quit on "Single Payer"

Indeed, many of them are "Single Payer" advocates.

Dr. Quentin Young claims credit for turning Barack Obama into a "Single Payer" advocate when the President was an Illinois State Senator.

It is clear that the Marxists who guided Obama's career in Chicago want a return on their investment.

It is also clear that the socialists

92-5 Quentin Young (l), Linda Rae Murray (2d l), Claudia Fegan (c), Barack Obama (r) at Quentin Young's 80th birthday celebration, 2003.

---

[596] http://www.socialistreview.org.uk/article.php?articlenumber=10628

and communists around Dr. Quentin Young and US Representative John Conyers will accept no compromise measures.

If the US Senate passes even the mildest of Healthcare Bills, the socialists will use the advantage to push for greater and greater changes until US medicine is under complete state control.

With one sixth of the US economy socialized, the far left will turn their attention to the rest.

It will be downhill coasting for the socialists and a downhill slide for America.

93. Obama's Marxist Doctor Once Supported Google Health Advisor

Trevor Loudon © Wednesday, December 09, 2009

As the world's largest search engine, Google is the planet's most powerful information provider. Google rankings can determine whether a story becomes "top of mind" for millions of people, or sinks without a trace.

Healthcare is a huge issue in the United States. President Barack Obama signing into law the Obama Healthcare Bill will affect the economic and political direction of the US.

A few years ago, Google established the Google Health Advisory Council:

> We often seek expertise from outside the company, and health is no exception. To help us think about the ways we can contribute to the healthcare industry, we formed the Google Health Advisory Council. The Google Health Advisory Council includes healthcare experts from provider organizations, consumer and disease-based groups, physician organizations, research institutions, policy foundations, and other fields.
>
> The mission of the Google Health Advisory Council is to help us better understand the problems consumers and providers face every day and to offer us feedback on product ideas and development. (Google Health Advisory Council)

93-1 John Lumpkin

This Council may have some impact on

the way Google handled the health debate - or else why have it?

Therefore, Americans should be concerned at the background and connections of one of Google's Health Advisory Board members, John R. Lumpkin.

He earned his M.D. and B.M.S. degrees from Northwestern University Medical School and his M.P.H. from the University of Illinois, School of Public Health. He has served on the faculty of University of Chicago, Northwestern University and University of Illinois at Chicago and has taught at Princeton University.

John Lumpkin is responsible for the overall planning, budgeting, staffing, management and evaluation of all program and administrative activities for the Robert Wood Johnson Foundation's Health Care Group.

He is a member of the Institute of Medicine of the National Academies and a fellow of the American College of Emergency Physicians and the American College of Medical Informatics. He has served on the Boards of directors for the Public Health Foundation and National Quality Forum, as President of the Illinois College of Emergency Physicians and the Society of Teachers of Emergency Medicine.

What his bio does not tell us is that John R. Lumpkin was once an identified supporter of the Communist Party USA.

John Lumpkin is the son of two Chicago Communist Party stalwarts, Frank and Bea Lumpkin.

In their day, the senior Lumpkins were leaders of the Illinois Party.

In the 1980s, both worked for the election of Chicago's first Black Mayor, the radical Harold Washington - the man who inspired Barack Obama to first move to the "Windy City."

Working through his "Save Our Jobs Committee," Lumpkin also helped elect communist connected US Senator Carol Moseley-Braun (D-IL) in 1992. Barack Obama contributed too, through his work with Project Vote.

According to the Communist Party USA's paper, the former *People's Weekly World* reported:

> Lumpkin also led Save Our Jobs Committee into independent political action. They played an important role

93-2 Frank and Beatrice Lumpkin, 2005

485

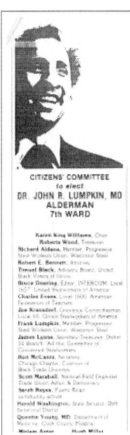

93-3 Dr. John E. Lumpkin, MD Campaign Poster

in the election of Harold Washington as Mayor of Chicago, a historic victory...Washington and Lumpkin had a special relationship ... Washington seemed to draw strength from Lumpkin's participation... (Wendland, Harold Washington: The People's Mayor 2008)

The Save Our Jobs Committee was important in the election of US Senator Carol Moseley-Braun (D-IL), the first Black woman to serve in the US Senate.

Barack Obama benefited from the same socialist/communist coalition when he won US Senator Carol Moseley-Braun (D-IL)'s former Senate seat in 2004.

In 1979, John R. Lumpkin ran for Alderman in Chicago's seventh Ward.

Leading members of the "Committee to elect John R. Lumpkin" included Harold Washington, Senator Carol Moseley-Braun, and Communist Party members Roberta Wood, Scott Marshall, Joe Kransdorf and Frank Lumpkin.

Timuel Black, now a member of both the Communist Party breakaway group Committees of Correspondence for Democracy Socialism and Democratic Socialists of America, was on the list. Black later became a close friend and supporter of Barack Obama.

Also there was Dr. Quentin Young, now a member of Democratic Socialists of America. For more than 20 years, Young has been a close friend, personal physician and political mentor to Barack Obama.

Though he has denied Party membership, Dr. Quentin Young was a member of the Young Communist League in his teens. A government commission investigating the 1968 Democratic Party Convention riots in Chicago accused Young of membership in the Bethune Club of the Communist Party (a party doctor's group).

Dr. Quentin Young has been the US' most active proponent of "Single Payer" or socialized healthcare for decades through his medical

93-6 Mark J. Almberg

93-5 List of signatories to an Illinois Communist Party to an electoral petition for the 1976 US Presidential Elections

committee for Human Rights, his Physicians for a National Health Program and his Health and Medicine Policy Research Group.

The next exhibit is a list of signatories on an Illinois Communist Party electoral petition for the 1976 US Presidential Elections.

John R. Lumpkin listed as are three prominent Party members, all of whom are active in the modern "Single Payer" movement and all of whom are close to Dr. Quentin Young: Mark J. Almberg, Peter Orris and Linda Rae Murray.

Mark J. Almberg is still a leading member of the Communist Party USA in Chicago. Mark J. Almberg is also the Communications Director of Dr. Quentin Young's Physicians for a National Health Plan, one the US's main "Single Payer" advocacy groups.

Dr. Peter Orris left the Communist Party in 1992 for the Committees of Correspondence, in which he now plays a leading role. While in the Communist Party, Orris helped Dr. Quentin Young establish the Physicians for a National Health Plan. Dr. Orris serves as Professor and Associate Director of the Great Lakes Center for Occupational and Environmental Safety and Health of the University Of Illinois School Of Public Health. Dr. Orris holds several union advisory roles, including SEIU and uses his positions to promote "Single Payer" at every opportunity.

Dr. Linda Rae Murray also left the Communist Party in 1992 and has since worked with Committees of Correspondence and Democratic Socialists of America. Dr. Linda Rae Murray is a prominent Chicago health professional and the immediate past President of Dr. Quentin Young's Health and Medicine Policy Research Group. She is a leading and active advocate for "Single Payer" and was elected President of the American Public Health Association - a post Dr. Quentin Young held in 1988.

John Lumpkin grew up in the Communist Party, including his extended family that were or are still Party members. All of them, in line with Communist Party policy, support "Single Payer'" socialized healthcare. John Lumpkin supported the Party. He benefited from the assistance of Party members in his own short political career. He worked in the incestuous "you scratch my back, I'll scratch yours" world of Chicago left politics.

Now his old comrades are making considerable progress towards their dream of socialized healthcare.

93-7 Dr. Linda Rae Murray

When the Healthcare Bill passes, socialization of the system is the primary goal of the Communist Party USA, Democratic Socialists of America and the Committees of Correspondence. Several of John Lumpkin's old allies are now vocal "Single Payer" advocates. One of them, Dr. Quentin Young, is the father of the US socialized healthcare movement and proudly admits to having tutored his friend Barack Obama in the subject.

John Lumpkin himself is an advocate of more government involvement in healthcare provision.[597]

The question is could John R. Lumpkin use his position at Google to influence the public health debate in a more socialist direction? Would his old friends and comrades approve the new direction?

---

[597] http://www.aarpmagazine.org/health/8_myths_about_health_care_reform.html

94. Concert or Coincidence? Obama and the Committees of Correspondence Connections

Trevor Loudon © Thursday, January 21, 2010

Committees of Correspondence for Democracy and Socialism (COCDS) are one of the US' most significant Marxist-Leninist parties.

The organization was born in 1992 out of a major split in the Communist Party USA, incorporating Trotskyites, former Maoists, socialists and anarchists to form a new party.

The party has strong ties to Cuba, Vietnam, Venezuela and the communist parties of France and the former East Germany.

Committees of Correspondence, was and is strong in Chicago. In Chapter 25, there are two leading CoC members that worked closely with Barack Obama.

Committees of Correspondence leader Manning Marable[598] wrote

 committees of **correspondence** for **democracy** and **socialism**

in British Trotskyist journal *Socialist Review* in December 2008:

> What makes Obama different is that he has also been a community organizer. He has read left literature, including my works, and he understands what socialism is. A lot of the people working with him are, indeed, socialists with backgrounds in the Communist Party or as independent Marxists. There are many people like that in Chicago who have worked with him for years... (D. M. Marable 2008)

94-1 British Trotskyist Journal Socialist Review

[598] http://www.socialistreview.org.uk/article.php?articlenumber=10628

He was referring to his Chicago COCDS comrades.

A Committees of Correspondence for Democracy and Socialism (COCDS) "Membership, Subscription and mailing list" dated October 14, 1994, has four hundred names on the list and many of the members on this list are members of the COCDS and have been identified from other reliable sources. The list does not prove COCDS membership per se, but it does indicate some degree of contact with the organization. What is striking are the names of several people who have promoted or influenced the political career of Barack Obama. They include:

CoC Membership, Subscription and Mailing List 10/14/94 IL				
Name	Address1	Address2 City 94-4 CoC List (cont.)	ST	J
Currie, Lamond	5122 S Ada	Chicago	IL	c
Curtin, Timothy	21 Oriole Lane	Glendale Hgts	IL	6

94-2 CoC Subscription and Mailing List

Carl Davidson

Carl Davidson is one of four co-leaders of the Committees of Correspondence, Davidson worked with Obama in the radical New Party in the 1990s. He later helped organize the famous 2002 peace rally in Chicago's Federal Plaza where Obama first became famous as an opponent of the Iraq War.

Representative Danny K. Davis

Dadrass, Fereidoun
Dardis, Lorraine
Davidson, Carl
Davis, Danny
Davis, Sara

94-3 CoC Subscription List (Cont.)

Davis is an Illinois Democratic Congressman and a member of Democratic Socialists of America with proven ties to the Communist Party and COCDS. Davis has been a long time Obama friend and political ally who campaigned with Obama in the New Party in 1995/96.

Bernardine Dohrn and Bill Ayers

Both are former leaders of the terrorist Weather Underground Organization (WUO). The couple hosted Obama's first known political gathering in their home in 1995. Bill Ayers[599] ties to Obama run deep:

> The two men were involved in efforts to reform the city's education system. They appeared together on academic panels, including one organized by Michelle Obama to discuss the juvenile justice system, an area of mutual concern. Mr. Ayers's book on the subject won a rave review in The Chicago Tribune by Mr. Obama, who called it "a searing and timely account." Mr. Obama further expanded his list of allies by joining the Boards of two well-known charities: the Woods Fund and the Joyce Foundation. These memberships have allowed him to help direct tens of millions of dollars in grants over the years to groups that championed the environment, campaign finance reform, gun control and other causes supported by the liberal network he was cultivating. Mr. Brazier's group, the Woodlawn Organization, received money, for instance, as did antipoverty groups with ties to organized labor like Chicago Acorn, whose endorsement Mr. Obama sought and won in his State Senate race. (Becker and Drew 2008)

Earl Durham

A former member of the Communist Party National Committee, Professor Durham later went into education reform in the 1970s and in the 1990s founded the organization Community Organizing and Family Issues. Barack Obama served on the organization's sponsoring committee in 1994-95.[600]

94-5 Earl Dunham

Marilyn Katz

Now a prominent Chicago public reactions professional and Democratic Party activist, Katz has a background in Students for a Democratic Society (SDS) and the socialist New American Movement. Katz, with Carl Davidson, helped organize Obama's appearance at the 2002 Chicago anti-Iraq War rally.

Marilyn Katz has worked closely with Barack Obama since meeting him through his position at Miner, Barnhill & Galland in the 1990s.

It was through the law firm that Mr. Obama met Marilyn Katz, who

---

599

http://www.nytimes.com/2008/05/11/us/politics/11chicago.html?pagewanted=3&_r=2
600 http://www.cofionline.org/about_cofi.php?id=11

gave him entry into another activist network: the foot soldiers of the white student and black power movements that helped define Chicago in the 1960s.

> "For better or worse, this is Chicago," said Ms. Katz, who has held fund-raisers for Mr. Obama at her home. "Everyone is connected to everyone." (Katz 2010)

Katz was a major fundraiser and a delegate at the Democratic Party convention for Obama. She was also an endorser of the Progressives for Obama (P40) website.

Fred Klonsky

Fred Klonsky is a former Students for a Democratic Society (SDS) activist, brother of Mike Klonsky and endorser of the Progressives for Obama (P40) website.

Mike Klonsky

94-6 Obama Campaign Website featuring Klonsky

Is a former leader of Students for a Democratic Society (SDS) and the pro-China Communist Party (Marxist-Leninist). Mike Klonsky is a longtime friend with Bill Ayers and was involved with some of the educational projects that Ayers and Obama worked together on. Until June 2008, Mike Klonsky ran a Blog on Barack Obama's campaign website. The blog was pulled on short notice after adverse publicity began surfacing in the blogosphere.

Alice Palmer

A long time Communist Party sympathizer, Alice Palmer has travelled extensively in the old Soviet Bloc and was a leader of the soviet front International Organization of Journalists. Obama was Alice Palmer's Chief of Staff when she ran for congress in the mid-1990s. She was the main sponsor of Obama's political career until he took her old Illinois State Senate seat in 1996. It was Alice Palmer who introduced Barack Obama to the meeting in the home of

Paidock, Charles A.
Palestine Sol Cmte,
Palmer, Alice & Buz
Pappademos, John
Pappademos, Melina

94-7 CoC List (cont.)

492

Bill Ayers and Bernardine Dohrn.

Lou Pardo

Lou Pardo is also a member of Democratic Socialists of America, Pardo worked with Obama on voter registration in 1992. In the mid-1990s Pardo was active with Obama in the Chicago New Party.

Dan Swinney

Swinney is a Chicago labor unionist and endorser of the Progressives for Obama (P40) website.

Kevin Tyson

A former member of the Communist Party, Kevin Tyson has been a longtime activist and co-parishioner with Obama in Rev. Jeremiah Wright's Trinity United Church of Christ.

94-8 Kevin Tyson

Mildred Williamson

A Chicago health professional, former Communist Party member and Committees of Correspondence leader. She is an endorser of the Progressives for Obama (P40) website.

Is it significant that all these people, several of them unconnected, all supported Barack Obama's career? Were they working, at least some of the time, in concert, to promote their mutual friend? On the other hand, are the Committees of Correspondence connections coincidental? What do you think?

95. Obama's Socialist Advisers Push Immigration Reform to "Create a Governing Coalition for the Long Term"

Trevor Loudon © Wednesday, January 27, 2010

Why, in a time of high US unemployment, is the Obama Administration considering US Representative Luis Gutiérrez's "Comprehensive Immigration Reform for America's Security and Prosperity" bill, which would grant citizenship to up to twelve million illegal immigrants?

95-1 US Representative Luis Gutiérrez

95-2 Eliseo Medina, Carl Marx Shier, Chicago 2004

The answer has little to do with humanity, national security or prosperity. It is all about power - raw socialist power. It is all about eight million more Democratic Party votes and the creation of a "governing coalition for the long term."

At the "progressive" America's Future Now! Conference in Washington, DC on June 2, 2009, SEIU International Executive Vice President Eliseo Medina addressed attendees on the issue immigration reform.

Speaking of Latino voters, Medina said, "When they voted in November, they voted for progressive candidates. Barack Obama got two out of every three voters that showed up"

Two things matter for the progressive community.

Number one: If we are to expand this electorate to win, the progressive community needs to be on the side of immigrants, that we'll expand and solidify the progressive coalition for the future..." When you are in the middle of a fight for your life, you will remember who was there with you. In addition, immigrants count on progressives to be able to do that.

Number two: We reform the immigration laws; it puts twelve million people on the path to citizenship and voters. Can you imagine if we have, even the same ratio, two out of three? If we have eight million new voters who care about and will be voting, we will be creating a governing coalition for the long term, not for an election cycle. (Medina 2009)

There you have the strategy. Fight for the illegal immigrants, grant them citizenship and exploit their gratitude in the form of votes to create a "governing coalition for the long term, not for one election cycle..."

Who is Eliseo Medina?

Medina is Vice President of the radical Service Employees International Union (SEIU) and has been the US' most effective immigration "reform" activist. His union, SEIU, is also the major backer of the Gutiérrez bill.

Selling the legalization of millions of illegal workers to the US labor movement has always been an uphill battle.

It was a huge turnaround in February 2000 when the AFL-CIO

reversed its long standing anti-illegal's policy, calling for a new amnesty for millions of undocumented workers and the repeal of the 1986 law that criminalized hiring them.

Eliseo Medina was one of the chief instigators behind that resolution.

Democratic Socialists of America, the Marxist organization to which Medina has long belonged, recognized that fact.

> Eliseo Medina is credited with playing a key role in the AFL-CIO's decision to adopt a new policy on immigration a few years ago, and was one of the organizers of the Immigrant Workers Freedom Bus Rides in 2003 (Democratic Socialists of America 2004)

Chicago Democratic Socialists of America honored Medina at their 2004 awards dinner; it was for his "vital role in the AFL-CIO's reassessment of its immigration policy."

Had Eliseo Medina not turned around the AFL-CIO and had the SEIU not supported it, US Representative Gutiérrez's bill would never have gotten off the ground.

Medina's first interaction with the forerunners of Democratic Socialists of America came in Chicago when, in 1969, he was sent by Cesar Chavez to lead the Chicago grape boycott campaign.

Medina contacted Carl Marx Shier, a member of the local Socialist Party of America chapter, later to be a key founder of the Democratic Socialists of America.

Shier connected Medina with the Chicago Labor movement, a decision

95-3 Eliseo Medina, second from left, Chicago DSA's 1975 awards dinner

that "propelled Medina's success with both the grape boycott and his career."

In 2004, Eliseo Medina became a Democratic Socialists of America honorary Chair.

In 2008, Eliseo Medina joined Barack Obama's National Latino

Advisory Council,[601] where he worked with Democratic Socialists of America (DSA) linked future Labor Secretary Hilda Solis, US Representative Luis Gutiérrez and the co-sponsor of Gutiérrez's immigration bill, the radical US Representative Nydia Velasquez (D-NY-12th District).

Representative Luis Gutiérrez is regarded in Chicago as one of Barack Obama's biggest supporters.

95-4 US Representative Luis Gutiérrez and Barack Obama

Eliseo Medina and Barack Obama both have ties to Chicago Democratic Socialists of America, so it is not surprising that Representative Luis Gutiérrez also has "connections."

When Representative Luis Gutiérrez ran for Congress in 1998, Democratic Socialists of America did not endorse any candidates, as they did Barack Obama in 1996.[602]

But he was "recommended" as worthy of a vote, because of his membership in the DSA/Institute for Policy Studies created Congressional Progressive Caucus and for his support of Progressive Challenge - also a DSA/IPS "baby."

In the mid-1990s, Luis Gutiérrez served on the Board of Illinois Public Action alongside Democratic Socialists of America (DSA) members Ron Baiman and Dr. Quentin Young, Democratic Socialists of America (DSA) supporters Representative Jan Schakowsky (D-IL-9th District), David Orr, Tom Balanoff and Communist Party member Frank Lumpkin and Soviet front leader Alice Palmer.

Representative Luis Gutiérrez got his start in politics as a Chicago Alderman elected as part of the Mayor Harold Washington "movement." Washington was elected Mayor of Chicago in 1983 by a coalition led by Chicago Democratic Socialists of America (DSA) and the Communist Party. Washington's election inspired the young Barack Obama to move

601 http://rootswire.org/conventionblog/patricia-madrid-named-obamas-national-latino-advisory-council
602 http://www.chicagodsa.org/ngarchive/ng45.html

to Chicago. He even applied for a job in the Washington administration.

In the '70s and '80s, Luis Gutiérrez was one of the leading US members of the Puerto Rican Socialist Party (PSP).

Marxist-Leninist PSP campaigned for Puerto Rican independence from the US. The organization maintained an unofficial "embassy" in Cuba and in the US was close to several revolutionary organizations including the terrorist Weather Underground Organization (WUO).

95-5 Jose LaLuz, right at Chicago DSA's 1992 awards dinner

Congressman Gutiérrez used his connections in the Chicago City government to secure government funds for the PSP sponsored cultural center and for Party sponsored social Services and ESL and GELD programs.

One of Eliseo Medina's comrades, Democratic Socialists of America (DSA) Vice Chair Jose Laluz[603] had also been a leading member of the Puerto Rican Socialist Party (PSP).[604]

In January 1976, Jose Laluz, representing the PSP Central Committee, attended the Weather Underground organized "Hard Times" Conference at the University of Chicago. The conference attempted to unify several radical groups into a new unified Communist Party.

In 2008, Jose Laluz was Chairman of Latinos for Obama,[605] a major Democratic Party effort to swing the Latino vote behind Obama.

LaLuz explained his tactics to the *Communist Party's People's Weekly World*:[606]

> "The Obama campaign is working in both New Mexico and Colorado, among other states, telling Latino voters about McCain's terrible stands on the economy and about the horrible role Republicans have played and continue to play on immigration... "We are showing how the

---

[603] http://keywiki.org/index.php/Jose_LaLuz
[604] http://keywiki.org/index.php/Jose_LaLuz
[605] http://www.ydsusa.org/news/2008-conference.html
[606] http://keywiki.org/index.php/Peoples_Weekly_World

companies and outfits that exploit Latino workers are the people behind McCain," (Key Wiki)

Between now and Election Day, LaLuz said, that the Obama campaign is registering voters in New Mexico and Colorado and developing lists of tens of thousands of Latino supporters for Obama. "Those lists will constitute the people we bring out on Election Day." (LaLuz 2008)

In 1999, Representative Luis Gutiérrez was one of a small group who lobbied President Clinton to pardon 14 imprisoned members of the Puerto Rican Separatists Fuerzas Armadas de Liberacion Nacional (FALN).

In September 2007, controversy erupted in Chicago when it was discovered that Illinois Governor Rod Blagojevich[607] had hired Steven Guerra as a $120,000 Deputy Chief of Staff for community Services.

It turned out that Guerra had spent two years in a federal prison for refusing a federal judge's order to testify before a grand jury investigating a wave of FALN bombings that terrorized Chicago and New York City in the 1970s and 1980s. Guerra chose conviction of contempt even though he was offered immunity from prosecution in exchange for his testimony.

A government informant had told investigators that Guerra was a member of FALN and recounted a June 1982 trip Guerra took to Puerto Rico to attend "a meeting of a cross section of terrorists."

"Guerra was identified at the meeting as "one of the leaders of the resistance in the United States".

"The discussion at the meeting included detailed plans for the ambush of police officers and the destruction of dams through the use of explosives." (Informant 1982)

Steven Guerra was hired by Chicago City in 2003, on the recommendation of Representative Luis Gutiérrez.

---

[607] http://keywiki.org/index.php/Rod_Blagojevich

Defending Guerra, Congressman Gutiérrez praised his long time acquaintance who "made what he considered a principled decision and he paid a heavy price for that decision." "I have known Steven for a long

time. He is a good man who cares about making our state a better place to live," said Gutiérrez.

The question is, will Gutiérrez and Medina's plans to "reform" immigration make the United States of America a better place?

95-6 Steven Guerra (c)

Is that even the intention?

Are illegal aliens pawns in a cynical fraud to give Obama's Democrats and their Marxist allies' indefinite power governing the coalition for the long term?

What do twelve million human beings matter, when a socialist America is at stake?

---

96. Coincidence? Obama, Frank Marshall Davis and the Earl Durham Connection

Monday, February 08, 2010

In Chapter 84, Why? It highlights the link between Barack Obama's communist childhood mentor, Frank Marshall Davis and Chicago journalist Vernon Jarrett, father-in-law of senior Obama adviser Valerie Jarrett.

The link is evidence that the communist networks that touched Obama in both Hawaii and Chicago were connected.

Vernon Jarrett and Frank Marshall Davis worked together in a communist front, the Citizen's Committee to Aid Packinghouse

96-1 Frank Marshall Davis

Workers in 1948 Chicago; the same year Davis moved to Hawaii.

More than forty years later, Vernon Jarrett followed Obama's career in Chicago and used his newspaper column to promote Obama's successful Senate campaign in 2004.

The question is, did some of Frank Marshall Davis' old Chicago comrades aid Barack Obama's career in Chicago more than four decades on?

This chapter looks at another link between Frank Marshall Davis and Obama's Chicago network.

The Abraham Lincoln School for Social Sciences was a Chicago institution of the 1930s and 1940s, run by the Communist Party USA.

The faculty members included known Party members Frank Marshall Davis, David Englestein, William L. Patterson, Geraldyne Lightfoot, Claude Lightfoot, Ishmael Flory and Earl Durham.

Frank Marshall Davis went off to work for the Hawaiian Communist Party, sinking into obscurity. His former comrade and colleague, Earl Durham, rose to the top of the communist ladder and went on to make a major impact on Chicago education and politics.

Earl Durham served in numerous leadership posts in the Communist Party USA. Elected to the Communist Party National Committee at the Party's 16th National Convention held in New York City on February 9-12, 1957, at which time he chose to serve on the party's eleven member national administrative committee.

At a meeting of the Party National Administrative Committee in May 1957, Durham was named as Youth Affairs Secretary of the party. He was appointed as one of nine party secretaries, who functioned as "a collective leadership" for the Communist Party USA.

After working and studying the psychopharmacology of heroin addiction, Earl Durham made the decision to earn a master's degree at the School of Social Service Administration at the University of Chicago. Upon graduation, the School hired him as a professor, where "he was able to influence many students to consider community organizing as a career."

One former student Ron Sanfield blogged:

96-2 Earl Dunham

I was a graduate student at the U of Chicago in the 1970s, and had Earl Durham for a professor.

Even though it was more than 30 years ago, I can still vividly remember those exciting sessions in his classroom. He challenged us to confront the realities of community organization, and what it REALLY meant. He challenged us to confront our feelings about race, about class, about the gap in America between rhetorical words and deeds.

One day, he told us, "If you really wanted to be doing community organization, you would be 'out there in the streets', not in here in this ivory-tower university" and taught us about Saul Alinsky who had walked those same streets of Hyde Park and other Chicago neighborhoods. (Sanfield 2007)

In the '80s, Earl Durham worked with the Communist Party and Democratic Socialists of America to elect Chicago's first black Mayor, long time communist front activist Mayor Harold Washington.

Washington's election in 1983 inspired Barack Obama to move to Chicago. Obama even wrote for a job in the Washington administration.

Earl Durham's brother, writer Richard Durham, served as Washington's speechwriter.

While never a confirmed party member, Richard Durham participated in several communist controlled organizations. In the 1950s, Durham worked as the national program director of the communist controlled United Packinghouse Workers of America. At the same time, he founded Chicago's Du Bois Theater Guild with Vernon Jarrett and Oscar Brown, Jr. Durham is a Communist Party member and a former official of Frank Marshall Davis' "Citizen's Committee to Aid Packinghouse Workers."

In the '80s, until Richard's death in 1984, both Durham brothers served on the Board of the Black Press Institute (BPI), the Chicago propaganda organization run by pro-Soviet Illinois State Senator, Alice Palmer.

96-3 Richard Dunham

In 1995, Alice Palmer launched the political career of her Chief-of-Staff Barack Obama at a meeting in the Hyde Park home of former Weather Underground terrorists Bill Ayers and Bernardine Dohrn.

In 1989, Earl Durham had served on the Board of the Chicago Committee in Solidarity with Southern Africa, along with Alice Palmer, another long time Obama friend and supporter Timuel Black.

Later, Timuel Black was a leader of the Communist Party breakaway group Committees of Correspondence.

A 1994 Chicago Committees of Correspondence "Membership, subscription and mailing" includes the names of Earl Durham, Alice Palmer, Bill Ayers and Bernardine Dohrn.

Earl Durham wrote the Chicago School Reform Act of 1988, which shifted decision making to the school level and created Chicago's unique Local School Councils.

These reforms created an opening exploited by radicals like Bill Ayers and Mike Klonsky and the up and coming Barack Obama.

In the '90s, Earl Durham and Barack Obama crossed paths in a new Chicago organization, Community Organizing and Family Issues (COFI).[608] Earl Durham was founding Board member of the organization, while Barack Obama served in 1994-95 on the COFI sponsoring committee.

COFI, like many Chicago community groups was a respectable "front" for radical activism. Some of Obama's radical COFI colleagues included:

- Ken Rolling - (signer of a 2008 statement in support of Bill Ayers)
- Jackie Grimshaw - (Obama's Hyde Park next-door neighbor, Democratic Socialists of America honoree Board member of the radical Democratic Socialists of America (DSA) controlled Midwest Academy)
- Barbara Engel - (served with Bernardine Dorhn in 1991 on a committee of the communist front organization, Chicago Committee to Defend the Bill of Rights)
- Anne Hallet - (signer of a 2008 statement in support of Bill Ayers, active with both Illinois and national ACORN)
- Judy Hertz - (involved with Illinois ACORN and the Midwest Academy)
- Elce Redmond[609] - (close to the Chicago Communist Party and active

[608] http://romantiCommunist Partyoet.wordpress.com/2010/02/23/obamas-communist-web-of-support-the-weissbourds-connection-to-frank-marshall-davis/
[609] http://communistpartyillinois.blogspot.com/2009/12/joy-and-inspiration-mark-chicago.html

in the Committees of Correspondence/Democratic Socialists of America dominated Chicago Political Economy Group)

- Mary Scott-Boria - (1998 co-President of the Democratic Socialists of America influenced Progressive Chicago Area Network (PROCAN))
- Ellen Schumer - (Board member of the Committees of Correspondence - Democratic Socialists of America infiltrated Obama, Ayers, Dohrn and Earl Durham supported *Crossroads Fund*)

That Barack Obama has mixed with Alinskyites, communists and socialists for his entire time in Chicago is beyond doubt.

The documentation shows that Communist Frank Marshall Davis mentored Barack Obama in Hawaii from the age of 11 to 18.

Vernon Jarrett and Earl Durham were both connected with Frank Marshall Davis.

Both men and their interconnected circles helped Barack Obama's rise through the world of Chicago far left politics.

Would Barack Obama be the leader of the Free World today had it not been for Frank Marshall Davis, Vernon Jarrett, Earl Durham and their Chicago comrades?

What do you think?

Does it matter?

97. Obama and the Weissbourds - Was There a Frank Marshall Davis Connection?

Trevor Loudon © Monday, February 22, 2010

Was there a Frank Marshall Davis Connection? Barack Obama has received the help of socialists and communists at every step of his political career - right back to his boyhood days in Hawaii, where the communist poet, Frank Marshall Davis, mentored him.[610]

Frank Marshall Davis, who was not a native of Hawaii, began his radical career in Chicago.

In 1985, Obama left New York for Chicago to work as a "community organizer."

---

[610] http://keywiki.org/index.php/Frank_Marshall_Davis

There is evidence that people with ties to Frank Marshall Davis supported Obama in his Chicago career.

Vernon Jarrett[611] was the father-in-law of senior Obama adviser Valerie Jarrett. The Chicago journalist promoted Obama's career through his newspaper columns. In the late 1940s, he worked with Davis on the publicity committee of a communist-controlled organization, the Citizen's Committee to Aid Packinghouse Workers.

Earl Durham[612] worked with Frank Marshall Davis in the Chicago Communist Party run Abraham Lincoln School for Social Sciences.[613]

In the mid-1990s, Earl Durham and Obama helped establish the radical dominated Community Organizing and Family Issues[614] organization.

This post looks at a third possible connection between the Frank Marshall Davis networks of the 1940s and the Obama movement of today.

In addition, teaching at Abraham Lincoln School for Social Sciences with Davis and Durham, was a woman named Bernice Targ.

97-1 Bernice Targ Weissbourd

Bernice Targ may be Bernice Targ Weissbourd, a Chicago activist and philanthropist. Born in 1923, she is the right age group and political inclination.

In March 2009, Bernice Targ Weissbourd[615] attended an 85th birthday tribute dinner for retired radical physician Quentin Young.[616]

According to the event program:[617]

Dr. Quentin Young began his activist life in the 1930s, as a teen, fighting fascism with his friend Bernice Weissbourd.

[611] http://keywiki.org/index.php/Vernon_Jarrett
[612] http://keywiki.org/index.php/Earl_Durham
[613] http://keywiki.org/index.php/Abraham_Lincoln_School
[614] http://www.cofionline.org/about_cofi.php?id=11
[615] http://keywiki.org/index.php/Bernice_Weissbourd
[616] http://keywiki.org/index.php/Quentin_Young
[617] http://keywiki.org/index.php/Quentin_Young_%28Summary%29

Dr. Quentin Young was a member of the Young Communist League in those days, so it is likely that Bernice Targ was also a comrade.

After World War II Quentin Young was an activist doctor and according to the House Un-American Activities Committee, was also a member of the Bethune Club of the Communist Party USA. (Weissbourd 2010)

97-2 Dr. Quentin Young (l) Barack Obama (r)

In the early 1970s, many Chicago communists left the party and linked up with ex-Students for Democratic Society (SDS) militants to create the Gramscian socialist, New American Movement (NAM).[618]

Dr. Quentin Young and his wife Ruth both supported NAM. When NAM and the Democratic Socialist Organizing Committee and NAM combined to form Democratic Socialists of America[619] in 1982, Dr. Quentin Young joined the new organization.

Young went on to meet, treat and mentor, over many years, an ambitious young Chicago lawyer/activist named Barack Obama.[620]

Meanwhile, Bernice Targ had married a young chemist-turned lawyer named Bernard Weissbourd.[621] As a chemist, Bernard Weissbourd had worked on the Manhattan Project to develop the Atomic Bomb and had contributed towards the discovery of Plutonium.

After the war, Bernard Weissbourd studied law and practiced as a lawyer for several years before becoming one of America's leading commercial property developers.

Despite his business success, Bernard Weissbourd was a man of the left. During the Civil Rights era, he held meetings of the radical Student Non-Violent Coordinating Committee in his backyard.

In 1983, Bernard Weissbourd served on the transition team of Chicago's Democratic Socialists of America (DSA)/Communist Party backed by Mayor Harold Washington[622] alongside, Dr. Quentin Young.

---

[618] http://keywiki.org/index.php/New_American_Movement
[619] http://keywiki.org/index.php/Democratic_Socialists_of_America
[620] http://keywiki.org/index.php/Barack_Obama
[621] http://keywiki.org/index.php/Bernard_Weissbourd
[622] http://keywiki.org/index.php/Harold_Washington

1983 was also the year that Obama first moved to Chicago, inspired by the victory of Mayor Harold Washington.

In 1992, Dr. Quentin Young, Ruth Young and Bernice Weissbourd were all members of the Chicago Committee to Defend the Bill of Rights[623] - the most successful Communist Party USA front ever. Earl Durham was also close to the organization in the late 1980s.

Democratic Socialists of America activists and members of the Committees of Correspondence[624], who had split from the Communist Party in 1991, dominated the Committee.

Dr. Quentin Young along with several leaders of the Chicago Committee to Defend the Bill of Rights, including Timuel Black,[625] Saul Mendelson[626] and Rabbi Arnold Jacob Wolf,[627] who joined with the Democratic Socialists of America and later became friends and supporters of Barack Obama.

In 2005, several of Obama's friends, colleagues and mentors including Earl Durham, Bernice Weissbourd, Quentin Young, Timuel

Black, Rev. Jeremiah Wright, Rev. Doctor Michael Pfegler, Alice Palmer, Abner Mikva and Leon Despres gathered together in the Chicago area with Friends of the Students Non-Violent Coordinating Committee, to commemorate the Civil rights movement of the 1960s.

Bernice Targ Weissbourd knows Earl Durham well. Did she know him at the Communist Party's Abraham Lincoln School with Frank Marshall Davis? The direct

97-3 Robert M. Weissbourd

Weissbourd-Obama connection comes through Bernard and Bernice's son, Chicago lawyer/businessman/activist Robert M. Weissbourd.[628]

---

[623] http://keywiki.org/index.php/Chicago_Committee_to_Defend_the_Bill_of_Rights
http://keywiki.org/index.php/Committees_of_Correspondence#6th_COCDS_Conventio
n.2C_San_Francisco.2C_July_2009
[625] http://keywiki.org/index.php/Timuel_Black
[626] http://keywiki.org/index.php/Saul_Mendelson
[627] http://keywiki.org/index.php/Arnold_Jacob_Wolf
[628] http://keywiki.org/index.php/Robert_M._Weissbourd

Like his wealthy parents, Robert Weissbourd has not let his commercial success dim his "social conscience."

Robert Weissbourd founded RW Ventures, LLC in 2000. He had served for ten years in executive positions at Shorebank Corporation, where he worked "to strengthen Chicago neighborhoods by investing in entrepreneurs, real estate and community organizations, and to help market institutions understand the benefits of returning to the inner city."

Before joining Shorebank, Weissbourd was a partner at Hartunian, Futterman & Howard, specializing in "federal constitutional and class action litigation, school desegregation and representation of government and non-profit agencies."

In 1981, Robert Weissbourd helped found the Chicago based Crossroads Fund[629] with socialists including Jean Hardisty[630] and Rona Stamm.

Crossroads is a major funder of the Chicago left and has been supported by a veritable who's who of Windy City radicals from Bill Ayers[631] and Bernardine Dohrn,[632] to the current US President Barack H. Obama.

In the late 1980s, Weissbourd was a Board member of the Progressive Chicago Area Network (PROCAN), alongside several prominent Democratic Socialists of America members, including current Illinois Representative Danny K. Davis,[633] Roberta Lynch,[634] Dr. Ron Sable[635] and Democratic Socialists of America (DSA) honoree and Obama's Hyde Park next-door-neighbor, Jackie Grimshaw.[636]

Later Grimshaw and Weissbourd were both Board members of the Center for Neighborhood Technology, a Chicago based Environmental group.

---

[629] http://keywiki.org/index.php/Crossroads_Fund
[630] http://keywiki.org/index.php/Jean_Hardisty
[631] http://keywiki.org/index.php/Bill_Ayers
[632] http://keywiki.org/index.php/Bernardine_Dohrn
[633] http://keywiki.org/index.php/Danny_K_Davis
[634] http://keywiki.org/index.php/Roberta_Lynch
[635] http://keywiki.org/index.php/Ron_Sable
[636] http://keywiki.org/index.php/Jackie_Grimshaw

97-4 Jackie Grimshaw,
Obama's Next Door Neighbor

Over a two year period in the US Senate, Barack Obama requested $3.2 Million in earmarks for the Center for Neighborhood Technology. Executives and Board members of the Center for Neighborhood Technology later contributed $20,688 to Obama's campaigns.

During the Presidential campaign, Robert Weissbourd served as Chair of Obama for America's Urban and Metropolitan Policy Committee. Also involved with this committee was Harry C. Boyte,[637] a veteran of the New American Movement and Democratic Socialists of America.

In 2009, Weissbourd also served on the Obama Transition Department of Housing and Urban Development Agency Review Team.

According to the Real Barack Obama (RBO),[638] Robert Weissbourd was an Obama bundler committed to raising a minimum of $50,000. He also contributed significant funds to Obama's campaigns from his own bank account: $3,600 in 2007 to Obama for America and $29,373 to the Obama Victory Fund (thereby achieving Mega-Donor Status in 2008),[639] $5,000 in 2005[640] to help launch Obama's Hopefund, Inc., with another $5,000 in 2006 and $9,113 in 2003-2004[641] to Obama for Illinois for Obama's US senatorial campaign.

That Barack Obama worked with Chicago communists and socialists is beyond doubt.

That some of these activists link to Obama's Hawaiian boyhood mentor, Frank Marshall Davis, is also becoming clear.

---

[637] http://keywiki.org/index.php/Harry_Boyte
[638] http://therealbarackobama.wordpress.com/2009/07/03/robert-weissbourd-obama-2008-urban-policy-committee-chair/
[639] http://www.whitehouseforsale.org/bundler.cfm?Bundler=25602
[640] http://www.campaignmoney.com/political/contributions/robert-weissbourd.asp?cycle=06
[641] http://www.campaignmoney.com/political/contributions/robert-weissbourd.asp?cycle=04

This raises several questions.

Did Obama come to Chicago because Davis's old friends could help him?

Did Obama seek these networks out, fall into them by accident or did he arrive with a list of introductions?

When was Obama first singled out for high office? Was it in 2004? Was it early in his Chicago days? Even earlier?

Are the answers to these questions important to you?

98. Obama Science Czar Holdren's Pro-Soviet Associations

Trevor Loudon © Tuesday, March 02, 2010

Obama's "Science Czar" John P. Holdren,[642] was once involved in a publication that included two accused Soviet informants as its founding sponsors.

Several other socialist and communist sympathizers worked for the publication, *the Bulletin of the Nuclear Atomic Scientists,* including some with family ties to Barack Obama. The publication is world famous for its ominous symbol, the Doomsday Clock.

Former scientists from the Soviet spy-riddled Manhattan Project and creators of the US Atomic Bomb founded *The Bulletin* in 1945.

98-1 John P. Holdren

From the start, *The Bulletin* and its associated organizations worked to weaken US nuclear superiority over the Soviet Union through

---

[642] http://www.keywiki.org/index.php/John_Holdren

East/West scientific exchanges, conferences and a steady stream of anti-nuclear propaganda designed to terrify the US public with tales of nuclear destruction and looming Armageddon.

It followed the Soviet propaganda line to a "T."

It was not surprising when in 1994, a former senior Soviet Intelligence officer named two of *The Bulletin's* sponsors, Leo Szilard[643] and Robert Oppenheimer,[644] as sources of atomic information to the Soviet Union.

98-2 Special Tasks, Memoirs of an Unwanted Witness-A Soviet Spymaster

According to Lieutenant General Pavel Anatolyevich Sudoplatov, a former wartime Director of the Administration for Special Tasks, an elite unit of the Soviet Intelligence Service, Leo Szilard, Robert Oppenheimer and Enrico Fermi, supplied information to the Soviets during their work on the Manhattan Project.

Pavel Sudoplatov claimed in his 1994 book "*Special Tasks, Memoirs of an Unwanted Witness - A Soviet Spy-master.*"

The most vital information for developing the first Soviet atomic bomb came from scientists engaged in the Manhattan Project to build the American atomic bomb - Robert Oppenheimer, Enrico Fermi, and Leo Szilard.

Oppenheimer, Fermi, Szilard, and Szilard's secretary were often quoted in the NKVD files from 1942 to 1945 as sources for information on the development of the first American atomic bomb. It is in the record that on several occasions they agreed to share information on nuclear weapons with Soviet scientists...

In 1940, a commission of Soviet scientists, upon hearing rumors of a super weapon being built in the West, investigated the possibility of creating an atomic bomb from uranium, but concluded that a weapon was a theoretical, not a practical, possibility. The same scientific commission recommended that the government instruct intelligence Services to monitor Western scientific publications.

---

[643] http://www.keywiki.org/index.php/Leo_Szilard
[644] http://www.keywiki.org/index.php/Robert_Oppenheimer

We were able to take advantage of the network of colleagues that Gamow had established. Using implied threats against Gamow's relatives in Russia, Elizabeth Zarubina pressured him into cooperating with us. In exchange for safety and material support for his relatives, Gamow provided the names of left-wing scientists who might be recruited to supply secret information...

98-3 Leo Szilard

Another route was from the mole who worked with Fermi and Pontecorvo. The mole in Tennessee was connected with the illegal station at the Santa Fe drugstore, from which material was sent by courier to Mexico. The unidentified young moles, along with the Los Alamos mole, were junior scientists or administrators who copied vital documents to which they were allowed access by Oppenheimer, Fermi, and Szilard, were part of the scheme.

We received reports on the progress of the Manhattan Project from Oppenheimer and his friends in oral form, through comments and asides, and from documents transferred through clandestine methods with their

full knowledge that the information they were sharing would be passed on. In all, five classified reports made available by Oppenheimer describing the progress of work on the atomic bomb.

Not only were we informed of technical developments in the atomic program, but we heard in detail the human conflicts and rivalries among the members of the team at Los Alamos. A constant theme was tension with General Groves, director of the project. We were told of Groves' conflicts with Szilard. Groves was

98-4 Robert Oppenheimer

outraged by Szilard's iconoclastic style and his refusal to accept the strictures of military discipline. The "baiting of brass hats" was Szilard's self-professed hobby. Groves believed that Szilard was a security risk and tried to prevent him from working on the Manhattan Project despite Szilard's seminal contribution to the development of the first atomic chain reaction with Fermi. (Sudaplatov 1994)

According to Pavel Sudoplatov, Oppenheimer and Szilard were also to play an important role after World War II.

We knew that Oppenheimer would remain an influential person in America after the war and therefore our relations with him should not take the form of running a controlled agent. We understood that he and other members of the scientific community were best approached as friends, not as agents. Since Oppenheimer, Bohr, and Fermi were fierce opponents of violence, they would seek to prevent a nuclear war, creating a balance of power through sharing the secrets of atomic energy. This would be a crucial in establishing the new world order after the war, and we took advantage of this.

After our reactor was put into operation in 1946, Beria issued orders to stop all contacts with our American sources in the Manhattan Project; the FBI was getting close to uncovering some of our agents. Beria said we should think how to use Oppenheimer, Fermi, Szilard, and others around them in the peace campaign against nuclear armament. Disarmament and the inability to impose nuclear blackmail would deprive the United States of its advantage. We began a worldwide political campaign against nuclear superiority, which kept up until we exploded our own nuclear bomb, in 1949. Our goal was to preempt American power politically before the Soviet Union had its own bomb. Beria warned us not to compromise Western scientists, but to use their political influence. (Sudoplatov, Sudoplatov and Schecter)

They started as antifascists and became political advocates of the Soviet Union.

Several of Oppenheimer's relatives were Communist Party members. The Manhattan Project identified Szilard as a "security risk" and considered sacking him. In the 1960s, he was involved with radical Washington DC "think tank," the Institute for Policy Studies[645] - infamous for its ties to foreign intelligence Services and a source of policy ideas[646] for the Obama administration.

Another *Bulletin* founding sponsor, Edward U. Condon, mentioned by FBI director, J. Edgar Hoover, in a May 1947 letter to US secretary of commerce Averill Harriman.

Hoover claimed that Condon was, as late as 1947, in contact with an alleged spy who had engaged in espionage for the Soviets in Washington

---

[645] http://www.keywiki.org/index.php/Institute_for_Policy_Studies
[646] http://newzeal.blogspot.com/2009/01/blog-post.html Chapter 60 - Institute For Policy Studies Plans Obama's America

from 1941 to 1944.

Condon was also close to Polish Embassy personnel, several members of the Communist Party USA and served on the Executive Board of an affiliate of the National Council of American-Soviet Science Friendship.

Other *Bulletin* founding sponsors included Harold C. Urey, a veteran of more than twenty Communist Party USA fronts, communist sympathizer Hans Bethe and "security risk" Isidor Rabi.

98-5 Edward U. Condon

By the time John Holdren was working on the *Bulletin's* Board of Editors in 1984, the situation had not improved.

Holdren's fellow Board member Deborah Shapley, was the granddaughter of astronomer Harlow Shapley, a veteran of dozens of Communist Party fronts.

Sponsors of the *Bulletin* at that time included the old hands, Edward U. Condon, Hans Bethe, Robert Oppenheimer, Isidor Rabi and Harold C. Urey.

Added to the roster were David Baltimore, an affiliate of the Institute for Policy Studies, Linus Pauling, a lifelong communist front activist and Jerome C. Wiesner, an Institute for Policy Studies affiliate and a Lyndon B. Johnson Arms Control appointee.

Serving on the *Bulletin's* Board of Directors in 1984 were:

- Aaron Adler[647] - (Board Chair in 1988, Adler also served on the Board was Board of Directors of the Chicago Center for US/USSR Relations and Exchanges)
- Larry McGurty (Communist Party USA and Betty Willhoite[648] later with Democratic Socialists of America[649] and Progressives for Obama (P40)[650] and a supporter of the Chicago Committee to Defend the Bill of Rights.[651] Adler was also a member of the Communist Party front Chicago Committee to Defend the Bill of Rights and was involved in

---

[647] http://www.keywiki.org/index.php/Aaron_Adler
[648] http://www.keywiki.org/index.php/Betty_Willhoite
[649] http://www.keywiki.org/index.php/Democratic_Socialists_of_America
[650] http://www.keywiki.org/index.php/Progressives_for_Obama
[651] http://keywiki.org/index.php/Chicago_Committee_to_Defend_the_Bill_of_Rights

a committee[652] to celebrate the 100th birthday of Communist Party member, Paul Robeson)

- Bernard Weissbourd[653] - (Chicago, a former Manhattan Project scientist, turned wealthy property developer. Weissbourd, a leftist was married to Bernice Targ Weissbourd[654] - the Bernice Targ, who taught at the Communist Party's Abraham Lincoln School[655] in Chicago in the late 1940s with Frank Marshall Davis,[656] later a mentor in Hawaii to the young Barack Obama. Bernice Targ Weissbourd was also a member of the Chicago Committee to Defend the Bill of Rights. The Weissbourds' son, Robert M. Weissbourd,[657] served as Chair of the Obama for America Campaign Urban and Metropolitan Policy Committee and on the Obama Transition Housing and Urban Development Agency Review Team in 2008)

Working with John Holdren on *The Bulletin* editorial team was:

- Bernard T. Feld – (Editor-in-Chief. Feld was an affiliate of the Peace Research Institute, which became the Institute for Policy Studies and number 11 on President Richard M. Nixon's famed "enemies" list)
- Ruth Adams[658] – (Editor. Adams was a Chair of the Institute for Policy Studies and supporter of the Chicago Committee to Defend the Bill of Rights. In the '60s, Adams served on the Advisory Committee of the Hyde Park Community Peace Center[659])

Other Council members included lifelong communist front activist:

- Robert Havighurst - (A founder of the Chicago Committee to Defend the Bill of Rights)
- Sydney Lens (aka Okun) - (A radical Trotskyist, later active in the Communist Party controlled Chicago Peace Council)
- Timuel Black[660]
- Quentin Young

Black and Young were accused of Communist Party membership

---

[652] http://www.keywiki.org/index.php/Paul_Robeson_100th_Birthday_Committee

[653] http://www.keywiki.org/index.php/Bernard_Weissbourd

[654] http://www.keywiki.org/index.php/Bernice_Weissbourd

[655] http://www.keywiki.org/index.php/Abraham_Lincoln_School_for_Social_Sciences

[656] http://www.keywiki.org/index.php/Frank_Marshall_Davis

[657] http://newzeal.blogspot.com/2010/02/obama-file-97-obama-and-weissbourds-was.html Chapter 97 - Obama and the Weissbourds – Was There a Frank Marshall Davis Connection?

[658] http://www.keywiki.org/index.php/Ruth_Adams

[659] http://keywiki.org/index.php/Hyde_Park_Community_Peace_Centre

[660] http://www.keywiki.org/index.php/Timuel_Black

by government investigative authorities. Timuel Black later joined the Communist Party offshoot, Committees of Correspondence. Both became officials of the Chicago Committee to Defend the Bill of Rights and the Democratic Socialists of America.

Both became friends, mentors and advisers to Barack Obama.

- Ruth Young[661] - (Managing Editor. The wife of Quentin Young and later also a member of the Chicago Committee to Defend the Bill of Rights)
- James Cracraft[662] - (Senior Editor. In 1988, Cracraft served on the Board of the Chicago Center for US/USSR Relations and Exchanges, under Aaron Adler. John Holdren worked in the 1980s in that milieu)

Jeff Jacoby has written in the Boston Globe:[663]

> "Holdren opposed the President Ronald W. Reagan administration's military buildup in the 1980s for fear it might "increase the belligerency of the Soviet government." He pooh-poohed any notion that "the strain of an accelerated arms race will do more damage to the Soviet economy than to our own." But that is exactly what happened, and President Reagan's defense buildup helped win the Cold War. (Jacoby 2010)

98-6 John Holdren and Barack Obama

Did the pro-Soviet, anti-American group influence John Holdren?

Today, John Holdren is President Obama's "Science Czar" - Director of the Office of Science and Technology Policy in the Executive Office of the President.

Holdren's brief encompasses global environmental change, fusion science and technology, comparative analysis of energy options, ways to reduce the dangers from nuclear weapons and materials, population control and the interaction of content and process in science and technology policy.

All these areas have huge implications for America's national

[661] http://www.keywiki.org/index.php/Ruth_Young
[662] http://www.keywiki.org/index.php/James_Cracraft
[663] http://www.jeffjacoby.com/2337/questions-for-obamas-science-guy

security, prosperity and future liberty.

Should a man with John Holdren's past associations be trusted with a position dealing directly with National Security?

Was Holdren given a proper security vetting or did he "slip through the cracks" like communist "Green Jobs Czar" Van Jones?

99. Security Risk? Obama "Science Czar" John Holdren and the Federation of American Scientists

Monday, March 08, 2010

Obama's "Science Czar" John Holdren has a history with the communist influenced journal, *The Bulletin, of the Atomic Scientists*.[664]

Of even more concern are Holdren's deep ties to a related organization, the Federation of American Scientists (FAS).[665]

Holdren has held important posts in the Federation and is still listed as a member of the FAS Sponsor's Board.

Like *The Bulletin of Atomic Scientists*, the F.A.S. was founded immediately after WW2 by left-leaning scientists, many of whom had worked in the Manhattan Project to create the U.S. atomic bomb. After the defeat of the Axis Powers, the scientists feared that the US would use their creation against their beloved Soviet Union.

Therefore, some of them worked to ensure that the Soviet Union was given every chance to develop better nuclear weapons, while American efforts where countered at every opportunity.

Original founders or sponsors of the FAS included:

99-1 Science Czar John Holdren (l)
Barack Obama (r)

[664] http://keywiki.org/index.php/The_Bulletin_of_the_Atomic_Scientists
[665] http://keywiki.org/index.php/Federation_of_American_Scientists

J. Robert Oppenheimer

Oppenheimer is the former head of the Manhattan Project.

99-2 J. Robert Oppenheimer

It was alleged that Oppenheimer was a secret Communist Party member[666] in Berkeley from 1938 to 1942. Oppenheimer's wife Kitty was an ex Party member and his mistress Jean Tatlock, was also a communist.

His brother Frank Oppenheimer, and Frank's wife Jackie, were both pre-War communists. Robert Oppenheimer's Los Alamos assistant, David Hawkins, had also been a Party member.

Oppenheimer admitted he knew by August 1943 that two of the scientists working under him were Communist Party members. Three scientists under Oppenheimer's direct supervision were later accused of leaking information to the Soviets. (Herken 2002)

Leo Szilard

Sziard is a key Manhattan Project scientist.

As a schoolboy in Hungary, Szilard founded the Hungarian Association of Socialist Students and was an enthusiastic supporter of Bela Kun's short lived 1919 communist revolution. Later, Szilard was involved in a Soviet study group in Germany, before emigrating to the USA. (Herken 2002)

99-3 Leo Szilard

In a 1994 book by Pavel Sudoplatov, a former wartime director of the Administration for Special Tasks and an elite unit of the Soviet intelligence Service and accused both Oppenheimer and Szilard of supplying atomic information to the Soviet Union.

Philip Morrison

Morrison was an assistant to Szilard in

99-4 Philip Morrison

---

[666] http://www.brotherhoodofthebomb.com/bhbsource/documents.html

the Manhattan Project.

A Communist Party member until at least 1942, Morrison was later accused of being a Soviet agent with the code name, "Relay." (Herken 2002)

Edward U. Condon

99-5 Edward U. Condon

Condon was the head of the US Bureau of Standards.

In May 1947, F.B.I. Director J. Edgar Hoover wrote that, as late as 1947, Condon had been in contact with an individual alleged, by a self-confessed Soviet espionage agent, to have engaged in espionage activities with Soviet agents in Washington, D.C. from 1941 to 1944.

Hoover added that Condon and his wife associated with several individuals from the Polish Embassy in Washington, including the wife of the Polish Ambassador, the secretary of the Embassy, and a former counselor of the Embassy. The latter, Ignace Zlotowski, a nuclear scientist, had worked as a Soviet espionage agent in direct contact with the Soviet Embassy in Washington. Condon was also active in at least one communist front and was an associate of several Communist Party members. (Wang 1998)

Harlow Shapley

99-6 Harlow C. Shapley

Shapley was a prominent astronomer.

Shapley had been involved in at least 25 Communist Party fronts. (Committee on Un-American Activities 1949)

Harold C. Urey

Urey was the Director of War Research, Atomic Bomb Project, Columbia University.

Urey was affiliated with at least ten Communist Party fronts and had attended a 1947 meeting in Paris, of the Soviet controlled World Federation of Scientific Workers.

In the late fall of 1945, the FAS scored a major political victory. While Congress was debating who should control atomic weapons, the FAS rented a room near the Capitol, equipped it with a typewriter, lobbied Senators and Representatives, and talked to reporters. Harold Urey, led the charge, promoting a bill calling for the creation of a civilian Atomic Energy Commission, led by a panel appointed by the

President- with no military representation. The debate continued into 1946, with the FAS working to make sure the bill passed.

> To the amazement of many observers, they won, though the bill was softened to allow some military input. (Activities 1956)

Moscow Center was happy. It was considered much easier to influence or infiltrate a civilian body than a military organization.

In October 1950, Senator Joseph McCarthy placed a statement in the Congressional Record charging that the Federation of American Scientists (FAS) was "heavily infiltrated with communist fellow travelers."

In the 1970's, FAS described itself as the "voice of science on Capitol Hill."

By the 1980s, FAS was working to oppose President Reagan's proposed space based missile defense system.

The Soviets were concerned about "Star Wars," knowing that if successful, it would make the US much less vulnerable to Soviet nuclear missile attack.

In 1983, a group of Soviet academics had sent an open letter to US scientists, asking whether, in the light of President Reagan's "Star Wars" speech of March that year, there had been a change in the professional consensus in the US regarding the feasibility of effective missile defenses.

FAS responded and received an invitation by senior Soviet scientist, Evgeny Velikhov, to visit the Soviet Union.

In November, FAS sent a party to the Soviet Union, which included FAS Chair David W. Hafemeister, Deputy Chairman John Holdren, President Jeremy Stone and staffer John E. Pike.

Velikhov told Hafemeister that the reason he decided to organize the Committee of Soviet Scientists was to educate a new generation of Soviet scientists about nuclear arms control and to re-open the US-Soviet dialog on strategic defense with the roles reversed.

The Soviet scientists tried to convince the US government, with US scientists as intermediaries, that the pursuit of ballistic missile defenses would be counterproductive.

John E. Pike

99-7 John E. Pike

Delegate John E. Pike went on to become "one of the country's most credible space industry observers" and an often quoted "security" expert.

In the 1980s, however, he was a key opponent of "Star Wars."

Pike helped form the Space Policy Working Group and the National Campaign to Save the ABM Treaty, to campaign against Reagan's missile defense policies.

In 1994, Pike wrote an article entitled *"Uncloaked Dagger: CIA Spending for Covert Action"* for *Covert Action Quarterly*, a journal founded by the US Central Intelligence Agency (CIA) renegade and Soviet Committee for State Security (Komitet Gosudarstvennoy Bezopasnosti (KGB)) contact Philip Agee.

Jeremy Stone

99-8 Jeremy Stone

Holdren's other co-delegate, Jeremy Stone, was also an interesting case. Stone, who led FAS from 1970 to 2000, has been an influential lobbyist and activist in the "peace" and foreign policy arena. He is the son of radical journalist I. F. Stone,[667] an identified Soviet agent of the pre -World War II period.

Like his father, Jeremy Stone has been close to the radical Washington D.C. based "think tank," the Institute for Policy Studies,[668] once notorious for its ties to Soviet operatives.

US Senator Mike Gravel of Alaska has written of his freshmen speech against Anti-Ballistic Missiles.

> Marcus Raskin, a co-founder of the Institute for Policy Studies, and Jeremy Stone helped the Senator to write the speech. Jeremy was I. F. Stone's son, who had been an expert opponent of ABM since 1963. His

---

[667] http://keywiki.org/index.php/I._F._Stone
[668] http://keywiki.org/index.php/Institute_for_Policy_Studies

opposition to Pentagon spending later earned Jeremy a place on Nixon's Enemies List. (Gravel 1969)

Evgeny Velikhov

99-9 President Vladimir Putin (l)
Evgeny Velikhov (r)

Velikhov was no gray Soviet bureaucrat either. The Soviet Union's top scientist-activist, Velikhov was an adviser to the Soviet leader Mikhail Gorbachev. Today he is close to Russia's de facto leader and former KGB chief, Vladimir Putin.

John Holdren later collaborated with Velikhov on a report on weapons grade Plutonium, writing in a June 1997 letter to Presidents Boris Yeltsin and Bill Clinton, on their findings:

> We respectfully submit the Final Report of the US-Russian Independent Scientific Commission on Disposition of Excess Weapons Plutonium. We strongly urge that the US and Russian governments, with support and cooperation from the international community, take additional steps - beyond those already underway - to more rapidly reduce the security risks posed by excess weapons plutonium, ensuring that this material will never again be returned to nuclear weapons.
>
> Our report recommends specific steps to meet this objective, including the technologies that can be used, a step-by-step plan of action for bringing these technologies into operation as rapidly as practicable, an international cooperative approach to financing the program, and establishment of an international entity to coordinate the necessary financing and implement the effort. Today, John Holdren remains listed on the FAS Board of Sponsors. His Co-sponsors include several interesting characters. (US Russian Independent Scientific Commission 1997)

Ann Druyan

99-10 Ann Druyan former wife of Carl Sagan

A former secretary of FAS, Druyan is an open Marxist. In 1998, she endorsed a New York event commemorating the 150th anniversary[669] of Karl Marx's "Communist Manifesto." (KeyWiki 2010)

---

[669] http://keywiki.org/index.php/Manifestivity

Stanley Sheinbaum

99-11 Stanley Sheinbaum

Sheinbaum was a West Coast philanthropist and a supporter of radical causes, including Democratic Socialists of America[670] and Progressives for Obama (P40).[671] In 1988 Sheinbaum led a delegation of American Jews that "persuaded" Palestinian terrorist leader Yasser Arafat to recognize Israel's right to exist and renounce terror. Arafat's promises, later proven insincere, helped earn Arafat the Nobel Peace Prize. (KeyWiki 2010)

Mark Ptashne

99-12 Mark Ptashne

Mark Ptashne was a Harvard geneticist. During the Vietnam War, Ptashne was involved in anti-war politics at Harvard and went to the extent of lecturing at the University of Hanoi.

In 1978, Ptashne attended a genetics conference in Moscow. In the 1980s, the scientific director of a Cuban genetics laboratory spent three months working with Ptashne at Harvard. (KeyWiki 2010)

In the 1940s, Mark Ptashne's father, Fred Ptashne,[672] was a tutor at the Communist Party's Abraham Lincoln School[673] in Chicago.

Coincidentally, several of Fred Ptashne's fellow tutors went on to intersect in some way with the career of Barack Obama,[674] including Earl Durham,[675] possibly Bernice Targ[676] and Obama's Hawaiian boyhood mentor, Frank Marshall Davis.[677]

---

[670] http://keywiki.org/index.php/Democratic_Socialists_of_America

[671] http://keywiki.org/index.php/Progressives_for_Obama

[672] http://keywiki.org/index.php/Fred_Ptashne

[673] http://keywiki.org/index.php/Abraham_Lincoln_School_for_Social_Sciences

[674] http://keywiki.org/index.php/Barack_Obama

[675] http://keywiki.org/index.php/Earl_Durham

[676] http://keywiki.org/index.php/Bernice_Weissbourd

[677] http://keywiki.org/index.php/Frank_Marshall_Davis

John Holdren

John Holdren held high office in two organizations with socialists, Soviet sympathizers and "security risks." Both organizations have worked with Soviet officials for policies beneficial to the former Soviet Union and detrimental to the US.

Holdren collaborated with a key figure in the Soviet-Russian scientific-political apparatus and traveled to the Soviet Union at the height of the "Cold War."

Now John Holdren holds the most important scientific post in the Western World and has the ear of the President of the United States of America.

Van Jones[678] resigned his White House post after his radical background was exposed.

John Holdren is in a position to do far more damage to US interests than Van Jones ever dreamed of. In the interest of National Security, shouldn't they scrutinize John Holdren?

100. Obama's "Faith Adviser" Jim Wallis Mixes With Socialists, Radicals and "Truthers"

Trevor Loudon © Monday, March 15, 2010

100-1 Barack Obama (l) Rev. Jeremiah Wright (r)

What could be a greater guide to a person's true nature than those from whom he seeks spiritual counsel?

President Barack H. Obama[679] spent twenty years under the ministry of Rev. Jeremiah Wright[680] on Chicago's South Side.

Rev. Jeremiah Wright is a Marxist and admirer of the founder of "Black Liberation Theology," James Cone,[681] who wrote in 1969:

[678] http://keywiki.org/index.php/Van_Jones
[679] http://keywiki.org/index.php/Barack_Obama
[680] http://www.keywiki.org/index.php/Jeremiah_Wright
[681] http://www.keywiki.org/index.php/James_Cone

100-2 Rev. Jim Wallis

"All white men are responsible for white oppression. Theologically, Malcolm X was not far wrong when he called the white man 'the devil.'" (Cone 1969)

In June 1998, Rev. Jeremiah Wright attended the Black Radical Congress[682] in Chicago where he shares a panel with Cornel West[683] and former parishioner, Michael Eric Dyson,[684] of the Democratic Socialists of America Religion and Socialism Commission, plus a former Communist Party member from his own Trinity United Church of Christ named Kevin Tyson.[685] The panel was entitled "Faith as a Weapon: Spirituality and the Role of the Church in the Radical Movement."

Maybe Rev. Jeremiah Wright even met another Congress participant - a young radical from Standing Together to Organize a Revolutionary Movement, named Van Jones.[686]

Today, President Obama gets his spiritual nourishment from another source, a leader of American "progressive" Christianity, named Jim Wallis.[687]

Jim Wallis is white, smooth and reasonable. He is no firebrand like Rev. Jeremiah Wright. He is a registered Democrat and the respectable face of the Christian left.

Rev. Jim Wallis has served on Obama's White House Advisory Council on Faith-based and Neighborhood Partnerships, or "Faith Council" since 2008, but the relationship is personal and goes back at least a dozen years.

In 2008, when Obama was queried over alleged Muslim allegiances, Rev. Jim Wallis wrote in defense of his friend:

> So let's set the record straight. I have known Barack Obama for more than 10 years, and we have been talking about his Christian faith for a

[682] http://www.keywiki.org/index.php/Black_Radical_Congress

[683] http://www.keywiki.org/index.php/Cornel_West

[684] http://www.keywiki.org/index.php/Michael_Eric_Dyson

[685] http://www.keywiki.org/index.php/Kevin_Tyson

[686] http://www.keywiki.org/index.php/Van_Jones

[687] http://www.keywiki.org/index.php/Jim_Wallis

decade. Like me and many other Christians, he agrees with the need to reach out to Muslims around the world, especially if we are ever to defeat Islamic fundamentalism. But he is not a Muslim, never has been, never attended a Muslim madrassa, and does not attend a black "separatist" church.

Rather, he has told me the story of his coming from an agnostic household, becoming a community organizer on Chicago's South Side who worked with the churches, and how he began attending one of them. Trinity Church is one of the most prominent and respected churches in Chicago and the nation, and its pastor, Rev Jeremiah Wright, is one of the leading revival preachers in the black church...

And one Sunday, as Obama has related to me and written in his book The Audacity of Hope, the young community organizer walked down the aisle and gave his life to Christ in a personal and real Christian conversion experience. We have talked about our faith and its relationship to politics many times since. And after Obama gave his speech at a Sojourners/Call to Renewal conference in June 2006, E.J. Dionne said that it may have been "the most important pronouncement by a Democrat on faith and politics since John F. Kennedy's Houston speech in 1960 declaring his independence from the Vatican." (KeyWiki 2008)

President Barack H. Obama and Rev. Jim Wallis, relationship is close. Nevertheless, who is this man who is committed to the Christian faith as the President himself claims to be?

Raised in a devout Plymouth Brethren household, Rev. Jim Wallis broke with the Church at fourteen over its failure to commit to political causes.

Wallis went on to join and lead the militant Students for a Democratic Society (SDS) at Michigan State University.

After College, Rev. Jim Wallis went on to attend Trinity Evangelical Divinity School in Illinois where he joined with other young seminarians in establishing the community that became Sojourner.[688] In 1979, Time magazine named Rev. Jim Wallis one of the *"50 Faces for America's Future"*.

In 1977, Rev. Jim Wallis moved his radical Sojourner community to Washington D.C., to a small district named Columbia Heights, a mile

---

[688] http://keywiki.org/index.php/Sojourners

from the White House.

Meanwhile, many of Rev. Jim Wallis' old Students for a Democratic Society comrades had founded a new Marxist organization with some older Communist Party veterans which they named the New American Movement (NAM). In 1982, NAM, in turn, merged with the Democratic Socialist Organizing Committee[689] to form Democratic Socialists of America.

The new organization made penetration of organized religion forming a Religion and Socialism Commission.[690]

A clipping from a July 1982 Democratic Socialists of America (DSA) newsletter, listing the three Religion and Socialism Commission co-Chairs:

The name Jim Wallace in Figure 100-3 is different from the spelling of Jim Wallis possibly a spelling typo, but the address on Quincy Street, one of five streets running through Columbia Heights in Washington D.C., is the same.

Was this Barack Obama's future spiritual adviser?

Step forward to 2010. Contributing editors to the *Sojourner* journal,

You will receive information on the commissions working with the New York office and the San Francisco office from them. These commissions include the Religion and Socialism Commission, the Hispanic Commission, the Anti-Racism Commission, and the Internationalism Commission all of which work with the New York office. The Urban and Community Commission works with the San Francisco Office. The Chairs of these commissions are as follows:

Religion and Socialism Commission Co-Chairs –

Barbara Van Buren   Jim Wallace   John Balzer
288 West 92nd St.   1311 Quincy St., N.E.   3528 Victor
New York, NY 10025   Washington, DC 20017   St. Louis, MO 63104

100-3 July 1982 clipping Democratic Socialists of America (DSA)

include Black Liberation theologian James Cone and two prominent members of Democratic Socialists of America (DSA)'s Religion and Socialism Commission, Cornel West[691] and Rosemary Ruether.[692]

---

[689] http://keywiki.org/index.php/Democratic_Socialist_Organizing_Committee
[690] http://www.dsausa.org/rs/
[691] http://keywiki.org/index.php/Cornel_West

In 1987, Democratic Socialists of America (DSA) member Joanne Landy, of Campaign for Peace and Democracy, circulated a statement Against Loans to Chile,[693] calling upon the Reagan Administration to oppose all loans to the anti-communist government in Chile.

Jim Wallis signed the statement as did DSA members Noam Chomsky, Michael Harrington, Adam Hochschild, David McReynolds, James Weinstein, Ed Asner and Rosemary Ruether, as well as "*Pentagon Papers*" leaker Daniel Ellsberg. In 2004, Asner, Ruether and Ellsberg signed another statement calling for an investigation into possible US government involvement in 9/11.

> An alliance of 100 prominent Americans announced today the release of the 911 Truth Statements, a call for immediate inquiry into evidence that suggests high-level government officials may have allowed the September 11 attacks to occur. (911 Truth 2004)

Van Jones also signed this statement, no doubt to his lasting regret.

Cornel West did not sign the "Truther" statement, but he, Adam Hochschild and Daniel Ellsberg were all later endorsers of the Progressives for Obama (P40)[694] website.

West went on to serve with yet another radical Obama mentor, Charles Ogletree[695] on Obama's Black Advisory Council in 2008. He refers to Obama as his "comrade."

100-4 Cornel West (l)
Rabbi Lerner (r)

West is close to William Julius,[696] who in February 1996 addressed a Democratic Socialists of America organized forum in Chicago alongside a young local lawyer named Barack H. Obama.

Cornel West has also long worked with Rabbi Michael Lerner[697] - another 9/11 "truth" petition signer. In 2005, West and Lerner set up the Network of Spiritual Progressives[698] to challenge "the Misuse of Religion,

---

692 http://keywiki.org/index.php/Rosemary_Ruether
693 http://www.keywiki.org/index.php/Against_Loans_to_Chile
694 http://keywiki.org/index.php/Progressives_for_Obama
695 http://www.keywiki.org/index.php/Charles_Ogletree
696 http://keywiki.org/index.php/William_Julius_Wilson
697 http://www.keywiki.org/index.php/Michael_Lerner
698 http://www.spiritualprogressives.org/

God and Spirit by the Religious Right."

Rabbi Michael Lerner, like Rev. Jim Wallis, is an old Students for a Democratic Society member. In the period after the formation of the Weather Underground Organization, Rabbi Michael Lerner and Weathermen Chip Marshall, Jeff Alan Dowd and Joseph H. Kelly, moved to Seattle to form the Seattle Liberation Front (SLF) "to bring the Revolution to Seattle."

A federal grand jury would later indict three of their SLF recruits for a February 17, 1970 attack on a government building.

The same year, Rabbi Michael Lerner was a founder of the New American Movement in Chicago and in the 1980s was active in Democratic Socialists of America.

In July 2005, Rev. Jim Wallis and Rabbi Michael Lerner were the keynote speakers at the launching of Cornel West and Lerner's "Network of Spiritual Progressives."

Rev. Jim Wallis used his talk to lambast the "religious right," arguing that the time has come for the left to take back American religion.

Rev. Jim Wallis condemned the "seduction" of key leaders of the religious right by the Republican Party. He remarked that conservatives have painted a picture of Jesus as "pro-rich, pro-war and pro-American," Wallis lamented, and "We need to take our religion back."

Rev. Jim Wallis also quoted a "young activist," who when asked where the new leaders were, was fond of remarking, "We are the ones we have been waiting for."

Sound familiar?

President Barack H. Obama has a more than twenty-five year history[699] with the Marxists of Democratic Socialists of America.

Barack Obama has several Democratic Socialists of America (DSA) personal friends, including Representative Danny K. Davis,[700] Dr. Quentin Young,[701] Timuel Black[702] and the late Rabbi Arnold Jacob

---

[699]
http://www.keywiki.org/index.php/Barack_Obama_and_Democratic_Socialists_of_Ame rica
[700] http://www.keywiki.org/index.php/Danny_Davis
[701] http://www.keywiki.org/index.php/Quentin_Young

Wolf[703] (also a member of Democratic Socialists of America (DSA)'s Religion and Socialism Commission).

The President has appointed several Democratic Socialists of America (DSA) connected activists to key positions, including:

- Ron Bloom[704] - (Manufacturing Czar)
- US Representative David Bonior (D-MI-12th District)[705]
- Rosa Brooks[706]
- Carol Browner[707] - (Energy Czar)
- US Representative Hilda Solis (D-CA-32nd District).[708]

Is the President's "spiritual advisor" cut from the same cloth?

Rev. Jim Wallis is socialist, a fervent believer in the state redistribution of wealth.[709] Wallis is connected to some of the most radical people in America.

Rev. Jim Wallis works hard to portray himself as moderate and a "bridge-builder." He is a Bible scholar and comes across as sincere and as trustworthy as the President himself does.

Nevertheless, maybe the millions of Christians and Jews who voted for Obama should remind them that it is not only men of God who can quote the Scriptures to suit their purpose.

101. Who's Been Fibbing Then? Evidence That Obama Was Deeply Involved in Socialist New Party "Sister Organization"

Trevor Loudon © Wednesday, April 07, 2010

Did President Barack H. Obama,[710] or someone close to him, mislead voters about the extent of the US president's involvement in the

[702] http://www.keywiki.org/index.php/Timuel_Black
[703] http://www.keywiki.org/index.php/Arnold_Wolf
[704] http://www.keywiki.org/index.php/Ron_Bloom
[705] http://www.keywiki.org/index.php/David_Bonior
[706] http://www.keywiki.org/index.php/Rosa_Brooks
[707] http://www.keywiki.org/index.php/Carol_Browner
[708] http://www.keywiki.org/index.php/Hilda_Solis
[709] http://www.bloggernews.net/118353
[710] http://keywiki.org/index.php/Barack_Obama

socialist Chicago New Party?[711]

In the run up to the November 2008 elections, evidence surfaced that Barack Obama had joined and been endorsed by the Chicago New Party during his successful 1995/96 Illinois State Senate run.

According to Obama's *"Fight the Smears"* website:[712]

> Right-wing hatchet man and conspiracy theorist, Stanley Kurtz is pushing a new crackpot smear against Barack falsely claiming he was a member of something called the New Party.

> However, the truth is Barack H. Obama has been a member of only one political party, the Democratic Party. In all six primary campaigns of his career, Barack has run as a Democrat. The New Party did support Barack once in 1996, but he was the only candidate on the ballot in his race and never solicited the endorsement (Fight the Smears 2008)

101-1 Barack Obama

Stanley Kurtz also queried Carol Harwell,[713] Obama's campaign manager at the time. She said:

> "Barack did not solicit or seek the New Party endorsement for state senator in 1995." (KeyWiki 2008)

This despite evidence that Obama was heavily involved in the New Party in 1995 and according to *New Party News* of Spring 1996, was a bona fide New Party member.[714]

The evidence is now presented that Obama was involved as early as 1993 with a New Party "sister" organization - Progressive Chicago.[715]

[711] http://keywiki.org/index.php/New_Party
[712] http://www.fightthesmears.com/articles/28/KurtzSmears.html
[713] http://keywiki.org/index.php/Carol_Harwell
[714] http://keywiki.org/index.php/Barack_Obama_and_the_New_Party
[715] http://keywiki.org/index.php/Progressive_Chicago

This organization was formed by members of the New Party for "progressive" candidates. Its main instigators included New Party members Madeline Talbott,[716] of Chicago ACORN[717] and Dan Swinney,[718] a Chicago labor unionist.

New Party members won three other primaries this Spring in Chicago: Barack Obama (State Senate), Michael Chandler, (Democratic Party Committee) and Patricia Martin (Cook County judiciary). Unfortunately, NP-endorsed State Representative candidate Willie Delgado lost a tight primary challenge, although he won 5 of the 6 precincts that the NP worked through the election.

101-2 Evidence Obama is involved in the New Party in 1995

In an April 27, 1993 letter to prospective Progressive Chicago members, Dan Swinney wrote in a circa 1993 Progressive Chicago introductory pamphlet:

Progressive Chicago was started by members of the New Party who wanted to be able to put together an organization strong enough to win

```
        I recently have become interested in the New Party as well
as committed myself to seeing if we can build a Progressive
Chicago network, working with Madeline Talbott of ACORN--the
local NP convener.

        I wanted to introduce you to the NP and Progressive Chicago
and would like to talk with you about it to see if there is a
role you want to play.

        Enclosed is a brochure, a longer description of NP and the
ideas behind it, and a flyer for a program on May 14 at Loyola.

        Let's talk either by taking advantage of some other event
where we both are, or I will give you a call shortly.

In Solidarity,


Dan Swinney
```

101-3 Dan Sweeney's 1993 letter for Progressive Chicago

started progressive Chicago: If that means supporting a candidate running as a Democrat, then fine. If that means running our own candidates in

[716] http://keywiki.org/index.php/Madeline_Talbott
[717] http://keywiki.org/index.php/ACORN
[718] http://keywiki.org/index.php/Dan_Swinney

aldermanic or state Representative races on whatever line that gives them the best chance of winning, fine. (Swinney 1993)

A Chicago New Party organizing report of June 2, 1993, named Progressive Chicago as a "sister organization:"

> At some point in the future we will have elections for a steering committee, but at this point we are concentra-ting on building up the internal organization...to build up our sister organization, Progressive Chicago. Once we have built up our membership for the two organizations, we will then elect a steering committee and move forward...

> Progressive Chicago would be a support organization for progressive political activity. This organization is modeled on Progressive

```
Future Plans  -  At  some point  in  the  future,  we  will have
elections for  a Steering Committee,  but, at this point,  we are
concentrating on building  up the  internal organization  through
staff  recruitment  and membership  recruitment; and the  external
organization through visits to different Community organizations,
unions,  constituency  groups,  etc.  to  build  up  our  sister
organization, Progressive  Chicago.  Once we  have built up  our
membership for  the  two  organizations:  The  New  Party  and
Progressive Chicago,  we will then elect a  steering committee and
move forward.
```

101-4 Future Plans for Progressive Chicago

Milwaukee and Progressive Dane.

> We hope that Progressive Chicago will be able to rebuild the shattered Harold Washington Coalition and be a leading force in supporting progressive coalitions and progressive change... (Chicago New Party 1993)

The New Party and Progressive Chicago were always intertwined

```
Send your  dues to  our office, call  us and  we'll let  you know
about meetings and  activities.  (Five  dollars is  the minimum.
Feel free  to send more --  we need it for  organizing expenses).
If you're already a member  of the New Party, we have an agreement
with them that $5 of the New  Party dues will automatically go to
Progressive Chicago.

****************************************************************
Return with check or money order to
Progressive Chicago
601 S. LaSalle, Room 200
Chicago, Illinois 60605                          ( w )_____
```

101-5 Agreement regarding dues

according to an undated Progressive Challenge call for members:

> If you're already a member of the New Party, we have an agreement with them that $5 of the New Party dues will automatically go to Progressive Challenge. (Chicago New Party 1993)

According to the organization's literature, Progressive Chicago aimed to unite progressive activists and organizations for progressive, grassroots electoral activity in local elections.

> Unite progressive activists and organizations for progressive, grassroots electoral activity in local elections.

> It is a renewal of the old Harold Washington coalition consisting of activists and academics, women, unemployed and union, gay and straight; community, organizations and churches, African American, Latino, Asian, Native American and white, seniors and people with disabilities, low income and middle income, west and south side. (Chicago New Party 1993)

It was the election of the leftist Mayor Harold Washington[719] in 1983, inspired Barack Obama to move to Chicago two years later. The Harold Washington coalition was led by an alliance of Chicago communists, socialists and "community activists," just like both of its direct descendants, the New Party and Progressive Chicago. Key Progressive Chicago leaders included:

- Ron Sable – (A member of Democratic Socialists of America and former associate member of the Marxist New American Movement)
- Dwayne Harris – (21st Century Vote)
- David Orr Cook - (County Clerk, closely tied to Democratic Socialists of America and once linked to the Communist party front US Peace Council)
- Ernestine Whiting – (ACORN)
- Madeline Talbott – (ACORN and New Party. Former colleague of Barack Obama in Project Vote)
- Bessie Cannon – (President SEIU Local 880)
- Keith Kelleher – (Head organizer SEIU Local 880. Husband of Madeline Talbott)
- Joe Gardner - (Commissioner, Metropolitan Water Reclamation District, former colleague of Barack Obama in Project Vote)

---

[719] http://keywiki.org/index.php/Harold_Washington

- Lou Pardo – (Northwest Voter Registration Project, an Obama associate, New Party and Democratic Socialists of America member and an affiliate of the Communist Party USA offshoot Committees of Correspondence)
- Dick Simpson – (a close associate of Democratic Socialists of America)
- Danny Davis – (New Party member with Obama. A member of Democratic Socialists of America and an associate of Committees of Correspondence and the Communist Party USA. Now an Illinois Congressman)
- Carol Harwell – (United Voter Registration League, later Obama's campaign manager)
- Barack Obama – (New Party member, long-time associate of Democratic Socialists of America, Committees of Correspondence and Communist Party USA)
- Carl Davidson – (Networking for Democracy, New Party member. A member of the Committees of Correspondence and a long time Obama associate and enabler. Later a founder of Progressives for Obama)
- Dan Swinney – (New Party member and an affiliate of Committees of Correspondence. Later a founder of Progressives for Obama)

People targeted or solicited to join Progressive Chicago included Obama political mentor and Communist Party affiliate Alice Palmer, Communist Party member Frank Lumpkin, Rev. Jim Reed of Christians for Socialism and Democratic Socialists of America associates Miguelle Del Valle, Carole Travis, Clem Balanoff, Sue Purrington and Jane Ramsey

Progressive Chicago on April 7, 1993, approached Barack Obama to join. The evidence is an unsigned handwritten note.

According to the same note, Obama was "more than happy to be involved."

By September 1993, Obama was one of seventeen people listed as a signatory on all Progressive Chicago letters according to page two of the September 22, Progressive Chicago letter to Joseph Gardner.

On December 31, 1993, Progressive Chicago wrote to all key

101-6 Unsigned Meeting Note 7 Apr 1993

101-7 Barack Obama, "...happy to be involved."

members, including Obama, inviting them to a January 19, 1994 meeting. Obama's involvement in Progressive Chicago was high level and lasted at least several months.

It appears beyond doubt that Barack Obama was involved, more

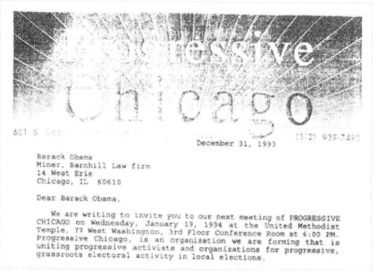

101-8 Joe Gardner to Barack Obama

than two years before his Illinois State Senate run, with a New Party founded sister organization "Progressive Chicago."

It is clear that ACORN and SEIU played a big role in Progressive Chicago, as did Marxist activists from Democratic Socialists of America and Committees of Correspondence.

In 2008, the US media went into a frenzy was alleged that Sarah Palin's husband had been involved in the Alaska Independence Party.

The same media believed the Obama's camp assurances that their candidate had never been involved in the New Party and even if he was, it was not socialist anyway.

Here is hard evidence that Obama was involved in a New Party "sister organization," founded by New Party members and run by hard-core socialists.

Perhaps some brave journalist might seek redemption and forgiveness from the American people by asking the President some tough questions.

It should not be too hard. The evidence is all here.

102. America's Little Lenin? Joel Rogers and the Obama Movement.

Trevor Loudon © Saturday, May 1, 2010

It is becoming increasingly clear that Barack Obama did not create a movement. A movement created Barack Obama.

One of the key leaders of that movement is a Madison, Wisconsin law professor and sociologist, Joel Rogers.

While not widely known outside "progressive" circles, few people have exercised more influence in more strands of the movement that selected and elected Barack Obama, than has Joel Rogers.

Obama's former "Green Jobs" Czar, the Marxist-Leninist Van Jones, has been part of Rogers' network for some years.

Rogers has served with Jones on the board of the Apollo Alliance, a radical led coalition of green groups and labor unions that had considerable input in writing Obama's massive "stimulus package."

102-1 Joel Rogers

Rogers has served as Senior Policy Adviser to Jones' Oakland based Green for All - the Northern California affiliate of the Apollo Alliance.

Van Jones took time in his address to the January 2009 Mayors Innovation Project conference to praise his friend Rogers.

Jones points out three "great gifts" that Joel Rogers "has given our movement:"

"A new economic model ...high road development ...the best thinking that he represents is now reflected in the White House."

."..the New Party, which is now the Working Families Party...the idea of a 'new politics' that you could actually have in this country bringing together labor, civil rights, feminists...and actually make a difference...is the basic framework for what took over the White House."

"His idea of a new energy paradigm. His founding the Apollo Alliance. I believe the stimulus is going to put something like $80 billion in this direction..." (V. Jones, Great Gifts from Joel Rogers 2009)

Jones credits Rogers with dreaming up the White House economic model, a 21st century "green" version of corporate socialism. Rogers also allegedly masterminded the electoral alliance that put Obama in the driver's seat. He then founded the organization that helped write the "stimulus bill," which is now funneling billions into a movement primarily designed to keep Obama and the Democrats in power.

That is a lot of influence for one man. Does Van Jones exaggerate?

Let us investigate.

The New Party which Rogers and Dan Cantor[720] founded in the early 90s, was an attempt to unite the poor, Blacks, Latinos, labor and "community groups" to work with, and inside, the Democratic Party to elect large numbers of leftist candidates to public office.

The party was essentially an amalgam of four organizations -radical Washington DC "think tank" the Institute for Policy Studies (IPS),[721] Democratic Socialists of America (DSA),[722] Service Employees International Union (SEIU)[723] and Association of Community Organizations for Reform Now (ACORN).[724]

The first strategic meeting to plan the New Party was held in Joel Rogers' home in Madison, Wisconsin in the very early 1990s. Present were Rogers' wife, Sarah Siskind,[725] Dan Cantor (now leading the New party spin-off Working Families Party[726] in New York), ACORN leaders Wade Rathke,[727] Zach Polett,[728] Steve Kest,[729] Jon Kest[730] and IPS linked activists Steve Cobble,[731] Harriet Barlow[732] and Sam Pizzigati.[733]

The very first meeting included Gerry Hudson[734] from Democratic Socialists of America (DSA) and SEIU, and early ACORN leader and IPS

---

[720] http://keywiki.org/index.php/Dan_Cantor
[721] http://keywiki.org/index.php/Institute_for_Policy_Studies
[722] http://keywiki.org/index.php/Democratic_Socialists_of_America
[723] http://keywiki.org/index.php/SEIU
[724] http://keywiki.org/index.php/ACORN
[725] http://keywiki.org/index.php/Sarah_Siskind
[726] http://keywiki.org/index.php/Working_Families_Party
[727] http://keywiki.org/index.php/Wade_Rathke
[728] http://keywiki.org/index.php/Zach_Polett
[729] http://keywiki.org/index.php/Steve_Kest
[730] http://keywiki.org/index.php/Jon_Kest
[731] http://keywiki.org/index.php/Steve_Cobble
[732] http://keywiki.org/index.php/Harriet_Barlow
[733] http://keywiki.org/index.php/Sam_Pizzigati
[734] http://keywiki.org/index.php/Gerry_Hudson

affiliate Gary Delgado.[735] When Anthony Thigpenn,[736] from Los Angeles was approached, he was supportive, but did not wish to play a leadership role.

Incidentally, both Delgado and Thigpenn were later supporters of Van Jones' anti-Iraq War magazine War Times.[737]

The party was socialist in character, but only revealed its true nature to friends.

On March 28-30, 1997, Democratic Socialists of America convened their annual Socialists Scholars Conference at Borough of Manhattan Community College, New York. Barack Obama, incidentally, attended some of these conferences[738] in the early 1980s.

The 1997 conference was themed "Radical alternatives on the eve of the millennium."

Invitees were asked to join the debate on "changes in the labor movement, Marxist theory, the state of the economy, market socialism and other areas where theory and practice meet" and listen to the United States only independent and socialist, US Senator Bernie Sanders (I-VT)[739] dialogue with Joel Rogers of the New Party.

Barack Obama joined the New Party[740] in Chicago during his 1995 Illinois State Senate run. As far back as 1993, Obama was a leader of the Chicago New Party sister organization, "Progressive Chicago."[741] Other Progressive Chicago leaders included Keith Kelleher[742] of SEIU and ACORN, Kelleher's wife, Madeline Talbott[743] of ACORN, Ron Sable,[744] US Representative Danny K. Davis[745] and Lou Pardo[746] of Democratic

---

[735] http://keywiki.org/index.php/Gary_delgado
[736] http://keywiki.org/index.php/Anthony_Thigpenn
[737] http://keywiki.org/index.php/War_Times
[738] http://keywiki.org/index.php/Barack_Obama_and_the_DSA
[739] http://keywiki.org/index.php/Bernie_Sanders
[740]
http://keywiki.org/index.php/Barack_Obama_and_the_New_Party/Progressive_Chicag o
[741] http://keywiki.org/index.php/Progressive_Chicago
[742] http://keywiki.org/index.php/Keith_Kelleher
[743] http://keywiki.org/index.php/Madeline_Talbott
[744] http://keywiki.org/index.php/Ron_Sable
[745] http://keywiki.org/index.php/Danny_K._Davis
[746] http://keywiki.org/index.php/Lou_Pardo

Socialists of America (DSA).

The New Party relied on "fusion" voting for its success. Candidates ran on both the Democrat and New Party lines, combining the vote totals from both. This practice was illegal in many states, so in 1997, Rogers and his wife Sarah Siskind took a case to the Supreme Court seeking to overturn the state bans.

According to the *"Milwaukee Journal Sentinel"* December 5, 1996:

102-2 Sarah Suskind, Esq. wife of Joel Rogers

> With allusions to possible electoral chaos, justices of the US Supreme Court expressed skepticism Wednesday over an effort to overturn forty state laws that forbid nominations of the same candidate by more than one political party.
>
> The high court heard arguments in a case from Minnesota that was orchestrated by a Wisconsin couple Joel Rogers, a University of Wisconsin-Madison law professor, and his wife, Madison attorney Sarah E. Siskind.
>
> Rogers is a co-founder and national Chair of the New Party, which describes itself as progressive and claims 10,000 members nationwide. The party has elected candidates for local offices in Wisconsin and elsewhere. (KeyWiki 2010)

The case failed and "'fusion" voting was ruled unconstitutional. Deprived of its main tactic, the New Party went into sharp decline, surviving under the Working Families Party banner in New York and a few other states.

Coincidentally, Sarah Siskind worked for the Madison Wisconsin office of Barack Obama's Chicago law firm, Miner, Barnhill and Galland.

In 2002, Sarah Siskind represented ACORN in a successful class-action lawsuit against sub-prime mortgage lender, "Household Finance Corporation."

According to Miner, Barnhill and Galland, for the last ten years, the firm (principally Sarah Siskind) has also represented individual consumers and organizational plaintiffs in class-action lawsuits challenging predatory lending practices. These include a series of deceptive practices and actions brought in Illinois, California and Massachusetts against Household Finance Corporation and recently consolidated in re Household Lending Litigation, Case No. C-02-1240 and Related Cases, N.D. Ca. They settled for $152 million in benefits and future desired relief.

Siskind won a settlement against Household Finance Corporation, which gave delinquent borrowers interest rate reductions, waivers of unpaid late charges, deferral of accrued unpaid interest and principal reductions.

It was a socialist "win-win" situation. Siskind and Miner, Barhill & Galland made money, ACORN was able to force another mortgage lender to make more soft loans to its "core constituency" and the 2008 sub-prime mortgage collapse was brought one-step closer.

Some commentators have surmised that some socialist's and leftists working through ACORN and similar groups may have deliberately promoted sub-prime lending as a way of creating economic chaos, thereby provoking a subsequent increase in government involvement in the economy.

They point to the now famous Cloward-Piven Strategy devised in the 1960s by Richard Cloward[747] and his wife Frances Fox Piven.[748] The "Cloward-Piven" plan involved enrolling as many people as possible onto state welfare programs. The point was to overload and collapse the state systems, leading to a Federal takeover of welfare.

Interestingly, when Richard Cloward died in 2001, 500 people gathered at the CUNY Graduate Center in New York City to celebrate his life and work. Speakers included:

- Frances Fox Piven
- Barbara Ehrenreich[749]
- Cornel West[750]

All New Party founders and Democratic Socialists of America (DSA) members:

- Gus Newport[751] (Democratic Socialists of America (DSA) member)

---

[747] http://keywiki.org/index.php/Richard_Cloward
[748] http://keywiki.org/index.php/Frances_Fox_Piven
[749] http://keywiki.org/index.php/Barbara_Ehrenreich
[750] http://keywiki.org/index.php/Cornel_West
[751] http://keywiki.org/index.php/Gus_Newport

- Howard Zinn[752] (New Party founder)
- Joel Rogers
- Miles Rapoport.[753]

Coincidentally, Rapoport was the President of the New York based "think tank" DEMOS,[754] an official partner organization of the Institute for Policy Studies and a close ally of ACORN.

102-3 Partners Demos, ACORN, and Project Vote

Barack Obama helped establish DEMOS in 1999-2000 and became a Trustee of the organization. Van Jones also later served as a DEMOS Trustee, but is currently on leave.

In 1998, Chicago Democratic Socialists of America (DSA) activist and IPS affiliate James Weinstein[755] presided over a major Chicago "Back to Basics" conference designed to re-align the US left back to "class politics." To explore how we (the Left) can increase our presence in the mainstream of American political and intellectual life.

Speakers included Dr. Quentin Young[756] (Democratic Socialists of America (DSA) member, New Party founder, Barack Obama long time friend, mentor and physician), Roxanne Dunbar-Ortiz[757] (a San Francisco based activist and comrade of Van Jones), plus Democratic Socialists of

---

[752] http://keywiki.org/index.php/Howard_Zinn
[753] http://keywiki.org/index.php/Miles_Rapoport
[754] http://keywiki.org/index.php/DEMOS
[755] http://keywiki.org/index.php/James_Weinstein
[756] http://keywiki.org/index.php/Quentin_Young
[757] http://keywiki.org/index.php/Roxanne_Dunbar-Ortiz

America (DSA) comrades Christine Riddiough[758], Joseph Schwartz[759] and Roberta Lynch.[760]

Joel Rogers, founder of The New Party, listed people's concerns: education, campaign finance reform, environment, raising the minimum wage and concern about global capitalism. Neither Democrats nor Republicans take this list seriously. Liberalism relied on favorable government regulation and mass politics to deal with problems. A new time calls for new politics, emphasizing economic strategy, citizen participation and electoral strategy.

In 2004, Joel Rogers from the Center On Wisconsin Strategy[761] and Robert Borosage[762] from IPS enlisted Democratic Socialists of America (DSA) friendly Steelworkers President Leo Gerard[763] and SEIU President Andy Stern,[764] to propose a new alliance of labor, environmental groups, business and "social justice" leaders - the Apollo Alliance. The Alliance, which soon included over 200 supporting organizations, released a report *"High Road or Low Road? Job Quality in the Green Economy"* which argues for a ten-year program investing in clean energy for a good jobs economy.

Joel Rogers, the Alliance's founding Chair, continues to serve on its board. Borosage is also a board member, as is Leo Gerard. John Podesta[765] from the Center for American Progress (CAP)[766] also serves, but took a break while co-Chairing President Obama's "transition," where he "coordinated the priorities of the incoming administration's agenda, oversaw the development of its policies and spearheaded its appointments of major cabinet secretaries and political appointees."

When Van Jones, an Apollo Alliance board member, was forced to exit the White House, Podesta gave him a job with the "Center for American Progress" (CAP).

---

758 http://keywiki.org/index.php/Christine_Riddiough
759 http://keywiki.org/index.php/Joseph_Schwartz
760 http://keywiki.org/index.php/Roberta_Lynch
761 http://keywiki.org/index.php/Center_On_Wisconsin_Strategy
762 http://keywiki.org/index.php/Robert_Borosage
763 http://keywiki.org/index.php/Leo_Gerard
764 http://keywiki.org/index.php/Andy_Stern
765 http://keywiki.org/index.php/John_Podesta
766 http://keywiki.org/index.php/Center_for_American_Progress

Besides Rogers, two old New Party affiliates are involved in the Apollo Alliance. Gerry Hudson of Democratic Socialists of America (DSA) and SEIU serves as a board member. Anthony Thigpenn serves on the Apollo Alliance advisory board and runs the Apollo affiliate in Los Angeles - which trains "anti-racist environmental organizers."

Thigpenn is a former member of the Maoist leaning Black Panther Party, but that is mild by Apollo standards. The former head of the New York Apollo Alliance Jeff Jones,[767] once led the terrorist Weather Underground Organization with he and President Obama's mutual friends, Bill Ayers[768] and Bernardine Dohrn.[769]

Former Democratic Socialists of America (DSA) youth leader and SEIU organizer Ron Ruggiero, serves as Apollo Alliance National Field Director.

It's a safe bet that a good portion of the $80 billion "stimulus package" will be going to Van Jones' "Green for All" in San Francisco, to Anthony Thigpenn "environmental anti-racism" trainers in Los Angeles and Jeff Jones' former crew in New York.

Any good Leninist will tell you, it is not gaining power that is important; it is the KEEPING of power.

Joel Rogers' New Party modeled the movement that put Obama in power. His Apollo Alliance provides a means for holding that power.

102-4 Any Good Leninist

It is essentially a massive patronage system, where a huge amount of taxpayer's money is channeled into radical led "green" camouflaged mass organizations.

These "green" armies will be the vote herders of the future. They will confront the Tea Party movement and other patriots on the streets of America. They will be the paramilitary armies used to intimidate the very

---

[767] http://keywiki.org/index.php/Jeff_Jones
[768] http://keywiki.org/index.php/Bill_Ayers
[769] http://keywiki.org/index.php/Bernardine_Dohrn

people who fund them.

In a January 2, 2009, tribute to Democratic Socialists of America founder Michael Harrington,[770] Gerry Hudson of the Apollo Alliance - SEIU - Democratic Socialists of America (DSA) wrote:

> It's tragic for so many reasons that Michael died too young; his voice and his wisdom are sorely needed. How he would marvel at the election of Barack Obama and the promise that this victory affords all of us on the democratic left! He is sorely missed. But were he alive, I would hope—and expect, that he and others who are informed by this vision of democratic socialism would join with us in SEIU as we seek to take advantage of a moment most of us have spent our lifetimes only dreaming of. (Hudson 2009)

Joel Rogers is the glue that ties many of these threads together - Institute for Policy Studies, Democratic Socialists of America, ACORN, SEIU, New Party, the Apollo Alliance - even possibly the sub-prime mortgage crisis.

I believe, had there been no Joel Rogers, there likely would have been no President Barack Obama. What do you think?

103. Barack Obama's "Respectable" Socialist Mentor, Abner Mikva

Trevor Loudon © Saturday, May 15, 2010

President Barack H. Obama[771] and his latest Supreme Court nominee Elena Kagan[772] have a friend in common -prominent former Congressman and Chicago lawyer, US Representative Abner Mikva (D-IL-2nd District).[773]

Fresh out of Harvard law School, Elena Kagan clerked for then Judge Mikva in Washington DC in 1986-87. In the 1990s, Obama, Kagan and Mikva were all on the Faculty of the University of Chicago Law School.

---

[770] http://keywiki.org/index.php/Michael_Harrington
[771] http://keywiki.org/index.php/Barack_Obama
[772] http://keywiki.org/index.php/Elena_Kagan
[773] http://www.blogger.com/Abner%20Mikva

Obama's relationship with US Representative Abner Mikva (D-IL-2nd District) is long and deep, but has been subject to little scrutiny. After all, US Representative Abner Mikva (D-IL-2nd District) is no radical; he is a highly respected "liberal" and Chicago elder statesman.

According to the *Chicago Sun-Times* April 14, 2009:

> Abner Mikva, a revered figure in Illinois politics, was an early Barack Obama booster and mentor. Mikva's backing–he is the gold standard for integrity in Illinois politics–was important in Obama establishing his credentials in the early days of his political career and in his US Senate run. (Sweet, Another Chicagoan, Laurie Mikva joins the Obama Administration 2009)

US Representative Abner Mikva (D-IL-2nd District) was one of Obama's early admirers, beginning in 1990 when he tried to hire the first black president of the Harvard Law Review for a coveted clerkship. (Obama turned him down, saying he was going to move to Chicago and run for public office). "I thought that showed a lot of chutzpah on his part," says Mikva.

103-1 Abner Mikva

The Obamas settled in Hyde Park and Barack became a lecturer at the University of Chicago Law School. Mikva, "whom Obama already knew from Washington," also taught there and the two renewed their acquaintance and became close. "We would have lunch and breakfast together and talk about a lot of things, different issues." How the pair knew each other "from Washington," where Obama never lived or worked or studied, is an interesting question.

When Barack H. Obama won the Presidency, Mikva summed up Obama's victory as also a victory for Chicago:

> Really what we will get out of this is, it will make clear for the last time Chicago is not just full of pork barrel, sleazy politicians who know only Machine politics... We also will have a very special president. (KeyWiki 2010)

Obama repaid those kind words by appointing Mikva's daughter, Laurie Mikva,[774] to the board of the Legal Services Corporation in June 2009.

103-2 Laurie Mikva

Nevertheless, who is US Representative Abner Mikva (D-IL-2nd District) really? This man mentored the President of the United States and employed a possible Supreme Court Justice. Is there anything in US Representative Abner Mikva (D-IL-2nd District)'s background that should concern us?

After Service in World War II, US Representative Abner Mikva (D-IL-2nd District) studied law at the University of Chicago. In 1949, communist led students went on strike at the City College of New York.

Twenty University of Chicago campus leaders met in April that year to show support for their New York counterparts, US Representative Abner Mikva (D-IL-2nd District) was among them. Several had communist connections including Elias Snitzer[775] and Sid Socolar,[776] both of whom later took the Fifth Amendment during government security hearings when questioned over alleged Communist Party membership.

103-3 Arthur Goldberg

In 1947, leftist lawyer Arthur Goldberg[777] became senior partner with US Representative Abner Mikva (D-IL-2nd District) in the Chicago law firm of Goldberg, Devoe, Shadur & Mikva.

Arthur Goldberg sponsored several local Communist Party fronts, including the Chicago Conference on Race Relations, the Conference on Constitutional Liberties in America and the National Emergency Conference. He was also president of the Chicago chapter of the National

[774] http://keywiki.org/index.php/Laurie_Mikva
[775] http://keywiki.org/index.php/Elias_Snitzer
[776] http://keywiki.org/index.php/Sid_Socolar
[777] http://keywiki.org/index.php/Arthur_Goldberg

Lawyers Guild,[778] accurately described in government hearings as "the foremost legal bulwark of the Communist Party." Surprisingly these affiliations did not stop Goldberg later from becoming a Supreme Court Justice and US Ambassador to the United Nations under Lyndon Johnson.

In the early 1950's, George Anastaplo, a classmate of Mikva's at the University of Chicago Law School, sparked controversy when he refused to deny Communist Party membership to a Character and Fitness Committee of the Illinois Bar. The Committee investigated and because he had not answered its questions, he could not become a lawyer.

Mikva was one of the first to come to Anastaplo's aid.

In 1954, "amicus curiae" briefs were filed on Anastaplo's behalf by two radical dominated organizations, the ACLU and the National Lawyers Guild. Mikva and Leon Despres[779] (a friend of Saul Alinsky,[780] an associate of Leon Trotsky and later a mentor to Barack Obama) signed the ACLU brief, filed in the Supreme Court of Illinois. Pearl Hart,[781] a veteran of several communist fronts, including the Chicago Committee to Defend the Bill of Rights,[782] signed the NLG brief.

Mikva too, would work with Alinsky, the legendary father of "community organizing."

In the 1966 Democratic primary election, US Representative Abner Mikva (D-IL-2nd District), then an Illinois State legislator, challenged the Daley machine-backed incumbent Barrett O'Hara for the second Congressional District. Liberal, independent forces and "The Woodlawn Organization" supported US Representative Abner Mikva (D-IL-2nd District).

To avoid jeopardizing the organization's nonpartisan tax exemption, TWO staffers went on the Mikva campaign payroll. They even recruited the notorious Blackstone Rangers street gang to put up yard signs warning against bribes offered by the "machine" team. Saul Alinsky was organizing TWO at the time and believed that a Mikva victory, made

[778] http://keywiki.org/index.php/National_Lawyers_Guild
[779] http://keywiki.org/index.php/Leon_Despres
[780] http://keywiki.org/index.php/Saul_Alinsky
[781] http://keywiki.org/index.php/Pearl_Hart
[782] http://keywiki.org/index.php/Chicago_Committee_to_Defend_the_Bill_of_Rights

VOICES

Hyde Park-Kenwood

Published monthly by Voices Press. **Mailing address:** 1525 E. 53rd Street, Chicago, Illinois 60615. Telephone **(312) 667-7838.** Offices open by appointment only. Subscriptions: $2.50 per year.

Co-Publishers: David S. Canter, Don Rose. **Editor:** Don Rose. **Managing Editor:** Jody Parsons. **General Manager:** David S. Canter. **Business Manager:** Ray Sherman. **Community Organizations Editor:**

103-4 Hyde Park - Kenwood VOICES

possible by TWO's political muscle, could have been a springboard to bigger things on the South Side.

Alinsky was reportedly furious when Mikva narrowly lost the primary.

In January 1969, the Chicago radical newspaper, *Hyde Park- Kenwood Voices*,[783] listed those who had helped produce its first sixteen monthly issues as "writers, researchers, photographers, artists and clerical workers."

The list included US Representative Abner Mikva (D-IL-2nd District), who wrote a regular column for the paper. The *"Voices"* was a mouthpiece for Students for a Democratic Society, Cuba sugar cane cutters, anti-Vietnam War activists and radicals of every stripe.

Proprietors were David S. Canter[784] and Don Rose.[785] Canter was a Communist Party member, importer and distributor of Soviet literature. He was once required to register as an official agent of the Soviet Union. Rose was equally as radical, but never a proven Party member. He was, however, a leader of the communist front, "Chicago Committee to Defend the Bill of Rights."

After the *"Voices"* folded in the mid-1970s, Rose and Canter went on to mentor a promising young journalist named David Axelrod[786] - the man who put Barack Obama in the White House and now serves as the President's chief adviser.

---

[783] http://keywiki.org/index.php/Hyde_Park_Kenwood_Voices
[784] http://keywiki.org/index.php/David_Canter
[785] http://keywiki.org/index.php/Don_Rose
[786] http://keywiki.org/index.php/David_Axelrod

In April 1975, the Communist Party controlled the Chicago Peace Council, which convened a "National Conference for a Drastic Cutback in Military Spending" in Chicago:

103-5 Institute for Policy Studies

> The purpose of the National Conference is to mount a national campaign and a vigorous program of action, which will speak to the hundreds of thousands who were part of the inspiring resistance to the war in Indo-China. The people of the US can and must turn this country around... (Chicago Communist Party 1975)

Speakers at the conference included Richard Criley[787] and Norman Roth[788] of the Communist Party and the Chicago Committee to Defend the Bill of Rights, Fr. Gerard Grant[789] and Frank Rosen[790] (also "Committee" members), Ed Sadlowski[791] of the United Steel Workers Union and later Democratic Socialists of America[792] and of course, US Representative Abner Mikva (D-IL-2nd District).

Mikva was elected to Congress in 1968. In Washington, Mikva became involved with the far left "Institute for Policy Studies."[793] At the time, the IPS was a magnet for "liberal" Democrats (and even a few Republicans), Marxists, third world radicals, Eastern Bloc diplomats and at least a few known KGB agents and contacts. It was (and remains) a center of subversion in the heart of the nation's capital.

In 1983, IPS celebrated its 20th anniversary with a giant "bash" at the National Building Museum, attended by approximately 1,000 staffers, politicians and supporters. US Representative Abner Mikva (D-IL-2nd District), of course, attended while his wife Zoe handled arrangements for the function.

IPS held regular seminars and schools, attracting people from all over the US and abroad. Could it have been through IPS that Mikva first met Barack Obama in Washington? Certainly, Obama was in the IPS

---

[787] http://keywiki.org/index.php/Richard_Criley
[788] http://keywiki.org/index.php/Norman_Roth
[789] http://keywiki.org/index.php/Gerard_Grant
[790] http://keywiki.org/index.php/Frank_Rosen
[791] http://keywiki.org/index.php/Ed_Sadlowski
[792] http://keywiki.org/index.php/Democratic_Socialists_of_America
[793] http://www.keywiki.org/index.php/Institute_for_Policy_Studies

103-6 Frank Wilkerson

"orbit." In 1999, IPS affiliate, Charles Halpern[794] recruited Obama from Chicago to help establish and serve as Trustee of the New York based "non-profit" DEMOS,[795] an official IPS partner organization.

Coincidentally, Obama's former "Green Jobs Czar" Van Jones[796] was also a DEMOS Trustee.

After his Congressional career, Mikva served as a judge in Washington DC (where he employed Elena Kagan) and later as White House counsel under Bill Clinton.

After leaving the White House, Mikva returned to his Chicago roots.

Not people to abandon old friends, Abner and Zoe Mikva[797] sent a message:[798] "Hooray for Progressives" to the Chicago Democratic Socialists of America 44th Annual Debs-Thomas-Dinner, held on May 10, 2002.

On Sunday October 29, 2006, the "Chicago Committee to Defend the Bill of Rights" held a "Celebration of The Dynamic Life of Frank Wilkinson (1914-2006)." Frank Wilkinson,[799] a founder of the "Committee," had been a forty year veteran of the Communist Party, before going on to join the almost as radical Democratic Socialists of America.

US Representative Abner Mikva served on the honoring committee with past or current Communist Party supporters Donna Wilkinson, Joan Elbert, Ruth Emerson, Yolanda Hall, Peggy Lipschutz, Bea Lumpkin, Frank Lumpkin, Harold Rogers, Mark Rogovin, Norman Roth, Emile Schepers, Studs Terkel and Tim Yeager.

Democratic Socialists of America members on the committee

---

[794] http://keywiki.org/index.php/Charles_Halpern
[795] http://keywiki.org/index.php/DEMOS
[796] http://www.keywiki.org/index.php/Van_Jones
[797] http://www.keywiki.org/index.php/Zoe_Mikva
[798] http://www.chicagodsa.org/2002Book.pdf
[799] http://www.keywiki.org/index.php/Frank_Wilkinson

included Representative Danny K. Davis,[800] Timuel Black,[801] and Dr. Quentin Young.[802] They all were coincidentally close friends and supporters of Barack Obama.

The left side of Chicago politics is so much a part of the mainstream, it is almost "respectable." Democrats, communists and socialists work together. They join each other's front groups and political parties.

Barack Obama and US Representative Abner Mikva (D-IL-2nd District) are steeped in this culture and Elena Kagan is peripherally connected to it. Young lawyers tend to clerk for those who share their outlook.

Chicago socialism has been a powerful force in Illinois politics since the election of far left Mayor Harold Washington[803] in 1983 and is now, spreading to Capitol Hill, the White House and threatens to infect the entire country.

104. Radical Royalty - Obama's Federal Reserve Pick - Sarah Bloom Raskin

Trevor Loudon © Wednesday, May 26, 2010

A seat on the US Federal Reserve Board carries tremendous power. The seven members of the Board of Governors of the Federal Reserve System are nominated by the President and confirmed by the Senate. A full term is fourteen years. During that time, a board member can influence the financial policies of the world's most powerful economy. In some ways, the seven men and women have more power than Congress or even the President himself.

That is why appointments to the Federal Reserve Board deserve as much scrutiny as those to the Supreme Court.

President Barack Obama recently made three nominations to the Federal Reserve Board: Janet Yellen, Peter Diamond and Sarah Bloom Raskin.

---

[800] http://keywiki.org/index.php/Danny_Davis
[801] http://keywiki.org/index.php/Timuel_Black
[802] http://keywiki.org/index.php/Quentin_Young
[803] http://keywiki.org/index.php/Harold_Washington

While most "Obama watchers" said little, some commentators from the left did take notice. Democratic Socialists of America[804] member, Larry Mishel of the Economic Policy Institute,[805] was pleased with the appointments:

> I think these are all great choices, and ones that will move Fed policy in the needed direction – responsive to the needs of middle-class and working families. (KeyWiki 2010)

104-1 Janet Yellen, Peter Diamond, Sarah Bloom Raskin

Of the three named, one stands out in particular - Sarah Bloom Raskin. That surname should ring alarm bells because Sarah Bloom married Jamin Raskin.

Sarah Bloom married into what is perhaps the closest America has to a radical "royal family."

Sarah Bloom Raskin is the wife of Jamin (Jamie) Raskin,[806] a legal academic, Maryland State Senator and the son of Marcus Raskin,[807] founder of the deservedly notorious Institute for Policy Studies (IPS).[808]

In 1963, Marcus Raskin and his partner, the late Richard Barnet[809] founded their radical "think tank" in Washington DC. IPS quickly grew to become a highly influential source of ideas, guidance and training for

---

[804] http://keywiki.org/index.php/Democratic_Socialists_of_America
[805] http://keywiki.org/index.php/Economic_Policy_Institute
[806] http://keywiki.org/index.php/Jamin_B._Raskin
[807] http://keywiki.org/index.php/Marcus_Raskin
[808] http://keywiki.org/index.php/Institute_for_Policy_Studies
[809] http://keywiki.org/index.php/Richard_Barnet

the US and international left. Its critics claimed that IPS consistently supported policies that aided the foreign policy goals of the Soviet Union and weakened the position of the United States.

Since its founding, IPS has consistently followed a pro-socialist line on foreign policy, defense and the economy and has spawned a large number of spin-offs, other think tanks and public affairs organizations following the same radical agenda.

104-2 Jamie Raskin

In 1978, in an article in National Review, Brian Crozier, director of the London-based Institute for the Study of Conflict, described IPS as the "perfect intellectual front for Soviet activities which would be resisted if they were to originate openly from the KGB."

IPS became a place where leftist Congressmen, Senators and Capitol Hill staffers could mingle with third world radicals, East Bloc diplomats and even a few identified KGB agents.

The FBI was intensely interested in Raskin's institute, until IPS sued the agency and extracted a written agreement forbidding any further FBI surveillance - an agreement that may still stand today.

In the early 1990s, IPS worked with Democratic Socialists of America and socialist US Senator Bernie Sanders (I-VT)[810] to establish the Congressional Progressive Caucus [811] with eighty members. In 2003, IPS also helped set up the communist dominated "peace" umbrella organization, United for Peace & Justice.[812]

Jamie Raskin admits that he grew up "in an environment of progressive politics."

A Harvard graduate and a "lifelong progressive Democrat," Jamie Raskin has brought "innovative ideas and a hands-on approach to government and politics at every level."

He has served on the Montgomery County Hate Crimes Commission, the Takoma Park Election Redistricting Task Force and the

---

[810] http://keywiki.org/index.php/Bernie_Sanders
[811] http://keywiki.org/index.php/Congressional_Progressive_Caucus
[812] http://keywiki.org/index.php/United_for_Peace_and_Justice

104-3 Cheriff Guellal, Markus Raskin, James L. Hudson

Takoma Park Gun Policy Task Force.

In 1992, he served on President Clinton's Justice Department Transition Team for the Civil Rights Division. Raskin was elected as a Kerry-Edwards Delegate to the Democratic National Convention in 2004.

A member of the board of "FairVote," the nation's leading electoral-reform group, Raskin was known as "a champion of voters' rights." In his 2003 book, *Overruling Democracy: The Supreme Court versus The American People,*" Raskin documented the Rehnquist Court majority's "assault on voting rights" in the 2000 election and "placed Bush v. Gore in the context of a series of Supreme Court decisions undermining the participatory rights of the people."

Focusing on the Rehnquist majority's statement that the "individual citizen has no federal constitutional right to vote" for president, Raskin argued for a constitutional amendment guaranteeing the right to vote (and to get one's vote counted) for all Americans.

Raskin has served as a Washington-area Board Member for the Rev. Jesse Jackson's[813] heavily communist infiltrated National Rainbow Coalition.

He has worked closely with far left US Representative Jesse Jackson, Jr.[814] to advance amendments in Congress and with IPS affiliated US Representative Eleanor Holmes Norton (DC-At Large)[815] to "advance a voting rights agenda for the people of Washington, D.C."

Unsurprisingly, Jamie Raskin has done pro bono legal work for SEIU,[816] ACORN,[817] Greenpeace and the radical led Students Against

[813] http://keywiki.org/index.php/Jesse_Jackson
[814] http://keywiki.org/index.php/Jesse_Jackson%2C_Jr.
[815] http://keywiki.org/index.php/Eleanor_Holmes_Norton
[816] http://keywiki.org/index.php/Service_Employees_International_Union
[817] http://keywiki.org/index.php/ACORN

Sweatshops. He has written for two Democratic Socialists of America and IPS affiliated journals, *"The Nation"*[818] and *"In These Times."*[819]

Raskin has also served on the board of Progressive Democrats of America,[820] an IPS spinoff, which is effectively the activist wing of the Congressional Progressive Caucus.

On March 10, 2006, IPS supporters, Yolande Fox[821] and former Algerian Ambassador, Cherif Guellal[822] hosted a book launch in their Washington home for Jamie Raskin's most recent book entitled *"Overruling Democracy: The Supreme Court Versus the American People."*

Fox was a former Miss America (1951) from Alabama. Cherif Guellal was a former top lieutenant to Algerian revolutionary leader Ahmed Ben Bella, winner of the 1964 Lenin Peace Prize. Guellal also had ties to the British Fabian Socialist Society in the early 1960s. During the 1967, Six-Day War, Algeria severed diplomatic relations to protest United States support for Israel. Instead of returning to Algeria, Guellal became a Fellow at IPS.

Other attendees included Jamie's father and Marcus Raskin, James L. Hudson[823] and Ira Lowe.[824]

Jim Hudson, a long time Washington "insider," was recently appointed by President Obama to the Directorship of the European Bank for Reconstruction and Development.

Ira Lowe is a trial lawyer and IPS supporter. He formerly represented IPS affiliate and Progressives for Obama[825] founder, Tom Hayden.[826]

Incidentally, IPS Trustee, Democratic Socialists of America member and Progressives for Obama co-founder, Barbara Ehrenreich[827] said of Raskin's book:

---

[818] http://keywiki.org/index.php/The_Nation
[819] http://keywiki.org/index.php/In_These_Times
[820] http://keywiki.org/index.php/Progressive_Democrats_of_America
[821] http://keywiki.org/index.php/Yolande_Fox
[822] http://keywiki.org/index.php/Cherif_Guellal
[823] http://keywiki.org/index.php/Jim_Hudson
[824] http://keywiki.org/index.php/Ira_Lowe
[825] http://keywiki.org/index.php/Progressives_for_Obama
[826] http://keywiki.org/index.php/Tom_Hayden
[827] http://keywiki.org/index.php/Barbara_Ehrenreich

This brilliantly argued and meticulously researched book both alarms and inspires. (Ehrenreich 2010)

Sarah Bloom has no known direct ties to the Institute for Policy Studies, but she did work for IPS connected Washington law firm Arnold & Porter from 1988 to 1993.

A current Arnold & Porter partner, Jeremy Karpatkin,[828] is a former Democratic Socialists of America youth organizer. Karpatkin directed field operations during the successful Senate run of far left Democratic Party operative Senator Carol Moseley-Braun[829] in 1992, in Chicago.

Coincidentally, Barack Obama ran the ACORN Project Vote [830] voter registration drive that year that helped Moseley-Braun to win. In 2004, Obama took over the same Senate seat.

Nearly three decades earlier, pioneering trial lawyer, Charles Halpern,[831] became involved with IPS through Arnold & Porter. The firm handled IPS' legal work and partner Thurman Porter had been an IPS trustee.

Halpern became corporate secretary to IPS, keeping minutes and records. He began to attend IPS seminars and parties at the Institute and at the home of founder Marcus Raskin, where he met radicals "like Paul Goodman and Ivan Ilich."

When Raskin and several other activists were arrested for conspiring to obstruct the military draft, Halpern helped with the defense. Halpern flew with Raskin to a meeting with the other defendants and their lawyers at the Greenwich Village home of radical lawyer and secret Communist Party USA member Leonard Boudin[832] - father of Weather Underground terrorist Kathie Boudin.[833] Fellow terrorist Bill Ayers[834] and Bernardine Dohrn[835] would later raise Kathie

---

[828] http://keywiki.org/index.php/Jeremy_Karpatkin
[829] http://keywiki.org/index.php/Carol_Moseley_Braun
[830]http://keywiki.org/index.php/Barack_Obama_Affiliated_Organizations#tab=ACORN_and_Project_Vote
[831] http://keywiki.org/index.php/Charles_Halpern
[832] http://keywiki.org/index.php/Leonard_Boudin
[833] http://keywiki.org/index.php/Kathie_Boudin
[834] http://keywiki.org/index.php/Bill_Ayers
[835] http://keywiki.org/index.php/Bernardine_Dohrn

Boudin's son Chesa Boudin[836] after she was jailed for her terrorist crimes.

Charles Halpern and three other lawyers founded the radical Center for Law and Social Policy (CLASP) in 1968, with the assistance of former US Supreme Court Associate Justice Arthur Goldberg,[837] who chaired the CLASP board.

A veteran of several communist fronts, Goldberg was, in the late 1940s, a Chicago law partner of Abner Mikva.[838] A lifelong associate of communists and socialists and an IPS affiliate, Mikva went on to employ a young law clerk named Elena Kagan.[839] Kagan mentors and befriends[840] a young Chicago lawyer named Barack Obama.

104-4 Charles Halpern

In 1999, Charles Halpern went on to found a New York based "think tank" DEMOS, an official partner organization of IPS. Among those recruited[841] to set up and join the first board of DEMOS included an obscure Illinois State senator named Barack Obama.

The DEMOS Board recruited several years later, a young San Francisco communist named Van Jones.[842]

DEMOS and IPS staffer Chuck Collins,[843] in an article written several months before the 2008 Presidential elections, suggested Jones as a possible "Green Jobs Czar" for the Obama

104-5 Robert Kuttner is a Distinguished Senior Fellow at Demos

---

[836] http://keywiki.org/index.php/Chesa_Boudin

[837] http://keywiki.org/index.php/Arthur_Goldberg

[838] http://keywiki.org/index.php/Abner_Mikva

[839] http://keywiki.org/index.php/Elena_Kagan

[840] http://newzeal.blogspot.com/2010/05/obama-file-103-barack-obamas.html Chapter 103 - Barack Obama's "Respectable" Socialist Mentor – Abner Mikva

[841] http://newzeal.blogspot.com/2009/08/obama-file-82-obama-communist-van-jones.html Chapter 82 – Exclusive! Obama, the Communist Van Jones and the Demos Connection

[842] http://keywiki.org/index.php/Van_Jones

[843] http://keywiki.org/index.php/Chuck_Collins

administration.

Robert Kuttner[844] is a Distinguished Senior Fellow at DEMOS and serves on the board of the Economic Policy Institute with Larry Mishel. The Democratic Socialists of America, described Kuttner as a "socialist."

Kuttner was very pleased when Obama nominated Sarah Raskin to the Federal Reserve Bank. He wrote in the March 14, 2010 "Huffington Post":

> Obama has also just appointed three relative progressives to the Federal Reserve, including Sarah Bloom Raskin of Maryland, widely considered the best of the state financial regulators. There is not a single businessman or banker in the lot. (Kuttner 2010)

Will Sarah Bloom Raskin sail into fourteen years at the helm of the US economy on a pleasant face and zero scrutiny?

On the other hand, will Senate Republicans and the media do their job and ask some serious questions?

---

[844] http://keywiki.org/index.php/Robert_Kuttner

The Choice: Freedom or Tyranny

105. "A Pattern of Socialist Associations" - Obama's Supreme Court Nominee, Elena Kagan (the Early Years)

Tuesday, June 29, 2010

President Barack H. Obama's[845] nomination to the US Supreme court, Elena Kagan, has been sold to the public as a "moderate" - yes, a little liberal leaning, but moderate none the less.

105-1 President Barack Obama (r), Associate Justice Elena Kagan (c) and Vice President Joe Biden (l)

Elena Kagan's patterns of association

If Elena Kagan is a moderate, why then has she long associated with people connected to three interrelated organizations - the Communist Party USA,[846] the Democratic Socialist Organizing Committee[847]/Democratic Socialists of America[848] and the far left

---

[845] http://keywiki.org/index.php/Barack_Obama
[846] http://keywiki.org/index.php/Communist_Party_USA
[847] Democratic Socialist Organizing Committee
[848] Democratic Socialists of America

Washington D.C. think tank, Institute for Policy Studies?[849]

Raised on New Yorks' Upper West Side, Elena Kagan's parents were both politically active in a place and era where politics was dominated by the Democratic, Socialist and Communist parties.

Elena's mother Gloria Kagan[850] campaigned to elect far left Democratic Congressman, William Fitts Ryan.[851] Her older brother Marc Kagan[852] was active in the socialist influenced New Directions movement in the Transport Workers Union. When one of its leaders, Roger Toussaint,[853] was elected union president in 2000, Mr. Kagan became his chief of staff, until a falling out occurred in 2003.

Marc Kagan's former comrade and boss, Roger Toussaint is prominent in the communist initiated Coalition of Black Trade Unionists which is now led by DSA member William Lucy.[854] He also serves in the leadership of the Center for the Study of Working Class Life[855] at Stony Brook University, alongside Ray Markey[856] from the Communist Party offshoot Committees of Correspondence[857] and Democratic Socialists of America leaders, Gerry Hudson,[858] Mark Levinson,[859] Stanley Aronowitz[860] and Frances Fox Piven,[861] co-originator of the infamous Cloward-Piven Strategy.[862]

Elena Kagan would later dedicate her Princeton history thesis on socialism in New York City to her activist brother.

> I would like to thank my brother Marc whose involvement in radical causes led me to explore the history of American radicalism and in the hope of clarifying my own political ideas. (Kagan 1981)

---

[849] http://keywiki.org/index.php/Institute_for_Policy_Studies
[850] http://keywiki.org/index.php/Gloria_Kagan
[851] http://keywiki.org/index.php/William_Fitts_Ryan
[852] http://keywiki.org/index.php/Marc_Kagan
[853] http://keywiki.org/index.php/Roger_Toussaint
[854] http://keywiki.org/index.php/William_Lucy
[855] http://keywiki.org/index.php/Center_for_the_Study_of_Working_Class_Life
[856] http://keywiki.org/index.php/Ray_Markey
[857] http://keywiki.org/index.php/Committees_of_Correspondence
[858] http://keywiki.org/index.php/Gerry_Hudson
[859] http://keywiki.org/index.php/Mark_Levinson
[860] http://keywiki.org/index.php/Stanley_Aronowitz
[861] http://keywiki.org/index.php/Frances_Fox_Piven
[862] http://newzeal.blogspottrevorloudon.com/2010/06/1966-cloward-piven-strategy-unveiled-at.html-socialist-scholars-conference/

Kagan first became interested in politics in high school and worked as a legislative intern for US Representative Ted Weiss (D-NY-20th District),[863] a Democrat from New York, during the summer of 1978 as a Deputy Press Secretary for US Representative Liz Holtzman (D-NY-16th District)[864] in the summer after her junior year.

The late Ted Weiss was very far to the left. In 1978, Congressmen Ted Weiss, John Burton, Ron Dellums (D.S.A. member), John Conyers (D.S.A. supporter), Don Edwards, Charles Rangel and others, attended a meeting organized for the Soviet front World Peace Council on Capitol Hill.

W.P.C. delegation members included President Romesh Chandra (Communist Party of India), KGB Colonel Radomir Bogdanov and Oleg Kharkhardin of the Communist Party of the Soviet Union International Department.

105-2 Ted Weiss

In 1981, another World Peace Council delegation led by Romesh Chandra, toured the US to publicize the "nuclear freeze" then being promoted by Leonid Brezhnev.

This group met with several far left Congressmen at the Capitol, including Weiss, John Conyers and George Crockett, Ron Dellums, Don Edwards and Mervyn Dymally.

During one of the meetings in these Congressmen's offices, an official of the Communist Party USA reportedly was present and made a speech recommending that the "peace movement" unite in supporting the cause of several terrorist groups including the Palestine Liberation Organization (PLO)[865] and the communist guerillas in El Salvador.

Weiss was also close to the Institute for Policy Studies. In 1983, IPS celebrated its 20th anniversary with an April 5 reception at the National Building Museum attended by approximately 1,000 IPS staffers and former staff.

---

863 http://keywiki.org/index.php/Ted_Weiss
864 http://keywiki.org/index.php/Liz_Holtzman
865 http://en.wikipedia.org/wiki/Palestine_Liberation_Organization

The Congressional I.P.S. committee members included Ted Weiss, Philip Burton, George Crockett, Ron Dellums, Tom Harkin and Leon Panetta, (later appointed by President Obama to head the Central Intelligence Agency). Liz Holtzman is also way left of center. In the late 1980s and early 1990's, the Marxist based Democratic Socialist Organizing Committee DSOC (later to become Democratic Socialists of America, or DSADSA) was highly influential inside the New York Democratic Party and city government - even Mayor David Dinkins[866] was a member.

On August 6 1993, a rally to commemorate Hiroshima Day was held in Dag Hammarskjold Park, New York. The rally was designed:

> "to kick off a national campaign to collect a million signatures supporting a Comprehensive Test Ban Treaty, commend president Clinton for extending the nuclear testing moratorium, urge renewal of the Non Proliferation Treaty, urge swift and complete nuclear disarmament." (KeyWiki 1993)

The radical Metro New York Peace Action Council sponsored the event.

Speakers included Liz Holtzman, (then NYC Comptroller,) leftist Congressmen Charles Rangel, Edolphus Towns, Leslie Cagan of Committees of Correspondence and the Cuba Information Project,

105-3 Liz Holtzman

Congressmen Major Owens (D.S.A. member) and Jerry Nadler (D.S.O.C. member,) NYC City Councilor Ruth Messinger (D.S.O.C./ D.S.A. member) and David McReynolds, a leader of the Socialist Party USA and also a D.S.A. member. Nearly 5 years later, in March 1998, McReynolds delivered a eulogy at a memorial Service for Chicago DSA activist Saul Mendelson.[867] Fellow DSA comrades Carl Marx Shier and Deborah Meier[868] also spoke, as did then IL State Senator Barack Obama.

At Princeton, Elena Kagan's political

---

[866] http://en.wikipedia.org/wiki/David_Dinkins
[867] http://keywiki.org/index.php/Saul_Mendelson
[868] http://keywiki.org/index.php/Deborah_Meier

beliefs emerged in an opinion piece she wrote for the Daily Princetonian a few weeks after Ronald Reagan's victorious 1980 election night. Kagan described her disappointment at Liz Holtzman's Congressional loss (Kagan had worked on her campaign) and her own "liberal views."

105-5 Professor Michael Walzer

"I absorbed ... liberal principles early," she said. "More to the point, I have retained them fairly intact to this day." (Kagan, Opinion 1980)

In the column, Kagan also expressed her despair at the state of the political left at the time, bemoaning the lack of:

105-4 Presentation Notice

"real Democrats — not the closet Republicans that one sees so often these days" and the success of "anonymous but Moral Majority-backed ... avengers of 'innocent life' and the B-1 Bomber, these beneficiaries of a general turn to the right and a profound disorganization on the left." (Kagan, Opinion 1980)

At Princeton, Elena Kagan's law school roommate was Sarah Walzer, [869] the daughter of Princeton social sciences professor Michael Walzer.[870]

Coincidentally, Michael Walzer was a leader of the Democratic Socialist Organizing Committee, both nationally and on campus.

In 1990, Michael Walzer was identified as a member of Democratic Socialists of America. Professor Walzer was also upset at Ronald Reagan's famous victory.

In her undergraduate thesis at Princeton entitled "*To the Final Conflict: Socialism in New York City, 1900-1933*," Kagan lamented the decline of socialism in the country as "sad" for those who still hope to "change America."

She asked why the "greatness" of socialism was not reemerging as a

---

[869] http://keywiki.org/index.php/Sarah_Walzer
[870] http://keywiki.org/index.php/Michael_Walzer

major political force:

> In our own times, a coherent socialist movement is nowhere to be found in the United States. Americans are more likely to speak of a golden past than of a golden future, of capitalism's glories than of socialism's greatness. Why, in a society by no means perfect, has a radical party never attained the status of a major political force? Why, in particular, did the socialist movement never become an alternative to the nation's established parties?

> "Americans are more likely to speak of a golden past than of a golden future, of capitalism's glories than of socialism's greatness," she wrote in her thesis. "Conformity overrides dissent; the desire to conserve has overwhelmed the urge to alter. Such a state of affairs cries out for explanation." (Kagan, To the Final Conflict: Socialism in New York City, 1900-1933)

Kagan called the story of the socialist movement's demise "a sad one, but also a chastening one for those who, more than half a century after socialism's decline, still wish to change America ... In unity lies their only hope."

Elena Kagan spent a year working on her 1981 thesis, under the direction of Princeton historian Sean Wilentz.[871]

When news of the thesis recently sparked controversy, Wilentz came out in defense of his former student.

Said Wilentz:

105-6 Sean Wilentz

> "Sympathy for the movement of people who were trying to better their lives isn't something to look down on... Studying something doesn't necessarily mean that you endorse it. It means you're into it. That's what historians do...

> Elena Kagan is about the furthest thing from a socialist. Period! And always had been, Period!" (KeyWiki 2010)

> Few would be more qualified to identify a socialist than Sean Wilentz.

---

[871] http://keywiki.org/index.php/Sean_Wilentz

In May 1980, Princeton University's Progressive Forum sponsored a May Day rally, opposite the Firestone Library. An advertisement for the event in the Daily Princetonian, "Workers of Princeton unite for a May Day rally" named speakers as Sean Wilentz and Stanley Aronowitz - a prominent DSA leader.

Today, Sean Willentz serves on the Board of "Dissent Magazine,"[872] which is effectively a mouthpiece for Democratic Socialists of America.

Dissent's masthead is Marxist heavy and lists several well-known D.S.A. affiliates including

- Irving Howe - (Deceased)
- Joanne Barkan
- David Bensman
- Mitchell Cohen
- Maxine Phillips
- Mark Levinson
- Bogdan Denitch
- Erazim Kohak
- Deborah Meier
- Harold Meyerson
- Jo-Ann Mort
- Carol O'Clearicain - (NYC Finance Commissioner under David Dinkins)
- Cornel West – (a member of Barack Obama's 2008 Black Advisory Council.)

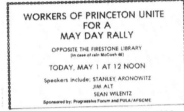

105-7 Daily Princetonian, May 1, 1980

One of Dissent's two editors is Elena Kagan's old roommate's dad, Michael Walzer. The other is Michael Kazin,[873] the historian of the Communist Party and a veteran of the 1969 Venceremos Brigade to Cuba.

At Princeton, Elena Kagan won a fellowship to Oxford University in England, where she studied "the history of British and European trade unionism." President Barack H. Obama himself has a long history with Democratic Socialists of America.[874]

[872] http://keywiki.org/index.php/Dissent
[873] http://keywiki.org/index.php/Michael_Kazin
[874] http://keywiki.org/index.php/Barack_Obama#tab=Democratic_Socialists_of_America

Is it possible that Elena Kagan shares similar associations? Should she be asked some questions on the subject?

106. Obama's Supreme Court Nominee, Elena Kagan's Socialist Associations (the Middle Years)

Trevor Loudon © Thursday, July 1, 2010

President Barack Obama's[875] Supreme Court appointment Elena Kagan[876] has a history of association with people tied to three interrelated organizations, the Communist Party USA,[877] Democratic Socialist Organizing Committee,[878] Democratic Socialists of America[879] and the far left Washington DC "think tank" Institute for Policy Studies.[880]

The previous Chapter looked at the radicals Kagan associated with during her college years at Princeton.

This post looks at two of Elena Kagan's employers post college:

Abner Mikva,[881] a former Congressman, Judge and White House official and Supreme Court Justice Thurgood Marshall.[882]

106-1 President Barack Obama (r), Elena Kagan (c), Vice President Joe

From 1986 to 1987, Elena Kagan worked as a Judicial Clerk for , Hon. Abner Mikva in the US Court of Appeals for the D.C. Circuit.

Usually regarded as a "liberal" or "progressive," Mikva in fact has a long history with the far left in both Washington DC and his Chicago base. Abner Mikva worked with Communist

[875] http://keywiki.org/index.php/Barack_Obama
[876] http://keywiki.org/index.php/Elena_Kagan
[877] http://keywiki.org/index.php/Communist_Party
[878] http://keywiki.org/index.php/Democratic_Socialist_Organizing_Committee
[879]
http://keywiki.org/index.php/Special:Search?search=democratic+Socialists+of+america&go=Go
[880] http://keywiki.org/index.php/Institute_for_Policy_Studies
[881] http://keywiki.org/index.php/Abner_Mikva
[882] http://keywiki.org/index.php/Thurgood_Marshall

Party supporters like Elias Snitzer and Sid Socolar, during his time at the University of Chicago Law School in the late 1940s.

From 1947, Mikva practiced labor law in Chicago in partnership with Arthur Goldberg,[883] general counsel for the communist dominated Congress of Industrial Organizations and the United Steelworkers of America.

Arthur Goldberg sponsored several Communist Party fronts in Chicago. These included the Chicago Conference on Race Relations, the Conference on Constitutional Liberties in America and the National Emergency Conference. Goldberg was also president of the Chicago chapter of the National Lawyers Guild,[884] accurately cited by Congressional investigators as "the foremost legal bulwark of the Communist Party."

106-2 Honorable Abner Mikva

President Lyndon Johnson later appointed Arthur Goldberg to the Supreme Court. In the 1950s, Mikva and his wife Zoe Mikva,[885] both worked with another communist infiltrated organization, American Civil Liberties Union (ACLU).

In the 1960s when first standing for Congress in South Chicago, Mikva worked closely with radical community organizer Saul Alinsky,[886] a man to whom President Obama owes a considerable intellectual debt.

Mikva also worked closely with two radical journalists who ran the *Hyde Park-Kenwood Voices*[887] newspaper, Don Rose[888] and his partner, Communist Party member David S. Canter,[889] who would become key Chicago power brokers. One whom they personally mentored and

[883] http://keywiki.org/index.php/Arthur_Goldberg
[884] http://keywiki.org/index.php/National_Lawyers_Guild
[885] http://keywiki.org/index.php/Zoe_Mikva
[886] http://keywiki.org/index.php/Saul_Alinsky
[887] http://keywiki.org/index.php/Hyde_Park_-_Kenwood_Voices
[888] http://keywiki.org/index.php/Don_Rose
[889] http://keywiki.org/index.php/David_Canter

106-3 Abner Mikva with Obama Poster 08'

promoted was a young journalist named David Axelrod,[890] who later became Barack Obama's key campaign strategist and now senior White House adviser.

In April 1975, the Communist Party controlled Chicago Peace Council[891] convened a "National conference for a drastic cutback in military spending" in the "Windy City."

The purpose of the National Conference is to mount a national campaign and a vigorous program of action which will speak to the hundreds of thousands who were part of the inspiring resistance to the war in Indo- China. The people of the US can and must turn this country around. (Chicago Peace Council 1975)

Speakers at the Conference included Congressman Abner Mikva, Richard Criley[892] and Norman Roth,[893] both members of the Communist Party and leaders of the very successful Party front group, Chicago Committee to Defend the Bill of Rights.[894] Ed Sadlowski,[895] of the United Steelworkers of America[896] and later identified as a member of Democratic Socialists of America, also spoke.

During the 1980s, Mikva was very close to the Institute for Policy Studies in Washington DC - a place where leftist Democrats and the occasional "liberal" Republican, mingled with socialists, communists, third world revolutionaries and East Bloc "diplomats."

Abner Mikva attended the organization's 20th anniversary celebrations on April 5, 1983. He was obligated, as his wife Zoe personally organized the affair. Abner Mikva was one of Barack Obama's early admirers, beginning in 1990 when he tried to hire the first Black president of the Harvard Law Review, for a clerkship. Obama turned Mikva down, saying he was going to move to Chicago and run for public

---

[890] http://keywiki.org/index.php/David_Axelrod
[891] http://keywiki.org/index.php/Chicago_Peace_Council
[892] http://keywiki.org/index.php/Richard_Criley
[893] http://keywiki.org/index.php/Norman_Roth
[894] http://keywiki.org/index.php/Chicago_Committee_to_Defend_the_Bill_of_Rights
[895] http://keywiki.org/index.php/Ed_Sadlowski
[896] http://keywiki.org/index.php/United_Steelworkers

office. Mikva was later close to both Barack Obama and Elena Kagan at the Chicago Law School where they all taught during the mid-1990s. Mikva acted as a mentor to Obama during his early political career.

Through all this, Abner and Zoe Mikva never forgot their Chicago communist and socialist friends. "Ab & Zoe Mikva" sent the message, ""Hooray for Progressives," to the Chicago Democratic Socialists of America 44th Annual Debs-Thomas-Harrington Dinner, May 10, 2002.

In 2006, Abner Mikva served on a committee to honor the life of Chicago Committee to Defend the Bill of Rights founder, Frank Wilkinson,[897] a forty-year Communist Party veteran turned Democratic Socialists of America comrade.

Serving on the Committee with Mikva were Obama friends, mentors and DSA members Dr. Quentin Young,[898] Timuel Black[899] and Congressman Danny Davis,[900] plus current or former Communist Party supporters Joan Elbert,[901] Ruth Emerson,[902] Yolanda Hall,[903] Peggy Lipschutz,[904] Bea Lumpkin,[905] Frank Lumpkin, Harold Rogers,[906] Norman Roth, Emile Schepers[907] and Tim Yeager.[908]

Congratulations Chicago DSA
On your Annual Debs-Thomas-Harrington Dinner.

Hooray for Progressives!!

Ab & Zoe Mikva

[897] http://keywiki.org/index.php/Frank_Wilkinson
[898] http://keywiki.org/index.php/Quentin_Young
[899] http://keywiki.org/index.php/Timuel_Black
[900] http://keywiki.org/index.php/Danny_Davis
[901] http://keywiki.org/index.php/Joan_Elbert
[902] http://keywiki.org/index.php/Ruth_Emerson
[903] http://keywiki.org/index.php/Yolanda_Hall
[904] http://keywiki.org/index.php/Peggy_Lipschutz
106-4 Celebrating Abner and Zoe Mikva

[907] http://keywiki.org/index.php/Emile_Schepers
[908] http://keywiki.org/index.php/Tim_Yeager

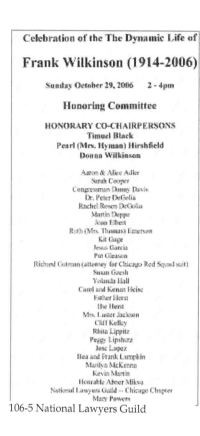

106-5 National Lawyers Guild

The National Lawyers Guild - Chicago chapter was also represented.

In 1987-1988 Elena Kagan worked as a Judicial Clerk for the Hon. Thurgood Marshall in the US Supreme Court.

Though sometimes mistakenly identified as an anti - communist, Thurgood Marshall had a radical past.

At the all Black Lincoln University in Chester County, Pennsylvania in the 1930s, Marshall's classmates included future socialist President of Ghana, Kwame Nkrumah and poet and author Langston Hughes,[909] later a close associate and fellow Communist Party comrade of Barack Obama's teenage mentor Frank Marshall Davis.[910]

In 1946, according to communist linked historian Herbert Shapiro,[911] Communist Party journalist Harry Raymond,[912] saved Marshall from a probable lynching near Columbia, Tennessee.

In the late 1940's, Thurgood Marshall was active in the leadership of at least two Communist Party infiltrated organizations, the American Civil Liberties Union (ACLU) and the National Lawyers Guild in which he served on the National Executive Board representing New York.

Other New York members of the National Lawyers Guild National Executive in 1949, included Communist Party members Leonard

---

[909] http://keywiki.org/index.php/Langston_Hughes
[910] http://keywiki.org/index.php/Frank_Marshall_Davis
[911] http://keywiki.org/index.php/Herbert_Shapiro
[912] http://keywiki.org/index.php/Harry_Raymond

Boudin,[913] Lee Pressman,[914] Henry (Harry) Sacher[915] and Abraham Unger.[916]

Lee Pressman was a fully-fledged Soviet spy, a member of the famous Ware Group,[917] which had operated inside the US government before and during World War II.

Leonard Boudin's daughter Kathie Boudin,[918] studied at Moscow University in 1966, before becoming a leader of the terrorist Weather Underground Organization with Bill Ayers[919] and Bernardine Dohrn.[920] After Boudin was jailed for her part in a botched 1981 robbery, which left three men dead, her son Chesa Boudin[921] was raised by Ayers and Dohrn.

It is likely that Barack Obama would have met Chesa Boudin through his friendship with Ayers and Dohrn.

In 1959, Kenyan independence activist and labor unionist, Tom Mboya, visited the US and met Thurgood Marshall. Mboya was so impressed with Marshall that he invited him to Kenya to help draft a new constitution for independent Kenya.

Marshall visited Kenya in 1960 on Mboya's invitation to attend a conference. His visit however did not impress the British and the American authorities, who considered him a radical. Under pressure from the British, the Kenyans barred Marshall from attending the conference.

However, it is Marshall's friendship with Mboya that is credited with a wave of Kenyan students coming to the US for further studies, beginning in the 1960s.

One of these students, a Marxist economist named Barak Obama Sr.,[922] studied in Hawaii, where he met 18-year-old Stanley Ann

---

[913] http://keywiki.org/index.php/Leonard_Boudin
[914] http://keywiki.org/index.php/Lee_Pressman
[915] http://keywiki.org/index.php/Henry_Sacher
[916] http://keywiki.org/index.php/Abraham_Unger
[917] http://keywiki.org/index.php/Ware_Group
[918] http://keywiki.org/index.php/Kathie_Boudin
[919] http://keywiki.org/index.php/Bill_Ayers
[920] http://keywiki.org/index.php/Bernardine_Dohrn
[921] http://keywiki.org/index.php/Chesa_Boudin
[922] http://keywiki.org/index.php/Barak_Obama

Dunham,[923] with whom he fathered a future president of the United States.

In 1965, President Lyndon Johnson appointed Judge Thurgood Marshall to the office of US Solicitor General, nominated to the United States Supreme Court in 1967.

Elena Kagan spent her youth in New York and Princeton mixing with people linked to the Communist Party, Democratic Socialist Organizing Committee/Democratic Socialists of America and the Institute for Policy Studies.

Elena Kagan's first two employers, Abner Mikva and Thurgood Marshall, also had similar connections.

Now Kagan is a Justice on the Supreme Court, chosen by a President with similar affiliations.[924]

Is there a pattern here?

107. Neil Abercrombie, Yet Another Covert Socialist in the Obama "Orbit"

Trevor Loudon © July 12, 2010

US Representative Neil Abercrombie[925] (D-HA-1st District) was a long time Hawaii Democratic Congressman and is currently running for the Governorship of that state.

While in Congress, Neil Abercrombie was one of Barack Obama's[926] earliest and most vocal supporters. This is not surprising, as there is a close Obama/Abercrombie family connection and seemingly many shared values.

107-1 President Obama and Governor Abercrombie

While studying at the University of Hawaii at Mānoa in the early 1960s,

---

[923] http://keywiki.org/index.php/Stanley_Ann_Dunham
[924] http://keywiki.org/index.php/Barack_Obama
[925] http://keywiki.org/index.php/Neil_Abercrombie
[926] http://keywiki.org/index.php/Barack_Obama

Abercrombie attended classes with and befriended current United States President Barack Obama's parents, Stanley Ann Dunham and the young Marxist economist Barak Obama, Sr.

107-2 Barak Obama Sr., and Barack Obama, Jr.

Neil Abercrombie claims to have been Barak Obama's "best" friend.

He also claims to have known young Barack Obama as a child and to know the values the future president of the United States was raised with.

There may be, however, another reason why Neil Abercrombie has been such a committed and zealous Obama supporter.

Barack Obama has close ties[927] to the US' largest Marxist based organization, Democratic Socialists of America (DSA).[928]

Obama attended socialist conferences in New York in the early 1980s at the Cooper Union the usual venue for the annual DSA organized Socialist Scholars Conferences.[929]

Barack Obama worked with DSA member Lou Pardo[930] on voter registration in Chicago in 1992. From 1993 to 1996, he was a member of the DSA influenced Progressive Chicago and its sister organization, the Chicago New Party.[931]

Obama addressed a DSA forum and the University of Chicago in February 1996 and earned a DSA endorsement for his Illinois State Senate run the same year.

Obama's friends and mentors include DSA members Quentin Young,[932] Timuel Black,[933] US Representative Danny K. Davis,[934] Cornel

[927] http://keywiki.org/index.php/Barack_Obama#tab=Democratic_Socialists_of_America
[928] http://keywiki.org/index.php/Democratic_Socialists_of_America
[929] http://keywiki.org/index.php/Socialist_Scholars_Conference
[930] http://keywiki.org/index.php/Lou_pardo
[931] http://keywiki.org/index.php/Barack_Obama#tab=New_Party.2FProgressive_Chicago
[932] http://keywiki.org/index.php/Quentin_Young
[933] http://keywiki.org/index.php/Timuel_Black
[934] http://keywiki.org/index.php/Danny_K_Davis

West[935] and the late Rabbi Arnold Jacob Wolf.[936]

Obama has appointed several DSA connected individuals to positions of authority including Transition Team member and former Democrat Party whip, US Representative David Bonior,[937] Labor Secretary Hilda Solis[938] and Senior Advisor to the Under Secretary of Defense and daughter of DSA leader Barbara Ehrenreich,[939] Rosa Brooks.[940]

Now it turns out that Neil Abercrombie also has DSA ties. He has almost certainly been a covert member of that organization.

According to the Nov/Dec. 1990, "*Democratic Left*" magazine on page 4, in 1990 the DSA Political Action Committee endorsed two Congressional candidates:

> "DSAer Democrat Neil Abercrombie seeking to regain the House seat representing Honolulu and Vermont independent candidate Bernie Sanders...." (Democratic Left 1990)

Does the phrase "DSAer Democrat" imply that Abercrombie was a member of that organization? Or was he simply a close associate and supporter like US Senator Bernie Sanders[941] -

Election Endorsements

The DSANPAC has endorsed two congressional candidates: DSA'er Democrat Neil Abercrombie seeking to regain the House seat representing Honolulu, Hawaii, and independent socialist Bernie Sanders making his second bid for Vermont's lone House seat against frosh congressman Republican Peter Smith, who beat Sanders in a close

107-3 Democratic Left Nov/Dec 1990, Page 4

also coincidentally a strong Obama supporter?

According to the Winter 2007, "*Democratic Left*" magazine, Neil Abercrombie and DSA and Communist Party USA[942] connected Congressman Dennis Kucinich[943] spoke at a Democratic Socialists of America Political Action Committee event in Washington DC at the

---

[935] http://keywiki.org/index.php/Cornel_West
[936] http://keywiki.org/index.php/Arnold_Jacob_Wolf
[937] http://keywiki.org/index.php/David_Bonior
[938] http://keywiki.org/index.php/Hilda_Solis
[939] http://keywiki.org/index.php/Barbara_Ehrenreich
[940] http://keywiki.org/index.php/Rosa_Brooks
[941] http://keywiki.org/index.php/Bernie_Sanders
[942] http://keywiki.org/index.php/Communist_Party_USA
[943] http://keywiki.org/index.php/Dennis_Kucinich

home of leftist "philanthropist" Stewart Mott.[944] The event was in support of Bernie Sanders.

> He (Sanders)flew to Washington and the next day attended the Washington, D.C., DSA PAC party at the home of Stewart Mott. Not only did Bernie Sanders speak; so did members of Congress Neil Abercrombie (HI) and Dennis Kucinich (OH). Christine Riddiough, former DSA National Director, served as host/ moderator'. (Democratic Left)

Neil Abercrombie was also a member of the radical Congressional Progressive Caucus,[945] which was founded by Bernie Sanders, with the help of DSA.

George (Skip) Roberts,[946] who has long served as a DSA rep to the Socialist International, has also worked as an aide to Congressman Abercrombie. In recent years, Roberts has been active in the Republican Party representing his boss, then SEIU[947] president, Andy Stern.[948]

More conclusive proof of Abercrombie's ties to DSA, is the fact that his wife Nancie Caraway,[949] an academic, noted for her far left views, has also been a DSA member.

Dr. Nancie Caraway

In 1985, Dr. Nancie Caraway of Hawaii was listed as a member of the Feminist Commission of the Democratic Socialists of America.

In 2008, Ehrenreich founded Progressives for Obama,[950] with DSA comrades Bill Fletcher, Jr.,[951] and Tim Carpenter.[952]

Nancie Caraway is also a big Obama supporter.

107-4 Dr. Nancie Caraway

At   Hawaii's   Democratic   Party

[944] http://keywiki.org/index.php/Stewart_Mott
[945] http://keywiki.org/index.php/Congressional_Progressive_Caucus
[946] http://keywiki.org/index.php/George_Roberts
[947] http://keywiki.org/index.php/Service_Employees_International_Union
[948] http://keywiki.org/index.php/Andrew_Stern
[949] http://keywiki.org/index.php/Nancie_Caraway
[950] http://keywiki.org/index.php/Progressives_for_Obama
[951] http://keywiki.org/index.php/Bill_Fletcher%2C_Jr.
[952] http://keywiki.org/index.php/Tim_Carpenter#Activism

headquarters, on Hawaii primary election night, February 2008, Caraway said there were upwards of 5,000 people in her polling station. She described the turnout as inspirational. "I'm a postmodernist cynic," she said. "This is a new page in American political culture." At the "request of the Obama Administration," Dr. Caraway currently serves as a consultant to US Ambassador Luis C. de Baca[953] in the Office to Monitor and Combat Trafficking in Persons.

107-5 Kurt Stand convicted Soviet spy

To my knowledge, US Representative Neil Abercrombie (D-HA-1st District) has never declared his affiliation with the DSA Marxists to the voters of Hawaii.

Perhaps he was concerned they might unnecessarily worry as to where his true allegiances lay.

While an ardent opponent of almost every US War from Vietnam to Iraq, Abercrombie finished his Congressional term as Chair of the Armed Forces Subcommittee on Air and Land Forces.

It would be interesting to know if Abercrombie ever declared his socialist affiliations to government security bodies before accepting this sensitive post.

It is worth noting that DSA affiliated senator Bernie Sanders addressed a conference of the Communist Party USA controlled and Soviet affiliated US Peace Council[954] in November 1989, with then DSA leader Manning Marable[955] and DSA affiliate Holly Sklar.[956]

It is also worth noting that 1990s DSA National Political Committee member and Obama admirer, Kurt Stand,[957] is currently serving a very long jail sentence for spying for the former Soviet Union and East Germany.

As an aspiring Governor of Hawaii, President Obama's old family

[953] http://keywiki.org/index.php/Luis_C._de_Baca
[954] http://keywiki.org/index.php/U.S._Peace_Council
[955] http://keywiki.org/index.php/Manning_Marable
[956] http://keywiki.org/index.php/Holly_Sklar
[957] http://keywiki.org/index.php/Kurt_Stand

friend and supporter, Neil Abercrombie, needs to answer some serious questions.

108. Pro Obama "JournoLista" Outed - New "Can of Worms" Opened

Trevor Loudon © Tuesday, July 27, 2010

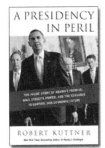

108-1 A Presidency in Peril

JournoList[958] was an email group of approximately four hundred journalists, bloggers and academics, who reportedly worked to influence news reporting in favor of US Senator Barack Obama[959] and the Democratic Party during and after the 2008 Presidential elections.

The latest list of alleged "Journolistas" has turned up a very interesting name - Robert Kuttner[960] of The

108-2 Robert Kuttner

American Prospect.[961] This man is no basement blogger or CNN hack. He is the author of two books on the President and is connected to some of Obama's most influential enablers.

Robert Kuttner's March 2008 *"Obama's Challenge: American's Economic Crisis and the Power of a Transformative Presidency"* is a call to use the Obama presidency to change America in a more "progressive" direction.

According to leftist "think tank" DEMOS:[962]

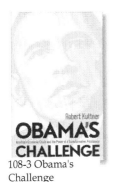

108-3 Obama's Challenge

In this urgent and important book, DEMOS Distinguished Senior Fellow Robert Kuttner, co-founder of The American Prospect, explains what a President Obama must do to solve America's economic crisis—the gravest since the Great

[958] http://newzeal.blogspottrevorloudon.com/2010/07/socialist-journolistas.html/
[959] http://keywiki.org/index.php/Barack_Obama
[960] http://keywiki.org/index.php/Robert_Kuttner
[961] http://keywiki.org/index.php/The_American_Prospect
[962] http://keywiki.org/index.php/DEMOS

Depression–and, in the process, become a truly transformative leader. (DEMOS 2010)

Kuttner's March 2010 book *"A Presidency in Peril"* , is an acknowledgement that Obama hasn't entirely lived up to some "progressive's" hopes, but that things could yet still be salvaged;

From DEMOS:

> In this hard-hitting, incisive account, DEMOS Distinguished Senior Fellow Robert Kuttner (author of the New York Times' Obama's Challenge Best-Selling) shares his unique, insider view of how the Obama administration not only missed its moment to turn our economy around-but deepened Wall Street's risky grip on America's future. Carefully constructing a one-year history of the problem, the players, and the outcome, Kuttner gives readers an unparalleled account of the president's first year. (DEMOS 2010)

Kuttner shows how we could, with swift, decisive action, still enact real reforms; and, how Barack Obama could redeem his promise.

The phrase "insider view" suggests DEMOS believes that Kuttner has some kind of access to Obama Administration thinking and policy.

That view is probably accurate. Back in 1999, then obscure IL State Senator Barack Obama, was brought to New York to help establish a new organization.

DEMOS was founded by "social entrepreneur" Charles Halpern.[963] Most of Halpern's recruits to DEMOS were well known politicians or activists - except Barack Obama.

By 1999, from the DEMOS website,[964] Halpern had assembled a talented working group to develop DEMOS. Among them were:

- David Callahan – (a fellow at the Century Foundation)
- Rob Fersh – (a long-time policy advocate)
- Stephen Heintz –(Vice-President of the East-West Institute)
- Sara Horowitz – (founder of Working Today)
- Arnie Miller – (a leading executive recruiter)
- Barack Obama – (then a state senator from Illinois)

---

[963] http://keywiki.org/index.php/Charles_Halpern
[964] http://www.DEMOS.org/backgrounder.cfm

108-4 Van Jones

- David Skaggs – (a congressional representative from Colorado)
- Linda Tarr-Whelan – (an internationally recognized expert on women and economic development)

This working group would eventually form the core of DEMOS' staff and Board of Trustees.

Barack Obama was an early DEMOS trustee, as was some years later another obscure young radical, this time from San Francisco, named Van Jones.[965]

Interestingly, DEMOS staffer, Chuck Collins,[966] in a September 26, 2008 article, posted several names he thought would make suitable appointments for an Obama administration.

One of them was:

"Van Jones, of the Ella Baker Center, to direct the Commerce Department's new "green jobs initiative..." (Collins 2008)

Collins was incidentally, a founder of the radical New Party,[967] which Obama joined[968] in the early/mid 1990s in Chicago.

Kuttner and Obama have something else in common - a close relationship to America's largest Marxist based organization Democratic Socialists of America.[969]

To quote DSA connected "JournoLista" Joel Bleifuss:[970]

In particular, Obama can be linked to the Democratic Socialists of America (DSA), the Democratic Party-oriented organization that is a member of the Socialist International (KeyWiki 2010)

Obama has been close to D.S.A., possibly back to the early 1980s. Certainly key Obama friends and allies such as Quentin Young, Timuel

---

[965] http://keywiki.org/index.php/Van_Jones
[966] http://keywiki.org/index.php/Chuck_Collins
[967] http://keywiki.org/index.php/New_Party
[968] http://keywiki.org/index.php/Barack_Obama_and_the_New_Party/Progressive_Chicago
[969] http://keywiki.org/index.php/Democratic_Socialists_of_America
[970] http://keywiki.org/index.php/Joel_Bleifuss

Black, the late Rabbi Arnold Jacob Wolf, Cornel West, Congressmen Danny K. Davis and Neil Abercrombie have been "DSAers." Other D.S.A types, such as Eliseo Medina, Harry Boyte and David Bonior, have worked on Obama's campaign or in his Administration.

Kuttner's ties to Democratic Socialists of America go back almost as far as Obama's.

In November 1989, Robert Kuttner addressed the DSA November 1989 National Convention in Maryland, on "the state of domestic politics."

In 1990, Democratic Socialists of America was selling a list of pamphlets, including "*Democratic Promise: Ideas for Turning America in a Progressive Direction,*" by DSA founder Michael Harrington,[971] William Julius Wilson[972] and Robert Kuttner.[973]

William Julius Wilson, incidentally, addressed a Democratic Socialists of America organized forum[974] at the University of Chicago, with Obama in early 1996.

> Over three hundred people attended the first of two Town Meetings on Economic Insecurity on February 25 in Ida Noyes Hall at the University of Chicago. Entitled "Employment and Survival in Urban America," the meeting was sponsored by the UofC DSA Youth Section, Chicago DSA and University Democrats.

> The panelists were Toni Preckwinkle, Alderman of Chicago's 4th Ward, Barack Obama, candidate for the 13th Illinois Senate District, Professor William Julius Wilson, Center for the Study of Urban Inequality at the University of Chicago, Professor Michael Dawson, University of Chicago and Professor Joseph Schwartz, Temple University and a member of DSA's National Political Committee. (Roman, A Town Meeting on Economic Insecurity: Employment and Survival in Urban America 1996)

In 1998, Robert Kuttner was honored at a Boston Democratic Socialists of America awards ceremony alongside DSA member

---

[971] http://keywiki.org/index.php/Michael_Harrington
[972] http://keywiki.org/index.php/William_Julius_Wilson
[973] http://keywiki.org/index.php/Robert_Kuttner
[974] http://www.chicagodsa.org/ngarchive/ng45.html

Deborah Meier.[975] In March that year, Deborah Meier spoke at a Chicago memorial Service for "DSAer" Saul Mendelson,[976] as did Barack Obama.

In 1998 Democratic Socialists of America described Kuttner as a "socialist."

> American Prospect The journal of "liberal" intellectual politics, though half of the writers, and one of the co-founders, Robert Kuttner, are socialists. This journal sees its mission as the reinvigoration of "liberalism," betraying a clear disregard for liberalism's expressed desire to accept death

> So far at least eight identified "JournoListas," have ties to Kuttner's, "The American Prospect." (The American Prospect 1998)

In 1996, Robert Kuttner helped found, with at least two dozen "D.S.Aers," the highly influential "progressive" umbrella group Campaign for America's Future (CAF).[977]

Fellow Campaign for America's Future founders Robert Borosage, John Cavanagh, Barbara Ehrenreich (D.S.A.), Frances Fox Piven (D.S.A.), Mark Ritchie (a Communist Party "friend") and Joel Rogers had helped establish Obama's New Party.

Campaign for America's Future founders Tom Hayden[978] and Barbara Ehrenreich went on to found, in 2008, Progressives for Obama,[979] which was supported by other CAF/DSA supporters Dick Flacks,[980] Todd Gitlin,[981] Adam Hochschild,[982] Frances Fox Piven[983] and Stanley Sheinbaum.[984]

Besides Kuttner, three other C.A.F. founders, James Galbraith,[985] Todd Gitlin[986] and Michael Kazin,[987] would later turn up as "JournoListas."

---

[975] http://keywiki.org/index.php/Deborah_Meier
[976] http://keywiki.org/index.php/Saul_Mendelson
[977] http://keywiki.org/index.php/Campaign_for_America%27s_Future
[978] http://keywiki.org/index.php/Tom_Hayden
[979] http://keywiki.org/index.php/Progressives_for_Obama
[980] http://keywiki.org/index.php/Dick_Flacks
[981] http://keywiki.org/index.php/Todd_Gitlin
[982] http://keywiki.org/index.php/Adam_Hochschild
[983] http://keywiki.org/index.php/Frances_Fox_Piven
[984] http://keywiki.org/index.php/Stanley_Sheinbaum
[985] http://keywiki.org/index.php/James_Galbraith
[986] http://keywiki.org/index.php/Todd_Gitlin
[987] http://keywiki.org/index.php/Michael_Kazin

Campaign for America's Future, has run for several years the successful Take Back America[988] and America's Future Now![989] Conferences, which annually attract the cream of the US "progressive" movement, including many "DSAers," "JournoLista's," Robert Kuttner and then Senator Barack Obama.

108-5 Take Back America

Earlier this year, Robert Kuttner was serving on the Advisory Board of the Cry Wolf Project.[990] This organization caused some controversy after it was found to be offering money to academics for articles countering conservative attacks on "progressive" programs.

Serving on the advisory board with Kuttner was Janice Fine[991] of Rutgers University, an early founder of the New Party and a member of the Editorial Advisory group of Wade Rathke's[992] DSA/ACORN[993] linked journal *Social Policy*.[994]

108-6 Robert Kuttner

Cry Wolf's three co-leaders were "DSAers" Peter Dreier,[995] Nelson Lichtenstein[996] and Donald Cohen,[997] a member of the Board of Directors of Van Jones' Oakland based Green for All.[998]

Another close tie to the Obama Administration comes through Kuttner's membership on the board of the Economic Policy Institute.[999]

The Washington based "think tank" is led by "DSAer" Larry

[988] http://keywiki.org/index.php/Take_Back_America
[989] http://keywiki.org/index.php/America%27s_Future_Now%21
[990] http://keywiki.org/index.php/Cry_Wolf_Project
[991] http://keywiki.org/index.php/Janice_Fine
[992] http://keywiki.org/index.php/Wade_Rathke
[993] http://keywiki.org/index.php/ACORN
[994] http://keywiki.org/index.php/Social_Policy
[995] http://keywiki.org/index.php/Peter_Dreier
[996] http://keywiki.org/index.php/Nelson_Lichtenstein
[997] http://keywiki.org/index.php/Donald_Cohen
[998] http://keywiki.org/index.php/Green_For_All
[999] http://keywiki.org/index.php/Economic_Policy_Institute

Mishel[1000] and boasts several DSA affiliates on its board, including Barry Bluestone, Teresa Ghilarducci (a Demos fellow), Julianne Malveaux and Bruce Raynor. New Party founder Larry Cohen[1001] and Campaign for America's Future founders Thomas Buffenbarger, Jeff Faux, Ray Marshall, Gerald McEntee, Robert Reich, Andy Stern (also Progressives for Obama) and Richard Trumka also serve.

Figure 108-7 Jared Bernstein

Two Economic Policy Institute board members have joined the Obama administration, William Spriggs[1002] as a Senior Adviser in the Department of Labor and Rebecca Blank[1003] as Under Secretary for Economic Affairs in the Department of Commerce.

More importantly long time EPI staffer and "JournoLista" Jared Bernstein[1004] has served as an Obama campaign adviser and currently works for Vice President Joe Biden.[1005]

Leftist economist and "Journalista" Paul Krugman,[1006] argued in November '08 that, given the "centrist makeup" of President Barack Obama's economic inner circle, the new Economic Recovery Advisory Board could be used to "give progressive economists a voice." Krugman also mentioned Jared Bernstein and fellow E.P.I economist, and E.P.I. president, "DSAer" Larry Mishel[1007] as "progressive economists" who might be suitable for the board.

The Biden appointment was a step in that direction.

Were the "Journolistas" really just a "chat group," or did they serve a larger role as a conduit of information to and from the Obama Administration?

1000 http://keywiki.org/index.php/Lawrence_Mishel
1001 http://keywiki.org/index.php/Larry_Cohen
1002 http://keywiki.org/index.php/William_Spriggs
1003 http://keywiki.org/index.php/Rebecca_Blank
1004 http://keywiki.org/index.php/Jared_Bernstein
1005 http://keywiki.org/index.php/Joe_Biden
1006 http://keywiki.org/index.php/Paul_Krugman
1007 http://keywiki.org/index.php/Lawrence_Mishel

Did some of their members actually have some influence on policy and/or appointments within the Obama Administration?

Was JournoList, an intelligence and influence brokering network for the Obama campaign and Administration?

Somebody needs to ask Robert Kuttner and other "Journolistas" some serious questions.

109. "JournoList" - the Soros, Google, Free Press and Obama Connections

Trevor Loudon © Monday, August 2, 2010

JournoList was an email group of up to four hundred prominent US journalists, academics and "new media" activists, who reportedly colluded in the run up to the 2008 election, to influence public opinion in favor of Barack Obama and the Democrats and against their Republican opponents.

Many "JournoListas" were involved with Marxist based organizations[1008] such as Democratic Socialists of America,[1009] or the far left Institute for Policy Studies.[1010]

Some, like Robert Kuttner[1011] of The American Prospect,[1012] had close ties to the Obama campaign and Administration.[1013]

An overlapping group of "JournoListas," at least eight strong were centered on another organization, which has close ties to the three highly influential power centers - financier and "change agent" George Soros,[1014] internet giant Google and DC based nonprofit Free Press[1015] - accused by its opponents of aiding Obama Administration attempts to censor and manipulate information on the internet.

[1008] http://trevorloudon.com/2010/07/socialist-journolistas/

[1009] http://keywiki.org/index.php/Democratic_Socialists_of_America

[1010] http://keywiki.org/index.php/Institute_for_Policy_Studies

[1011] http://keywiki.org/index.php/Robert_Kuttner

[1012] http://keywiki.org/index.php/The_American_Prospect

[1013] Chapter 108 - Pro Obama "JournoLista" Outed – New "Can of Worms" Opened

[1014] http://keywiki.org/index.php/George_Soros

[1015] http://keywiki.org/index.php/Free_Press#Board

109-1 New America Foundation

The organization in question, the Washington DC based New America Foundation[1016] has close ties to the Obama Administration, stretching back to Obama's alma mater Occidental College in the early 1980s.

While claiming to be non-partisan, New America clearly leans left:

The New America Foundation is a nonprofit, nonpartisan public policy institute that invests in new thinkers and new ideas to address the next generation of challenges facing the United States. The foundation's mission is animated by the American ideal that each generation will live better than the last. That ideal is today under strain. Our education and health care systems are struggling with problems of quality, cost and access. The country requires creative means to address its fiscal challenges and pay for needed public, social and environmental investments. Abroad, the United States has yet to fashion sustainable foreign and defense policies that will protect its citizens and interests in a rapidly integrating world. (New America Foundation 1999)

109-2 Frida Berrigan

This is "progressive" code for domestic socialism, paid for out of a decreased defense budget.

Frida Berrigan[1017] is Senior Program Associate of the Arms and Security Initiative at the New America Foundation.[1018]

In 2007, Berrigan represented the socialist dominated War Registers League[1019] on the Steering Committee of the communist dominated United for Peace and Justice.[1020] In 2009, Frida Berrigan was a Contributing Editor and a member of the Editorial Board of Chicago

---

[1016] http://keywiki.org/index.php/New_America_Foundation
[1017] http://keywiki.org/index.php/Frida_Berrigan
[1018] http://keywiki.org/index.php/New_America_Foundation
[1019] http://keywiki.org/index.php/War_Resisters_League
[1020] http://keywiki.org/index.php/United_for_Peace_and_Justice

based socialist journal, *"In These Times."*[1021]
There she served alongside former Weather
Underground terrorists and Obama associates
Bill Ayers[1022] and Bernardine Dohrn.[1023] Also
Sid Hollander[1024] of Democratic Socialists of
America and David Moberg,[1025] a veteran of
the Gramsci-Marxist New American
Movement.[1026] Moberg organized the 1976
Weather Underground "National Hard Times
Conference."[1027]

109-3 Parag Khanna

Parag Khanna,[1028] Senior Research Fellow,
American Strategy Program and Director,
Global Governance Initiative, at New America, provided "expert" foreign
policy advice and opinion to Barack Obama's Presidential campaign.[1029]

Khanna also spoke at the "Change the World" conference, hosted by
British Fabian Socialist Society[1030] on January 19, 2008.

The eight known "JournoListas" affiliated to the New America
Foundation are:

- Shannon Brownlee[1031] - (Senior Research Fellow, Economic Growth
  Program, N.A.F. A former senior editor at *US News & World Report*,
  her work has appeared in a wide variety of publications including
  the *Atlantic Monthly, Discover, Glamour, More, Mother Jones, New York
  Times Magazine, The New Republic, Slate, Time, Washington Monthly,
  Washington Post* and the *Los Angeles Times*)

- Michael A. Cohen[1032] - (Former Co-Director, Privatization of Foreign
  Policy Initiative, N.A.F. Cohen's work has appeared in the
  Washington Post, Christian Science Monitor, the *St. Petersburg Times,*

[1021] http://keywiki.org/index.php/In_These_Times
[1022] http://keywiki.org/index.php/Bill_Ayers
[1023] http://keywiki.org/index.php/Bernardine_Dohrn
[1024] http://keywiki.org/index.php/Sidney_Hollander
[1025] http://keywiki.org/index.php/David_Moberg
[1026] http://keywiki.org/index.php/New_American_Movement
[1027] http://keywiki.org/index.php/Hard_Times_Conference
[1028] http://keywiki.org/index.php/Parag_Khanna
[1029] http://keywiki.org/index.php/Barack_Obama
[1030] http://keywiki.org/index.php/UK_Fabian_Society
[1031] http://keywiki.org/index.php/Shannon_Brownlee
[1032] http://keywiki.org/index.php/Michael_A._Cohen

the *World Policy Journal*, the *New York Times, Foreign Policy*, the *New York Daily News, Forbes.com, Courier de la Planete, Talkingpointsmemo.com, Politico, Worth Magazine* and he is a frequent blogger at www.democracyarsenal.org. During the 2008 US presidential campaign he was a regular contributor to the *New York Times Campaign Stops blog*. He has also been featured on *ABC News, Fox News, BBC TV* and radio, *South African television, Al Jazeera, Air America* and XM Radio's *Potus '08*)

- Tim Fernholz[1033] - (Research Fellow, Asset Building Program N.A.F., Writing Fellow of The American Prospect[1034])

- Christopher Hayes[1035] - (Christopher Hayes: Schwartz Fellow N.A.F. Former senior editor of *In These Times*,[1036] Washington editor of *The Nation*.[1037] In April 2010, Hayes spoke at a Georgetown University, seminar *"Labor, the Left and Progressives in the Obama Era"* with Barbara Ehrenreich,[1038] Gerry Hudson[1039] and Harold Meyerson[1040] of Democratic Socialists of America and fellow "JournoLista" and DSA associate Michael Kazin.[1041])

- Daniel Levy[1042] - (Senior Research Fellow, American Strategy Program and Co-Director, Middle East Task Force N.A.F. During the Barak Government of 1999-2001, Levy worked in the Israeli Prime Minister's Office as special adviser and head of Jerusalem Affairs, following which Mr Levy worked as senior policy adviser to then Israeli Minister of Justice, Yossi Beilin. In this capacity he was responsible for coordinating policy on various issues including peace negotiations, civil and human rights, and the Palestinian minority in Israel. He is a Founder of the Democratic Socialists of America influenced JStreet[1043] organization)

- Sara Mead[1044] - (Senior Research Fellow, Education Policy Program and Workforce and Family Program, N.A.F)

[1033] http://keywiki.org/index.php/Tim_Fernholz
[1034] http://keywiki.org/index.php/The_American_Prospect
[1035] http://keywiki.org/index.php/Christopher_Hayes
[1036] http://keywiki.org/index.php/In_These_Times
[1037] http://keywiki.org/index.php/The_Nation
[1038] http://keywiki.org/index.php/Barbara_Ehrenreich
[1039] http://keywiki.org/index.php/Gerry_Hudson
[1040] http://keywiki.org/index.php/Harold_Meyerson
[1041] http://keywiki.org/index.php/Michael_Kazin
[1042] http://keywiki.org/index.php/Daniel_Levy
[1043] http://keywiki.org/index.php/JStreet
[1044] http://keywiki.org/index.php/Sara_Mead

- Mark Schmitt[1045] - (Senior Research Fellow, American Strategy Program N.A.F. Former Director of Policy and Research at George Soros' Open Society Institute[1046])

- Steven Teles[1047] - (Schwartz Fellow N.A.F., writer for *The American Prospect*. Associate Professor of Political Science at Johns Hopkins University. He is currently writing a book on how politics affects policymaking)

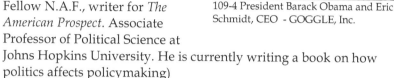

109-4 President Barack Obama and Eric Schmidt, CEO - GOGGLE, Inc.

- Tim Wu – (Another New American Foundation Schwartz fellow is a professor at Columbia Law School and the Chairman of Free Press. He is the co-author of *Who Controls the Internet?*)

Marxist Robert W. McChesney founded Free Press in 2002.[1048] Free Press[1049] has the ear of the Obama Administration and is responsible for a report written by McChesney and Democratic Socialists of America associate and "Free Presser" John Nichols entitled, "*National Journalism Strategy*" which calls for "massive public intervention" into the news business.

At Chicago D.S.A's 2006 awards dinner, John Nichols of The Nation, spoke to the "need to go beyond taking back our country, beyond things just not getting worse and the need for a progressive agenda."

Chair of the New American Foundation Board of Directors and a member of the N.A.F. Leadership Council is none other than Eric Schmidt,[1050] Chairman & CEO, Google, Inc.

Schmidt is a member of President Obama's Council of Advisors on Science and Technology.

There is another, more obscure Obama/Google connection. A

[1045] http://keywiki.org/index.php/Mark_Schmitt
[1046] http://keywiki.org/index.php/Open_Society_Institute
[1047] http://keywiki.org/index.php/Steven_Teles
[1048] http://keywiki.org/index.php/Robert_McChesney
[1049] http://en.wikipedia.org/wiki/Free_Press_(organization)
[1050] http://keywiki.org/index.php/Eric_Schmidt

109-5 Johnathan Soros

couple of years ago, Google appointed Dr. John Lumpkin[1051] to its Health Advisory Council. John Lumpkin came from a well-known Chicago Communist Party family. However, John Lumpkin unsuccessfully stood for Alderman in Chicago's seventh Ward in 1979. Several Communist Party members, as well as activists Timuel Black[1052] and Dr. Quentin Young,[1053] led the "Committee to Elect Dr. John R. Lumpkin."

Black and Young both went on to join Democratic Socialists of America. Both also became friends, mentors and political supporters of Barack Obama. Quentin Young was Obama's personal physician at one stage and attended the famous meeting where Obama's political career began in the home of Bill Ayers and Bernardine Dohrn.

Serving with Eric Schmidt on the N.A.F. Leadership Council is Jonathan Soros,[1054] President & Co-Deputy Chairman, Soros Fund Management, LLC.

Jonathan Soros serves on the board of directors of his father's Open Society Institute (OSI).[1055] Before graduate school, Johnathan was a program manager at O.S.I. in Budapest. He also served as a staff member on the Clinton/Gore '92 campaign and inaugural committees.

The Open Society Institute funded the New America Foundation to the tune of at least $250,000 in 2008.

President and CEO of the New America Foundation is Steve Coll.[1056]

[1051] http://keywiki.org/index.php/John_Lumpkin
[1052] http://keywiki.org/index.php/Timuel_Black
[1053] http://keywiki.org/index.php/Quentin_Young
[1054] http://keywiki.org/index.php/Jonathan_Soros
[1055] http://keywiki.org/index.php/Open_Society_Institute
[1056] http://keywiki.org/index.php/Steve_Coll

It turns out the Steve Coll and his wife, Susan Keselenko Coll[1057] were good friends of Barack Obama back at Occidental College in the 1980s.

In February 2008, in response to accusations that Obama had used drugs while a student journalist and blogger at *"The Washington Note,"* Steve Clemons,[1058] interviewed Steve and Susan Coll about Obama's drug use at the time without mentioning his connection to Steve Coll.

> A separate couple I found on my own and who knew Barack Obama at Occidental College are New America Foundation President and New Yorker staff writer Steve Coll and his wife, Susan. I asked Coll what the depth of his and his wife's relationship with Obama was – and whether he'd seen the presidential aspirant get "wild."

> Coll told me that he was two years, and his wife one year ahead of Barack and that they were all good friends.
>
> They are friends now, but at a more pronounced distance and do not see each other much.
>
> Coll recounted that he and Susan were impressed with Obama then and saw absolutely nothing on the drug front with him -

109-6 Steve Coll President-CEO New America Foundation

> - though he can't say the same about a lot of his other Oxy pals. He said that his one wild thing that got him many accolades was his hard lobbying to get the trustees to divest Occidental College holdings from South Africa, which they did.

Steve Clemons is the Senior Fellow and Director of the American Strategy Program at the New America Foundation. Could he be one of the more than 200 unidentified "JournoListas?"

Clemons is also contributor to the website Havana Notes, which is dedicated to easing US government sanctions against Cuba, alongside one time Democratic Socialists of America member Patrick Doherty,[1059]

[1057] http://www.keywiki.org/index.php/Susan_Coll
[1058] http://keywiki.org/index.php/Steven_Clemons
[1059] http://www.keywiki.org/index.php/Patrick_C._Doherty

Anya Landau French,[1060] (both of the New America Foundation) and longtime pro-Cuban propagandist Gail Reed.

109-7 Susan Keselenko

Had Clemons delved a little deeper, he might have found that Steve and Susan Coll hung around with leftists like Caroline Boss[1061] and Rick Cole[1062] at Occidental. Many of their friends were involved with Occidental's "Democratic Socialist Alliance," which in turn had ties with the radical New American Movement and the Democratic Socialist Organizing Committee[1063] - which amalgamated to form Democratic Socialists of America in 1982.

Susan Keselenko took classes with Barack Obama from Prof. Roger Boesche[1064] who is also a socialist, a proponent of the radical philosopher John Rawls.

Today Susan Coll is a writer, the author of novels *"Rockville Pike"* and *"KarlMarx.com."*

It seems that the concept of leftist journalists and writers covering their friends is not limited to confirmed "Journolistas."

The "JournoListas" who helped Barack Obama into the White House are not unique. They are merely part of a movement to promote a promising young leftist that may have begun more than thirty years ago.

Without sympathetic socialist journalists, it is unlikely that Barack Obama would be President of the United States today.

[1060] http://www.keywiki.org/index.php/Anya_Landau_French
[1061] http://www.keywiki.org/index.php/Caroline_Boss
[1062] http://www.keywiki.org/index.php/Rick_Cole
[1063] http://keywiki.org/index.php/Democratic_Socialist_Organizing_Committee
[1064] http://keywiki.org/index.php/Roger_Boesche

110. Collusion! How Socialist Harold Meyerson Kick Started the Obama Propaganda Machine

Trevor Loudon © Tuesday, August 3, 2010

Barack Obama owes his political career to three Marxist organizations, Communist Party USA, Committees of Correspondence for Democracy and Socialism and Democratic Socialists of America.

Of the three, Obama's decades of old ties to Democratic Socialists of America are documented.

Part of this support has come in the form of favorable media stories about Obama and in orchestrated attacks against his opponents. It is no coincidence that several members of the recently exposed, pro-Obama JournoList had close ties to DSA.

Harold Meyerson[1065] is both a leading US journalist and a Vice Chair of Democratic Socialists of America.

110-1 Collusion!

Meyerson is an op-ed columnist for the *Washington Post* and is the editor-at-large at *The American Prospect*.[1066]

While not an identified member of JournoList, Meyerson is professionally and politically associated with several members.

- *Washington Post* "JournoListas" so far identified include - Alec McGillis, Greg Sargent, and Dave Weigel,
- *The American Prospect* "Journolistas" include - Spencer Ackerman, Dean Baker, Sam Boyd, Tim Fernholz, John Judis, Ezra Klein (JournoList founder), Mark Schmitt, Adam Serwer, Robert Kuttner (author of two books

110-2 Harold Meyerson

[1065] http://keywiki.org/index.php/Harold_Meyerson
[1066] http://keywiki.org/index.php/The_American_Prospect

on the Obama Administration) and Paul Waldman
- Democratic Socialists of America affiliated "JournoListas" include - Joel Bleifuss, Todd Gitlin, a Progressives for Obama supporter), John Judis, Michael Kazin, Scott McLemee, Rick Perlstein, Katha Pollitt (Feminists for Peace and Barack Obama) endorser and Robert Kuttner

On April 6, 2010, a seminar *"Labor, the Left, and Progressives in the Obama Era"* was held at Georgetown University - further evidence of D.S.A.-JournoList collusion in favor of Obama.

> After the success of health care reform, what's next on labor's agenda? How can the labor movement grow and engage with a progressive movement that speaks to the Obama era? What is the role of younger workers, workers of color, and women? Is there a new "New Deal" on the horizon? (Eggers 2010)

Speakers included;
- Barbara Ehrenreich – (D.S.A. leader, Progressives for Obama founder)
- Christopher Hayes – (Washington editor of *The Nation*, JournoList member, affiliate of D.S.A. linked publication *In These Times*)
- Gerry Hudson – (D.S.A. member, executive Vice-president of the very pro Obama SEIU)
- Michael Kazin - (co-editor of *Dissent*, JournoList member, close to D.S.A.)
- Harold Meyerson.

One of the speakers above, Gerry Hudson has written how the late founder of D.S.A., Michael Harrington would view the election of Barack Obama.

> It's tragic for so many reasons that Michael died too young; his voice and his wisdom are sorely needed. How he would marvel at the election of Barack Obama and the promise that this victory affords all of us on the democratic left! He is sorely missed. But were he alive, I would hope—and expect, that he and others who are informed by this vision of democratic socialism would join with us in SEIU as we seek to take advantage of a moment most of us have spent our lifetimes only dreaming of. (KeyWiki 2010)

It should come as no surprise to learn that Harold Meyerson was one of the first, if not THE FIRST, journalist to promote Barack Obama outside his adopted state of Illinois.

From the *Washington Post* February 25, 2009:

> In March of 2004, a few days before the Illinois Democratic senatorial primary, I wrote a column for this page headlined "A Bright Hope in Illinois." It was, I believe, the first column for a daily newspaper outside Illinois devoted to a rising young pol named Barack Obama. Bolstered by polling that showed Obama to be the clear leader in the race, I fearlessly predicted that he'd become Illinois' next senator and quoted the assessment of Jan Schakowsky, the Democratic member of Congress from Chicago's Gold Coast district, that Obama would "march right onto the national stage and the international stage." (Meyerson 2009)

Jan Schakowsky, also a major Obama supporter, is of course also a very close friend of Chicago Democratic Socialists of America.

At Chicago D.S.A's 2004 46th Annual Debs-Thomas-Harrington Dinner, Jan Schakowsky told the story of a meeting in Washington with US president George Bush.

The Congressional Black Caucus had demanded a meeting with President Bush to discuss the situation in Haiti.

Schakowsky had also been invited because of her strong interest in the issue.

According to Chicago DSA's *New Ground*, May/June 2004:

> Bush finally, at the insistence of caucus members, made it to this meeting and spent enough time to display his ignorance of the issue. He noticed Jan, a lone white face, and seemed to "jump back" when he saw her button. Osama? No, Mr. President. Barack Obama, and you'll be hearing from him when he becomes the Senator from Illinois. (Baiman, The Dump Bush Dinner 2004)

Congratulations Chicago DSA
On your Annual Debs-Thomas-Harrington Dinner.

Congresswoman Jan Schakowsky
Paid for and authorized by Schakowsky for Congress

110-3 Jan
Schakowsky

This is what Harold Meyerson wrote about Barack Obama in the original March 12, 2004, *Washington Post* article. The narrative that would put Obama in the White House is clearly already in play. Meyerson touches all the bases that are repeated endlessly in the media from 2006 to 2008:

> You'd think his name alone would keep him from winning: Barack Obama. Put an "Obama for Senate" bumper sticker on your car and the dyslexic or myopic might just try to punch you out.
>
> Yet, three days ago, in its last pre-election poll before Tuesday's primary for the open US Senate seat in Illinois, the Chicago Tribune

reported that Obama, a 42-year-old state senator, had opened a wide lead over the six other candidates vying for the Democratic nomination to succeed the departing Peter Fitzgerald...

Organization men are a staple of Illinois politics, of course, and investment bankers seem poised to take over the Senate in our plutocratic age. Obama, by contrast, is a candidate who all but defies categorization – and who would certainly mark a radical departure for the stodgy Senate...

But that scarcely begins to describe the distinctiveness of Obama. His father was Kenyan, his mother a white girl from Kansas. The two met and married at the University of Hawaii in 1960 (when miscegenation was still a felony in more than half the states). His father disappeared from his life when Obama was 2; his mother raised him in Hawaii and Indonesia. Obama went to college at Columbia University, then moved to Chicago for five years of community organizing in a fusion of civil rights crusading and Saul Alinsky house-to-house plodding. He then went to Harvard Law School, where he became the first black president of the Law Review; returned to Chicago to run a program that registered 100,000 voters in the '92 elections, entered a civil rights law firm and became a senior lecturer in constitutional law at the University of Chicago. ..

Seven years ago Obama was elected to the state Senate from a district in Chicago's South Side. In Springfield, he developed a reputation as an impassioned progressive who was able to get support on both sides of the aisle...

In October 2002, Obama made an eloquent case against the impending war in Iraq at a rally in downtown Chicago. Declaring repeatedly that "I don't oppose all wars," he distinguished what he termed "a dumb war, a rash war" from a string of just and necessary wars in which the United States had engaged. He is surely the progressives' darling in the field, drawing enthusiastic support from white Lake Shore liberals as well as the African American community. But he's also won the endorsements of virtually all the state's major papers, many of which – such as Chicago's Tribune and Sun-Times – note their disagreement with him on the war but hail him as a brilliant public servant nonetheless. Should Obama win, says Rep. Jan Schakowsky of Evanston, who backs his candidacy, he'd "march right onto the national stage and the international stage..."

While practicing law in the early 1990s, Obama wrote *"Dreams From My Father,"* a memoir and meditation of genuine literary merit that depicts his understandable quest for his identity – a quest that immersed him in the world of Chicago's poor and that took him to a Kenyan village in search of a father he never knew. It's a story of worlds colliding, fusing and redividing, of a life devoted to re-creating in a grittier world the idealism and sense of community of the early civil rights movement, which provided the backdrop for his parents' marriage.

If by "American" we mean that which is most distinctive about us and our ideals, if we mean it to refer to our status as a nation of immigrants that could yet become the world's first great polyglot, miscegenetic meritocracy, then Barack Obama, if elected, would not only become the sole African American in the Senate: He would also be the most distinctly American of its members. (Meyerson, A Bright Hope in Illinois 2004)

Harold Meyerson was taped plugging Obama outside the Democratic Party convention in Denver in 2008.

Yes, Barack Obama is Harold's man alright!

It is clear that DSA has had "the fix" in for Obama, for some years.

Would Barack Obama be President of the United States today, without JournoList and a sympathetic "progressive" media?

Would JournoList have existed, or have been as influential, without Democratic Socialists of America?

Does America owe its current president, at least partly, to DSA, a few thousand strong Marxist organizations, that most voters have never heard of?

111. Degrees of Separation – Obama, Socialist Scholars and the East German Spy

Trevor Loudon © October 13, 2010

Stanley Kurtz's new book "*Radical-in-Chief: Barack Obama and the Untold Story of American Socialism*", finally proves that Barack Obama attended the Democratic Socialists of America - run Socialist Scholars Conferences in 1983 and 1984.

He also reveals how some of the Marxists participating in those conferences would influence Obama's career in later years.

Look at the 10th annual Socialist Scholars Conference held at the Borough of Manhattan Community College in April 1992.

One panel in particular was important: "Towards a New Party", with Elaine Bernard,

TENTH ANNUAL
SOCIALIST SCHOLARS
Conference

WHOSE NEW WORLD ORDER?
WHAT'S LEFT?

April 24 - 26, 1992 ◆ Friday 7 - 9 p.m. ◆ Saturday & Sunday 9 a.m. - 6 p.m.
Borough of Manhattan Community College ◆ New York City

111-1 Socialist Scholars Conference

Towards a New Party

sponsor: Democratic Socialists of America, CUNY
chair: Elaine Bernard *Harvard University, NDP*
Arthur Lipow *Michael Harrington Center, London*
Kurt Stand *Democratic Socialists of America*
Judy Page *New Party*

111-2 Towards a New Party

Arthur Lipow, Kurt Stand and Judy Page.

The panel was openly sponsored by D.S.A., and Elaine Bernard and Kurt Stand who are both leading D.S.A. comrades. Lipow is at the very least a supporter.

At this time, the New Party was in its infancy. The first strategic meetings to plan the New Party were held in the Madison Wisconsin home of radical academic Joel Rogers in the very early 1990s.

Present at the meeting were Rogers' wife Sarah Siskind, (a lawyer who worked for the same firm as Barack Obama), Dan Cantor (now a leader of the D.S.A. infiltrated New York Working Families Party), ACORN leaders Wade Rathke, Zach Polett, Steve Kest and Jon Kest, Steve Cobble (from the far left Institute for Policy Studies, (there in an advisory role), Sandy Morales Pope (for the first 18 months), and at least at the first meeting Gerry Hudson from D.S.A. and SEIU.

Of the conference panelists Judy Page was obviously a New Party activist, while Elaine Bernard went on to become a key builder of the New Party.

Stand
(Sketch by Dana Verkouteren)
111-3 Kurt Stand

Kurt Stand

The most interesting of the panelists however, was Kurt Stand.

At the time Stand was member of the D.S.A. Racial Diversity Task Force – charged with finding ways of recruiting (and retaining) more "people of color" into the organization. He would also soon become a member of the D.S.A.'s "steering committee" and later, its "national political committee".

In other words he was a key leader of the organization.

Kurt Stand was the son of Mille Stand, a long time Communist Party USA member.

Inspired by his family's beliefs, Kurt Stand was politically active from his teens – defending Angela Davis and Philip Berrigan and Daniel Berrigan and joining the Young Workers Liberation League; youth-wing of the Communist Party.

Kurt Stand was also a long standing spy for East Germany and possibly the Soviet Union.

The young Kurt Stand began his spying activities in 1972 after being recruited by East Germany to cultivate other spies in the Washington, DC, area. He was introduced to East German intelligence officers (the Stasi) through his father Mille Stand, a chemical engineer who fled Nazi Germany in the 1930s.

An FBI affidavit said East Germany's relationship with the Stand family goes back to Stand's father (Mille Stand), who recruited his son as a communist agent.

Stand and his wife, co-conspirator Theresa Squillacote frequently traveled to Mexico, Germany, and

Canada during which time Stand would meet with their East German handlers.

When the two Germanys united in 1990, Stand's controllers attempted to recruit him to spy for the Soviet Union and then for the Russian Federation. Although he never gained access to classified material, his role in the operation was to recruit agents and to provide information about the non-governmental groups with which he worked. Stand allegedly received $24,650 for his recruiting and coordinating efforts.

On 23 Oct 1998, he and wife Squillacote were convicted of conspiracy to commit espionage, attempted espionage, and illegally obtaining national defense documents. On 22 Jan 1999, a US District Judge sentenced Squillacote to 21 years and 10 months in prison and Stand to a sentence of 17 years and six months.

What role if any Kurt Stand played in the New Party is unknown, but the role of its most famous recruit, Barack Obama is becoming increasingly clear.

In 1993, the Chicago New Party founded an equally radical "sister organization", Progressive Chicago. New Party members, ACORN activist Madeline Talbott and labor unionist Dan Swinney played a key role in this new organization's formation.

Barack Obama was a member of both organizations.

In an April 27, 1993 letter to prospective Progressive Chicago members, Swinney wrote:

> I recently have become interested in the New Party as well as committed myself to see if we can build a Progressive Chicago network, working with Madeline Talbott of ACORN – the local New Party convener.
>
> I wanted to introduce you to the NP and Progressive Chicago and

111-5 Letter regarding Jan 1994 meeting

> would like to talk to you about it to see if there is a role you want to play. (Swinney 1993)

Barack Obama was probably approached to join Progressive Chicago as early July 7, 1993 and was among key members invited to a

111-4 Barack Obama's Invitation to attend

January 1994, meeting in this December 31 1993 letter.

Numerous documentary sources have confirmed that Obama went on to also join the New Party including this clipping from *New Party News* Spring 1996, page 1.

Barack Obama went on to win an Illinois State Senate seat, then a US Senate seat, followed by the Presidency of the United States of America.

Kurt Stand languishes in prison, a convicted traitor to his country. However he still remains committed to "changing America".

In June 2008 Kurt Stand wrote an essay in prison entitled *"Supporting Barack Obama: A Prison-Eye View of the Presidential Campaign"*:

> As to Obama, I vacillated, knowing of his past activism, but not seeing enough in his Senate record or campaign approach to sufficiently differentiate himself from Edwards or Clinton.

> To go back to Obama, nobody knows what he will do, but if he is able to overcome our country's racism and actually win election we can expect some initial efforts to rein in the excesses of the Bush Administration, some measures to ameliorate the worst conditions which people are experiencing in terms of rights, in terms of insecurity.

> It will be up to those who want genuine social justice to build movements that give him the possibility of pushing further; finding out then whether he will or won't remembering that the key will not be him but us (defined as those who worked for his election, for social justice activists, the left) and what we do, how we organize. How we use the social solidarity the campaign is developing as the basis of a renewed social solidarity. Will that be enough—no, the structural roots of the wars in Iraq/Afghanistan, of neo-liberal economics, of the authoritarian aspects of our political culture won't go gently in the night.

> Only, however, by working in good faith with attempts to improve what is, is it even possible to imagine the building of the necessary, broad-based, independent, radical formations able to press for deeper changes.

> In sum, radicals and progressives ought to join those—including those in prison— who have already decided to back Obama, see where the campaign can take us, and see what can then be accomplished. (Stand 2008)

Interesting indeed that that Kurt Stand should claim knowledge of Obama's "past activism."

Bibliography & Attributions

911 Truth. "Repsected Leaders and Famlies Launch 9/11 Truth Statement Demanding Deeper Investigation into the Events of 9/11." *911 Truth.* 26 Oct 2004. http://www.911truth.org/article.php?story=20041026093059633 (accessed Mar 8, 2010).

About Time. "Former Black Panthers considered terrorists under the Patriot Act." *Its About Time.* 25 Dec 2005. http://www.itsabouttimebpp.com/Announcements/Former_Black_Pant hers.html (accessed Jul 24, 2009).

ACORN, et al v. Household International, Inc. 2002 WL 1563805 (Superior Court of California, 2002).

Activities, House Committee on Un-American. *Trial by Treason.* Committee Findings, Washington, DC: US House of Representatives, 1956.

Alarcon, Evelina. "Cesar E. Chavez: The Farm Worker Leader honored with a California Legal Holiday." *Cesar Chavez Holiday.* Aug 2000. http://www.cesarchavezholiday.org/aboutcesarechavez.html (accessed Mar 5, 2009).

—. "Communist Support." *Hilda Solis, Key Wiki.* Nov 2000. http://www.keywiki.org/index.php/Hilda_Solis (accessed Dec 20, 2008).

—. "Evelina Alarcon." *KeyWiki.* Mar 2009. http://keywiki.org/index.php/Evelina_Alarcon (accessed Mar 5, 2009).

—. "On the Work of Districts and Clubs." *Communist Party USA.* 22 Sep 2001. http://www.cpusa.org/on-the-work-of-districts-and-clubs/ (accessed Mar 5, 2009).

Albano, Teresa. "Prospects for Black and Latino unity." *OEN OpEdNews.com.* 1 Feb 2008. http://www.opednews.com/articles/opedne_pepe_loz_080131_prospects _for_black_.htm (accessed Feb 1, 2008).

Albano, Terrie. "Will Progressives respond?" *PA Political Affairs, People's Weekly World* . 31 Jan 2008. http://paeditorsblog.blogspot.com/2008/01/will-progressives-respond.html (accessed Feb 1, 2008).

American Civil Liberties Union of Illinois. "Prominent Chicago Area Organizations and Social Justice Activists ask FBI to Make Spy Files Public." *American Civil Liberties Union of Illinois.* 2 Dec 2004. http://www.aclu-il.org/news/press/2004/12/prominent_chicago_area_organiz.shtml (accessed May 16, 2009).

Andrew, Christopher, and Oleg Gordievsky. *KGB: The Inside Story of its Foreign Operations from Lenin to Gorbachev.* London: Hodder & Stoughton, 1990.

Apollo Alliance. "Apollo Board of Directors." *Apollo Alliance*. 2008. http://web.archive.org/web/20080118101719/www.apolloalliance.org/about_board.php (accessed Aug 9, 2009).

Arm the Spirit. "Black Radical Congress (BRC) June 19-21, 1998." *World History Archieves*. 15 Jun 1998. http://www.hartford-hwp.com/archives/45a/228.html (accessed Oct 4, 2008).

Ayers, William. "The Forgotten Communist Manifesto: Prairie Fire." *The Obama File*. 9 May 1974. http://www.zombietime.com/prairie_fire/ (accessed Oct 4, 2008).

Bachetell, John. "Special District Meeting on African American." *Communist Party USA*. 24 Oct 2007. http://www.cpusa.org/special-district-meeting-on-african-american-equality (accessed Jun 1, 2009).

Bachtell, John. "Illinois Senate Race offers Historical Opportunity." *People's World*. 17 Oct 2007. http://peoplesworld.org/illinois-senate-race-offers-historic-opportunity/ (accessed Sep 2, 2008).

—. "Speical District Meeting on African American." *Communist Party USA*. 24 Oct 2007. http://www.cpusa.org/special-district-meeting-on-african-american-equality/ (accessed Oct 17, 2008).

Bacon, David. "El Valiente Chicao." *David Bacon Stories: Portraits*. 19 Jan 2001. http://dbacon.igc.org/Portrait/07Corona.htm (accessed Mar 4, 2009).

Baiman, Ron. *New Ground 56*. Jan/Feb 1998. http://www.chicagodsa.org/ngarchive/ng56.html#anchor1041720.

—. "The Dump Bush Dinner." *New Ground 94*. May/Jun 2004. http://www.chicagodsa.org/ngarchive/ng94.html#anchor346820 (accessed Feb 10, 2008).

—. "The Dump Bush Dinner." *New Ground 94*. May - Jun 2004. http://www.chicagodsa.org/ngarchive/ng94.html#anchor346820 (accessed Aug 3, 2010).

Balanoff, Betty. "2008 Hall of Honor: Leon Depres." *Illinois Labor History Society*. 2008. http://www.illinoislaborhistory.org/hall-of-honor/201-2008-hall-of-honor.html (accessed May 16, 2009).

Barnes, James A. "Obama's Inner Circle." *National Journal*. 31 Mar 2008. (accessed Jul 2009).

Bechtel, Marilyn, and Dorothy Johnson. "PWW events to salute peoples leaders." *People's Weekly World*, 15 Dec 2006.

Becker, Jo, and Christopher Drew. "Pragmatic Politics, Forged on the South Side." *The New York Times*. 11 May 2008.

http://www.nytimes.com/2008/05/11/us/politics/11chicago.html?page wanted=1&&%2359;_r=2 (accessed Jan 20, 2010).

Bentley, Bruce. "Chicago New Party News Update." *New Ground 42*. Sep/Oct 1995.

—. "Chicago New Party Update." *New Ground 42*. Sep/Oct 1995. http://www.chicagodsa.org/ngarchive/ng42.html (accessed Jan 18, 2008).

—. "New Ground 42." *Chicago DSA*. Sep/Oct 1995. http://www.chicagodsa.org/ngarchive/ng42.html#anchor792932 (accessed Aug 19, 2008).

—. "New Ground 42." *Chicago New Party Update*. Sep/Oct 1995. http://www.chicagodsa.org/ngarchive/ng42.html#anchor792932 (accessed Oct 11, 2008).

—. "Where Does the Left Go from Here?" *New Ground 39*. Mar/Apr 1995. http://www.chicagodsa.org/ngarchive/ng39.html#anchor354294 (accessed Oct 11, 2008).

Bently, Bruce. "New Party Update." *chicagodsa.org*. Jul/Aug 1996. http://www.chicagodsa.org/ngarchive/ng47.html#anchor781435.

Berkowitz, Jeff. "The Barack Obama Watch: Today's Labor Rally."." *Public Affairs*. 3 Mar 2007. http://jeffberkowitz.blogspot.com/2007/03/barack-obama-watch-todays-labor-rally.html (accessed Feb 27, 2008).

Bhargava, Deepak. "How Do Progressives Connect Ideas to Action?" *Open Society Foundation*. 29 Nov 2006. http://www.soros.org/resources/events/progressives_20061129 (accessed Oct 1, 2009).

—. "Key Wiki Deepak Bhargava." *Center for Community Change*. 7 Oct 2009. http://www.keywiki.org/index.php/Deepak_Bhargava (accessed Oct 7, 2009).

Black Press Institute. "Socialism is the Only Way Forward." *Black Press Institute - KeyWiki*. 1983. http://keywiki.org/index.php/Black_Press_Institute (accessed Nov 17, 2009`).

Black Radical Congress. "Black Radical Congress Program." *Final Program for Black Radical Congress*. 18 Jun 1998. http://mailman.lbo-talk.org/1998/1998-June/002946.html (accessed Oct 4, 2008).

Black, Curtis. "Milt Cohen: A Life in the Movement." *New Ground 33*. Mar/Apr 1994. http://www.chicagodsa.org/ngarchive/ng33.html (accessed Oct 17, 2008).

Black, Timuel. Woodson Regional Library Auditorium, Chicago. 11 Feb 2007.

Bloom, Ron. "If I Ran the Zoo: A Win-Win Solution for the Steel Industry." *Democratic Left*. Fall 2006. http://www.dsausa.org/dl/Fall_2006.pdf (accessed Sep 16, 2009).

Blount, Donald. "Valerie Jarrett." *Take Political Action*. 24 May 2008. http://blog.takepoliticalaction.org/main/2008/05/valerie-jarrett.html (accessed Oct 27, 2008).

Bonior, David. "David Bonior Calls for a North American Parliament." *Democratic Left*. Winter 2003. http://www.dsausa.org/dl/Winter_2003.pdf (accessed Nov 21, 2008).

Bonior, David E. "David E. Bonior." *Wikipedia, The Free Encyclopedia*. 21 Nov 2008. http://en.wikipedia.org/w/index.php?title=David_E._Bonior&oldid=4478 51492 (accessed Nov 21, 2008).

Boyd, Sam. "Hilda Solis is Great." *Tapped: The group blog of The American Prospect*. 18 Dec 2008. http://www.prospect.org/csnc/blogs/tapped_archive?month=12&year= 2008&base_name=hilda_solis_is_great#111685 (accessed Dec 20, 2008).

Bruck, Connie. "Can Mayor Antonio Villaraigosa Keep Control of L.A.'s Battling Factions?" *The New Yorker*. 21 May 2007. (accessed Mar 4, 2009).

Buhle, Paul, and Dan Georgakas. "History of the Comintern Sections Communist Party USA." *Encyclopedia of the West*. 1992. (accessed Jun 1, 2009).

Buhle, Paul, and George Georgakas. "Communist Party USA." *University of Illinois Press*. 1992. http://eprints.cddc.vt.edu/marxists/history/usa/parties/cpusa/encyclop edia-american-left.htm (accessed Oct 17, 2008).

Cabral, Amilcar. "Tell No Lies, Claim No Easy Victories." *Newritings*. 11 Feb 2009. http://newritings.wordpress.com/2009/02/11/cabral-tell-no-lies-claim-no-easy-victories/ (accessed Apr 6, 2009).

Campbell, Duane. "San Francisco Bay Area Democratic Socialists of America." *San Francisco Bay Area Democratic Socialists of America*. 14 10 2001. www.rawbw.com/~ross/dsa.

Canter, Marc. "50-42." *Marc's Voice*. Chicago: Broad Band Mechanics, 30 Sep 2008.

—. "Who was David S. Canter #1." *Marc's Voice*. 23 Sep 2004. http://blog.broadbandmechanics.com/2004/09/23/who_was_david_s/ (accessed Oct 31, 2008).

Carty, Sharon Silke. "Task Force Exec Ron Bloom can see All Sides in Auto Fight." *USA Today*. 19 Mar 2009. http://www.usatoday.com/money/autos/2009-03-18-auto-task-force-ron-bloom_N.htm (accessed Sep 16, 2009).

Cavanagh, John. "27th Annual Letelier-Moffitt Human Rights Awards." *TNI.* Nov 2005. http://www.tni.org/article/27th-annual-letelier-moffitt-human-rights-awards (accessed Apr 30, 2009).

Center for Community Change. "Community Organizers Welcome One of their Own to the White House." *Community Change.* 5 Nov 2008. http://www.keywiki.org/index.php/Center_for_Community_Change (accessed Oct 7, 2009).

Cereijo, Dr. Manuel. "Third World War." *Lanuevacuba.* 23 May 2006. http://www.lanuevacuba.com/archivo/manuel-cereijo-114.htm (accessed Apr 4, 2009).

Chapman, Frank. "Is Barack Obama a Marxist Mole?" *USA Survival.* 2 Feb 2008. http://www.usasurvival.org/ck2.22.08.html (accessed Apr 25, 209).

—. "Letter to Communist Party USA Peoples Weekly World." *Keywike.* 19 Jan 2009. http://www.keywiki.org/index.php/Frank_Chapman (accessed Feb 4, 2009).

"Chicago 2005 Debs-Thomas-Harrington Dinner." *Chicago DSA.* 5 May 2005. http://www.chicagodsa.org/d2005/index.html (accessed Sep 2, 2008).

Chicago Communist Party. "Chicago Peace Council." *National Conference for a Drastic Cutback in Military Spending.* 5 - 6 Apr 1975. (accessed May 1, 2010).

Chicago Democratic Socialist of America. "1992 Eugene V. Debs - Norman Thomas - Michael Harrington Dinner." *Chicago DSA.* 1 May 1992. http://www.chicagodsa.org/d1992/index.html (accessed Feb 18, 2008).

Chicago DSA. "1983 Norman Thomas - Eugene V. Debs Dinner." *Debs Dinner.* 7 May 1983. http://www.chicagodsa.org/d1983/index.html (accessed Oct 17, 2008).

—. "1983 Norman Thomas - Eugene V. Debs Dinner." *Chicago DSA.* 7 May 1983. http://www.chicagodsa.org/d1983/index.html (accessed Oct 31, 2008).

Chicago DSA Debs Dinner. "1992 Eugene V. Debs - Norman Thomas - Michael Harrington Dinner." *Chicago Democratics Socialists of America.* 1 May 1992. http://www.chicagodsa.org/d1992/index.html (accessed Sep 13, 2008).

Chicago New Party. *ProgressiveChicago Organizing Report.* Chicago: Chicago New Party, 1993.

Chicago Peace Council. "National Conference for a Drastic Cutback in Military Spending." *Chicago Communist Party.* Chicago: Chicago Communist Party, 1975. 5 - 6.

Chicago Sun Times. *AFSCME backs Obama, Breaks for National Endorsement.* Chicago, 1 Dec 2007.

—. "Obituaries." *Chicago Sun Times*. 30 Aug 2004. (accessed Sep 11, 2009).

City Room. "Illinois Delegates Call Obama Rise the Culmination of a Dream." *City Room Politics*. 29 Aug 2008. http://www.chicagopublicradio.org/Content.aspx?audioID=28572 (accessed Sep 2, 2008).

Cohan, William D. "Can these men save Detroit?" *Fortune*. 25 Feb 2009. http://money.cnn.com/2009/02/25/autos/Obama_car_czar.fortune/index.htm (accessed Sep 17, 2009).

Collins, Chuck. "Twenty Two to know." *In These Times*. 26 Sep 2008. http://www.inthesetimes.com/article/3933/twenty_two_to_know/ (accessed Jul 26, 2010).

Committee on Un-American Activities. *Review of the Scientific and Cultural Conference for World Peace*. Review, Washington D.C.: US House of Representatives, 1949.

Committees of Correspondence for Democracy and Socialism. *A Critical Moment*. Letter to Membership, Chicago: COCDS, 2008.

Cone, James. *Black Liberation Theology*. Maryknoll, NY: ORBIS Bookss, 1969.

Corona, Bert. "Bert Corona." *KeyWiki*. n.d. (accessed Mar 4, 2008).

Daily Kos. "Jackie Grimshaw: Next Door Neighbor." *Daily Kos*. 15 Feb 2008. http://www.dailykos.com/story/2008/2/15/233425/277/462/456189 (accessed Oct 23, 2008).

Damore, David. *PolitickerNV.com*. 12 Jan 2008. Link Down.

Data Center. "Data Center Research for Justice." *Data Center*. 8 Apr 2009. http://www.datacenter.org/ (accessed Apr 9, 2009).

Davidson, Carl. "Carl Davidson on Barack O'bomb em'." *Marxism Mailing List archive*. 21 Jan 2007. http://www.archives.econ.utah.edu/archives/marxism/2007w03/msg00182.htm.

—. "Carl Davidson replies to Trevor Loudon." *New Zeal Blog*. Feb 2008. (accessed Sep 28, 2008).

—. "Discover the Networks." *Carl Davidson*. 2009. http://www.discoverthenetworks.org/individualProfile.asp?indid=2322 (accessed Aug 27, 2009).

—. "Keep on Keepin' On." *Carl Davidson Blogspot*. 5 Aug 2009. http://carldavidson.blogspot.com/2009/08/socialism-and-emerging-progressive.html (accessed Aug 27, 2009).

Davis, Angela. "Angela Davis: Not another prison." *People's World*. 21 Apr 2009. http://www.peoplesworld.org/angela-davis-not-another-prison/ (accessed Apr 25, 2009).

Davis, Danny. "Chicago DSA Endorsements in the March 19th Primary Election." *New Ground* 45. Mar/Apr 1996. http://www.chicagodsa.org/ngarchive/ng45.html#anchor1078925 (accessed Jan 12, 2008).

Davis, Danny K. "United States House Committee on Ways and Means." *Wikipedia: The Free Encyclopedia.* 7 Dec 2008. http://en.wikipedia.org/w/index.php?title=United_States_House_Commi ttee_on_Ways_and_Means&oldid=440611276 (accessed Dec 12, 2008).

Davis, Renne. "Ethan Youngs sojurn in Cuba with the Venceremos Brigades." *Hyde Park - Kenwood VOICES.* Nov 1967. (accessed Sep 11, 2009).

Democracy for New Mexico. "Patricia Madrid Named to Obama's National Latino Advisory Council." *Democracy for New Mexico.* 22 Aug 2008. http://www.democracyfornewmexico.com/democracy_for_new_mexico /2008/08/patricia-madr-2.html (accessed Dec 20, 2008).

Democratic Left. "Election Endorsements - Spring 2006." *Democratic Left*, 1990: 4.

—. "Send a student to Minnesota." *Democratic Left*. Fall 2002. http://www.dsausa.org/dl/Fall_2002.pdf (accessed Nov 21, 2008).

Democratic Socialist of America. "What is Democratic Socialism." *Democratic Socialists of America.* 21 Nov 2008. http://www.dsausa.org/pdf/widemsoc.pdf (accessed Nov 21, 2008).

Democratic Socialists of America. "Chicago 1983 Norman Thomas - Eugene V. Debs Dinner." *Chicago DSA.* 7 May 1983. http://www.chicagodsa.org/d1983/index.html (accessed Sep 11, 2008).

—. "Eliseo Medina named an Honorary Chair of DSA." *Democratic Socialists of America.* 9 August 2004. http://www.dsausa.org/LatestNews/2004/medina.html (accessed Jan 27, 2010).

—. "Hilda Solis Keynote Speaker." *Twenty First Century Socialism conference.* 5 November 2005. http://keywiki.org/index.php/DSA (accessed Sep 26, 2009).

—. "Illinois Blazes Progressive Paths." *New Ground* 28. Dec 1992. http://www.chicagodsa.org/ngarchive/ng28.html#anchor410524 (accessed Oct 17, 2008).

DEMOS. "A Presidency in Peril." *DEMOS.* Mar 2010. http://www.demos.org/publication.cfm?currentpublicationID=6818F9D7 %2D3FF4%2D6C82%2D5107212EB1E76E82 (accessed Jul 26, 2010).

—. "Backgrounder." *DEMOS website.* 2000. http://www.demos.org/backgrounder.cfm (accessed Aug 17, 2009).

—. "Obama's Challenge." *DEMOS.* 2010. (accessed Jul 26, 2010).

Dixon. "Barack Obama Hypocrisy on Healthcare." *Thomas Paine's Corner.* Feb 2007. http://civillibertarian.blogspot.com/2007/02/barack-obama-hypocrisy-on-health-care.html (accessed Feb 20, 2008).

Down iwth Tyranny. "Desperate Lieberman Campaign being Investigated by FBI for Posting Forged Documents from Obama & Reid." *Down with Tyranny.* 1 June 2006. http://downwithtyranny.blogspot.com/2006/06/desperate-lieberman-campaign-being.html (accessed Oct 4, 2008).

Dreyer, T, and D Hamilton. "The Left and Barack Obama." *The Rag Blog.* 23 Mar 2008. http://theragblog.blogspot.com/2008/03/left-and-barack-obama-t-dreyer-and-d.html (accessed Sep 23, 2008).

DSA. "DSA PAC ESTABLISHED." *Democratic Socialists of America.* Spring 2006. http://www.dsausa.org/dl/Spring_2006.pdf (accessed Nov 21, 2008).

Ebel, Eric. *Democratic Socialists of American Greater Detroit Local.* Apr 2007. http://kincaidsite.com/dsa/meetings.html.

Eggers, Dave. "Labor, the Left, and Progressives in the Obama Era." *Literacy, Literature and Democracy.* Washington D.C.: Lannan Symposium, Georgetown University, 2010.

Ehrenreich, Barbara. "Barbara Ehrenreich." *Discover the Networks.* 1 May 2010. http://www.discoverthenetworks.org/individualProfile.asp?indid=1058 (accessed May 26, 2010).

Elliott, Brenda J. "Labor "Reunification"." *The Real Barack Obama.* 21 Apr 2009. http://therealbarackobama.wordpress.com/2009/04/21/labor-reunification/ (accessed Apr 30, 2009).

Embree, Alice. "Movement for a Democratic Society, Austin Chapter." *Front Page.* 29 Mar 2008. http://mds-austin.pbworks.com/ (accessed Sep 23, 2008).

Farberov, Snejana. "The Red League rallies around a blue party canidate." *Columbia News Service.* 27 Feb 2008. http://jscms.jrn.columbia.edu/cns/2008-02-19/farberov-obamacommies.html (accessed Feb 29, 2008).

Federal Election Commission. *Political Campaign Contributions 2006 Election Cycle.* Campaign Report, Washington, DC: Federal Election Commission, 2006.

Fight the Smears. "Fightthesmears.org." 2008. http://www.fightthesmears.org/?page_id=12 (accessed Apr 2010).

Fishman, Joelle. "CT People Before Profits." *Connecticut Communist Party USA.* 2 Nov 2008. http://ctpeoplebeforeprofits.blogspot.com/2008/11/merrilee-milstein-day-puts-working.html (accessed Nov 20, 2008).

Flory, Ishmael. "Illinois Communist Party USA." Chicago: Malcolm X College, 21 Sep 1991.

Free Republic LLC. "54 Socialists are in the US Congress." *Free Republic.* 19 Aug 2008. http://www.freerepublic.com/focus/news/763360/posts (accessed Aug 19, 2008).

Freedom Road Socialist Organization. *Freedom Road Socialist Organization.* 16 Feb 2008. http://freedomroad.org/ (accessed Feb 16, 2008).

Friedman, Larry. *Identity's Architect: A Biography of Erik H. Erikson.* New York, NY: SCRIBNER, 1999.

Friedman, Max. "A View from the Right: The Post and Me." *Augusta Free Press.* 13 Jun 2008. (accessed Oct 31, 2008).

Gaboury, Fred. "An interview with William McNary." *People's World.* 5 Oct 2002. (accessed Sep 2, 2008).

Gage, Kit, and Lewis Myers Jr. "Civil Liberties: The Next Four Years." *THE CHICAGO COMMITTEE TO DEFEND THE BILL OF RIGHTS.* 8 Dec 2004. http://www.ccdbr.org/events/041208.html (accessed Dec 17, 2008).

Garnace, Princess. "Cal State-Sacramento Professor Shows Support for Obama." *CBS News.* 11 Dec 2007. http://www.cbsnews.com/stories/2007/12/11/politics/uwire/main3608004.shtml (accessed Feb 29, 2008).

Garskof, Bert. "Bert Garskof Bethany CT." *The Nation.* 21 Sep 2008. http://www.thenation.com/letter/empty-title-3097 (accessed Oct 21, 2008).

—. "Former Terrorists Bill Ayers and Bernardine Dohrn Involved in Key Pro-Obama Organisation." *Trevor Loudon Blog.* 21 Sep 2008. Chapter 30 – Former Terrorists Bill Ayers and Bernardine Dohrn Involved in Key Pro-Obama Organisation (accessed Oct 17, 2008).

Gilbert, David, and David Loud. "Communism in Chicago and the Obama Connection." *Discover the Network, America's Survival.* Feb 2008. http://www.discoverthenetworks.org/Articles/chicago-obama[1].pdf (accessed Aug 19, 2008).

Good, Thomas. "Underground: My Life in SDS and the Weathermen." *Next Left Notes*. 23 Mar 2009. http://nextleftnotes.org/NLN/index.php?s=Mark+Rudd (accessed Mar 28, 2009).

Goodman, Amy. "Dr. Quinton Young, Longtime Obama Confidante and Physician to MLK." *Democracy Now!* 11 Mar 2009. http://www.democracynow.org/2009/3/11/dr_quentin_young_obama_confidante_and (accessed Feb 19, 2008).

GOP. *GOP.com*. 25 Oct 2008. http://www.gop.com/index.php (accessed Oct 25, 2008).

Gravel, US Senator Mike. "Maurice Robert "Mike" Gravel." *Wikipedia The Free Encyclopedia*. 1969. http://en.wikipedia.org/wiki/Mike_Gravel (accessed Mar 8, 2010).

Green, David. "Detroit DSA Celebrate at 10th Annual Douglass-Debs Dinner." *Talking Union*. 6 Dec 2008. http://talkingunion.wordpress.com/2008/12/06/detroit-dsaers-celebrate-at-10th-annual-douglass-debs-dinner/ (accessed Apr 30, 2009).

—. "The Employee Free Choice Act - A Democratic Socialist of America Priority." *Democratic Left - the Magazine of the Democratic Socialists of America*. Spring 2007. (accessed Sep 11, 2009).

Grossman, Ron. "Palling around with street toughs convinced Alinsky." *Chicago Tribune*. 30 Jan 2009. (accessed May 16, 2009).

Gruenberg, Mark. "Union Activits Energized for 2008 Elections." *Political Affairs*. 16 Nov 2007. http://politicalaffairs.net/union-activists-energized-for-2008-elections/ (accessed Nov 11, 2008).

Guthrie, Woody. *This Land is Your Land*. Performed by Pete Seeger. Lincoln Memorial, Washington, DC. 20 Jan 2009.

Hayden, Tom. "Key Task: Isolate and Divide the Right." *zcommunications*. 18 Sep 2008. http://www.zcommunications.org/key-task-isolate-and-divide-the-right-by-tom-hayden (accessed Oct 26, 2008).

—. "Progressives for Obama." *The Nation*. 7 Apr 2008. http://www.thenation.com/article/progressives-obama (accessed Sep 11, 2008).

—. "ROOTING FOR THE NEW WORLD ORDER." *The New Block Magazine*. 7 Apr 2008. (accessed Dec 12, 2008).

Hayes, Christopher. "Obama's Media Maven." *The Nation*. 6 Feb 2007. http://www.thenation.com/article/obamas-media-maven (accessed Oct 31, 2008).

Herken, Gregg. *Brotherhood of the Bomb.* New York, NY: Henry Holt and Company, LLC, 2002.

Herszenhorn, David M. "Public Lives: This Green isn't Blue About Nader or Gore." *The New York Times.* 17 11 2000. http://www.nytimes.com/2000/11/17/nyregion/public-lives-this-green-isn-t-blue-about-nader-or-gore.html?sec=&spon=&pagewanted=all (accessed Oct 21, 2008).

Holderness, Peter. "Bronzeville oral history engages new generation." *Windy Citizen.* 20 Feb 2008. http://www.windycitizen.com/2007/02/21/bronzeville-oral-history-engages-new-generation (accessed Feb 20, 2008).

Holland, Jesse J. "Obama comes up short on union support." *USA Today.* 18 12 2007. http://www.usatoday.com/news/politics/2007-12-18-1318792961_x.htm (accessed Jan 12, 2008).

Horowitz, David. "Alice Palmer." *Freedom Center.* Jun 1986. http://www.discoverthenetworks.org/individualProfile.asp?indid=2325 (accessed Aug 19, 2008).

—. "Barbara Ehrenreich." *Discover the Network.* 11 Sep 2008. http://www.discoverthenetworks.org/individualProfile.asp?indid=1058 (accessed Sep 11, 2008).

—. "Carl Davidson." *Discover the Networks.* 28 Sep 2008. http://www.discoverthenetworks.org/individualProfile.asp?indid=2322 (accessed Sep 28, 2008).

—. "Danny Glover." *Discover the Networks.* 11 Sep 2008. http://www.discoverthenetworks.org/individualProfile.asp?indid=1119 (accessed Sep 11, 2008).

—. "Jan Schakowsky." *Discover the Networks.* 8 Feb 2008. http://www.discoverthenetworks.org/individualProfile.asp?indid=1506 (accessed Feb 8, 2008).

—. "Robert Borosage." *Discover the Networks.* 28 Mar 2009. http://www.discoverthenetworks.org/individualProfile.asp?indid=1170 (accessed Mar 29, 2009).

—. "Tom Hayden." *Discover the Networks.* 11 Sep 2008. http://www.discoverthenetworks.org/individualProfile.asp?indid=1334 (accessed Sep 11, 2008).

Household International, Inc. *Household, ACORN and consumers reach proposed settlement.* News Release, Bufflo, NY: Household News Archieves, 2003.

Hudson, Gerry. "SEIU VP Explains Strategy: Build a Progressive Movement with Labor at its Core." *Talking Union.* 22 Jan 2009.

http://talkingunion.wordpress.com/2009/01/22/building-a-new-progressive-movement-with-labor-at-its-core/ (accessed May 1, 2010).

Informant, Government, interview by Government Investigator. *Steven Guerra* (June 1982).

Jackson, David, and Ray Long. "Obama knows his way around a ballot." *Chicago Tribune Politics.* 20 Feb 2008. http://www.chicagotribune.com/news/politics/obama/chi-070403obama-ballot-archive,0,5297304,full.story (accessed Feb 20, 2008).

Jacoby, Jeff. "Questions for Obama's Science Guy." *The Boston Globe.* 18 Jan 2010. http://www.jeffjacoby.com/2337/questions-for-obamas-science-guy (accessed Mar 2, 2010).

Jarrett, Vernon. "Project Vote brings Power to the People." *Chicago Sun Times.* 11 Aug 1992. http://www.encyclopedia.com/doc/1P2-4124205.html (accessed Oct 11, 2008).

—. "Project Vote brings Power to the People." *Encyclopedia.com.* 11 Aug 1992. http://www.encyclopedia.com/doc/1P2-4124205.html (accessed Jun 1, 2009).

Jensen, Trevor. "In Memory of Marian Despres: 1909 - 2007." *Hyde Park History.* 6 Jan 2007. http://www.hydeparkhistory.org/InMemory.pdf (accessed May 16, 2009).

Jones, J. "Good Jobs, Clean Energy." *Jeff Jones Strategies.* Sep 2008. http://www.jeffjones-strategies.com/index.htm (accessed Sep 28, 2008).

Jones, Jeff. "The Audacity of Obama: Centrist Appointments a Smoke Screen." *The Rag Blog.* 28 Nov 2008. http://theragblog.blogspot.com/2008/11/obama-centrist-appointments-are-smoke.html (accessed Dec 3, 2008).

Jones, Van. "Challenging White Supremacy Workshop." *Collective Liberation - The Catalyst Project.* 6 Apr 2009. http://collectiveliberation.org/index.php?option=com_content&task=view&id=15&Itemid=27 (accessed Apr 6, 2009).

—. "Great Gifts from Joel Rogers." *Mayor's Innovation Conference.* Washington, DC, 2009.

—. "Second Annual Banquet Gathers to Build Progressive." *Portside.* 25 Jan 2006. http://lists.portside.org/cgi-bin/listserv/wa?A2=ind0601d&L=portside&P=1708 (accessed Aug 27, 2009).

Kagan, Elena. "Opinion." *Daily Princetonian.* 1980. (accessed June 26, 2010).

Kagan, Elena. *To the Final Conflict: Socialism in New York City 1900 - 1933.* Undergraduate Theses, Borough of Princeton, NJ: Princeton University, 1981.

Kaplan, Lee. "Duke University's Weekend Hate Fest." *Front Page Mag.* 15 Oct 2004. http://97.74.65.51/readArticle.aspx?ARTID=11021 (accessed Sep 28, 2008).

Katz, Marilyn. "Marilyn Katz." *Key Wiki - Marilyn Katz.* 20 Jan 2010. http://keywiki.org/index.php/Marilyn_Katz (accessed Jan 20, 2010).

KeyWiki. "Bleifuss, Joel." *Key Wiki.* 26 Jul 2010. http://keywiki.org/index.php/Joel_Bleifuss (accessed Jul 26, 2010).

—. "Canter, David." *KeyWiki David Canter.* 2009. http://www.keywiki.org/index.php/David_Canter (accessed Sep 11, 2009).

—. "Druyan, Ann ." *Key Wiki - Ann Druyan.* 8 Mar 2010. http://keywiki.org/index.php/Ann_Druyan (accessed Mar 8, 2010).

—. "Harwell, Caroll." *Key Wiki - Carol Harwell.* 2008. http://keywiki.org/index.php/Carol_Harwell (accessed Apr 2010).

—. "Holtzman, Liz ." *Key Wiki.* 6 Aug 1993. http://keywiki.org/index.php/Liz_Holtzman (accessed Jun 29, 2010).

—. "Hudson, Jerry." *Key Wiki.* 2 Aug 2010. http://keywiki.org/index.php/Jerry_Hudson (accessed Aug 10, 2010).

—. "Meeks, Gregory." *Key Wiki.* 26 Sep 2009. http://www.keywiki.org/index.php/Gregory_Meeks (accessed Oct 17, 2009).

—. "Mikva, Abner." *Key Wiki - Abner Mikva.* 1 May 2010. http://keywiki.org/index.php/Abner_Mikva (accessed May 1, 2010).

—. "Mishel, Lawrence ." *Key Wiki - Lawrence Mishel.* 1 May 2010. http://keywiki.org/index.php/Lawrence_Mishel (accessed May 26, 2010).

—. "Ptashne, Mark." *Key Wiki.* 8 Mar 2010. http://keywiki.org/index.php/Mark_Ptashne (accessed Mar 8, 2010).

—. "Rogers, Joel." *Key Wiki - Joel Rogers.* 1 May 2010. http://keywiki.org/index.php/Joel_Rogers (accessed May 1, 2010).

—. "Sheinbaum, Stanley ." *Key Wiki - Stanley Sheinbaum.* 8 Mar 2010. http://keywiki.org/index.php/Stanley_Sheinbaum (accessed Mar 8, 2010).

—. "Wallis, Jim ." *Key Wiki - Jim Wallis.* 2008. http://keywiki.org/index.php/Jim_Wallis (accessed Mar 8, 2010).

—. "Wilentz, Sean." *Key Wiki: Sean Wilentz.* 29 Jun 2010. http://keywiki.org/index.php/Sean_Wilentz (accessed Jun 29, 2010).

—. "Working Families Party." *Key Wiki*. 7 Oct 2009. http://keywiki.org/index.php/Working_Families_Party (accessed Oct 7, 209).

Klein, Aaron. "Another Weatherman Terrorist a play in the Obama Campaign." *World Net Daily*. 26 Sep 2008. http://www.wnd.com/index.php?fa=PAGE.view&pageId=76234 (accessed Oct 11, 2008).

Kupendua, Marpessa. "Black Radical Congress [Mission]." *Black Radical Congress, Enorsers of the Call*. 17 Mar 1998. http://www.hartford-hwp.com/archives/45a/524.html (accessed Oct 4, 2008).

Kuttner, Robert. "The End of an Illusion." *Huffington Post*. 14 Mar 2010. http://www.huffingtonpost.com/robert-kuttner/the-end-of-an-illusion_b_498467.html (accessed May 26, 2010).

Kyle, Sharon, and Dick Price. "Barack's Sister Brings the Heat to El Sereno." *LA Progressive*. 22 Jun 2008. http://www.washingtonpost.com/wp-dyn/articles/A53239-2004May24.html (accessed Mar 5, 2009).

LaLuz, Jose, interview by People's Weekly World. *Chirman of Latinos for Obama* (19 Sep 2008).

Lamb, Yvonne Shinhoster. "Vernon Jarrett, 84, Journalist, Crusader - Obituaries." *The Washington Post*. 25 May 2004. http://www.washingtonpost.com/wp-dyn/articles/A53239-2004May24.html (accessed Oct 17, 2008).

—. "Vernon Jarrett, 84, Journalist, Crusader - Obituaries." *Washington Post*. 24 May 2004. http://www.washingtonpost.com/wp-dyn/articles/A53239-2004May24.html (accessed Jun 1, 2009).

Lenin and National Liberation. "Amilcar Carbral - Outstanding Leader of African Liberation Movement - A Tribute." *Africa Speaks*. Apr/Jun 1970. http://www.africaspeaks.com/reasoning/index.php?topic=2741.0 (accessed April 4, 2009).

Lewis, Bertha, and Patrick Gaspard. "Run WFP Run! Run WFP Run!" *The Nation*. 2 Jul 2001. http://www.thenation.com/article/run-wfp-run-run-wfp-run (accessed Oct 2009).

Litvinsky, Marina. "One in Five Children Sinking into Poverty." *People's World*. 5 Jun 2009. http://www.peoplesworld.org/one-in-five-children-sinking into poverty (accessed Sep 9, 2009).

Lizza, Ryan. "The Political Scene." *The New Yorker*. 12 Jan 2008. http://www.newyorker.com/reporting/2008/07/21/080721fa_fact_lizza?currentPage=all (accessed Aug 23, 2008).

Lozano, Pepe. "Harold Washington wore a Union Label." *People's World*. 23 Feb 2008. http://www.peoplesworld.org/harold-washington-wore-a-union-label/ (accessed Oct 17, 2008).

—. "Harold Washington Wore a Union Label." *People's World*. 20 Feb 2008. http://blogs.myspace.com/index.cfm?fuseaction=blog.ListAll&friendId=2 01214108 (accessed Feb 22, 2008).

Lozono, Pepe. "Latino voters key to Obama win in battleground states." *CPUSA People's World*. 18 Sep 2008. http://www.peoplesworld.org/latino-voters-key-to-obama-win-in-battleground-states/ (accessed Sep 18, 2008).

Machtinger, Howard. "Obama and the Left." *Progressives for Obama Forum*. 15 Apr 2008. http://progressivesforobama.lefora.com/2008/04/15/obama-and-left/ (accessed Sep 30, 2008).

Marable, Dr. Manning. "The four legged stool that won the US presidential election." *Facebook*. Dec 2008. http://www.facebook.com/note.php?note_id=52209419748 (accessed Jan 11, 2009).

Marable, Manning. "The four legged stool that won the US presidential election." *Socialist Review*. Dec 2008. http://www.socialistreview.org.uk/article.php?articlenumber=10628 (accessed Dec 8, 2009).

Margolis, Dan. "Super Sunday events for People's World." *Peoples Weekly World*. 2 Dec 2006. http://www.peoplesworld.org/super-sunday-events-for-pww/ (accessed Aug 28, 2008).

—. "Young Communist League." *People's World*. 2 Jun 2006. (accessed Aug 28, 2008).

Markowitz, Norman. "Edwards Withdraws: Some Thoughts About What it Means." *PA Political Affairs, People's Weekly World*. 30 Jan 2008. http://paeditorsblog.blogspot.com/2008/01/edwards-withdraws-some-thoughts-about.html (accessed Feb 1, 2008).

—. "Obama's Mandate for Change." *Political Analysis*. 22 Nov 2008. http://peoplesworld.org/opinion-obama-s-mandate-for-change/ (accessed Nov 17, 2009).

—. "Senator Obama Continues to Mobilize People for Progressive Change." *Political Affairs Editors Blog, People's Weekly World*. 10 Feb 2008. (accessed Feb 13, 2008).

Marshall, Scott. "Obama Wins! Labor Wins! Working Families Win! The American people reject policies of greed and union-busting!" *Labor UpFront*. 7 Nov 2008. http://laborupfront.blogspot.com/search?updated-min=2008-01-01T00%3A00%3A00-06%3A00&updated-max=2009-01-01T00%3A00%3A00-06%3A00&max-results=50 (accessed Nov 20, 2008).

McClelland, Edward. "Chicago is Barack Obama's kind of Town." *Salon.com*. 14 Jan 2008. http://www.salon.com/news/opinion/feature/2008/01/14/obama/print.html (accessed Oct 30, 2008).

McNary, William. "Presidents proposal protects drug profits." *CPUSA Newspaper People's World*. 16 Feb 2002. http://transitional.pww.org/president-s-proposal-protects-drug-profits/ (accessed Sep 8, 2008).

—. "Women's Voices, Women Vote." *The Huffington Post*. 1 May 2008. http://www.huffingtonpost.com/william-mcnary/womens-voices-women-vote_b_99548.html (accessed Sep 2, 2008).

Medina, SEIU International Vice President Eliseo. "America's Future NOW!" *SEIU*. Washington D.C.: SEIU, 2009.

Meeropol, Michael. "Obama and the Left: Shout Loud and Clear." *The Rag Blog*. 4 Dec 2008. http://theragblog.blogspot.com/2008/12/obama-and-left-shout-loud-and-clear.html (accessed Dec 12, 2008).

Meyerson, Harold. "A Bright Hope in Illinois." *Washington Post*. 12 Mar 2004. http://www.washingtonpost.com/wp-dyn/content/article/2008/08/13/AR2008081303273.html (accessed Aug 3, 2010).

—. "Another Star in Chicago." *The Washington Post*. 25 Feb 2009. http://www.washingtonpost.com/wp-dyn/content/article/2009/02/24/AR2009022403017.html (accessed Aug 3, 2010).

Moberg, David. "Obama's in the Eye of the Beholder." *In These Times*. 7 Sep 2007. http://www.inthesetimes.com/article/3329/ (accessed Sep 2, 2008).

Munoz, Rosalia. "Arizona Conference." *People's Weekly World*. 6 Mar 2004. (accessed Feb 6, 2008).

Munoz, Rosalio. "Southern California Latinos Rally for Obama." *PA Political Affairs, People's Weekly World*. 5 Feb 2008. http://paeditorsblog.blogspot.com/2008/02/southern-california-latinos-rally-for.html (accessed Feb 6, 2008).

Murray, Dr. Linda Rae. "Acceptance Speech President of the APHA." *American Public Health Association*. APHA, 2009.

Murray, Dr. Linda Ray. "The Medicare, Spirit of 1848, Women's and Socialist Caucuses." *American Public Health Association*. San Diego: APHA, 2008.

Myles, Dee. "Vernon Jarrett: A Partisan Journalist Giant." *People's World*. 5 Jun 2004. http://www.peoplesworld.org/vernon-jarrett-a-partisan-journalistic-giant/ (accessed Oct 17, 2008).

Neff, Gina. "Socialist Scholars Conference." *PEN-L Mailing List Archieve*. 20 Mar 1997. http://archives.econ.utah.edu/archives/pen-l/1997m03.d/msg00084.htm (accessed Oct 26, 2008).

New America Foundation. "About." *New America*. 1999. http://www.newamerica.net/about (accessed Aug 2, 2010).

New Party News. *New Party News*. Spring 1996.

Newman, Nathan. "Defending Van Jones from the McCarhyites." *Daily Kos*. 4 Sep 2009. http://www.dailykos.com/story/2009/9/4/776855/-Defending-Van-Jones-from-the-McCarthyites (accessed Oct 2009, 2009).

Newsletter, Greater Detroit Local DSA. "DSA National Convention." *Greater Detroit Local DSA Newsletter*. 13 Nov 2009. http://kincaidsite.com/dsa/newsletter.html (accessed Nov 21, 2008).

Nolan, Michael D. "A Cuban Revolutionary and a Cuban Exile Reunite." *The Rag Blog*. 4 Apr 2009. http://theragblog.blogspot.com/2009/04/cuban-revolutionary-and-cuban-exile.html (accessed Apr 8, 2009).

Norris, Chuck. "A Dirty Secret within Obamacare Bill: Government coming into Homes and Usurping Parental Rights over Child Care and Development." *Romanticpoet's Weblog*. 11 Aug 2009. http://romanticpoet.wordpress.com/2009/08/12/ (accessed Sep 9, 2009).

Nowell, Bob. "The Role of the International Organization of Journalists (IOJ) in the Debate about the "New International Information Order." *http://www.eric.ed.gov/ERICWebPortal*. n.d. http://www.eric.ed.gov/ERICWebPortal/search/detailmini.jsp?_nfpb=true&_&ERICExtSearch_SearchValue_0=ED189654&ERICExtSearch_SearchType_0=no&accno=ED189654 (accessed 2009).

—. "The Role of the International Organization of Journalists in the Debate about the "New International Information Order," 1958-1978." *International Organization of Journalists*. 1978. http://www.keywiki.org/index.php/International_Organization_of_Journalists (accessed Nov 17, 2009).

Nuisance Industry. "RIP Leon Depres (Obit with Obama statement)." *Daily Kos*. 6 May 2009. http://www.dailykos.com/story/2009/5/7/728648/-RIP-Leon-Despres-(obit-with-Obama-statement) (accessed May 16, 2009).

Obama, Senator Barack. "Tone, Truth, and the Democratic Party." *Daily Kos*. 30 Sep 2005. http://www.dailykos.com/story/2005/09/30/153069/-Tone,-Truth,-and-the-Democratic-Party (accessed Oct 31, 2008).

O'Brian, Mary, and Livingston, Martha. *10 Excellent Reasons for National Health Care*. New York, NY: The New Press, 2008.

Ogletree, Charles. "Trial Advocacy Workshop." *Harvard Law.* 1986. (accessed Jun 17, 2009).

O'Leary, Brad. "Obama's sweatheart - deal home loan." *World Net Daily.* 15 Oct 2008. http://www.wnd.com/index.php?fa=PAGE.view&pageId=77971 (accessed Sep 19, 2009).

PA Staff Writers. "Labor Solidifies Victory for Obama." *Political Affairs.* 1 Nov 2008. http://politicalaffairs.net/search/SphinxSearchForm?Search=1+Nov+2008 &action_results=search (accessed Nov 11, 2008).

Pallasch, Abdon M. "Obama shows caution on Middle East, Rabbi says." *Chicago Sun Times.* 27 Jul 2008. http://www.suntimes.com/news/politics/obama/1076922,CST-NWS-rabbi27.article (accessed Oct 28, 2008).

Palmer, Alice. "Palmer's trip to the Soviet Union." *People's Daily World.* 24 Dec 1986. http://www.peoplesworld.org/><a rel="cc:attributionURL" property="cc:attributionName" href="http://www.peoplesworld.org">www.peoplesworld.org</a> / <a rel="license" href="http://creativecommons.org/licenses/by-nc-nd/3.0/us/">CC BY-NC-ND 3.0</a> (accessed Nov 2009).

Palmer, Alice, interview by Mike Giocondo. *People's Daily World* (24 Dec 1986).

Pattberg, Mike. "More Stuff on Trade." *Boston Democratic Socialists of America.* 27 Sep 2007. http://www.dsaboston.org/yradical/yr2007-09.pdf (accessed Nov 21, 2008).

Pazniokas, Mark. "Obama Kickoff is SRO, Hillary Announces Malloy Endorsement." *Capital Watch.* 12 Jan 2008. http://blogs.courant.com/capitol_watch/2008/01/obama-kickoff-is-sro-hillary-a.html (accessed Oct 4, 2008).

PBS Online Newshour. "Obama Learned Lessons on the Path to the National Stage." *PBS Online Newshours.* 28 Aug 2008. http://www.pbs.org/newshour/bb/politics/july-dec08/obamaprof_08-28.html (accessed Oct 25, 2008).

People's Daily World. "Chicago Alderman Danny K. Davis." *People's Daily World,* 28 Jul 1990.

People's World. "Communists call for Urgent Action on Crisis." *People's World.* 22 Nov 2008. http://www.peoplesworld.org/communists-call-for-urgent-action-on-crisis/ (accessed Nov 21, 2008).

—. "Opinion: Obamas mandate for change." *People's World.* 22 Nov 2008. http://www.peoplesworld.org/opinion-obama-s-mandate-for-change/ (accessed Nov 11, 2008).

Perazzo, John. "Ron Bloom, Manufacturing Czar." *Front Page Mag.* 21 Oct 2009. http://frontpagemag.com/2009/10/21/ron-bloom-manufacturing-czar/ (accessed Sep 16, 2009).

Phelps, Christopher. "The New SDS." *The Nation.* 16 Apr 2007. (accessed Oct 2008).

Piana, Della. "NY Labor Day: Time to Make a Change." *CPUSA People's World Blog.* 5 Sep 2008. http://peoplesweeklyworldblog.blogspot.com/2008/09/ny-labor-day-time-to-make-change.html (accessed Sep 11, 2008).

—. "PA Editors Blog." *CPUSA Political Affairs Blog.* 5 Feb 2008. http://peoplesweeklyworldblog.blogspot.com/2008/09/ny-labor-day-time-to-make-change.html (accessed Sep 11, 2008).

Ponte, Lowell. "How Socialist Unions Rule the Democratic Party." *Front Page Mag.* 14 Jul 2004. http://archive.frontpagemag.com/readArticle.aspx?ARTID=12216 (accessed Feb 16, 2008).

Prados, Adrian Bleifuss. "Obama for a Participatory Democracy." *The Activist.* 28 Jan 2008. http://theactivist.org/blog/obama-for-a-participatory-democracy (accessed Feb 27, 2008).

Publiese, Michael. "Name the System." *Mailman-lbo-talk.* 1 Dec 1999. http://mailman.lbo-talk.org/1999/1999-December/021208.html (accessed Feb 27, 2008).

Ransby, Barbara. "What is the Black Radical Congress (BRC)?" *Hartford-hwp.* 10 Jun 1998. http://www.hartford-hwp.com/archives/45a/228.html (accessed Apr 25, 2009).

Rauh, Grace. "Former Brooklyn Congressman Barack Obama." *The New York Sun.* 17 Oct 2007. http://www.nysun.com/new-york/former-brooklyn-congressman-backs-obama/64690/ (accessed Aug 28, 2008).

Reardon, Patrick T. "The Agony and the Agony." *Chicago Tribune.* 24 Jun 2007. http://www.chicagotribune.com/news/local/chi-070620axelrod-htmlstory,0,7217326.htmlstory (accessed Oct 30, 2008).

Rebel-PWCM-JLA, The. "New curriculum glorifies communist who called for 'resistance' against cops." *Original from Leftist Blog Machete 48.* 3 Mar 2009. http://www.sodahead.com/united-states/students-taught-to-emulate-van-jones-anti-police-activism-new-curriculum-glorifies-communist/question-1565771/ (accessed Apr 4, 2009).

Reynolds, Gretchen. "Vote of Confidence." *Chicago Magazine.* Jan 1993. http://www.chicagomag.com/Chicago-Magazine/January-1993/Vote-of-Confidence/ (accessed Oct 17, 2008).

Roman, Bob. "A Town Meeting on Economic Insecurity: Employment and Survival in Urban America." *New Ground* 45. Mar/Apr 1996. http://www.chicagodsa.org/ngarchive/ng45.html#anchor1078705 (accessed Dec 20, 2008).

—. "A Town Meeting on Economic Insecurity: Employment and Survival in Urban America." *New Ground* 45. Mar - Apr 1996. http://www.chicagodsa.org/ngarchive/ng45.html (accessed Jul 27, 2010).

—. "Chicago Anti-FTAA Action." *Chicago DSA.* May/Jun 2001. http://www.chicagodsa.org/ngarchive/ng76.html#anchor427305 (accessed Sep 16, 2009).

—. *New Ground 39.* March/April 1995. http://chicagodsa.org/ngarchive/ng39.html.

—. "A Town Meeting on Economic Insecurity: Employment and Survival in Urban America." *New Ground 45,* Mar/Apr 1996.

—. "New Party Organizes." *New Ground* 38. Jan/Feb 1995. http://www.chicagodsa.org/ngarchive/ng38.html.

—. "Other News." *New Ground* 120. Oct 2008. http://www.chicagodsa.org/ngarchive/ng120.html (accessed Sep 16, 2009).

—. "Progressive Potential." *New Ground* 62. Jan/Feb 1999. http://www.chicagodsa.org/ngarchive/ng62.html (accessed Oct 25, 2008).

—. "Where Do We Go From Here?" *49th Annual Debs - Thomas - Harrington Dinner.* 7 May 2007. http://www.chicagodsa.org/d2007/index.html (accessed Sep 17, 2009).

Romerstein, Herbert, and Levchenko, Stanislav. *The KGB Against the Main Enemy - How the Soviet Intelligence* Service *Operates.* New York, NY: Lexington Books, 1989.

Romerstein, Herbert, and Stanislav Levchenko. *The KGB Against the "Main Enemy": How the Soviet Intelligence* Service *Operates Against the United States.* New York, NY: MW Books, 1989.

Roosevelt, President Franklin D. "Presidential Directive." Washington, DC: White House, 6 Sep 1939.

—. "Presidential Directive of September 6, 1939." *National Counterintelligence Center.* 1944. http://www.fas.org/irp/ops/ci/docs/ci1/ch4d.htm (accessed Sep 11, 2009).

Rucker, Philip. "Potential Obama Appointees Face Extensive Vetting." *The Washington Post.* 18 Nov 2008. http://www.washingtonpost.com/wp-dyn/content/article/2008/11/17/AR2008111703037.html?hpid=topnews (accessed Nov 20, 2008).

Rudd, Mark. "How to build a Movement." *Mark Rudd*. 2008. http://www.markrudd.com/?organizing-and-activism-now/how-to-build-a-movement.html (accessed Sep 30, 2008).

—. "Let's Get Smart About Obama." *The Rag Blogg*. Nov 2008. http://www.markrudd.com/?organizing-and-activism-now/lets-get-smart-about-obama-nov-2008.html (accessed 3 2008, Dec).

Sanfield, Ron. "District 299 The Chicago School Board." *Earl Dunham RIP*. 27 Oct 2007. http://district299.typepad.com/district299/2007/10/earl-durham-rip.html (accessed Feb 8, 2010).

Sargent, Greg. "Labor Leaders Hail Obama's Pick for Labor Secretary." *TPM Election Central*. 18 Dec 2008. http://tpmelectioncentral.talkingpointsmemo.com/2008/12/andy_stern_on_obamas_labor_sec.php (accessed Dec 20, 2008).

Schaps, Margie. "A Perfect Storm Rising:." *2005 Debs - Thomas - Harrington Dinner*. 6 May 2005. http://www.chicagodsa.org/d2005/index.html#anchor291968 (accessed Dec 8, 2009).

Schlussel, Debbie. "The Company He Keeps: Obama Hangs with Hezbollah's Iranian agent Imam." *Debbie Schlussel*. 16 May 2008. http://www.debbieschlussel.com/3770/the-company-he-keeps-obama-hangs-with-hezbollahs-iranian-agent-imam/ (accessed Apr 30, 2009).

Schultz, Burt. *Obama's Rhetoric, Pragmatism and the University of Chicago*. Thesis, Chicago: University of Chicago, 2003.

SEIU. "SEIU Members Endorse Sen. Barack Obama." *SEIU.org*. 19 Feb 2008. http://www.seiu.org/political/presidential/barack-obama/ (accessed Feb 13, 2008).

Sherman, Steven. "The Democratic Left and Cuba." *Counterpunch*. 21 Apr 2003. http://www.counterpunch.org/2003/04/21/the-democratic-left-and-cuba/ (accessed Sep 22, 2009).

Shier, Carl Marx. "39th Annual Dinner Makes the Organization Proud." *New Ground 52*. May/Jun 1997. http://www.chicagodsa.org/ngarchive/ng52.html#anchor311557 (accessed Sep 17, 2009).

Shier, Carl Marx. *Saul Mendelson Memorial*. Performed by Carl Marx Shier. First Unitarian Church, Chicago. 29 Mar 1998.

Shier, Carl. "Setting the Terms for Globalization." *New Ground 64*. May/Jun 1999. http://www.chicagodsa.org/ngarchive/ng64.html#anchor713759 (accessed Feb 23, 2008).

Shier, Carl, and Bob Roman. "New Ground 30." *Chicago DSA*. Jul/Aug 1993. http://www.chicagodsa.org/ngarchive/ng30.html (accessed Dec 8, 2009).

Smiley, Erica. "Bi-Annual Report to YCL National Council." *Political Climate*. 6-7 Oct 2007. http://www.yclusa.org/article/articleview/1805/1/6/ (accessed Feb 29, 2008).

Solis, Hilda. "The New Capital of Progressive Politics?" *Los Angeles DSA National Convention*. Winter 2006. http://www.dsausa.org/dl/Winter_2006.pdf (accessed Dec 20, 2008).

Solomon, John. "John Edwards Hair." *Post Politics Hour*. 25 Jul 2007. http://www.washingtonpost.com/wp-dyn/content/discussion/2007/07/21/DI2007072100807.html (accessed Feb 4, 2009).

Spitfire. 2008. (accessed Sep 28, 2008).

Staub, Michael E. "Torn at the Roots: The Crisis of Jewish Liberalism in Postwar America." *Questia Media America*. 2002. http://www.dsausa.org/dl/Winter_2006.pdf (accessed Oct 28, 2008).

Strickland, Eliza. "The New Face of Environmentalism." *Truth-Out.org*. 2 Nov 2005. http://www.truth-out.org/article/eliza-strickland-the-new-face-environmentalism (accessed Apr 6, 2009).

Sudaplatov, Pavel. *Special Tasks, Memoirs of an Unwanted Witness - A Soviet Spymaster*. New York, NY: Little, Brown and Company, 1994.

SUP Auckland Regional Newsletter. *SUP Auckland Regional Newsletter*. Auckland, NZ: SUP Auckland Regional Newsletter, 12 Nov 1980.

Sweeney, Michael. "Leon M Depres 1908 - 2009: The LIberal Conscience of Chicago." *Stonecipher*. 7 May 2009. http://stonecipher.typepad.com/the_stonecipher_report/2009/05/leon-m-despres-19082009-the-liberal-conscience-of-chicago.html (accessed May 16, 2009).

Sweet, Lynn. "Another Chicagoan, Laurie Mikva joins the Obama Administration." *Chicago Sun Times*. 18 Apr 2009. http://blogs.suntimes.com/sweet/2009/04/another_chicagoan_laurie_mikva.html (accessed May 1, 2010).

—. "Obama's Ayers Connection never Bugged Anyone." *Chicago Sun Times*. 14 Apr 2008. http://www.suntimes.com/news/sweet/901879,CST-NWS-sweet18.article (accessed Oct 28, 2008).

Swinney, Dan. *Introductory Pamphlet*. Chicago: Progressive Chicago, 1993.

Targ, Harry. "Midwest CCDS Discusses How Venezuelan Policies Increase Public Services While Cook County Destroys Them." *CCDS Forum & Discussion Board*. 8 Apr 2007. http://www.cc-ds.org/discussion/midwest_ccds_meeting_mar07.html (accessed Dec 8, 2009).

The American Prospect. "About - The American Prospect - Our Mission." *Prospect*. 1998. http://www.prospect.org/cs/about_tap/our_mission (accessed Jul 27, 2010).

The Independent. "David Axelrod: Political Strategist." *The Independent Profiles*. 25 Oct 2008. http://www.independent.co.uk/news/people/profiles/david-axelrod-guiding-light-972796.html (accessed Oct 30, 2008).

The Traditional Values Coalition. "Who is David Axelrod - Obama's Political Advisor?" *Traditional Values Coalition*. 5 Mar 2008. http://www.traditionalvalues.org/read/3275/who-is-david-axelrod—obamas-political-advisor/ (accessed Oct 30, 2008).

The White House. "President Barack Obama." *Huffington Post*. 30 Jan 2009. http://www.huffingtonpost.com/robert-kuttner/pesident-obama-wants-you_b_162975.html (accessed Apr 6, 2009).

Thomas, Monifa. "David Canter 81, Lawyer, Activist." *Chicago Sun Times*. 30 Aug 2004. http://nl.newsbank.com/nl-search/we/Archives?p_product=CSTB&p_theme=cstb&p_action=search&p_maxdocs=200&s_dispstring=rest(Mr.%20Canter's%20father%20moved%20the%20family%20from%20Boston%20to%20Russia)%20AND%20AND%20date(all)&p_field_advanced-0=&p_text_advan (accessed Oct 30, 2008).

Tom, Hayden, Glover, Danny, Bill Fletcher Jr., and Barbara Ehrenreich. "Barack is Our Best Option - And You're Needed Now!" *Progressive America Rising*. 24 Mar 2008. http://www.progressivesforobama.net/?page_id=2 (accessed Sep 11, 2008).

Topo, El. "Report from the Chicago MDS-SDS convergence, 11/9." *The Sixties*. 17 Nov 2007. http://sixties-l.blogspot.com/2007/11/report-from-chicago-mds-sds-convergence.html (accessed Sep 21, 2008).

TPM Cafe. "Compendium of Hillary's Dirty Tricks." *TPM Cafe*. 1 May 2008. http://www.talkingpointsmemo.com/talk/2008/05/compendium-of-hillarys-dirty-t.php (accessed Sep 2, 2008).

Trevor, Jensen, and Ron Grossman. "Leon Despres, council foe to first Daley, Dies." *Chicago Breaking News*. 6 May 2009.

http://www.chicagobreakingnews.com/2009/05/leon-despres-council-foe-to-first-daley-dies.html (accessed May 16, 2009).

Trib Live Opinion. "Barack Obama's Closet." *Pittsburgh Tribune Review*, 14 Jan 2007.

Tyner, Jarvis. "Obama for President." *Maine Owl*. 7 Feb 2008. http://maineowl.net/blog/item/322 (accessed Aug 16, 2008).

—. "Obama for President." *Maine Owl*. 7 Feb 2008. http://maineowl.net/blog/item/322 (accessed Aug 16, 2008).

US Action. "US Action Board of Directors Meeting." *1 Sep 2008*. Chicago: US Action, 2008.

US House of Representatives. "Communist Outlets for the Distribution of Soviet Propaganda in the United States." *Committee on Un-American Activities*. Washington D.C.: US Government Printing Office, 1962.

US Russian Independent Scientific Commission. *Final Report of the USRIS Commission on Disposition of Excess Weapons Plutonium*. Public Policy Report, Washington, DC: US Government, 1997.

Wald, Alan. "African Americans, Culture and Communism Part 2: National Liberation and Socialism." *Against the Current #86*. May/Jun 2000. http://www.hartford-hwp.com/archives/45a/436.html (accessed Oct 17, 2008).

Wang, Jessica. *American Science in an Age of Anxiety*. Chapel Hill, NC: The University of North Carolina Press, 1998.

Washington, Laura S. "The Whole World was Watching." *In These Times*. 23 Aug 2008. http://www.inthesetimes.com/article/3876/the_whole_world_was_watching/ (accessed Oct 2008, 2008).

Washington, Laura S. "Debunking the 60s with Ayers and Dohrn." *In These Times*. 17 Aug 2006. http://www.inthesetimes.com/article/2785/ (accessed Dec 12, 2008).

—. "The Whole World was Watching." *In These Times*. 23 Aug 2008. http://www.inthesetimes.com/article/3876/the_whole_world_was_watching/ (accessed Sep 11, 2009).

Waters, Maxine, Hilda Solis, and Elena Henry. "Greetings to the Communist Party." *KeyWiki: Hilda L. Solis*. June 1996. http://keywiki.org/index.php/Hilda_L._Solis (accessed Dec 20, 2008).

Webb, Sam. "A Springtime of Possibility." *People's World Communist Party USA*. 15 Nov 2008. http://www.keywiki.org/index.php/Sam_Webb (accessed Nov 28, 2008).

Webb, Sam. *Off and Running: Opportunity of a Lifetime*. National Chairman's Speech, Cleveland, Ohio: Communist Party USA, 2009.

—. "Pass the Budget! Grassroots Coalition Demands Action." *Peoples World*. 26 Mar 2009. http://www.peoplesworld.org/pass-the-budget-grassroots-coalition-demands-action/ (accessed Mar 28, 2009).

—. "The Impossible becomes Possible." *People's World*. 23 May 2009. http://www.peoplesworld.org/speech-the-impossible-becomes-possible/ (accessed May 23, 2009).

Weissbourd, Bernice. "Bernice Weissbourd." *Key Wiki* . 22 Feb 2010. http://keywiki.org/index.php/Bernice_Weissbourd (accessed Feb 22, 2010).

Wendland, Joel. "Harold Washington: The People's Mayor." *Political Affairs*. 28 Feb 2008. http://www.politicalaffairs.net/article/articleview/6528/ (accessed Feb 28, 2008).

—. "Marxist Thought Online." *Political Affairs*. 28 Feb 2008. http://www.politicalaffairs.net/article/articleview/6528/1/318/ (accessed Feb 2008, 2008).

—. "SEIU Backs Obama." *PA Political Affairs, People's Weekly World*. 15 Feb 2008. http://paeditorsblog.blogspot.com/search?q=Andy+Stern (accessed Feb 13, 2008).

Westerfield, David. "Reclaiming Revolution - History and Summation of STORM." *David Westerfield*. Sep 2009. http://www.davidwesterfield.net/2009/09/reclaiming-revolution-history-and-summation-of-storm/ (accessed Aug 27, 2009).

Wheeler, Tim. "2008 Take back America Conference." *People's Weekly World*. 2008. (accessed Sep 2, 2008).

—. "Live Blogging from South Carolina." *PA Political Affairs, People's Weekly World*. 26 Jan 2008. http://paeditorsblog.blogspot.com/2008/01/live-blogging-from-obamas-campaign-in.html (accessed Jan 28, 2008).

—. "Obama wins big in South Carolina." *PA Political Affairs, People's Weekly World*. 26 Jan 2008. http://paeditorsblog.blogspot.com/2008/01/obama-wins-big-in-south-carolina.html (accessed Jan 28, 2008).

—. "Kucinich: the most unreported story of 2004." *People's World*, 26 Feb 2004.

—. "Whose World is it?" *Angelfire.com*. 25 Dec 1999. http://www.angelfire.com/la/cominternet/pww99.html (accessed Oct 20, 2008).

Wikipedia contributors. "Jan Schakowsky." *Wikipedia, The Free Encyclopedia*. 8 Feb 2008. http://en.wikipedia.org/w/index.php?title=Jan_Schakowsky&oldid=4346 54047 (accessed Feb 10, 2008).

Wikipedia. "Jesse Jackson, Jr." *Wikipedia*. 23 Dec 2003. http://en.wikipedia.org/w/index.php?title=Jesse_Jackson,_Jr.&oldid=3663 70498 (accessed Aug 22, 2008).

Willamette Reds of Oregon. "Tyner on the Presidential Election." *Willamette Reds of Oregon*. 16 Aug 2008. http://willamettereds.blogspot.com/2008/08/jarvis-tyner-on-presidential-election.html (accessed Aug 16, 2008).

Williams, Jim. "Committees of Correspondence Meet in Chicago." *New Ground 36*. Sep/Oct 2000. http://www.chicagodsa.org/ngarchive/ng36.html#anchor810069 (accessed Aug 19, 2008).

—. "Committees of Correspondence Meet in Chicago." *New Ground 36*. Sept/Oct 2000. http://www.chicagodsa.org/ngarchive/ng36.html#anchor810069 (accessed Dec 17, 2008).

Wojcik, John. "Change to Win." *People's Weekly World*. 23 Feb 2008. http://www.peoplesworld.org/change-to-win-endorses-obama/ (accessed Feb 23, 2008).

Wolf, Rabbi Arnold Jacob. "My Neighbor Barack." *Jews for Obama*. 2008. http://jews4obama2008.wordpress.com/my-neighbor-barack-by-arnold-jacob-wolf/ (accessed Oct 28, 2008).

Wright, Rev. Jeremiah. "Rev. Jeremiah Wright." *KeyWiki*. 25 Apr 2009. http://keywiki.org/index.php/Jeremiah_Wright (accessed Apr 25, 2009).

Yearwood, Pauline Dibkin. "Bar Mitzvah, Old Man: At age 83, Rabbi Arnold Jacob Wolf is his Big Day." *The Chicago Jewish News Online*. 23 Mar 2007. http://www.chicagojewishnews.com/story.htm?sid=1&id=250469 (accessed Oct 28, 2008).

Young M.D., Quentin, Don McCanne M.D., David Himmelstein M.D., and Mark Almberg. "Doctors, citing mandate for change, call on Obama, Congress to 'do the right thing' on health reform." *Physicians for a National Health Program*. 5 Nov 2008. http://www.pnhp.org/news/2008/november/doctors_citing_mand.php (accessed Nov 11, 2008).

Zagaroli, Lisa. "Congressman Gleefully Admits he was Wrong about Obama." *McClatchy Newspaper*. 19 Jan 2009. http://www.modbee.com/2009/01/19/569796/congressman-gleefully-admits-he.html (accessed Jun 24, 2009).

Zunes, Stephen. "Obama's Right Turn." *Foreign Policy in Focus*. 11 Jun 2008. http://www.fpif.org/articles/obamas_right_turn (accessed Sep 23, 2008).

Index

12th World Festival of Youth and Students, 88

1937 Memorial Day Massacre at Republic Steel, 361

21st Century Vote, 533

911 Truth Statement, 527

Abercrombie, Neil, 573, 574, 575, 576, 577, 578, 581

Abraham Lincoln School, 149, 500, 504, 506, 522

Abt, John, 362

Abu Ghraib, 210

Abunimah, Ali, 140

ACORN
  Association of Community Organizations for Reform Now, 12, 74, 380
  Foreclosure Avoidance Program (FAP), 184
  Illinois Project Vote, 398, 399, 412
  Project Vote, 155, 156, 163, 164, 196, 197, 375, 380, 399, 412, 420, 421, 485, 556

Acosta, Jerry, 266, 267, 316

Adams, Elliott, 111

Adams, Richard, 391

Adler, Aaron, 513, 515

Administration for Special Tasks, 510, 517

Advancing Change in the Age of Obama, 459

Affirmative Action, 59, 65, 82, 212, 288, 307, 464

African American Agenda 2000, 130, 343

African American Equality and Building Communist Party USA, 154

African American Police League, 341

African American Student Affairs, 80

African National Congress, 405

Agee, Philip, 335, 520

Agenda for Change, 454, 460

Aguilar, Antonio, 267, 316

AIG, 275

Aiyetoro, Adjoa, 387

al Qaeda, 357

Alarcon, Evelina, 266, 268, 315, 316, 317, 318

Alarcon, Richard, 267, 317

Alaska Independence Party, 535

Alawan, Eide, 357

Albano, Terrie, 26

Alderman (Chicago)
  Burrell, Sam, 163
  Chandler, Michael, 76, 171
  Davis, Danny K, 75, 144
  Preckwinkle, Toni, 165, 176, 271

Alderwoman (Chicago)
  Helen Schiller, 78
  Shiller, Helen, 176, 260

Al-Hanooti, Muthanna, 353

Ali, Tariq, 281

Alinsky, Saul, 43, 176, 303, 361, 501, 547, 568

Alinskyism, 43, 176

Alkalimat, Abdul, 130, 131, 343

Alliance to End Repression, 191, 194, 350, 418

Almberg, Mark J., 473, 487

Always Bring a Crowd, 61

America Coming Together, 451

American Civil Liberties Union (ACLU), 568, 571

American College of Emergency Physicians, 485

American College of Medical Informatics, 485

American Committee for Protection of Foreign Born (ACFPFB), 150

American Crescent, 357

American Public Health Association, 471, 482, 483, 488

American Rights at Work, 236, 263, 351, 352, 358

American Strategy Program, 587, 591

Americans for Democratic Action, 31, 87

Americans United for Change, 319

America's Future Now!, 494

America's Urban and Metropolitan Policy Committee, 508

Anastaplo, George, 547

Anderson, Kurt, 13, 143

Anderson, Sam, 130, 344

Annenberg Challenge, 110, 122

ANWR
   Arctic National Wildlife Refuge, 38

Apartheid South Africa, 159

Apollo Alliance, 355, 388, 389, 432, 450, 536, 542, 543, 544

Apollon, Mael, 450

Appelbaum, Stuart, 263

Applied Research Center, 453

Aptheker, Herbert, 159

Arab-Israeli conflict, 357

Arafat, Yasser, 522

Ariyoshi, Koji, 311

Arnold & Porter, 556

Aronowitz, Stanley, 561

Asian Law Collective, 312

Associated Press, 104

Atomic Bomb, 505, 518

Audacity of Hope, 252, 525

Axelrod, David, 192, 193, 195, 197, 198, 199, 204, 205, 350, 366, 400, 416, 418, 420, 421, 422, 548, 569, 625

Axelrod, Myril, 192

Ayers, Bill, 79, 110, 112, 114, 115, 119, 120, 122, 123, 125, 126, 128, 133, 135, 136, 139, 140, 146, 153, 162, 167, 168, 173, 178, 179, 180, 181, 188, 194, 222, 248, 256, 277, 280, 281, 286, 322, 324, 329, 338, 343, 344, 345, 348, 349, 389, 392, 414, 440, 461, 471, 490, 491, 492, 493, 501, 502, 507, 543, 556, 572, 587, 590, 611

Ayers, Rick, 139

Ayers, Tom, 414

Bachtell, John, 154, 374, 411

Back of the Yards Neighborhood Council, 43, 176

Baiman, Ron, 496

Baker, Ella J, 331, 332, 343, 346, 389, 390

Baker, General, 130, 344

Balanoff, Clem, 534

Balanoff, Tom, 9, 10, 92, 496

Baldridge, Jim, 24

Baldridge, Margaret, 24, 25

Baltimore for Barack, 24

Baltimore, David, 513

Bank Street College of Education, 343

Baraka, Amina, 130, 131, 344

Baraka, Amiri, 131, 344

Barclay, Bill, 140

Barkan, Joanne, 566

Barlow, Harriet, 537

Barnet, Richard, 552

Barnett (Frappier), Nancy, 332

Barragan, Senia, 111

Barsamian, David, 112

Baxandall, Rosalyn, 101, 114

Bay Area Marxist-Leninist-Maoist Organization, 390

Bay Area Police Watch,, 327
Bayer, Henry, 9, 380
Bear Stearns, 275
Becerra, Xavier, 32
Becker, George, 431, 432
Beilin, Yossi, 588
Belafonte, Harry, 101
Bell, Debbie, 131
Bella, Ahmed Ben, 555
Benjamin, Medea, 474
Bennis, Phyllis, 396, 458
Bensman, David, 566
Bernard, Elaine, 13, 75, 145, 172, 597, 598
Bernardin Amendment, 46
Bernstein, Jared, 584
Berrigan, Daniel, 599
Berrigan, Frida, 586
Berrigan, Philip, 599
Bethe, Hans, 513
Bethune Club, 79, 222, 470, 486, 505
Bhargava, Deepak, 454, 455, 456, 457, 458, 459, 460
Bild, Bernice, 208, 366, 428
Bishop, Maurice, 462, 463
Bitter Fruit: Black Politics and the Chicago Machine, 1931-1991, 174
Black Advisory Council, 146, 271, 285, 347, 388, 452, 527, 566
Black Freedom Movement: A Radical Democratic Vision, 346
Black Panthers, 332, 383
Black Press Institute (BPI)_, 80, 81, 462, 464, 467, 501
Black Press Review, 462, 464
Black Radical Congress, 22, 98, 100, 101, 129, 130, 134, 140, 257, 285, 343, 345, 346, 439, 524
Black Student Union, 383
Black Workers for Justice, 130, 343

Black, Timuel, 47, 48, 49, 83, 89, 102, 140, 161, 191, 194, 203, 207, 208, 261, 285, 297, 327, 345, 348, 350, 364, 365, 372, 414, 417, 418, 428, 438, 460, 479, 486, 502, 506, 514, 515, 528, 551, 570, 574, 581, 590
Blackshere, Margaret, 9
Blackstone Rangers, 547
Blank, Rebecca, 584
Bleifuss, Joel, 580
Blue Diamond Workers Organizing Committee, 20
Blue Dog Democrats, 319
Bobo, Kim, 380
Boesche, Roger, 592
Bond, Julian, 236, 263, 354, 445
Bonior, John, 436
Bontemps, Arna, 152
Books Not Bars, 336, 407
Booth, Heather, 42, 43, 56, 57, 93, 95, 175, 176, 443, 455
Booth, Paul, 56, 176, 417
Borosage, Robert, 319, 320, 355, 542
Boss, Caroline, 592
Boston Communist Party, 199, 422
Boudin, Cathy, 399
Boudin, Chesa, 557, 572
Boudin, Kathie, 556, 557, 572
Boudin, Leonard, 399, 556, 572
Boudreaux, Ray, 387
Bowman, Barbara Taylor, 414
Bowman, John, 387
Bowman, Valerie, 413
Boyd, Sam, 593
Boyte, Harry C., 508
Braden, Anne, 348
Braden, Carl and Anne, 150
Breira Organization, 190, 280
Brezhnev, Leonid, 562
Bridges, Harry, 150, 311, 313

Brie, Andre, 78, 144, 260
Brisben, Quinn, 32, 165
Brit Shalom, 189
British Fabian Socialist Society, 555, 587
British Labour Party, 475
Brock, Lisa, 131
Brooklyn Democratic Party, 86
Brooks, Rosa, 441, 529
Brower, Elaine, 115
Brown Jr., Oscar, 157, 372, 409, 501
Brown, Humberto R, 131
Brown, Oscar C., 371, 372, 376, 409, 413
Brownlee, Shannon
  Atlantic Monthly, 587
  Discover, 587
  Glamour, 587
  Los Angeles Times, 587
  More, 587
  Mother Jones, 587
  New York Times, 587
  New York Times Magazine, 587
  Slate, 587
  The New Republic, 587
  Time, 587
  US News & World Report, 587
  Washington Monthly, 587
  Washington Post, 587
Brownlee, Shannon, 587
Buber, Martin, 189
Buck, Marilyn, 338
Buffenbarger, Thomas, 584
Buffington, Docia, 71
Buhle, Paul, 101, 111, 114, 123, 137, 153, 179, 182, 255, 280, 281, 283, 324, 373, 410, 440
Bulletin of the Nuclear Atomic Scientists, 509
Bunch, Lonnie, 345

Burger, Anna, 41, 55, 262
Burlage, Robb, 281
Burnham, Linda, 131, 402, 403, 405
Burns, Haywood, 138, 348
Burnstein, Malcolm, 101
Burroughs, Margaret, 152, 157, 376, 413
Cabasso, Jackie, 20
Cabasso, Jacqueline, 404
Cabral, Amilcar, 328, 329, 453
Cagan, Leslie, 452, 457
California Nurses Association, 473
California State University, 69
Callahan, David, 398, 579
Cameron, John D, 93
Camp Galil, 434
Campaign for America's Future, 319, 320, 439, 456, 582, 584
Campbell, Dolores Delgado, 266, 446
Campbell, Duane, 69, 102, 237, 265, 266, 446
Campbell, James E, 131
Campbell, Jim, 102
Campo, Frank del, 404
Canida, Innocenta, 329
Cannon, Bessie, 533
Canter, Marc, 205, 207, 208
Canter, David S., 193, 195, 350, 365, 416, 417, 418, 419, 422, 423, 424, 425, 426, 427, 548, 568
Canter, David Simon, 199, 200, 203, 204, 205, 207, 208, 366, 615, 625
Canter, Harry, 199, 200
Canter, Harry J, 199, 422, 423
Canter, Marc, 205, 426, 427
Canter, Miriam, 204
Cantor, Dan, 537
Cape Verde Islands, 328
Caraway, Dr. Nancie, 576
Carew, Jan, 466

Casey, Leo, 444
Casoy, Flavio, 474
Cassel, Douglass, 133, 345
Castafieda, Jorge, 391
Castro, Fidel, 38, 403
Castro, Victoria, 267
Cavanagh, John, 276, 278, 279, 582
Center for American Progress (CAP), 251, 298, 324, 394, 542
Center for Community Change (CCC), 454, 457, 458, 459
Center for Constitutional Rights, 138, 348
Center for International Human Rights, 133, 345
Center for Law and Social Policy (CLASP), 557
Center for Neighborhood Technology, 177, 507
Center for the Study of Working Class Life, 561
Center On Wisconsin Strategy, 542
Central America Free Trade Agreement, 11
Central Committee of the Communist Party of China
   Deputy Minister Zhang Zhijun, 290
Century Foundation, 398
Cesaire, Aime, 447, 453
Cesar E. Chavez National Holiday, 314, 315
Challenging White Supremacy Workshop, 327, 328, 390, 391
Chandler, Alderman Michael, 14
Chandra, Romesh, 467
Change the World Conference, 587
Chapman, Frank, 81, 300, 301, 348, 350
Charney, Alan, 93
Chavez, Cesar, 37, 269, 314, 315, 316, 317, 318, 364, 495

Chavez, Hugo, 38, 101
Chicago ACORN, 531
Chicago Alderman
   Chandler, Michael, 142, 143
   Colon, Ray, 97
   Davis, Danny K, 78, 260
   Davis, Danny K., 48
   Despres, Leon, 359
   Dick Simpson, 63, 64
   Moore, Joe, 97
   Preckwinkle, Toni, 22
Chicago Alderwoman
   Schiller, Helen, 144
Chicago Center for US/USSR Relations and Exchanges, 513, 515
Chicago City Clerk
   Valle (D), Miguel del, 382, 479
Chicago Coalition for Voter Registration, 162
Chicago Committee on Southern Africa, 374, 411
Chicago Committee to Defend the Bill of Rights, 47, 140, 194, 203, 260, 418, 502, 506, 513, 514, 515, 547, 548, 549, 550, 569, 570
Chicago Communist Party, 60, 70, 144, 151, 154, 155, 159, 162, 166, 191, 282, 300, 311, 349, 366, 370, 424, 466, 485, 502, 504
Chicago Conference on Race Relations, 546
Chicago Daily Observer, 429
Chicago Defender, 152, 156, 371, 372, 376, 408, 410, 412
Chicago Democratic Party Convention, 195, 419
Chicago Historical Society, 345
Chicago Housing Authority, 414
Chicago Maroon, 423
Chicago Mayor

Richard J. Daley, 51, 376
Washington, Harold, 54
Chicago Mobilization Committee, 419
Chicago New Party, 141, 142, 248, 256, 530, 532, 538
Chicago NOW, 109, 161
Chicago Peace Council, 60, 81, 514, 569
Chicago Red Squad, 191, 194, 204, 365, 418
Chicago School Reform Act of 1988, 502
Chicago Socialist Party, 10
Chicago Sun-Times, 156, 157, 375, 376, 412, 413, 423
Chicago Tribune, 133, 152, 157, 193, 345, 360, 373, 376, 410, 413, 418, 491
Chicago Young Communist League, 26, 50, 65
Chicagoans Against the War in Iraq, 197, 421
Chicagoans Against War & Injustice, 15
Chicago's Citizen Action Program, 176
Chicago's Malcolm X College, 468
Chicago's South Shore Cultural Center, 157, 376, 413
Chicago's South Side Community Art Center, 152
Chief of Staff
  Barack Obama (Alice Palmer), 171, 301, 381, 492
  Patrick Gaspard (Margarita Lopez), 448
  Rahm Emanuel (Barack Obama), 366
  Sonya Sanchez (Jesse Garcia), 171
  Steven Guerra (Governor Rod Blagojevich), 498

Vallerie Jarrett (Mayor Harold Washington), 376
William Delgado (Miguel del Valle), 171
Children and Family Justice Center, 345
China Communist Party, 492
Chinese Communist Party, 112, 122
Chomsky, Noam, 43, 48, 74, 112, 121, 145, 147, 161, 172, 178, 180, 255, 279, 281, 297, 346, 349, 356, 378, 527
Chris Matlhako, 404
Christian Coalition, 13
Christians for Socialism, 534
Christopher Hayes
  In These Times, 588
  The Nation, 588
CIA Diary, 335
Citizen Action/Illinois, 92, 93, 97
Citizens Committee, 280
Citizens Party, 451
City College of Chicago, 161
City University of New York, 21, 87
Civil Rights Congress, 148
Clark, Ed, 237
Clark, Jack, 443
Clarke, Yvette, 451
Claypool, Forest, 205, 427
Clemons, Steve, 591
Clinton, Hillary, 5, 17, 103, 268, 324
Cloward, Richard, 540
Cloward-Piven Strategy, 452, 455, 540, 561
Coalition for Education on Sexual Orientation, 139
Cobble, Steve, 102, 145, 147, 276, 277, 278, 279, 283, 537, 598
Cochran, Johnnie, 387
Code Pink, 299, 474
Cohen, Barry, 102

Cohen, Cathy, 130, 133, 344, 345
Cohen, Donald, 583
Cohen, Hannah, 161
Cohen, Larry, 584
Cohen, Michael A.
  ABC News, 588
  Air America, 588
  Al Jazeera, 588
  BBC TV, 588
  Christian Science Monitor, 587
  Courier de la Planete, 588
  democracyarsenal.org, 588
  Forbes.com, 588
  Foreign Policy, 588
  Fox News, 588
  New York Times, 588
  New York Times Campaign Stops, 588
  Politico, 588
  Privatization of Foreign Policy
    Initiative, 587
  South African television, 588
  St. Petersburg Times, 587
  Talkingpointsmemo.com, 588
  Washington Post, 587
  World Policy Journal, 588
  Worth Magazine, 588
  XM Radio's Potus '08, 588
Cohen, Michael A., 587
Cohen, Michael A. Foreign Policy, 587
Cohen, Milton, 48, 162, 191, 194, 207,
261, 365, 366, 418, 428
Cohen, Mitchell, 566
Colbert, Lenore, 450
Colburn, Bruce, 13
Cole, Johnetta, 101, 386
Cole, Rick, 592
Coll, Steve, 590, 591
Coll, Steve, 590
Coll, Susan, 591, 592
Coll, Susan Keselenko, 591

Collins, Chuck, 396, 397, 580
Colombian Communist Party, 38
Color of Change, 325
Columbia University, 8, 20, 67, 102,
126, 196, 238, 283, 303, 343, 378, 420,
518, 596
Committee for Protection of Foreign
Born (CFPFB), 311
Committee of Soviet Scientists,
519
Committee on Chicago Police
Torture, 139
Committees of Correspondence for
Democracy and Socialism (COCDS),
15, 17, 95, 116, 129, 178, 285, 299, 402,
478, 561
Communication Workers of America
(CWA), 73
Communist Manifesto, 101, 482, 521
Communist Party of the Soviet Union
Congress, 464
Communist Party USA, 12, 15, 17, 19,
25, 26, 32, 50, 54, 58, 70, 72, 73, 78, 79,
81, 86, 92, 98, 104, 107, 115, 129, 130,
135, 142, 156, 167, 170, 177, 183, 187,
191, 219, 223, 225, 227, 230, 234, 243,
247, 255, 258, 262, 266, 270, 278, 299,
300, 307, 311, 313, 314, 316, 318, 319,
320, 322, 327, 341, 342, 343, 349, 351,
359, 362, 367, 370, 377, 383, 386, 390,
392, 399, 402, 404, 408, 412, 425, 438,
440, 449, 462, 463, 466, 468, 474, 475,
478, 485, 487, 488, 489, 500, 505, 506,
513, 560, 567
Communist Party USA Mexican
American Equality Commission, 33,
34
Communist Prty USA, 158
Communist Takeover Of America -
45 Declared Goals, 194

Communist Workers Party, 112
Community Organizing and Family Issues (COFI), 502
Community Voting Project, 455
Comprehensive Immigration Reform for America's Security and Prosperity, 493
Condon, Edward U., 512, 513, 518
Cone, James, 523, 526
Conference on Alternative State and Local Policies, 400
Conference on Constitutional Liberties in America, 546
Confronting the Low-Wage Economy, 455
Congress of Racial Equality, 47
Congressional Black Caucus, 35, 87, 120, 462, 595
Congressional Progressive Caucus, 18, 19, 31, 36, 86, 234, 235, 258, 265, 268, 269, 291, 298, 301, 451, 477, 553, 555
Connecticut Communist Party, 228, 229
Conrad, Earl, 193
Cook County Commissioner
    Danny K. Davis, 78, 260
Cooper Union for the Advancement of Science and Art, 21
Cop Watch, 330
Corona, Bert, 312, 313, 314, 316
Corporate Profile Project, 335, 406
Council on Environmental Quality (CEQ), 325
Council on Foreign Relations, 398
Councilman of Los Angeles
    Alarcon, Richard, 316
Councilwoman
    New York, NY – Nargaruta Lopez, 448
Cracraft, James, 515

Creamer, Robert, 176
Criley, Richard, 151, 191, 194, 261, 418, 549, 569
Crocket, George, 153, 373, 411
Crossroads Fund, 139, 140, 503, 507
Crozier, Brian, 553
Cry Wolf Project, 583
Cuba Project/Conexiones, 336, 406
Cuban American, 110
Cuban Intelligence (DGI), 299, 335, 352, 353, 403, 439
Cuban Interest Section, 78, 144, 260
Cultural Club, 149
Cunningham, Otis, 81, 300
Currie, Barbara Flynn, 31, 208, 428
Daily Kos, 209, 453
Daily World, 81, 155, 463, 464
Daniel Levy
    American Strategy Program, 588
    Middle East Task Force N.A.F, 588
Daniels, Ron, 387
Darrington, Michael, 175
DataCenter, 335, 336, 389, 405, 406, 407
Davidson, Carl, ii, 89, 90, 91, 102, 112, 119, 120, 172, 178, 181, 182, 197, 248, 255, 277, 278, 286, 404, 421, 490, 534, 608, 613
Davidson, Carl, 13, 15, 17, 95, 112, 113, 114, 119, 136, 140, 142, 143, 145, 147, 172, 181, 182, 197, 248, 249, 256, 281, 285, 286, 301, 303, 322, 337, 349, 350, 392, 393, 394, 403, 404, 405, 421, 440, 490, 491
Davis, Angela, 19, 25, 48, 78, 132, 139, 144, 159, 161, 179, 255, 260, 297, 327, 344, 346, 347, 348, 383, 403, 599, 609
Davis, Angela Y, 131, 132
Davis, Angela Y., 130, 344
Davis, Attieno, 457
Davis, Danny, 62, 144, 365, 534, 570

Davis, Frank Marshall, 74, 113, 132, 148, 151, 152, 158, 193, 296, 311, 313, 314, 367, 370, 371, 372, 377, 408, 409, 410, 413, 416, 499, 500, 501, 503, 504, 506, 508, 514, 522, 571

Davis, Rennie, 417

Dawson, Michael, 22, 131, 132, 271, 581

Dean, Howard, 450

Debs, Eugene, 51, 94, 153, 175, 363, 432

Debs-Thomas-Harrington Dinner, 7, 10, 18, 37, 45, 57, 94, 95, 154, 175, 380, 432, 433, 482, 595

Delgado, Gary, 279, 538

Delgado, William, 7, 76, 143

DeMauro, Rose Ann, 473, 474

Democracy Now, 470

Democratic Convention, 93, 94, 95, 380

Democratic Leadership Council, 13, 286

Democratic National Convention, 49, 108, 147, 177, 182, 197, 385, 421

Democratic Party, 6, 9, 12, 14, 24, 25, 26, 30, 36, 50, 58, 63, 70, 71, 74, 75, 77, 78, 86, 87, 94, 96, 105, 106, 116, 117, 118, 143, 145, 149, 157, 161, 166, 169, 173, 180, 185, 186, 196, 197, 198, 209, 212, 214, 221, 223, 224, 225, 229, 235, 240, 243, 244, 253, 256, 272, 274, 279, 286, 288, 300, 301, 309, 318, 321, 322, 349, 376, 381, 410, 413, 417, 419, 420, 421, 422, 433, 439, 455, 470, 475, 486, 491, 492, 494, 497

Democratic Socialist Organizing Committee (DSOC), 236, 363, 560, 567, 592

Democratic Socialists of America, 6, 9, 11, 12, 15, 17, 18, 20, 27, 30, 32, 36, 37, 38, 40, 42, 43, 44, 45, 48, 50, 51, 56, 58, 62, 64, 66, 69, 74, 75, 77, 79, 86, 87, 92, 93, 98, 107, 129, 135, 141, 153, 170, 174, 178, 187, 226, 234, 236, 255, 258, 263, 270, 278, 342, 363, 373, 383, 388, 410, 429, 437, 448, 476, 478, 486, 490, 495, 496, 506, 508, 526, 528, 535, 544, 550, 553, 555, 558, 560, 561, 567, 580, 585, 592

DEMOS, 397, 398, 399, 400, 439, 450, 453, 458, 459, 541, 550, 557, 558

Denitch, Bogdan, 21, 566

Despres, Leon, 208, 359, 360, 361, 362, 363, 364, 366, 367, 417, 479, 547

Detroit Jewish Labor Committee, 434

Diallo, Amadou, 448

Die Linke (The Left Party) of Germany, 404

Diehl, Kim, 346

Dinkins, David, 566

Dissent, 566

Doherty, Patrick, 591

Dohrn, Bernardine, 110, 112, 114, 115, 119, 125, 126, 128, 135, 136, 137, 139, 140, 141, 146, 153, 159, 162, 167, 168, 173, 178, 179, 180, 181, 182, 188, 248, 255, 256, 277, 280, 286, 331, 338, 341, 343, 344, 345, 346, 348, 389, 414, 440, 461, 471, 490, 493, 501, 502, 507, 543, 556, 572, 587, 590, 611

Dohrn, Jennifer, 136, 138, 182, 332, 333, 348

Domino Publications, 425

Dorfman, Ron, 61

Douglass, Frederick, 343

Dowd, Jeff Alan, 528

Doyle, Angela, 450

Dr. Linda Rae Murray, 481, 482, 483, 488

Dr. Peter Orris, 481, 487

Dr. Quentin Young, 483, 484, 486, 487, 488

Dreams from My Father, 20, 251, 378, 448

Dreier, Peter, 102, 265, 432, 445, 583

Dreyer, Thorne, 102, 114, 116, 119, 249

Druyan, Ann, 521

DSA Low Wage Justice Project, 455

DuBois, W.E.B., 157, 376, 413

Dunbar-Ortiz, Roxanne, 390, 391, 405, 414, 415, 541

Dunham, Stanley Ann, 573

Durham, Earl, 491, 500, 501, 502, 503, 504, 506, 522

Durham, Richard, 501

Dyson, Michael Eric, 134, 347, 524

Earth Day, 257

East German Communist Party, 78, 144, 260

East-West Institute, 398

Economic Development Administration, 61

Economic Policy Institute, 432, 439, 552, 558, 583, 584

Edel, Eric, 237

Education Commission of the Communist Party USA, 375

Edwards, John, 29

Ehrenreich, Barbara, 43, 75, 90, 100, 114, 120, 121, 136, 145, 147, 172, 179, 180, 181, 186, 187, 249, 255, 256, 277, 278, 279, 281, 282, 285, 286, 303, 320, 322, 324, 378, 393, 400, 431, 432, 440, 441, 457, 458, 540, 555, 575, 582, 588, 594, 610, 613, 625

Eisenscher, Michael, 404

Elbaum, Max, 391, 403, 405, 415

Elbert, Joan, 570

Ella J Baker Center for Human Rights, 325, 327, 330, 336, 389, 401, 405, 407, 453, 458

Ellsberg, Daniel, 139, 283, 527

Emanuel, Rahm, 264

Emergency Civil Liberties Committee, 348

Emerson, Ruth, 570

Employee Free Choice Act, 105, 106, 264, 306, 612

Encyclopedia of the American Left, 153, 373, 410

Engel, Barbara, 502

Environmental Advocates of New York, 389

Epstein, Barbara, 391

Erikson Institute, 414, 415

Erikson, Erik, 415

European Bank for Reconstruction and Development, 555

Fadlallah, Sheikh Mohammed Hussein, 357

Fair Immigration Reform Movement, 454

Fairness Doctrine, 467

FairVote, 554

Faith as a Weapon, 134, 524

FALN, 498

Fannie Mae, 275

Fanon, Frantz, 448, 453

FARC
  Colombian Revolutionary Armed Forces, 38

Farrakhan, Louis, 173

Faux, Jeff, 584

Federal Art Project, 152

Federation of American Scientists (FAS), 516, 519

Fegan, Claudia, 480

Fein, Oliver, 472, 473, 474

Feinglass, Abe, 151, 191, 194, 200, 350, 418, 424

Female Storytellers Igniting Revolution to End Violence, 139

Feminist Response in Disability Activism, 139
Feminists for Peace, 133
Feminists for Peace and Barack Obama, 594
Fermi, Enrico, 510
Fernholz, Tim
  Asset Building Program N.A.F., 588
  The American Prospect, 588
Fernholz, Tim, 588
Fersh, Rob, 398, 579
Fight the Smears, 530
Figueroa, Hector, 453
Filner, Bob, 439
Fishman, Joelle, 34, 229, 231
Fitzgerald, Peter, 596
Flacks, Dick, 582
Flacks, Mickey, 102
Flacks, Richard, 102, 283
Fletcher Jr., Bill, 75, 112, 113, 119, 121, 130, 131, 132, 136, 147, 172, 180, 181, 186, 187, 249, 256, 280, 281, 282, 285, 286, 303, 322, 324, 343, 344, 345, 349, 387, 393, 400, 404, 440, 576
Fletcher, Bill, 75, 90, 100, 114, 120, 121, 130, 131, 132, 145, 172, 179, 255, 276, 277, 278, 303, 343, 378, 387, 404, 480, 576, 625
Flory, Ishmael, 47, 409, 468
Flowers, Elwood, 52, 155
FMLN, 404
Fonda, Jane, 102
Foreign Policy, 113, 629
Fox News, xix, 388
Fox, Yolande, 555
Frappier, Diana, 330, 331, 336, 338, 390, 407
Frappier, Jon, 335, 336, 337, 389, 390, 391, 406, 407

Frappier, Nancy, 330, 332, 333, 346, 389
Freddie Mac, 275
Free Press, 585, 589
Freedom Road Socialist Organization, 42
French Communist Party, 448
French, Anya Landau, 592
Freud, Sigmund, 415
Friedman, Larry, 415
Friedman, Paul, 449
Friends of Alice Palmer, 460
Fry, Pat, 395
Fugitive Days, 133, 345
Funny, Kashim, 346
fusion voting, 185, 539
Futorian, Aviva, 102, 140
Galbraith, James, 582
Gamble, Rory, 441
Gannon, Dennis, 9
Garcia, Arnoldo, 415
Garcia, Marcos, 404
Garcia, Marshall, 449
Gardner, Joe, 533
Gardner, Joseph, 164, 534
Garskof, Bert, 112, 113, 166, 167, 168, 179, 255, 611
Gaspard, Patrick, 447, 448, 450, 451, 452, 453
Gates, Henry Louis, 383
Generation Change, 455
Geoghegan, Tom, 367
George, Christine, 102
Gerard, Leo, 431, 432, 433, 473, 542
Gerson, Simon, 466
Giocondo, Mike, 466
Gitlin, Todd, 102, 582
Givat Haviva Educational Institute, 190
Global Governance Initiative, 587

Glover, Danny, 114, 147, 181, 282, 386, 387, 400
Goff, Fred, 335, 406
Gold, Adam, 328, 403
Goldberg, Arthur, 546, 568
Goldberg, Devoe, Shadur, & Mikva, 546
Goldwater, Barry, 201
Gonzalez, Antonio, 34
Gonzalez, Jorge, 102
Good, Thomas, 102, 114, 115, 136, 137, 180, 182, 323
Good, Tom, 123, 126, 323, 324
Goode, Selma, 434
Goodman, Amy, 470
Goodman, Paul, 399, 556
Google, 484, 488
Google Health Advisory Council, 484
Gorbachev, Mikhail, 521
Gosse, Van, 457
Graeber, David, 112, 179, 255
Graff, Gerald, 345
Gramsci, Antonio, 68
Grant, Fr. Gerard, 549
Great Lakes Center for Occupational and Environmental Safety and Health, 487
Great Society, 224, 225, 425
Greater Detroit Democratic Socialists of America (DSA), 434
Green Collar Economy, 325
Green for All, 325, 338, 389, 390, 394, 536, 583
Green Jobs, 325, 338, 394, 395, 396, 450, 516
Green Left Weekly of Australia, 78, 144, 260
Green Party, 166, 168, 439
Green, David, 237, 430, 434, 437, 438
Greenhouse, David, 352

Greens-for-Gore, 166
Griffiths, Arturo, 131
Grimshaw, Bill, 174
Grimshaw, Jackie, 173, 174, 175, 177, 187, 238, 438, 479, 502, 507
Guellal, Cherif, 555
Guerra, Steven, 498
Guinea-Bissau, 328
Guinier, Lani, 458
Gustin, Felicia, 403
Guthrie, Woody, 295, 296
Haber, Al, 123, 168, 179
Haber, Alan, 115
Habonim, 433
Hafemeister, David W., 519
Halern, Charles, 579
Hall, Yolanda, 261, 478, 480, 550, 570
Hallet, Anne, 502
Halpern, Charles, 398, 399, 550, 556, 557
Hamas, 357
Hamilton, David, 102, 114, 115, 116, 119
Hammonds, Evelynn, 130, 344
Harber, Al, 281
Hardisty, Jean, 507
Harold Meyerson, 264, 432, 593, 594, 595, 597
Harriman, Averill, 512
Harrington, Michael, 7, 42, 51, 56, 95, 154, 363, 364, 456, 527, 544, 581, 594, 607
Harris, Dwayne, 533
Harris, Pat, 450
Hartford Courant.com, 137
Hartunian, Futterman & Howard, 507
Harvard, 8, 163, 355, 379, 454, 522
Harvard Black Law Student Association, 385
Harvard Business School, 434

Harvard Law Review, 545

Harvard Law School, 22, 67, 384, 478, 596

Harvard Legal Aid Bureau, 384

Harvard Medical School, 473

Harvester, 60

Harwell, Carol, 530

Havana Notes, 591

Havighurst, Robert, 514

Hawaiian Communist Party, 113, 149, 370, 408, 500

Hawaiian Democratic Party, 149

Hayden, Tom, 90, 99, 100, 102, 112, 113, 114, 119, 120, 124, 136, 139, 147, 179, 181, 249, 255, 256, 277, 281, 282, 283, 303, 322, 324, 393, 400, 403, 404, 417, 440, 458, 555, 582, 613

Hayes, Charles, 52, 200, 204, 206, 365, 424, 426

Hayes, Christopher, 588, 594

Haynes, Robert J, 444

Healey, Dorothy, 415

Health and Medicine Policy Research Group, 487, 488

Healthy Schools Network, 389

Healy, Dorothy, 415

Heartland Democratic Presidential Forum, 454

Heintz, Stephen, 398, 579

Hellander, Ida, 474

Helphand, Ben, 177

Henderson, Wade, 355

Henry, Elena, 266, 446

Hertz, Judy, 502

Hezbollah, 357

Hickey, Roger, 320

Higginbottom, Heather, 443

High Road or Low Road? Job Quality in the Green Economy, 542

Hightower, Jim, 283

Hill, Joe, 254

Hill, Patricia, 341

Himmelstein, David, 474

Ho, Mei-ying, 403

Hochschild, Adam, 237, 527, 582

Hollander, Sid, 587

Holly Sklar, 577

Holtzman, Liz, 563, 564

Homes, Robert Taylor, 414

Honolulu Record, 149, 311

Hoover, J. Edgar, 512, 518

HOPEFUND, 157, 376, 413

Horne, Gerald, xvi, 112, 113, 119, 131, 132, 179, 187, 255

Horowitz, Sara, 398, 579

House Un-American Activities Committee, 79, 193, 200, 201, 203, 204, 260, 296, 417, 424, 425, 449, 505

Household Finance Corporation, 183, 184, 539, 540

Howe, Irving, 566

Huberman, Leo, 192

Hudson, Gerry, 43, 56, 131, 133, 355, 388, 432, 450, 537, 543, 544, 561, 588, 594, 598

Hudson, James L., 555

Hudson, Jerry, 43

Huerta, Dolores, 269, 364

Huffington Post, 93

Hughes, Langston, 571

Hull, Blair, 96

Hurd, Maude, 145, 172

Hyde Park Kenwood Voices, 203

Hyde-Park Herald, 79, 193, 416

Hyde-Park Kenwood Voices, 193, 204, 417, 425, 548, 568

IL State Controller Dan Hynes, 96

Ilich, Ivan, 399, 556

Illinois College of Emergency Physicians, 485
Illinois Communist Party, 60, 154, 372, 374, 409, 411, 468, 473, 487
Illinois Issues, 8
Illinois Project Vote, 8
Illinois Public Action (IPA), 82, 92
Illinois Safe Schools Alliance, 139
Immigrant Workers Freedom Bus Rides, 495
In These Times, 94, 114, 133, 186, 197, 256, 279, 345, 421, 452, 555, 587
Independent Voters of Illinois, 11, 31, 166, 366, 427, 428
Independent Voters of Illinois (IVI), 207, 428
Industrial Areas Foundation, 43, 176
Industrial Workers of the World, 199
Inside the Company, 335
Institute for America's Future, 320
Institute for Policy Studies, 102, 112, 191, 278, 283, 286, 297, 303, 319, 320, 324, 352, 353, 358, 386, 397, 399, 439, 457, 512, 513, 514, 520, 537, 541, 544, 549, 556, 561, 567, 569, 573, 598
Institute for Policy Studies (IPS), 276, 277, 279, 283, 353, 358, 396, 552
Institute of Medicine of the National Academies, 485
International Association of Democratic Lawyers, 138, 348
International Organization of Journalists, 463, 465, 492
International Organization of Journalists (IOJ), 464, 465
International Publishers, 88
Interreligious Foundation for Community Organization., 475
Iraq War, 16, 35, 47, 54, 95, 113, 155, 181, 197, 249, 252, 256, 327, 328, 350, 352, 355, 357, 358, 390, 403, 421, 441, 457, 490, 491
Isaacs, Amy, 31
Islamic Center of America, 357
Izvestia, 467
Jackson, James, 300
Jackson, Jesse, 17
Jackson, Rev. Jesse, 62, 98, 196, 320, 360, 420, 448, 554
Jackson, Sandi, 83
Jackson, Santita, 82
Jacobs, Harold, 102
Jacoby, Jeff, 515
James, Clara, 267
James, Michael, 102, 112, 182
James, Mike, 114, 123, 255
Jaques, Geoffrey, 449
Jarrett, Valerie, 157, 158, 173, 376, 377, 407, 408, 413, 414, 416, 499, 504
Jarrett, Vernon, 152, 153, 155, 156, 157, 371, 372, 373, 375, 376, 377, 408, 409, 410, 412, 413, 416, 419, 499, 501, 503, 504
Jewish Labor Committee, 434, 440
Jobs with Justice, 140, 354, 439
John Birch Society, 425
John Marshall Law School, 423
Johnson, J.J., 131
Johnson, Zenobia, 102
Johnson's "Great Society", 425
Jones, Absalom, 134
Jones, Anthony (Van), 324
Jones, Hank, 387
Jones, Jeff, 125, 126, 128, 136, 139, 153, 167, 179, 182, 251, 252, 255, 281, 338, 344, 389, 392, 432, 440, 543, 614
Jones, Van, 325, 326, 329, 330, 331, 336, 337, 338, 346, 388, 389, 390, 391, 394, 395, 396, 397, 400, 401, 402, 403, 405, 407, 414, 415, 432, 446, 450, 453, 458,

459, 516, 523, 524, 527, 536, 537, 538, 541, 550, 557, 580
JOURNAL INQUIRER, 138
JournoListas
  DSA Affiliated
    Gitlin, Todd, 594
    Judis, John, 594
    Kazin, Michael, 594
    McLemee, Scott, 594
    Perlstein, Rick, 594
    Pollitt, Katha, 594
    Robert Kuttner, 594
  The American Prospect, 593
    Ackerman, Spencer, 593
    Baker, Dean, 593
    Fernholz, Tim, 593
    Judis, John, 593
    Klein, Ezra, 593
    Waldman, 594
    Robert Kuttner, 593
    Schmitt, Mark, 593
    Serwer, Adam, 593
  Washington Post
    McGillis, Alec, 593
    Sargent, Greg, 593
    Weigel, Dave, 593
JournoListas, 582, 585, 587, 591, 592
  Washington Post:, 593
JournoListas, 594
JournoListas
  DSA Affiliated
    Bleifuss, Joel, 594
JStreet, 588
Julius, William, 271, 383, 527
Justice Coalition of Greater Chicago, 47
Kagan, Elena, 544, 550, 551, 557, 563, 565, 567
Kagan, Gloria, 561
Kagan, Marc, 561
Kahlo, Frida, 362
Karpatkin, Jeremy, 163, 556

Katz, Marilyn, 102, 113, 114, 121, 123, 181, 182, 195, 197, 249, 256, 419, 421, 491, 615
Kazin, Michael, 566, 582, 588, 594
Kelleher, Keith, 533, 538
Kelley, Robin D. G., 130, 344
Kelley, Robin D.G., 112, 114, 119, 132, 133, 182, 187, 344
Kelley, Robin DG, 131, 179
Kelly, Joseph H., 528
Kelly, Robin D G, 102
Kendall, Jackie, 43, 57, 177, 438
Kerry, John, 108, 443
Kerry, Teresa Heinz, 12
Keselenko, Susan, 591, 592
Kest, Jon, 452, 537, 598
Kest, Steve, 537, 598
KGB, 299, 424, 425, 465, 549, 553
Khalidi, Rashid, 114, 123, 180, 322, 392
Khanna, Parag, 587
King, Dr. Martin Luther, 159, 194, 364, 418
King, Martin Luther, 45, 94, 134
King, Rodney, 325
Kling, Jack, 159
Klonsky, Fred, 103, 295, 296, 492
Klonsky, Michael, 112, 113, 122, 136, 140, 179, 182, 256, 281, 295, 337, 392, 492, 502
Klonsky, Mike, 119, 120, 122, 123, 136, 179, 182, 255, 295, 392, 502
Klonsky, Robert, 112, 295
Klonsky, Susan, 103, 140
Knuttenen, David, 237
Kohak, Erazim, 566
Kotchergine, Vadim, 128
Kramer, Steve, 449
Kransdorf, Joe, 486
Kranz, David, 450
Krugman, Paul, 584

Kucinich, Dennis, 25, 211, 575, 576
Kurtz, Stanley, 530
Kushner, Sam, 267
Kuttner, Robert, 558, 578, 585
LA City Board of Education, 267
LA City Councilor
  Alarcon, Richard, 267, 268
La Raza National Lawyers Association (LRNLA), 312
Labor Party, 226, 475
Laguerra, Socorro, 450
Laluz, Jose, 107, 108, 109, 110, 162, 497
Landy, Joanne, 472, 527
Lansana, Quraysh Ali, 346
Latin American Medical School (ELAM), 355
Latinos for Obama, 107, 162, 497
Lawyers Committee for Human Rights, 325
Lazard Freres, 434
Leadership Conference on Civil Rights, 355
League of American Writers, 148
League of Conservation Voters, 97, 290
League of Women Voters, 366
LeBlanc, Judith, 457
Lefley, Harriet, 31, 165
Left Forum, 186, 378, 395
Lenin, 40, 249, 252, 328, 436
Lenin and National Liberation, 328
Lenin Peace Prize, 555
Lens (aka Okun), Sydney, 514
Lerner, Rabbi Michael, 271, 527, 528
Letelier, Orlando, 353, 358
Letelier-Moffitt Memorial Human Rights Domestic Award, 353
Levchenko, Stanislav, 202, 425, 622
Levinson, Mark, 561, 566
Levison, Stanley, 331

Levy, Daniel, 588
Lewis, Bertha, 451
Liberty Hill Foundation, 459
Lichtenstein, Nelson, 583
Lightfoot, Claude, 47, 159
Lighty, Michael, 109, 161, 474, 481
Lincoln School, 311
Line of March, 390, 391
Lipow, Arthur, 598
Lipschutz, Peggy, 570
Lipshutz, Peggy, 261
Lizza, Ryan, 42
Llewellyn, Frank, 95, 266, 446
Lorde, Audre, 343
Los Angeles Alliance for a New Economy, 265
Lou Pardo, 538
Lowe, Ira, 555
Low-Income Home Energy Assistance (LIHEAP), 381
Lozano, Pepe, 26, 27, 50, 65, 155, 347
Lozano, Rudy, 26, 27, 53, 54, 64, 65
Lucy, William, 561
Lumpkin, Bea, 60, 61, 93, 570
Lumpkin, Beatrice, 60
Lumpkin, Dr. John, 590
Lumpkin, Frank, 60, 61, 82, 93, 160, 261, 486, 496, 534, 550, 570
Lumpkin, Frank and Bea, 485
Lumpkin, John R., 485, 486, 487, 488
Lumumba, Patrice, 447
Lux, Mike, 458, 459
Luxemburg, Rosa, 441
Lynch, Bill, 449
Lynch, Roberta, 479, 507, 542
Lyons, Eugene, 192
Machen Center, 331
Machete 48, 326
Machtinger, Howard, 136, 139, 182
Machtinger, Howie, 125, 126, 128

Macomb Community College, 357
Magnes, Judah, 189
Malcolm X, 134, 343, 524
Malcolm X College, 80
Malveaux, Julianne, 130, 344, 584
Mandate for Change-Policies and Leadership for 2009 and beyond, 298
Manhattan Project, 505, 510, 511, 512, 514, 517, 518
Mann, Bob, 208, 366, 428
Maoists, 15, 21, 136, 390, 396, 400, 457, 489
Marable, Manning, 48, 74, 121, 123, 130, 131, 132, 133, 145, 147, 172, 179, 180, 186, 187, 255, 280, 281, 283, 284, 285, 286, 288, 289, 324, 343, 344, 346, 349, 370, 392, 408, 414, 483, 489, 577
Marder, Alfred, 457
Mark Schmitt
    American Strategy Program, 589
    Open Society Institute, 589
Markey, Ray, 561
Markowitz, Norman, 28, 39, 225, 475
Marshall, Chip, 528
Marshall, Ray, 584
Marshall, Scott, 227, 232, 486
Marshall, Thurgood, 571
Marshall, Togi, 131
Martin, Judge Patricia, 77
Martin, Patricia, 11, 14
Martinez, Betita, 327, 337, 346, 390, 392, 403, 405, 414, 415
Marxist, 6, 9, 11, 14, 15, 17, 20, 30, 36, 37, 38, 44, 50, 58, 86, 92, 94, 107, 108, 112, 114, 115, 135, 142, 167, 170, 186, 219, 224, 249, 259, 278, 283, 287, 288, 289, 312, 327, 359, 448, 455, 469, 470, 475, 477, 482, 495, 499, 521, 523
Marxist based Organizations, 585
Marxist-Leninist, 489, 492, 497

Marxist-Leninist Puerto Rican Socialist Party, 332
Marxist-Leninist-Maoist, 324
Mass Party Organizing Committee, 331, 332
Massachusetts Coalition for Full Employment, 434
Max, Steve, 42, 43, 56, 443, 452
Maxwell, Mary Beth, 263, 354
Mayor
    Berkeley, CA - Gus Newport, 81, 83, 101, 153, 300, 373, 411, 540
    Chicago, IL - Harold Washington, 6, 7, 21, 27, 28, 30, 44, 45, 47, 50, 51, 53, 58, 59, 60, 61, 65, 66, 79, 80, 151, 153, 154, 157, 158, 159, 160, 161, 162, 174, 175, 198, 350, 360, 366, 373, 375, 376, 410, 411, 412, 413, 422, 485, 486, 496, 501, 505
    Chicago, IL - Jane Byrne, 63, 64
    Chicago, IL - Richard J. Daley, 59, 413
    Detroit, MI - Coleman Young, 153, 373, 411
    Los Angeles, CA - Antonio Villaraigoza, 267, 268, 310, 312, 313
    New York, NY - David Dinkins, 448, 563
    New York, NY – Rudy Giuliani, 448
    Newark, NJ - Cory Booker, 286
    Stamford, CT - Dannel Malloy, 137
Mayors Innovation Project, 536
Mazur, Jay, 103, 452
Mboya, Tom, 572
McChesney, Robert W., 589
McDonnell, Brian V., 125
McDowell, Leila, 466
McEntee, Gerald, 67, 176, 219, 220, 432, 584
McGurty, Larry, 513

McKinney & McDowell, 466
McKinney, Gwen, 466
McKnight, John, 478
McNary, Bill, 82
McNary, William, 92, 93, 94, 95, 96, 97, 187, 238, 319, 321, 479
McReynolds, David, 32, 165
Mead, Sara, 588
Medical Committee for Human Rights, 471
Medicine Policy Research Group (HMPRG), 478
Medina, Eliseo, 36, 37, 44, 56, 269, 446, 494, 495, 496, 497
Meeropol, Abe, 254
Meeropol, Mike, 253, 254, 258
Meeropol, Robert, 254
Meier, Deborah, 31, 165, 458, 563, 566
Mendelson, Saul, 30, 31, 165, 166, 208, 238, 365, 366, 428, 438, 458, 506, 563, 582, 623
Messinger, Ruth, 448
Metro New York Peace Action Council, 563
Metropolitan Pier and Exposition Authority, 164
Metropolitan Water Reclamation District, 164
Meyerson, Harold, 264, 265, 445, 566, 588, 593
Michigan State University, 168, 525
Midwest Academy, 12, 42, 43, 56, 57, 93, 175, 176, 177, 263, 452, 455, 502
Midwest-Northeast Voter Registration Education Project, 379, 380
Mikva, Abner, 567, 569
Mikva, Honorable Abner, 261
Mikva, Laurie, 546
Mikva, Zoe, 568, 570

Miller, Arnie, 398, 579
Miller, Ethelbert, 112, 179, 281, 324
Mills, Pam, 450
Milstein, Merrilee, 450
Miner, Barnhill & Galland, 183, 539
Miner, Judson, 159
Minnite, Lorraine, 399
Mishel, Larry, 432, 552, 558, 584
Mitchell, Charlene, 112, 119, 130, 131, 132, 179, 255, 344, 348
Moberg, David, 94, 587
Moffitt, Ronni Karpen, 353
Mohawk Hudson Land Conservancy, 389
Mondale, Walter, 206
Montague, Ann, 73
Montgomery County Hate Crimes Commission, 553
Moore, Alderman Joe, 141
Moore, Joe, 95, 103, 208, 366, 428
Mora, Elena, 88
Morales-Pope, Sandy, 598
Morcum, Judge Claudia, 236
Morice, Devra, 115
Morris, Calvin, 479
Mort, Jo-Ann, 566
Moscow Center, 519
Moseley, William (Bill), 237
Mothers on the Move, 43
Movement for a Democratic Society, 115, 116, 129, 132, 135, 146, 153, 167, 178, 186, 247, 254, 280, 281, 297, 322, 327, 337, 344, 414, 440, 441
Movement for A Democratic Society (MDS), 392
Movimiento Estudiantil Chicano de Aztlán, 312
Muhammad Ahmad, 123, 130
Muhammad, Akbar, 132
Mullings, Leith, 130, 132, 133, 343

Muñoz, Alderman Ricardo, 95
Muñoz, Rick, 78, 144, 260
Muñoz, Rosalío, 32, 457
Murray, Linda Rae, 487
Mustin, Ronelle, 143
Muwakkil, Salim, 130, 132, 133, 186, 344, 345
Myerson, Mike, 81, 300
Myles, Dee, 62, 133, 156, 157, 375, 412
Myles, Denice (Dee), 131
NAACP Legal Defense Fund, 466
Nader, Ralph, 166, 211
Nathan Cummings Foundation, 398
Nathan Cummings Fund, 399
Nation of Islam, 173
National Alliance Against Racial and Political Repression (NAARPR), 25, 81, 341
National Alliance of Black Journalists, 463
National Association of Black Journalists, 152, 373, 410
National Campaign to Save the ABM Treaty, 520
National Conference for Alternative State and Local Public Policies, 281, 283
National Conference of Black Lawyers, 138, 312, 348
National Emergency Conference, 546
National Federation for Constitutional Liberties, 148
National Hard Times Conference, 587
National Hispanic Leadership Council, 268
National Labor Relations Act, 40, 272
National Latino Advisory Council, 269, 446, 496
National Lawyers Guild, 101, 138, 312, 348, 547, 568, 571

National Mexican American Equality Commission, 315
National Negro Congress, 148
National Physicians Alliance, 472
National Preparatory Committee, 88
National Quality Forum, 485
NATO Multilateral Nuclear Force (MLF), 425
Negro American Labor Council, 47
Negro Newsfront, 372, 410
Negro People's Front, 152
Negro Story, 193
Nesbitt, Prexy, 132, 140
Network of Spiritual Progressives, 527
New Afrikan People's Organization, 130, 343
New America Foundation, 586, 587
New American Movement, 101, 109, 162, 236, 363, 470, 491, 505, 508, 528, 587, 592
New American Movement (NAM), 526
New Deal, 29, 59, 98, 224, 225, 227, 245, 253, 257, 272, 275, 276, 287, 298, 308, 367
New Deal era, 253
New International Information Order, 465
New Masses, 296
New Mexico State Legislature, 251
New Party, 6, 7, 11, 12, 13, 14, 15, 16, 43, 74, 75, 76, 77, 129, 132, 141, 142, 143, 144, 145, 146, 147, 164, 169, 170, 172, 180, 181, 182, 183, 185, 186, 238, 248, 259, 279, 284, 285, 297, 301, 349, 381, 382, 388, 397, 400, 403, 450, 451, 452, 458, 479, 490, 493, 580
New York Daily News, 588
New York Times, 166, 325, 579, 604, 613

New York Working Families Party, 103, 451

New York Working Families Party (WFP), 284

New York's Tammany Hall, 40

Newman, Nathan, 453

Next Left Notes, 126, 136, 182, 323, 612

Nicaraguan Sandinistas, 439

Nichols, John, 303, 476

Nixon's Enemies List, 521

Nkrumah, Kwame, 571

Nolan, Michael D, 336, 337

Norquist, Grover, 212

North American Congress on Latin America (NACLA), 335, 406

North American Free Trade Agreement, 235

North American Free Trade Agreement (NAFTA), 234

North American Political Union, 235

Northwestern Law School, 341

Northwestern University, 80, 133, 137, 345, 485

Northwestern University Law School, 345

Northwestern University Medical School, 485

Novick, Bob, 73

Nowell, Bob, 465

Noyd, Captain Dale, 168

Nqukula, Charles, 78, 144, 260

Nuestro Mundo, 20, 96

NY Democratic Socialists of America, 452

Obafemi, Ahmed, 130, 344

Obama Transition Housing and Urban Development Agency Review Team, 514

Obama, Barack, ii, x, xi, xvi, xvii, 5, 6, 7, 8, 9, 10, 11, 12, 14, 15, 17, 18, 20, 21, 22, 24, 26, 27, 28, 29, 30, 31, 32, 34, 35, 37, 39, 40, 41, 43, 44, 47, 48, 49, 50, 52, 53, 54, 56, 57, 59, 62, 65, 66, 67, 69, 70, 72, 73, 74, 75, 76, 79, 80, 82, 86, 88, 89, 90, 92, 93, 94, 95, 98, 99, 102, 103, 104, 107, 108, 109, 110, 113, 115, 116, 117, 118, 119, 120, 122, 124, 125, 129, 132, 133, 134, 135, 141, 142, 143, 146, 148, 151, 153, 154, 155, 156, 157, 158, 159, 163, 164, 170, 171, 173, 174, 176, 177, 178, 180, 181, 182, 183, 184, 185, 187, 189, 191, 192, 193, 194, 196, 198, 199, 203, 207, 208, 209, 219, 220, 223, 228, 230, 235, 239, 261, 262, 264, 270, 271, 280, 283, 284, 289, 290, 313, 317, 320, 322, 327, 342, 343, 345, 346, 347, 348, 350, 353, 359, 361, 366, 367, 368, 370, 372, 374, 375, 376, 377, 378, 379, 380, 382, 384, 387, 396, 397, 398, 400, 407, 408, 410, 411, 412, 413, 414, 415, 416, 418, 420, 422, 427, 428, 429, 437, 444, 446, 450, 452, 453, 454, 458, 460, 468, 469, 470, 471, 477, 478, 479, 480, 483, 484, 485, 486, 488, 489, 490, 491, 492, 493, 494, 495, 496, 499, 500, 501, 502, 503, 505, 506, 508, 509, 514, 515, 522, 524, 526, 528, 530, 533, 534, 535, 536, 538, 539, 541, 544, 545, 547, 548, 549, 551, 556, 557, 566, 567, 569, 570, 571, 572, 573, 574, 578, 579, 580, 581, 582, 583, 584, 585, 590, 591, 592, 593, 594, 595, 597, 598, 599, 600, 601, 605, 607, 610, 618, 621, 623, 625, 626

Obama, Barack and Michelle, 157

Obama, Barak, 572

Obama, Michelle, 82, 159, 174, 199, 208, 428, 491

Obama, Michelle and Barack, 383, 384

Obama, Senator Barack, 329

Occidental College, 102, 265, 303, 445, 586, 591

O'Clearicain, Carol, 566

October League, 122

Ogletree, Charles, 383, 387, 527

O'Leary, Brad, 414

O'Neil, Dennis, 458

Open Society Institute, 442, 456, 457, 590

Operation PUSH, 62, 366

Oppenheimer, Robert, 510, 513, 517

Oregon, 73, 147, 181

Organizing for America, 305, 306, 319

Orr, David, 141, 208, 366, 428, 479, 496, 533

Orris, Leo, 471

Orris, Maxine, 471

Orris, Peter, 471, 472, 474, 479, 487

Ortiz, Roxanne Dunbar, 405

Outlaws of Amerika, 332

Overruling Democracy
  The Supreme Court versus The American People, 554

Overruling Democracy: The Supreme Court Versus the American People, 555

Pace University, 395

Packinghouse Workers Union, 200, 205, 423, 424, 426

Page, Judy, 598

Palestine liberation Organization, 190

Palestine Liberation Organization (PLO), 562

Palestinian Liberation Organization, 114, 280

Palevsky, Max, 283

Palin, Sarah, 446, 535

Palmer, Alice, 534

Palmer, Edward "Buzz", 462

Panel IV. Intellectuals in Times of Crisis, 345

Panetta, Leon, 286, 324

Pardo, Lou, 262, 285, 379, 382, 438, 493, 534, 574

Party National Administrative Committee, 500

Party of Democratic Socialism of Germany, 78, 144, 260, 404

Pascal, Oskar, 237

Pastors for Peace Caravans, 475

Patrice Lumumba Friendship University, 82

Patrinos, Sandi, 13, 143

Patterson, Louise T., 371, 372, 409

Patterson, William L., 372, 409

Pauling, Linus, 513

Peace Action Committee, 47

Peace and Freedom Party, 451

Pearson, Ted, 140, 349

Peery, Nelson, 346

People Organized to Win Employment Rights (POWER), 327

Peoples College of Law, 312

People's Daily Word, 462

People's President, 59, 66

Peoples Weekly World, 25, 44, 50, 78, 95, 96, 97, 105, 108, 144, 260, 297, 301, 316, 319, 485, 497

Pereira, Dulce Maria, 78, 144, 260

Perkins, Marion, 152

Perlo, Victor, 228

Phillips, Maxine, 566

Physicians for a National Health Plan, 487

Physicians for a National Health Program, 109, 161, 221, 223, 469, 470, 476, 487

Physicians for a National Health Program (PNHP), 471

Piana, Libero Della, 104, 105, 106
Pike, John E., 519, 520
Piven, Frances Fox, 75, 103, 145, 147, 172, 182, 186, 187, 280, 283, 378, 432, 452, 455, 540, 561, 582
Pizzaro, Raphael, 74, 146, 172, 449
Pizzigati, Sam, 537
Podesta, John, 324, 542
Podesta, Leon, 251, 323, 394
Polett, Zach, 537, 598
Political Affairs, 28, 39, 104, 112, 132, 133, 219, 221, 225, 475
Pope, Carl, 355, 388
Porter, Thurman, 556
Portuguese Communist Party, 329
Power, Samantha, 444, 445
POWER-People Organized to Win Employment Rights (POWER), 403
Prairie Fire Organizing Committee, 138, 331
Preckwinkle, Alderman Toni, 31
Preckwinkle, Toni, 208, 428, 581
President
 Franklin D. Roosevelt, 29, 40, 253, 287
 George W. Bush, 35
 John F. Kennedy, 323, 456, 525
 Lyndon B Johnson, 224, 225, 256, 257, 272, 425, 456, 513, 547
 Richard Nixon, 257
 Ronald Reagan, 20, 61, 225, 336, 406
 William J. Clinton, 166, 521, 550
President
 Ronald Reagan (R), 564
President
 Lyndon B. Johnson, 573
President
 George W. Bush, 595
President Elect

Obama, Barack, 225, 226, 227, 229, 230, 233, 239, 240, 248, 253, 258, 262, 268, 270, 278, 283, 310, 313, 321
President-elect
 Barack Obama, 221
Pressman, Lee, 362, 572
Prince, Rob, 80, 81, 300
Princeton University, 68, 388, 485
Progressive Caucus, 36
Progressive Change, 39
Progressive Chicago, 503, 507, 530, 531, 532, 533, 534, 535, 538, 574, 600, 625
Progressive Chicago Area Network (PROCAN), 503, 507
Progressive Democrats of America, 98, 100, 102, 298, 431, 476, 555
Progressive Majority, 402, 458
Progressive Majority Political Action Committee, 320
Progressive Party, 47, 194, 372, 418
Progressives For Obama (P4O), 98, 100, 101, 113, 114, 115, 116, 129, 134, 136, 139, 140, 147, 153, 169, 172, 173, 181, 182, 186, 187, 197, 247, 249, 256, 282, 285, 288, 295, 297, 301, 303, 320, 322, 327, 338, 349, 386, 387, 393, 400, 403, 404, 417, 421, 440, 441, 452, 458, 481, 492, 493, 513, 527
Progressives in an Obama World
 The Role of the Progressive Movement in a Democratically Controlled Washington, 458
Project Vote, 163, 164, 375, 379, 412, 533, 614
Project Vote (ACORN), 399
Prosten, Jesse, 191, 194, 350, 418
Ptashne, Fred, 522
Ptashne, Mark, 522
Public Health Foundation, 485

Puerto Rican Separatists Fuerzas Armadas de Liberacion Nacional (FALN), 498
Puerto Rican Socialist Party (PSP), 108, 466, 497
Puerto Rican Support Committee, 331
Puerto Rican Support Group, 332
Pugliese, Michael, 68
Purrington, Sue, 109, 161, 208, 366, 429, 534
Putin, Vladimir, 521
Putsch, Birch, 425
Qazwini, Imam Hassan, 357
Quinnipiac University, 166
Rabi, Isidor, 513
'Race Matters', 132
Racial Diversity Task Force, 598
Radical alternatives on the eve of the millennium, 538
Radical America, 137
Rahman, Saif, 458
Raley, Jane, 341
Ramirez, Celina, 407
Ramsey, Jane, 479, 534
Randolph, Philip, 288
Ransby, Barbara, 130, 132, 133, 140, 342, 343, 344, 345, 346
Rapoport, Miles, 399, 400, 450, 458, 459, 541
Raskin, Jamie, 552, 553, 554, 555
Raskin, Marcus, 283, 356, 399, 458, 520, 552, 555, 556
Raskin, Sarah Bloom, 552, 558
Raskin's institute, 553
Rathke, Wade, 265, 537, 583, 598
Rawls, John, 592
Raynor, Bruce, 57, 58
Real Barack Obama (RBO), 508
Red Squad, 260
Redmond, Elce, 502

Reed, Gail, 592
Reed, Rev. Jim, 534
Reich, Robert, 584
Religion and Socialism Commission, 134, 524, 526, 529
Religious Socialism, 189
Reparations Coordinating Committee, 386
Representative
    Davis (D-IL), Danny K, 260
    Jan Schakowsky (D-IL-9th District), 176
Reuther, Walter, 42
Revolution in the Air - Sixties Radicals Turn to Lenin, Mao and Che, 391
Rezko, Tony, 173, 460
Richard, Bruce, 450
Riddiough, Christine, 103, 542
Right-to-know Project, 336
Rivera, Dennis, 449
Rivera, Diego, 362
Rivera, Jackeline, 404
Robert Kuttner, 578, 579, 581, 582, 583, 585
Robert Wood Johnson Foundation's Health Care Group, 485
Roberts, George (Skip), 576
Robeson, Paul, 74, 157, 343, 376, 413, 514
Robinson, Michelle, 376, 413
Robinson, Randall, 387, 466
Rogers and Dan Cantor, 537
Rogers, Harold, 261, 365, 550, 570
Rogers, Joel, 185, 186, 187, 388, 432, 536, 537, 538, 539, 541, 542, 543, 544, 598
Rogovin, Mark, 261, 550
Rojas, Don, 462, 463
Rolling, Ken, 502
Roman, Bob, 13, 143, 433

Romero, Gloria, 33
Romerstein, Herbert, 202, 300, 425
Roosevelt University, 362
Rorty, Richard, 345
Rose, Don, 191, 193, 194, 195, 196, 197, 198, 199, 203, 204, 205, 206, 208, 249, 350, 365, 367, 400, 416, 417, 418, 420, 421, 425, 429, 548, 568
Rosemont, Franklin, 123
Rosen, Frank, 261, 300, 549
Rosen, Pauline, 81, 300
Rosenberg, Julius, 254
Rosenberg, Julius and Ethel, 253
Ross, Bob, 137
Ross, Dennis, 304
Rossman, Michael, 112
Roth, Norman, 191, 194, 261, 349, 418, 549, 550, 569, 570
Rubenstein, Bruce, 136, 137, 167, 180, 255
Rubenstein, Bruce D., 136, 137, 138, 167
Rudd, Mark, 103, 112, 114, 119, 123, 125, 126, 127, 128, 136, 137, 139, 153, 167, 179, 182, 247, 249, 252, 255, 322, 323, 324, 338, 344, 389, 390, 392, 393, 394, 440, 623
Ruether, Rosemary, 526
Russell, Myra, 31, 165
Russian Federation, 599
Rutgers University, 39, 225
RW Ventures, LLC, 507
Ryan, William Fitts, 561
Sable, Dr. Ron, 507
Sable, Ron, 507, 533, 538
Sacher, Henry (Harry), 572
Sadlowski, Ed, 549, 569
Salazar, Coqui (Pedro Enrique), 336
Salazar, Pedro, 337
Salazar, Pedro Eusebio, 337

Salazar, Peter E., 337
Saltzman, Bettylu, 140, 479
Salud, 481
San Francisco Committees of Correspondence, 453
Sanchez, Sonia, 130, 344
Sanchez, Sonya, 14, 76, 143
Sanders, Bernie, 18, 19, 186, 290, 291, 431, 443, 538, 553, 575, 576, 577
Saturday School Program, 384
Save Our Jobs (SOJ), 160
Save Our Jobs Committee, 485
Schaffner, Jay, 103
Schakowsky, Jan, 35, 36, 37, 38, 44, 57, 66, 67, 68, 82, 92, 176, 187, 238, 270, 285, 358, 437, 438, 439, 479, 480, 496, 595, 596, 613, 628
Schepers, Emile, 570
Schiller, Alderwoman Helen, 141, 261
Schloop, Phillip, 441
Schlussel, Debbie, 357
Schmidt, Eric, 589
Schmidt, John, 164
Schmitt, Mark, 589
Scholz, Helmut, 404
School of Unity and Liberation (SOUL), 327
Schulman, Jason, 457
Schuman, Michael, 280
Schumer, Ellen, 503
Schwartz, Joseph, 22, 43, 271, 542
Scott-Boria, Mary, 503
Seattle Liberation Front (SLF), 528
Second Baptist Church, 267
Secretary of State Colin Powell, 37
Seeger, Pete, 48, 295, 296, 297, 327
SEIU
    Local 880 (Chicago, IL), 76
    President Andy Stern, 576

Service Employees International Union, 36
Shaiken, Harley, 263, 356, 445
Shapiro, Herbert, 571
Shapiro, Lucas, 457
Shapley, Deborah, 513
Shapley, Harlow, 513, 518
Sheinbaum, Stanley, 522, 582, 615
Shier, Carl Marx, 30, 48, 154, 165, 177, 495, 563, 623
Shier, Nancy, 177
Shoemaker, Richard, 237
Shorebank Corporation, 507
Shriek, Maumelle, 18
Sierra Club, 97, 355
Simpson, Dick, 64, 208, 366, 428, 534
Sims, Joe, 132, 133
Single Payer, 45, 46, 221, 226, 236, 469, 470, 471, 472, 473, 475, 476, 477, 478, 480, 481, 483, 486, 487, 488
Single-Payer Healthcare Alliance, 476
Siskind, Sarah, 183, 184, 185, 537, 539, 598
Skaggs, David, 580
Sklar, Holly, 455
Small Schools Workshop, 122
Smiley, Erica, 457
Smith, Barbara, 130, 344
Smith, Betty, 88
Smith, Lasker, 132
Smith, Paul, 177
Snitzer, Elias, 546
Sobell, Morton, 254
Social Policy, 583
Socialist International, 266, 289, 433, 439, 446
Socialist International (SI), 289, 290
Socialist International Commission for a Sustainable World Society, 443
Socialist International Migrations Committee, 266
Socialist Party of America, 363, 495
Socialist Review, 283, 321, 489
Socialist Scholars, 473
Socialist Scholars Conference, 284
Socialist Scholars Conference (SSC), 21, 378
Socialist Scholars Conferences, 453
Socialist Workers Party, 332
Socialists Scholars Conference, 87
Society of Teachers of Emergency Medicine, 485
Socolar, Sid, 546
Soetoro-Ng, Maya, 317
Sojourner, 134, 525, 526
Soler, Jose, 466
Solomon, Mark, 81, 299
Solomon, Prof. Mark, 301
Soros Fund Management, LLC, 590
Soros, George, 442, 450, 454, 456, 585
Soros, Jonathan, 590
South African Communist Party, 78, 144, 260, 328, 329, 403, 404, 405, 439
Southern California Communist Party, 316
Southern California Democratic Party, 34
Southwest Organizing Project, 336, 407
Southwest Voter Registration Project, 34
Soviet KGB, 193
Soviet Lieutenant General Sudoplatov, Pavel Anatolyevich, 510
Soviet Politburo, 465
Soviet Socialist Republic of Kazakhstan, 329
Soviet spy, 150, 228, 362

Space Policy Working Group, 520
Special Interest or Class Consciousness? How Labor Put Obama in the White House, 219
Special Tasks, Memoirs of an Unwanted Witness-A Soviet Spymaster, 510
Spiegel, Jack, 191, 194, 350, 418
Spirit of 1848, 482
Spirituality and the Role of the Church In The Radical Movement, 134, 524
Spriggs, William, 584
Springer, Kim, 346
Squillacote, Theresa, 439, 599
Stab, Michael E., 190
Staggs, Sarah, 81, 300
Stalinism, 362
Stamler, Dr. Jeremiah, 204
Stamler, Jeremiah, 480
Stamm, Rona, 507
Stand, Kurt, 234, 439, 577, 598, 599, 601
Stand, Mille, 599
Standing Together to Organize a Revolutionary Movement, 326, 346, 524
Standing Together to Organize a Revolutionary Movement (STORM), 346, 390, 401
Stanford University, 345, 383
Stanford, Max, 123
Stasi, 599
State Governor
  California Gray Davis, 314
  IL Governor
    Pat Quinn (D), 478
  Illinois Rod Blagojevich, 498
  Massachusetts Deval Patrick, 286
  New York David Paterson, 286
State legislature
  IL Representative

Harold Washington (D), 156
State Legislature
  CA State Assemblyman
    Antonio Villaraigoza, 316
    Villaraigoza, Antonio, 267
  CA State Senate
    Solis, Hilda, 267
  CA State Senator
    Cedillo, Gill, 266
    Gilbert Cedillo, 312, 316
    Hilda Solis, 316
  GA State Representative
    Julian Bond (D-GA), 432
  IL State Representative
    Cynthia Soto (D), 97
    House Majority Leader Barbara Flynn Currie (D), 165
    Mary Flowers (D), 380
    Miguel del Valle (D), 14, 76, 97, 143, 171
    William Delgado (D), 45
  IL State Senate
    Alice Palmer (D), 8, 14, 48, 49, 76, 77, 79, 80, 81, 82, 83, 92, 110, 143, 146, 162, 171, 173, 300, 301, 348, 381, 460, 461, 462, 463, 464, 466, 467, 468, 469, 471, 492, 496, 501, 502
    Barack Obama (D), 11, 14, 16, 17, 22, 30, 31, 35, 43, 44, 46, 77, 79, 82, 96, 129, 133, 158, 164, 165, 166, 180, 185, 222, 238, 279, 291, 345, 379, 398, 492, 530, 538, 563, 579
    David Delgado, 382
    Jesse Garcia (D), 14, 76, 143, 171
    Miguel del Valle (D), 380, 382
Steel Workers Union
  George Becker, President, 431
Steinberg, Brian, 450
Steinem, Gloria, 75, 146, 172
Stern, Andy, 41, 42, 56, 103, 263, 264, 542, 576, 584
Stone I.F., 193
Stone, Jeremy, 519, 520
Strharsky, Loretta & Harry, 335, 406

Struik, Dirk J, 150
Stuart, Judith, 341
Student Non-Violent Coordinating Committee, 505
Students for a Democratic Society (SDS), 15, 42, 56, 93, 98, 115, 116, 129, 135, 147, 153, 166, 178, 195, 247, 255, 271, 278, 286, 334, 354, 355, 388, 403, 405, 417, 419, 443, 455, 471, 491, 492, 505, 525
Sudoplatov, Pavel, 510, 511, 517
Summers, Lawrence, 250, 393
Sunstein, Cass, 445
Sustainable World Society, 289
Sutley, Nancy, 325
Sweeney, John, 9, 38, 42, 67, 68, 103, 219, 220, 226, 236, 263, 357, 358, 431, 434, 445
Swinney, Dan, 493, 531, 534, 600
Szilard, Leo, 510
Szold, Henrietta, 189
Takoma Park Gun Policy Task Force, 554
Talbott, Madeline, 531, 533, 538, 600
Tamarin, Henry, 9
Tambor, Milton, 237
Tappis, Steve, 136, 139, 140, 182
Targ, Bernice, 504, 505, 506, 514, 522
Targ, Harry, 103
Tarr-Whelan, Linda, 580
Tasini, Jonathan, 103
Teles, Steven, 589
Temple University, 22, 271
Terkel, Studs, 157, 261, 282, 366, 376, 413, 550
The American Prospect, 578, 582, 585, 589, 593, 606, 625
The Battle for Guatemala
  Rebels, Death Squads, and US Power, 391
The Center for Public Intellectuals, 133
The Chicago Ida B. Wells Forum, 130, 343
The Coalition of Black Trade Unionists, 64
The Cry for Unity: Communists and African Americans, 1917-1936, 300
The Godfather, 29
THE KGB AGAINST THE MAIN ENEMY, 425
The Labor Party, 130, 343
The Malcolm X Grassroots Movement, 130, 343
The Nation, 99, 100, 136, 137, 169, 451, 452, 454, 458, 555
The Other America, 456
The Progressive Revolution
  How the Best in America Came to Be, 459
The Reagan File, 336, 406
The Real News, 383
The Red Decade: The Stalinist Penetration of America, 192
The Sopranos, 29
the Takoma Park Election Redistricting Task Force, 553
The Washington Note, 591
Thigpenn, Anthony, 538, 543
Thindwa, James, 97
Thinking Big: Progressive Ideas for a New Era, 459
Thomas, Linda, 134, 347
Thomas, Norman, 35, 51, 95, 154, 175, 363, 432
Thompson, Mike, 353
Tikkun Magazine, 271
Together United Recommitted Forever TURF, 331
Torrez, Lorenzo, 33
Totten, Gloria, 458
Toussaint, Roger, 561

Toxic Nightmare, 336

TransAfrica Forum, 386, 400

Translation World Publishers, 200, 201, 203, 424

Transport Workers Union, 561

Travis, Carole, 534

Trial Lawyers of America (ATLA), 38

Tribble, James, 57

Tricontinental Congress, 334

Trinity Evangelical Divinity School, 525

Trinity United Church of Christ, 341, 493, 524

Trinkl, John, 103

Troope, April, 380

Trotsky, Leon, 362

Trotskyists, Socialist Party, 195, 419

Trotskyites, 15, 31, 362, 489

Trumka, Richard, 480, 584

Truth, Sojourner, 134

Tubman, Harriet, 343

Turner, Nat, 134

Tynan, Roxana, 265

Tyner, Jarvis, 72, 73, 74, 130, 132, 133, 231, 344, 368

Tyson, Kevin, 347, 493, 524

Ucelli, Juliet, 458

UCLA Labor Center, 265

UIC, African-American Studies, 133, 345

UIC, College of Education, 133, 345

Uncloaked Dagger: CIA Spending for Covert Action, 520

Unger, Abraham, 572

Union

    AFL-CIO, 42, 52, 96, 108, 219, 220, 257, 262, 263, 266, 298, 299, 319, 352, 358, 431, 437, 439, 476, 494, 495

    John Sweeney, President, 9, 38, 42, 67, 219, 220, 227, 236, 262, 358, 431, 445

    Margaret Blackshere, President, 9

    Massachusetts

      Robert Haynes, President, 444

Amalgamated Clothing and Textile Workers Union, 109

Amalgamated Meatcutters & Butcherworkmens' Union, 424

AmalgamatUnion.othing and Textile Workers Union, 161

American Federation of Labor – Chicago (AFL-C)

    Dennis Gannon, President, 9

American Federation of Labor (AFL), 42

American Rights at Work (ARW), 354, 431, 441, 445

California Nurses Association, 473, 476

Change to Win, 41, 54, 55, 56, 257, 298, 437

Chicago Federation of Labor, 52, 64

Chicano Farm Workers Union, 314

Citizen's Committee to Aid Packinghouse Workers, 371, 408, 409, 499, 501, 504

Coalition of Black Trade Unionists (CBTU), 52, 561

Congress of Industrial Organizations (CIO), 42, 313, 362, 371, 408

Employee Free Choice Act, 11, 226, 227, 232, 275, 352, 430, 441

Employee Free Choice Act (EFCA), 430

Hotel Employees and Restaurant Employees, 97

International Brotherhood of Teamsters, 471

International Longshore Workers and Warehouse Union (ILWU) Local 26

    Bert Corona, President, 313

International Longshore Workers Union (ILWU), 149, 311
International Typographical Union Chicago Local 16, 423
International Union of Operating Engineers, 441
Labor Council for Latin American Advancement, 404
People Organized to Win Employment Rights (POWER), 404
Public Sector
    International Association of Fire Fighters, 471
    American Federation of State, County, and Municipal Employees (AFSCME), 97, 108
    Council 31
Henry Bayer, Executive Director, 9
    American Federation of Teachers, 97
    Chicago Teachers Union, 51, 52, 97
    Colorado Federation Teachers, 80
    National Teacher Corps, 47
    SEIU
        Gary Hudson, Vice President, 450
        Illinois State Council
Tom Balanoff, President, 9
    Local 1, 9
    Local 1199
Angela Doyle, Vice President, 450
Bruce Richard, Vice President, 450
Geoffrey Jaques, Associate Editor 1199 News, 449
Lenore Colbert, Vice President, 450
Marshall Garcia, Vice President, 449
Nelson Valdez, Vice President, 450
Pat Harris, Vice President, 450
Paul Friedman, Vice President, 449
Raphael Pizzaro, Organizer, 449
    Local 1199 Child Care Fund, 450
    Local 1199 New York, 448, 449
Milstein Merrilee, Vice President, 450

    Local 1199 Seattle
Pam Mills, Vice President, 450
    Local 503, 73
    Local 660 Los Angeles, CA, 266
    Local 880 (Chicago, IL), 13, 14, 142, 143, 171
    Service Employees International Union, 38, 41, 56, 133, 269
    Service Employees International Union (SEIU), 494
    Teachers Committee for Quality Education, 47
SEIU
    Doctors Council, 472
Teamsters
    Local 705, 97
The Citizen's Committee to Aid Packing House Workers, 371
The Coalition of Black Trade Unionists, 52
UNITE HERE, 55
UNITE HERE Local 1
    Henry Tamarin, President, 9
United Auto Workers, 439, 441
    Local 600, 356
    Region 4, 52
United Farmworkers Union, 364
United for Peace & Justice, 257
United Packinghouse Workers Union, 52
United Steel Workers of America
    Leo Gerard, President, 431, 433
United Steelworkers of America, 473, 569
US Labor Against the War, 404
United for Peace & Justice, 15, 98, 120, 277, 298, 299, 321, 452, 454, 457, 553
United for Peace and Justice, 586
United Nations Centre on Transnational Corporations, 335, 406

United Power for Action and Justice (UPAJ), 93
United States House Committee on Ways & Means, 258
University of California, 139, 356, 415
University of California, Berkeley, 356
University of Chicago, xvii, 22, 44, 132, 133, 174, 175, 176, 189, 193, 200, 204, 271, 345, 361, 416, 485, 497, 500, 544, 545, 546, 547, 574, 581, 596, 623
University of Illinois, 80, 133, 342, 343, 345, 485
University of Illinois at Chicago, 485
University Of Illinois School Of Public Health, 487
University of Miami Medical School, 31, 165
University of Pennsylvania, 42
University of Wisconsin-Madison, 185
Urey, Harold C., 513, 518
US Action, 92, 93, 94, 96, 97, 98, 229, 257, 319, 321, 439
US Ambassador
  Luis C. de Baca, 577
  UN Ambassador John Bolton, 212
US Attorney General
  Kennedy, Bobby, 257
US Catholic Conference, 319
US Czar
  Energy Czar Carol Browner, 289, 290, 298, 443, 529
  Green Jobs-Van Jones, 330, 388, 396, 400, 429, 550, 557
  Manufacturing Ron Bloom, 429, 431, 432, 433, 434, 440, 529
  Regulatory – Cass Sunstein, 445
  Science - John P. Holdren, 509, 513, 514, 515, 516, 519, 521, 523
US Deputy Assistant to the President for Domestic Policy

Heather Higginbottom, 443
US Federal Election Commission (FEC), 237
US Federal Reserve Board, 551
US Federal Reserve System, 551
US Labor Secretary
  Hilda Solis, 316, 436, 496, 575
US Marine Barracks - Biert, 357
US National Security Council
  Samantha Powers, Director for Multilateral Affairs, 444
US Peace Council, 60, 80, 81, 109, 110, 159, 300, 348, 374, 411, 463, 466, 577
US President
  Barack H. Obama, 38, 115, 295, 302, 306, 325, 359, 360, 523, 529, 560, 566
  Richard M. Nixon, 514
  Ronald W. Reagan, 515
  William J. Clinton, 498
US President Elect
  Barack H. Obama, 256, 288, 289
US Representative
  Abercrombie (D-HA-1st District), Neil, 573, 577
  Barney (D-MA-4th District), Frank, 19
  Becerra (D-31st-District), Xavier, 269
  Bonior (D-MI-12th District), David, 234, 235, 236, 237, 238, 263, 268, 286, 289, 290, 291, 352, 356, 357, 441, 445, 529
  Bonior (D-MI-17th District), David, 239, 352, 353, 431
  Conyers (D-MI-14th District), John, 86, 87, 159, 222, 223, 286, 439, 469, 473, 476, 477, 480, 484
  Davis (D-IL-7th District), Danny K, 7, 11, 14, 62, 77, 78, 79, 87, 95, 141, 144, 145, 159, 187, 235, 238, 258, 261, 262, 285, 342, 349, 426, 438,

439, 460, 479, 480, 490, 507, 528, 538, 551, 570

Davis (D-IL-7th District), Danny K, 7

DeLacy (D-WA-1st District), Hugh, 150

Delgado (D-IL), David, 11

Dellums (D-CA-9th District), Ronald Vernie "Ron", 17

Emanuel (D-IL-5th District), Rahm, 366

Ford Jr. (D-TN-9th District), Harold, 286

Grijalva (D-AZ-7th District), Raul, 269

Gutiérrez (D-IL-4th District), Luis, 269, 493, 496, 497, 498

Hayes (D-IL-1st District), Charles, 160, 424

Holmes Norton (DC-At Large), Eleanor, 554

Holtzman (D-NY-16th District), Liz, 562

Jackson Jr. (D-IL-2nd District), Jesse, 82, 366, 554

Kucinich (D-OH-10th District), Dennis, 25, 211

Lee (D-CA-9th), Barbara Jean, 17, 18, 19, 20, 66, 81, 86, 87, 300, 301, 348

McDermott (D-WA-7th District), Jim, 353

Mfume (D-MD-7th District), Kweisi, 236

Mikva (D-IL-2nd District), Abner, 286, 400, 417, 544, 545, 546, 547, 548, 549, 551

Nadler (D-NY-8th District), Jerrold, 439

Owens (D-NY-11th District), Major, 86, 87, 88, 451

Pelosi (D-CA-8th District), House Speaker Nancy, 36, 38, 476

Rangel (D-NY-15th District), Charles, 259

Sánchez (D-CA-39th District), Linda T., 269

Savage (D-IL-2nd District), Gus, 62

Schakowsky (D-IL-9th District), Jan, 35, 36, 37, 38, 44, 57, 66, 67, 68, 82, 92, 187, 238, 358, 438, 439, 479, 480, 496

Skaggs (D-CO-2nd District), David, 398

Solis (D-CA-32nd District), Hilda, 236, 262, 263, 264, 265, 268, 269, 270, 289, 291, 310, 354, 445, 446, 529

Torres (D-CA-38th District), Esteban, 267

Velasquez (D-NY-12th District), Nydia, 269, 496

Washington (D-IL-1st District), Harold, 160, 162, 163, 165, 195, 196, 363, 419, 420

Waters (D-CA-35th District), Maxine, 267, 268

US Secretary of Labor
Solis (D-CA-32nd District), Hilda, 312

Solis, Hilda, 309, 355

US Secretary of State
Clinton (D-NY), Hillary, 323

Clinton, Hillary, 252, 324

US Senator
Bayh (D-IN), Evan, 319

Boxer (D-CA), Barbara, 320

Chisholm (D-NY), Shirley, 87

Clinton (D-NY), Hillary, 9, 25, 26, 28, 32, 55, 70, 83, 86, 104, 241, 250, 268, 310, 393

Clinton (D-NY), Hillary Rodham, 137

Conrad (D-ND), Kent, 319

Durbin (D-IL), Dick, 67, 68, 212, 478

Edwards (D-NC), John, 25, 237

Feingold (D-WI), Russ, 211

Goldwater (R-AZ), Barry, 425

Gravel (D-AK), Mike, 520

Hart (D-CO), Gary, 196

Leahy (D-VT), Pat, 211

Lieberman (ID-CN), Joe, 138, 166

McCain (R-AZ), John, 32, 198, 422

McCarthy (D/R-WI), Joseph, 70, 519

McCarthy (D-MN), Eugene, 257

McGovern (D-SD), George, 87

Mondale (D-MN), Walter, 196

Moseley Braun (D-IL), Carol, 27

Moseley-Braun (D-IL), Carol, 8, 31, 44, 50, 58, 62, 154, 155, 156, 159, 160, 161, 196, 320, 360, 412, 420, 428, 485, 486

Obama (D-IL), Barack, 9, 10, 17, 20, 22, 23, 24, 25, 26, 27, 28, 30, 31, 32, 34, 35, 37, 39, 40, 41, 44, 49, 50, 52, 54, 55, 58, 59, 65, 66, 69, 70, 72, 73, 79, 86, 88, 93, 94, 98, 104, 105, 107, 108, 110, 115, 116, 117, 118, 133, 134, 137, 138, 141, 155, 158, 161, 166, 169, 173, 174, 175, 177, 178, 183, 192, 196, 198, 209, 210, 211, 212, 213, 214, 215, 219, 259, 270, 315, 317, 341, 342, 347, 357, 377, 578, 587

Reid (D-NV), Harry, 138

Sanders (I - VT), Bernie, 18, 19, 186, 290, 291, 443, 538, 553

Simon (D-IL), Paul, 198, 214, 215, 320, 421

Wellstone (D-MN), Paul, 214, 215, 432

US Supreme Court
 Associate Justice Arthur Goldberg, 557
 Associate Justice Elena Kagan, 560, 561, 567, 573
 Associate Justice Thurgood Marshall, 567, 571
 Chief Justice John G Roberts, 209

US Under Secretary of Defense
 Rosa Brooks, 575

US Under Secretary of Defense for Policy
 Michele Flournoy, 441

US Vice President
 Joseph Robinette Joe Biden Jr., 584

US White House
 Office of Energy and Climate Change Policy, 443
 Office of Science and Technology Policy, 515

Valdez, Nelson, 450

Valle, Miguelle Del, 534

Vaughn, Jackie, 52, 53

Velikhov, Evgeny, 519, 521

Venceremos Brigades, 110, 313, 354, 390, 402, 403, 405, 417, 566

Venezuelan Embassy, 404

Veterans for Peace, 111, 200

Vietnam War, 100, 167, 168, 399, 429, 471

Villar, Tony, 311

Wagner, Robert, 40

Wallace, Henry, 194, 418

Wallace, Howard, 457

Wallerstein, Immanuel, 103, 139, 282, 283

Wallis, Rev. Jim, 524, 525, 526, 528, 529

Walzer, Michael, 564, 566

Walzer, Sarah, 564

War Council, 332

War Registers League, 586
War Times, 328, 390, 401, 403, 538
Ware Group, 572
Ware ring, 362
Warren, Dorian, 141
Washington Post, 152, 233, 265, 373, 410, 445, 593, 595, 616, 618, 622
Washington, Harold, 151, 362
Waskow, Arthur, 190, 191, 280, 458
Watt, Addie, 53
Weather Underground, 102
Weather Underground Organization (WUO), 15, 79, 110, 112, 115, 129, 135, 146, 153, 159, 173, 177, 222, 247, 255, 278, 286, 313, 322, 329, 330, 331, 332, 338, 343, 344, 346, 389, 390, 392, 396, 399, 400, 405, 406, 414, 417, 432, 440, 461, 471, 497, 501, 528
Webb, Sam, 231, 239, 240, 241, 242, 243, 244, 245, 246, 307, 310, 367
Weinstein, James, 541
Weissbourd, Bernard, 505, 514
Weissbourd, Bernice Targ, 504, 506, 514
Weissbourd, Robert, 507, 508
Weissbourd, Robert M., 506, 514
Welbon, Yvonne, 141
Wells, Ida B., 130, 131, 132, 343
Wellstone Action, 432
Wendland, Joel, 59
Wesleyan University, 434
West, Cornel, 68, 69, 75, 103, 114, 130, 132, 134, 146, 147, 173, 271, 285, 344, 347, 349, 378, 383, 387, 388, 431, 452, 524, 526, 527, 528, 540, 566, 575
Western States Legal Foundation, 404
Wheeler, Tim, 23, 24, 97, 160
Whiting, Ernestine, 533
Who's Building the New Party?, 145
Wiesner, Jerome C., 513

Wilder, Solveig, 77
Wilentz, Sean, 565
Wilhoitte, Betty, 208, 366, 460
Wilkins, Fanon Che, 346
Wilkinson, Frank, 151, 261, 550, 570
Willamette Reds of Oregon, 73
Willentz, Sean, 566
Willhoite, Betty, 103, 513
Williams, Ian, 452
Williams, Mei-ying, 403
Williams, Rev. Pierre, 23
Williams, Steve, 401, 403, 404
Williamson, Mildred, 103, 478, 481, 493
Wilson, William Julius, 22, 271, 443, 581
Wing, Bob, 403, 405, 415
Winpisinger, William, 48
Wisconsin Steel, 60, 61
Wise, Tim, 103
Wittner, Lawrence S, 80
Wolf, Rabbi Arnold, 187, 188, 189, 190, 191, 192, 194, 280, 418
Wolf, Rabbi Arnold Jacob, 188, 189, 203, 350, 438, 506, 575, 581, 628
Wolf, Rabbi Jacob, 238
Wolins, Leroy, 200
Wolins, LeRoy, 424
Women of Color Resource Center, 401, 403
Women's Strike for Peace and Council, 81
Wonder, Stevie, 62
Wong, Kent, 265
Wood, Roberta, 486
Woodlawn Organization, 491
Woods Fund for Chicago, 12, 491
Woolhandler, Steffi, 473
Workers Party of Brazil, 78, 144, 260
Workers World Party, 332

Working Families Center, 452
Working Families Party, 6, 439, 451, 452
Working Today, 398
World Federation of Democratic Youth, 88
World Peace Council, xiii, 81, 109, 159, 200, 300, 305, 424, 463, 465, 467, 562
World Publishers, 424, 425
Wright, Jim, 52
Wright, Rev. Jeremiah, 134, 175, 286, 341, 346, 347, 493, 523, 524, 525
Wright, Richard, 152
Wu, Tim, 589
Wyatt, Addie, 52
Yale University, 137, 325
Yarbrough, Karen, 341, 342
Yeager, Tim, 262, 550, 570
Yeltsin, President Boris, 521
Yes We Can!, 310, 364
YMCA, 319
Young Communist League, 69, 70, 71, 88, 154, 166, 364, 374, 411, 470, 478, 486, 505

Young Peoples Socialist League, 10, 291
Young Workers Liberation League, 599
Young Worker's Liberation League, 347
Young, Dr. Quentin, 45, 46, 48, 67, 68, 75, 79, 82, 92, 109, 110, 140, 146, 161, 162, 173, 187, 191, 194, 203, 221, 222, 223, 238, 262, 274, 280, 285, 286, 348, 349, 350, 364, 366, 367, 417, 418, 438, 461, 469, 470, 471, 472, 473, 474, 477, 478, 479, 480, 483, 486, 487, 496, 504, 505, 506, 514, 515, 528, 541, 551, 570, 574, 580, 590
Young, Ruth, 506, 515
Youth Force Coalition, 336, 407
Youth United for Community Action, 336, 407
YWCA, 319
Zapatista rebels, 234
Zinn, Howard, 112, 146, 147, 179, 180, 541
Zlotowski, Ignace, 518

Made in the USA
Charleston, SC
30 January 2014